Chinese on the American Frontier

Pacific Formations: Global Relations in Asian and Pacific Perspectives
Series Editor: Arif Dirlik

What Is in a Rim? Critical Perspectives on the Pacific Region Idea, 2nd edition
edited by Arif Dirlik

Inside Out: Literature, Cultural Politics, and Identity in the New Pacific
edited by Vilsoni Hereniko and Rob Wilson

Teaching Asian America: Diversity and the Problem of Community
edited by Lane Ryo Hirabayashi

Encounters: People of Asian Descent in the Americas
edited by Roshni Rustomji-Kerns with Rajini Srikanth and Leny Mendoza
Strobel

Displacing Natives: The Rhetorical Production of Hawai'i
by Houston Wood

The Geography of Encounters: People of Asian Descent in the Americas
edited by Roshni Rustomji-Kerns

After Postcolonialism: Remapping Philippines–United States Confrontations
by E. San Juan, Jr.

Voyaging through the Contemporary Pacific
edited by David L. Hanlon and Geoffrey M. White

Forthcoming Titles

The Pacific Rim Becomes Borderless
by Xiangming Chen

Diversifying the State: American Grassroots Groups and Japanese Companies
by Tomoji Ishi

Surviving the City: The Chinese Immigrant Experience in New York, 1890–1970
by Xinyang Wang

Chinese on the American Frontier

Edited by Arif Dirlik

with the assistance of Malcolm Yeung

ROWMAN & LITTLEFIELD PUBLISHERS, INC.
Lanham • Boulder • New York • Oxford

ROWMAN & LITTLEFIELD PUBLISHERS, INC.

Published in the United States of America
by Rowman & Littlefield Publishers, Inc.
4720 Boston Way, Lanham, Maryland 20706
www.rowmanlittlefield.com

12 Hid's Copse Road
Cumnor Hill, Oxford OX2 9JJ, England

British Library Cataloguing in Publication Information Available

Library of Congress Cataloging-in-Publication Data

Chinese on the American frontier / edited by Arif Dirlik, with the assistance of
Malcolm Yeung.
    p. cm. — (Pacific formations)
Includes bibliographical references and index.
ISBN 0-8476-8532-2 (alk. paper)
1. Chinese—United States.   I. Dirlik, Arif.   II. Yeung, Malcolm.   III. Series.

E184.C5 C496 2001
973.04′951—dc21

00-034199

Printed in the United States of America

♾™The paper used in this publication meets the minimum requirements of American
National Standard for Information Sciences—Permanence of Paper for Printed Library
Materials, ANSI/NISO Z39.48-1992.

For Nicki,
And His Many Frontiers

Contents

Preface

This reader is the culmination of an interplay of professional interests in and a personal fascination with the nineteenth-century U.S. western frontier; I do not dare say which of these elements has played the more significant part in the production of this book. My work as a historian of China has led over the last few years to an interest in Chinese Overseas, stimulated by the increasing global visibility (especially in the United States) of the diaspora of Chinese populations, which in numerous ways challenges received notions of China and the Chinese. My new interest has resulted in scholarly forays into Asian American studies; it has led also to the incorporation of the Asian American experience in my teaching.

As Asian American studies have developed over the last three decades, Asian American scholars have focused most of their attention on the two coasts, especially California. There have been tantalizing hints of the importance of Asians in the history of the western frontier. Particularly intriguing in my case was a reference by the Chinese American writer Frank Chin (in his introduction to *The Big Aiieeeee!* a collection of Asian American writing) to Wong Sam's *An English-Chinese Phrase Book together with the Vocabulary of Trade, Law, etc. Also a Complete List of Wells Fargo & Co's Offices in California, Nevada, etc.* (San Francisco, 1875), which listed Wells Fargo offices throughout the West of interest to Chinese customers, in the process indicating also the presence of hundreds of "Chinatowns" scattered throughout the region. It had been a matter of concern to me in teaching the Asian American experience — which for most of the nineteenth century meant the Chinese American experience — that we did not even have a clear mapping of the Chinese presence in the United States; Chin's reference pointed to possibilities in filling the gap.

I began to look into these possibilities during a sabbatical year I spent in the Ethnic Studies Department at the University of Colorado. While at work on a project on the revolutionary movement in Guangzhou (Canton) in the 1920s, I took occasional rest from my project to go through western historical journals to see what might be available on the Chinese in the nineteenth century. What I found came as a big surprise: voluminous scholarship published in state journals that not only included mapping for individual states, but revealed much else about Chinese activity on the frontier. Much of this work has been done by state historians or historians of the West, some had been done by China specialists like myself (the selections below by Edward Rhoads, Gary Tipton, and Loren Chan), and some by amateur local historians, drawing on local sources, more often than not sponsored by state historical societies. Asian American scholars or historians of the West may be familiar with this work; but to my knowledge (and judging by bibliographical references) little of it has found its way into scholarship addressing questions of national scope. It was not difficult to decide that a compilation of sampling of this scholarship would not only bring attention to this significant body of literature, but would be valuable for teaching purposes as well. This collection is the result. The mapping is there, but the literature takes us beyond mapping into important questions of Asian American history, the history of the frontier, and even nineteenth-century Chinese history.

It would be disingenuous of me to suggest, however, that scholarship and teaching played the only—or perhaps even the primary—parts in this undertaking. My interest in the Chinese of the frontier was piqued over two decades ago, when in the gift shop of the Crazy Horse Monument near Custer, South Dakota, I picked up a pamphlet by Mildred Fielder, entitled *The Chinese in the Black Hills.* I was already a historian of China at the time, but I was not in the Black Hills out of scholarly interests. The Crazy Horse Monument is a monument to a great Indian chief; it is in some ways also a monument to the fascination of many foreigners, or foreign-born Americans, with the American West. Korczak Ziolkowski, the Polish-born sculptor, moved West after a fairly successful career in New York to undertake this monumental project; his faith and vision come closest to a living example of the "Foolish Old Man" in the Chinese parable made famous by Mao Zedong during the Cultural Revolution, who set out to remove a mountain even if it would take his descendants thousands of generations to complete the task. Ziolkowski's task continues today in the Black Hills, though he himself is deceased.

While few may be able to match Ziolkowski in his commitment to the West and its indigenous peoples, many share his fascination, including myself. Growing up in a Third World country, Turkey, absorbing Hollywood fare without (I hope) sharing its ideology, I have long viewed the American West as the ultimate in exotic places. I realized this after I came to the United States as a graduate student and found I had a compulsion to drive back and forth across the country whenever possible. My trip to the Black Hills in 1979, when I picked up Fielder's pamphlet, was one of many such trips. The discovery that there had been Chinese in the Black Hills (Chinese Overseas conventionally have not been part of the Chinese historian's training) only added to my fascination, now bolstered by professional curiosity, with the West. I would like to think that both strands, the professional and the personal, have gone into the making of this volume.

This volume was compiled while I was on a fellowship from the Chiang Ching-kuo Foundation to work on a study of the Canton Commune of December 1927;

I would like to express my gratitude, to the foundation for (unintentionally) making this volume possible as well. I thank Evelyn Hu-DeHart, chair of the Department of Ethnic Studies (then the Center for the Study of Ethnicity and Race in America) at the University of Colorado and a friend, for suggesting that I spend my sabbatical year as a visiting scholar in the department. When she extended the invitation, this project was not a part of any conscious plan in my mind; I merely wished to get acquainted with some of the scholars in that department with whose work I was familiar. The acquaintance has been pleasant and rewarding in many unforeseen ways.

Finally, when this project appeared on my intellectual horizon, I was able to count on the assistance of a former student from Duke University, presently a graduate student in history at the University of Colorado, Malcolm Yeung. While I am chiefly responsible for the selections, Malcolm did the "mapping"—putting together the maps and the tables—and compiled the bibliography. Malcolm is rare among Chinese American students of my acquaintance in his courage to abandon a promising career in science to take the plunge into Asian American history. This project stands, I hope, as one of the first intellectual fruits of his courage.

Arif Dirlik

Introduction
Mapping the Chinese Presence on the U.S. Frontier

Arif Dirlik

This reader brings together an impressive body of work on Chinese in the western states during the nineteenth century, making possible a mapping of Chinese presence and activity on the U.S. frontier.[1] The Chinese presence between the two coasts has received only marginal attention from specialists on Asian America. The primary goal of this collection is to bring attention to a body of scholarship that may help fill a lacuna in our knowledge and understanding of the history of Chinese in a region they played an important part in forming. We hope also that what this scholarship reveals will stimulate further work on the region.

Written mostly by scholars with a primary interest in the history of the U.S. frontier and histories of the western states, these histories of Chinese are intended to bring greater clarity to our understanding of the social legacy of the frontier. We hope that the collection, by bringing together work on individual states, will also make a contribution to the study and teaching of the nineteenth-century frontier in general. Finally, in surprising ways, the frontier experience of Chinese has dimensions that involve nineteenth-century Chinese state and society; and even historians of China may find elements of interest in these writings.

If one may judge by work published in state historical journals, most of the work on Chinese in the western states (and the majority of the selections in this collection) is a product of the last two decades. It coincides, in other words, with the emergence of Asian American studies as a discrete field. While there are no doubt individual reasons for scholarly interest in frontier Chinese among historians of the West, it is quite probable that the noticeable proliferation of work on the Chinese over the last two decades owes at least some of its stimulus to the increasing awareness of the Chinese propagated by Asian American studies, and the increasingly prominent roles Chinese in particular and Asians in general have come to occupy in the American consciousness.

Mainstream Chinese American scholarship, however, has remained focused almost exclusively on the coastal populations.[2] This may be understandable on demographic grounds, as the population of Chinese in the frontier West at its height (1870–80) did not exceed 15 percent of the total Chinese population in the western states and quickly declined thereafter, until few traces were left in most locations of the once-important Chinese presence. I think, however, that the question is not merely demographic. Chinese American studies, as Asian American studies in general, were initially stimulated by strong community interests and focused therefore on the locations of such communities, which for the most part excluded those western states that had long been denuded of their Chinese populations. Transformations in the field as it unfolded further marginalized the history of frontier Chinese. As new immigration has swollen the numbers of first-generation Chinese, there has been a shift of interest to the Asian roots of Chinese Americans at the expense of interest in historical roots in the United States, including the community interests that had informed the work of earlier scholars. There may be a class element as well. Unlike earlier Chinese immigrants, the new generation of immigrants include, most prominently, professionals and upscale entrepreneurs, to whom the histories of successful Chinese American role models may be more relevant than the histories of the working-class Chinese of the nineteenth century. As early as the 1980s, Asian American specialists expressed uneasiness about the emphasis in Asian American history on "railroads and concentration camps."[3] Without miners and railroad workers, of course, there is little in the way of early Asian American history, especially in the regions covered here.

The work of the historians included in this collection is important, therefore, in recovering the history of Chinese on the nineteenth-century frontier. But this work is also important in ways that may not be so readily apparent: as place-based histories that offer a critical counterpart to the globalizing tendencies of the present, which pervade Asian American studies as well. I am referring here to recent preoccupation with "diasporas," of which the Chinese diaspora is most pertinent. Interest in the Chinese diaspora has shifted attention to the global migrations of Chinese and its cultural consequences. This interest is a quite legitimate product of an increasingly important global phenomenon and raises fundamental economic, social, political, and cultural questions, including the most crucial in my view: what do we understand by the terms China and Chinese? This is the point of departure for the way we organize inquiry and research, not to speak of more fundamental issues of politics and community.

Unless it is place-grounded, however, the study of disapora in its very naming ("Chinese") invites the return of reified racial and cultural identifications to mark diverse populations—a "Chineseness," in other words, that exists independently of time and place. While presently economic success endows these markers with positive value, we need to remember that it was these same markers that were the cause of prejudice and discrimination against the Chinese at an earlier time. National historiography for some time provided something of an antidote by substituting identity defined by the nation-state for racially or culturally conceived identities. But the nation-state itself, while more grounded territorially and historically, suffered from its own reifications by abolishing differences within its own spaces and, more pertinently here, by excluding populations outside of its boundaries. Chinese overseas always presented problems to a Chinese nationalist historiography; the history of Chinese overseas was excluded from the national history of China and left to specialists of regions or countries where the overseas populations were located. The same, incidentally, was also the case for foreign historians of China: so long as the nation-state has provided the unit of historical analysis, its boundaries have also shaped the study of history; the history of Chinese Overseas has not been part of the training of the historian of China.

The turn to the study of diasporas, while it shares much in common with earlier race- or culture-based identification, also differs from the latter because it is post-nationalist (and questions the nation-state as a locus of identity) and globalist. Nevertheless, its very globalism tends to erase differences based on place and the different histories that are articulated through place. This has given rise in recent years to a concern with the local against the global. If I prefer "place" over "local" in describing this phenomenon, it is for two reasons. First, local itself was a product of nationalist historiography, as in "local history," and was thus an extension of a nationalist historiographical project. Second, place has to my mind more concrete associations with the locality. Not to quibble too much over words, history informed by a sense of place not only resists erasure by globalist reification but serves also as a reminder of the very concrete experiences and activities through which people have constructed and defined their activities.

These conceptual and methodological problems with important ideological and political consequences may not be an explicit concern of any of the selections below. On the other hand, these histories are consciously place-based to the extent that they ground their analyses in the concrete interactions of locations on the frontier, not only thwarting reified and homogenizing notions of "Chineseness," but complicating the meaning of what it "is" to be Chinese American, because these frontier experiences distinguished frontier Chinese from their coastal counterparts as well. As such, they offer instances of a kind of analysis that may be crucial at a time when Asian American studies are caught up in the conflicting demands of globalism and localism.

If bringing the frontier experience into Chinese American historiography may have significant conceptual consequences, the reverse is also the case. Studies of the frontier and the western states have suffered from a blindness where the Chinese population is concerned. The work included in this collection obviously has gained professional recognition, but it is fair to say that it has yet to find its way into broader conceptualizations of the frontier. A perusal of state histories indicates that references to Chinese populations are still extremely rare, and even recent revisionist frontier historiography, such as Patricia Limerick's *Legacy of Conquest*, which explicitly addresses issues of ethnicity on the frontier, draws for the most part on literature from the Pacific states.[4]

I have suggested elsewhere that recognizing the Chinese (and the Asian) presence also compels a recognition of an "eastern" frontier, challenging the long-standing Eurocentric myth of the western expansion of Europeans.[5] While Chinese on the frontier were few in number, the selections in this collection indicate nevertheless that their presence made a significant impact on the formation of the frontier. Chinese, of course, did not come from the West alone; there was also Chinese immigration to the frontier from the South (Mexico) as well as, in the case of Colorado, from the Southeast. The point, however, is that Chinese made more than an exotic addition to the frontier—they were crucial in certain areas of economic activity. The Chinese experience also confirms a dynamic view of the frontier against official demographic definitions, which historians such as Limerick have challenged.[6] The frontier was where the action was, so to speak, and was characterized by certain kinds of economic activity: mining chief among them. It is interesting that the height of the Chinese presence on the frontier, roughly 1860–90, coincided with the most intense period of activity in the formation of the frontier.

On the other hand, while recent historiography such as Limerick's challenges the myth of the frontier by bringing frontier historiography into mainstream U.S. historiography, the erasure of the uniqueness of the frontier may possibly produce its own blind spots. Seen through the eyes of the Chinese populations, the frontier did afford certain unique opportunities that were unavailable in the more settled parts of the country; indeed, Chinese were driven out of the frontier once frontier society gave way to more settled social patterns. The "uniqueness" of the frontier was also reflected in the social life of the Chinese and their relations with other groups.

Finally, attention to the Chinese frontier experience has some surprises for the historian of China as well. Phenomena that have been interpreted in the historiography of China as signs of Chinese inability to cope with a new historical situation appear differently when placed against the frontier experience of emigrant Chinese. There were Chinese investments in U.S. railroads, such as those of the Guangzhou (Canton) merchant, Howqua. U.S. railroads builders recruited Chinese laborers directly in Guangdong and managed them through labor practices of Chinese origin, which was a major cause of white labor hostility to the Chinese. What such phenomena implied for social dynamics back in China is a question that is yet to be addressed by historians of China.

There are also more direct inferences to be drawn from the Chinese frontier experience. Chinese anti-foreignism in the nineteenth century has long been a staple of the historiography of China. What do we make of this if we place next to it the anti-foreignism that Chinese suffered in the American West? The Los Angeles massacre of Chinese in 1871 followed closely on the heels of the Tianjin massacre of 1870 in China (when a number of French missionaries were killed). While the latter has been taken as a sign of Chinese "barbarism," few historians of China are even familiar with the former.[7] In terms of numbers killed and the level of viciousness, nineteenth-century anti-foreignism in China was easily matched by the Rock Creek (1885) and Snake River (1887) massacres (see selections below). Conversely, the Qing Dynasty officials' responses to these anti-Chinese activities on the frontier challenge the conventional view of the dynasty's in-competence in dealing with a new international situation; Qing officials in the United States and China responded promptly to these events, calling on interna-tional law to hold the U.S. authorities responsible for such atrocities.[8]

While I have no wish to exaggerate the conceptual breakthroughs exemplified by studies of the kind below, it is fair to say nevertheless that they point to the pos-sibilities of a more comprehensive inter-referential historiography that may en-rich historical understanding, and evaluation, where both Chinese and U.S. his-tories are concerned, not to speak of Asian American historiography. I, for one, would no longer care to teach the modern history of China without reference to the above-mentioned events.

It is important in considering these historiographical possibilities to read the literature on frontier Chinese critically. As I will elaborate below, Chinese were to become during these years part of frontier lore, and it is possible that in some cases the stories told about them in contemporary sources may be apocryphal. It is also possible to detect in some of the writings below, especially those pro-duced by amateur local historians, a nostalgic romanticized view of Chinese–white relations; while these writings show a great deal of sympathy for the Chi-nese and bemoan the racism to which they were subjected on the frontier, the au-thors themselves often perpetuate the racist vocabulary of the frontier in their ref-erences to "Chinamen" and "celestials." Even some of the professional historians, as historians of individual states, may be vulnerable in their interpretations to the frontier lore inscribed in their documentation, not to speak of a tendency to the beautification of social relations in their states against what was happening else-where. In at least one case (the selection on Idaho by Liping Zhu), it is possible also that the author's own dim view of life in China leads to an exaggerated representation of Chinese welfare in Idaho. Place-based history, in other words, has its own pitfalls and oversights, exacerbated in this case by the folklore of the frontier.

Did the frontier make a difference in the Chinese American experience? The answer on the basis of the material presented here is a qualified yes. Qualified, because the Pacific coast and the frontier states shared a common history in fun-damental ways—not only through extensive communications but also in terms of human flows: the frontier, after all, was peopled by migrations from the two coasts, and the migrants brought with them attitudes and prejudices that had already taken shape before they arrived on the frontier. On the other hand, the frontier was not a replica of the coasts, and its unique circumstances allowed for variations that need to be taken into account in confronting the complexities in the Chi-nese experience of the United States in the nineteenth century.

Readers may draw from the selections below a multitude of questions of interest pertinent to the Chinese experience on the frontier. It seems important, however, to highlight here a few of the prominent issues they present from the perspective of Chinese American historiography. Five issues seem to be of primary significance:

the reconfigurations on the frontier of coastal patterns; oppression, resistance, and violence on the frontier; social relations on the frontier; the dynamics of frontier Chinatowns; and interethnic relations. It is important to bear in mind in discussing these issues that a distinction between stable, settled areas and new settlements may be a more significant difference than that between coast and frontier; indeed, what primarily distinguished the frontier from the coast was its unsettledness. The Chinese presence in the Great Plains and western states came to an end by the settlement of the frontier by the last decade of the century. On the other hand, in the already settled urban areas of the "frontier," differences from the coast in social relations between whites and Chinese were possibly less marked than in the many small settlements that dotted the nineteenth-century frontier.

CHINESE ON THE FRONTIER

Like others that set out from the Pacific coast, the Chinese moved northward and eastward in pursuit of economic opportunities once the mining boom had ended in California: partly in response to news of newly discovered goldfields but also as workers employed in the building of railroads. Unlike in the case of the initial move to California (and, to a lesser extent, Washington), however, the eastward expansion of the Chinese was in some ways by "invitation."[9] There is some lack of clarity in available materials over the nature of the eastward migration of Chinese laborers: it was at once the organized movement of laborers and the search for opportunity by individual entrepreneurs; while details are hazy, both processes were at work. Chinese laborers were certainly recruited in great numbers by the railroads, which actually did their recruiting in China.[10] Recruitment of Chinese for labor needs was fairly common in the burgeoning territories of the West, which sought both economic development and population growth. Chinese laborers were recruited through labor contractors, who might have been whites or Chinese. Chinese entrepreneurs, most prominently those of the Six Companies in San Francisco, were involved in the organization of labor for others or for their own undertakings. Saxton writes that the laboring Chinese "was at the mercy of the Chinese merchants, the associations, agents, contractors, who had fetched him over from Canton, who arranged for his employment, collected his wages, fed him 'protected' him, and determined when, or if he would ever return to his homeland."[11] The same pattern operated on the frontier, whether the recruitment was for others or for the recruiters themselves. The numbers could be significant even in the latter case. Sometime in 1875, in Pioneer, Montana, "Tim Lee, an Oriental, brought a company of 800 Chinese to the gulch. For several years he directed these laborers, who patiently washed gold from the tailings and carried away the waste rock in baskets to restack it on new dumps. Finally, when they could no longer uncover any gold, they left. Tim Lee remained, a highly respected resident of the gulch and perhaps the only Oriental to be admitted to membership by the Masons."[12]

Where Tim Lee's army of laborers went in anyone's guess. They presumably joined other Chinese who set out individually or in small groups seeking their fortunes as independent entrepreneurs. The Chinese who peopled the Chinatowns of Idaho, Utah, and Colorado were mostly former laborers of the central Pacific region. In some cases, however, these laborers did not wait for their contracts to run out. Liping Zhu writes that

> The mining frontier not only welcomed "free" laborers, it helped to *create* "free" laborers. . . . If a person were too poor to go to Idaho, he could join a Chinese company in California or Nevada, which would often pay his travel expenses. On arrival in the Boise Basin, he simply broke the contract by running away. . . . In 1883 two Chinese miners, Chow Kung Lein and Loo Hue, of Sing Hop & Co., slipped away with fourteen hundred dollars worth of supplies. These runaways angered company officials, who could do nothing except place a notice in the local newspaper smearing their names and proclaiming them "opium addicts and swindlers."[13]

Another author notes that "as these Chinese miners spread over the western territories in the wake of the white miners, the hold of the Chinese district companies was somewhat weakened and some Chinese gained a measure of freedom. With the decline of mining many Chinese moved into other occupations such as laundering, domestic service, vegetable gardening and operating restaurants."[14] The statement points to another aspect of the Chinese experience on the frontier: Chinese as participants in the making of the frontier. Except in such already settled urban centers as Salt Lake City and Denver, Chinese were participants from the beginning in the creation of settlements, a contribution remarked in most of the discussions below. In many places outside these urban areas, Chinese, in spite of their small numbers, nevertheless constituted a significant portion of the population. The Chinese presence was the most conspicuous in Idaho (which may also account for the exaggerated claims made for Chinese welfare in Idaho), where around 1870 they constituted nearly 30 percent of the total population. In Montana and Wyoming, Chinese made up a majority or a significant portion of the population. In Prescott, Arizona, a major center in that state's formation, "one of Prescott's founding fathers [Quon Clong Gin] was an Asian, a fact perhaps deliberately overlooked since."[15]

Numbers, however, tell only part of the story. If I may leave aside in this context the implications of the term "civilization" (the cause of so much mischief and cruelty on the frontier), the Chinese, for all they were denied "civilized" status, played a major part in "civilizing" the frontier. The occupational diversity to which Sister Elsensohn refers in the statement above filled a crucial economic and social need in many parts of the frontier, including major population centers. Railroads and mining may have been the major reasons for the eastward expansion of the Chinese, but they quickly branched out into the "tertiary" sector of the economy, filling a real economic need. The tables in the appendix indicate the diversity of Chinese occupations. Suffice it to say here that social oppression, which ruled out involvement in large-scale agriculture or industry, drove the Chinese into service occupations that were of strategic importance in frontier communities. Chinese as truck farmers, laundrymen, restaurant owners, pharmacists, or even managers of opium dens contributed to the formation and sustenance of such communities.

The gender aspect of this activity is no less significant. Chinese communities all over the United States were "bachelor" communities, since Chinese women were few in number, and antimiscegenation laws in most states precluded marriage between Chinese and whites. While this made Chinese unusual in the settled urban centers (coastal or otherwise), under frontier conditions, Chinese bachelor communities did not differ significantly from those of others—most communities on the frontier were predominantly single-sex. On the economic side, the service occupations into which Chinese branched out in order to minimize competition with whites, and therefore avoid suppression, were those considered "women's occupations." The Chinese, in other words, answered those crucial needs that ordinarily had been met by women's work, which was missing on the frontier. It is not surprising, therefore, that as the male-dominated frontier society turned into settled family society, this Chinese economic contribution became marginal. The effect was felt most evidently by Chinese laundrymen: with wives to wash their clothes, white males no longer needed the services of Chinese laundries. As I will note below, the Chinese laundry on the frontier also brought Chinese men into conflict with white women, to whom washing clothes was one way of earning a living: Chinese men and white women, together among the disadvantaged on the frontier, were nevertheless pitted against one another in a struggle for survival. In Helena, Montana, "Committee of Ladies," the laundrywomen, notified the "sons of Cathay" that "they must suspend the washing or laundry business immediately."[16] The conflict also typified Chinese relations with similarly placed minority or colored groups on the frontier, of which more below.

Although the differences of frontier conditions opened up new possibilities in the Chinese experience of America, it is important not to exaggerate them. I will discuss below the commonality of the coastal and frontier experiences in the context of prejudice against and oppression of Chinese. The Chinese on the frontier were themselves tied to their coastal counterparts by everyday needs as well as through organized activity. While the frontier may have afforded the spaces to break contracts and run away into a different way of life, this kind of motion only served to confirm the already established image of the Chinese as "sojourners," with little interest in settling down and becoming Americans. On the other hand, to the extent that Chinese societies of the frontier retained their ties to the coastal areas, it confirmed the equally powerful image of Chinese cultural insularity. The latter found confirmation in the organizational networks, which voluntarily or involuntarily also limited Chinese integration into their newfound places.

These organizational networks seem to have been all the more powerful where Chinese settled in Chinatown. Chinatowns were as nodes in a network of Chinese around the West that served purposes of economic transactions and social control. While there is considerable uncertainty over the amount of wealth that Chinese mining activity produced, the amounts were significant enough to make Chinese into valued customers of Wells Fargo.[17] Wells Fargo catered to Chinese needs other than financial, as it also transported opium to Chinese communities around the West.[18] Networks were required also for everyday needs, for the Chinese populations on the frontier had food preferences that could be supplied only from the coast or from China. Remote Blackfood City (near Marysville, Montana) "received large shipments of rice direct from China . . . [which was] brought in from Helena by ox-team."[19] Chinese pharmacies and stores in Chinatowns all over the western states imported goods from China for the Chinese and white population alike.[20] Material goods were not the only needs; spiritual requirements also had to be imported from China, more often than not by intermediaries on the coast. A Butte, Montana, newspaper reported in 1882 that "The great Chinese Joss arrived last night by express from California, and is being feasted to-day with all the delicacies of the season."[21] Chinese on the frontier also had access to coastal publications that kept them informed of national developments as well as news from across the Pacific.[22]

But needs were only part of the story. Over the same networks, it would seem, prevailed a chain of organization and supervision. The Six Companies were active over this network; so were Chinese merchants of the coast who invested in the interior: following the lynching of Chinese in Pierce City, Idaho, "Chinese merchants from Portland, Oregon, immediately sent agents upriver to Lewiston and into northern Idaho, both to safeguard the property of their people and to check the facts in the case."[23] The overseas branch of the Triad Society, the Chee Kung Tong (Zhigong tang, referred to in the literature as the Chinese Masonic Lodge), which served purposes ranging from mutual aid to politics to criminal activity, was active over the network and commanded a huge membership; in Prescott, Arizona, 80 percent of local Chinese belonged to the society.[24] Also active were the various "tongs," which created divisions among frontier Chinese as they did along the coast.

OPPRESSION, RESISTANCE, VIOLENCE

The commonality between the Pacific coast and the western frontier is nowhere more evident than in the racist discrimination and persecution of Chinese. While anti-Chinese prejudice may have been a "California import,"[25] the "import" was readily assimilated on the frontier. The persecution of Chinese took especially tragic forms around the years surrounding the passage of the first Chinese exclusion law in 1882 (that barred the immigration of all but a few Chinese into the

United States), when the "Chinese question" became a national issue. John Wunder suggests that the exclusion law made a real difference in legal cases involving Chinese when he writes that:

> Prior to 1883, the first year of the passage of national legislation limiting Chinese migration to the United States, five decisions were rendered by the Montana Territory Supreme Court dealing with Chinese-related disputes. Three of those decisions favored Chinese litigants. After 1883, however, this trend reversed. Ten cases were heard, and seven resulted in unfavorable opinions for Chinese Montanans.[26]

The numbers here may be too small to justify speaking of "trends," but Wunder's suggestion is confirmed by other, more tragic, evidence of anti-Chinese racism. The anti-Chinese riots in Denver occurred in 1880, when the national debate over the "Chinese question" heated up in connection with the presidential election. The most widely known massacre of Chinese took place in Rock Springs, Wyoming, in 1885, when twenty-eight Chinese were butchered by a mob, nearly six hundred were driven into the inhospitable countryside, and their homes were burned down. Less well known but greater in numbers killed (thirty-one), and even more shocking in its brutality, was the murder of Chinese miners in the Hell's Canyon area of the Snake River in 1887 by a band of outlaws. Initial efforts to blame these tragic incidents on new immigrants (such as Italians) or professional outlaws was contradicted by the evidence. News of Rock Springs was accompanied by threatened massacres of Chinese in locations ranging from Utah to Wyoming.[27] The brutal deed of the outlaws in Hell's Canyon was matched in grisliness by the "Chinese skull fashioned into a sugar bowl [that] graced the kitchen table of one ranch house for many years."[28] In historical perspective, which was available to Isaac Bromley in 1886, these incidents were part of a widespread mass agitation against Chinese across the western states.

Disturbance over the "Chinese question" may have authorized, rather than caused, the intensified persecution of the Chinese. Historians have pointed to economic depression as a cause of increased intra-labor conflict. Anti-Chinese violence, however, was anything but new, and is not to be attributed to material causes alone. Anti-Chinese prejudice followed Chinese from California and persisted in the face of evidence contrary to the "reasons" that justified it. It became part of the frontier ideology in the form of a frontier folklore.

The lynchings of Chinese in Pierce City, Idaho, in 1885 may have been the most visible of a long history of lynchings in the West. Chinese were sometimes lynched for alleged criminal activity; such was the case with Ah Chow, hanged by vigilantes in Helena, Montana, in 1870 for having killed three men.[29] On other occasions Chinese were lynched for sport, as in the case of a white miner who hanged a Chinese in Silver Bow County near Butte in 1868. A report three decades later stated that "it was not a judicial execution. It was simply the cold, premeditated act of a disheartened, yet patriotic and Fourth-of-July conscious miner who hanged the Chinaman to a cottonwood tree just for the devilment and in the hopes that it might bring luck."[30] The Texas judge Roy Bean's statement that he did not know of any laws against killing Chinese was echoed by law enforcement officials elsewhere. The numbers of Chinese lynched may have been in the hundreds; exact numbers are unavailable as most cases went untried and unreported.[31]

In a situation where race provided a fundamental principle of social organization and politics, racially based violence was only the visible articulation of attitudes that pervaded society; and Chinese were only one group of its victims, although they were possibly the most uniformly persecuted group on the frontier. If Chinese were initially "invited" to the frontier states in the 1860s and 1870s, the invitation did not preclude racist discrimination. Mobs protesting against Chinese turned back arriving Chinese laborers even before they could begin work, as in Nederland, Colorado, in 1874.[32] Discriminatory laws that targeted the Chinese were passed as they arrived on the frontier. And Chinese were frequently forced by vigilantes out of communities where they had settled. The pathos of the Chinese on the frontier comes through loud and clear in the following newspaper announcement by a group of Chinese in Helena, Montana, under the title, "Good Chinamen":

> This is to certify that we, the undersigned, are good Chinamen and have lived in California and other parts of the United States, and that we have at all times been willing to abide by all the laws of the United States, and the States and Territories in which we have lived. And are now willing to deport ourselves as good law abiding citizens of Montana Territory, and ask but that protection that the liberal and good government of this country permits us to enjoy. We pay all our taxes and assessments, and only ask that the good people of Montana may let us earn an honest living by the sweat of our brow.[33]

Racism against the Chinese was part of the "folklore" of the frontier, built into the very language of the frontier. Hollon writes that "'Not having a Chinaman's chance' quickly took on a grim, literal meaning, and derogatory jokes about 'chinks' became part of the folklore of the West."[34] It was not merely in the jokes that racism was expressed, but in the everyday naming of the Chinese, which rendered male Chinese into "John Chinaman" and females into "China Mary," thereby denying them their individuality. The Cantonese term of affection, "Ah," was made into a surname for Chinese because it was easy to pronounce; in Prescott, Arizona, "half of the Chinese men and one woman tabulated in the 1880 . . . went by that name, one even being Ah Ah."[35]

Chinese were not passive victims of racist violence. While they made an effort to avoid competition and confrontation with whites, when pushed, they could and did fight back. In the 1897 boycott against Chinese businesses in Butte, Chinese took the boycotters to court and won, although they were unable to collect the indemnity awarded to them by the courts due to the insolvency of the defendants.[36] Where there were large numbers of Chinese, as in Boise Basin, Chinese got quite litigious, frequently using the courts against both other Chinese and whites for cases that ranged from the significant to the trivial. In this same area, Chinese were able to wage a successful battle to overcome legal discrimination. In 1866, they won the right to testify against whites. They also were victorious over the is- sue of oath-taking, which had been a problem in the courts not just for Chinese but for other non-Christians as well: how to judge the veracity of the oaths of non-Christians in giving testimony. The so-called chicken-oath represented an ac- commodation by the courts of Chinese practices: "In front of the judge each Chi- nese witness cut off a live chicken's head to draw blood on a platter. The witness, who had written his oath on a piece of paper, dipped it in the blood. The paper then was properly burned with a candle."[37]

Nor was litigation the only means Chinese used to defend themselves against racist violence. Chinese developed a reputation for fighting: "The Chinese was something of a fighter. Perhaps his method of fighting, knife in one hand, hatchet in the other, discouraged many white bully b'hoys. Their duals resulted in lopped off ears and gouged cheeks if not death."[38] Chinese, moreover, were quick to adjust to the ways of the frontier. According to Liping Zhu, "at least some Chinese in the Boise Basin possessed an awesome arsenal of firearms, ranging from an 1857 Smith & Wesson revolver to an 1873 Springfield army rifle. Similar to other nineteenth-century westerners, many young Chinese males carried bowie knives and Colt re- volvers on their hips in public. . . . Arrests of Chinese most commonly were for bat- tery and assault, for showing deadly weapons, and for 'disturbing the peace.'"[39]

As a group, "Chinese did not back down from a fight when provoked. On one occasion in Nevada in 1878, they fought with axes, pitchforks, and whatever other weapons they could lay their hands on when whites threatened them."[40] Individ- ually, too, they were prepared to defend themselves:

> When Mike Kelly tried to jump the claim of a Chinese miner, the two went to Fightn' Bar to shoot it out. Each hid behind a tree and for some minutes noth- ing happened. Mike got tired of waiting and cautiously peeked out. Bang, went his opponent's pistol, shooting Mike in the face. After he recovered, he claimed that he had been hit by his own bullet which struck that of the Chinaman and ricocheted.[41]

Chinese laundrymen often seem to have had altercations with customers who were careless with their payments or ticket stubs. An anonymous ditty went, "Mel- ican man is all okay—Wears stiff hat and big bouquet. Melican man no payee wash bill—Melican man can go to————."[42] The altercations frequently turned physical. An incident reported in Spokane Falls in 1884 shows that laundrymen, too, could fight back fiercely:

"Say you yaller skinned Chinee, I left two flannel shirs an' a pair o' overalls here to be washed t'other day, an' when I sent my boy around here to get 'em an' tell yer I'd lost the check, yer said 'no checky, no washy' to 'im."

"No checkee, no washee. Dlat lite; me no yalle-skin. Me Chinee man. Me lun washee house. No checkee, no washee."

"Then I'll smash your mug all over your face," and the irate patron of Tung Lung began to work his arms. A moment later he was so mixed up with the Chinaman that he could hardly tell which was which. He got an awful thrashing, and when he came out of the laundry with one ear partly bitten off, and with his nose bashfully retired from view within his face, with one eye hanging down on his cheek and the other closed for repairs he mournfully said to a man who asked what ailed him: "Ther rule o' that wash house air 'no checky, no washy,' and I'm dad gummed if they don't enforce it."[43]

While it is important to note that Chinese did fight back in ways that the frontier made possible, such resistance, and its effectiveness, should not be exaggerated. In the end, racial persecution and violence played a significant part, if not the only part, in the Chinese retreat from the frontier by the later 1880s. The image of the fighting Chinese probably derived more from intra-Chinese fighting than from Chinese fights with whites. While some of this intra-Chinese fighting was a direct product of social organization among the Chinese, the conditions created by racial oppression played a part there, too. Theft and women were frequent causes of violence among individual Chinese. In the predominantly male (and patriarchal) Chinese society, "stealing" another's woman often led to violence, on occasion against the women but more often among the males. Most impressive, however, were the pitched battles among groups of Chinese, sometimes as part of national tong wars, at other times over local competition for supremacy. These battles had a tendency to become local spectacles, edged on and enjoyed by whites. Hollon describes one in California that had many parallels across the western states:

Everyday for three weeks before the battle, there were public parades and drills with flying dragon banners in the streets of the mining towns throughout the district. Excitement mounted and thousands of spectators gathered as the date for the pitched battle approached. When the Cantons and the Hong Kongs finally met on the battle field, instead of commencing the fight immediately, they preferred to stand and hurl insults at one another across a neutral zone. But the Angols had not come to witness a war of words; they wanted to see blood. By three o' clock in the afternoon it was obvious that nothing was going to happen without forceful encouragement on the part of the spectators. Consequently, they swarmed onto the field and literally pushed the two sides together, at which time a drunken Swede began firing into the crowd. Another white man immediately killed the Swede. In the general melee that followed, the Hong Kongs suffered eight dead, while the Cantonese lost two of their members. Twelve others later died of wounds. Had the spectators exhibited the "coolness and courage" of the Chinese, no one would have been killed.[44]

SOCIAL RELATIONS

An event such as the above may seem particularly bizarre, but it was such unusual occasions that brought Chinese and whites together even in the small frontier communities. Given the importance of Chinese enterprises to frontier communities, there was considerable economic contact between Chinese and others, but histories of the frontier agree that economic interaction was not matched by social intercourse. Racial and cultural distrust divided the communities. Where Chinese were tolerated, racism and prejudice still distanced them from their social environment. The organizational affinities of Chinese exacerbated this distance by making them into part of a social and cultural network that enhanced a Chinese culturalism; as Liestman puts it, "although Chinatowns remained segregated from the communities in which they existed, they did not live in isolation from one another."[45] These distances confirmed the prejudicial views of many whites that Chinese had no interest in becoming part of and contributing to the local community, even when there was much evidence to the contrary.

There was some interaction, to be sure, marked by class features. Prominent Chinese were dubbed unofficial "mayors" of Chinatowns—"Mayor" Dick in Phoenix, Mayor "Chin" in Salt Lake City, Mayor "Leu" in Butte—who owed their honorific titles to the esteem they commanded in both the white and the Chinese communities, which enabled them to serve as intermediaries between the two groups.[46] In these cases, it was possible for Chinese and whites to intermingle on social occasions. Even then, however, such occasions were unusual ones. Chinese New Years, the rare Chinese wedding, and Chinese funerals were the most important occasions to bring together the two groups. One report on a New Year's celebration noted that "judging from the crowd of miners present in China Alley each evening at the celebration, one might be led to believe that the Chinese Joss might have Hibernian or Cornish relatives."[47] It was not the food, which was not yet widely appreciated on the frontier, but Chinese generosity with whiskey that was a major attraction for the whites. Chinese weddings, in their very rarity, provided other occasions for intermingling: "A number of American friends (James Murray, mining magnate and uncle of the present United States senator from Montana, a judge, professor, prominent lawyer, three prosperous merchants and Senator Tom Carter) were entertained the evening of February 13 at an elaborate dinner held at the Shanghai Cafe in Chinatown, and given by Dr. Huie Pock and Tom Lee in honor of Dr. Huie Pock's newly acquired bride, recently arrived from China."[48] These events were matched in the mirthful celebrations they occasioned by Chinese funerals:

> L. A. York recalled the funeral of Song Lee, a well-known merchant, as one of the most colorful Chinese celebrations held in Silver City. Before the deceased was laid to rest in the Chinese cemetery, a hog roasted with various delicacies was served to a multitude of jovial Chinese and American friends. After much revelry a funeral pro-

cession proceeded to the cemetery to the tune of "There'll Be a Hot Time in the Old Town Tonight" played by an American band hired for the occasion. A Chinese band consisting of a beer-keg drum, a piccolo, and cymbals beat out a wailing oriental tune, while the mourners whistled heartily, scattering red strips of paper along the trail to frighten any devils that might be lurking about. Eatables were buried with the departed Celestial to insure happy festivities upon his meeting with his ancestors. As the body was lowered into the grave, the band obliged with another tune: "Down Went McGinty."[49]

While such "festivities" invited broad participation by both the elite and the ordinary men on the street, it was generally the latter who frequented the Chinese restaurant and the opium den: the most common locations for social encounters between Chinese and whites. Chinese opium-smoking was a common cause for white complaint about the Chinese, but it was when whites developed the habit that the concerns became most conspicuous.[50] Chinese noodle shops also "did a standout business day and night." Already in some places it became fashionable to end an evening's entertainment with a visit to a noodle shop. Opium dens and noodle shops seem also to have brought together different classes; in the noodle ship, a "West side millionaire might rub elbows with Cabbage Patch bum, and Galena Street harlot might be found sitting in a booth across from a prominent society matron, with miners generously interspersed throughout the room."[51]

A court statement by the proprietor of an opium den, Yung Lee, might well serve as a metaphor for the social and cultural relationship of Chinese to their frontier environments: "Yung Lee sell dleams—velly nice dleams—if China boy or 'Melican boy or girl want to have nice, pletty dleam—Yung Lee, he fix 'em up. They pay Yung Lee money, he bling 'em one—to-hour dleam—pletty dleams— no disturbance—no botha anybody—just lay down—sleep—dleam. Much blettah then spend money for Ilish whiskey and want to kill evlybody. Much better dleam—no hurt anybody!"[52]

The Chinese presence became a visible and integral part of frontier society and culture. The Chinese pursued their own ambitions, but with their laundries, restaurants, pharmacies, vegetable gardens, and opium dens, they also provided crucial services to the communities in which they lived. Chinatowns and joss houses became part of the physical space of these communities. Chinese speech (as heard by whites) and unusual Chinese personalities became part of frontier lore. Chinese social ceremonies became major occasions for the whole community. While we know much less about the Chinese perception of their environment, there is sufficient evidence to indicate that they, too, were changed by interaction. They adopted frontier garb, they carried six-shooters, and they got into litigation as well as brawls. When asked what he was going to do for the Chinese New Year's celebration, a young Chinese called "Kid" replied that he was going to "do like Melican man. Get dlunk, go out on street, fight and laisee hellee."[53] The Chinese in their turn participated in "American" festivals; Deadwood was proud of its "world champion Chinese hose team," which won the championship in the 1888 Fourth of July celebrations. Bachelor Chinese men, without children of their own, became famous for their kindness to white children.[54] The Chinese laundryman Fun Gee, "king of the Chinese 'washee-washee' houses" in Dublin Gulch, Montana, was known for his kindness: "A white widow of Dublin Gulch with about ten small children was in competition with Fun at one time—or was she: The lady wasn't strong physically and frequently became ill. Whenever this happened her competitor, Fun Gee, sent his men over to her house to do her washing, wringing and ironing, and distributed dimes and quarters among her children."[55] The point here is not cultural adaptation by one side and assimilation by the other, which are bad questions to begin with. The point rather is that their co-presence in frontier societies induced in each community new cultural constructs and formations.

Chinese presence became integral to the societies and cultures of the frontier, but there was no real integration. In spite of their very real contribution to the formation of these societies, and the presence they acquired in western folklore, Chinese remained exotics. A remarkable example of this contradictory place they held in the consciousness of Westerners is Joe Sulentic's book on Deadwood's Chinatown. What is most remarkable about this book is that it makes Chinatown the site of a telling of some of the most venerated legends of Deadwood: "Big Ears Jack and China May walked the same streets with Wild Bill Hickok and Calamity Jane."[56] While Sulentic recognizes the everyday presence of the Chinese, however, his placing of the Chinese with these legends of the West ironically also distances the Chinese from everyday life by rendering them as part of frontier folklore. Sulentic's book is marked by Chinese characters on the upper corners of every page, which according to the author are "used for appearance only."[57] What is remarkable is that in many cases, the characters are upside down and Chinese phrases mistranslated. Admission of Chinese into local folklore is not the same thing, obviously, as social integration or overcoming cultural exoticism.

In the sympathetic accounts of Chinese in the West, there is considerable nostalgia. Unfortunately, the same folklore that affirmed the Chinese presence was marked by racism. Even where the racism was not overt or intentional, the almost uniform representation of Chinese as exotics nourished the more overt kinds of racism by portraying them ultimately as outsiders, distant from the communities in which they lived.

RISE AND FALL OF CHINATOWNS ON THE FRONTIER

There has been some debate on the dynamics of Chinatowns. The explanations have ranged from the functionalist one of Chinatowns as defensive communities necessary for self-protection against a racist environment, at the one extreme, to the culturalist one of Chinatowns as products of Chinese "clannishness." I have no wish to engage in what I think to be a fruitless debate that must in the end be resolved empirically and circumstantially. Race is an important question here, too; while there is no shortage of ethnic communities living in their own enclaves, the exotic image of the Chinese has led to an exaggeration of Chinese unwillingness to integrate with and assimilate into American society.

Such was the case also with Chinatowns on the frontier. Coercion, as well as defense and protection, obviously did play some part in the formation of Chinatowns. Where Chinese gathered in large numbers, in some cases, the white population sought to "quarter" them in their own enclave.[57] On the other hand, Chinese social legacy is not to be ignored in Chinatown formation. Even where there were no restrictions on Chinese landownership, as in the Boise Basin in Idaho, Chinese tended to cluster together in enclaves. Within Chinatowns, there was a further inclination to establish subenclaves along district and surname lines.[58]

One element that appears with greater clarity in the smaller Chinatowns of the frontier than in the larger population centers is that of everyday life. For one thing, Chinese brought to the frontier in labor gangs were not merely inclined but required to live together. Even where this was no longer the case, meeting the necessities of everyday life, from foods imported form the coast to opium dens, encouraged the Chinese populations to cluster together (especially since they were, for the most part, single males unwanted by the communities around them). This element of the "everyday," I think, needs to be distinguished from culturalist explanations of abstract cultural tendencies.

The decline of Chinatowns on the frontier was also the product of complex circumstances, but infusing the whole was the one constant of racial persecution, which intensified after the passage of the Chinese Exclusion Law of 1882. The law cut off the flow of new immigrants, even as it led to greater harassment of Chinese. As numbers of scholars have remarked, and the evidence below supports, Chinese on the frontier joined Chinese on the coast in legally contesting the Exclusion Law and its requirements. Their abandonment of the struggle may have something to do with declining economic and social opportunities in the western states. In the activity that still occupied most Chinese into the 1880s, mining, there was a shift from individually based placer mining to large-scale corporate hard-rock mining, from which the Chinese were excluded by labor opposition. Hand-washing laundries met increasing competition from steam laundries. These changes affected Chinese livelihood at a basic level and encouraged migration back to the Pacific states where larger Chinese enclaves offered greater opportunities. There were also social aspects to this migration. As the frontier turned into settled society, Chinese bachelor communities appeared more out of place and less desirable (in addition to the now-serious competition from wives doing the laundry at home!). For bachelor Chinese, the coastal areas held forth at least some possibility of marriage and family. It appears, in other words, that there was no longer anything to fight for. Chinatowns of the frontier did not decline gradually but disappeared abruptly from the western scene from 1890.[59]

CHINESE AND OTHER PEOPLES OF COLOR

The frontier experience also highlights the Chinese relationship to other peoples of color, especially the American Indians. Already in California, anti-Chinese attitudes had spread from white laborers to the African American and the Mexican populations. While there were few African Americans in the frontier states, in the Southwest at least, Chinese continued to suffer Mexican and Chicano resentment of their presence.[60]

The new experience on the frontier was with American Indians. Indian massacres of Chinese was a commonplace experience on the frontier, the most notable being "the legendary slaughter by Paiute Indians of forty to sixty Chinese miners in 1866."[61] The long queue of the Chinese apparently provided a temptation for scalp-hunting Indians. More importantly, in some regions, the two groups entered economic competition; in Nevada, the Chinese–Paiute conflict arose form the Chinese outcompeting and displacing the Paiutes as wood-retailers.[62] A frequent complaint about Chinese was that they sold liquor to the Indians, which increased the possibilities of conflict.

At the individual level, once again, relations could be otherwise. Chinese males married Indian women,[63] and in Deadwood, "Chief Two Sticks, a Brule Indian, was married to a 'Chinese' woman who was called China Mary."[64] Then there was the case of the prominent Chinese merchant Wong Sing in Duchesne, Utah, who spoke the Ute language and was so respected that when he died, "sixty Ute men assembled at the office of the Indian agency to mourn his passing."[65]

It would be reductionist to suggest that economic reasons were the only, or even the most fundamental, ones for these group conflicts in every case. And yet, the competition for livelihood on the frontier was an important element in Chinese/Indian or Chinese/Mexican relations, as well as in Chinese relations with white women or with minority laborers such as Italians and French Canadians. Such competition had been present ever since the Chinese arrival on the Pacific coast, which quickly pitted white labor against the Chinese. This competition, in the social conditions of the nineteenth century, unfortunately expressed itself in the language of racism. In this sense, there was little difference between coast and frontier, for race pervaded politics and social consciousness in both areas, overwhelming commonalities of class and/or gender.

The selections below cover the areas east of the Sierra Nevada and the Cascades, through the Great Plains. They are restricted to the years 1860–90, which were the years of the greatest Chinese presence in this region, coinciding with the formation of the frontier and its eventual replacement by settled society.

These readings are intended for undergraduate and graduate classes as well as for the interested public. We have provided a rather extensive bibliography that may serve as the point of departure for further research into the Chinese experience in the western states. These selections, we hope, illustrate the possibilities for, and the promise of, such research.

NOTES

1. I realize that the "coast/frontier" distinction is at best a tenuous one, justifiable mainly on temporal grounds, since the Pacific coast itself was something of a frontier — especially for the Chinese. I use frontier here to distinguish those areas that were in the initial stages of settlement, where Chinese were participants in the settlement from the beginning rather than latecomers, so that whites could hardly claim priority except on the grounds that they were white. In many locations, Chinese constituted a substantial portion of the population, if not a majority, and contributed significantly to the frontier as compared, say, to California, which already had a Chinese population of nearly 80,000 by 1880, which may have affected the dynamics of their relationships with other groups.

2. It is problematic, needless to say, to speak of a "mainstream" in a young field in flux. On the other hand, there is no reason why work on the Western states should not be considered an integral part of the growth of Chinese American studies and mainstream in its own right. I am making the distinction partly on the grounds that the latter work has been done mostly by historians of the West and published in state journals as part of the discourse on the American West. Much of this work has not found its way into the literature of Chinese American studies. A revealing example is the recent collection by Sucheng Chan, in which the selections focus almost entirely on California, Oregon, and Washington, with hardly a reference to the interior. See Sucheng Chan, ed., *Peoples of Color in the American West* (Lexington, Mass.: D. C. Heath and Co., 1994).

3. Michael Omi, "It Just Ain't the Sixties No More: The Contemporary Dilemma of Asian American Studies," in Gary Okihiro, et al., eds., *Reflections in Shattered Windows: Promises and Prospects for Asian American Studies* (Pullman: Washington State University Press, 1988), 35.

4. Patricia N. Limerick, *The Legacy of Conquest: The Unbroken Past of the American Frontier* (New York: Norton, 1987).

5. Arif Dirlik, "Asian Pacific in Asian American Perspective," in A. Dirlik, ed., *What Is in a Rim? Critical Perspectives on the Pacific Region Idea* (Boulder: Westview Press, 1993).

6. I am referring here to the static definition of the frontier in terms of population: two persons per square mile.

7. For the Tianjin massacre, see John K. Fairbank, "Patterns behind the Tianjin Massacre," *Harvard Journal of Asiatic Studies* 20, 3–4 (December 1957): 480–511. For the Los Angeles massacre, see C. P. Dorland, "Chinese Massacre in Los Angeles in 1871," *Annual Publication of the Historical Society of Southern California*, no. 3 (1894): 22–26.

8. This comes up frequently in the selection below. See also Robert R. Swartout, Jr., "In Defense of the West's Chinese: Denny's Brief for Li Hung-chang," *Oregon Historical Quarterly* 83, 1 (spring 1982): 25–35.

9. Liping Zhu, "The Chinese on the Rocky Mountain Mining Frontier: The Boise Basin, Idaho, 1863–1910" (Ph.D. diss., University of New Mexico, 1994), 67. The welcoming attitude toward the Chinese was quite prevalent in the 1860s and early 1870s.

10. George Kras, "Chinese Laborers and the Construction of the Central Pacific," *Utah Historical Quarterly* 37, 1 (winter 1969): 41–57; Edward J. M. Rhoads, "The Chinese in Texas," *Southwestern Historical Quarterly* 81, 1 (July 1977): 2–2.

11. Alexander Saxton, "The Army of Canton in the High Sierra," *Pacific Historical Review* 35, 2 (May 1966): 151.

12. Muriel Sibell Wolle, *Montana Paydirt: A Guide to the Mining Camps of the Treasure State* (Denver: Sage Books, 1973), 221.

13. Liping Zhu, "'A Chinaman's Chance' on the Rocky Mountain Mining Frontier," *Montana: The Magazine of Western History* 45, 4 (autumn/winter 1995): 43.

14. Sister M. Alfreda Elsensohn, *Idaho Chinese Lore* (Cottonwood: Idaho Corporation of Benedictine Sisters, 1970), 13.

15. Florence C. Lister and Robert H. Lister, "Chinese Sojourners in Territorial Prescott," *Journal of the Southwest* 31, 1 (spring 1989): 2.

16. Larry Barsness, *Gold Camp: Alder Gulch and Virginia City, Montana* (New York: Hastings House, 1962), 240.

17. Harold P. Anderson, "Wells Fargo and Chinese Customers in Nineteenth Century California," in Frank H. H. King, ed., *Eastern Banking: Essays in the History of the Hong Kong and Shanghai Banking Corporation* (London: Athlone Press, 1983), 735–52.

18. Ibid., 750–51.

19. Wolle, *Montana Paydirt*, 115.

20. Patricia K. Ourada, "The Chinese in Colorado," *Colorado Magazine* 29 (1952): 280.

21. Quoted in Robert R. Swartout, Jr., "Kwangtung to Big Sky: The Chinese in Montana, 1864–1900," *Montana: The Magazine of Western History* 38, 1 (winter 1988): 49. Joss was derivative of "deos," god. "Joss house" was the term used to describe Chinese temples.

22. Liping Zhu, "How the Other Half Lived: Chinese Daily Life in Boise Basin Mining Camps," *Idaho Yesterdays* 38, 4 (winter 1995): 27.

23. Kenneth Owens, "Pierce City Incident, 1885–1886," *Idaho Yesterdays* 3, 3 (fall 1959): 11.

24. Lister and Lister, "Chinese Sojourners," 51.

25. Barsness, *Gold Camp*, 238.

26. John R. Wunder, "Law and the Chinese in Frontier Montana," *Montana: The Magazine of Western History* 30, 3 (summer 1990); 23.

27. Isaac H. Bromley, *The Chinese Massacre at Rock Springs, Wyoming Territory* (Boston: Franklin Press, 1886), 3–5.

28. David H. Stratton, "The Snake River Massacre of Chinese Miners, 1887," in Duane A. Smith, ed., *A Taste of the West* (Boulder: Pruett Publishing Co., 1887), 119.

29. Wolle, *Montana Paydirt*, 72. A contemporary pointed out that Ah Chow, a cripple, had engaged in justifiable homicide. Ibid.

30. Writers' Program of the Work Projects Administration in the State of Montana, *Copper Camp: Stories of the World's Greatest Mining Town, Butte, Montana* (New York: Hastings House, 1943), 198.

31. W. Eugene Hollon, *Frontier Violence: Another Look* (New York: Oxford University Press, 1974), 91–92.

32. Richard E. Lingenfelter, *The Hardrock Miners: A History of the Mining Labor Movement in the American West, 1863–1893* (Berkeley: University of California Press, 1974), 119.

33. Quoted in Wunder, "Law and Chinese," 20.

34. Hollon, *Frontier Violence*, 91.

35. Lister and Lister, "Chinese Sojourners," 23.

36. Stacy A. Flaherty, "Boycott in Butte: Organized Labor and the Chinese Community, 1896–1897," *Montana: The Magazine of Western History* 37, 1 (winter 1987): 35–47.

37. Liping Zhu, "'A Chinaman's Chance,'" 44. The "chicken-oath" was also an accepted practice in the courts in Montana and Oregon. For Montana, see Barsness, *Gold*

Camp; 243. For Oregon, see Nancy K. Feichter, "The Chinese in the Inland Empire during the Nineteenth Century" (Master's thesis, State College of Washington, 1959), 51–52. For the question of oaths, see John R. Wunder, "Chinese in Trouble: Criminal Law and Race on the Trans-Mississippi West Frontier," *Western Historical Quarterly* 17, 1 (January 1986): 25–41. Chinese, classified with American Indians as "Mongolians," had been denied the right to testify against whites since the case of *People v. Hall* in California in 1854.

38. Barsness, *Gold Camp*, 240.

39. "'A Chinaman's Chance,'" 47.

40. Loren B. Chan, "The Chinese in Nevada: An Historical Survey, 1856–1970," *Nevada Historical Society Quarterly* 25, 4 (winter 1982): 280.

41. Wolle, *Montana Paydirt*, 224.

42. Joe Sulentic, *Deadwood Gulch: The Last Chinatown* (Deadwood, S.D.: Deadwood Gulch Art Gallery, 1975), 65.

43. Quoted in Feichter, "Chinese in the Inland Empire," 7.

44. Hollon, *Frontier Violence*, 87.

45. David Liestman, "Utah's Chinatowns: The Development and Decline of Extinct Ethnic Enclaves," *Utah Historical Quarterly* 64, 1 (winter 1996): 76.

46. Gary P. Tipton, "Men Out of China: Origins of the Chinese Colony in Phoenix," *Journal of Arizona History* 18, 3 (autumn 1977): 349–50; Liestman, "Utah's Chinatown," 85–86; Writer's Program, *Copper Camp*, 119.

47. Quoted in Writer's Program, *Copper Camp*, 115.

48. Ibid., 116. For festivities occasioned by the arrival of another Chinese bride, this time in Deadwood, South Dakota, see Estelline Bennett, *Old Deadwood Days* (New York: Charles Scribner's Sons, 1935), 29.

49. Betty Derig, "The Chinese of Silver City," *Idaho Yesterdays* 2, 4 (winter 1958–59): 3–4.

50. Liestman, "Utah's Chinatowns," 77.

51. Writer's Programs, *Copper Camp*, 116.

52. Quoted in ibid., 112.

53. Quoted in Sulentic, *Deadwood Gulch*, 59.

54. Don C. Conley, "The Pioneer Chinese of Utah," in Helen Z. Papanikolas, ed., *The Peoples of Utah* (Salt Lake City: Utah State Historical Society, 1976), 255–56. See also the story of Butt Cut in Elsensohn, *Idaho Chinese Lore*, 63–65. The children did not return the favor, as they, too, were "famous for harassing Chinese."

55. Quoted in Writer's Program, *Copper Camp*, 115.

56. Sulentic, *Deadwood Gulch*, 10. Big Ears Jack was a Chinese restaurant owner who was famous for his physical prowess, the big portions he served, and stuffing the coins he collected in his ears. See p. 45.

57. Lawrence Michael Fong, "Sojourners and Settlers: The Chinese Experience in Arizona," *Journal of Arizona History* 21, 3 (autumn 1980): 230, 251.

58. Ibid., 238.

59. In addition to the selections below, Rose Hum Lee provides a detailed account of the dynamics of Chinatowns in her pioneering *The Growth and Decline of Chinese Communities in the Rocky Mountain Region* (New York: Arno Press, 1978).

60. Leigh D. Johnsen, "Equal Rights and the 'Heathen Chinee': Black Activism in San Francisco, 1865–1875," *Western Historical Quarterly* 11, 1 (January 1980): 57–68; Evelyn Hu-DeHart, "Immigrants to a Developing Society: The Chinese in Northern Mexico, 1875–1932," *Journal of Arizona History* 21, 3 (autumn 1980): 275–312; Leo M.

Dambourges Jacques, "The Chinese Massacre in Torreon (Coahuila) in 1911," *Arizona and the West* 16, 3 (autumn 1974): 233–46. The Mexican experience was an element in the Chinese cooperation with the armies of General Pershing against Pancho Villa, which earned them citizenship in Texas. See Edward Eugene Briscoe, "Pershing's Chinese Refugees in Texas," *Southwestern Historical Quarterly* 4 (April 1959): 467–88.

61. Stratton, "Snake River Massacre," 113.

62. Russell M. Magnaghi, "Virginia City's Chinese Community, 1860—1880," *Nevada Historical Society Quarterly* 24, 2 (summer 1981): 134. A similar conflict over wood-retailing brought Chinese into conflict with French Canadians in Montana, which led to a "battle that raged for weeks." Writer's project, *Copper Camp*, 109.

63. Feichter, "Chinese in the Inland Empire," 113.

64. Sulentic, *Deadwood Gulch*, 40. I am unable to explain the quotation marks around Chinese. There seems to be little question that she was Chinese. Sulentic relates that "just before Two Sticks was to be hung for the murder of four white men in 1893–94, the story says, he told his wife: 'I'm going to die and go to heaven.' She replied: 'You go to heaven, I'll go to China.'"

65. Conley, "Pioneer Chinese," 271–73.

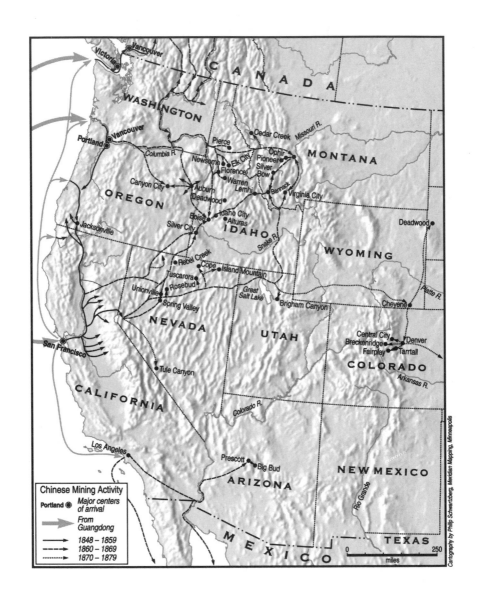

Chinese Mining Activity

Portland ● Major centers of arrival

From Guangdong

1848 – 1859
1860 – 1869
1870 – 1879

CANADA

Victoria
Vancouver
WASHINGTON
Portland Vancouver
Columbia R.
Pierce
Cedar Creek
Missouri R.
Ophir
Pioneer
Silver
Bow
MONTANA
Newsome
Elk City
Florence
Warren
Canyon City
Auburn
Deadwood
Lemhi
Bannack
Virginia City
OREGON
Boise
Idaho City
Alturas
Jacksonville
Silver City
IDAHO
Snake R.
Deadwood
WYOMING
Rebel Creek
Cope Island Mountain
Tuscarora
Unionville
Rosebud
Great
Salt Lake
Brigham Canyon
Platte R.
Cheyenne
Spring Valley
NEVADA
UTAH
Central City
Breckenridge
Fairplay
Denver
Tarrtall
San Francisco
Tule Canyon
COLORADO
Arkansas R.
CALIFORNIA
Colorado R.
Los Angeles
Prescott
Big Bud
ARIZONA
NEW MEXICO
Rio Grande
MEXICO
TEXAS

0   250
miles

Cartography by Philip Schwartzberg, Meridian Mapping, Minneapolis

Part I

Chinese on the Eastern Frontier

1

After the Gold Rush: Chinese Mining in the Far West, 1850–1890

Randall E. Rohe

The best available statistics suggest that the major gold rushes in the American West attracted from 10,000 to 100,000 persons per year. Each gold rush clearly reflected its importance, world or regional, in the origin of its participants, and while the foreign element formed a noticeable portion of some gold rushes, Americans invariably comprised the primary component of any goldfield population. But American dominance of the goldfields often ended or considerably lessened with the end of the flush production period, usually the placer period.

With the exhaustion of the rich surface placers, came an increasing necessity for the employment of capital on a large scale and corporate methods to work the deep diggings. As a result, hired labor became the rule in most types of mining and many of the original miners turned to other occupations or moved to new mining regions. Almost ritually, in area after area, men of foreign birth replaced the original miners. In the placer areas, it was the Chinese who usually supplanted the original miners. A government report in 1871 noted:

> Very few Chinese engaged in lode mining. The Chinese almost completely restricted themselves to placer mining, especially working areas abandoned by whites and reworking tailings. In some quartz mines and stamp mills, however, the Chinese did supply the labor for "certain inferior purposes such as dumping cars, surface excavation, etc."[1]

As yields declined, almost every placer region of note received its complement of Chinese, and they became, in fact, a ubiquitous feature of the mining West.[2]

The omnipresence of the Chinese on the mining frontier is well known, but their role in mining, except in California, is sparsely and inadequately understood. The dynamics and direction of the Chinese movement through the mining regions of the West need examination as well. Most existing studies fail to examine the factors that influenced the magnitude and timing of their migrations, and no work attempts to depict cartographically Chinese activities on the mining frontier. More than one writer has equated the Chinese arrival with a mining district's decline, describing them as a useful index of worn-out mines and low-level technology or as harbingers of decline. But this commonly held view may be in error. Chinese migration may have corresponded to a technological change, as mining moved from an individual, labor-intensive operation to a corporate, capital-intensive one. The generalization that the Chinese movement into mining occurred immediately after the flush production period seems based largely on the pattern of California and the Northwest. Does the history of the Chinese experience in the remainder of the West lend further support to this generalization?

The vast majority of works on the Chinese stress prejudice and discrimination, perhaps to the point of overstatement. Of all the minority groups that participated in the mining frontier the Chinese certainly received the harshest and most inequitable treatment, but studies emphasizing racial discrimination may overlook the importance of Chinese actions on the frontier. Economic competition is the commonly given reason for the harassment felt by the Chinese. But did the Chinese compete with white miners or complement them? Moreover, what in fact did most Chinese do on the western mining frontier?

CALIFORNIA BEGINNINGS

Before the California goldrush, Chinese immigration to the United States was almost negligible, but soon, like others attracted to the goldfields, the Chinese came in numbers. On February 1, 1849, fifty-four Chinese resided in California: by January 1, 1850, the number had reached 791; and by the end of 1850 it had passed 4,000. After 1850–1851, Chinese immigration increased dramatically. Internal turmoil and economic instability in China provided, the "push," gold in California, the "pull." In 1851, 2,400 to 2,700 Chinese arrived and a year later, the peak period of Chinese immigration, between 18,000 and 20,000 Chinese reached California. The immigration of 1852 brought the number of Chinese in California to about 25,000, a nearly four-fold increase in population in one year.[3]

The bulk of the Chinese emigration to California depended on a credit-ticket system, which paid their passage in turn for a stated term of labor. Six Chinese companies or district associations, headquartered in San Francisco with branch offices in Sacramento and Stockton, administered this system in accordance with Chinese laws. Up to 1854, the majority of Chinese came from about fifteen of seventy-two districts in Kwangtung Province in southern China. Eventually, twenty-one districts in Kwangtung Province supplied 99 per cent of all the Chinese immigrants to the United States. With minor exceptions, Hongkong served as point of departure.[4]

The long crossing lasted forty-five to sixty days, sometimes longer. Under

cramped conditions, meager provisions, primitive sanitary facilities, and poor ven-
tilation, it is surprising how many survived the Pacific crossing. Chinese immigrants landed in San Francisco and often remained but a few days there before
boarding steamers that transported them to Sacramento, Stockton, Marysville,
and other points on the Sacramento and San Joaquin rivers. In these towns,
agents of the Six Companies directed the indentured immigrants to points
throughout the mining region. This pattern of Chinese migration was the result
of several factors: fluctuations in the economy, how long the migrants might stay,
and the changing population level as new arrivals came to the United States. All
of this was within the framework of the Six Companies.[5]

Only a few Chinese reached the gold region immediately following Marshall's
discovery. In 1850, Chinese constituted only about 500 out of 57,787 miners in
California.[6] As Chinese immigration increased, however, the number of Chinese
in the goldfields rose significantly. Beginning in 1851, contemporary writers, like
the following, mentioned the increasing presence of Chinese in the goldfields:

> Followed up the Yuba at the foot of the mountains about three miles to Missouri Bar,
> Found a great many Chinese rocking with cradles, making from three to eight dol-
> lars a day.[7]

The large immigrations of 1852–1854 coincided with a mass entry into mining.
As the *San Francisco Herald* reported in 1852:

> The Chinese hive has swarmed here [Middle Fork of Yuba] as elsewhere this Spring
> [1852] — at least 5000, off and on have visited the locality.[8]

> Among the rush of miners into our country [Shasta] . . . we observed our Oriental
> friend "John" frequently multiplied.[9]

Within two years of their heaviest immigration, the Chinese had penetrated to
practically every mining district in California. In fact, the Chinese already dominated some districts, and as early as 1855 contemporary newspapers placed the
number of Chinese miners in California at 20,000.[10]

The Chinese generally set up camps near their claims along the streams they
worked, with small tents and primitive brush structures serving as houses. In 1850
there were few large settlements of Chinese, but later groups of one hundred or
more Chinese miners banded together in short-lived villages throughout the mining region. Some established their own settlements, while others occupied camps
deserted by white miners. In 1852, almost one-third of the Chinese lived in large
camps and only a few hundred resided in localities with large foreign, non-Chinese populations; the Chinese tended to band together.[11]

Some California towns restricted Chinese residents to specific districts or sections
of their municipalities; other towns achieved the same result by *de facto* custom.

Wherever the Chinese resided, however, the tight, almost self-segregated, nature of their settlements was dominant, providing the Chinese a measure of protection and the ability to retain their culture and social institutions. Characteristic of the larger Chinese settlements was the presence of a joss house or temple. In California, the towns of Weaverville, Shasta, Yuba, Placerville, Coloma, Grass Valley, and many others contained "Chinatown" sections. One of the largest Chinese mining settlements, Chinese Camp, had a population of 2,000 and was located near Sonora.[12]

By the end of the 1850s, Chinese represented perhaps a quarter of the state's miners. During this period, Chinese turned almost exclusively to mining as an occupation. In February 1859, for example, the *Sacramento Daily Union* reported that 75 per cent of the Chinese population of California were employed in mining. Census enumerators in 1860 found that 24,282 Chinese out of a total Chinese population of 34,935 worked as miners, and two years later some 30,000 of the 48,391. Chinese in the state worked as miners. A year later, probably the peak of Chinese mining, 80 to 85 per cent of the Chinese population engaged in mining.[13]

Within a few years, however, many Chinese left mining regions. The burden of the Foreign Miners' Tax, coupled with numerous outrages perpetrated upon them, drove the Chinese from the California mines. In 1867, only 35 per cent to 50 per cent of the more than 50,000 Chinese in California engaged in mining.[14] Yet, as mining declined as an occupation among Chinese, they still had a significant presence in California's goldfields because the number of white miners declined even faster. An exodus of white miners to the Northwest goldfields in the 1860s left the Chinese as the largest single ethnic or national group of miners. By 1870, Chinese accounted for over half of the total mining population and according to one report, they accounted for three-fifths of the miners in 1873.[15]

Over the course of the 1870s, however, the total number of Chinese miners continued to decrease. They either followed the mining frontier or found other employment in towns. By 1876, less than 12,500 Chinese miners remained and the decline persisted, leaving only 10,024 in 1880. Yet, mining ranked second only to common laboring as the major occupation of the Chinese, well above most other occupational categories. In 1884, the number of Chinese miners rose to 15,000, but the figure represented only approximately 15 per cent of the Chinese population. Five years later, Chinese miners constituted less than a third of the mining population, and after the turn of the century, their proportion dropped to only about 15 per cent.[16]

As a general rule, the Chinese worked for themselves or Chinese companies, although there is documentation of white and Chinese miners working side-by-side and even co-operating in joint ventures. Especially during the early years, most Chinese worked as independent miners and were never a significant portion of the labor employed by white companies. Over the years, however, whites employed more and more Chinese so that by the late 1880s whites had nearly one-third of California's Chinese miners in their employ. Whites paid Chinese $1.00 to $1.25 a day in the 1860s, increasing it to $1.75 to $2.00 by the 1870s.[17]

For their own protection, Chinese miners often worked together in groups of a dozen or more. Their equipment, in the 1860s, consisted of little more than shovels, picks, pans and cradles. Diarist Alpheus Richardson described what were probably a typical California Chinese miners in 1852 near Bidwell Bar, California:

> This morning as we was [*sic*] about to start several Chinamen passed along the road with their mining tools such as cradles, picks, pans and shovels, all tied to the middle of a pole and a man at each end of the pole. This is the way—two and two with their implements and with broad brimmed hats, short breeches, wooden shoes, pipe in the mouth, and long hair plaited and laying down on their backs—quite a show for a green Californian.[18]

Chinese miners continued to use the cradle or rocker long after their white counterparts had abandoned it. Its long employment by the Chinese was probably because of its cheapness and portability. For the Chinese, mobility was important, especially when hostility from whites forced them to move quickly from one mining district to another. The long use of the rocker also seems to have forestalled the Chinese from using larger, more sophisticated equipment. A description in 1850 of Chinese miners building river dams for mining purposes demonstrates their involvement in relatively large-scale operations early on, but most Chinese miners did not improve beyond the use of the ricker until after whites had departed and Chinese formed mining companies of their own.[19]

The Chinese mining companies of the early 1860s typically consisted of fewer than five workers and were co-operative ventures for river mining. This type of mining involved building dams, ditches and flumes to divert streams from their natural beds, enabling miners to work the streambeds. Chinese miners normally constructed wing dams in these operations. On the American River, where river mining began in California, the Chinese dominated river mining activity by 1850, and within four years they had inherited the greater part of the river claims in the entire state.[20] As a government reported commented in 1875:

> The river-bars, once noted for their great yield are now nearly exhausted. Having ceased to pay the demands of white labor, this class of mining has been abandoned to the patient and plodding Chinese, who are still engaged on the banks and bars of the Yuba in washing ground which has been worked three or four times by white labor. Their system of operation is to turn rivers from their beds by means of long flumes and run the dirt through boxes.[21]

The main exception to the Chinese monopoly in river mining was in the "Northwest Mines" where whites were still a significant force in this form of mining through the 1880s. But here as well, the Chinese acquired more and more of a monopoly so that by 1890 the State Mineralogist reported that Chinese held numerous river claims and several thousand of them were using wing dams. The old wing dams on the Feather, Yuba and American rivers were gone by 1890, the mineralogist wrote, "except where small companies of Chinese are at work."[22]

The typical Chinese river mining operations in the late 1880s and 1890s consisted of a company of four to ten men using derricks, dams, pumps, and ditches along with traditional placer tools. Yuba River operations were described by census enumerators in 1890 as a small but profitable enterprise:

> there were about 100 Chinese employed in river mining on the North Yuba river, which flows by the town of Downieville, scattered, in about a dozen companies, 10 miles each way from the town. The average time worked each year is 120 days, in 1889 probably 150, and the aggregate product between $35,00 and $45,000 annually. about half of this is sold at the bank of Messrs. Scammon & Co., at Downieville; the other half to a Chinese buyer in the same town or taken direct to San Francisco. The aggregates amount of capital invested by the Chinese in their operations is not more than $25,000. The plant consists of temporary dams in the river, one or more water wheels, and Chinese rotary pumps, derricks, ditches and sluices to each claim.[23]

Although the river mining activities of the Chinese attracted considerable attention, most Chinese companies during the 1865 to 1880 period worked in hydraulic mining, with a few working drift mines. Chinese often avoided drift mining except when employed by whites, as in 1884 when nearly 200 worked for whites in this form of mining near Oroville on the Feather River. A court decision that outlawed dumping mine tailings into streams halted much hydraulic mining, but a leading engineering publication claimed that this did not stop the Chinese.[24]

> [M]ost of these mines are operated, under leases obtained by the Chinese, who, through recourse to their peculiar methods, manage to escape arrest, or, if arrested, manage, by these same methods, to keep their leased claims, and also those they purchase, running all the same.[25]

Some Chinese worked for whites in hydraulic operations such as in Siskiyou County, California, in the early 1890s where half of the miners were Chinese. Whites sometimes employed Chinese in hauling away large boulders. The Chinese moved these large rocks with slings attached to poles and then neatly stacked them in piles near mining sites; many of these stacks remain today as physical reminders of Chinese involvement in California hydraulic mining.[26]

NORTH TO OREGON

From California, many Chinese followed the advance of the mining frontier into the Northwest, where they duplicated patterns established in the Golden State.

As production declined and original miners moved on, the claims passed to the Chinese. From mining region to mining region, singly or in groups, the Chinese usually travelled by foot, occasionally by mule or horseback, and sometimes by stage. It was in the Northwest that the Chinese established a base for their further movement into the Rocky Mountains.[27]

Control remained in the hands of the "Six Companies." Commercial agents or storekeepers in constant contact with the headquarters of their district companies directed the movement. Perhaps as early as 1852, the Chinese reached the gold-fields of southwestern Oregon. Apparently, the number of Chinese remained small until 1856,[28] but in the next year, the *Oregonian* alleged that:

> The Chinamen are about to take the country. There are from one thousand to twelve hundred in this country [Josephine] engaged in mining. They are buying out the American miners, paying big prices for their claims.[29]

In the summer of 1859, the *Sacramento Daily Union* reported the dominance of Chinese in some Oregon mining areas, but the census of 1860 gave Oregon a total of only 425 Chinese, although 370 of them did work as miners.[30] Through the 1860s, the number of Chinese in the goldfields of southwestern Oregon continued to increase. "Many of the mining districts in this county [Jackson]," the *Oregon Sentinel* reported, "are fast being filled up with Chinamen. There are at least 100 on Jackass Creek, 175 on Applegate, 60 on Sardine Creek, 30 on Kiota Creek and 15 or 20 on the bars of Rogue River."[31] Another writer described what seemed to be a great increase of Chinese in the Rogue River Valley.

> We observed in squads, the ubiquitous Chinamen, moving from mining locality to mining locality, fleeing from the kicks of one to the cuffs of the other, with no fixed abiding place to be called his permanent home.[32]

As early as 1864, and probably earlier, the Chinese dominated some districts.[33] "Chinese are working over many old digging," the *Daily Oregonian* noted in 1868, "and along the bars of Rogue river these people may be seen in numerous places employing their patient industry in washing out the gold which white labor has neglected as too small pay."[34] Rossiter Raymond, who compiled a government report on western mining districts, noted in 1869 that Chinese mainly worked the once very productive mines of southwestern Oregon, and the decennial census in the following year indicated that southwestern Oregon accounted for over a quarter of the Chinese in the state.[35] The dominance of the Chinese in the mines of southwestern Oregon continued in the 1870s and 1880s, as Raymond reported:

> The western districts, once the scene of a busy placer mining industry, have relapsed into comparative idleness, though the ancient diggings are still reworked here and there by Chinese.[36]

From California and Oregon, the Chinese followed the advance of mining into British Columbia in 1858 when news of gold on the Fraser River filtered southward. By July of 1859, the goldfields of the Fraser contained some 400 to 800 Chinese, and during 1860 an estimated 4,000 Chinese engaged in mining. A correspondent reported that "small Chinese mining-camps dot the banks and bars" of the Fraser.[37] Meanwhile, the Chinese spread to other districts. In 1861, Chinese represented 75 per cent of the miners in the Similkameen area of south central British Columbia and a year later the Caribo contained over 5,000 Chinese. There were reports that the Chinese almost exclusively controlled the Hope and Yale areas by 1865.[38] A year later, a correspondent of the *Colonist* reported the Kootenay almost abandoned by whites and the coming of the Chinese. A sizeable migration of Chinese had reached the Kootenay during the year and by fall the Chinese outnumbered the whites two or three to one in some areas.

The season of 1867 saw hardly any whites mining on the Kootenays and by 1868, as a government report stated, "The Big Bend country and Kootenay have been quite deserted, and we hear of only a few Chinamen and prospectors being in these districts."[39] Although British Columbia's Chinese population had declined to less than 2,000 by 1870, throughout the 1880s and 1890s small numbers of Chinese continued mining in British Columbia.[40] As late as 1890, in fact, Chinese accounted for 90 percent of the gold recovered on the Fraser River for the year. Many of the Chinese who left the mines of British Columbia spread to newly opened goldfields in the United States, eventually reaching the mining areas of Washington, northeastern Oregon, Montana and particularly Idaho.[41]

TO IDAHO'S OWYHEE DISTRICT

The Chinese advancement into Idaho began in 1864. That year newspapers noted the presence of Chinese along the Snake River and the South Fork of the Clearwater. At first, the Chinese encountered hostile resistance, but as each district declined more and more claims transferred from white to Chinese ownership. Oro Fino was the first. After considerable opposition, the claim holders at Oro Fino favorable to Chinese labor gained the ascendancy and finally in September 1864, the miners of the Oro Fino District adopted a resolution to invite the Chinese into the camp.[42] The *Walla Walla Statesman* immediately perceived the significance:

> Heretofore the miners have very generally prohibited Chinamen from working the mines of the upper country, by their local district laws, but it is apparent that those laws will not exclude them much longer.
>
> As the mining camps become less productive and laborers follow up the richest diggings, it may be safely assumed that other mining localities will shortly follow the example of Oro Fino in the motion of introducing Chinese labor. . . . it will not be long before that whole upper country will be overrun with them.[43]

The prophecy proved true. Within the next few years, the Chinese appeared in almost every mining district of northern Idaho. In early 1865, one newspaper reported that the estimate of the Chinese agents of the movement of Chinese into the "upper country" during the coming season ranged from 2,000 to 5,000. Two years later, several newspapers commented on the great number of Chinese in some of the northern districts.[44]

The movement of Chinese did not stop at the northern mines. In the middle sixties, the Chinese extended southward into the mining districts of central Idaho, reaching the Owyhee District in the spring of 1865.[45] As early as May of that year, the *Idaho World* noted that:

Our camp [Silver Creek] is likely to be taken, subdued and occupied by the celestial. A large gang lately arrived here, and hundreds more are on their way . . .[46]

The comments of this contemporary proved remarkably correct. Almost within a year, the omnipresence of the Chinese in the Owyhee District led the *Owyhee Avalanche* to comment that "Almost every abandoned claim or gulch in which the color of gold can be found has its gang of Chinamen at work.:[47] In 1867, the *Walla Walla Statesman* expected over 500 Chinese to work just Jordan Creek.[48]

Almost simultaneously with Chinese activities in the Owyhee District came their advance into the Boise Basin. The first Chinese miners in the Boise Basin, only fifty or sixty, arrived in 1865.[49] The *Idaho World*, on November 11, 1865, reported large numbers of Chinese crowding into the Basin, and a week later the newspaper predicted the intended introduction of thousands of Chinese into Idaho the next spring. They would, according to the *World*, "buy up all the old, good-for-nothing claims in the country."[50] It was another prediction time proved correct; two years later the *Idaho World* announced the probable presence of fully 5,000 Chinese in the Basin in the ensuing mining season.[51] The real figure probably was closer to 2,000, but by 1868 the Chinese accounted for fully one-third of the mining population in the vicinity of Idaho City.[52] The next year the Chinese population of Boise County reached 3,000, compared to a white population of about 7,000, and Idaho City contained "about as many Chinese as whites."[53] The Chinese, by 1870, held the greater portions of the creek and gulch claims of the Boise Basin. The same year saw the introduction of Chinese labor into the Warren District, which attracted some 1,200 Chinese in the space of only two years. These Chinese, according to a government report, "monopolized the gravel workings, going over the mining grounds as second and a third time."[54]

The discoveries of 1863–1864 in the Kootenay of British Columbia and in Montana, coupled with declining production, drew many miners away from the northern Idaho districts. Mining district laws against Chinese miners, which had been poorly enforced anyhow, became more relaxed, and finally, on January 11, 1866, the Idaho territorial legislature passed an act allowing the Chinese to mine on payment of a license fee of five dollars per month.[55] These conditions accelerated the movement of Chinese into Idaho in the latter 1860s.[56]

The census of 1870 disclosed that the Chinese represented almost a third of the people in Idaho and, even more revealing, the census showed that the Chinese constituted almost 60 percent of the miners.[57] Rossiter Raymond, in his mining report of 1872, estimated that "Probably two-thirds of all the claims now worked are in the hands of the Chinese."[58] His report for the following year graphically reiterated the dominance of the Chinese in the goldfields of Idaho:

> [F]or every well paying claim worked by white men, we find at present probably not less than five or six which return profit only to Chinamen, and a few camps are almost exclusively worked and owned by them.[59]

The census of 1880 showed a decrease in the number of Chinese, although they continued to engage chiefly in mining and to dominate many placer areas.[60] The exodus of Chinese from Idaho continued through the 1880s; the census of 1890 disclosed that 2,007 Chinese remained, with perhaps 40 per cent of them working as miners.[61]

Mining areas in northeastern Oregon's Blue Mountains, opened in 1861–1864, represented a contemporaneous extension of Idaho mining activity. As the placer yield declined in northeastern Oregon in the later 1860s, the Chinese became prominent, expanding successively into the John Day, Powder River and Burnt River Districts in 1866, 1867, and 1868. By the end of the decade, they predominated, sometimes to the extreme, in many of the mining districts of the Blue Mountains.[62] In 1868, for instance, the North Fork of the John Day contained some 200 Chinese, "they having bought up nearly all the old river claims."[63] Rossiter Raymond, in his report for 1870, evaluated their importance in these districts:

> Meager returns from Canon City and neighboring districts indicate a somewhat increased production . . . mainly by reason of the influx of Chinese, who succeed . . . by their superior patience and economy [to] continue the production of gold in many localities where it would otherwise cease.[64]

Chinese miners, over the next two decades, continued to increase in the mining districts of northeastern Oregon, but by the 1890s the attraction of mining for the Chinese declined. Many left the mines and northeastern Oregon or turned to other occupations.[65]

Almost immediately following the Chinese advancement into Idaho and adjacent Oregon, came their expansion into Montana. As early as 1866, the *Walla Walla Statesman* reported the arrival of Chinese near Virginia City for the purpose of mining. A year later they had extended their field of operation to Helena.[66] James W. Taylor, in a government report describing the conditions of mining in Montana for 1867, noted:

The bulk of the auriferous treasure is now exhausted . . . the placers once worked over, are said to be exhausted . . . the diggings now fall into the hands of the Chinese, who patiently glean the fields abandoned by the whites.[67]

The latter 1860s brought increasing mention of Chinese entrance into mining. Of the approximately 800 Chinese in Montana in 1868, about 60 per cent of them worked as miners. A contemporary estimate set the Chinese population for 1869 at between 2,000 and 3,000, although the census of 1870 reported slightly less than 2,000 Chinese in the territory. As in other states and territories, mining employed the overwhelming majority of Chinese. The census listed over 70 per cent of Montana's Chinese as miners, even though they accounted for only slightly more than 20 per cent of all miners.[68]

Newspapers and the Mining Commissioner's Reports of the 1870s noted the presence of Chinese in many of the placer areas.[69] Despite their widespread presence, however, the total Chinese population apparently remained small. The census of 1880 recorded less than 2,000 Chinese in Montana.[70] During the 1880s the Chinese continued to increase and spread throughout the territory, with the result that by 1885 almost every placer district in the major mining counties contained some Chinese, notably Deer Lodge, Lewis and Clark, Jefferson, Choteau, Meagher, Beaverhead, Madison, and Gallatin counties. Although the census in 1890 gave the number of Chinese in Montana as 2,532, perhaps only a little more than 10 per cent of them worked as miners.[71]

Of the northwestern states, Washington attracted the fewest Chinese. The meager placers of the state offered only limited opportunities for mining, but Chinese miners worked throughout central Washington, in the mining districts of the Wenatchee Mountains, and along the Yakima, Wenatchee and Columbia rivers. The upper Columbia probably attracted the first significant movement of Chinese into Washington. In 1862, an influx of Chinese from British Columbia came into the Fort Colville mines and along the Columbia and Pend Oreille rivers. After the initial penetration to the Columbia Basin from British Columbia, the great movement of Chinese was from California. Within a year, the Upper Columbia already contained a fair number of Chinese and after two years hundreds of Chinese worked the Columbia above Rock Island. The *Walla Walla Statesman* reported in 1867 that only the Chinese, some three or four hundred in all, still mined along the Columbia and Pend Oreille rivers near Colville. That same year the *North Idaho Radiator* reported Chinese mining along the Snake River in Washington.[72]

Less than 20 per cent of Washington's 234 Chinese were miners, according to the census in 1870, but they represented over 25 per cent of all miners. Fewer than 100 of these Chinese were in the Columbia region of eastern Washington; one author, however, his estimated that the Chinese population here approached 1,500.[73] During the 1870s Chinese continued their mining operations at various points on the Columbia and Snake rivers, and one source claimed that in 1880 the Kettle River and the upper stretches of the Columbia alone contained more than 1,000 Chinese, a sizable proportion of Washington's 2,186 Chinese.[74] A Corps of Engineers report in 1881 mentions Chinese miners all along the Columbia as far as Rock Island. The upper portions of the river especially contained large numbers of Chinese, sometimes engaged in rather substantial mining operations, as a government report noted:

> There are quite a number of Chinamen engaged in mining on the river bars. . . . In some instances the Chinamen have put in flumes several miles in length and constructed quite extensive works to obtain the precious mental.[75]

Through the middle 1880s, the Columbia region continued to attract some Chinese, but few of them continued mining in Washington by the end of the decade. The census for that year recorded 3,260 Chinese, but probably less than 7 per cent of these worked as miners.[76]

COLORADO AND THE SOUTHWEST

Unlike the other major placer areas of the West, those of Colorado did not receive an influx of Chinese immediately following its flush production period. Even when the Chinese did arrive, their numbers remained relatively insignificant. Probably the quite limited extent of its placers, compared to those of California, Idaho, and Montana, primarily accounted for the restricted Chinese migration to Colorado.

Apparently, the first Chinese arrived in Colorado in 1869 after completion of the transcontinental railroad. The census of 1870 did not list any Chinese as engaged in mining in Colorado, although some Chinese probably first mined in Gilpin County sometime prior to 1873. In 1873, additional Chinese arrived in Gilpin County and worked as miners on Clear Creek below Central City.[77] The *Mining Review* reported:

> The Cameron diggings below Black Hawk have been leased to a party of Chinamen for the winter. It is also reported that some owners of ground further down the creek propose importing Chinese labor in the spring to reopen their long forsaken patches.[78]

In 1878, between 100 and 200 Chinese worked the placers of Gilpin County.[79] The following year a contemporary writer described the Chinese activities along North Clear Creek. "As the ground becomes too 'lean' for the average miner the Chinamen steps in and makes from one to three dollars per day. We can see large gangs of the Celestials at work, and have an opportunity of studying gulch mining practically."[80] The census for 1880 gave Gilpin County only 124 Chinese, 91 per cent of them employed as miners.[81] Despite their limited numbers, the Chinese made their presence felt:

> The placer mines of Gilpin County are gradually passing into the hands of the Chinese. Russell, Leavenworth, Illinois, and Lake Gulches are almost entirely controlled by them at this time and some of them are branching out to the old abandoned gulches to the west and northwest of Central. This class of miners has produced the bulk of placer gold for the year.[82]

The Chinese population in Gilpin County dropped to 82 in 1885 and five years later only 49 resided in the county.[83]

The only other Colorado mining areas to attract significant numbers of Chinese were in South Park. Fairplay first attracted a contingent of Chinese in 1874 and 1875, and in the spring of 1876 the *Mining Review* reported that the Fairplay Mining Company planned to hire 200 to 400 Chinese that year. Within a few months a reported 160 Chinese miners were working at Fairplay.[84] The Fairplay Gold Mining Company leased ground to the Chinese at a royalty of 25 per cent of their daily earnings. The company housed them and provided food and clothing at its store, where a Chinese clerk was employed to fill their orders.[85]

The nearby Tarryall placers contained two or three dozen Chinese by 1878; two years later abut 100 Chinese worked at Fairplay and 25 at Tarryall. As late as 1884 a contemporary observer remarked that the placers of Park County employed mostly Chinese. The Chinese population, however, continued to decline. The decennial census in 1890 registered only 62 Chinese in Park County, although a few Chinese continued to mine the Tarryall and Peabody placers until after the turn of the century.[86]

Besides the mining districts of Gilpin and Park counties, lesser numbers of Chinese engaged in mining near Idaho Springs, Breckenridge, Alamosa, Gunnison, Ouray, Silverton, Lake City, Rico, and Telluride.[87] Except in isolated cases, the Chinese never accounted for a significant proportion of Colorado's mining population.

Shortly after the Chinese achieved a notable, if somewhat limited, presence in Colorado their advance reached still farther eastward. In 1875 the Chinese arrived in the newly discovered goldfields of the Black Hills, although they did not engage in mining until 1878. A year later the *Engineering and Mining Journal* reported Chinese reworking several claims along lower Whitewood Gulch; in 1880 Chinese worked a dozen or so of the fifty claims in Deadwood and Whitewood Gulches. The Black Hills, however, attracted relatively few Chinese. Census reports in 1880 and 1890 gave Dakota Territory some 200 Chinese and only a few were miners.[88] The relatively limited placer deposits of the Black Hills, the declining appeal of mining as an occupation, and probably, too, the always present discrimination toward the Chinese explain the fewer Chinese miners in the Dakotas.

On a much smaller scale than the Chinese advance into the Northwest and the Rocky Mountains was their parallel movement into the Southwest.[89] The first contingent of Chinese to reach the Southwest arrived in 1856; that year Chinese laborers worked on a mining ditch at Gold Canyon near Dayton, Nevada. Recognizing the possibilities of mining, some fifty Chinese began working the claims abandoned (or thought unproductive) by whites. Although the Chinese formed the majority of miners working the Gold Canyon placers by 1850, their numbers remained small.[90]

The building of the Virginia and Truckee, and the Central Pacific railroads, however, brought many more Chinese to Nevada, and with the compliance of these railroads some of the unemployed Chinese turned to mining and spread throughout the northern half of the state. The Chinese population stood at 3,152 in 1870, with 240 of these working as miners, or only approximately 8 per cent of the Chinese population and 3 per cent of all miners. Ten years later Nevada's Chinese population reached its peak at 5,416,[91] although probably less than 10 per cent worked as miners and they accounted for less than 10 per cent of all miners. Despite the small percentage of Chinese miners, the Chinese did dominate some districts, such as the Spring Valley (or Paradise) District where the Director of the Mint reported that "seventy-five or eighty Chinamen were profitably working the old Placer mines"[92] in 1883. Between 1884 and 1895, an estimated 3,000 Chinese worked the Spring Valley District in north central Nevada. The Chinese population of Nevada had declined to less than 3,000 by 1890, of which perhaps 15 per cent found employment as miners. Their population decline continued during the 1890s and by the turn of the century only 1,352 Chinese remained in Nevada,[93] very few of whom were miners.

Several factors combined to retard and limit the Chinese advancement throughout much of the Southwest. The placers there generally proved to be widely scattered and not particularly rich. Scarcity of water also limited mining operations. The presence of potentially hostile Indians, at least initially, proved an important factor in parts of the Southwest. Anti-Chinese discrimination, likewise, played its usual role. But in many parts of the Southwest it was competition from Mexicans that proved to be the major factor.

In most of the Southwest, it appears that Mexicans served as counterparts to the Chinese. As with the Chinese in the rest of the West, Mexicans in the Southwest worked the less valuable deposits or those areas worked out and abandoned by white miners. New Mexico and Arizona especially attracted large numbers of Mexicans.[94] The placers along the Colorado River in Arizona provide a typical example of the Mexican role in mining in the Southwest. "For several years these Colorado placers," Hubert Howe Bancroft wrote in 1889, "attracted a crowd of Californians . . . but as a rule the dry washing processes were too tedious for the permanent occupation of only but Mexicans and Indians."[95]

During the 1860s, Mexicans gained control of more and more of the placer areas of the Southwest. The major placer districts of Arizona were described in 1871 as dominated by Mexican miners.[96] Little change took place in the next ten years and a description of placer mining in Arizona in 1881 still emphasized the omnipresence of Mexicans:

> Gold placers have also been found in many portions of the Territory, which after yielding large amounts . . . were abandoned. . . . . Considerable quantities of gold are, however, still obtained from them by individual enterprise of Mexicans.[97]

During the same period, the *Engineering and Mining Journal* reported of the major placer areas of New Mexico, "all the districts have been worked for some years, mostly by Mexicans."[98]

Despite stiff competition from Mexicans, the Chinese did participate in placer mining in both Arizona and New Mexico. The first Chinese perhaps reached Arizona in 1869.[99] Within a few months, the *Arizona Miner* reported an influx of Chinese miners near Prescott:

> The flight of ye Chinamen is Big Bugwards. Two, three and four cents to the plan were found by one of them recently. The finder sent word to his fellow countrymen in Prescott, who . . . resolved to start immediately . . .[100]

Apparently, the number of Chinese engaged in mining in Arizona and New Mexico until the 1890s was few. They probably reached their peak in the late 1890s and just after the turn of the century. Of the two states, the placers of Arizona received by far the greatest number of Chinese.[101]

CHINESE AND GOLD

Of all the ethnic groups represented in the placer areas of the West, perhaps none proved more ubiquitous and significant than the Chinese. They excelled in saving gold, especially fine gold, under difficult conditions. They complemented rather than competed with white miners; competition between whites and Chinese miners was generally in terms of hired labor and was probably more implied than real. Many times the movement of independent Chinese miners into a mining district was encouraged. As the rich, surface placers declined and the original miners moved on, the Chinese almost without fail replaced them, and this movement of Chinese brought about a new concentration of miners in areas abandoned by whites. In effect, the Chinese slowed population declines by settling recently abandoned mining areas, and maintained gold production in those same areas.

During their first decade in the West, most Chinese worked in the mines, about 75 per cent of them by the early 1860s. By the 1870s they had spread to almost every major placer area in the West, and the late 1860s and early 1870s, in fact, probably marked the peak of Chinese mining activity. In 1870 mining employed less than a third of the Chinese population, but the Chinese represented over 25 percent of all miners, and in some individual states the Chinese accounted for one-half to almost two-thirds of all miners. Over the next two decades the Chinese in increasing numbers turned away from mining, so that by 1890 they probably represented less than a tenth of all miners in the West. By the end of the century, the Chinese had for the most part abandoned mining; in fact, by this date, most had died, returned to China, moved east, or settled in the large cities of the West Coast.[102]

The amount of gold recovered by the Chinese will never be known, and the meager statistics available preclude even an educated guess. More than one government official lamented the impossibility of getting any details on Chinese mining operations or the amount of gold they produced. The Chinese were very secretive and seldom mined at only one location for an extended time. Most of the gold passed into the hands of Chinese merchants and a good part of it went on to China. A few scattered references, like the following, are all we have.

> [T]he reports from sixty four placer claims in Grant County [Oregon, 1870] eleven . . . worked by white men with paid labor, and the remainder by Chinese . . . show for the former a yield of $4 per day per hand, and for the latter only $1.30. There is no doubt that the Chinese have in this case concealed the actual amount of their production, reporting an aggregate of about $126,000, when the real amount must have been at least twice as great.[103]

Contrary to the prevailing opinion of the day, the Chinese did not send all of their gold to China and they were an important factor in the economic development of many areas.

> Colville [Washington] feels the loss of her Chinamen, they having been the principal consumers of her productions. They worked and took out . . . on the Columbia and Pend Oreille rivers, where white men would not work, and nearly every dollar they made was money put into circulation, and the benefit of which would never have been felt had it not been for them.[104]

The Chinese paid their share of taxes—miner's taxes, property taxes, poll taxes, and other assessments—and they received none of the services their tax money provided. They made significant purchases of mining equipment and mining claims.

Almost without exception, the Chinese appeared on each successive mining frontier. The Chinese role in mining, despite their omnipresence, remains largely unexamined. The majority of existing works have stressed the discrimination and prejudice felt by the Chinese almost to the point of distorting reality. Many of the generalizations on the Chinese require re-examination. The low level technology (rocker syndrome) attributed to the Chinese needs restatement; many examples of extensive Chinese mining operations exist. The influx of Chinese into a district did not necessarily correspond with a district's decline. Often it coincided with the exhaustion of the rich surface placers and the change to methods that enabled the working of lower-grade deposits and increased production.

Hopefully researchers will move away from the overworked theme of anti-Chinese discrimination and investigate other aspects of the Chinese experience on the western mining frontier. Details in the diffusion of Chinese miners throughout the West in the late nineteenth century, for example, need clarification, and little is known of Chinese mining activities in southwestern states and the less important placer areas of the West.

The distribution of Chinatown settlements in the mining West and their morphology, layout, location within mining towns, and more, needs examination. How distinctive was the cultural landscape of the Chinese and what were its characteristics? And there are numerous other questions that must be asked. Do Chinese place names suggest the location and intensity of Chinese mining activity in the West? Apparently, the Chinese purposely introduced and spread a particular plant species—"Trees of Heaven" (*Ailanthus altissima*)—in the West. Why did they plant these trees and does the present range of the trees have any relationship to the extent of Chinese mining activity in the West? Why did the Chinese avoid lode mining, or did they avoid it completely? And, finally, what role did the Chinese play in labor conflicts in the lode mining industry in the last two decades of the nineteenth century?

Chinese mining in the American West is not what we have previously thought it to be. But because we do not know enough about it, generalizations are hazardous. There is no question however, that much remains to be discovered. As perhaps the most important of ethnic groups involved in western gold mining, the Chinese deserve a full re-examination.

NOTES

1. Rossiter W. Raymond, "Statistics of Mines and Mining in the States and Territories West of the Rocky Mountains." 42d Cong. 1st Sess., *House Ex. Doc. no. 10*, serial 1470 (Washington: GPO, 1871), p. 4.

2. The majority of works on the Chinese in the West focus on racial discrimination. Of the major exceptions, the best are David V. DuFault, "The Chinese in the Mining Camps of California: 1848–1870," *Historical Society of Southern California Quarterly*, 41 [June, 1959], pp. 155–170; and Ping Chiu. *Chinese Labor in California 1850–1880* (Madison: State Historical Society of Wisconsin, 1963). Of lesser value are: Pauline Minke, *Chinese in the Mother Lode 1850–1870* (San Francisco: R & E Research Associates, 1974) and Stephen Williams. "The Chinese in the California Mines, 1848–1880" (unpublished M.A. thesis, Stanford University, 1930). On the mining frontier, the Chinese constituted by far the most notable and significant minority group. Compared to the Chinese, blacks only infrequently appeared in notable numbers. Blacks, however, did participate in mining from

California to the Black Hills. See for instance, Rudolph M. Lapp, *Blacks in Gold Rush California* (New Haven: Yale University Press, 1977). The Mexicans, especially in California, formed a notable part of the mining population and like the Chinese felt discrimination. See William Robert Kenny, "Mexican-American Conflict on the Mining Frontier 1848–1852," *Journal of the West*, 6 (October 1967), pp. 582–592 and "Nativism in the Southern Mining Region of California," *Journal of the West*, 12 (June 1973), pp. 126–138.

3. In the 20 years, 1820–1840, only eleven Chinese immigrated to the United Sates, and from 1840 to 1850 but 335. Of the latter, 300 arrived in California during 1840. In the 1850s and 60s, the Chinese population of the United States was concentrated almost entirely in California with approximately 80 per cent of that in the gold field. (R. Guy McClellan, *The Golden State: A History of the Region West of the Rocky Mountains.* [San Francisco: Flint & Co., 1974], p. 421; Thomas W. Chinn (ed.), A *History of the Chinese in California* (San Francisco: Chinese Historical Society of America, 1969), pp. 13, 22. William Hoy, *The Chinese Six Companies* (San Francisco: Chinese Consolidated Benevolent Association, 1942), p. 1; H. H. Bancroft, *History of California*, Vol. VI, 1848–1859 (San Francisco: The History Co., 1889), p. 124.

4. Hoy, *Chinese Six Companies*, p. 6.

5. Gunther Barth, *Better Strength: A History of the Chinese in the United States, 1850–1870* (Cambridge, Mass.: Harvard University Press, 1964), p. 113; Townsend Walter. "Gold Mountain Guests: Chinese Migration to the United States, 1848–1882," *Journal of Economic History*, 37 (March 1977), pp. 264–267.

6. Chinn, *Chinese in California*, p. 30; Chiu, *Chinese Labor*, p. 12.

7. Kenneth Haney (ed.), *Gold Rush by Sea from the Journal of Garrett W. Low* (Philadelphia: University of Pennsylvania Press, 1941), p. 166.

8. *San Francisco Herald*, September 17, 1852.

9. *San Francisco Herald*, December 2, 1852.

10. Walton Bean, *California: An Interpretive History* (New York: McGraw-Hill, 1968), p. 163; Hoy, *Chinese Six Companies*, p. 6; Chinn, *Chinese in California*, p. 30: Barth, *Better Strength*, p. 114; *Daily Alta California*, September 13, 1854; *Sacramento Daily Union*, October 10, 1855.

11. Chiu, *Chinese Labor*, p. 11, 13, 22: Alexander McLeod, *Pigtails and Gold Dust* (Caldwell, Idaho: Caxton Printers, 1948), p. 49.

12. Chinn, *Chinese in California*, p. 31. See Marianne Kaye Wells, "Chinese Temples in California" (unpublished M.A. thesis, University of California, Berkeley, 1962).

13. The census gave 24,282 Chinese out of a total mining population of 82,573. Chiu, *Chinese Labor*, pp. 27, 64; *Sacramento Daily Union*, February 10, 21, 1850; *Population of the United States in 1860*, p. 620; B. S. Brooks, *Appendix to the Opening Statement and Brief of B. S. Brooks on the Chinese Question* (San Francisco: Women's Co-operative Printing Union, 1877), p. 73.

14. Katherine Coman, *Economic Beginnings of the Far West.* Vol. II (New York: Macmillan Company, 1912), p. 382, gives 35 per cent: Chiu, *Chinese Labor*, p. 64, 45–50 per cent; Raymond "Mineral Resources," (Washington: 1868), p. 268, gives 40 percent: Browne, "A Report upon the Mineral Resources," (Washington: 1867), p. 382 gives 45 per cent.

15. Chiu, *Chinese Labor*, p. 27; *Ninth Census Volume I 1870*, p. 722; *Daily Alta California*, February 25, 1873. Many of the Chinese employed by the Central Pacific when released returned to California and took up mining. Thus, the number of Chinese miners

increased from 15,000 in 1868 to some 17,000 in 1870 (Chiu, p. 49). The *Sacramento Daily Union.* November 27, 1869, reported only 6,500 Chinese miners in a total Chinese population of 41,000.

16. Chiu, *Chinese Labor,* p. 64; California State Mining Bureau, *Fourth Annual Report of the State Mineralogist* (Sacramento: State Office, 1884), p. 35; *Ninth Annual Report of the State Mineralogist* (1890), p. 23; *Mining and Scientific Press,* April 11, 1903, p. 227. A much higher percentage is given in "Immigration," 57th Cong., 1st Sess. *House Ex. Doc. no. 184.* serial 4345 (Washington: GPO, 1901), p. 753.

17. Chiu, *Chinese labor,* p. 37; California State Mining Bureau. *Ninth Annual Report of the State Mineralogist* (San Francisco: State Office, 1890), p. 23; Rodman W. Paul, *California Gold* (Lincoln: University of Nebraska Press, 1967), pp. 351–352.

18. Herbert Eaton, *The Overland Trail to California in 1852* (New York: G. P. Putnam's Sons, 1974), p. 283.

19. Robert F. G. Spier, "Tool Acculturation among the 19th Century California Chinese," *Ethnohistory,* 5 (Spring 1958), pp. 101–102.

20. Chiu, *Chinese Labor,* p. 31; *Ninth Annual Report of the State Mineralogist* (1890), p. 23; Paul, *California Gold,* p. 130.

21. Rossiter W. Raymond, "Statistics of Mines and Mining in the States and Territories West of the Rocky Mountains," 43d Cong., 2d Sess., *House Ex. Doc. no. 77,* serial 1651 (Washington: GPO, 1875), p. 150.

22. *Engineering and Mining Journal,* September 12, 1885: *Ninth Annual Report of the State Mineralogist* (1890), pp. 262–263, 266.

23. "Eleventh Census of the United States 1890, Mineral Industries," 52d Cong., 1st Sess., *House Misc. Doc. no. 340* pt 1, pp. 111, 109.

24. Chiu, *Chinese Labor,* p. 31; *Ninth Annual Report of the State Mineralogist* (1890), p. 23: H. C. Burchard, *Report of the Director of the Mint* (Washington: 1885), p. 76.

25. *Engineering and Mining Journal,* September 12, 1885.

26. California State Mining Bureau. *Eleventh Annual Report of the State Mineralogist* (San Francisco State Office, 1893), pp. 443–444.

27. Barth, *Better Strength,* p. 186. Of the Rocky Mountain states, research revealed no evidence of Chinese mining in the placer areas of Wyoming. However, Wyoming did contain Chinese and they undoubtedly engaged in gold mining though probably on a very limited scale.

28. Barth, *Better Strength,* p. 185; Chinn, *Chinese in California,* p. 33: Viola N. Currier, "The Chinese Web in Oregon History" (unpublished M.A. thesis, University of Oregon, 1925), p. 26; *Sacramento Daily Union,* August 23, 1858: *Daily Alta California,* October 4, 1856.

29. *Oregonian,* October 31, 1857; see also *Daily Alta California,* September 26, 1857.

30. *Sacramento Daily Union,* July 27, 1859; see also *Oregon Sentinel,* February 19, 1859; *Population of the United States in 1860,* p. 620; Christopher H. Edson, *The Chinese in Eastern Oregon, 1860–1890* (San Francisco: R & E Research Associates, 1974), p. 29.

31. *Oregon Sentinel,* December 20, 1862.

32. *Washington Statesman,* December 6, 1862.

33. Chinn, *Chinese in California,* p. 33.

34. *Daily Oregonian,* August 8, 1868.

35. Raymond, "Statistics of Mines and Mining" (Washington: 1870), pp. 213–214; *A Compendium of the Ninth Census* (June 1, 1870), pp. 84–85.

36. Raymond, "Statistics of Mines and Mining" Washington: 1874), p. 252; see also Raymond, "Statistics of Mines and Mining" (Washington: 1870), p. 213. See also H. C. Burchard, *Report of the Director of the Mint* (Washington: 1882), p. 166; (Washington: 1883), p. 191, 193.

37. Robert Edward Wynne, "Reaction to the Chinese in the Pacific Northwest and British Columbia 1850–1910" (unpublished Ph.D. dissertation, University of Washington, 1946), pp. 106, 112, 120, 129–130; H. S. Palmer, "Remarks upon the Geography and Natural Capabilities of British Columbia, and the condition of Its Principal Gold Fields," *Journal of the Royal Geographical Society*, CXXXIV (1894), p. 194. See also Bancroft, *History of British Columbia*, pp. 444, 450.

38. Matthew Macfie, *Vancouver Island and British Columbia* (London: Longmen, Green, Longman, 1865), pp. 241–242: W. E. Willmott, "Some Aspects of Chinese Communities in British Columbia Towns," *British Columbia Studies I* (Winter, 1868–69), p. 28.

39. John Willis Christian, "The Kootenay Gold Rush: The Placer Decade 1862–1872" (unpublished Ph.D. dissertation, Washington State University, 1967), p. 105: Wynne, "Reaction to Chinese," pp. 145, 138–139; William J. Trimble, "The Mining Advance into the Inland Empire," *Bulletin of the University of Wisconsin*, no. 638 History Series III (1914), p. 58; "Commercial Relations 1868," *Annual Report on Foreign Commerce for the Year Ended September 30, 1868* (Washington: 1860), pp. 296–297.

40. Wynne, "Reaction to Chinese," pp. 145, 357. This represented 18 per cent of the total population.

41. British Columbia Department of Mines, *Bulletin 21* (1952), p. 24; according to Betty Derig, "Celestials in the Diggings," *Idaho Yesterdays* (Fall 1972), p. 2, up to 1870 an estimated 20 percent of the Chinese of Idaho came from British Columbia.

42. *Walla Walla Statesman*, September 30, 1864, October 7, 1864.

43. *Walla Walla Statesman*, October 7, 1864.

44. *Walla Walla Statesman*, February 17, May 5, 12, 1865; *Daily Oregonian*, March 1, 21, 1865, February 17, 1865, May 24, 1867; *Owyhee Avalanche*, June 1, 1867; *Idaho World*, February 2, 1867.

45. Fran Coble Trull, "The History of the Chinese in Idaho from 1864 to 1910" (unpublished M.A. thesis. University of Oregon, 1946), p. 10, says Chinese were in Silver City by 1864.

46. *Idaho World*, May 6, 1865; see also *Owyhee Avalanche*, August 19, 1865.

47. *Owyhee Avalanche*, June 23, 1866.

48. *Walla Walla Statesman*, May 3, 1867.

49. *Idaho World*, October 7, 1865.

50. *Idaho World*, November 11, 18, 1865.

51. *Capital Chronicle*, September 4, 1869; *Idaho World*, February 23, 1867.

52. *Capital Chronicle*, December 1, 1869; *Boise Democrat*, May 27, 1868.

53. *Capital Chronicle*, October 27, August 4, 1869.

54. Rossiter W. Raymond, "Statistics of Mines and Mining" 42d Cong., 1st Sess., *House Ex Doc. no. 10*, serial 1470 (Washington: GPO, 1871), p. 187; *Walla Walla Statesman*, February 12, 1869; *Owyhee Tidal Wave*, December 16, 1869; Raymond, "Statistics of Mines and Mining" (Washington: 1870), p. 250; H. C. Burchard, *Report of the Director of the Mint* (Washington: 1882), p. 194; Waldemar Lindgren, "The Gold and Silver Veins of Silver City, De Lamar and Other Mining Districts in Idaho," U.S. Geological Survey 2nd

Annual Report 1898–99, pt. 111 (Washington: 1900), p. 238. Trimble, "The Mining Advance into the Inland Empire" *Bulletin of the University of Wisconsin*, no. 638 History Series, III (1914), p. 208, says 1872; Bancroft, *History of Washington, Idaho and Montana, 1845–1889*, p. 552.

55. H. C. Burchard, *Report of the Director of the Mint* (Washington: 1882), p. 194.

56. *An Illustrated History of North Idaho Embracing Nez Perces, Idaho, Latah, Kootenay and Shoshone Counties* (Western Historical Publishing, 1903), p. 42; *Lewiston Journal*, July 4, 1867; *Idaho Tri-Weekly Statesman*, April 30, 1867; *Walla Walla Statesman*, April 5, August 9, 1867; April 9, 1869; *Daily Oregonian*, April 4, May 24, 1867; *Capital Chronicle*, September 22, October 13, 1869; *Montana Post*, March 26, 1869; Raymond, "Mineral Resources of the States and Territories West of the Rocky Mountains" (Washington: 1868), p. 580; John Haily, *The History of Idaho* (Boise: Syms-York, 1910), p. 128. Nancy Koehler Feichter, "The Chinese in the Inland Empire during the Nineteenth Century" (unpublished M.A. thesis. State College of Washington, 1959), p. 131, gives Idaho 4,274 Chinese in a total population of 20,000 for 1869. *The Daily Oregonian*, June 16, 1869, estimated that Idaho contained 1,500 Chinese out of a population of 25,600.

57. *Compendium of the Ninth Census (June 1, 1870)*, pp. 551, 546; *Ninth Census Volume 1*, 1870, p. 730; Trull, "Chinese in Idaho," p. 17, states: "Many . . . connect the Chinese only with the placer mines of Idaho . . . the majority of the Chinese were not miners." A statement typical, unfortunately of much research on the Chinese. The facts just do not substantiate such statements. According to the census of 1870 Idaho contained 4,274 Chinese of which 3,853 worked as miners (*Compendium of the Ninth Census [June 1, 1870]*, p. 18; *9th Census Volume 1*, 1870, p. 730).

58. Rossiter W. Raymond, "Statistics of Mines and Mining in the States and Territories West of the Rocky Mountains," 42d Cong., 3d Sess., *House Ex. Doc. no. 210*, serial 1561 (Washington: GPO, 1873), p. 198.

59. Rossiter W. Raymond, "Statistics of Mines and Mining in the States and Territories West of the Rocky Mountains," 43d Cong., 1st Sess., *House Ex. Doc. no. 141*, serial 1608 (Washington: GPO, 1874), p. 243.

60. *Compendium of the Tenth Census*, p. 3. Paul, *Mining Frontiers*, p. 144, felt the proportion of Chinese miners for 1880 remained about the same as in 1870.

61. *Compendium of the Eleventh Census*, p. 517; *Report of Eleventh Census*, 1890. Part II, p. 550.

62. *Daily Mountaineer*, May 21, 1866; *Walla Walla Statesman*, June 14, 1867, April 24, 1868; Raymond, "Statistics of Mines and Mining in the States and Territories West of the Rocky Mountains" (Washington: 1870), pp. 222–224, 228.

63. *Boise Democrat*, September 23, 1868; *Walla Wall Statesman*, September 18, 1868.

64. Raymond, "Statistics of Mines and Mining" (Washington: 1871), p. 177.

65. *Engineering and Mining Journal*, March 16, 1875, p. 188, September 13, 1879, p. 191; *Black Hills Journal*, June 14, August 9, October 18, 1879, January 24, 1880; Raymond, "Statistics of Mines and Mining (Washington: 1875), p. 318; H. C. Burchard, *Report of the Director of the Mint* (Washington: 1883), pp. 180, 186–188, 400.

66. *Walla Walla Statesman*, September 21, 1866; *Helena Herald*, June 26, 1867; A. K. McClure, *Three Thousand Miles through the Rocky Mountains* (Philadelphia: Lippincott & Co., 1869), pp. 312, 372.

67. "Report of James W. Taylor on the Mineral Resources of the United States East of the Rocky Mountains" (Washington: 1868), p. 49.

68. *Walla Walla Statesman*, May 1, 1868; *New North-West*, August 27, December 10, 1869; Raymond, "Statistics of Mines and Mining" (Washington: 1870), pp. 260–282; *Montana Post*, August 7, 1868; Raymond, *Mineral Resources of the States* (Washington: GPO, 1869), pp. 140–141; *Compendium of the Ninth Census*, p. 441; *9th Census Volume 1*, 1870, p. 744.

69. *New North-West*, January 28, May 6, June 10, 1870; F. W. Warner, *Montana and the Northwest Territory* (Chicago: Blakely, Brown & March Printers, 1879), p. 57, and *Montana Territory History and Business Directory, 1879* (Helena: Fisk Bros., 1879), p. 182: Raymond, "Statistics of Mines and Mining in the States and Territories West of the Rocky Mountains" (Washington: 1872), pp. 272–274, 288, 292 (Washington: 1877), pp. 238, 260.

70. *Compendium of the Tenth Census*, p. 557.

71. James P. Kimball, *Report of the Director of the Mint* (Washington: 1886), p. 151; *Compendium of the Eleventh Census*, p. 519; *Report of Eleventh Census*, 1890, p. 578.

72. Warren Wilson Tozier, "The History of Gold Mining in the Swank, Peshastian, and CleClum Mining Districts of the Wenatchee Mountains, 1853–1899" (unpublished M.A. thesis, Washington State University, 1965) pp. 80–81; *Oregon Statesman*, June 30, 1862; *Washington Statesman*, August 30, 1862; Wynne, "Reaction to Chinese," pp. 50–51; N. W. Durham, *History of the City of Spokane and Spokane County* (Spokane: S. J. Clark, 1912), p. 272; *Walla Walla Statesman*, April 7, 1865; *North Idaho Radiator*, March 4, 1865.

73. *Compendium of the Ninth Census*, p. 551; *9th Census Volume 1*, 1870, p. 762; John P. Esvelt, "Upper Columbia Chinese Placering," *The Pacific Northwesterner*, 3 (1959), p. 6.

74. *Black Hills Journal*, August 9, October 25, 1879; Esvelt, "Upper Columbia Chinese," pp. 7–8; *Compendium of the Tenth Census*, p. 557.

75. "The Upper Columbia River and the Great Plan of the Columbia," 47th Cong., 1st Sess., *Senate Ex. Doc. no. 186*, serial 1991 (Washington: GPO, 1882), p. 27.

76. H. C. Burchard, *Report of the Director of the Mint* (Washington: 1885), pp. 432–433: *Compendium of the Eleventh Census*, p. 523; *Report of the Eleventh Census*, 1890, part II, p. 620.

77. Ross Hum Lee, *The Chinese in the United States of America* (Hong Kong: Hong Kong University Press, 1960), p. 75; Patricia K. Ourads, "The Chinese in Colorado," *Colorado Magazine*, 29 (1952), pp. 276–277.

78. *Mining Review*, November 1873, p. 35; *The Engineering and Mining Journal*, September 1, 1877, p. 165, reported some 75 to 85 Chinese working along North Clear Creek.

79. *Engineering and Mining Journal*, March 16, 1878, p. 188.

80. Robert E. Strahorn, *To the Rockies and Beyond* (Omaha: The New West Publishing Co., 1879), p. 55.

81. Gerald E. Rudolph, "The Chinese in Colorado 1869–1911" (unpublished M.A. thesis, University of Denver, 1964), p. 41.

82. H. C. Buchard, *Report of the Director of the Mint* (Washington: 1881), p. 145.

83. Rudolph, "The Chinese in Colorado," p. 31; *Compendium of the Eleventh Census*, p. 516.

84. *Mining Review*, March 6, 1876, p. 197, April 3, 1876, p. 223, May 15, 1876, p. 276.

85. *Engineering and Mining Journal*, December 29, 1877; *Mining Review*, May 15, 1876.

86. Virginia McConnell, *Bayou Salado: The Story of South Park* (Denver: Sage Brooks,

1966), p. 162; Frank Fossett, *Colorado, Its Gold and Silver Mines* (New York: C. G. Crawford, 1880), p. 507; H. C. Burchard, *Report of the Director of the Mint* (Washington: 1885), p. 223; *Compendium of the Eleventh Census*, p. 516; George E. Roberts, *Report of the Director of the Mint* (Washington: 1902), p. 130.

87. Rudolph, "The Chinese in Colorado," p. 80.

88. *Cheyenne Daily Leader*, April 23, 1877; *Black Hills Daily Times*, April 14, 1877, February 1, March 27, August 5, August 7, 1878, April 24, 1880; *Engineering and Mining Journal*, July 26, 1879; L. P. Brockett, *Our Western Empire: Or the New West Beyond the Mississippi* (Philadelphia: Bradley & Co., 1881), p. 762, *Compendium of the Tenth Census*, p, 557; *Compendium of the Eleventh Census*, p. 522.

89. Research revealed little information on Chinese mining activities in the Southwest. The only work located on the Chinese in Utah, for instance, Kate B. Carter ("The Early Chinese of Western United States," *Our Pioneer Heritage* (1976), pp. 429–496) does not mention Chinese mining. According to Raymond ("Statistics of Mines and Mining in the States and Territories West of the Rocky Mountains" [Washington: 1877], p. 275). However, the Chinese worked the placers of Bingham Canyon at least as early as 1875.

90. J. Wells Kelly, *First Directory of Nevada Territory* (San Francisco: Valentine & Co., 1862), p. 213; J. Ross Browne and James W. Taylor, *Report upon the Mineral Resources of the United States* (Washington: GPO, 1867), p. 87; Dan De Quille, *The Big Bonanza* (Hartford, Conn.: American Publishing Co., 1878), pp. 10–11. Numerous sources give 1856 as the date of the earliest Chinese mining in Nevada. However, at least one diarist traveling to California in 1852 noted the presence of Chinese miners at Gold Canyon, Nevada, that year (Eaton, *Overland Trail*, p. 292); *Population of the United States in 1860*, p. 620.

91. *A Compendium of the Ninth Census*, p. 551; *9th Census Volume 1*, p. 746; *A Compendium of the Tenth Census*, pp. 2–3.

92. H. C. Burchard, *Report of the Director of the Mint* (Washington: 1884), p. 529.

93. William A. Vanderburg, "Placer Mining in Nevada," University of Nevada, *Bulletin XXX* (1936), p. 158: *Compendium of the Eleventh Census*, p. 520; *Report of the Eleventh Census*, 1890, p. 582; *Census Report*, Volume I, Twelfth Census, p. 568.

94. See *The Arizona Miner*, September 21, 1864, December 7, 1876; *Rio Abajo Weekly Press*, September 29, 1863; *The New Mexican*, April 20, 1866, June 15, 1867; *Rocky Mountain News*, January 6, 1864; *Mining and Scientific Press*, November 9, 1863; H. C. Burchard, *Report of the Director of the Mint* (Washington: 1882), pp. 328–329 (Washington: 1885), p. 59; James P. Kimball, *Report of the Director of the Mint* (Washington: 1888), p. 142; George E. Roberts, *Report of the Director of the Mint* (Washington: 1898), p. 104; Sylvester Mowry, *Arizona and Sonora: The Geography, History and Resources of the Silver Region of North America* (New York: Harper & Bros., 1864), p. 87.

95. H. H. Bancroft, *History of Arizona and New Mexico 1530–1880* (San Francisco: The History Company, 1889), p. 580.

96. *Weekly Arizona Miner*, January 21, 1871.

97. H. C. Burchard, *Report of the Director of the Mint* (Washington: 1882), pp. 249–250.

98. *Engineering and Mining Journal*, June 14, 1879, p. 434.

99. *Arizona Miner*, October 2, November 27, 1869.

100. *Arizona Miner,* January 15, 1870.

101. "Immigration," 57th Cong., 1st Sess., *House Ex. Doc. no. 184,* serial 4345 (Washington: GPO, 1901), p. 754. These figures must seem high, but research revealed no others to refute or substantiate them.

102. Robert V. Hine, *The American West* (Boston: Little, Brown & Co., 1963), p. 215; 9th Census, Volume I, 1870, pp. 722–723, 730, 744, 746, 749, 753, 759, 762, 765.

103. Raymond, "Statistics of Mines and Mining" (Washington: 1871), p. 177.

104. *Walla Walla Statesman,* March 15, 1865.

2

The Army of Canton in the High Sierra

Alexander Saxton

On the day the golden spike at Promontory, Utah, completed America's first transcontinental railroad, the celebrations in California began early and continued late. Eighteen special trains steamed into the state capital that morning bearing delegations, drums, trumpets, whiskey, banners, prostitutes, artillery and detachments of the National Guard. The parade went on for hours. First were brass bands and state dignitaries. Then came the railroad company, led by nine carriage loads of triumphant Central Pacific executives. After them followed the machinists and ironworkers, the coppersmiths, boilermakers, blacksmiths. Eight of the famous crew of Irish tracklayers who had set a national record by spiking down ten miles of rail in a single day marched by with their mauls on their shoulders.[1] Yet oddly, the men who had dug the grade and set the ties upon which the rails were spiked, who had, in short, contributed four-fifths of the labor of building the railroad,[2] took no part in the festivities at Sacramento. These of course were the Chinese; and the story of the Central Pacific's tattered army of Canton—how it came to be employed at railroad building, how it clawed its way across the Sierra Nevada—provides one of the more ambiguous chapters of California's golden age.

The transcontinental line had begun as a wartime undertaking. Prior to the Civil War, Theodore Judah's engineering studies and his tireless agitation of the project in California and Washington had inspired some preliminary steps of organization; but it was only the threatened dismemberment of the Union, coupled with removal of Southern opposition to the north-central route, which finally brought Congress in 1862 to the point of voting out franchises and federal money. Appropriately, since the railroad had been a major plank of the Republican platforms, the franchise for the western portion went to a group of rising young California Republicans, most of whom, at the time, were still small businessmen in Sacramento. Having come west as gold-hunters in '49 or soon after, they had, like many others, done better at storekeeping than at mining. Judah was the only one among them with knowledge of railroad construction, and they lost little time in forcing Judah out of the enterprise. However, they did have other assets, not least of which were that they had helped hold the state against the secessionists; and that one of their number, Leland Stanford, was serving simultaneously as first Republican governor of California and first president of the Central Pacific Railroad.[3]

Two gigantic problems immediately confronted the young entrepreneurs: scarcity of capital and scarcity of labor. These they must resolve somehow before they could come to grips with the third and even larger problem—the Sierra Nevada. As to the first difficulty, Congress had partially solved it for them by loans of government bonds and outright grants of public land along both sides of the projected right of way.[4] Here was security for borrowing needed capital. But the solution of the first difficulty tended to aggravate the second. Because of the bonds and land grants were to be issued per mile of track constructed, and because no meeting point for the eastern and western lines was designated in the act of Congress, the two companies were thrown into a race for mileage, and for survival.[5] Success would hinge on speed of construction. In a time of national crisis such an arrangement doubtless seemed appropriate; but construction speed in that pre-bulldozer era varied more or less directly with the size of the labor force. And the labor force available in California in the early 1860's appeared meager indeed. Of the men offering for hire—white men, that is—most were, like the promoters of the railroad themselves, slightly over-age forty-niners, still gold-diggers at heart. There was, in addition, a sprinkling of laborers and skilled mechanics beginning to drift out from the East. But they too seem to have been infected upon arrival in the golden state with a touch of the poet. "Mining was more to their taste than the discipline of railroad work," wrote Lewis Clement who served as assistant chief in the Central Pacific engineering department. "They were indifferent, independent and their labor high-priced . . . The first mining excitement meant a complete stampede and consequent abandonment of all work."[6] The company would hire men in San Francisco, pay their expense to the railhead, where promptly they vanished over the skyline in the direction of the latest diggings.[7]

Responsibility for solving the Central's construction problems fell to one of its four top directors, Charles Crocker. Innocent though he was of any training in engineering, Crocker believed he held a firm grip on the essential ingredient: knowledge of how to handle workingmen. "There was no need for sympathy for those men," he reminisced afterwards. "Why I used to go up and down that road in my car like a mad bull, stopping along the way wherever there was anything amiss and raising old Nick."[8] Even Crocker's assaults, however, failed to squeeze much mileage out of the boomers and grubstakers who were willing to handle an occasional shovel for the transcontinental railroad. The months rolled into years and the great California project seemed to have bogged down hopelessly in the mud flats and oak thickets of the lower foothills. After two years of effort, the railhead stood less than fifty miles from its starting point. The High Sierra was not yet even in sight.

To make matters worse—far worse—the Central's eastern rival, the Union Pacific, which had gotten off to a slow start, was now hitting full throttle. With easy assess to materials by way of the Missouri River, and ample labor supply from the waves of Irish immigrants coming through the Atlantic seaports, the Union Pacific in the spring of 1866 was laying track at the pace of a mile a day. It was outbuilding the Central by something like eight to one.[9] The Central Pacific directors had engaged in endless discussions of their paralyzing labor problem. Before Appomattox they had toyed with the idea of having Confederate prisoners shipped out under guard. Later they investigated the possibility of importing Negro freedmen from the South. One of the first suggestions for using Chinese seems to have come from Crocker's brother, E. B. Crocker, former Chief Justice of the Supreme Court of California, and legal counsel to the railroad. But the construction department was unimpressed. Chinese might do well as cigar makers, houseboys, laundrymen; might even be successful at combing the tailings of abandoned placer mines. But for heavy construction they were too small, too frail. Many of them, it was reported, weighed only a hundred pounds full grown. To send such midgets into the Sierra was obviously absurd.[10]

The decision to hire Chinese was finally taken in 1865. There were, by that time, plenty available. Chinese had been coming into California since 1849; in the mid-fifties they had been driven out of the gold camps by the American miners; but as the surface deposits were skimmed off and the Americans moved on to richer diggings elsewhere, the Chinese, drifting back into the foothills, had set to reworking the gravel heaps and tailings of the old placer mines. By 1865 there wasn't much left even for Chinese miners.[11] According to the legend, Charles Crocker ordered up a gang of fifty, largely for the purpose of frightening his white workers who had threatened a strike.[12] The results were so gratifying to him that he sent out a general call. Up from the gold camps and the valley towns, and from Sacramento and San Francisco, they came trooping into the mountains. Crocker, despite the protests of his white employees, had 3,000 at work before the end of the year. "Without them," wrote the Central's president, Leland Stanford, "it would be impossible to complete the western portion of this great national highway within the time required by the acts of Congress." Stanford described the Chinese as "quiet, peaceable, industrious, economical—ready and apt to learn all the different kinds of work required in railroad building.[13] They were, in fact, a construction foreman's dream. The number rapidly increased to ten or eleven thousand, and from then till the golden spike at Promontory, four men in every five hired by the Central Pacific were Chinese.[14]

In the spring of 1866—three years after the start of construction—the Central finally came up against its first major outpost of the High Sierra. This was Cape Horn, a rocky buttress around the base of which the American River rumbled through its thousand foot deep canyon.[15] No detours were feasible. The only route was the half-circle traverse across the slabs and angles of rock. Chinese laborers were lowered in baskets. They chipped and drilled, scrambled up the lines while charges of gunpowder roared beneath them; drilled again. Inch-by-inch they hacked out a ledge wide enough for men to walk on; wide enough for a wheelbarrow; wide enough at last to receive the eight-foot sleepers. As the gangs moved forward, the work train came nosing after them, its grab irons and journal boxes literally hanging over space.[16]

All summer the cars from Sacramento and schooners creaking up out of the valley brought more Chinese.[17] They trudged past the railhead, spreading out for forty miles through the canyons and over the granite escarpments. At night the fires of their camps glowed on the heights and by day the smoke of burning timber and the black clouds from powder blasts drifted across the blue Sierra sky. "The work goes bravely on," Crocker wrote to the editor of the *Gold Hill News* on the Comstock Lode in Nevada. "In the fall of 1867, I will meet you at Truckee Meadows and pass you through to Sacramento by rail in seven hours."[18]

But Crocker was to miss this guess by almost a year. As the army moved into the high country, its rate of progress diminished. Records of the engineering department indicated that it sometimes took 300 men ten days to clear and grub a mile of right of way. After that came grading which might hold up an even larger gang for weeks or months. Each yard of dirt and rock had to be dug down by hand and carried away in baskets and wheelbarrows. In August, Crocker moved part of his force up to Donner Summit to begin drilling the tunnel.[19] Dynamite had not yet made its appearance and explosives then available were inadequate to the work in hand. Sierra granite was so hard that gunpowder simply spurted back out of the blast holes. Nitroglycerin, recently invented by the Swedish chemist Nobel, was unreliable and frightfully dangerous. But as it was cheap, smokeless, potent, Central presently had a man employed full time compounding the new explosive.[20] "A terrible explosion at Camp 9 near Gold Run," the Sacramento *Union* reported. "Six men were killed, three whites and three Chinamen. The foreman was blown to pieces and part of him not found."[21] Such accidents became almost casual occurrences. Even Crocker's second-in-command, the line boss James Strobridge, lost his right eye to a premature nitroglycerin blast.

While the drilling crews labored at the summit, the railhead crept from Cape Horn to Cisco, fourteen miles below the western portal of the unfinished tunnel. Here in early December the first snows overtook Crocker's army.[22] The directors had been hoping for a winter as mild as those of the previous several years, but 1866 brought one of the heaviest on record. Storms rolled in from the ocean in endless succession. The north wind howled over the granite slopes, drifting snow into the gullies and hollows, filling the newly graded cuts. Snow plows bogged down and the shovel brigades were sent to their rescue. Out over those enormous oblique white surfaces moved the zigzag processions of tiny figures in their cotton jackets and blue jeans. The snow fell faster than they could dig it out. Then a sudden thaw would send runoffs waters rampaging into the lower canyons, tearing out trestles, sweeping away embankments. "The fall of snow above this place is immense," wrote the Dutch Flat *Enquirer*. And again: "we are now in the midst of one of the most severe winters we have experienced. . . . In one or two places, the fills, we hear, are so completely washed out that nothing but the rails are to be seen suspended in the air resembling telegraph wires."[23]

It was scarcely possible to continue; yet it now seemed equally impossible to retreat. Each week lost meant the loss of hundreds of thousands in land and subsidy. But even more crucial was the over-riding question of control. For the California line to be operable afterwards as an independent and profitable enterprise, it would have to have something better within its territory than granite peaks and uninhabited desert. But eastward, the nearest lands of sufficient fertility to provide some volume of freight and passenger traffic were the Mormon settlements in Utah. This meant that whichever road first reached Salt Lake basin would probably come to dominate the entire system.[24] Crocker, ridden raw by his fellow directors who besieged him over the telegraph from rose-arbored Sacramento, hurled his forces into this battle in a cold, continuing frenzy.[25] He would not pull back from the summit. The portals of the tunnel were buried under fantastic drifts, the Chinese encampments were snowed under. They dug chimneys and air shafts, lived by lantern light, huddling, freezing. They tunnelled in from the camps to reach the portals of the tunnel itself, and the work continued, although materials now had to be lowered forty feet or more by steam hoist from the surface of the snow, and the waste from the digging removed in the same way.[26] On Christmas Day, 1866, the Dutch Flat *Enquirer* reported that

> a gang of Chinamen employed by the railroad were covered up by a snow slide and four of five died before they could be exhumed. . . . The snow fell to such a depth that one whole group of Chinamen was covered up during the night and parties were digging them out when our informant left.[27]

Crocker at last shifted part of his army across the divide. Boxcars, flatcars, locomotives, rail and ties were loaded on sleds and dragged over the summit by teams of horses wallowing in the snow and long lines of Chinese on the tow ropes. This advance detachment set to work near the Nevada line where the climate was a few degrees warmer. But at first sign of spring, he fetched them back up to the crest again. Snow removal alone consumed weeks. After that, the damage to the roadbed, the washed-out fills and trestles, had to be repaired before new work could begin.[28] Meanwhile Crocker had his survey teams running the line east to the Utah border, and graders at work halfway across the state of Nevada. Everything was ready for the big push into the open desert, where, Crocker promised the Central would match the Union Pacific's pace of a mile a day,[29] and make up the mileage and the subsidy lost. Huge depots of supplies and equipment were accumulating in Sacramento and along the line to Cisco. But Donner Summit held fast.

The Chinese assaulted the tunnel at both ends, then sunk a shaft in the center and worked back in opposite direction. They were thus digging four faces simultaneously, in shifts twenty-four hours a day. Boring the tunnel required thirteen months; and when the drillers holed through at last, it was not midsummer, but well on into September.[30] Before tracks could be laid, winter had shut in upon them. Once again the camps were snowed under. For the second time the railhead fell back to Cisco, and again Crocker drove his labor force into the desperate struggle to keep a trickle of supplies moving by sled over the summit.[31] Crocker's chief lieutenant, James Strobridge, testifying twenty years later before a federal investigating commission, recalled the details of both those winters with an almost agonized clarity:

> That was the winter when the Dutch Flat stage stuck in the mud for six weeks in the streets of Gold Run. . . . There was a good deal of the winter that the (rail)road was blocked, and then in those bad winters we did not keep it open. . . . We hauled over that snow to Donner Lake the material for a railroad track of forty miles, with all the trimmings, three locomotives and forty cars. We built forty miles of railroad in the Truckee Canyon before the connection was made by way of the summit. . . . In that manner we forced our way across the mountains at an enormous cost. It cost nearly three times what it would have cost to have done it in the summertime when it should have been done. But we shortened the time seven years from what Congress expected when the act was passed.

And then, although the commission had made clear that it was inquiring only into the cost in dollars, James Strobridge told them:

> The snow slides carried away our camps and we lost a good many men in those slides; many of them we did not find until the next season when the snow melted. . . .[32]

It was spring again before the tunnel was finally opened for traffic,[33] and by this time the race with the Union Pacific was almost ended; but the Central had not lost. With supply trains puffing at hourly intervals over the hump from California, the construction gangs marched eastward, out from the Truckee into the barren, dry-bone valley of the Humboldt. Now, making up for lost time, the gangs hit the line before daybreak and worked on after dark by the flaring yellow light of sagebrush bonfires. The railhead moved forward, month after month, at the relentless pace of a mile a day.[34] By the end of January, in 1869, the Central had set its feet solidly in the Great Salt Lake basin, while not far to the east, the Union Pacific was rolling down out of the Rockies. The contest was a tie; and it was clear that the incredible two year storming of the summit had saved the day for the Sacramento shopkeepers.

But the Chinese had not only saved the day. They had saved the railroad a great deal of money as well. In 1865 the going rate for white unskilled labor had been thirty dollars a month plus board and lodging. Chinese received the same sum in cash but fed and housed themselves. While the Central's estimate of seventy-five cents to a dollar a day as the cost of maintaining their white workers was probably a good deal too high, it would appear, even if the dollar were cut in half, the company was able to purchase Chinese labor for something like two-thirds the price of white. And the comparison remains incomplete, as there is evidence that Chinese were frequently used on jobs falling within the skilled ratings (masonry, tracklaying, blacksmithing, handling explosives); and these, for white men, would have commanded a wage of three to five dollars a day.[35]

Beyond this, Chinese labor offered the advantage of being simpler to manage. The men hired out not as individuals, but in gangs of fifty to a hundred. Each gang furnished its own cooks, set up its own camp, and was represented, in dealings with the company, by its own "agent." These agents—generally English-speaking Chinese—received the wages for the entire gang in monthly lump sums. They purchased food, then distributed individual earnings after deducting for any debts owed.[36] Presumably the agents were in business for profit, or worked for men who were; and as most of the laborers under their care would have come not long since from the hungry coast of South China where people were accustomed to make do on a few handfuls of rice a day,[37] the profits involved in feeding them out of thirty dollars per man per month gold coin could have been—and doubtless were—spectacular.

And finally, in addition to being cheap and easy to manage, Chinese labor had the great merit of being expendable. All laborers in heavy construction in those days had to be to a degree expendable; but Chinese were more so than most because the initial investment was small and because there were no anxious relatives living near by. As to the cost in human life of crossing the Sierra, little record remains; although newspaper reports of the two winters at the summit and James Strobridge's recollections suggest that it must have been high. Crocker reputedly kept 10,000 or more on the line.[38] But what the rate of replacement may have been to keep that many there we do not know. Apparently there were regular shipments of new recruits from South China. "We had a good deal of difficulty getting labor," Lewis Clement, the assistant chief in the engineering department, testified afterwards. "The labor was not in the country and had to be imported."[39]

The importation was carried in British and American vessels fitted with barred steerage holds. Largest broker in this traffic seems to have been a Dutch trader named Cornelius Koopmanschaf whose headquarters were in San Francisco. Generally the immigrants remained under bond for their passage and other debts that might accrue to Chinese merchants living in California, and the merchant associations in San Francisco's Chinatown—the so-called Six Companies—served as enforcement agencies. The imported labor was then rented out in gangs; and to complete this circle, an unofficial but firm agreement between the Six Companies and west coast ship operators prevented any Chinese from taking passage out of California unless he carried a clearance from the Six Companies. It was a tight system. As for the Central Pacific, it secured most of its Chinese gangs through the agency of the firm of Sisson and Wallace, in which, by convenient coincidence, one of the Crocker brothers, Clark W., became a leading member.[40]

The question of whether all this constituted free or servile labor was sharply debated at the time. Slavery in the United States presumably had been abolished by 1865—an accomplishment for which the Republicans claimed considerable credit; and indentures of any kind were unenforceable at law. Speaking for the Central Pacific, and perhaps for the Republican party of California as well, railroad president Leland Stanford asserted that, "No system similar to slavery prevails." He went on to argue that because men might choose to work in gangs under the orders of *agents* was no reason to suppose the principles of free contract and free labor were being violated.[41]

Historians have continued the debate. But however the semantics may be deployed, the substance of the matter seems fairly obvious. The Chinese laborer could not escape his Chinese-ness in America. He had knowledge neither of the language nor of the law. In effect he was at the mercy of the Chinese merchants, the associations, agents, contractors, who had fetched him over from Canton, who arranged for his employment, collected his wages, fed him, "protected" him, and determined when, or if he would ever return to his homeland. Export of labor from South China was already an old institution by 1865, and had furnished workers under long terms of servitude for the plantations of the West Indies and for the Pacific islands.[42] Chinese laborers may have been better off in the Sierra Nevada than their fellows elsewhere; but it is unlikely they were *much* better off.

The legacy that all this left to California (and to America)—aside from the physical fact of the railroad across the mountains—has been an enduring distortion of reality, a masking of social roles. Those who derived the most immediate benefit from a system that was in fact very similar to slavery would take the high ground of generosity and brotherhood. One of the very few credit lines recorded for the Chinese during the California celebrations of the transcontinental railroad came from E. B. Crocker, brother of Clark W., the gang labor contractor, and brother of the redoubtable construction superintendent, Charles E. B. Crocker, himself a director of the Central Pacific, and former Chief Justice of the State Supreme Court (a post to which he had been appointed by Governor Leland Stanford), was reputedly the man who had first suggested hiring Chinese. On the day of the golden spike, champagne glass in hand, the Judge mounted the rostrum of the Assembly in Sacramento to offer a toast to "the greatest monument of human labor." Then he added, "I wish to call your minds that the early completion of this railroad we have built has been in large measure due to that poor, despised class of laborers called the Chinese—to the fidelity and industry they have shown."[43]

But the note that prevailed more generally through the celebrations—and as it turned out, the prophetic note—was sounded by the orator of the day in San Francisco, Judge Nathaniel Bennett. For Judge Bennett, this triumph of railroad construction was wholly owing to the fact that his fellow Californians were "composed of the right materials, derived from the proper origins. . . . In the veins of our people," he declared, "flows the commingled blood of the four greatest nationalities of modern days. The impetuous daring and dash of the French, the philosophical and sturdy spirit of the German, the unflinching solidity of the English, and the light-hearted impetuosity of the Irish, have all contributed each its appropriate share. . . ." Without pausing to mention any share for the Chinese, Judge Bennett moved along to his peroration: "A people deducing its origins from such races, and condensing their best traits into its national life, is capable of any achievement."[44] The achievement of burning Chinese laundries and hanging their proprietors was not far in the future. It would prove, in fact, only a short step from ignoring the accomplishment of the Chinese laborers, as Judge Bennett had done, to denying their humanity.

NOTES

1. Sacramento *Union*, May 8, 1869.
2. U.S., Pacific Railway Commission, *Report and Testimony Taken*, 50th Cong., 1st sess., Sen.Ex.Doc.51 (Washington, 1888), VI, 3139–3140.
3. E. L. Sabin, *Building the Pacific Railway* (Philadelphia, 1919), 13–40. George T. Clark, *Leland Stanford* (Stanford, 1931), 194.
4. Sabin, 13–40.
5. Testimony of Leland Stanford, Pacific Railway Commission, V, 2523.
6. John D. Galloway, *First Transcontinental Railway* (New York, 1950), 144.
7. Pacific Railway Commission, VI, 3225–3226.
8. Charles Crocker, "Facts ... regarding ... identification with the Central Pacific Railroad," dictation to H. H. Bancroft (typescript in the Bancroft Library, University of California, Berkeley), 49–52.
9. Galloway, 160, 299–300.
10. Oscar Lewis, *The Big Four* (New York, 1938), 69–70. Dutch Flat *Enquirer*, July 5, 1867.
11. Ping Chiu, *Chinese Labor in California, 1850–1880* (Madison, 1963), 27–30.
12. Chiu, 44.
13. Figures on Chinese employment in 1865 and the Stanford statement are quoted in Sabin, 110–111.
14. Pacific Railway Commission, VI, 3139.
15. Galloway, 84.
16. Sabin, 114–115.
17. Sacramento *Union*, June 18, 1866.
18. Reprinted in the Sacramento *Union*, June 6, 1866.
19. Galloway, 160.
20. Pacific Railway Commission, V, 2577; and VI, 3206.
21. Sacramento *Union*, April 18, 1866. Robert L. Fulton, *Epic of the Overland* (Los Angeles, 1934), 33–35.
22. Sacramento *Union*, Nov. 29, Dec. 12, 1866.
23. Dutch Flat *Enquirer*, Jan. 36, Feb. 3, 1867.
24. Testimony of Leland Stanford, Pacific Railway Commission, V, 2523.

25. Clark, 223.

26. Pacific Railway Commission, V, 2577–2579.

27. Reprinted in the Sacramento *Union*, Dec. 18, 1866.

28. Pacific Railway Commission, VI, 3150.

29. Sabin, 160.

30. Lewis, 77. Dutch Flat *Enquirer*, Oct. 30, 1867.

31. Fulton, 36–37. Pacific Railway Commission, V, 2522–2523.

32. Pacific Railway Commission, V, 2580–2581, and VI, 3150.

33. Dutch Flat *Enquirer*, May 23, 1868.

34. Dutch Flat *Enquirer*, Aug. 15, 1868.

35. Fulton, 33–35; Pacific Railway Commission, VI, 3139–3140; Dutch Flat *Enquirer*, Dec. 28, 1867.

36. Galloway, 144–145; Lewis, quoting Leland Stanford, 71.

37. Gunther-Barth,"Chinese Sojourners in the West: The Coming," *Southern California Quarterly*, XLVI (March 1964), 55–56.

38. Testimony of Charles Crocker, U.S. Congress, *Report of the Special Joint Committee to Investigate Chinese Immigration*, 44th Cong., 2nd sess., Senate Report 689 (Washington, 1877), 675.

39. Pacific Railway Commission, VI, 3224.

40. Persia Crawford Campbell, *Chinese Coolie Immigration* (London, 1923). On Koopmanschaf, see Gunther Barth, *Bitter Strength* (Cambridge, 1964), 117, 192–193. For Clark W. Crocker and Sisson Wallace & Co., see H. L. Wells, *History of Nevada County* (Oakland, 1880), 215–216. Also, *Report of the Special Joint Committee*, testimony of former Governor Low of California, 82; testimony of Charles Crocker, 674–676; and testimony of James Strobridge, 724.

41. From the president's annual reports as quoted in Lewis, 71.

42. Barth, *Southern California Quarterly*, XLVI (1964), 55–68.

43. Sacramento *Union*, May 8, 1869.

44. San Francisco *Bulletin*, May 8, 1869.

Part II

Chinese in the Southwest
(Arizona, Nevada, New Mexico, Texas)

3

Sojourners and Settlers: The Chinese Experience in Arizona

Lawrence Michael Fong

Much of the literature on early Chinese immigrants to the western United States focuses on their experiences in California and as laborers on the great railroad construction projects of the late nineteenth century. Their role in Arizona Territory, however, has been largely neglected and bears deeper examination. The earliest Chinese settlers came to Arizona just after it had become a Territory of the United States in 1863. They had reached a land of frontier opportunities and values, where cultures were ethnically diverse and the Anglo segment was becoming numerically dominant. Arizonans were, for the most part, preoccupied with controlling the large Hispanic population politically and the native Indian population militarily. The Chinese did not enter the Territory in sufficient numbers to be viewed as a significant social threat and thus were not confronted with the discriminatory legislation or the violent expressions of prejudice that had greeted them in California, Colorado, Wyoming and Montana.

Initially the Chinese were drawn from their troubled homeland to the sparsely settled western frontier after news had reached them of the vast natural resources and beauties of the region; it was a land to be conquered, then exploited by ingenuity and business acumen. Gold strikes attracted Asians and Anglos alike, but the false dream of unlimited and undiscovered mineral wealth left many disheartened and without any hope of income. First regional, then national legislation was directed at the Chinese, taking them out of circulation and direct competition with the Anglos. But with the need for transportation and for communication with the industrial Northeast came the construction of transcontinental railroads. The Chinese were available, they were disciplined laborers, and again they were brought to the expanding western territories. The railroads, in turn, helped them escape persecution in northern California and brought them to less developed and populated territories. Arizona was one such place.

39

Here they were accommodated within a similarly restrictive, but far less hostile, social and political atmosphere. The new arrivals tended to conform generally to existing political notions: they aligned themselves with traditional parties, voted along party lines, supported party issues, and presented no barrier to Anglo determination of policy. Through adaptability they were able to fare much better in the harsh Arizona environment of the 1870s than in other locales. They took on a number of occupations after the railroad construction played out; they were willing to take jobs few others wanted and to work for lower wages as well. Many achieved success and remained as permanent residents.

To understand the Chinese experience in Arizona it is necessary to examine their treatment in California, the port of entry for the majority of Oriental arrivals. The Chinese presence there was notable in 1848. As news of the gold discoveries attracted prospectors from throughout the continent, word also reached the provinces of southeastern China through the Chinese already in California.

Seaports like Canton and Shanghai had developed into commercialized urban centers. The declining hegemony of Mandarin elitism and foreign Manchurian rule had made survival for the common Chinese uncertain. These factors, coupled with civil unrest and alternating seasons of floods and droughts, made passage to the gold fields worth any investment and any discomfort in steerage travel across the Pacific Ocean.

Having arrived, the immigrants, for a while, did very well. Initially, the quiet, industrious Asian goldseekers were able to work placers alongside Europeans, Mexicans, South Americans and Anglos. Much of the gold, however, had been extracted by the late 1850s, and the only other sources of income were in the developing cities. Migration of prospectors to Sacramento and San Francisco created competition between Chinese and others for jobs. The Foreign Miners' Tax of 1850 already had led many Chinese to the cities to seek employment in domestic services, laundries and small mercantile enterprises.[1]

As the country developed, new opportunities attracted new waves of immigrants. The year 1860 saw an influx of Chinese as contract laborers, or "coolies," who disembarked in San Francisco. Existing manpower needs for large construction projects like the railroads might have been met by native Indian and Mexican groups, but the Chinese were contracted with despite growing prejudice against them. In the West, a large force of workers was necessary for rapid development, and increasing Chinese immigration helped to fill the need, bringing their total numbers to near 50,000 by 1860. Still, they represented less than one percent of the total California population.

Chinese labor was cheap and easy to handle. Men working on the construction of the Central Pacific Railroad received ten to twenty dollars per month, a food allowance or rations of rice, fish, beef or pork, vegetables and oil, as well as eating utensils. They furnished their own bedding and the railroad companies provided a "comfortable, water-proof quarter."[2] Laborers were segregated and the Chinese worked among themselves with one of their group acting as the section foreman and as liaison with the construction supervisors.

The meeting of the Central Pacific and the Union Pacific Railroads at Promontory Point, Utah, in 1869, again sent the unemployed into the cities. This time California, as well as the nation, was in an economic depression, primarily caused by wildcat speculation and declining gold production. (The stock market was based on the gold standard.) Periods of drought in California affected agricultural production adversely. The economy, therefore, was a major issue in the political platforms of Pacific states politicians. Chinese immigration was claimed to be closely related to fiscal problems in the United States. The Chinese were accused not only of working for lower wages but also of taking away work that others deserved. Women, for example, began seeking employment as domestics, an occupation once left solely to the Chinese. For Dennis Kearny and the Workingman's Party, however, the Chinese were a threat to unionism and the unions' monopoly of labor in California. Cigar, shoe and food manufacturers in San Francisco continued to need labor as their enterprises developed and expanded, but pressures against hiring Chinese prevailed. Circulars from San Francisco's office of the Cigarmakers' International Union reached Tucson at the turn of the century, listing manufacturers who continued to employ Chinese, "which is a great injury to our white working men and women." The union asked readers to boycott these firms and, like the food manufacturers, they attached special labels to their products proclaiming "Made by white labor," or "Made by white man."[3]

San Francisco officials, reacting to pressure from unions and those political factions that wanted to rid California of the "Chinese problems," as they phrased it, "quartered" the Orientals in a segregated area. Ironically this isolation created a self-sufficient community, supported through voluntary associations, schools, hospitals and commercial networks.

The prevailing prejudice against Orientals began to be reflected in legislation by 1880. George Seward in that year negotiated a treaty with China that permitted the United States to regulate, limit or suspend the immigration of Chinese laborers.[4] Others, however, were not to be included in the restriction. "Chinese subjects, whether proceeding to the United States as teachers, merchants or from curiosity, together with their servants; and Chinese laborers who are now in the United States shall be allowed to go and come of their own free will and accord, and shall be accorded all the rights, privileges, immunities and exemptions which are accorded to citizens of the most favored nation."[5]

The Exclusion Law of 1882 quickly followed. It provided for the rejection of laborers—"skilled and unskilled and those engaged in mining"—over the next ten years."[6] All other Chinese, except diplomats, were required to bring a certificate from their government and any found to be in the United States unlawfully were to be deported. Treaties between the United States and China in 1884 and 1885 said nothing about the rights of Chinese already living or trading in the United States.

The Geary Act of 1892 extended the Exclusion Law for another ten years and required certificates of residency with detailed particulars about the person, including a photograph.[7] Regulations called for the arrest of any Chinese without one. In 1902, these restrictive laws were extended indefinitely. Arizona, too, had felt the influences of this federal legislation and of popular prejudice.

Nevertheless, the Chinese kept coming. In 1852, twenty-nine ships arrived in San Francisco bearing Chinese immigrants who hoped to find wealth and security in the California gold fields. One vessel had come from Mazatlán, Sonora, Mexico.[8] The migration of Chinese to Arizona and the Southwest not only followed routes from California, but included direct immigration from China to Mexico, where immigrants set out on overland trails from the interior to the Sonora-Arizona border.

Those who came to Arizona found themselves in difficulties created by tension existing between Anglos and Hispanics. The Territory of Arizona was the result of Anglo occupation of Mexican land lost after the Mexican War (1846–48). Issues surrounding enfranchisement of Territorial residents, however, did not emerge until 1863, when Arizona and New Mexico became separate Territories. Anglo settlers in Arizona feared a consolidated Mexican vote.[9] Since an increase in population and in the number of registered voters was of fundamental importance for gaining statehood, the Mexican majority represented a potential obstacle to Anglo domination of growth and development. In this historical setting, the experience of the Chinese was one of relative accommodation during their initial migrations and settlement throughout the Territory. They made no trouble and at first encountered little opposition. They even made progress in conforming to the ways of the western frontier. Although segregated, they adjusted to American dress and eating habits, even though their contact with Anglos, Mexicans and Indians was minimal. Furthermore, working on a section of the railroad often brought them into cities and towns. As their appearances in centers of population became more frequent, they began to encounter prejudice.

A number of early Chinese pioneers came to Prescott, arriving after the completion of the Central Pacific Railroad in 1869. In November 1869, a few of these new immigrants were received with journalistic bias.

> MORE CHINAMEN—Three more Chinamen arrived here during the week, and have gone to work. There are now four of them which is quite enough.[10]

In spite of opposition, they established groceries, laundries and a joss house, or shrine, along Goodwin and Granite streets. George Ah Fat ran local advertisements for his laundry in the *Daily Arizona Miner* in the 1870s.

Others were reported on June 13, 1868, in the employ of the Vulture mining works near Wickenburg. A *Miner* article of that date states that these twenty-one Chinese pioneers did most of the work there. Many still felt their hearts flutter when the discovery of gold or silver was mentioned.

> The flight of ye Chinamen is Big Bugwards. John thinks he has struck a big thing there, and is bound to go. Two, three and four cents to the pan were found by one of them, recently. The finder sent word to his countrymen in Prescott . . . and they im-

mediately resolved to start immediately. "Me no likee cookee, no likee washee, any more. Me go Big Bug light away, where one Chinaman telle me he find gleat deal coarse gold."

Editorializing, the article continued:

Now, John, as you have gone out into the woods, we tell you to beware of the Apache.[11]

Chinese prospectors were known to rework old Spanish claims dating back to the eighteenth century and their methods for extracting gold were similar to placer techniques acquired in California. They were well acquainted with the speculative nature of this type of mining, and, accordingly, were not unfamiliar with incidents of fraud and conniving. In the 1870s some Chinese who were interested in investing in a mining operation came upon a claim being worked by Anglos west of Tubac. While a few of the miners were showing them a site which wasn't producing well, the others salted a bank and mixed fine gold dust with loose earth around the area. The Chinese were convinced of its wealth after washing out about eight dollars in gold and bought the claim for ten dollars. They became discouraged, however, after getting only about two ounces — the amount of gold salted in the bank. Realizing that there was no more of the metal, they gathered up their belongings, rice and tea, and set off for Tucson only to be attacked by Apaches, who killed the entire party of ten. The Chinese were fine subjects for scalping, as their hair was shaved close to the crown of the head and then tied in a pigtail.[12]

New opportunities arose for the Chinese in the late 1870s when Collis P. Huntington decided to build a southern transcontinental railroad through Arizona. The need for experienced railroad workers presented the Chinese of California a chance to escape prejudice in the coastal cities. Survival for the new arrivals in the Territory, however, often depended on cooperation with other Arizonians. Though they themselves did not eat fish, Yuma Indians willingly sold them to Chinese when the construction camps reached the Colorado River in 1877. There also existed an informal business relationship between Chinese launderers and local Indians. Frontier laundries needed wood to fuel the fires for boiling vats of water and soap. Indians would gather chunks of mesquite, oak and ironwood and sell them to the Asian launderer.

By the spring of 1877, Huntington's track-laying crews had pushed across southern California and were at the Colorado River. Among the laborers, of course, were the Chinese immigrants. The Yuma *Arizona Sentinel* reported on April 14, 1877, that "on Monday a force of Chinamen was put to work near the river at Hanlon's Ferry. During the week their numbers have been increased and the lot of horses and carts sent over to them. . . . The main Chinese camp is about a mile above Hanlon's on the California side. . . ." Salary and provisions during the construction of the Southern Pacific Railroad were comparable to those on the Central Pacific. Although for those Chinese sojourners who had, in fact, indentured their labor with an agent in China or California for passage, the one-dollar-per-day salary went mostly toward repaying their debt. On November 23 of the same year, the *Arizona Sentinel* reported that "249 Chinamen came in six cars. . . . On Thursday came eight cars with over 300 Chinamen, and yesterday 21 more came [into Arizona]."

When the Southern Pacific reached Tucson on March 20, 1880, it had become directly responsible for the largest settlement of Chinese in the Territory. The 1880 United States Census, for example, lists 1630 Chinese residents, of which 1153 lived in Pima County, 159 of them in Tucson. Within the Pima County total, 850 Chinese (a few with Hispanic surnames) were enumerated as laborers. Across all these pages is written "Railroad Workers."[13]

Following the completion of the SP line, a few Chinese remained in Arizona and continued to work as cooks and waiters. Others worked as section hands. These occupations presented less strenuous demands than construction had at a time when most of the Chinese laborers were section graders, leveling the terrain upon which tracks would later be laid.

Again, if there was an opportunity to leave monotonous construction work, Chinese would take the chance for better employment. Wherever they went, friends and relatives were apt to follow. Before the Southern Pacific had reached Gila Bend, Arizona, for instance, three men who shared the family name Wong left the work gangs and came to Tucson. They arrived in the late 1870s and established the O.K. Restaurant on the southeast corner of Church Plaza and Mesilla Street. A laundry basket was used instead of a cash register and meals were seventy-five cents each.[14] At a later date the Wongs became involved in litigation and needed the services of an interpreter. It was common for Chinese to appear in court to substantiate their legal status as bona fide immigrants under the exclusionary laws. With three immigrants of the same surname before the court, testimony may have required their answering questions about immediate blood relationships and family ties within their native village in China. Many immigrants had memorized answers to these questions prior to coming to America. Others who had immigrated before them would write home with a detailed question and answer dialogue based on their own interrogation. Native settlement maps were drawn giving full details about location of dwellings, rice fields and other villagers to aid the immigrants' memories. Chan Tin-Wo, a railroad cook, provides an example. He came to Tucson on the request of the Wongs and, after their case was resolved, Chan opened a general merchandise store on North Main.[15] Unlike the Wongs, he became politically active. In the 1880 Great Registers there are no recorded Chinese who voted and in the Pima County register for 1882, Chan Tin-Wo is the only one listed. His native "village" is given as "China" and it is shown that he was naturalized the year before. It appears that in Pima County there were no social or political barriers for Chinese who wished to participate in deciding county or municipal issues. Of course, one had to be able to speak the institutional language, English.

The *Arizona Daily Star* of November 9, 1884, lists Chan Tin-Wo as a "most prosperous groceryman in this city. Chan is a Republican striker and may be said to be on the wrong side of the fence, but he has the reputation of being about as honest and square in his dealing as men are generally made." In 1895, before his return to China, Chan requested that a brother, Don Doan-Yook, and nephew, Don Chun-Wo, come to Tucson. As a legal resident and businessman he could sponsor relatives for immigration to the United States. Again, migration and settlement were dependent on relationships, and Chan Tin-Wo's ability to speak English was paramount to gaining the rights and privileges given to others.

Don Sing, another successful Chinese merchant, operated a small grocery on the Pima Indian reservation near Casa Grande. In *A Pima Remembers*, George Webb relates that one afternoon a few Pimas were in the store searching for some kind of sweet. Don Sing, came up and asked what they wanted. They told him and he picked up a strawberry preserve and to their surprise he said in plain Pima: "Go 'ep sitoli we' nega 'i-da," meaning, "This is pretty good. It has syrup on it."[16] Don had learned to speak the language by growing up with Pimas and Papagos.[17] Another grocer spoke of his early experiences in the 1900s. Until he was able to speak either English or Spanish with some fluency, his customers would bring with them bags of empty cans and packages to help identify what they wanted to purchase.

Lee Wee-Kuan, whose route of migration to Arizona took him through northern Mexico, settled and ran a grocery in the Yaqui village outside of Tucson. His choice to settle initially among the Spanish-speaking Yaquis was based on his experience in northern Mexico and his ability to speak their language.[18]

Language and blood ties helped to determine settlement, but another important factor was the relationship of native villages with neighboring communities in China. This may have influenced Lee, who was from southeastern China, in his decision. There existed intense rivalry, for example, between members of two districts in Kwangtung, the Sam Yap and Sze Yap. The antagonism was so great that in Arizona immigrants from these two regions would not live in the same area. This concept of territory was reflected in migration and settlement patterns based on personal relationships. Kinship, as stated in the exclusionary laws, was a legal avenue for Chinese immigration. Chinese businesses were dependent on similar familial relationships which offered social and economic support.

Chinese immigrants in Arizona were primarily from the Sam Yap and Sze Yap Provinces, and in Tucson the earliest arrivals were from the former. Almost simultaneously others came from Toy San of the Sze Yap district. As their numbers increased, Sam Yap immigrants left. Lee Wee-Kuan was from Sun Wui and this may be the reason he first settled on the outskirts of Tucson. Sun Wui and Toy San residents in China were amiable since they were from the same district in southern Kwangtung province. With the influx of Sun Wui immigrants to

Tucson, Lee Wee-Kuan eventually relocated within the city. This process of displacing one Chinese group with another based on native regionalism expresses solidarity along more subtle lines than ethnic grouping. As individuals, pioneer Chinese were usually more concerned with economic survival than with ethnic consolidation.

After their initial settlement, these newcomers found other occupations available in copper mining, domestic services and truck gardening. Not far from most towns were Chinese-tended vegetable gardens. In the Clifton area the men coordinated their efforts in cultivating fresh produce along the banks of the Gila River near Guthrie. Every two weeks, six Chinese from Clifton would go out to the gardens to relieve another group of six, who would then return to town.[19] The gardens at Fairbank, in southern Arizona, provided fresh produce for Tombstone and Benson. Along the Santa Cruz River near Tucson several parcels of land were leased in the 1880s to Chinese farmers.

Over one hundred acres in the Tucson area were being cultivated by the Chinese at this time. Much of the land was owned by Leopoldo Carillo, Samuel Hughes, Solomon Warner and the Sisters of St. Joseph. During one of the water-rights hearings in 1883, a witness compared Chinese and Mexican gardens. A Mr. Stephens testified that the Chinese gardener "raises cabbages, garlic and in fact everything in the vegetable line from an artichoke to the biggest cabbage, and the chinaman makes it a matter of business and he produces all he can, and as often as he possibly can. The Mexican garden produces a few chili peppers, onions, garbanzos, beans, melons & etc. . . ."[20]

These fresh produce plots were irrigated from acequias twice as often as fields of wheat, barley and cotton. The Chinese gardens south of Sisters' Lane required water continuously, and several of the townspeople thought this distribution of water was unfair. Anglo landowners, however, were eager to lease available lands to the Chinese for cultivation, sometimes to the dissatisfaction of others. In a letter to the Presbyterian Home Mission in New York, Superintendent Howard Billman of the Tucson Indian School wrote on June 26, 1889, that he personally inspected the irrigation practices of the Chinese. "Some thieving Chinese above us were simply robbing us," he complained.[21]

Thus Chinese gardeners became the suppliers of fresh produce that no other pioneer settler felt it profitable enough to market in northern, central and southern Arizona. An interesting location for a garden was even found at the Territorial Prison at Yuma. The *Arizona Republic* on November 10, 1893, reported the institution was in "shipshape order, the lawns kept well and green with grass, the garden, where formerly calabasas [pumpkins] had been raised, is now transformed into a regular French vegetable garden attended by a Chinaman who is lodged there for life, and [who] deserves credit as a good vegetable gardener."

As businessmen the Chinese were well organized. Clara Ferrin of Tucson observed in 1897 that adjoining their gardens are small huts built of adobes and ornamented by tin-cans, barley sacks and bushes, in which two or three partners or "cousins" as they call each other live together. . . . They do most of the work by hand, pushing steadily along behind the plow until the ground has been laid in smooth furrows. . . . As soon as the plants begin to grow they are covered with coal-oil cans to protect them from the sun. . . . The man who sells the product comes into town as early as five o'clock in the morning so that the vegetables will not be withered by the sun and will be fresh when they arrive in the market. . . . All that morning he goes house to house selling vegetables from a strong, but shabby wagon. Their methods of business are very exact. . . . They have their special customers and keep the account by marking down on the casement of the door the amount bought each day and at the end of the month they have not the trouble of making out bills. After selling nearly all their vegetables they breakfast with one of their city "cousins" in a grocery store.

Miss Ferrin wondered about the "great disadvantage it would be to us if the vegetable chinamen were all removed from Tucson."[22]

The Chinese were an asset as well to early copper mining in the Territory. In 1879, forwarding agents Barnett and Block imported a trainload of the Asians to build a railway from the Longfellow mines to the smelting works in Clifton.[23] Henry Lesinsky, owner of the operation, desired to use Chinese labor, although he did not want to be responsible for starting a "Mongolian invasion of the territory." These laborers were assigned work that "even Mexicans cannot be got to do."[24]

Chinese had been employed by Lesinsky a year earlier in the narrow ravines of the hills over thirty-five miles from the copper mines. Here they gathered and burned mesquite for charcoal used in the reduction process. They carried it with back packs for a mile to a location where the product could be transferred to wagon teams for shipment to the Mexican furnaces. To the discontent of the other miners, some Chinese eventually were employed in the underground shafts, although Lesinsky clearly stated that their labor would be separate from that of the others.[25]

In Clifton, all the Chinese ultimately met with resistance from the Anglo residents of the mining camps. Most of them again sought refuge in other occupations available to them. Although they were not met with repressive measures such as the California Foreign Miners' Tax, Chinese miners were nevertheless unwelcome in Arizona. Had they learned from similar experiences in California? By the turn of the century those Asians in Clifton had already established themselves in other sectors of commerce that allowed them to expand with the developing Territory. In retail trades, credit was one feature which helped to establish Chinese businesses in the mining regions.

Nevertheless, in an atmosphere of anti-Chinese sentiment, these Oriental pioneers had to "withdraw from overt competition by engaging in occupations and businesses which supplemented the economic order."[26] To do this, they banded together to promote mutual business and social pursuits. Voluntary associations, called "tongs" by the Anglos were not only business-oriented but acted as a support for the local elders in settling intra-group conflicts. For many early Chinese businesses, extended lines of credit and trade were arranged with already established firms in California and Arizona. Such forms of mutual aid were the mechanisms used to counteract external threats from western institutions.

An essential component in the Arizona economy was ranching. The Chinese, ever alert to opportunity in their new home, were raising cattle in the Territory as early as 1891. Brand registers in that year list Lim Kee as a stock owner in southern Arizona. In Pima County, You Chang of Lochiel registered his brand in 1898. You Cang had married a Mexican woman, Esperanza, in Lordsburg, New Mexico, in the 1890s. Their son Ernest, who was an American citizen by virtue of his birth in Arizona in 1897, was later considered one of the better ranch hands in southern Arizona.

In the northern section of the Territory, Louie Ghuey was one of the "progressive Chinese." He was the builder of the first brick building in Holbrook, and ads promoting the businesses of this enterprising pioneer appear in the Holbrook *Argus* from 1895 to 1898, when he owned a grocery, restaurant, bakery and photographic studio. It seems that Louis Ghuey rented his businesses to others in order to devote most of his time to real estate and photography. In the latter pursuit his reputation was that of a "celestial artist." In 1896, Louie Ghuey was commissioned by the *Argus* to photograph important businessmen, residences and reservoirs in Holbrook and surrounding towns.

By the late nineteenth century, Chinese settlers had participated in the major sectors of the Arizona economy: mining, railroad construction, agriculture, retail businesses, and ranching. They were now permanent residents and an established part of the Arizona scene; they could point to their contributions in the development of the region. Yet they still faced instances of discrimination and prejudice, even as they achieved a general acceptance within this desert society.

The family of Lee Kwong and Lai Ngan became the first Chinese to settle in Nogales, Arizona, and their experiences can be termed typical of those who came to the Territory and stayed.[27] They were the children of actors in a touring opera company that appeared in San Francisco theaters in the 1870s. Lee Kwong, many years older than Lai Ngan, had settled in San Francisco during the gold strike. At the time of the opera company's departure, Lai Ngan was left with relatives in California instead of returning to China with her parents. She became the wife of Lee Kwong in an arranged marriage. In 1884, she gave birth to her first son, Percy; then two daughters, Carmen in 1886, and Aurelia in 1888. In 1890 Kee Kwong traveled to Guaymas, Sonora, to prospect for gold. He took with him their six-year-old son Percy. Lai Ngan set out to meet them, sailing from San Francisco to Guaymas with her two infant daughters. During this period the family lived in Guaymas, where Kwong hoped to discover wealth in gold. Lai Ngan worked in a

Chinese-owned shoe factory, where she ironed the upper parts of shoes to be sewn onto the soles. The children were cared for by her Indian friend and companion, Doña García.

Lai Ngan gave birth to four more children. In Guaymas, Concepcion was born in 1897. Louise was born near her father's mine at La Colorada in 1899, as was Marian in 1901, and Frank in 1903. Marian recalls the determination of her mother after her father sold their house out from under them:

> Lai Ngan, my mother, started a little grocery store in La Colorada where she bought a house so we would have someplace to stay. One day a man came over and said to her, "You owe me some rent." She said, "What do you mean I owe you some rent? I bought this house myself." My mother got so mad. She got a stick and told him, "You get out of her and don't you ever come back looking for rent because I'm not going to give it to you. This is my house and I don't care how many times he sold it, it's mine." So the man never came back. When we left La Colorada, my mother just left the house and never got any money for it; maybe my father did.[28]

Not wanting the children to be raised in Mexico, Lai Ngan returned to the United States in 1903 and settled in Nogales, Arizona. There she rented a big house for $25 a month. She also ran another small grocery. Lee Kwong followed. He sold lottery tickets morning, noon and night. They were the only Chinese family in Nogales, although there were several single Chinese men. Marian attended school with her brothers and sisters.

> We used to have problems in Nogales when we were going to school. The Mexican kids used to tease us because we were Chinese. There were some Mexican boys in our neighborhood who would always take my brother and beat him up. My brother Frank, who was smaller and younger, would cry. One day I told them that if they didn't stop bothering him I was going to go after them. So they didn't believe me. One day they teased my brother so much I went after them and I beat one up something terrible. Oh, I just beat him to a "fare thee well." He was crying and crying and his brother asked him, "Aren't you ashamed of yourself? You let a girl beat you up?" He said, "I'm not crying 'cause it hurt me, I'm crying 'cause I'm mad." After that they never bothered Frank anymore.[29]

In 1907 the family took in and nursed Rita, a young girl of Chinese-Mexican parentage who was stricken with malaria. The family and Rita developed a strong attachment. Rita's father, a conservative Chinese, wanted her raised in the Chinese tradition and speaking the Chinese language. He had followed Rita and her mother into Mexico, where they had fled with a Mexican man. After stealing Rita away, he brought her to the Lee household to live. After only a few years, she was taken away from the Lees and again given to another Chinese family who knew more of the traditional customs.

One evening, the family my sister Rita was living with invited us to stay for dinner. They set the table with chopsticks. We didn't know how to use chopsticks. It was really embarrassing. The people kept saying, "You're Chinese and you don't know how to use chopsticks? You might as well not be Chinese." Then they gave us forks to eat with. When we got back to Nogales, we told our mother that we were ashamed to be Chinese and not be able to do things Chinese people do. She said, "Hereafter you are going to learn to eat with chopsticks." So she bought the bowls and chopsticks and the spoons and everything else and showed us how to do it.[30]

In 1914 Lee Kwong visited his eldest son Percy, who had moved to San Francisco where he worked for an import-export firm. Lee had longed to return to San Francisco and the Chinese community in which he spent his early days as an immigrant. While there, he suffered a stroke and died. The entire family then moved to San Francisco and they stayed until 1917, when Lai Ngan remarried. They then returned to Nogales, remaining there until 1918, when, upon the request of Mrs. Lim Goon, they decided to move to Tucson. The Lim Goons had bought rental property called the Moore Cottages on the northeastern edge of downtown, and offered the Lees room and board in exchange for managing them. That same year, Lai Ngan gave birth to Tom. After her death in 1940, a few family members remained in Tucson.

The Lee Kwong story emphasizes the role of the family, which within Chinese tradition is thought of as the most revered institution. It represents the ideal unit for maintaining one's identity and culture. In Arizona, Chinese bachelors, or men separated from their families, frequently adopted one. This filled the need for the several generations of relatives who maintained and observed traditional Chinese rituals. In Tucson, ethnic identity was often strengthened by the "tong," meaning association or clique. Here men could talk of the old days and of current Chinese affairs, play traditional games, and discuss the difficulties in adjusting to the West. Other places for interaction were at joss houses, opium dens and Chinese groceries and businesses. It was common for the building which housed a business to serve also as a residence, especially in the case of groceries and laundries, and most Chinese communities in Arizona prior to the 1900s could be described generally as "rooming house cultures."[31]

Rituals performed in China were often re-enacted in the joss house, a landmark in most Arizona towns. To the residents of Clifton, Nogales, Phoenix and Tucson, the temples and rituals (which were a mystery to the Anglos) provided a source for racist slander. For the Chinese, the world of spirits is like the world of men. Ancestral worship would be observed during the New Year celebration and other Chinese festivals and holidays. Material subsistence was as necessary in the netherworld as it was in the realm of the living. In the *Journal Miner* for October 10, 1879, an article on such beliefs was headlined, "Feeding the Dead."

R. J. Rutherford, the pioneer expressman, this morning performed the pious duty of taking two of the followers of Confucius, with a lot of roast pig, peaches, grapes and a bottle of brandy to Lynx Creek to feed a dead countryman, who has lain beneath the cold gravel of the lonely canyon, where he was murdered, a whole year, without a morsel of food or a drop of anything to cheer him on his journey to that flowery kingdom where all good Chinamen at last bring up. Rutherford says there was no throw off about the food: they left plenty of it and that which was good, on the grave, and as the two live celestials returned to town with him, there is no probability of their returning to bring away what their defunct friend may leave after satisfying his appetite.

Other cultural traits were regarded with suspicion by the Anglo community. Particular forms of dress, and foods, fruits and flowers held symbolic significance and had the power to avert or overcome evil for the Asians. The Chinese queue worn by all men until 1911 was a symbol of allegiance to the Ch'ing dynastic rule of the Manchurians, who dominated China from 1644 to 1911. The bound feet of the Chinese women was aesthetically pleasing and implied that a woman's position was stationary and in the home. White narcissus flowers brought good fortune and the peach blossoms long life. Arizona shopkeepers frequently gave their best customers flower bulbs during celebrations of Chinese holidays. All these customs and observances set the Chinese apart and made them different.

Family relationships were also a mystery to the white settlers and became the basis for discriminatory legislation. Because of restrictive immigration laws in force until 1943, the primary bond among Chinese did not usually extend beyond father-son, uncle-nephew or brother-to-brother connections. Few Chinese women made their way to the Territory. Those who did were usually reunited with husbands who had immigrated earlier. In 1871, the first Chinese women—one of ten to live in the Territory—arrived in Prescott. Even within all-male groups, however, the function of kinship was vital in the maintenance of culture and in introducing immigrants to new geographical territories. Although most of the bachelor Chinese remained single, some married women of other races. A 1901 Arizona law prohibited Chinese from marrying Anglos, stating "the marriage of a person of Caucasian blood with a Negro or Mongolian is null and void."[32] Marriage between Chinese and Mexicans was accepted, as were relationships between them and members of other minority groups. Chinese with families were more readily acceptable to residents of the Territory than were single men. For the Chinese, marriage also dispelled the distrust and dislike of the "sojourner," who was only in the country temporarily to take advantage of its opportunities and wealth. Hi Wo, of Benson, was one immigrant who established an American family rather than return to China. In 1900 he married Emeteria Morena and raised four daughters: Isabel, Soledad, Victoria and Felicia; and one son, José. These children spoke no Chinese, celebrated none of their father's native festivals and took Spanish names. Their dominant language was Spanish and all were confirmed Catholics.

Their lack of numbers was one reason the Chinese in Tucson, Phoenix and other communities in Arizona did not develop into self-sufficient units familiar in

San Francisco's Chinatown. Yet, it is important to note that the mandatory segregation of tens of thousands of the Asians in the 1860s laid the framework for this independent community. In Tuscon, a petition to "quarter" the Chinese was judged unconstitutional in 1893.[33] Although in the 1880s there were Anti-Chinese Leagues in every major town in the Territory, Arizonans actually felt no threat from the "yellow peril."

The great problem for every Chinese community was to be apart from, yet part of, the larger society. Culturally distinguishable from Mexico, Indian, Negro and Anglo in the plural society of the greater Southwest, the Chinese soon learned to communicate in English and Spanish. Christian mission schools were institutions that helped them in this need. In Tucson the Chinese Mission School was located on Ott Street in the 1800s. Later, English was taught at the Chinese Evangelical Church on Meyer Street. One of the first mission schools established in the Territory was at Prescott in 1880. T. W. Otis, a pioneer merchant, was also one of the founders of the Presbyterian and Congregational churches in the old capital. Wanting to help the Chinese, he organized classes to instruct them in English, using the Bible and the hymnal as texts. In 1895, his ten Chinese students held a special service conducted entirely in English, singing hymns and reciting passages from the New Testament.

As a result of such programs the children began to lose their native culture. To the distress of their pioneer parents and grandparents, second and third generation children grew up without knowing how to speak Chinese. Some families could afford to send their children to China for instruction, thus reestablishing familial ties and maintaining an ethnic identity for the Arizona-born Orientals. In 1930, the Chinese Evangelical Church brought a minister from China to Tucson who was hired to conduct services in Chinese and to teach the children their ancestral language.

By the 1920s, however, many of the younger Orientals were participants in the mainstream of Anglo society. Their background was still visible in allegiances to political parties in China, and to family and business associations and commercial networks in Arizona and California, but they also contributed to the needs of their adopted state and country. Lee Park Lin was an interpreter for the United States Immigration and Naturalization Service and also served on civic committees in Tucson. Teamed with prominent Tucsonan Herbert Drachman, he promoted the sales of World War I bonds. Lee was also a deacon in the First Baptist Church until the 1920s, when he returned to California. Several Arizona Chinese were drafted into service during the war. In the 1930s, a traditional Chinese orchestra performed for community picnics at the Elysian Grove in Tucson. Throughout the state, they joined others in the celebration of Cinco de Mayo and Fourth of July holidays.

Politically, the Chinese were slow to become active. At the time of their arrival in the 1860s, the dominant Anglo institutions had decisively dealt with a varied population that included native Indians and a Hispanic majority. Promotion by

Anglos of Mexican enfranchisement might have slowed development of the Territory and the granting of statehood. The course taken was one of political non-inclusion and cultural indifference. The early Chinese immigrants to the Territory were also political nonentities. Their numbers, and those seeking full participation in voting rights, were minimal. It was Chan Tin-Wo, however, who cast the decisive vote in favor of a bond issue for the construction of Drachman School in the 1890s. At the time, his business and home were located in today's "Barrio Historico" of Tucson. Chan, Heng-Lee, Gee Soon and a handful of others were registered prior to the turn of the century, and they always followed party lines and supported popular issues. As an ethnic group, consolidated voting would never threaten the power of Anglo political institutions.

It is within this diverse economic, political and social climate that the Chinese pioneers settled in Arizona. Many came but left no lasting mark. Discrimination, undesirable working conditions, or the hardships of frontier life drove them out. Many stayed, however, and prospered. They made the most of very little, providing services or goods that the existing population began to depend on, and over the years they gave much toward the development of the Territory. The Chinese shared in the Arizona fortune and found a lasting place within the unique cultural plurality of the Southwest.

NOTES

1. The bill specified that all who wished to mine, and who were not native-born citizens of the United States, or who had become citizens under the Treaty of Guadalupe Hidalgo, were required to pay a license fee of twenty dollars a month. Many of the Chinese miners, either unwilling or unable to pay the tax, went into these other occupations.

2. *The Railroad Gazette*, September 19, 1870.

3. Circular in Julius Goldbaum Collection, Arizona Historical Society (AHS), Tucson.

4. H. Mark Lai and Philip P. Choy, *Outlines: History of the Chinese in America* (Privately published, 1972. Distributed by Everybody's Bookstore, San Francisco), pp. 89–90.

5. Cheng-Tsu, ed., *Chink!* (New York: World Publishers, 1972), pp. 17–19.

6. Mary Coolidge, *Chinese Immigration* (New York: H. Holt & Co., 1909), p. 183.

7. *Ibid.*

8. Stan Steiner, *Fusang* (New York: Harper & Row, 1979), p. 88.

9. Rodolfo Acuna, *Occupied America* (San Francisco: Canfield Press, 1972), pp. 93–94.

10. *Daily Arizona Miner*, November 27, 1869.

11. *Daily Arizona Miner*, June 13, 1868.

12. Captain James Hobbs, *Wild Life in the Far West* (Hartford, Conn.: Wiley, Waterman and Eaton, 1973).

13. Figures based on the 1870 and 1880 Federal Census for New Mexico and Arizona Territories (Washington: Government Printing Office).

14. Chun-Wo Don to Joseph A. Roberts, January 22, 1935, biographical file at AHS, Tucson.

15. *Ibid.*

16. George Webb, *A Pima Remembers* (Tucson: University of Arizona Press, 1959), pp. 74–75.

17. James Don, interview with LMF in Florence, Arizona, February, 1978.

18. Lee Kim Wah, interview with LMF in Tucson, Arizona, March, 1977.

19. Al Fernandez, interview with LMF in Clifton, Arizona, September, 1978.

20. Manuscript in Charles Rivers Drake Collection, AHS, Tucson.

21. Reverent Howard Billman to B. Boyd, June 26, 1889, in Tucson Indian Training School Collection, Letter Press, p. 282, at AHS, Tucson.

22. Unpublished and untitled manuscript to Clara Ferrin Collection, dated June 5, 1897, AHS, Tucson.

23. *The Arizona Citizen* (Tucson), July 18, 1879.

24. *The Arizona Enterprise* (Prescott), July 31, 1878.

25. *The Post* (San Francisco), July 25, 1878.

26. Rose Hum Lee, *The Chinese in the United States of America* (Hong Kong: Hong Kong University Press and Oxford University Press, 1960), pp. 252–253.

27. Marian Lim, fifth child of Lee Kwong and Lai Ngan, interviews with LMF, 1979, in Tucson, Arizona.

28. *Ibid.*

29. *Ibid.*

30. *Ibid.*

31. Rose Hum Lee, *The Chinese in the United States of America*, p. 330.

32. Arizona Legislative Assembly, *Revised Statutes of Arizona Territory, 1901* (Columbia, Mo.: Press of E. W. Stephens, 1901), #3092, p. 809.

33. The 1890 Sanborn maps for Tucson locate a Chinese and Mexican settlement north of Alameda Street. The 1883 Sanborn map shows that a few general stores operated by Chinese were located in the Barrio Libre. The areas bordered by Main, Pennington and Pearl Streets included Chinese businesses and dwellings and it is believed that Mexicans and other members of minority groups lived nearby.

4

Chinese Sojourners in Territorial Prescott

Florence C. Lister and Robert H. Lister

THE CHINESE ARE HERE

It may be no coincidence that in 1869, when the first contingent of Chinese to follow Quon Clong Gin to Prescott appeared, the Union Pacific Railroad was completed. In that year tracks laid from northern California eastward with the help of Chinese laborers, variously estimated between six and twelve thousand, connected at Promontory in northern Utah with the line punched through from the opposite direction. With this long-distance rail network finally completed, large numbers of Chinese were stranded in the sparsely inhabited interior West with no means of support. Up to this time they had lived in communal work camps along the survey route and had been provided with customary foodstuffs and supplies imported from China by the agents who had contacted for their services.[1] But on May 10, 1869, their job finished, they were dismissed disinterestedly to fend for themselves as best they could. Most returned to the Pacific coast. A few others traveled eastward on the new rails, eventually to congregate in urban ghettos. Still others gradually dispersed in small groups throughout the spacious intermountain region and moved along with the growing mining frontier.[2] Of these, the greatest number settled temporarily in Idaho, where by 1870 they comprised a third of the population. Some made their way to Wyoming, to Colorado, or to other places in Utah. News of mineral strikes traveled with mysterious but lightning speed through the camps of the West, so it is surmised that those who showed up in Prescott were part of this body of anchorless men.

If so, they could have made their way south through the sagebrush flats of central Utah and southern Nevada to Hardyville or Fort Mohave, where it was possible to cross the formidable barrier of the Colorado River, in 1869 just being explored further upriver by John Wesley Powell. From these minuscule clusters of buildings at the northern limit or river navigation from the Gulf of California, a toll road cut overland in a southeasterly direction to Prescott (Map 1). Stages and freight wagons were available to bring the Chinese men to town.[3]

In the same period other Chinese were moving along the western border of the Arizona Territory. They may have prompted fellow villagers or relatives to follow them. The 1870 federal census tabulated one Chinese at La Paz and seven at Arizona City (changed to Yuma in 1873) on the Colorado River. Two of them worked on river steamers. One had opened a hotel. Another five Chinese men resided in Vulture City, with one at the Vulture Mine, both located south of Prescott on the desert near modern Wickenburg. One Chinese was recorded in a sweeping southwestern sector of Yavapai County which included Date Creek, Kirkland Valley, and Skull Valley.[4] All these Chinese then in southern Arizona are believed to have moved by steamer across the Gulf of California or to have crossed the Colorado Desert on muleback from the California jumping-off place of San Bernardino. That land route would have brought them to the supply depot of Ehrenburg on the river, where a semiweekly stage made its way 213 miles up through the tiers of rocky arid mountains to Camp Date Creek and then on to evergreen Prescott.[5]

However they came, the local press for the first time confirmed that Chinese were present in the community. Moreover, if one can assume that the reporter reflected popular opinion, it is obvious that negative attitudes toward the Chinese already existed.

> We have heretofore neglected to inform our readers that a veritable young Celestial arrived at Fort Whipple a short time ago. Should he live long enough to become a man, Yavapai county will contain one Chinaman.
>
> A real live Chinaman, with tail and other appendages. . . . For our part, we have seen as many of them as we care to see.
>
> Three more Chinamen arrived here during the week, and have gone to work. There are now four of them in this vicinity, which is quite enough.
>
> Since our last, some ten or twelve more Chinamen have arrived.[6]

The report of a lone Chinese youth at Fort Whipple, a post adjacent to Prescott and one of a line of small, insufficiently staffed military installations across territorial Arizona whose purpose was to keep the warlike Indians in check, points to an underlying tragedy behind the overseas movement of the Chinese. Many of those who made the hellish journey in dank vessel holds from China to America were mere children. A comparison of census data giving current age with stated years of residence in the United States shows that it was not uncommon for boys of eight to twelve years of age to have left home and family in the urgent need to earn money abroad. It was the lot of Chinese peasant boys to take a full role in providing for the common good as soon as they were physically capable, but overseas residency meant the added burden of insecurity and loneliness. Many such youngsters never lived to make it back to their homeland. For others, the return trip was delayed for years. For all, it was a too-rapid transition from childhood to manhood.

It was the 1863 discovery of gold which had lured Euro-Americans into this Arizona region, until then an unexplored wilderness. With their previous experience among the mines of California, it was predictable that some of the newly arrived Chinese would hope to share in Prescott's mineral riches. In the condescending prose of the time, a local paper told its readers of one such effort being made in a mining district to the east of town.

> The flight of ye Chinamen in Big Bugwards. John thinks he has struck a big thing there, and is bound to go. Two, three, and four cents to the pan were found by one of them, recently. The finder sent word to his fellow countrymen in Prescott, who, upon learning the glad tidings, held a meeting, discussed the "subject" and resolved to start immediately, if not sooner. They waited upon their employers and each one said: "Me no likee cookee; no likee washee, any more. Me go Big Bug light away, where one Chinaman telle me he find gleat deal coarse gold. Sabe John. You pay me; me go." They were paid, and went, on their way rejoicing, leaving their employers in the lurch. Now, John, as you have gone out into the woods, we tell you to beware of the Apache.[7]

Placer mining was attractive to the Chinese sojourners because little capital was required beyond the purchase price of shovel, rocker, and pan. Placering already had proved profitable in Prescott's satellite districts, such as Big Bug, Lynx Creek, and the Hassayampa drainage, although the diggings left for the Chinese were worked over and abandoned or those regarded as sterile. From this disadvantageous practice came the phrase "Chinaman's chance," meaning little chance at all. Ignoring the white miner's snickers, a handful of Chinese workers nevertheless gained a meager livelihood at local placering until the resources were exhausted. With no hint of rancor, the press graciously noted this modest success.

> Eight or ten Chinamen are working some placers in the vicinity of the old Ramos farm on Lynx Creek and are doing well.[8]

The farm of pioneers Cornelio and Mary Ramos had been purchased in the 1870s by Chinese Sam Lee and several partners for the sum of three hundred dollars in gold.[9] That considerable investment suggests combined savings accrued over a period of time, perhaps from sustained employment such as railroad construction. When the riffles on Lynx Creek were cleaned out or the seasonal stream went dry, the enterprising Lee and his associate, Ah Fork, opened a one-room saloon and stage station (Figure 2). While living there, Lee is credited with having provided materials to repair wagons of a Euro-American party which had been wrecked during an Apache attack.[10]

Such encounters with Indians were part of daily life on this frontier. Unknowingly, Prescott had been placed in the heart of the traditional lands of the Yavapai, a seminomadic people who expectedly resented Euro-American intrusion and took advantage of every opportunity to eliminate it. Constantly seeking some weakness in Euro-American defenses, the Yavapai hoped to unnerve, if not kill, the settlers, and the Indians' owl hoots and coyote howls could be heard nightly as they communicated with each other from lookouts in the valley around the town. Whenever troops rode out of the tiny Whipple Barracks, Yavapai smoke signals curled along the horizon.[11] To the west of the Yavapai were river tribes, notably the Yuma and Mohave, who made travel through their domain precarious. Several of their massacres of wagon trains received extensive publicity. Even more fearsome was the band of western Apache sweeping through the craggy rim country of central Arizona. Throughout the late 1860s and early 1870s they indiscriminately picked off isolated individuals and subjected them to horrible mutilations and deaths.[12] Ranchers, miners, stagecoach passengers, and military scouts were their fair game. The Chinese, too, became victims of these ruthless warriors, who did not recognize the Asians as racial brothers. It is said that the long queues of Chinese black hair merely enhanced the taking of scalps.[13]

The limited number of soldiers skilled in Indian warfare, the rough terrain, and the cleverness of the Native Americans allowed a state of war to continue for years. Not until 1873, when Lieutenant Colonel George Crook and his Whipple Barracks stalwarts finally brought the western bands to reservation life, was there temporary respite from these depredations in the Prescott region. However, within a few years in other districts of the Arizona Territory, the culpability of government Indian agents and contractors wiped out this brief peace. A band of Chiricahua Apaches bolted in rebellion against abuse, fled to the Mexican mountains, and opened a new chapter of conflict that was not ended until 1886. At that time the ringleader, Geronimo, and his men finally surrendered. Prescott was not affected in the second phase of the Apache campaigns except that, until he was replaced, Crook again operated out of Whipple Barracks.

Danger on the frontier notwithstanding, the 1870s saw an increasing influx of Chinese straggling into the remoteness of central Arizona, perhaps drawn there by relayed messages of little open hostility toward others of their race. With an apparent feeling of helplessness and alarm, Euro-American newspapermen kept their readers aware of the oncoming Asian tide. The Prescott *Enterprise* carried such items on September 15 and October 10, 1877.

> Nearly all the stages which have arrived here recently have brought Chinamen as passengers. We hope we are not to be victims of this barbarous horde. We don't admire the Chinese, anyway.
>
> Still they come! Two more Chinese arrived in Prescott on the stage last Sunday morning. The Chinese population of Prescott is getting to be pretty numerous, and unless something is done to stop this immigration they soon will overrun everything.

The rival *Arizona Weekly Minor* noted, on October 26, 1877,

> A wagon load of Chinese arrived, today, from the Colorado River, and took up their residences at Mongolian Headquarters on Granite Street. Prescott has over fifty of these pig-tail celestials who live on rice and opium.

Two years later we read,

> Prescott has about 75 or 80 Chinamen, which is 75 or 80 too many. Now is a good time to get rid of them.[14]

And the following year:

> The coach was loaded down this morning with one Chinaman and emptiness— agreeable companions.[15]

Part of the 1870s surge of Chinese immigrants to the Prescott region was due to construction of the Southern Pacific Railroad, which was planned to run along the thirty-second parallel from Los Angeles to New Orleans. By mid-1877 the tracks had reached the west bank of the Colorado River at Yuma. During a year-long delay while a bridge was being put across the river and permission was being sought to traverse the military reservation on the east side, some of the large Asian labor force deserted camp. Prescott, several hundred miles to the northeast, pre-sented the opportunity for less physically demanding jobs out of the desert heat.

Typically, the Chinese in the American West lived, worked, and relaxed to-gether. That communal settlement pattern often was necessary because of the lack of available or affordable housing in communities just being carved out of the fron-tier. The Chinese were probably not disturbed by such an arrangement, because men's and boys' houses were commonplace in the south China region from which they had come.[16] Perhaps more important in the West, such houses served as a de-fense against an unfamiliar and often unfriendly outside world. All these factors may have been at work in Prescott, where in 1870 there were just 151 widely dis-persed dwellings. One might have been on the lot on the east side of Granite Street between Gurley and Goodwin streets which had been purchased by Quon Clong Gin. Several ramshackle buildings across Granite Street were available for rent, one formerly a butcher shop operated by Euro-American pioneer Guilford Hath-away. Thus when other Chinese began drifting into town, this is the district to which they were attracted and where they were to remain concentrated during their entire stay. Although no residential restrictions were placed on the new Asian migrants, it conveniently happened that the area they favored already was consid-ered by Euro-Americans to be a less desirable part of town, even though it was just one block from the plaza, and the seat of territorial government at times would be immediately across the stream to the west of Granite Street. A map of 1890 con-firms earlier references to the block on Granite Street between Gurley and Good-win streets as Prescott's small Chinatown (Map 2, Fig. 4.1).

The Chinese occupied a half dozen frame buildings on the west side of Gran-ite Street. In each case a small room opening onto the dirt street in front served as a place of business. In the rear, a variable number of men lived in one or more rooms modified with wooden bunks along the walls and pegs upon which clothes could be hung. A wood stove provided heat, essential in the brief winters typical

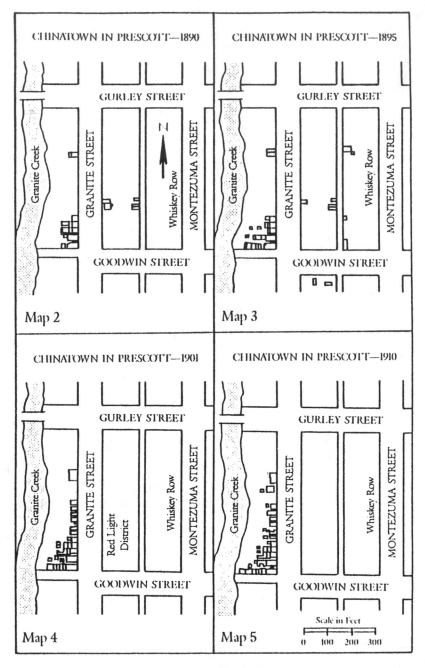

Figure 4.1 Maps of Chinatown in Prescott, 1890–1910. Based upon Sanborn Fire Insurance Maps, Sanborn–Perris Map Co., New York.

of the five-thousand-foot elevation. A simple, common kitchen contained cooking stove, table, chairs, storage shelves, and utensils. Probably there was some sort of a small altar in the bedroom and an image of the kitchen god in the cooking area to whom cursory recognition was offered. A few family pictures, cheap prints torn from Chinese-language publications, or lunar calendars adorned walls. Otherwise, the cellular rooms were devoid of ornamentation but were cluttered from overcrowding and infrequent housecleaning. Privies stood our back along the creek. Kitchen gardens, stray chickens, and stables shared the yards. In general, these meager quarters were no better, and certainly no worse, than those the Chinese knew in their homeland. Nor were they appreciably inferior to others occupied by much of the Euro-American bachelor population.

At some undetermined period the building on the second lot on Granite Street north from Goodwin acquired the distinction of a second story fronted by a porch. An elevated false roofline across the facade bearing simple scrolled decoration was the only modification hinting at anything other than the usual building to be found in any western frontier town. Presumably, this upper level and its elaboration were ordered and paid for by Chinese tenants to serve as their meeting hall, where both religious and social activities could take place. Such installations were common in their native villages of south China. They assumed even greater importance in the American West as group rallying places.

Inside the rooms, considered by Euro-Americans to be a temple, was undoubtedly a clay or wooden image of the god Kuan Yu (also Kuan Ti or Kuan Kung), one of a hierarchy of idols termed *josses*. Kuan Yu was a legendary military hero of the Three Kingdoms believed to exemplify masculinity. Usually he was portrayed as a red-faced, bewhiskered individual in a seated position. Kuan Yu likely was accompanied by one or more altars and votive tables, banners with inscriptions, lanterns, long sandlewood tapers (or joss sticks) stuck into brass urns of sand to be slivered as incense, red candles, perhaps a barrel-shaped umbrella (a symbol of respect or purity), red paper prayer slips and a furnace for their burning, and a gong and drum on a wooden stand.[17] The most educated man of the group probably was the guardian of the so-called temple, with responsibilities for burning incense, lighting candles, pouring rice wine, and interpreting divination signs for determining propitious dates for burial of the dead or for proposed activities.

Opposite this complex of structures, on the east side of Granite Street, was a boardinghouse indicated by Sanborn fire-insurance mappers as Chinese, and at least three additional Chinese-occupied dwellings faced the alley behind. They are believed to have been on what was once the Quon Clong Gin land. By 1890, scattered to the north and south of this core of Chinatown were ten other buildings used by the Asians as joint work and sleeping space. Their locations may have been determined by those of the clients served. Other Chinese were provided spartan housing at their places of employment. Everywhere, whether on Granite Street or more removed, it was mere subsistence-level survival, uncomfortable as it was unhealthful. But as the Chinese wanted, or perhaps as social and economic conditions mandated, it was together.

The Chinese who settled in Prescott were quick to see that the resident Euro-American population, in a ratio of five males to one female, routinely got hungry and dirty but had no inclination to tend to these needs. Recognizing that cooking and washing required little specialized skill and only a minimal command of English, these migrants, like other Chinese throughout the mountain West, formed small-scale food and laundry service industries that were to flourish for the entire lifetime of the local Chinese community. As the enterprises expanded, they included related activities ranging from dishwashing to raising vegetables, from ironing to delivering cleaned garments. The 1870 federal census revealed that, out of a total Prescott population of 668 persons, there were six Chinese already engaged in these tasks. A. He Sing, Ali Tung, and Wo Sam said they were cooks. Whether they had found work in kitchens of boardinghouses, restaurants, or private homes is not known. Ah Lee, Ah Poy, and Ah Hin were laundrymen, who may have plied their trade in private homes. The average age of these immigrants was between twenty-nine and thirty years. All had been born in China. Because clan or village members customarily colonized together, it is assumed they had been personally acquainted before they reached Arizona. It is also assumed that they were speakers of the Sze Yap dialect, inasmuch as those persons were most numerous among the incoming lower-class migrants. The devastating Taiping Rebellion centered in south China had driven them out of their homeland.

Even though terrorized by Indians and suffering prolonged effects of national economic depression, in the 1870s Prescott was a lively place where day or night at any number of bars a thirsty man could get a shot of liquor. The block along the west side of the plaza on Montezuma Street was becoming a wooden wall of rowdy drinking, gambling, and cavorting establishments known to one and all as Whiskey Row and peopled with the cast of mismatched characters that made the Old West the stuff of drama. Many saloonkeepers added eateries in the knowledge that even cowboys in town for relaxation, off-duty soldiers, or miners celebrating a find could not live by drink alone. The eager Chinese were in luck, being in the right place at the right time. In short order, they took over management or operation of these saloon restaurants, either employed by Euro-American owners or leasing their facilities. A talent for pleasing American palates cheaply added the phrases "chop house" and "noodle joint" to the upland vocabulary.

Daily, another growing corps of Chinese laundrymen worked in shabby, frame washhouses, their yards filled with drying platforms and pools of sudsy water. The more aggressive of the washermen displayed a characteristic Chinese taste for partnerships, with three or four men forming a joint business venture.[18] Combined resources provided the necessary funds for supplies of soap, firewood, and a few pieces of equipment. Partners were apt to have been related by clan or village. Proprietorship gave them the satisfaction of self-employment, a desirable status enhancement for those who formerly may have known only peasant background. It also allowed the option of the requisite trip back to China for family visits, while the endeavor continued to function in the hands of the others. These instances of group effort usually involved a division of labor in which some men washed, some ironed, and an apprentice, generally newly arrived in America, learned how to do both satisfactorily.

One solo laundry owner was Ah Sam, who had the foresight to set up shop next to the town jail. An entry in the Proceedings of the Board of Supervisors shows his receipt of $16.45 for washing done for prisoners confined there.[19]

As Paul Siu points out,[20] each laundry was a microcosm of China. Men tied by blood or territorial relationships worked side by side all day, ate and slept side by side at night, were concerned for each other's welfare, and together recalled home and times past. Except for sporadic encounters with Euro-American customers, they were out of touch with the culture around them. In the absence of their own firsthand impressions, their personal reactions to that situation remain unknown. If they fit the sojourner profile described by Siu, they considered themselves outsiders, and the Euro-Americans thought of them only in relation to their jobs and not to their individual personages.

George Ah Fat was one of the few early immigrants to Prescott who can be viewed as an up-and-coming entrepreneur. With several partners, he placed what may have been the first commercial advertisement of a Chinese-owned business in Prescott. He likely had a ghost writer, but there is no doubt that he had learned the value of western-style promotion. The advertisement, which appeared in the September 2, 1871, edition of the *Arizona Weekly Miner*, read,

New Laundry

GRANITE STREET   PRESCOTT, ARIZONA
GEORGE AHFAT & CO.

Wash every class of fabric at their New Laundry Ladies' clothing flooted by flooting machine [*sic?*] in a manner to suit the most fastidious. Shirt bosoms, etc. polished and made to show well. Terms reasonable. Public patronage solicited.

The Ah Fat enterprise must have prospered, because on February 16, 1877, the same paper told its readers,

George Ah Fat gave a new year's dinner today, at which, he informed us yesterday, he intended among other delicacies to serve tea that costs $10 per pound.

Success, however, had its price. For unknown reasons, the industrious Ah Fat had acquired an enemy. The *Enterprise* of March 21, 1877, carried this brief item.

An attempt was made last Saturday to blow up the wash-house belonging to George Ah Fat. It is supposed to have been made by another Chinaman. There was no harm done, beyond the charring of some timbers.

Then reenter Sam Lee, as a follow-up article revealed.

> Sam Lee, the Lynx Creek Chinaman, who was arrested on a complaint made by
> George Ah Fat, to the effect that said Lee tried to blow up said Ah Fat's house, with
> a can of powder, has been held to answer to the charge before the next Grand Jury.
> Bail was set at $1,000 and not being able to produce the necessary bonds he was re-
> manded to jail.[21]

That matter apparently resolved, at summer's end Sam Lee's troubles were to
come to a violent conclusion.

> On Sunday afternoon an altercation took place between two almond-eyed sons of the
> Flowery Land, named, respectively Sam Lee and Ah Fork. The disturbance was
> about ownership of some property, and as usual, there was a woman mixed up in the
> affair. Sam Lee commenced the trouble and struck Ah Fork three times with a knife,
> severely wounding him. Ah Fork, having procured a knife, struck Sam Lee with it,
> killing him instantly. Coroner Day, with a jury, held that the homicide was justifi-
> able.[22]

The bits of information available strongly suggest that the two men shared the
attentions of one of the rare Chinese women in the northern territory. Anxieties
over pleasures, rather than business, may have led to the fracas. To continue the
Sam Lee saga,

> Ah Fork, who it will be remembered killed Sam Lee, his brother Celestial, at Lynx
> Creek recently, has been re-arrested and is now in jail. Ah Fork was allowed to go free
> upon the verdict of the coroner's jury, but subsequent investigation has revealed the
> fact that his release was the result of crooked swearing or interpretation. The Grand
> Jury, on reassembling, will have a chance at him.
>
>   The case of Ah Fork for the murder of Sam Lee was examined on Tuesday by Jus-
> tice Cate. The prisoner was discharged, there being no evidence to convict him of
> the offense. The prosecuting witness, Ah Key, testified that the reason he had sworn
> out a warrant charging Ah Fork with murder was that he had a dispute with him about
> a wagon.
>
>   The property of Sam Lee, recently killed on Lynx Creek, will be sold tomorrow
> evening by C. F. Cate, public administrator. There is a good span of horses and wagon
> in the outfit.[23]

Two years later a touching postscript to the sad Lee affair was reported by the
local paper.

> R. J. Rutherford, the pioneer expressman, this morning performed the pious duty of
> taking two of the followers of Confucius, with a lot of roast pig, peaches, grapes and
> a bottle of brandy to Lynx Creek to feed a dead countryman, who has lain beneath
> the cold gravel of that lonely canyon, where he was murdered, a whole year (*sic*],

without a morsel of food or a drop of anything to cheer him on his journey to that flowery kingdom where all good Chinamen at last bring up.

Rutherford says there was no thrown off about the feed: they left plenty of it, and that which was good, on the grave, and as the two live celestials returned to town with him, there is no probability of their returning to bring away what their defunct friend may have left after satisfying his appetite.[24]

Placing food in or on the graves of the dead for the soul's journey to the nether world was a customary practice in China going back at least as far as the Bronze Age.[25] Uninformed Euro-American associates of the Chinese were merely bemused that costly edibles could be squandered by men having little money. They did not realize it was one more expression of the unquestioning adherence on the part of the Chinese to their Confucian moral obligations to friends and family. The men who went out to the Lynx Creek grave may well have shared the Lee surname.

As for George Ah Fat, whose house the deceased allegedly torched, he gave up laundering and went into the restaurant business next to a saloon owned by D. C. Thorne. The 1880 census showed him managing a Montezuma Street eatery and overseeing four Chinese cooks, who probably shared his investment. That change of trade would have been considered by both Euro-Americans and Asians as a step up the social and economic scale. Unfortunately, the following item suggests that abuse by Euro-American customers drove him and his colleagues away and that the racial prejudice present from the beginning of the Prescott Chinese colony had not been eradicated through greater familiarity.

George Ah Fat & Co., of the Cabinet Chop House, desire us to state that they have concluded to make an unconditional surrender, and will, after this evening, cease to run the boarding department of the Cabinet.[26]

Cooking was an honorable profession in China requiring long apprenticeship, but most of those who initially took up this occupation in America had no such training. Adaptable and ingenious, they generally were peasants or small tradesmen whose lives on the borderlands of famine had taught them how to make something palatable out of virtually nothing. This experience stood them in good stead in frontier kitchens. In contrast, laundering, as practiced by Chinese in the West, carried with it the stigma of having been nonstop woman's work in the homeland. When men engaged in such work went back to China, they often were scorned.[27] However, on the west coast both these trades became strictly controlled by Chinese guilds regulating, apprenticeships, wages, prices, and locations. The first bloody riot within the San Francisco Chinatown was between laundrymen protesting areal restrictions imposed by a guild.[28] Additionally, Chinese district or clan associations had the power to sanction or deny a person's participation in either line of work.[29] Records are lacking to confirm the presence of any similar work structure in Prescott, but it is evident that a labor stratification based upon white racial attitudes was operative, and it essentially denied the Chinese much opportunity to demonstrate their true worth.

Some of the Euro-American attitudes toward the cooking and washing occupations were unyielding. This was tough country, where manliness was equated with wielding a pick or ax, riding herd, fighting Indians, or beating a team of mules into obedience. In the code of time and place, slaving over the proverbial hot stove or scrub board was not manly. Doing these tasks placed the Chinese in the most lowly servile status, even though the services rendered were essential to the daily functioning of the bachelor-dominated, roominghouse culture. "No tickee, no launlee" stereotyped the overseas Chinese to many Americans, even after they had graduated to other work.

It was not merely the means by which these immigrants at the bottom rungs of the ladder were existing and flourishing that fueled anti-Chinese sentiment. One root problem was, on the one hand, a perplexing lack of interest on the part of Asians in what to most red-blooded Euro-American citizens were the obvious benefits of Americanization and Christianity, and, on the other, a staunch belief among Euro-Americans in the necessity of racial, cultural, linguistic, and religious conformity in order for the nation to prosper. These feelings were intensified by many highly visible physical and ethnic distinctions between themselves and the Chinese. The frontier's towering, brawny Swedes, Germans, or Irishmen often interpreted the generally short stature, slight build, straggling whiskers, scurrying gait, and hand gestures of the southern Chinese as signs of weakness. The weak were not countenanced in this environment.

Furthermore, Chinese dialects were harsh to western ears; their several thousand written characters, brushed rather than penned, were incomprehensible. In the early years, many overseas Chinese did not learn English, nor did they have any motivation for doing so inasmuch as they operated within their own sphere. That caused resentment among Euro-Americans, a feeling irrationally heightened by their own lack of understanding of the Chinese language. Most of the immigrants who in the course of a day had to deal with Euro-Americans managed to learn a few key English words or phrases, but their difficulties of pronunciation provided the basis for endless belittling imitations. The biased frontier press, among them the Prescott newspapers, fueled this cruel parody.

Chinese names also were a constant source of confusion for westerners, as well as for those now attempting to reconstruct overseas Chinese history. Not only were they difficult to transcribe into English, but often it was not realized that the Chinese reversed the order so that surnames typically preceded personal names.[30] This was the Chinese way of immediate clan identification. Moreover, for a variety of reasons, the immigrants sometimes chose not to go by the appellations given them in China. As a consequence, many names surviving in records are corruptions, reversals, nicknames, anglicizations, and outright falsifications.[31] Strings of aliases litter extant documents. It appears that if a Chinese man was called

Charley or Joe by some chance Euro-American acquaintance, he kept that name for the duration of his stay in the United States. Or he simply took the name of some Euro-American of whom he may have heard. How else can one explain the fact that a Cantonese who worked as a cook in La Paz in 1870 was known as Joseph Smith unless he had passed through Zion or met a waggish Mormon en route to the Colorado River? How can one account for a Prescott caterer's being Fong Murphy? It is particularly intriguing that a high percentage of the immigrants told paymasters, census takers, or other Euro-American recordkeepers that their personal names were Ah. Actually, Ah is not a proper name but a term of endearment or a nickname used by Cantonese. Perhaps simply because it was easy for English speakers to write and spell, the Ahs definitely had it. Half of the Chinese men and one woman tabulated in the 1880 Prescott census went by that name, one even being Ah Ah.

The typical garb of the Chinese laborer and his mandatory queue starkly signaled his uniqueness to the Euro-American frontiersman (Figure 5). Usual clothing consisted of a dark blue, loose cotton tunic (*san*), untailored cotton pants (*koo*), soft dark sandals, white socks, and either a skull cap or a conical rice-straw hat. Added warmth was supplied by a quilted, waist-length, cotton jacket fastened down the front with loops. These clothes were ideal for sub-tropical southern China, but they did not suit more severe climates or rugged labors in thorny or rocky terrain. Chinese men faced with these conditions in western America gradually acquired mixed assortments of sturdy boots, denim trousers, wool jackets, and broad-brimmed, black felt hats, but traditional Chinese garments were retained for festive occasions.

Because ingrained food habits generally are relinquished only under duress, the local Chinese surely made every effort to eat as they did in Guangdong or Fujian provinces. With trade channels expanding during the territorial period, they were able to secure their preferred supplies from intermediaries on the west coast who depended upon Asian business. Red meat, potatoes, fried eggs, and boiling coffee may have been dished out by Chinese cooks on Whiskey Row, but on Granite Street the diet undoubtedly was rice, soy sauce, peanut oil, bean sprouts, preserved duck eggs, dried sea creatures, barbecued pork, pickled cabbage, and gallons of green tea. As if that were not affront enough to Euro-American sensitivities, chopsticks replaced forks, cups had no handles, flat saucepans gave way to round-bottomed woks, and razor-sharp cleavers sliced through bone and gristle.

With their often-recounted ethnocentrism, the sojourners in Prescott, like their countrymen trying to survive in other sectors of the western frontier, can be interpreted as outwardly indifferent to what Euro-Americans thought of them and their ways as long as it did not involve personal harm or forfeiture of dreams. Because most anticipated being away from their homeland just long enough to accumulate a stake, they seemed to cultivate a detachment from American affairs which made Euro-American associates edgy. Luck and ability both played a part in their monetary success, but in the meantime, the overseas Chinese demonstrated their intention of pursuing familiar paths, making accommodations to American lifestyles only as necessary for existence or to accomplish certain ill-defined economic goals.

For many, those goals became increasingly vague and unachievable through time.[32] Opportunities in a small, out-of-the-way town like Prescott, without agricultural, fishing, lumbering, or manufacturing potential, always were limited. Added to the narrow economic base was the fact that racial stereotypes already in place before the Chinese appeared on the local scene restricted them to a few services. Thus, partly by choice and partly because of racism, the immigrants were essentially isolated, although at the same time they were symbiotically dependent on a dominant society that was itself economically undiversified and struggling to survive. Here were seeds for future trouble.

Regardless of race, the way of life for many men on the frontier was stressful. For members of all groups, social control often broke down into crimes against each other. The Chinese had a further burden: they had come to America with a deep-rooted habit of intragroup quarreling. Lineages, villages, secret societies, and individuals typically were enmeshed in feuds and vendettas that had bloodied generations.[33] That resort to easy violence was transferred to the American West, although the immigrants did not wear guns strapped about their hips as did their Euro-American contemporaries. Instead, in fits of rage they had no hesitancy about grabbing any object—ax, pick, or knife—and taking after an enemy. Some proved to be fair shots once guns were acquired. Eventually, the salaried soldiers of the Chinese tongs became the fiercest of all fighting men in the West.[34]

For the Chinese, the difference between home and the Arizona Territory was that disputes in the latter, especially those involving personal attacks, ideally were settled in court. Even though they distrusted courts, lawyers, and officials, the sojourners found the American law beneficial. In China there was no leniency toward commoners who disturbed the public order, only savage physical punishment meted out without due process.[35] In contrast, the bulk of the Chinese in the United States were self-proclaimed transients and without citizenship. Yet they were given the protection of American law. That necessarily also entailed the obligation to observe it, often something of a problem for these aliens who were prone to resort to extralegal methods against their countrymen.[36]

Prescott's newspapers vacillated between straightforward reporting of such internal Chinatown troubles and patronizing verbiage. In either case, there was a quality of small-town gossip. The following selection indicates the range of conflict but is not intended to imply any greater degree of lawlessness on the part of the Asians than among fellow Euro-Americans, some of whom seemed bent on giving Prescott a reputation for wildness. A relevant statistic is that in 1899 there were 228 prisoners in the territorial prison in Yuma, of whom only two were Chinese.[37] Even in California, where the infamous tong wars raged during the late nineteenth century, relatively few Chinese were incarcerated. The offenses noted by the Prescott press pale by comparison.

Hee King was find $50 and costs last Saturday in Justice Ottis's court, for stealing $25 from another Chinaman.

This week, Justice Fleury has recorded an unusual amount of criminal business. On Wednesday, he completed the examination of two chinamen, charged with applying a hatchet to the head of another Celestial, and which case had been on the docket for several days. After having listened to the conflicting stories usual in such cases, and finding that he lacked jurisdiction to guillotine the whole outfit, discharged one of the defendants, and suffered the other, together with the complainant, to pay a fine of fifty dollars each, with the alternative of fifty days in the county jail.

Two Celestials with unpronounceable names, last night got into a difficulty in the rear of Tompkins' saloon, which resulted in one of the combatants receiving an ugly wound on the head from a shovel in the hands of his adversary. Arrest was made late last night by Marshal Dodson of the Chinaman who used the shovel and an examination will be held to-day before Justice Fleury.
 The Chinaman who committed the assault last night and whose name in Ah Fun, was examined to-day before Judge Fleury, plead guilty to the charge, was find $100 and not responding with the amount levied will spend the ensuing fifty days in the county jail. He is reported to have recently come here from Los Angeles, is a Chinese desperado of the highbinder type, and the court felt the necessity of making an example of him to deter future lawlessness among his compatriots.

Joe Jung, who committed an assault on Tung Young this morning, was brought before Judge Fleury and fined $50. In default of the necessary funds, wherewith to pay the fine, he was politely escorted to the county jail, with permission to assist in watering the young shade trees around the plaza, for a term of fifty days.[38]

While generally on peaceful but impersonal terms, Prescott's Euro-Americans and Chinese experienced some minor clashes that took on racial overtones. Although the papers tended to side with the former, it is to their credit that this was not invariably the case, particularly in instances such as the one recounted below when Asians obviously were victimized.

Monday night last, at a Chinese wash-house, on Granite Street, three tea and opium inspired devils from the Flowery Land, attacked a countryman of theirs, who had sawed off his tail, cut him up horribly and would have killed him outright had not Jennings, the night watchman, rushed in and stopped the war. The tailless Chinaman's wounds were dressed by Dr. Kendall, who informs us that they were sufficiently numerous and dangerous to have put an end to any man or living thing save a Chinaman. Arrests were made by Jennings, but we believe that all the flesh-chopping scoundrels are now at large.
 In connection with this affair, there is considerable talk among citizens, regarding Jennings' action, to get possession of certain cash belonging to one or more of the Chinese—said action, some say, being very similar to that in vogue among burglars and highwaymen.

Nightwatchman Jennings wishes us to state that in taking money from Chinese depositories, on the night of the fracas, he had acted according to the urgent request of the Chinaman whom the others had tried to kill, and who, by the way, is now at the point of death.

One of our citizens made several "honest pennies" out of the recent Chinese row, in this way: one "John" wished some arrests made, the citizen in question pretended to be a peace officer, and would not move in the matter until the complaining heathen paid him $10, which he did. Our cute cit. [citizen] then went and button-holed one of the pugnacious "Johns" until said "John" paid him $5, when Mr. Cit. let him go. While this action cannot be claimed as legitimate, it will, perhaps, prove to be good experience to the Celestials.

Private Peter Ness, of Company C, 23d Infantry, died at Fort Whipple hospital, on the 10th inst., from the effects of a gunshot wound recently inflicted upon him by a Chinaman, at this place, which Chinaman was, on Thursday last, examined by Justice Otis and remanded to jail, to await trial for the killing of Ness.

The Chinaman who is accused of killing the later Peter Ness, is now out on bail. His counsel, Capt. J. P. Hargrave, applied to district court commissioner, Ed. W. Wells, for a writ of habeas corpus, on the ground of unlawful imprisonment, when, after Hargrave, for the writ, and those of Judge Carter against, admitted the prisoner to bail in the sum of $1,500, with J. E. G. Mitchell and Guilford Hathaway as sureties.

This action will save some county expense. There are no fears that the Chinaman will skedaddle, it being pretty generally conceded that it will be hard to convict him of murder.

Kim Wa, a Celestial, and a U.S. soldier had a dispute and skirmish on the street this morning, over a wash bill. The Chinaman got the best of the fray.

Last Monday night three Chinamen attacked the cook of the Fort Whipple band, and were about converting him into a gelatinous mass, when several chivalric Frenchmen, who were standing in front of Eymarie's saloon, came boldly to the rescue, drove the Chinese horde away and rescued the unfortunate from the clutches of the heathen. Vive la France.

Hon. J. H. Behan had occasion to call at the Chinese laundry this P.M., when a controversy arose, leading to some half dozen of the pig-tail race making an assault on him with clubs. He tried to defend himself with a revolver, which unfortunately, failed to work. He received several severe cuts about the head. Four of his assailants were arrested and lodged in jail.

The Chinese washermen, some ten or twelve, who attacked J. H. Behan yesterday were on trial to-day before Justice Cate. After considerable testimony was taken the case went over until to-morrow.[39]

Lonely and far from familiar places and the family that was the hub of their social organization, the Chinese of the West turned to three principal forms of recreation: paid sex, gambling, and smoking opium. Participation in one or all sometimes absorbed the monies being saved for home. Prescott's papers had little to say about the first two activities; they also were standard attributes of Euro-American frontier life.[40]

The Chinese movement to America was primarily one of young men. It has been estimated that in California about half of them were married, but statistics for Prescott reveal that in the initial period of Chinese presence there were more than twice as many single than married sojourners.[41] Wives of the latter had been left in China for economic and social reasons. At the outset, there was not enough money to pay two passages. Few lower-class women wanted to venture beyond the customary security of their husband's extended family circle, and they were unprepared to withstand the physical rigors of frontier life.[42] Whereas almost thirty-five thousand Chinese men had reached the west coast early in the 1860s, only sixteen Chinese women had braved the journey.[43] Lyman states that between 1850 and 1882 one hundred thousand Chinese men were in America, as opposed to 8,848 women.[44] Married men, thus, were faced with an unnatural sexual curtailment. The chances for single sojourners to meet respectable Chinese female companions in the United States were virtually nil. Theoretically, mates for them could not be sought in other races because miscegenation was legally prohibited in thirty states, as well in the Arizona Territory.[45] One consequence of the gender imbalance was prostitution.[46]

At first the Chinese men sought out Euro-American, Negro, and Hispanic women who did not maintain racial barriers among their customers. Then, beginning in the middle of the nineteenth century, numerous Chinese women were sold into slavery, kidnapped, or duped into coming illegally into the United States under the auspices of secret societies reaping tremendous financial profits from a fleshpot traffic that was permitted to flourish by corrupt or indifferent American officials. For decades, these so-called singsong girls[47] represented virtually the total immigration of Chinese females. One exception was a limited number of merchant wives, who were kept in tight seclusion because they, too, were preyed upon by slavers.[48]

One protest came from a Prescott reporter.

> The importation of Chinese women for immoral purposes is a crying disgrace to the United States and to American civilization. It is a so-called civilized Government acting the part of procuress, but although the better sense of the country has long cried out against it, the infamous traffic still continues.[49]

The scarcity of Chinese women led to other deviant behavior. Cases of polyandry, more than one man to a wife, are known. That may have been the circumstance behind the murder of Sam Lee on Lynx Creek. Probably more common were jealous squabbles of the sort described below in the journalistic sarcasm of the day.

> Lots of fun for the whites of Prescott, this week, and heap vexation of spirit for the Chinese portion of our population. The business came up in this way: Several months ago, there dwelt at Los Angeles, California, a rather prepossessing damsel, of small stature, and (county recorder Wells informs us), smaller feet. So-Sing-Sing-Hoy, the feminine in question, was seen and admired by Ah-Own, who, according to his tale (no allusion to his pig-tail) presented himself before her, and, offering her his heart, hand and the largest part of his "licy", had his proposed accepted, took So-Sing-Sing-Hoy home with him and put her in his little bed. Weeks rolled on, as a novel donkey would say, and the happy twain grew unhappy in each other's bosoms. The climate, or something else, was not favorable to the growth of love between them, besides the terrible Los Angeles riot, in which so many Chinese were slaughtered, scared these two Celestials out of their sandals, and they turned their faces toward Arizona; arrived, in due time, at Wickenburg, and were there living as harmoniously as two rival Tom Cats, until a Prescott Chinaman named Sam Horne [Sam hon, a laundryman on Gurley Street in the 1880 census] went down there one day, and tooted his horn in the ear of the damsel, who jumped into his wagon, and rode with him to Prescott, to the great disgust of her several Wickenburg husbands, but more especially to Ah-Own, the dreamy Chinaman who claimed her as his own. Well, Mr. Horne, the female, and the white escort arrived here in good season, Horne and the woman lived together and swore by each other, until the discarded Wickenburger arrived in this camp and commenced playing little games, the object of which was to get possession of his "wifey". To settle the question, Ah-Own appealed to the officers of the law, when the case was tried before recorder Ed. W. Wells, who, after hearing the testimony on both sides, and all that the lawyers—Judge Carter and Frank Ayers—had to say, ordered Mr. Horne to return the China woman over to her first husband. Ah-Own, in as good condition as he (Horne) had found her. This, too, after Horne had been married to So-So, or So-Sing—have forgotten her right name. Yielding, very reluctantly, to this distasteful decree, the female accompanied Ah-Own and party to headquarters at their wash-house, where, not liking the smell of the soapsuds, she screamed for her dear Horne, who, with his party, was about to freeze on to her, when Sheriff Thomas came up, escorted the female and male Chinaman to the recorder's office where Judge Wells tested the woman's love, and finding that it flowed in the direction of Sam Horne's horn spoon, permitted her to go 'mit Sam, who, at this writing, is in jail, serving a term of imprisonment for assaulting the sheriff.
> We had almost forgotten to state the Judge Otis came nigh marrying the woman to another Chinaman; also, that upon being asked if she would take a (Sam) Horne for her lawful husband, she replied, in mingled Chinese and Californian, "You bet-tee."[50]

In 1874 a woman who quite probably was Prescott's first Chinese prostitute made her appearance (Figure 6). Her loose-fitting silk pants outfit, groomed chignon, thin eyebrows, and rice-powdered face were typical of her class, although the reporter announcing her arrival was unaware of her occupation.

Wickenburg stage arrived at about half past six, Thursday evening, with several passengers, and seven packs of mail. Among the passengers was a Chinese female, the first that has ever visited this town, and section of country, and, we hope, the last.[51]

By 1880, there were four more Chinese singsong girls at work beside Euro-Americans and Hispanics in the red-light district that had grown up along the corner of Granite and Goodwin streets adjacent to Chinese roominghouses. All the women indicated they were married, and one still lived with her husband. Probably they had been purchased by prospective mates, only to be resold as the opportunity presented itself. Since three thousand dollars was a common going rate, the temptation was strong for dealing in females.[52] The local singsong girls were under the supervision of Ah Yong, a thirty-five-year-old brothel operator assumed to have been a member of one of the west-coast tongs that controlled the Chinese prostitution racket.[53] Organized crime had come to Prescott.

In a few years child slavery had arrived as well. As background, it should be noted that in times of severe need Chinese peasant families considered female offspring more a liability than an asset. They were routinely disposed of. During the demoralizing crises of the nineteenth century, Chinese female infanticide may have ranged as high as seventy percent.[54] Hundreds of other young girls were sold into slave gangs brought surreptitiously into the United States. Preteens were used as domestics until they had matured enough to engage in sexual acts. The situation had become so deplorable that in 1871 the Methodist Church opened an asylum in San Francisco, and in 1873 the Presbyterian Woman's Occidental Board of Foreign Missions launched a campaign for the rescue of these youngsters. One child beyond their reach turned up in Prescott.

She was June Wong. Fearing for her safety, June ran away from her Chinese "foster father," a local resident, to be taken in by Theodore W. Otis and his wife. Otis had driven into town in 1874 with a freight wagon load of groceries with which he opened a store. In addition to running this enterprise for three and a half decades, at various times he also served as postmaster and district court judge and was active in founding the Presbyterian and Congregational churches.[55] No doubt he was aware of the efforts being made in California to help victims like June. Eventually legally adopted by the Otis couple, June Wong worked as a servant in their household. Her wages were to educate her as a missionary so that in due time she could return to China on the church's behalf.

In addition to actively supporting prostitution, the Chinese were habitual gamblers. This form of recreation may have especially flourished in America because of the circumstances surrounding the sojourns.[56] In the back rooms of their temporary Chinatowns as well as in more formal gambling parlors, with time on their hands and a consuming eagerness to make a quick fortune, they enjoyed fantan, dominoes, checkers, a lottery called *pak hop piu*, and similar diversions.[57] Fantan, a game in which participants bet on the number of objects from one to four a dealer put in a container, was a favorite social affair.

There is just one record of a Chinese-run gambling parlor in Prescott, but along with most of the male Euro-American residents, the Chinese also frequented Prescott's many public gaming tables. Poker was preferred in those places. As noted by the *Enterprise*, March 27, 1886, "the Chinese are good patrons of all games of chance."

In March 1880, Prescott imposed a gambling tax of fifteen dollars. If no license was obtained, offenders were subject to a fine of twenty-five to three hundred dollars.[58] Very shortly, the local Chinese were in trouble.

> The celestial portion of our inhabitants were congregated this afternoon at the office of Justice A. O. Noyes, at which place some of their forces were being tried for the offense of carrying on gambling without a license. Capt. Hargrave appeared for the prisoners.[59]

The most pernicious habit the Chinese brought with them to America was the use of opium. The drug was obtained from the dried juice of the poppy *Papaver somniferum*, which was processed, rolled into balls, graded for several qualities, and packed into small, flat, brass tins. For centuries known in China for medicinal purposes, opium gained widespread popularity among all levels of society with the sixteenth century introduction of tobacco. The two substances were smoked together to produce a state of dreamy euphoria. Soon opium was being used alone and proving particularly addictive. The British generally are considered responsible for encouraging the drug's demoralizing use because opium harvested in their holdings in India was a critical commodity in the large-scale trade for Chinese tea.

Recognizing the physical, emotional, and moral ravages among the populace caused by opium, in 1796, 1813, 1814, and 1838 the Chinese government outlawed its importation from regions such as India and tried to suppress its cultivation and use at home.[60] The collusion of smugglers, administrative officials, the producing British colonial empire, and Chinese addicts and pushers prevented eradication of the underground trade. In 1858 opium again was legalized owing to the badly needed high revenues involved. Chinese merchants openly dispatched the drug to overseas Chinese outlets. The first shipment of fifty-two boxes of opium reached San Francisco in 1861 on the ship *Ocean Pearl* out of Hong Kong.[61] In 1880 raw gum opium and opium prepared for smoking, together valued at more than one and a half million dollars, passed through United States Customs.[62] Once in the country, it was under the control of the various fighting tongs parlaying its distribution into high-stakes power and profit.

Like every other Chinese settlement in the West, Prescott had one or more opium dens. They were not the dark holes of iniquity the press made them out to be but were merely bare frame rooms behind a couple of grubby stores or washhouses on south Granite Street. Undoubtedly cramped and filthy, they were the dismal homes-away-from-home of some of the local Chinese. In their privacy, for many reasons that may be presented to have included monotony, alienation, tension, or physical disabilities, some residents found relief or languor in the debilitating opium fumes.

The way in which this narcotic was consumed contributed to non-users' vague suspicions of indecency, for an opium smoke was not a loud convivial affair in a public place. The procedure began by lying on one's side, which, of course, dictated certain surroundings. A bed of sorts and semidarkness provided the right atmosphere. Then, on a long metal needle, one took a bit of the prepared, syrupy opium mass from its brass container, held it over the flames of a kerosene lamp until it bubbled, rolled it into a tiny pea, and forced it into the small hole of the warmed, flat-topped, ceramic bowl of a long-stemmed pipe. A deep drag produced an immediate peaceful sensation. Several further pipesful sometimes led to stupor.

Although agitated Euro-American neighbors were disgusted at what they thought went on in the dens, for a time they tolerated them as a Chinese eccentricity. After all, there were wide-open liquor parlors just a block away where a segment of the host society was similarly addicted to whiskey. The Euro-Americans likely also were cognizant of the problems some soldiers had experienced as an aftermath of the Civil War, when opium used recklessly as an ingredient in morphine, codeine, and patent medicines had created dependencies.[63] Regardless, it remained for the seduction of local innocents to bring the citizenry to attention. Out to make money any way possible and many themselves being users, the Chinese did not consider the supplying of opium to Euro-Americans as anything irregular. Outraged, strait-laced citizens thought differently. Matters began to come to a had before the end of the 1870s.

Among the many evils and vices which the influx of Mongolian immigration has brought to the shores of the Pacific one of the worst is, without doubt, the detestable habit of opium-smoking, which is slowly and steadily growing upon our youths of both sexes. . . . Prescott being a live town, anxious to adopt all the innovations of the age, both good and bad, could not be long without its opium smoking. It was necessary for its proper growth and standing among the towns of the Pacific coast that it should have a half-lighted, stifling rookery, presided over by a cadaverous-looking heathen, in which our "way up" boys and fast young men—and we are sorry to say, representatives of the other sex—might waste away their money and their brains by puffing away at a drag, which would turn their stomach were it prescribed by a physician; but then you know "it's the fashion, and you ain't a sport if you can't stand a half dozen pipes of opium." Many of our citizens would be astonished to see the number of men and women who visit these Granite Street hovels, at all hours of the day and night, and if they want to satisfy themselves of the correctness of our assertions let them take a stand for a few hours at the corner of Granite and Goodwin streets. They will see hurrying in, stealthily, quite a number of habitees [sic] of both sexes, from some of our leading citizens to the lowest harlot who plies her vocation on that street, and if they can manage to be passed in they will be able to feast their eyes with the disgusting sight of this powerful narcotic. Something should be done to stop this detestable failing, which seems to possess such enticing qualities.

The Chinese dens of Prescott carry on quite an extensive business in the way of opium smoking. There are several persons, not altogether Chinese in nationality, who pay for the privilege of inhaling the intoxicating fumes from opium pipes in the celestial dens of Prescott.[64]

Finally, in 1880, the authorities took action against those who provided the drug and bunks and those who took advantage of the service.

Any person who shall hereafter, within the corporate limits of the Village of Prescott, keep or maintain, or become an inmate of, or shall in any way contribute to the support of any place, house or room, where opium is smoked, or where persons assemble for the purpose of smoking opium or inhaling the fumes thereof, shall be declared guilty of a misdemeanor and shall be fined in the sum of not less than ten or more than one hundred dollars.[65]

Even so, the practice of opium smoking continued.

Ah Jim [a cook in the 1880 census] the Chinaman arrested yesterday for selling opium, and also for keeping an opium fumigating den, was tried before a jury in Recorder Rush's Court, found guilty as charged, and sentenced to pay a fine of $25 or serve 12 ½ days in the City Calaboose. Other cases of a similar nature will come up on Saturday.

Dodson has several Chinese gentlemen in limbo for an infringement of a certain City ordinance prohibiting the smoking of opium within the city limits.[66]

At that point, a prominent lawyer who had made a specialty of defending the civil rights of the immigrants contested the legality of the ordinance.

Judge Hargrave, counsel for the Chinese prisoner, charged with violating a city ordinance in regard to the use of opium, swore out a warrant and caused the arrest of City Recorder C. B. Rush and City Marshal J. M. Dodson this morning, for violation of Chinese rights and for overreaching their official duties. They were taken before Justice Noyes, and upon their petition the case was postponed until to-morrow morning or Saturday. There seems to be a difference of opinion in regard to the constitutionality of the Opium Ordinance.[67]

Apparently, Hargarve lost the argument; the ordinance was reissued three years later, with the fine raised to three hundred dollars and a possible penalty added of one year's imprisonment.

In 1887 the United States Congress passed an act prohibiting the importation of opium for other than medical purposes. Laws or not, opium smoking went on unchecked, as was noted in the *Prescott Weekly Courier* of February 17, 1893.

Night before last Constable Miller, with the aid of two citizens, raided a Chinese opium joint of middle Granite Street, capturing twelve opium smokers, four pipes, and several cans of opium. There were three whites and nine Chinamen captured. Thirteen persons were in the room at the time of the raid, but one got away. The constable states that when the room was entered the fiends were all lying in bunks arranged around the walls, one above another, and each prisoner was in a stupefied state until they had walked a short distance in the open air. They were brought before Judge Noyes, who held them in $50 bail each, trial to take place before him at 10 o'clock tomorrow. A white man and woman gave the bail and were released. The other ten prisoners went to jail.

Leading Chinamen rustled around all day yesterday and finally gave bonds for their opium-smoking brethren in jail, who were released about 6 o'clock last evening.

The following year nine Chinese were arrested for the same offense.[68] They pleaded guilty and were fined $22.85.

Other communities and states likewise were clamping down on opium users. On the international scene, public sentiment mounted against the havoc caused by the drug. Chinese rulers imposed a heavy tax on opium and secured a treaty with the British, in which the latter agreed to decrease their exports from India to China. Health conferences encouraged greater worldwide surveillance to curtail smuggling. All these efforts helped reduce, but not eliminate, the opium menace. The dens of Prescott remained local fixtures.

A recreational activity not usually considered in relation to the overseas Chinese was drinking. At home Chinese males were known to have been heavy users of alcoholic beverages of high potency and to have enjoyed drinking games and clubs.[69] It might be thought that in America, as with the Euro-Americans, social consumption of wines, brandy, or whiskey was another pleasure in which they indulged. However, eyewitness descriptions of nineteenth-century western life frequently mentioned the sobriety of the Chinese, with the implications that liquor was something they did not consume. In the boozy milieu of the frontier the drinking habits of the Chinese may not have been extraordinary enough to warrant comment, or perhaps their imbibing was done within the privacy of Chinatown. That extensive drinking did occur has been suggested by archaeological research carried out in the last several decades in areas formerly occupied by Chinese. Quantities of globular stoneware spirits bottles of a type still made in China, as well as discarded glass American liquor and beer containers, have been unearthed. It should be noted that there was only one term in Chinese for alcoholic beverage. That was *pai chiu,* usually translated as "wine" but actually more closely resembling vodka in being distilled, made from a starch base such as sorghum, millet, or rice, and ninety-five to one hundred proof.[70] Some Chinese merchants in Prescott purchased other spirits from a local white wholesaler.

The Prescott Chinese also continued to be Chinese in several recreational celebrations that intrigued the Euro-American community. These included seasonal religious and social festivals commencing in the second-story hall on Granite

Street but always spilling out into the surrounding neighborhood. No matter the occasion, the accompanying deafening noise from fusillades of exploding strings of fire-crackers and what to western ears was exotic, discordant music provided by gong, drum, cymbals, and flute could not have failed to attract the attention of the whole town. The most elaborate celebration was that commemorating Chinese New Year.[71] This was primarily a social event but had religious overtones. An early description follows.

> People living within hearing of the Chinese quarters, need not be told, this morning, that China New Year began at midnight last night. Such another pandemonium as was maintained all along the line, from two o'clock until daylight, is not often heard in this well organized Christian land.
>
> Pistols, bombs, fire-crackers, in short, everything that could command, that would make a noise, was brought into requisition.
>
> This morning the whole China male population went out making New Year's calls, dressed in silk attire, and we observed that in front of some of their residences they had difficulty in wading through the husks from bursted fire-crackers.
>
> The fire-cracker business is a dangerous nuisance, and although it may be a part of their religion, as a means of frightening away the Devil, it is at the same time a source of many conflagrations, and ought to be a subject of police regulation.[72]

As inventors of gunpowder, the Chinese expectedly were fond of firecrackers and used them exuberantly. These noisemakers, laced into strings, were routinely included in stocks shipped from the west coast. If carelessly used, they did pose a threat to the huddle of frame buildings that already had experienced cyclic fires and re-erections. After 1880 the village council required a permit from the mayor before fireworks could be ignited, with noncompliance carrying a fine of ten to one hundred dollars. The penalty later was raised to three hundred dollars.[73]

The serving of special foods was an essential part of all the observances, even those carried out in the most removed corners of the Chinese world such as that at Prescott. Hospitable and with a gnawing but unacknowledged longing to be accepted, as well as reaffirming their own ethnicity to the world at large, Chinese of all economic levels opened many of their festive indulgences to whomever would join in. The Chinese labor class did not fully comprehend the distinctiveness of its cuisine on these occasions, since it took its way of life for granted. The local paper noted:

> Visitors will be welcome, and will be served with bird nest soup, shark's fins, fish maws, chop suey, Chinese candies, and many other concoctions strange to the American tastes.[74]

A week later the paper provided a fuller account:

> Inside the Joss House the stranger, no matter of what nationality, was welcomed, treated to choice Chinese delicacies, and sent on his way with the "Kong Hac Fat

Tsi" greeting. The decorations in the Chinese house of worship were elaborate. Chinese lanterns hung everywhere, crimson silk draperies hid the otherwise bleak walls, scrolls of Chinese prophecies and sayings of Confucius were profusely scattered about, and myriads of lighted candles and burning punk and incense lent aid to the air of orientalism which pervaded the place.

On one side of the big room, at the end of which stood the Chinese altar, adorned by the immobile Joss, the Chinese musicians were seated, all wearing hats or some other head covering, as did the visitors who entered from time to time, in groups of three and four, to stand chatting awhile, discussing the music which struggled, piecemeal from the several performers, and then to go on to the "Noodle Joint," where Chinese refreshments awaited them.[75]

Because Chinese music was not harmonious and the instruments used to produce it were unfamiliar, Euro-American observers frequently commented upon performances of Chinese bands at ceremonial functions. It is unknown whether music was also a form of entertainment when the sojourners gathered socially.

Occasions such as the New Year's festivities were attended by Euro-American townsmen, as the paper noted, but there is no clue that the Prescott Chinese ever were similarly invited to Euro-American civic or social functions. Some of what the Euro-Americans regarded as Chinese clannishness obviously resulted from their own thoughtlessness. Such rejection, whether intentional or not, surely served to drive the sojourners deeper into their own ethnicity in defense against psychological damage. Had families been permitted to join these men, it is possible that Euro-American rebuff would not have produced such self-defeating reaction.

THE CHINESE ARE ENTRENCHED

At the end of the 1870s the Prescott Chinese population had increased from the original six men to ninety-six males and five females, according to the federal census.[76] Population figures relative to Chinese are only suggestive because of the extreme fluidity of this group. A few men settled in for decades interspersed with home visits to China, but the majority were rootless, restive, unburdened by worldly goods, and drifted from place to place, job to job. Nevertheless, records reveal that in 1880 there was just one married couple in the Prescott colony. They were Ah Chong, a cook, and Chow Aie, a prostitute. They lived on Granite Street with Ah Can, a miner. All the immigrants had been born in their homeland, but no data on their prior length of stay in the United States are available. They ranged from fifteen to sixty-two years of age and worked at thirteen different low-level vocations. Not one was unemployed. Nor was one of what might be considered a professional, white-collar class. Laundering was by far the most common occupation, but cooking also engaged a sizable percentage of the immigrants.

Some participants in these trades counted on advertising to bring in Euro-American customers, indicating one kind of adjustment to circumstances the Chinese were ready to make.

> Wong Lee, all same Melicano [American] man, runs the wash house near the foot bridge at the crossing of Granite Creek. Call and see his laundry and procure one of his cards, printed in American after the style of the 19th century.

> New Restaurant, Open Monday, February 3. Ah Wah, late cook at the Cabinet, has rented the Dining Rooms attached to P. M. Fisher's Saloon, where by good cooking and attention to business, he hopes to merit a share of the public patronage. Board per week, $8.00; Single meals .50. Chicken and eggs three times a week.[77]

Servants, gardeners, and laborers comprised the next most numerous groupings. All five women were prostitutes. The youngest two were twenty years old; the eldest was forty-five.

Almost half of the Asians lived on two blocks of Granite Street, confirming that it was their principal quarter (Table 4.1). Ten had found employment and lodging at Whipple Barracks. Twenty-eight others roomed either at the rear of the restaurant-saloon complex along Montezuma Street or in an upstairs boarding-house there.

No address is indicated in the 1880 census for ten of those engaged full time in gardening. It is believed they likely had begun to develop vegetable plots, predictably known as the Chinese Gardens, at the north end of Granite Street across from the confluence of Granite and Miller creeks, and resided in several huts near them. In this locality, the pine-clad hills flattened out into gravelly terraces suitable for small-scale farming. Four other gardeners are noted as dwelling on Granite and Montezuma streets. Either they walked the short distance to their out-of-town fields or they cared for kitchen plots located around some of the Chinese-occupied buildings or Euro-American gardens within the settlement proper.

Table 4.1 Places of Chinese Residence in Prescott

Location	1880	1900	1910
Granite Street	46	37	128
Montezuma Street	28	119	5
Gurley Street	9	6	5
Cortez Street	1	11	—
Goodwin Street	1	18	5
Willis Street	—	4	—
Whipple Barracks	10	—	5
Miller Valley	10?	—	8

Source: U.S. Federal Census, Arizona Territory.

These Chinese had seen another need in the economic network of the town and were alert enough to take advantage of it. Home gardens were sufficient only for individual families, and Prescott's removal from major transportation routes made it difficult to procure any substantial amounts of fresh produce for commercial use or for the military messes. In this instance, the Chinese had the benefit of an agrarian heritage extending back four thousand years to the rise of the Neolithic. From that time on, labor-intensive manual farming had brought most of the arable eastern Asian continent under control and had fed millions. Intimate knowledge of soils, plants, and microclimates became the aggregate legacy of generations of land-bound masses. It was a priceless fund of knowledge upon which local Chinese could draw.

It was the older elements of the Chinese community in Prescott who turned to agriculture as a means to their common end. Perhaps their age made them less adaptable to taking on new trades. At any rate, on the outskirts of the village they broke virgin sod, hauled off boulders, weeded, put down wells because the nearby creeks ran only during summer showers, and sowed the vegetable and fruit crops familiar to Euro-Americans. Had they followed their ancient method of using nightsoil as fertilizer, there surely would have been howls of protest from horrified observers, as in California.[78] The common products were brought by one-horse wagon to be sold primarily to the town's eating establishments. Since many of these restaurants and boardinghouse kitchens were operated by countrymen, it was a distribution chain from Chinese gardener to Chinese cook to Euro-American consumer. Chinese vegetables, such as bok choy, snow peas, winter melons, or long, hot, white radishes, supplied their own ethnic group. Very possibly the men also raised hogs and chickens for the same clients.

The cooks provided services using American products for the dominant Euro-American society and therefore were on the front lines of cultural interaction. The washermen and gardeners were less so. However, the two merchants and one clerk counted in the 1880 census functioned exclusively within Chinatown. As ethnic entrepreneurs, they moved in to establish businesses geared to the needs felt by the local Chinese for maintaining their homeland pattern of living as much as possible. Probably they never bothered to learn English because both their suppliers and customers communicated in Chinese, and they had no set prices since bargaining was the norm in their experience. Use of United States currency was essential for business conducted with Euro-Americans, but there is some evidence that coins minted in China in small denominations circulated within the overseas Chinese enclaves.[79] The ageless abacus, its bells clinking rapidly along vertical wires, was more efficient than an adding machine for the Chinese merchants. There may have been some specialization in inventories. To judge from better-known circumstances in similar communities, the cramped, dingy Chinese stores, filled with odors unfamiliar to most westerners, were crammed to the rafters with an amazing variety of foodstuffs, spices, teas, wine, herbal medicines, culinary herbs, tobacco, clay pipes, opium paraphernalia, paper and silk lanterns, musical instruments, playing cards and wooden or ivory counters, candles, joss sticks, double-edge wooden combs, baskets of various sizes, hardware, clothes, kitchen gear, soup spoons, and serving dishes. Perhaps even more important than the familiar articles from China was the role of the store as a place where Chinese men could congregate to discuss the events of their day, much as Euro-American colleagues were doing in other emporiums. For the illiterate, the shopkeeper may have served as a scribe, writing occasional letters to families across the ocean.

In a few years a third shopkeeper had arrived. He, too, opened a store in the Chinese quarter, but it is obvious he hoped to sell some of his imported stock of both Chinese and Japanese derivation to Euro-American residents. The *Arizona Journal Miner*, October 9, 1889, reported,

> Queng Sing, the enterprising Chinese crockery and tea merchant on Granite Street has just received a large invoice of elegant flowered china wares from the land of Confucius. Also a lot of pure Orlang tea, which will be sold cheap.[80]

NOTES

1. Kraus 1969: 41–57.
2. Robe 1982: 5.
3. Walker and Butkin 1979: 41.
4. U.S. Federal Census, Arizona Territory, 1870.
5. Walker and Butkin 1979: 41.
6. *Arizona Weekly Miner*, May 29, November 27, December 4, 1869; Yoder 1951: 38.
7. *Arizona Weekly Miner*, January 15, 1870.
8. *Arizona Journal Miner*, February 9, 1877.
9. Ramos, of Mexican ancestry, had become a naturalized citizen on October 14, 1868. Index to Minute Record of Orders and Naturalization, 1865 to September 13, 1906, Yavapai County Court House. Potter 1964: 59.
10. *Arizona Journal Miner*, December 29, 1876.
11. Yoder 1951: 27.
12. Walker and Butkin 1979: 38.
13. Fong 1980: 7; 1984: 198–99.
14. *Arizona Weekly Miner*, October 3, 1879.
15. *Arizona Weekly Miner*, July 16, 1880.
16. Prazniak 1984: 124.
17. Culin 1890a: 40–41; Lee 1960; Wells 1971.
18. Light 1972; 93.
19. *Arizona Weekly Miner*, October 7, 1871.
20. Siu 1952: 34–44; 1964: 429–42.
21. *Enterprise*, March 21, 1877.
22. *Enterprise*, August 22, 1877.
23. *Enterprise*, August 29, September 1, September 5, 1877.
24. *Arizona Weekly Miner*, September 5, 1879.

25. Culin 1890b: 195.

26. *Arizona Weekly Miner*, July 16, 1880.

27. Lee 1960: 81.

28. Dillon 1962: 100–101.

29. Light 1972: 91–92.

30. Lee 1960: 135.

31. Lyman 1974: 110.

32. Sin 1952: 34–44.

33. Culin 1890b: 193; Kraus 1969: 56–57; Lyman 1974: 15, 50–52.

34. Dillon 1962: 167.

35. Bluden and Elvin 1983: 148; Clayre 1984: 9.

36. Culin 1890b: 193.

37. *Arizona Republican*, October 24, 1899.

38. *Arizona Weekly Miner*, September 3, 1875; March 5, 1880; August 6, 1880. A highbinder was a Chinese urban hired gun in the employment of a group, or tong, engaged in criminal activities. The term may have derived from the custom of binding the queue to the top of a man's head so that it could not be grasped by an assailant. Dicker 1979; 15.

39. *Arizona Weekly Miner*, January 20, 27, 1872; January 25, March 15, March 22, December 19, 1873; August 1, October 3, 1879.

40. In 1864, of 36 adult females in the Third Judicial District that encompassed Prescott, 44 were known prostitutes. U.S. Federal Census, Arizona Territory, 1864. Historical Records Survey, Phoenix, 1938.

41. U.S. Federal Census, Arizona Territory. Prescott, 1880: married Chinese males 29, single Chinese males 62; 1900: married Chinese males 111, single Chinese males 121; 1910 married Chinese males 74, single Chinese males 53.

42. Lyman 1970: 18.

43. Lee 1949: 422–32; Wegars 1984.

44. Lyman 1970: 18.

45. Lyman 1974: 91.

46. Wegars 1984.

47. Dillon 1962: 141, 169.

48. Lyman 1974: 89.

49. *Enterprise*, August 26, 1877.

50. *Arizona Weekly Miner*, February 15, 1873.

51. *Arizona Weekly Miner*, March 11, 1874.

52. Dillon 1962: 231.

53. U.S. Federal Census, Arizona Territory, 1870.

54. Wegars 1984.

55. Obituary, Archives, Sharlot Hall Museum.

56. Culin 1891: 14.

57. Culin 1890b: 196.

58. Village of Prescott, Ordinances, No. 21. Archives, Sharlot Hall Museum.

59. *Arizona Weekly Miner*, April 2, 1880.

60. Gernet 1982: 534.

61. Dillon 1962: 61.

62. Kane 1976: 16.

63. Dai 1964: 645.

64. *Enterprise*, August 13, 1877; *Arizona Weekly Miner*, October 24, 1879.

65. Village of Prescott, Ordinances, No. 22. Archives, Sharlot Hall Museum.

66. *Arizona Weekly Miner*, June 4, 1880.

67. Ibid.

68. Register of Criminal Action, Third Judicial District Court, Proceedings, June 1894, Yavapai County Court House.

69. Chang 1977: 278.

70. Chang 1977: 342.

71. Chinese New Year was on the first moon after the sun entered the sign of Acquarius, therefore never earlier than January 21 or later than February 19.

72. *Arizona Weekly Miner*, February 1, 1878.

73. Village of Prescott, Ordinances Archives, Sharlot Hall Museum.

74. *Arizona Journal Miner*, February 1, 1908.

75. *Arizona Journal Miner*, February 8, 1908.

76. U.S. Federal Census, Arizona Territory, 1870.

77. *Arizona Weekly Miner*, April 2, 1880.

78. Spier 1958: 81.

79. Greenwood 1980: 113–23; Olsen 1983: 118.

80. Oolong tea is a semi-fermented green variety.

5

The Chinese in Nevada: An Historical Survey, 1856–1970

Loren B. Chan

On October 27, 1855, John Reese and his associates were granted a franchise to build a watch ditch along the Carson River to bring water to nearby Gold Canyon for mining and other purposes. To construct the ditch, Reese hired forty to fifty Chinese laborers from California in 1856. That marked the initial entry of Chinese into what would become the state of Nevada.[1]

These Chinese congregated in a settlement at the mouth of a ravine which the whites called Chinatown (later renamed as the town of Dayton, now located northeast of Carson City in Lyon County). More Chinese were added to the original work crew later in 1856 and 1857. When the ditch was completed in August 1858, some of the workers moved back to California, but in 1859 there were some thirty-five Chinese still living in small stone, mud, and tule huts at Dayton.[2]

From this humble beginning, persons of Chinese descent have lived in Nevada continuously to the present. During the second half of the nineteenth century they participated in the economic development of the state, often in the face of discrimination and persecution, and limited opportunities. In China's Guandong province, the "decline" phase of the traditional historical cycle was beyond immediate redemption: there was no way to determine when the cycle would run its course, and whether a new dynasty would quickly improve the quality of life.[3] In the meantime, life must go on. Work had to be secured, and families had to be fed even if it meant that many able-bodied men had to go abroad to earn their livelihoods.

Because of their social and economic backgrounds (from the peasantry, with limited educations), and the prevailing discriminatory laws and feelings in the United States, the range of occupational pursuits open to the Chinese in Nevada during the frontier period was quite limited. They could mine only with white permission. Most of the Chinese males became itinerant laborers, cooks, or domestic servants. A small number were doctors, merchants, gamblers, or skilled craftsmen. Virtuous Chinese women were expected to remain in China, so that the few who made their way to Nevada often became prostitutes. In a male dominated frontier society, that was to be expected.[4]

Nevada's frontier society was an extension of California's. After the discovery of the Comstock Lode in 1859, the bulk of the newcomers in the new mining district came by way of California. The white Americans and European immigrants carried with them the prevailing anti-Chinese attitudes of the new Pacific coast state. As Chinese immigration became a political issue in California during the 1870s and 1880s, it also became an issue in Nevada. Ultimately the outcries of the western congressional delegations were enough to persuade the federal government to suspend and then to prohibit the immigration of Chinese laborers. The Chinese thus became the first ethnic group to be barred from immigrating to the United States. Moreover, no first generation resident alien of Chinese descent was eligible to apply for naturalized United States citizenship before 1943 because of racial considerations.

Certainly their different racial appearance set them off as a group apart. Their dress, language, and customs did not allow them to blend in easily with the rest of the population. At first they were few in number. In the 1860 federal census, there were only twenty-three persons of Asian descent (probably Chinese) in Carson, Humboldt and St. Mary's counties, Utah Territory (Nevada Territory was not organized until the following year). From 1860 to 1880, the Chinese population in Nevada steadily increased, until an all-time high of 5,416 was reached in 1880.

Thereafter and until 1950, the number of Chinese in the state decreased in a linear fashion regardless of the ups and downs in Nevada's total population. The initial settlement of the state was due to the discoveries on the Comstock Lode and the subsequent interest in mining which they spawned. After the Comstock went into decline, it was not until the Tonopah and Goldfield mining booms that the state's population again increased. By the time those booms ended, Nevada had passed from its frontier stage of development to its modern economic dependence on agriculture, gaming and related tourism, and federal spending.

The precipitous decline in the Chinese population after 1880 may be attributed to a number of reasons. First, there was the sojourner mentality of the Chinese. They left their homeland to earn their living, but they expected to live out their final days in China. Second, American laws discouraged further immigration and the settlement of entire Chinese immigrant families; and finally, there was the quality of life in Nevada itself. Being the objects of discriminatory laws, periodic racist violence, and scapegoating for economic depressions did not make the Chinese look forward to spending the rest of their lives in the Sagebrush State.

In 1950, Nevada's Chinese population reached its smallest size since statehood had been achieved; there were only 281 persons of Chinese descent still residing in the state: 82 in Washoe County, 56 in Clark, 26 in Elko, 24 in White Pine, and the rest scattered throughout the state. Since 1950, the state's overall population has increased dramatically and its Chinese population has kept pace, even though it accounts for only two-tenths of one per cent of the total from 1950 to the present. In the post–World War II period, the Chinese must be considered as one of the state's smaller minority groups.

Even so, whatever growth the Chinese community in Nevada has had since 1945 can in part be explained by the lessening of anti-Chinese attitudes nationally and in the state. Chinese can now immigrate legally. Separated families can be reunited. Chinese aliens can apply for naturalized American citizenship. And discrimination laws affecting employment, housing, and marriage have been dropped nationally and in Nevada. In other words, it is only within relatively recent times that the social atmosphere in the state has been conducive to the development of stable, family-oriented, long-term residence by persons of Chinese descent.

The purpose of this article is to survey the historical presence of the Chinese in each of Nevada's seventeen counties from 1856 to 1970. The pictures which emerge are far from complete, because they are based on fragmentary evidence. Even incomplete pictures, however, are better than none at all.

Carson City (Ormsby County)

On August 29, 1861, Territorial Secretary Orion Clemens reported to the editors of the *Missouri Democrat* that the population of Carson City was 1,466, including 16 Chinese.[5] The Chinese population increased continually until 1880, when Ormsby County had the greatest number of Chinese residents of any county in the state, and when Nevada ranked behind California and Oregon in having the third largest concentration of Chinese in the nation. At its peak in 1880, the Chinese population numbered around 800 in Carson City, and the state capital's Chinatown stretched for five blocks.[6] It was the largest Chinese quarter of any town or city in Nevada. One could find hotels, restaurants, gaming houses, laundries, houses of prostitution, and even some temples in which traditional Confucian, Buddhist, and Taoist rites were performed.[7] So numerous were the Chinese that Ah For, a Christian convert, raised funds to build the Chapel of the Good Shepherd, the Protestant Episcopal Mission in Carson City. It was completed on September 23, 1874, had a seating capacity of fifty, and cost $500. The Chinese in western Nevada donated $300, and the remainder came from sympathetic whites. Attendance at the chapel was spotty. The few who attended services wanted to learn to speak English more than to listen to the Christian gospel. The mission was soon abandoned.[8]

Carson City's Chinese colony was largely self-sufficient. Most of its population worked as laborers, cooks, or launderers for Caucasians. To meet the needs of that large working-class population, a broad range of individuals engaged in service occupations, including jewelers, watchmakers, tinsmiths, doctors, dentists, and teachers. One must not conclude, however, that the size of the county's Chinese population was necessarily directly correlated to the size of its white population. In 1880, Ormsby County was only the fifth most populous county in Nevada (after Storey, Eureka, Elko, and Washoe counties), yet it had the largest number of Chinese.[9]

Actually, there were good reasons why the Chinese were concentrated in Carson City. First, they were banned from mining on the Comstock Lode because of the opposition of the white miners' unions. Second, the building of the Virginia and Truckee Railroad introduced Chinese to the area. And third, there was employment to be found in the area.

As first the territorial and later the state capital, Carson City attracted politicians and others who could tolerate the Chinese, benefit from their presence, and not feel threatened by them. That was not the case elsewhere in Nevada. During the late nineteenth century, anti-Chinese agitation in Carson City and elsewhere in the state was usually led by men who themselves were immigrants, and who felt so insecure about their own places in Nevada's frontier society that they seized upon the issue of race to make places for themselves.

When E. D. Sweeney, an Irishman, and Robert Fulstone, an Englishman, cried that "the Chinese must go" in 1860, they were but the first of a nineteenth-century procession of European immigrant rabblerousers. Eight years later when the so-called "Woodchoppers War" occurred, it was the Irish and the French-Canadian immigrants who tried to drive the Chinese from cutting timber in the Sierra and to expel all of the Chinese from Carson City and the state of Nevada.[10]

Under the United States naturalization law of 1870, however, white immigrants were eligible to become naturalized American citizens and thus voters. The Chinese immigrants, on the other hand, were barred from obtaining American citizenship until 1943. European immigrants and native-born white working-class Americans often made a common cause of hating the Chinese. When such hatred was expressed at the polls, the politician listened and acted accordingly. In the 1880 general election in Nevada, 17,259 voters indicated their approval of abolishing further Chinese immigration. Only 193 voters opposed such an abolition.[11]

Generally speaking, Nevada's white politicians joined their California counterparts in the incessant late nineteenth-century clamor for Chinese exclusion. Their demands bore fruit in the forms of the 1882 Chinese Exclusion Act, the Scott Act (1888), the Geary Act (1892), the 1902 Chinese Exclusion Act, and subsequent anti-Chinese measures down to the time of World War II. Nevada's senior United States Senator Francis G. Newlands best summarized white Nevada's racial and political attitudes when he wrote in 1909:

> History teaches that it is impossible to make a homogeneous people by the juxtaposition upon the same soil of races differing in color. Race tolerance, under such conditions, means race amalgamation, and this is undesirable. . . Our country, by law to take effect upon the expiration of treaties, should prevent the immigration of all

peoples other than those of the white race, except under restricted conditions relating to international commerce, travel, and education.[12]

In the case of Ormsby County, the anti-Chinese laws accomplished their intended effects. After 1880, the Chinese started leaving—slowly at first, but then in droves apparently between 1890 and 1900. By the latter year, all of Nevada was economically depressed. The free coinage of silver was no longer a hot national political issue, and the Comstock was well into its period of decline as a mining district.

Between 1900 and 1950, Carson City's Chinese continued to leave—most likely either for northern California or Guangdong province. By 1950, only six persons of Chinese descent were left living in Ormsby County. After 1800, more Chinese left the county than entered it. The Chinese surnamed population could not increase because of Nevada's anti-miscegenation law, and because of the exclusion laws which inhibited the reuniting of Chinese husbands with their wives and families in America.

As late as 1910 and 1920, Carson City still had a Chinatown, but it was only a shadow of its former self. About the biggest news in the community during the 1920s was the sparing of the life of Hughie Sing, a Chinese-American teenager, who was involved in a tong murder in 1921. His confederate Gee Jon, the actual murderer, was executed in 1924 in the gas chamber at the Nevada State Prison as the first man to be executed by lethal gas in the United States.[13]

By the decade of the 1930s, the Chinese population of Ormsby County was down to somewhere between 20 and 31 inhabitants. In August of 1938, Thomas W. Chinn of San Francisco visited Carson City, and recorded his impressions of what he saw and the Chinese people with whom he conversed. Only two rows of dilapidated wooden buildings remained in Chinatown. Most of the structures were empty and abandoned. Chinn concluded that most of the Chinese inhabitants had died or moved elsewhere between 1888 and the time of his visit.[14]

The Chee Kung Tong building still stood, complete with its two Chinese altars. It was in a sorry state of repair, and the inside was covered with grime and dust. Since taxes had not been paid on the building for years, the city assumed ownership of the property.[15] Eighty-one-year-old Wong Toy slept in the building and acted as its caretaker. A former laborer, he arrived in the United States in 1882, and by 1938 was a recipient of county welfare relief funds.[16]

Chinn saw other buildings in the Chinese quarter which indicated how lively it had been in the past. The Wui Hsien Low building, a ranshackle two-story structure, was once used as a house of prostitution. Yee Bong, a man over 70 years of age and who claimed to have been born in Virginia City, still ran his restaurant, although it was usually devoid of customers. And the Sun Quong Chong merchandise store, a surviving building from the early days of Chinese settlement in Carson City, still was there despite being abandoned by the Lai family, who left for San Francisco in 1936.[17]

All of the Chinese with whom Chinn conversed were oldsters. In addition to Wong Toy and Yee Bong, he also talked to an old lady around 75 years old with the surname of Ho. These old-timers recalled when Dr. Sun Yat-sen visited Carson City's Chinatown to raise money for the 1911 republican revolution in China. He stopped at the Chee Kung Tong building in his quest for funds and political support from the Nevada Chinese.[18]

At the cemetery, Chinn found twenty Chinese buried. The plot where the burials were located belonged to the Yan Wo District Association, the organization of the Hakka-speaking people from Guangdong province. Apparently none of the Guangdong district associations (including the Yan Wo group) had visited Carson City since 1923 to disinter the remains of the dead for shipment back to China for the customary final burial.[19]

Three years after his first visit, Chinn visited Carson City's Chinatown. By 1941 several of the old wooden structures were razed. He saw Wong Toy again, and met Mrs. Lau Kau On, then 90, who had once been a prostitute in Virginia City. Naturally the handful of old-timers respun a few of their old yarns, but they also told Chinn a few new ones. They mentioned two of the Chinese temples which were once in Carson City, as well as the many brothels, four lottery shops, and over twelve opium dens which Carson's Chinatown boasted in its heyday.[20]

After 1940, Carson City's few remaining old-timers either succumbed to old age or moved away. The 1950 census showed only six Chinese inhabitants still living in Ormsby County. Since then the number of Chinese has increased. The number of persons of Chinese descent living in Carson City (Ormsby County was consolidated with Carson City in 1968), however, still remains small. In 1970, only 25 Chinese lived in Nevada's capital city: 16 males and 9 females.

Clark County

Clark County was not established as a separate political entity until 1909. Its creation was in response to the rapid growth of the city of Las Vegas, which itself was not founded until 1905. Prior to the county's creation, that part of southern Nevada that bordered on the Colorado River was part of Lincoln County.

Las Vegas was established as a fueling and watering stop on the newly completed San Pedro, Los Angeles and Salt Lake Railroad. At first it was just a tent town, but it quickly grew to be a stable (albeit small) town. Chinese pioneers were present when the town was founded. When Charles P. ("Pop") Squires, founder of the *Las Vegas Age*, arrived in February of 1905 and when Leon H. Rockwell arrived in the following year, both men observed Chinese businessmen already established.[21] Among the first Chinese in Las Vegas were Wong Kee and Ong Loy, restaurant owners; and Ying Lee, a laundryman.[22]

Ying Lee tried his hand at the restaurant business briefly. In February of 1908 he and his partners, Man Ying and Chin Yee, purchased the Arrowhead Restaurant from Mrs. Albert Simmons. After only four months as a restaurateur, however, Lee sold his share in the partnership and returned to his laundry, which was located on an alley running from Fremont to Carson Street between First and Second.[23]

Wong Kee gained his food service experience in Las Vegas by first conducting the restaurant at the Colorado Hotel. In August of 1909 he purchased the Arrowhead Restaurant, which became a popular eating place frequented by railroad workers.[24] In 1913 he was fined for providing liquor to minors.[25] Also in that year, Clark County canceled its contract with Wong, whereby the restaurant owner had fed the county jail inmates for twenty cents per meal. Sheriff Sam Gay complained that Wong's stingy portions of food were insufficient and even cause of illness in some of the prisoners. Wong apparently ignored the sheriff's complaints, and the matter was brought to the attention of the county commissioners, who promptly canceled the contract. The commissioners then ordered Gay to feed his prisoners elsewhere at a cost not to exceed twenty-five cents per meal.[26]

In addition to the few Chinese in Las Vegas, there were also a small number involved in cooking and the restaurant business at Goodsprings. In 1916 the *Las Vegas Age* reported that Fong Don, Mon Gow, and Lee Ping had a restaurant there and that Charley Ching, an old-time cook, was in charge of the Bullion boarding house.[27]

The decade of the 1920s did not bring any drastic change. There were a few Chinese restaurant owners in Las Vegas including Woo Weget, proprietor of the A. C. Kitchen,[28] and the first of the Fong clan, Sui Mon Fong and Gim Fong, who arrived in the city in 1926 and opened the Silver Cafe. Fewer than twenty Chinese lived in the county at any time during the decade.

As Nevada entered the depression years of the 1930s, the Chinese population remained numerically constant in the Las Vegas area. The great public works project in Clark County, the building of Hoover Dam, induced thousands of Americans to move to the state in search of work. Federal specifications, however, prohibited the use of Asian labor.[29]

The overall size of the Chinese population in Clark County, therefore, remained quite small until relatively recently. From 1910 to 1950, there were fewer than 100 Chinese in Las Vegas and environs at any one time. Not until 1960 did the number of Chinese exceed 100. By then there were 225 Chinese in the county (154 males and 71 females), with the incorporated area of the city of Las Vegas accounting for 170 of them (117 males and 53 females). In the years since 1960, the Chinese population has kept up the area's overall population growth and has remained at about two-tenths of one per cent of the total population. Nevertheless, by 1970 Clark County achieved the distinction of having the largest Chinese population of any Nevada county in the twentieth century.

Elko County

The first Chinese entered what became Elko County as laborers constructing the Central Pacific Railroad across Nevada in 1868. Many had been recruited in the mining districts of northern California (about 65 per cent), and others were new immigrants hired in China expressly for the purpose of building the railroad. While construction of the railroad took place in Nevada, they were paid $36 per month (not including meals) for working six days a week from sunrise to sunset.[30] Usually they were assigned to work gangs of twelve to twenty men each.[31]

After laying the rails through the Sierra from California with considerable loss of life due to cliff falls, avalanches, and tunneling with high explosives, the work across the Great Basin was considerably easier and quicker. Clad in blue denim overalls and shirts, and wearing straw hats, thousands of Chinese workers drilled, graded, leveled, laid ties, drove spikes, and built culverts. They were responsible for erecting several timber bridges across the Humboldt River.[32]

The Chinese workers were fed a varied diet of Chinese foods. The railroad camps were well stocked with Chinese provisions: dried oysters and fish, sweet rice, crackers, dried bamboo shoots, salted cabbage, Chinese sugar, dried fruits and vegetables, vermicelli, dried seaweed, Chinese bacon, dried abalone, dried mushrooms, peanut oil, tea, rice, pork, and poultry. Most of these provisions were dried; prior to the age of refrigeration, only these types would keep well in Nevada's harsh desert climate. White railroad workers usually consumed a monotonous diet of beef, beans, bread, butter, and potatoes. The Chinese drank lukewarm tea, whereas the whites frequently drank contaminated stream water. All in all, the Chinese railroad laborers probably had a more balanced diet than the white workers did. They certainly did not have a lower living standard.[33]

After completion of the Central Pacific to Utah, the railroad's approximately 10,000 Chinese workers were *not* suddenly discharged to flood the western labor market, to serve as unfair competitions to white workingmen, and thus to stimulate growth of the anti-Chinese movement in the west. No such things occurred. Instead, a boom in railroad construction occurred in California after the completion of the first transcontinental line. After Leland Stanford drove the celebrated golden spike at Promontory Point, the demand for Chinese railroad builders continued unabated for at least one more decade.

At times, it seems there were relatively few reliable, industrious white workers willing to blast rock, shovel dirt, and perform the rest of the drudgery of railroad building. After 1869, the Chinese built the Southern Pacific line linking San Francisco to Los Angeles by way of the San Joaquin Valley through Tehachapi Pass (completed in 1876). They also built the Southern Pacific line linking Los Angeles with Yuma, Tucson, Lordsburg, Deming, and El Paso, where the connection was made in 1882 with the Texas and Pacific Railroad. By that time the second transcontinental railroad was completed.

Not more than a quarter to a third of the Chinese who laid the rails across Nevada elected to stay in the state after 1869. During the 1870s, approximately 5,000 Chinese were employed by the railroad in California. Most were veterans of building the Central Pacific across Nevada. In addition, California offered employment opportunities to the returning railroad workers in other industries like agriculture (seasonal planting and harvesting, sharecropping, truck gardening) and the manufacturing of shoes and cigars. The increase in Nevada's Chinese population from 1870 to 1880 had more to do with the state's general economic growth which completion of the Central Pacific created, rather than to a horde of former railroad workers suddenly becoming enamored with Nevada. Moreover we must remember that after the Central Pacific was completed four other important railroads in Nevada were built by the Chinese: the Virginia and Truckee, Eureka and Palisade, Carson and Colorado, and Nevada-California-Oregon. Constructing these shorter railroads, along with the rather limited opportunities in mining, hard manual labor, cooking, laundering, domestic service, and ethnically oriented businesses were enough to keep the state's Chinese population growing through immigration.

After 1869, the Chinese who remained in Elko County settled either in the towns along the railroad (Carlin, Elko, Wells, Toano, and Montello) or headed north of the railroad to the mining camps (Cornucopia, Tuscarora, Mountain City, Gold Creek, and Contact).

RAILROAD TOWNS

Carlin

Even before the town was started in December 1868, Chinese railroad workers were present at Carlin meadows on the Humboldt River. They planted vegetable gardens in the area, and the town in its early days was sometimes referred to as "Chinese Gardens." A considerable number settled in town, including railroad workers, cooks, laundrymen, and even a few women.[34] When the Chinese Minister to the United States, Ch'en Lan-in, passed through Carlin on the train in 1876 on his way to Washington, D.C., he observed three hundred or more Chinese in the town, including wives and families.[35] Most likely many of the Elko County Chinese learned that Ch'en would be passing through, and were present in Carlin to welcome the visiting dignitary.

Elko

Because it was the biggest town along the Central Pacific in the county as well as the county seat, Elko was sure to attract a fair number of Chinese settlers. In Myron Angel's *History of Nevada*, five homicides involving Chinese in Elko were recorded in 1870. Most of the early Chinese lived on Commercial Street between Fourth and Fifth. This area, which also including a portion of Silver Street, was Elko's first Chinatown. It was struck by fire on October 19, 1871.[36]

During the 1870s the Chinese colony in town grew in size. Sun Wah established a laundry in 1875; and the Hi Loy general store, established in 1878 at the corner of Fifth and Silver, was one of the largest in town. Whites as well as Chinese patronized it, and its proprietor did a brisk business in importing and exporting in cooperation with Chinese firms in San Francisco.[37]

In addition, the Chinese had their own hospital in Elko attended by a Chinese physician. White patients were admitted to it, since it was quite common for Caucasians to place greater faith in traditional Chinese medicine than in conventional American medicine.[38]

The Chinese also contributed to frontier Elko's well-being in another way. They grew almost all the vegetables which the townspeople consumed during the 1870s and 1880s. Potatoes, carrots, and turnips were the principal crops. The most successful of the early gardeners was Wah Sing, a potato grower. After his sojourn in Elko, he returned to China.[39]

Despite their contributions to the community, however, the Elko Chinese were not spared from anti-Chinese feeling. In April of 1876 the town's whites passed a resolution opposing further Chinese immigration, but no violence or other direct action was aimed at any of Elko's Chinese.[40] Nevada historian Wilbur S. Shepperson has pointed out that "When aroused, Nevadans could show great feeling for a particular man and yet condemn hundreds of his fellow nationals."[41] The experience of the Chinese in Elko during the 1870s supports this contention. Whites accepted and even praised the Chinese in town as individuals, yet were almost universal in their condemnation of the Chinese as a national group.[42]

Wells, Toano, and Montello

Each of these railroad towns had temporary Chinese populations in the 1870s; nearly all of the Chinese worked on section gangs, as members of roundhouse crews, and on railroads. In Wells, the Chinatown was located near the roundhouse, and it included cafes, stores, a Chinese temple (joss house), and laundries; Montello had a Chinese store, temple, and several Chinese homes.[43]

MINING CAMPS

Tuscarora

During the 1870s, Tuscarora had the largest Chinese population in Nevada outside of the Comstock area, and its Chinatown was the largest one in the state. In 1869, approximately two hundred Chinese released by the Central Pacific were introduced into the area to work some white-held placer claims. Other Chinese arrived later to work placer claims which whites had abandoned.[44]

In 1870, they built a water ditch for their placers, and were making about five to twenty dollars per day for their work. Tales about the early days in Tuscarora abound, but their factual accuracy cannot be confirmed. According to one account, Chinese miners supposedly extracted $500,000 in gold there in 1872.[45] After 1876, however, the area became the destination of a stampede of white miners, as boom conditions developed. From that point onward, the Chinese changed from a majority to a slightly tolerated minority.[46]

In 1880, only five per cent of the 214 Tuscarora Chinese listed in the manuscript census were miners. Because placer mining was declining and the white anti-Chinese movement in town was trying to curtail economic opportunities for nonwhites, the Chinese started to move into other occupations. The greatest number became servants or cooks in white households. Other occupations besides mining represented in Tuscarora's Chinese community in 1880 were wood-chopping, laundering, gambling, retail trade, traditional medicine, and barbering. There were only sixteen Chinese women residing in Tuscarora's Chinese quarter, more than half of whom were employed in Chinese-owned brothels.[47]

Those who worked as woodchoppers had to cut sagebrush on the desert and haul it by team and wagon to the white-owned mines; it was used to fuel the steam-operated machinery at the mines. Competition developed between the Chinese and white woodchoppers, and the Chinese did not back down from a fight when provoked. In 1878, they fought with axes, pitchforks, and whatever other weapons they could lay their hands on when whites threatened them. By 1881, the areas closest to Tuscarora were almost completed cleared of sagebrush, and it became necessary to scour the countryside up to fifteen to twenty miles away.[48]

By the 1880s, Chinese mining was on the decline in the Tuscarora area, but it was not completely dead. The last significant activity occurred in 1884, when a Chinese company built an hydraulic machine for washing gold in Eagle Ravine. More than a thousand feet of flume were used to bring water to the placers. Other Chinese companies built sluices in Gardner, Canton, and Half Moon ravines. For their labors, the Chinese recovered about $30,000 in gold; but that was not enough for them to break even. Thereafter the placers and Old Tuscarora (the Chinese quarter) were gradually abandoned.[49]

From a high of about 500 people in 1880, Tuscarora's Chinese population steadily decreased in size as mining and other related activities declined. In 1890 there were about 250; in 1893 the number was down to 85; and six years later, only 12 Chinese were left. The water ditches were abandoned by 1900, and the last Chinese miner in Tuscarora died in 1927.[50]

Mountain City, Gold Creek, and Contact

During boom periods in these mining camps, a few Chinese were active. In the 1870s, former Chinese employees of the Central Pacific operated placer mines; only one remained by the early 1890s. Chinese prospectors joined the rush to Gold Creek beginning in 1873, and engaged in rudimentary placer mining. Some Chinese merchants were active there also; the Li family operated a general store for almost forty years, doing its greatest volume of business during the late

1870s and 1880s, when Gold Creek was a flourishing camp. Finally, a few Chinese mined at Contact for copper, silver, and gold on a commission basis.[51]

As can be gleaned from the above accounts, the Chinese played important roles in railroading and mining in Elko County during the late nineteenth century. With the passing of time, however, their number steadily decreased. As the railroad workers grew older, they yearned for the companionship of other Chinese and especially for their families. Many of them moved to San Francisco or returned to Guangdong province.

The Chinese miners also moved elsewhere when placer mining no longer paid adequate returns for diligent labor and group investments in equipment and supplies. Added to these considerations were the various Chinese exclusion acts of the late nineteenth and early twentieth centuries. It should come to us as no surprise that Elko County's Chinese population has remained at under 100 at any one time since 1920, and under 30 since 1940.

About the only occupational pursuits which the small number of Chinese in the county have embraced in recent years have been in the food and beverage businesses (especially the operation of small Chinese restaurants, cafes, and bars) in Carlin and Elko, and dealing at the several casinos in Elko. Because of the county's relatively small overall population, the size of its Chinese population has remained small and in the future will probably continue to be small.

Esmeralda County

Until 1911, Esmeralda County also included the area that now comprises Mineral County. Chinese were present in the area around Aurora, the first county seat, during the early 1860s. In Myron Angel's *History of Nevada*, mention is made of a homicide committed by a Chinese near the town. On April 17, 1863, a Chinese stabbed an Irishman with the surname of McKinty at Winters' Mill, located half a mile south of Aurora. McKinty died on April 24.[52] This incident helps shatter the stereotype of the meek, passive, nonresistant Chinese. The Chinese could fight, brawl, seek vengeance, and kill just as well as anyone else on the Nevada mining frontier; as with any ethnic group, the Chinese had their share of thieves, murderers, and rogues.

Besides Aurora, Chinese also lived in Candelaria and Columbus. Their presence at the latter location had to do with the Pacific Coast Borax Company, which began its operations at the Columbus Salt Marsh in 1872. Several hundred Chinese workers toiled at the marsh, where borax and other minerals were concentrated by heating the marsh water in evaporation boilers. Borax mining started to decline in 1875, but production in the area went on until about 1890.[53]

In the early twentieth century, the Chinese were largely excluded from participating in the mining boom at Goldfield. Labor unions like the American Federation of Labor, the Western Federation of Miners, and the Industrial Workers of the World were all active in the new mining district, and all were unabashed advocates of white supremacy. As a consequence, the Chinese were banned from working in the mines or in related activities.

Anti-Chinese feeling was so strong that Minnie P. Blair, a participant in the Oral History Project conducted by the University of Nevada Library (Reno), recalled that during the period from about 1909 to 1918, no Chinese were allowed to get off the trains of the Las Vegas and Tonopah Railroad at Goldfield. The town followed a strict policy of "no Chinese allowed."[54]

The United States census figures for Esmeralda County for 1920 show the size of the population after the detachment of the old north county area (which became Mineral County in 1911) and the 1919 mill closure of the Goldfield Consolidated Mines Company.[55] By 1920 the county seat, Goldfield, was already declining as a significant gold mining center. No persons of Chinese descent were reported as residents of Esmeralda County in the decennial federal censuses after 1920.

Eureka County

Eureka County was not organized until 1973. Its formation had to do with the discovery of silver and lead in the area where the town of Eureka was later built. According to Nevada historian Russell R. Elliott, the Eureka mining district was the most productive region in the state outside of the Comstock Lode between the 1860s and 1880.[56]

Chinese first entered what later became Eureka County in the early 1860s. White prospectors established a silver mining camp at Cortez (about sixty-eight miles northeast of Austin) just at about the time people were rushing to Austin in the hopes of finding another Comstock. Simon Wenban, a mining entrepreneur, discovered deposits of silver chloride and silver bromide near Cortez. He started preliminary mining operations, and hired a Chinese foreman. However, Wenban lacked the capital to mine his claim in earnest. He approached some Chinese merchants in San Francisco, who grubstaked him to the tune of $20,000.[57]

Wenban's operations at Cortez lasted from the early 1860s well into the 1870s. His mine workers were mainly Chinese, and he paid them at fixed wage rates: $1.50 a day for mines; $2.50 for twelve hours for millmen; and $2.50 per cord of wood for woodcutters.[58]

In addition to work in mining, the Chinese were very much involved in railroad construction and maintenance in Eureka County. They were responsible for building the Central Pacific and the Eureka and Palisade railroads, which gave the county east to west and north to south transportation links. Along the Central Pacific, Chinese resided in towns like Beowawe and Palisade, where in 1880 they accounted for ten to twenty percent of the townsfolk.[59]

From the Central Pacific line in the northern part of the county, Chinese laborers built the narrow gauge Eureka and Palisade Railroad, which ran from the

Humboldt River Palisades (ten miles southwest of Carlin) south to the county seat at Eureka—a total of ninety miles. Work on the roadbed began in December of 1873 with a crew of 58 whites and over 100 Chinese veterans of the Central Pacific. By January of 1875, 52 miles of track were in place.[60]

Further grading of the roadbed resumed in June of 1875, with a work force of 500 men. Almost all were Chinese, except for the scraper drivers. During construction, the Chinese staged a strike. It was broken by withhholding their drinking water. The railroad was completed to Eureka on October 22, 1875.[61]

Even before completion of the railroad, the county seat, Eureka, had a significant Chinese population. The Chinese worked as cooks, domestics, and laborers. Five of them lost their lives in the disastrous flood which struck the town on July 24, 1874.[62]

Along with their compatriots elsewhere in Nevada, the Eureka Chinese had to endure racist persecution. Anti-Chinese feeling in the county started heating up in February of 1876. By March it became a crusade. At that time, two Chinese were killed in Eureka, and another one suffered a similar fate on a wood ranch in Diamond Valley (about twenty-five miles northeast of Eureka). On May 23 and December 15, anti-Chinese public meetings and demonstrations were held, and a number of Chinese were driven from their work on the Eureka and Palisade Railroad.[63]

But despite the racism and the decline in mining output, a steadily decreasing number of Chinese remained in the county seat and elsewhere. A longtime resident of the county, Peter Merialdo, remembered the existence of a Chinese temple (joss house) on Bateman Street in Eureka as late as 1912 or 1913.[64] Since 1930, there have been fewer than ten Chinese residents in the entire county at any one time. They have usually resided in the town of Eureka, and have operated small restaurants, cafes, or bars there.

Humboldt County

Humboldt County was established in 1861 before Nevada attained statehood. Until 1919, it also included what is now Pershing County. During the nineteenth century, most of the important mining activity in the county was in the vicinity of Unionville.

That town became the county seat in 1861. It was the site of a mining boom from 1863 to 1870, during which time its white inhabitants distinguished themselves by exhibiting an especially virulent variety of anti-Chinese racism. For example, the Democratic party organ in town, the *Humboldt Register,* equated "Chinamen, baboons and trained monkeys."[65] A segment of Unionville's population was also responsible for forcibly expelling all of the town's Chinese residents in the middle of January 1869. The Chinese, outnumbered and outgunned, did not resist. The sheriff and the various white social, religious, and fraternal organizations in town did nothing to prevent the expulsion. Charges against the perpetrators of the unlawful act were subsequently dropped.[66]

This kind of experience, however, did not permanently dissuade persons of Chinese descent from working and living in the county. After Unionville declined as a white mining center, scattered Chinese returned to the environs to mine. In American Canyon, Wong Kee (most likely not directly related to any other person with the same romanized name) placer mined from the 1880s onward with the help of many fellow Chinese. They tunneled through 10 to 90 feet of bedrock, and hit a vein in the first half of a claim that stretched for 10,000 feet in the canyon. Water was at a premium at the mine site. With only enough water to achieve a depth of six inches, sluices could not be used. Instead, Wong and associates used rockers. As late as 1905 there were still Chinese mining in the canyon. By that time there were fewer than ten, and all were quite elderly. Remains of the once-flourishing mine littered the hillsides: scraps of rock, mud, adobe, lumber, and a few dugouts.[67] In addition, one or two other old Chinese were still placer mining in Barber Canyon in 1905.[68]

Elsewhere in Humboldt County, the Chinese lived in Winnemucca, near Golconda, and even in remote McDermitt. A Chinese tenant farmer grew vegetables on a small parcel of ranch land near Golconda. His produce was well received in Winnemucca. Seventy-five miles to the north of Winnemucca, Tom Low and his wife owned a general store at McDermitt. They supplied the many sheep camps and ranches in the area. Not only did the Chinese merchant sell supplies, but he also bought what the local ranchers and rangelands produced: hay, grain, and wool. Mrs. Tom was also an unusual lady on the Nevada frontier. She was fluent in Cantonese, English, and Paiute, and thus was a great help to her husband in the conduct of the family-owned business.[69]

In the southern half of Humboldt County prior to its organization as Pershing County, a small Chinese population lived in Lovelock. In 1870, there were 18, and ten years later the town had 31 Chinese residents. Most were railroad workers or farm laborers. By the turn of the century, the number of Lovelock Chinese increased to 39, and by far the majority of them were cooks or restaurant operators.[70]

Among the early Chinese merchants in Lovelock were Ah Foo, who ran a restaurant during the late 1880s, and the Lee family, which operated the cafe at Young's Hotel. Between 1900 and 1919, several Chinese laundries operated in town: the Lovelock Laundry (owned by Kim Lung), the Wah Lung Company, and other establishments run by Hop Lee, Wong Kee, and Kee Kin.[71]

Undoubtedly old age and the Chinese exclusion laws took their toll on Humboldt County's Chinese population. Since 1950 the county's number of Chinese residents had dwindled to the point of insignificance, and the few who have been occasionally counted in the decennial censuses since 1950 are not old-timers, but instead scattered representatives of a new generation.

Lander County

The history of Lander County is largely a tale of two towns: Austin in the south, and Battle Mountain in the north. The distance between them is about ninety miles.

Austin, located close to the geographic center of Nevada, got its start as a silver mining camp in 1862. It became the center of the new Reese River mining district, and was made the county seat in 1863. Most of its early inhabitants came from the Comstock, including the Chinese. An English visitor to the town during the period from 1866 to 1867, Sir Charles Wentworth Dilke, observed several Chinese laundries and a small Chinese temple (joss house) in town. Most of the Chinese worked as peddlers, cooks, or laundrymen. This member of Parliament arrived at the following conclusion regarding the Austin Chinese: "All were quiet, quick, orderly, and clean."[72]

Such a sweeping observation by a traveler was bound to be inaccurate. Approximately one decade after Dilke visited Austin, one of the town's more notorious killings took place in June of 1877 when Mann Tonn killed Ah Hoy. The killer was sentenced to serve twenty-five years in the Nevada State Prison.[73] Based on these types of fragmentary evidence, it is difficult to piece together an accurate picture of Chinese life in frontier Austin. Most likely past reality is to be found elsewhere between these two types of images. To assume that the town's Chinese were either all angelic or all plagued by internecine feuding would be perhaps to miss the ordinary for the unusual or the spectacular.

Five years after the Ah Hoy affair, a Jewish visitor to Austin estimated the town's total population at around 2,300, including 6 blacks and approximately 100 Chinese. The Chinese had a virtual monopoly on the laundry business, and also worked as servants and cooks. Austin had a Chinese temple and at least one of the tongs maintained a branch in town. This description of Austin depicts the Lander county seat at the historical height of both the county's total population and Chinese population. While lacking in minute details, it is nevertheless generally accurate.[74]

In the northern portion of Lander County, the Chinese first arrived in Battle Mountain as railroad construction workers for the Central Pacific. After completion of the rail line to Utah, Thomas Nelson hired some of the former railroad employees to tend his flocks of sheep in the vicinity of Battle Mountain. So adept did the Chinese become at herding that other sheepmen began hiring Chinese. For a good number of years during the late nineteenth century it was common to see Chinese herders and camp-tenders in Nevada where sheep were grazed on the open range. Their role as immigrant herders was later assumed by the French and Spanish Basques.[75]

In the town of Battle Mountain, a small Chinese quarter developed. Its few businesses served the Chinese shepherds and miners who worked in the area. Apparently there were quite a few Chinese miners in Lander County at one time, because when the Chinese Minister to the United States, Ch'en Lan-pin, passed through Battle Mountain in 1876 on his way to Washington, D.C., he was definitely impressed by the number of Chinese who arrived in town to greet him.[76]

Fire destroyed Battle Mountain's Chinese quarter during the autumn of 1878, but most likely it was rebuilt.[77] Throughout the decade of the 1880s, the town had a relatively large Chinese population for a settlement of its size. White merchants considered the Chinese as good credit risks, because most of their debts were ultimately paid in full. Moreover, it was a Chinese custom to pay off all loans each year before the arrival of Chinese New Year.[78] According to Chinese belief, failure to do so could bring about misfortune during the new year.

During the twentieth century, the Chinese have not been numerous in Austin and Battle Mountain. Since 1920, the decennial federal censuses have consistently reported fewer than 20 Chinese residents at any one time in Lander County.

Lincoln County

Before 1909, Lincoln County also included the land area of what is now Clark County. Never did the county's Chinese population exceed 100 at any one time. Even in 1880 at the peak of Nevada's nineteenth-century population growth and when the Chinese accounted for 8.7 per cent of the total population, Chinese only accounted for 3.8 per cent of Lincoln County's population.

Most of the Chinese lived in the county seat, Pioche, and smaller numbers resided in mining camps like Bullionville, Delamar, Fay, and Caselton as new mineral discoveries were made at those sites.[79] During the 1870s, Pioche's Chinese residents lived in two parts of town: on Pioche Street, and on lower Main Street. Almost all of them hailed from the Taishan (Toishan) district of Guangdong province. In 1874, a newspaper article reported only two members of the Hop Wo District Association living in Pioche, which meant that they were most likely from either the Kaiping (Hoiping) or Enping (Yanping) districts.[80]

Principal occupations of the early Pioche Chinese were washing and ironing. To break the monotony of everyday life, the town's Chinese smoked opium, gambled, and patronized the few Chinese prostitutes on lower Main Street. Seldom did they encroach upon the "turf" of other ethnic groups. Instead, they stayed to themselves, and often even fought with each other.[81]

One such fight, which perhaps was typical, was reported in the *Pioche Daily Record* on August 30, 1873:

Yesterday afternoon, at three o'clock, a Chinaman named Ah Cue, and familiarly called "Sam," was seen approaching the rear end of Sam Wo's washhouse on Lacour Street, north of the court-house. He bore in one hand a pistol, in the other hand an eight-inch knife, and under one of his arms another pistol. When he had approached to within a short distance of the house another Chinaman named Ah Fan, and commonly known as "Charley," fired at him, the ball striking within two or three yards of Ah Cue's feet. Ah Cue stood his ground and fired five shots at his opponent, none of them, however, taking effect. Just then officer McManus laid hands on him, and he was prevented from using the other pistol and the knife. The whole affair did not take more than a minute; and within three minutes after the first shot [,] the fiery Ah Cue was safe within prison walls. Ah Fan, however, had fled to some place unknown, and no one saw him more.

The cause of the difficulty was, as near as we could learn, as follows: Ah Fan had been a cook in a restaurant. By some means he lost his place, and Ah Cue was engaged to fill it. In consequence of this a quarrel occurred between the parties in Chinatown, and shortly after Ah Cue "heeled" himself with the weapons described, and with a laudable desire of imitating Caucasian manners as practiced in Pioche, went after his enemy. . . . Verily the "Heathen Chinee" is becoming civilized.[82]

Altercations between whites and Chinese, however, were a different matter. On October 6, 1877, the *Record* carried a story about a Chinese cook whose arm had been wounded after he had been shot at by a white assailant. The newspaper commented: "No action was taken in this matter to find out the perpetrator of the outrage as our officials don't get paid salaries to bother about whether a Chinaman is shot and killed or whether he is allowed to live and eat rice."[83]

But even though the Chinese were not considered the equals of whites in Pioche, that did not preclude development of friendships between individual whites and Chinese. The editor of the *Record* reflected the ambivalence of one who frequently employed anti-Chinese clichés in his writing, yet still had to admit that the Chinese and whites could coexist amiably once they became more familiar with each other. For example, the 1877 marriage of a Pioche Chinese merchant nicknamed "Charley Beene" to Miss Sen Choy proved to be one of the great social events in town. The white participants in the wedding ceremony—including the witnesses, justice of the peace, and the newspaper editor who covered the story—all took turns kissing the bride. Then it was the turn of "the rest of the boys," and a champagne party followed.[84]

In addition, it seemed the Pioche's Caucasians looked forward to the annual Chinese New Year celebrations with almost as much anticipation as the Chinese. In 1887 when Miss Fong Chop was named queen of that year's celebration, the *Record's* editor remarked that "during their New Year, the Chinese are social beasts even if they are heathens. Many of our beaux and belles joined in the festivities with a vim."[84]

These and other news items in the *Record* show that the Chinese were fair game to be stereotyped as a group, but often were respected as individuals and friends.

This dichotomy between word and deed was also illustrated by the case of Wo Ling, a Pioche Chinese associated with the Ong Chung Lung store, who in 1887 left for a visit to China. In his absence from the United States, the American government approved of the Scott Act, which prohibited the re-entry of Chinese laborers to this country from abroad unless the Chinese had families in this country or property in the United States valued at one thousand dollars. When Wo Long tried to return to Pioche in the fall of 1888, he was detained in San Francisco by American immigration officials and threatened with deportation. Upon learning of his plight, his compatriots in Pioche promptly approached Lincoln County officials and asked them to issue an affidavit with Wo Ling's photograph on it attesting to his eligibility to re-enter the country and to return to Pioche as a Chinese merchant and property owner.[84] The county authorities, known for their support of the anti-Chinese movement, complied with the Chinese request. After more than a month of detention in San Francisco, Wo Ling was allowed to land and return to Nevada.[87]

As the decade of the 1890s approached, the number of Chinese residing in Pioche started to decline. The first Chinese Exclusion Act (1882) and Scott Act (1888) were both taking effect by that time. After passage of the Geary Act (1892), the true effect of these various laws was felt. In compliance with the new law, all Chinese laborers in the county had to be registered. In Pioche, that meant that about 25 to 30 persons by 1894.[88] Two years later the *Pioche Weekly Record*, commenting on the depressed state of mining in the area, the effects of the panic of 1893, and the gradual departure of the Chinese from town said:

> The celestial observance of Chinese New Year has not been so demonstrative this year as in the past. This is due to the prevailing hard times and the comparatively few Chinamen left hereabouts. The joss house has been repainted however, a flag pole erected and the dragon on the yellow ground has floated over the place for a number of days past.[89]

After the turn of the century, the Chinese population of Lincoln County decreased as the years passed. Only a few still remained, such as Tom Wah and his wife Gue Gim Wah, who operated a boarding house and restaurant for the mine workers of the Combined Metals Reduction Company at Caselton. Tom Wah was many years older than his wife, and after he died she continued to operate the boarding house and restaurant. As late as 1980 she was still residing in Caselton, and operating Wah's Cafeteria there. During the decade of the 1970s, Gue Gim Wah accounted for one of only two Chinese known to be living in Lincoln County.

Lyon County

Mention has already been made of the first Chinese introduced to Nevada and Lyon County in 1856. The northern portion of the county was on the periphery of the Comstock mining excitement, and settlements like Dayton (previously known as Chinatown), Silver City, and Johntown (named after the white label for "John Doe" Chinese as "John Chinaman") all had small Chinese populations.

The early Chinese sojourners worked as laborers, woodchoppers, fruit and vegetable peddlers, and also placer mined for gold in areas abandoned by whites.

After the decline of Comstock mining, a small number of Chinese remained in Dayton working as domestic servants in white households and as cooks in the town's hotels. There were also two Chinese laundries operating in town during the late 1890s.[90]

Elsewhere in the county, the Chinese helped to build the Carson and Colorado Railroad. In June of 1880, labor contractor Ah Quong provided 200 Chinese laborers who joined with about 300 whites in starting construction east of Mound House. These Chinese workers were hired in Reno, but because of the strongly anti-Chinese feelings which the white population on the Comstock still harbored, they could not travel to the construction site by way of the Virginia and Truckee Railroad (a line that had already been built by Chinese laborers). Instead, they were transported from Reno to Wadsworth and then south to the work camp in Churchill Canyon.[91] Eventually the railroad connected Reno and the Comstock region (via the Virginia and Truckee Railroad) with northern Esmeralda County (later detached as Mineral County) and the Owens Valley in eastern California.

Besides working in occupations directly or indirectly linked to mining in the northern parts of the county, a small number of Chinese also worked as cooks on some of the many farms and ranches in the Smith and Mason valleys in the southern portion of the county. In the twentieth century, however, the Chinese did not participate in the greatest mining enterprise in Lyon County, the Anaconda Copper Corporation's open pit operations at Weed Heights (just outside of Yerington). Copper mining at Week Heights lasted from 1952 until 1978.[92] By then the Chinese population in the county had declined numerically to the point of insignificance.

Mineral County

Prior to 1911, the land area of what is now Mineral County constituted the northern half of Esmeralda County. The presence of Chinese at Aurora and Candelaria has already been mentioned (see the section of this article about Esmeralda County). The Chinese worked as laundrymen, cooks, servants, and laborers in the various mining camps which dotted the region from the 1860s onwards.

When the Carson and Colorado Railroad was built through northern Esmeralda County in the 1880s, more Chinese entered the region as railroad workers. At Mina, a stop on the railroad, a small Chinese community existed during the period from about 1905 down to the 1920s.[93] It was there in 1921 that Gee Jon, a member of the Hop Sing Tong, murdered Tom Quong Kee, a seventy-four-year-old laundryman and nominal member of the Bing Kung Tong. That notorious incident marked the last occurrence of "tong warfare" in Nevada.[94]

By the decade of the 1930s there were very few Chinese still residing in Mineral County. From 1930 to 1970 only a half dozen or fewer Chinese have lived in the county at any one time.

Nye County

Nye County never had a large Chinese population. Even during peak periods of mining activity, the county had fewer than one hundred Chinese residents at any one time. Traditionally, life in the county meant working at some task connected with mining or ranching. During the late nineteenth century, the county's small number of Chinese were dispersed at the various mining camps which sprang up. The Chinese worked at the few occupations open to them like cooking and laundering. A few were miners, but they usually only worked claims which whites had abandoned. Even at the height of Chinese residence in Nevada in 1880 when the Chinese accounted for 8.7 per cent of the state's total population, only 3.5 per cent of Nye County's population was Chinese. In cases when the Chinese tried to join whites in developing new mining districts in the county (as occurred at Tybo in 1888), the white miners rudely and violently excluded them from participating.[95]

After the turn of the century, a small number of Chinese moved to the new boom town of Tonopah. A small Chinatown developed, complete with laundries, food stores, and lottery shops. The Chinese were not allowed to work in the mines; instead, they were expected to work as cooks, laundrymen, and domestic servants in white households. Among the members of Tonopah's newly rich elite it was "quite the thing" to have at least one Chinese servant.[96]

Tonopah was also the scene of the last outbreak of anti-Chinese mob violence in Nevada. On the night of September 15, 1903, a mob of white workingmen destroyed Chinese homes, inflicted bodily harm on individual Chinese, and was responsible for the death of Chinese laundryman Chong Bing Long, age 66. Fifteen Caucasians were arrested after the incident. Ultimately nine of them were released, and the remaining six were acquitted of charges of wrongdoing supposedly because of insufficient evidence.[97]

Not all of the town's whites approved of what happened. After the mob action, the more solid citizenry passed a resolution condemning what had happened. In addition to showing some concern for the unfortunate Chinese, these more stable elements of the white community were fearful of the possibly negative effect that the incident might have on potential investors in the area's mines.[98]

Tonopah's silver mines reached their peak period of production between 1910 and 1914. Thereafter they declined, even though four of them continued in operation until World War II.[99] Reflecting these facts, Nye County's total population declined between 1920 and 1950, as did its Chinese population.

Aside from employment in Tonopah, a few Chinese worked as cooks and hired hands on the ranches in the Smoky and Monitor valleys; and in more recent times, a small number of persons of Chinese descent have been employed at the

Nevada Test Site at Mercury. During the decade of the 1970s, about the only visibly Chinese-owned business in Nye County was a small restaurant in Tonopah.

Pershing County

Before 1919, the land area of what is now Pershing County comprised the southern half of Humboldt County. During the late nineteenth century, Chinese resided at Unionville and mined in American Canyon (east of Oreana Station), Barber Canyon (northeast of Mill City), and Spring Valley (east of Oreana Station and north of American Canyon).[100]

After 1919, the small Chinese population of the new county was concentrated in Lovelock. The Woo, Chang, and Yup families were all active in running various business enterprises. During the 1920s, many of the town's Chinese lived in family households with several children.[101]

The Woo family originated in the Kaiping (Hoiping) district in Guangdong province. During the 1920s and 1930s, it owned a bar, the Savoy Restaurant, the Lacey Barbershop, the Pershing Hotel restaurant in Lovelock, and shared ownership in an eighty-acre farm in the area with a Chinese farmer, Hom Slew.[102]

The Chang family centered around Jim Chang On, who was born in San Francisco in 1876, and his China-born wife, Chae See. Chang moved to Lovelock shortly after China's 1911 republican revolution, and engaged in many types of business activity. He owned the Elite Hotel, the Northern Cafe, and the Wing Lee Company (which specialized in Chinese products and general merchandise); operated a *bak gop biu* (Chinese lottery or keno) game in partnership with the Woo family; developed mining properties in partnerships with white miners, and made investments in landholdings in Pershing County. His three sons (Lewis, William, and Frank) were all born in Nevada.[103]

The Yup family traced its origins to Yap Shen Soon, a partner of the Woo family. During the 1920s, the Yups operated the Temple Cafe, located on Main Street (near Broadway) in Lovelock.

These three families formed the backbone of the small Chinese community in Lovelock during the 1920s and 1930s. From 1920 onwards the size of the community gradually decreased, due perhaps to the exclusion laws, a lack of social acceptance of Chinese in Lovelock, and the urges of the American-born to seek their futures elsewhere. Overall, the Chinese left very little in the way of an enduring legacy in the history of Pershing County. Their number was quite small. At best they were tolerated as merchants and laborers.

Storey County

Much has been written about the place of the Chinese on the Comstock during the region's bonanza days. Unfortunately, a good deal of it is inaccurate. Most common is exaggeration of the size of the Chinese population. Never did the resident Chinese population exceed one thousand at any one time. In fact, if federal census figures are to be believed, Storey County never achieved the historical distinction of having the largest Chinese population in Nevada. At best it only had the second largest concentration of Chinese, and that only during the 1870s and early 1880s.

The Chinese entered Storey County during the year of the initial Comstock discovery in 1859. Fearing Chinese competition, the white Gold Hill Mine Workers' Union passed a resolution on June 11, 1859, prohibiting Asians from holding claims in the new district.[104] Nevertheless there were tasks other than mining which had to be performed, and the Chinese moved in to do the laundering, cooking, vegetable gardening, and woodchopping.

The plans were made to link the main Central Pacific Railroad tracks in Reno with Carson City and the Comstock cities (Silver City, Gold Hill, and Virginia City), it was assumed that the Chinese would help construct the new line. In this regard the *Territorial Enterprise* remarked on June 5, 1869:

> in case a company is formed to make a railroad or dig a canal, outsiders do not trouble themselves much about it—they are allowed to use Chinamen, jackasses or whatever is best and cheapest for them. . . . On this coast it is quite certain that the Chinese will be our railroad builders: in fact, there are few white men who care to work as common laborers on railroads for railroad wages, as they can do better. . . .[105]

Work began on April 1, 1869. Four hundred and fifty Chinese, just released from constructing the Central Pacific as far east as Reno, were hired. Whites served as superintendents and bosses, and Chinese served as work gang overseers and laborers. The overseers were paid one dollar per day per laborer, but oftentimes they did not pass on the full amount to each worker.[106]

Construction of the railroad was not easy. Timber for the ties had to be cut from nearby mountainsides; and erection of the Crown Point trestle, which measured some 500 feet in length and was 85 feet high, required the full energies of many men. The difficulty of building the Virginia and Truckee Railroad can only be partially fathomed today. There was no modern grading or track-laying equipment in 1869. Seven tunnels had to be blasted and dug.[107]

On September 29, 1869, approximately 350 Virginia City and Gold Hill miners marched to the Chinese construction camp near the Overman Mine. They drove the Chinese out of their wooden huts despite a warning from the Storey County sheriff. None of the Chinese were injured, but their huts were all destroyed. The mob leaders were mostly Irish immigrant miners active in the white labor union on the Comstock. William Sharon, who was building the Virginia and Truckee, finally had to make a deal with the union: he promised that none of his Chinese laborers would ever be allowed to work in the mines.[108]

With that assurance, construction was allowed to continue. The railroad reached Gold Hill on November 12, 1869, and Virginia City on January 29, 1870.

After the new line was in operation, the Chinese were routinely discriminated against. The railroad's management provided regular passenger coaches for whites, but Chinese passengers could only ride in cabooses. In fact, the Virginia and Truckee Railroad made a point of retaining cabooses on its passenger trains in order to provide segregated seating.[109]

Life on the Comstock for the Chinese during the 1860s and 1870s was in some respects far from attractive. Life in Storey County was at times rude, crude, and violent. The Chinese themselves sometimes settled their differences with fists and guns.

For example, Yuk Lee was shot and killed by another Chinese on Ophir Road four miles from Gold Hill on October 26, 1863.[110] And in 1872, it was necessary for authorities in Virginia City to arrest fifteen Chinese for brawling. Apparently an argument developed between some men from the Taishan and Xiangshan (Zhongsham) districts, resulting in two of them being wounded. Even though most of the Comstock Chinese were confronted with the indignities of racial discrimination, that in itself did not mean that all Chinese got along well with each other. Differences in their places of geographic origin in Guangdong province were enough to keep the Comstock Chinese from developing any strong sense of racial solidarity.[111]

Most of the Chinese on the Comstock resided in Virginia City. In 1870 the federal census showed 749 Chinese living in Storey County, and 539 were inhabitants of Virginia City. The majority were itinerant laborers or cooks. There was a small elite of doctors, merchants, gamblers, and skilled craftsmen who owned personal property of value. Probably the most highly esteemed Chinese were the physicians, who treated Chinese and white patients alike. At the bottom of the class structure were the Chinese prostitutes, who were segregated from their white counterparts and held as virtual slaves. Most of them had been sold once in China, and again on their arrival in California. In Virginia City their earnings were kept by Chinese male brothel keepers who were members of the San Francisco-based tongs. Besides prostitution, opium addiction was also a bane in Virginia City, as it was in China.[112]

It seems that only a minority of the Comstock's white population showed much sympathy for the Chinese, or tried to understand them, but there were attempts. In 1875, the Episcopal Church encouraged a Chinese convert, Ah For, to build a chapel in Virginia City. Ah For translated gospel messages into Cantonese, preached on alternate Sundays, and taught religion classes on weekday evenings. Part of the cost of maintaining his chapel was assumed by the Sunday school of St. Paul's Episcopal Church. This unique experiment in missionary work, however, only lasted for about one year. Fire struck the chapel in October of 1875, and the structure was not rebuilt. Ah For later received a missionary appointment from the Church of England, and returned to China.[113]

In addition to the Episcopal Church, the Chinese had a friend in Mark Twain, who during the 1860s worked as a reporter for the *Territorial Enterprise*. He later wrote about the Chinese in *Roughing It*, published in 1872. Twain's sympathy for the Chinese was certainly unusual for the time, but in compensating for the slurs of his fellow whites he tended to stereotype the Chinese *positively*:

> They are a harmless race when white men either let them alone or treat them no worse than dogs; in fact, they are almost entirely harmless anyhow, for they seldom think of resenting the vilet insults or the cruelest injuries. They are quiet, peaceable, tractable, free from drunkenness, and they are as industrious as the day is long. . . .[114]

> Any white man can swear a Chinaman's life away in the courts, but no Chinaman can testify against a white man. Ours is the "land of the free"—nobody denies that—nobody challenges it. (Maybe it is because we won't let other people testify).[115]

> A disorderly Chinaman is rare, and a lazy one does not exist. . . .[116]

> All Chinamen can read, write, and cipher with easy facility—pity but all our petted *voters* could. . . .[117]

> They are a kindly disposed, well-meaning race, and are respected and well treated by the upper classes all over the Pacific coast. No Californian *gentleman or lady* ever abuses or oppresses a Chinaman, under any circumstances, an explanation that seems to be much needed in the East. Only the scum of the population do it—they and their children; they, and, naturally and consistently, the policemen and politicians, likewise, for these are the dust-licking pimps and slaves of the scum, there as well as elsewhere in America.[118]

What Twain had to say about California also applied to Nevada. The Comstock's frontier society was little more than an extension of California's.

Virginia City's Chinese community similarly was tied to San Francisco's Chinatown. Chinese foodstuffs, herbal medicines, and other products from the homeland all had to pass through San Francisco. The Bay City was also where all the Chinese social organizations were headquartered: the Chinese Consolidated Benevolent Association (or Chinese Six Companies) and its component district associations; the clan (family or surname) associations; and the tongs. San Francisco was probably the first place in America that a Nevada-bound sojourner would see. It was the city that financed the Chinese businesses on the Comstock. It was also the city through which the remains of Nevada's deceased Chinese passed on the way home to final burial in Guangdong province.

In 1878, Virginia City's Chinese community consisted of nineteen businesses, including the following:

1) Restaurants:
    a) Hong Hing Low, 4 "I" Street
    b) Yune Fong Low, 5 North "H" Street

2) Herb shops:
   a) Hin Sang Hong, 103 Union Street
   b) Hoy Yuen Tong, 111 Union Street
   c) Man Fook Tong, 6A North "H" Street
   d) Quong Song Tong, 6 North "H" Street
   e) Yet Song Tong, 105 Union Street
3) Groceries:
   a) Quong Wo Lung, 110 Union Street
   b) Yuen Lung, 6 "I" Street
4) Physician:
   Dr. Gin Hin, 9 North "C" Street
5) Other businesses:
   a) Fook Sing, 101 Union Street
   b) Gung Wo, 1 "H" Street
   c) Kwong Hi Loy, 2 "H" Street
   d) Po Chin, 6A "I" Street
   e) Quong Yuen, 107 Union Street
   f) Ty Chong, 8 North "H" Street
   g) Wo Chong, 106 Union Street
   h) Yee Chung, 15 "I" Street
   i) Yee Lon, 4A "I" Street[119]

Between 1878 and 1882, the city's Chinese population decreased due to decreasing yields from the Big Bonanza mines, which affected all sectors of the Comstock's economy. By the latter year, only four businesses from 1878 remained: Fook Sing, Gung Wo, Hin Sang Hong, and Kwong Hi Loy. In addition, three new businesses had been started since 1878: Chung Lee, On Tai, and Sam Sing. Overall, the number of Chinese-owned businesses declined—an accurate reflection of the decreasing size of Virginia City's Chinese population. Aside from operating businesses, of course, the Chinese continued to work as cooks in the white-owned hotels and as domestics in well-to-do white households. Some even were bold enough to engage in quartz mining when there were no immediate threats from whites.[120]

From the 1880s onward, the size of the Chinese population in Storey County began to decline quite precipitously. The Chinese, like others on the Comstock, remained in the area in considerable numbers only when there were chances for economic advancement. As the ore bodies became exhausted, people left Virginia City in droves, including the Chinese.

In the 1970s, the history of the Chinese on the Comstock as presented to tourists who visited Virginia City was little more than a hodgepodge of distorted, stereotyped, commercialized schlock.[121] On page 372 of the "Yellow Pages" in the 1979–1980 *Nevada Bell Telephone Directory* there was an entry under the "Historical Places" heading that read:

CHINATOWN VIRGINIA CITY: ORIGINAL OLD CHINESE TOWN BUILT IN
1860's—bordellos, gen. stores, laundries, blacksmith shop, graveyards, old casino
halls, original artifacts, famous Tong dynasty building—tickets at Red Garter Saloon—
FOR TICKETS CALL 115 South C VCty . . . . 847 0655.

In 1964, Woo Loung Wah, age 105, was honored in Reno as the sole survivor
of the Central Pacific Railroad's Chinese work crew which laid the tracks through
the Sierra from California to Nevada. He symbolized the thousands of Chinese
who built the steel road which enabled Nevada to develop her rich mineral resources during the late nineteenth century. The Reno section of the Central Pacific was officially placed in use on June 19, 1868, and the presence of Chinese
in the Reno area dates from that time onward.[122]

When Ch'en Lan-pin, Chinese Minister to the United States, passed through
Reno in 1876 on his way to Washington, D.C., he observed that there were one
hundred or more Chinese living in Reno.[123] Two years later, a white Workingmen's Party convention held in the city called for a prohibition on the use of Chinese laborers in the city.

Prejudice against the Chinese, however, did not prevent the Nevada-California-Oregon (N-C-O) Railway from hiring dependable Chinese railroad builders
to help connect Nevada and California with the Pacific Northwest. Reno was the
base of operations during construction. Work began during the spring of 1881
with a work force of 80 Chinese out of a total of 240 men. Labor contractor Ah
Jack supplied the Chinese workers. The Chinese did most of the grading of the
roadbed. After the railroad was in operation, the N-C-O Railway continued to employ Chinese to work on its track crews. Their job was to clear winter snows off
the tracks with shovels.[124] Partially because of the labor of the Chinese, Washoe
County was linked to the towns of northeastern California and eastern Oregon
(table 5.1).

The county did not achieve the distinction of having the largest Chinese population in the state until 1900. It was second to Humboldt County in that regard
in 1910, but regained and held its primacy in every decennial census thereafter
from 1920 to 1960. To a great degree the growth of Washoe County's Chinese
population reflected Reno's position as Nevada's largest urban center from 1900
until the 1950s, with only chief challenges from Tonopah and Goldfield while
those cities enjoyed mining booms. Also, Reno's Chinese community survived because it was an extension of San Francisco's, and supplied virtually all of the Chinese scattered throughout the Nevada hinterland with ethnic goods and services.

But Reno was also the scene of the last overtly anti-Chinese incident occurring
in Nevada. In November of 1908, city officials ordered most of the buildings in
Chinatown (located east of Virginia Street and north of the Truckee River) destroyed, supposedly for reasons of public health. Many elderly Chinese were left

Table 5.1　Washoe County

Year	Total population, Washoe County	Chinese population, Washoe County	Chinese percentage of total
1870	3,091	221	7.1
1880	5,664	526	9.3
1890	6,437	217	3.4
1900	9.141	246	2.7
1910	17,434	155	0.9
1920	18,627	155	0.8
1930	27,158	195	0.7
1940	32,476	119	0.4
1950	50,205	82	0.2
1960	84,743	249	0.3
1970	121,068	411	0.3

homeless as the winter season began. Curiously though, Chinese-owned houses of prostitution frequented by whites were allowed to remain.[125]

After the turn of the century, Reno was viewed in San Francisco's Chinatown as a city that was especially amenable to gambling. Depending on the honesty or corruptibility of Bay Area police forces, gambling was not always a "sure thing" in California. In Nevada, public acceptance of gambling was much more widespread than in California, and a considerable number of Chinese gamblers moved to Reno to ply their craft.

The Chinese were responsible for introducing their lottery game, *bak gop biu* ("white pigeon ticket") to Nevada. Tickets used in the game originally used Chinese characters. Today, the game flourishes in virtually every major Nevada casino, and is known as keno. Numbers have replaced the Chinese characters on the lottery tickets, but the game is still basically the same.[126]

As early as 1918, Bo Wah ran a lottery game in Reno at the corner of Second and Lake Streets. He held two drawings per day at eight o'clock in the morning and eight o'clock at night. Needless to say, his players were not limited to Reno's small Chinese community.[127]

The modern methods of conducting the game using numbers pellets, and a drum were not common in Reno until about 1925. During the 1930s and 1940s, *bak gop biu* as played by non-Chinese in Nevada was known as "race horse keno," since the Nevada state constitution prohibited lotteries. In 1951, the state passed a law placing a wagering tax on off-track horse race betting, and the "race horse" part of the Chinese-invented Nevada lottery game was dropped. Since 1951, *bak gop biu* has been known as keno in virtually all the state's major gaming establishments.[128]

From 1910 until 1950, Washoe County's Chinese population was less than two hundred. Besides gamblers, there were a small number of merchants, craftsmen, manual laborers, domestic servants, cooks, railroad maintenance men, and occasionally a few Chinese physicians. The community was big enough to support a branch of the Chinese Consolidated Benevolent Association (Chung Wah Wui Gwoon *Zhonghua huiguan*, or Chinese Six Companies); a local unit of the Hop Sing Tong; a temple (joss house); and a Chinese language school. Most of the Chinese-occupied buildings during those years were either on the west side of North Virginia Street, on East First Street, or on Lake Street between First and Second.

In August of 1938, Thomas W. Chinn of San Francisco visited Reno's Chinatown, and dined on chow mein at a restaurant called Choy Bux, owned by a Mr. Choy. The proprietor was originally from the Zhongshan (Chungshan) district, of China'a Guangdong province, and had lived for eighteen years in Carson City before purchasing his business from another Reno Chinese. Chinn observed that Reno had a total of four Chinese restaurants at that time.[129]

By then, of course, China and Japan were at war. The War of Resistance to Japanese Aggression (the Chinese phase of World War II) lasted from 1937 to 1945. Since 45 per cent of Reno's Chinese were resident aliens ineligible to become naturalized American citizens, it was only natural for them to be active in patriotic activities on behalf of their mother country.[130] Led by the older men who were community leaders, the Reno branch of the Chinese Consolidated Benevolent Association engaged in war relief fund-raising on China's behalf throughout the wartime period.

During and after the war, however, Washoe County's Chinese population decreased to its lowest numerical level since the time the Chinese first settled in the Truckee River region. The 1950 census showed only 82 Chinese still residing in the county (with 68 of them living in Reno). A Chinese-American study, conducted about 1946, arrived at a figure of only 56 Chinese residents in the city of Reno, divided among seven families.[131] Many of the older first generation Chinese immigrants died, returned to China, or moved to San Francisco. Leadership of the Benevolent Association passed to the American-born second generation, some members of which were not fluent in Cantonese, unable to read the Chinese written language, and more interested in being Americans than being concerned with China and things Chinese. Whatever cohesion the Benevolent Association has provided for Reno's small Chinese community began to crumble during the 1950s as the Association's building—the Chinese temple at 46½–48½ East First Street—fell into disuse. Nature supplied the finishing blow in 1958 when the Truckee overflowed its banks and did irreparable damage to the brick building. It was later declared structurally unsound, and demolished.

Since 1950, the Chinese population of Washoe County has steadily increased. Most of this growth has been due to immigration from Hong Kong, Taiwan, and California. The old, immigrant, Cantonese-speaking Chinese community is no more. The surviving members of the old branch of the Benevolent Association (many of whom are American-born and whose deceased parents were once members) associate with each other as friends rather than as members of an organization. The Hop Sing Tong still has members in Reno, but the organization no longer has its own building in the downtown area; in fact, there is no longer an identifiable Chinatown in Reno. Its last vestiges, the New China Club building and the adjacent Hop Sing Tong building, both located at the corner of Lake Street and Commercial Row, were razed during the 1970s to make way for parking for Harrah's downtown casino complex. By 1970, Washoe County finally lost to Clark County the distinction of having the largest Chinese population in the state — a distinction which the northern county had held continuously since 1920.

For the most of its history, White Pine County has had a small Chinese population (see table 5.2). The greatest number of Chinese were present during the 1970s, the period when the Hamilton mining district was booming. Occupations open to them included cooking, laundering, woodchopping, water-carrying, and vegetable gardening.[132]

A few hardy Chinese pioneers in the county were merchants. Among them was Charles Wab, who arrived at Cherry Creek in 1874. He was one of the first merchants to settle there, and started the town's first restaurant and Chinese merchandise store. Thereafter he was identified with the town for fifty years, making a reputation for himself as a grubstaker of prospectors and a charitable feeder of penniless men.[133]

During the late nineteenth century, White Pine County's Caucasian population reacted to the Chinese in two ways. It scorned the Chinese as a group for political reasons, yet tolerated and even respected individual Chinese. For example, when President Chester A. Arthur vetoed a twenty-year Chinese exclusion bill in 1882, he was burned in effigy throughout the White Pine mining district.[134] Yet the Chinese continued to work in the county unmolested.

Table 5.2 White Pine County

Year	Total population, White Pine County	Chinese population, White Pine County	Chinese percentage of total
1870	7,189	292	4.1
1880	2,682	107	4.0
1890	1,721	46	2.7
1900	1,961	31	1.6
1910	7,441	25	0.3
1920	8,935	32	0.4
1930	11,771	40	0.3
1940	12,377	18	0.1
1950	9,424	24	0.3
1960	9,808	19	0.2
1970	10,150	9	0.1

In the 1890s and early 1900s, most of the county's Chinese were cooks. There was a Chinese cook working at the McGill Ranch, and virtually all of the hired cooks in Ely were Chinese. There were enough Chinese living in Ely for the town to support a small Chinatown prior to 1900.[135]

Aside from the cooks, there were also a few Chinese herb doctors. These physicians were highly regarded by whites, since they offered alternatives to western medicine in the treatment of disease. Some whites felt that Chinese doctors were more effective than their white counterparts. Moreover, Chinese doctors were usually consulted as physicians of choice by those whites afflicted by venereal diseases. Such individuals would be too embarrassed to face a white doctor, and generally knew that the Chinese doctors had better reputations for effecting cures. Since demand for the services of the Chinese doctors far outran the small number of such physicians present in the county, it was necessary for the herbalists to circuit-ride the county in order to reach as many patients as possible.[136]

Since 1900, there have been forty or fewer Chinese residents in White Pine County at any one time. Some of them have engaged in the restaurant business. Most, however, have moved elsewhere because of the limited economic opportunities which the county has to offer. This has been especially true since termination of the Kennecott copper mining operations at Ruth and McGill in 1978.[137]

The records of the past as summarized in this article serve to illustrate the bitter-sweet nature of the historical experience of the Chinese in the state. Most of today's Chinese residents of Nevada, however, do not have any direct ties to that experience for they, like the vast majority of other Nevadans, are recent immigrants from somewhere else. Nevertheless as Chinese and Nevadans they *should* know about the history of their ethnic predecessors in the Silver State. The Chinese still comprise a small minority of the population, and they occasionally encounter other people whose mistaken attitudes toward and images of the Chinese — based on past stereotypes — still persist. If any of the information presented in this article can shed some light on such mistaken attitudes and images, then its major purpose will have been achieved.

NOTES

1. Fanny G. Hazlett, "Historical Sketches and Reminiscences of Dayton, Nevada." *Nevada Historical Society Paper* 3 (1932–1922): 21–22.

2. Ibid., pp. 22, 24–26.

3. Traditional Chinese historians generally adhere to the cyclical interpretation of history. They believe that every dynasty goes through a cycle of strengthening, stability, and decline, and that a repetition of this cycle explains China's historical development.

4. Gregg Lee Carter, "Social Demography of the Chinese in Nevada: 1870–1880," *Nevada Historical Society Quarterly* 18 (Summer 1975): 77–78, 83.

5. Franklin R. Rogers, ed., *The Pattern for Mark Twain's Roughing It: Letters from*

Nevada by Samuel and Orion Clemens. University of California English Studies, no. 23 (Berkeley: University of California Press, 1961), p. 56.

6. Phyllis Zauner and Lou Zauner, *Carson City, Nevada* (South Lake Tahoe, Calif.: E-Z Publishing Co., 1977), p. 22.

The authors exaggerate a bit and assert that at its peak, Carson City had a Chinese population of almost two thousand. Ormsby County's population reached a peak of 988 in 1880. In that year, Carson City accounted for 802 of them, and the other 186 Chinese were spread out in other parts of the county. See Pei Chi Liu, *Meiguo huaqiao shi [A History of the Chinese in the United States of America, 1848–1911]* (Taipei: Overseas Chinese Affairs Commission, 1976), p. 85.

7. Pei Chi Liu, *Meiguo huaqiao shi* p. 84.

8. Myron Angel, ed., *History of Nevada* (Oakland, Calif.: Thompson and West, 1881; reprint ed., Berkeley, Calif.: Howell-North Books, 1958), pp. 197–198.

9. Carter, "Social Demography," *Nevada Historical Society Quarterly* 18 (Summer 1975): 82.

Carter concludes that in late nineteenth-century Nevada history there is a positive correlation between the size of a white population and its Chinese "satellite." He asserts that the relationship was directly proportional: the larger the number of whites, the larger the number of Chinese. Statistics from the 1880 census disprove his assertion. Carson City's population serves as the best example.

10. Wilbur S. Shepperson, *Restless Strangers: Nevada's Immigrants and Their Interpreters* (Reno: University of Nevada Press, 1970), pp. 117–119.

11. Ibid., p. 118.

12. Francis G. Newlands, "A Western View of the Race Question," *Annals of the American Academy of Political and Social Science* 34 (September 1909): 50–51.

13. Loren B. Chan, "Example for the Nation: Nevada's Execution of Gee Jon," *Nevada Historical Society Quarterly* 18 (Summer 1975): 90–106.

14. Thomas W. Chinn, "Notes on California Chinese, 1935–1941," *Chinese Historical Society of America Bulletin* 7 (December 1972): 7.

15. Ibid.

16. Chinn, "Observations: 1935–1941." *Chinese Historical Society of America* 7 (December 1972): 7–8.

17. Chinn, "Notes on California Chinese," *Chinese Historical Society of America Bulletin* 7 (December 1972): 7–8.

18. During the Ch'ing (Manchu) dynasty, no overt political opposition was tolerated. In south China, people loyal to the overthrown Ming dynasty, a Han Chinese ruling house, organized the Triad Society in 1674. As an underground, secret society, its slogan was "Overthrow the Ch'ing and restore the Ming." It was organized along the lines of a fraternity or brotherhood, complete with its own ritual and veneration of Kuan Kung, a Confucian deity (the "god of war") and patron of the society.

The Triads established their first lodge in the United States at San Francisco in 1853. The organization was incorporated in that California city in 1879 as the Chee Kung Tong. The word "tong" itself means "hall." Other tongs were formed in the United States as offshoots of the Chee Kung Tong. During the late nineteenth century, the tongs shared an interest in overthrowing the Manchus; but they also engaged in gambling, narcotics, prostitution, extortion, murder-for-hire, and other criminal activity. They feuded with each other to control specific areas ("turf"), and by and large might be considered roughly analogous to the Sicilian Mafia, albeit on a much more modest scale and within the limits of American Chinese society. On the positive side, the tongs provided their members with personal and business protection, medical care, payment of funeral costs and widow's pensions, and also offered them job opportunities.

But as the Chinese exclusion acts started to take effect, memberships in these organizations gradually declined. The last repercussions of a California-initiated "tong war" in Nevada occurred in 1921, where Gee Jon, a Hop Sing Tong gunman, was sent to murder Bing Kung Tong member Tom Quong Kee at Mina. Gee was later executed in the gas chamber at the Nevada State Prison for his crime.

Since the 1920s, the tongs have largely curtailed their involvement in illegal activities and violence. In the 1970s, they function primarily as social and fraternal organizations for older, Cantonese-speaking immigrants. In the twentieth century, the Chee Kung Tong was active in Carson City, the Hop Sing Tong in Reno (it became somewhat of a guild of Chinese gaming operators), and most recently, the Ying On Tong in Las Vegas. None of the tongs refer to themselves anymore as "tongs" per se, but instead label themselves as Chinese Free Masons or merchants' and laborers' associations.

For further reading consult John King Fairbank, Edwin O. Reisehauer, and Albert M. Craig, *East Asia: Tradition and Transformation* (Boston: Houghton Mifflin Co., 1978), pp. 467–486; Immanauel C. Y. Hsu, *The Rise of Modern China*, 2d ed. (New York: Oxford University Press, 1975), pp. 117–181; Him Mark Lau and Philip P. Choy, *Outlines: History of the Chinese in America* (San Francisco: Chinese-American Studies Planning Group, 1973), pp. 123–125; Stanford M. Lyman, *The Asian in the West*, Social Science and Humanities Publications, no,. 4 (Reno and Las Vegas: Desert Research Institute, University of Nevada System, 1970), pp. 33–46; Betty Lee Sung, *Mountain of Gold: The Story of the Chinese in America* (New York: Macmillan Co., 1967), pp. 137–138; Chün-tu Hsüch, *Huang Hsing and the Chinese Revolution* (Stanford, Calif.: Stanford University Press, 1961), pp. 77, 84, 86; and Chan, "Example for the Nation," *Nevada Historical Society Quarterly* 18 (Summer 1975): 90–106.

19. Chinn, "Notes on California Chinese," *Chinese Historical Society of American Bulletin* 7 (December 1972): 7–8.

20. Chinn, "Observation," *Chinese Historical Society of America Bulletin* 7 (November 1972): 7.

21. Stanely W. Paher, *Las Vegas: As It Began—As It Grew* (Las Vegas: Nevada Publications, 1971), pp. 70–71; Leon H. Rockwell, "Recollections of Life in Las Vegas, Nevada, 1906–1968," typed transcript, Oral History Project, University of Nevada Library, Reno, 1968, pp. 27, 74–75.

22. *Las Vegas Age*, 14 April, 3 June, 15 July, 21 October 1905; Rockwell, "Recollections," pp. 74–75.

23. *Las Vegas Age*, 1 February 13, 27 June 1908.

24. Ibid., 21 August 1909; Paher, *Las Vegas*, p. 129.

25. *Las Vegas Age*, 5 July 1913.

26. Ibid., 8 November 1913.

27. Ibid., 22 January, 15 April 1916.

28. Ibid., 19 June 1928.

29. Loren Briggs Chan, *Sagebrush Statesman: Tasker L. Oddie of Nevada*. Nevada Studies in History and Political Science, no. 12 (Reno: University of Nevada Press, 1973), p. 143.

30. Lai and Choy, *Outlines*, p. 57.

31. Thomas W. Chinn, H. Mark Lai, and Philip P. Choy, eds., *A History of the Chinese in California: A Syllabus* (San Francisco: Chinese Historical Society of America, 1969), p. 44.

32. Richard G. Lillard, *Desert Challenge: An Interpretation of Nevada* (New York: Alfred A. Knopf, 1942), p. 158.

33. Chinn, Lai, and Choy, eds., *A History of the Chinese in California*, pp. 44–45.

34. Edna B. Patterson, Louise A. Ulph, and Victor Goodwin, *Nevada's Northeast Frontier* (Sparks: Western Printing and Publishing Co., 1969), p. 592.

35. Pei Chi Liu, *Meiguo huaqiao shi*, p. 85.

36. Angel, ed., *History of Nevada*, pp. 349, 397.

37. *Elko Independent*, 10 November 1876.

38. Lester W. Mills, *A Sagebrush Saga* (Springville, Utah: Art City Publishing Co., 1956), p. 89.

39. *Elko Free Press*, 6 March 1886.

40. Ibid., 23 April 1876; Mills, *A Sagebrush Sage*, p. 90.

41. Wilbur S. Shepperson, "Immigrant Themes in Nevada Newspapers," *Nevada Historical Society Quarterly* 12 (Summer 1969): 20.

42. For example:

"The Chinaman is a problem. He is all over the Pacific Coast, in every State and Territory which comprises that region, and forms the most undesirable and disturbing element of the population. His good qualities are very few, and may be summed up in three words: Industry, frugality, and patience. His vices are legion, and comprise, in part, dishonesty, cruelty, filth, idolatry, and opium smoking. He has no home ties, and seeks none; he lives in a hovel in the villages and towns, and, crowded like sheep in a pen, in filthy buildings in Chinese quarters in the large cities. His women are all prostitutes, brought from China as slaves. To steal is his creed; to lie, his religion. I will not say that there are no Chinamen whatever better than this picture; but where there are such, they form notable exceptions to a general rule. . ."

The above passage may be found in Fred H. Hart, *The Sazerac Lying Club: A Nevada Book* (San Francisco: Henry Keller & Co., 1878), p. 210.

43. Patterson, Ulph, and Goodwin, *Nevada's Northeast Frontier*, pp. 581, 653, 638.

44. Ibid., p. 660; Pai and Choy, *Outlines*, p. 51.

45. *Elko Independent*, 23 October 1870; Lai and Choy, *Outlines*, p. 51.

46. John M. Townley. "The Tuscarora Mining District." *Northeastern Nevada Historical Society Quarterly* 2 (Summer and Fall 1971): 26.

47. Ibid., p. 27.

48. Patterson, Ulph, and Goodwin, *Nevada's Northeast Frontier*, p. 662; Townley, "Tuscarora," *Northeastern Nevada Historical Society Quarterly* 2 (Summer and Fall 1971); *Elko Independent*, 3 March 1878.

49. *Elko Free Press*, 25 April 1884; Patterson, Ulph, and Goodwin, *Nevada's Northeast Frontier*, pp. 658–659.

50. Townley,"Tuscarora," *Northeastern Nevada Historical Society Quarterly* 2 (Summer and Fall 1971): 11, 28; Patterson, Ulph, and Goodwin, *Nevada's Northeast Frontier*, p. 659.

51. B. F. Miller, "Nevada in the Making: Being Pioneer Stories of White Pine County and Elsewhere," *Nevada State Historical Society Papers* 4 (1923–1924): 360; Angel, ed., *History of Nevada*, p. 394; Patterson, Ulph, and Goodwin, *Nevada's Northeast Frontier*, pp.

606, 615; Nell Murbarger, *Sovereigns of the Sage* (Palm Desert, Calif.: Desert Magazine Press, 1958), 178–179.

52. Angel, ed., *History of Nevada*, p. 344.

53. Ibid., p. 419; Chinn, Lai, and Choy, eds., *A History of the Chinese in California*, p. 36.

54. Minnie P. Blair, "Days Remembered of Folsom and Placerville, California: Banking and Farming in Goldfield, Tonopah, and Fallon, Nevada," typed transcript, Oral History Project, University of Nevada Library, Reno, 1967, p. 45.

55. Guy Louis Rocha, "Radical Labor Struggles in the Tonopah-Goldfield Mining District 4 of 1922." *Nevada Historical Society Quarterly* 20 (Spring 1977) 26.

56. Russell R. Elliott, *History of Nevada* (Lincoln: University of Nebraska Press, 1973), p. 106.

57. Angel, ed., *History of Nevada*, pp. 428–429; Charles Labbe, *Rocky Trails of the Past* (Las Vegas: Charles Labbe, 1960), p. 93.

58. Labbe, *Rocky Trails*, pp. 93–94.

59. Angel, ed., *History of Nevada*, pp. 438, 443.

60. Gilbert H. Kneiss, *Bonanza Railroads* (Stanford, Calif.: Stanford University Press, 1941), pp. 84–85.

61. Ibid., pp. 87–89.

62. Angel, ed., *History of Nevada*, p. 441.

63. Ibid., p. 437.

64. Peter Merialdo, "Memories of a Son of Italian Immigrants, Recorder and Auditor of Eureka County, Nevada State Controller, and Republican Party Worker," typed transcript, Oral History Project, University of Nevada Library, Reno, 1967, p. 6.

65. *Humboldt Register* (Unionville), 27 April 1867.

66. Shepperson, *Restless Strangers*, p. 118; *Humboldt Register* (Unionville), 16 January 1968.

67. Allen C. Bragg, *Humboldt County.* 1905 (Winnemucca: North Central Nevada Historical Society, 1976), 20–21; *Silver State* (Winnemucca), 23 April 1905.

68. Bragg, *Humboldt County*, p. 32; *Silver State* (Winnemucca), 27 April 1905.

69. Bragg, *Humboldt County*, pp. 58, 66; *Silver State* (Winnemucca), 15 May, 5 June 1905.

70. Mary K. Rusco, "Counting the Lovelock Chinese," *Report of archaeological and historical investigations at Ninth and Amherst, Lovelock, Nevada*, ed. E. M. Hattori, M. K. Rusco, and D. R. Tuohy (Carson City: Nevada State Museum, 1979).

71. Philip D. Hart, "Chinese Community in Lovelock, Nevada: 1870–1940," *Report of archaeological and historical investigations at Ninth and Amherst, Lovelock, Nevada*, ed. E. M. Hattori, M. K. Rusco, and D. R. Tuohy (Carson City: Nevada State Museum, 1979).

72. Wilbur S. Shepperson, ed., "Sir Charles Wentworth Dilke: A Republican Baronet in Nevada," *Nevada Historical Society Quarterly* 3 (October–December 1960): 19–20.

73. Angel, ed., *History of Nevada*, p. 354.

74. "The Rise and Fall of the Jewish Community of Austin, Nevada," *Western States Jewish Historical Quarterly* 9 (October 1976): 88.

75. Clel Georgetta, "Sheep in Nevada," *Nevada Historical Society Quarterly* 8 (Summer 1965): 15–39; Dale L. Morgan, *The Humboldt: Highroad of the West* (New York: Farrar and Rinehart, Inc., 1943), p. 316.

76. Pei Chi Liu, *Meiguo huaqiao shi*, p. 85.

77. Angel, ed., *History of Nevada*, p. 471.

78. Murbarger, *Sovereigns of the Sage*, pp. 37–38.

79. *Pioche Daily Record*, 20 February 1874, 30 January 1896; *Lincoln County Record* (Pioche), 19 October 1900; Georgia Lewis, "The Dragon that Rides the Wind," *Nevadan Magazine, Las Vegas Review-Journal*, 5 March 1972.

80. *Pioche Daily Record*, 4 December 1872; 12 March 1874.

81. Ibid., 4 December 1872; 17 May 1873.

82. Ibid., 30 August 1873. The expression "Heathen Chinee" comes from a poem by the late nineteenth-century American writer Bret Harte (1936–1902) entitled, "Plain Language from Truthful James." First published in 1870, it was frequently quoted throughout the ensuing decade by both the advocates and opponents of Chinese immigration.

The poem's plot was quite simple: deceivers can be deveived. Truthful James and Bill Nye, both Caucasian, attempted to swindle a supposedly naive Chinese, Ah Sin, out of his money by cheating him in a card game. Ah Sin, although seeming to be unaware of the conspiracy, was completely prepared to beat the cheaters at their own game by even better cheating! After being beaten, Nye yelled the familiar battle cry, "We are ruined by Chinese cheap labor," which had utterly no relevance to the card game.

Harte's poem showed the universality of evil and served as a satire on Caucasian selfishness and racism, which indeed were the main elements behind the various anti-Chinese slogans which were so popular in late nineteenth-century America. Those who participated in harassing and persecuting the Chinese, however, felt that the poem supported their view of the Chinese as inherently treacherous and sinful. They quoted the lines from the poem which said: "That for ways that are dark. And for tricks that are vain. The Heathen Chinee is peculiar. ..."

The full text of the poem may be found in any of the many editions of Harte's collected works. For an insightful analysis of the place of the Chinese in late nineteenth- and early twentieth-century American literature, consult William Purviance Fenn, *Ah Sin and His Brethren in American Literature* (Peiping: California College in China, 1933).

83. *Pioche Weekly Record*, 6 October 1877.

84. Ibid., 1 December 1877.

85. Ibid., 29 January 1887.

86. Ibid., 1 December 1888; 17 September 1896; Lewis, "The Dragon that Rides the Wind," *Nevadan Magagine, Las Vegas Review-Journal*, 5 March 1872.

87. *Pioche Weekly Record*, 15 December 1888.

88. Ibid., 12 April 1894.

89. Ibid., 13 February 1896. The term "celestial" refers to the Celestial Empire, a name commonly used by American writers for China when it was under the rule of the Ch'ing (Manchu) dynasty.

"Chinaman" was the way most whites referred to the Chinese during the late nineteenth century and a good part of the twentieth century. Use of the term is now considered in poor taste, and offensive to Chinese ancestry. The proper term is "Chinese."

Mention of "the dragon on the yellow ground" refers to the design of the Chinese national flag during the time of the Ch'ing dynasty.

90. Clark J. Guild, "Memories of My Work as a Lyon County Official, Nevada District Judge, and Nevada State Museum Founder," typed manuscript, Oral History Project, University of Nevada Library, Reno, 1967, pp. 33, 37–38.

91. David F. Myrick, *Railroads of Nevada and Eastern California*, 2 vols. (Berkeley: Howell-North Books, 1962), 1:168.

92. Lee Adler, "Anaconda Closure Doesn't Dampen Yerington's Spirit," *Nevada State Journal* (Reno), 2 July 1978.

93. Stanley W. Paher, *Nevada Ghost Towns and Mining Camps* (Berkeley: Howell-North Books, 1970), pp. 437–439.

94. Chan, "Example for the Nation," *Nevada Historical Society Quarterly* 18 (Summer 1975): 91–92.

95. Labbe, *Rocky Trails*, p. 64.

96. Henry Hunt Atkinson, "Tonopah and Reno Memories of a Nevada Attorney," typed transcript, Oral History Project, University of Nevada Library, Reno, 1967, pp. 36–37; Marjorie Moore Brown, interview with author, San Francisco, Calif., 22 August 1970.

97. Shepperson, *Restless Strangers*, p. 120; *Tonopah Times-Bonanza*, 4 November 1977.

98. *Tonopah Times-Bonanza*, 4 November 1977.

99. Paher, *Nevada Ghost Towns*, p. 341.

100. Ruseo, "Counting the Lovelock Chinese," *Report of archaeological and historical investigations*; Hart, "Chinese Community in Lovelock," *Report of archaeological and historical investigations*.

101. Hart, "Chinese Community in Lovelock," *Report of archaeological and historical investigations*. See two recent articles by Mary Rusco: "Counting the Lovelock Chinese," *Nevada Historical Society Quarterly* 24 (Winter 1981): 319–328; and "Chinese in Lovelock, Nevada: History and Archaeology, *Halcyon* (1981): 141–151.

102. Ibid.

103. Ibid.

104. Pei Chi Liu, *Meiguo huaqiao shi*, p. 84. For a recent, comprehensive treatment see Russell M. Magnaghi, "Virginia City's Community, 1860–1880," *Nevada Historical Society Quarterly* 24 (Summer 1981): 130–157.

105. *Territorial Enterprise* (Virginia City), 5 June 1869; Cecil G. Tilton, *William Chapman Ralston: Courageous Builder* (Boston: Christopher Publishing House, 1935), p. 151.

106. Tilton, *Ralston*, p. 151; Gordon A. Sampson, "Memoirs of a Canadian Army Officer and Business Analyst," typed transcript, Oral History Project, University of Nevada Library, Reno, 1967, p. 142.

107. Sampson, "Memoirs," pp. 142, 149.

108. Shepperson, *Restless Strangers*, p. 117; Kneiss, *Bonanza Railroads*, pp. 57–58.

109. Kneiss, *Bonanza Railraods*, 61, 63, 65.

110. Angel, ed., *History of Nevada*, p. 345.

111. *Territorial Enterprise* (Virginia City) 19 June 1871, 25 June 1872; Francis P. Weisenburger, "God and Man in a Secular City," *Nevada Historical Society Quarterly* 14 (Summer 1971): 6.

112. Pei Chi Liu, *Meiguo huaqiao shi*, p. 85; Carter, "Social Demography," *Nevada Historical Society Quarterly* 18 (Summer 1975): 83; William Wright (Dan De Quille), *The Big Bonanza* (Hartford, Conn.: American Publishing Co., 1876; New York: Alfred A. Knopf, 1947), p. 291; Marion Goldman, "Sexual Commerce on the Comstock Lode," *Nevada Historical Society Quarterly* 21 (Summer 1978): 110, 113; Hubert Howe Bancroft, ed., *The Works of Hubert Howe Bancroft*, vol. 25: *History of Nevada, Colorado, and Wyoming, 1540–1888* (San Francisco: The History Company, Publishers, 1890), p. 292.

113. Angel, ed., *History of Nevada*, pp. 197–198.

114. Samuel Langhorne Clemens (Mark Twain), *Roughing It* (Hartford, Conn.: American Publishing Co., 1872; New York: New American Library, 1962), pp. 291–292.

115. Ibid., p. 292.

116. Ibid.

117. Ibid., p. 293.

118. Ibid., p. 297.

119. Wells Fargo and Company, *Directory of Chinese Business Houses* (San Francisco, 1878), pp. 84–86; idem, *Directory of Chinese Business Houses* (San Francisco, 1882), p. 132.

120. Bancroft, ed., *Nevada*, p. 292: Wells Fargo and Company, *Directory of Chinese Business Houses* (San Francisco, 1882), p. 132.

121. There are two excellent studies on this subject: Jeffrey Schrank, *Snap, Crackle, and Popular Taste: The Illusion of Free Choice in America* (New York: Dell Publishing Co., Inc., 1977); and Gillo Dorfles, *Kitsch: An Anthology of Bad Taste* (London: Studio Vista Ltd., 1969).

122. H. K. Wong, "Forging a Link," *Chinese Historical Society of America Bulletin*, 15 January 1966; Pei Chi Liu, *Meiguo huaqiao shi*, p. 85.

123. Pei Chi Liu, *Meiguo huaqiao shi*, p. 85.

124. Myrick, *Railroads of Nevada*, 1:342, 344, 352.

125. *Reno Evening Gazette*, 11 November 1908.

126. Stewart Culin, *The Gambling Games of the Chinese in America*, Publications of the University of Pennsylvania. Series in Philology, Literature and Archaeology, vol. 1, no. 4 (Philadelphia: University of Pennsylvania Press, 1891; reprint ed., Las Vegas: Gambler's Book Club, 1969), p. i.

127. Raymond I. Sawyer, *Reno, Where the Gamblers Go!* (Reno: Sawston Publishing Co., 1976), p. 12.

128. Culin, *Gambling Games*, p. i.

129. Chinn, "Notes on California Chinese," *Chinese Historical Society of American Bulletin* 7 (December 1972): 7.

130. According to the 1940 census, 106 Chinese lived in Reno, and another 13 resided elsehwere in Washoe County. Of the Reno Chinese, 48 (45.28%) were foreign-born, and 58 (54.72%) were American-born.

131. Lew Ling, ed., *The Chinese in North America: A Guide to Their Life and Progress* (Los Angeles: East-West Culture Publishing Association, c. 1946), appendix.

132. *White Pine News* (Treasure City), 11 August 1869; *White Pine News* (Hamilton), 18 June 1870; W. Turrentine Jackson, *Treasure Hill: Portrait of a Silver Mining Camp* (Tucson: Univerity of Arizona Press, 1963), p. 92.

133. Miller, "Nevada in the Making," *Nevada State Historical Society Papers* 4 (1923–1924): 311, 322–323.

134. Russell R. Elliott, ed., "Letters from a Nevada Doctor to His Daughter in Connecticut," *Nevada Historical Society Quarterly* 1 (September 1957): 24–25. Later the same year, President Arthur signed a ten-year exclusion bill.

135. Charles D. Gallagher, "Autobiography and Reminiscence," typed transcript, Oral History Project, University of Nevada Library, Reno, 1965, pp. 18, 50.

136. Ibid., p. 45.

137. *Nevada State Journal* (Reno), 30 June 1978.

6

Virginia City's Chinese Community, 1860–1880

Russell M. Magnaghi

Historical analysis of the role of Chinese on the Comstock Lode has been neglected. In part because of historical circumstances that attended their arrival and departure too little has been preserved or even written about the Chinese past. Contemporary accounts often reveal a considerable misunderstanding of Chinese culture and life-styles; only the newspapers of the Comstock communities remain to provide detailed views, but these sources must be used with extreme care because of their inherent bias. Yet during the heyday of the Big Bonanza, about a thousand Chinese lived in the vicinity of Virginia City, and any history of the region and the era which neglects their role is necessarily incomplete. It is the object of this study to help fill this gap in our knowledge of the role of minorities and the handicaps they faced in the development of Nevada.[1]

The first Chinese to arrive in western Nevada came from California to the mouth of Gold Canyon in the late 1850s. Eventually there were between forty and fifty Chinese employed digging a ditch to carry water from the Carson River to the placer mines in the canyon. Upon completion of the ditch in 1858 many Chinese remained and were allowed to work banks and bars abandoned by the white miners. With a little luck and plenty of hard work they could collect an ounce of gold per day, and under these conditions other Chinese followed until there were nearly two hundred Chinese in the vicinity. Their settlement was called China Town until it was later renamed Dayton.[2]

The discovery of silver on the Comstock Lode in 1859 began a great rush eastward from California; it attracted hundreds and then thousands of people, all seeking their fortunes. On March 27, 1860, the *Alta California* noted that "All are going—rich and poor, miners, merchants, doctors, lawyers, bummers, loafers, gamblers and Chinamen."[3] The typical Chinese who made the trip was usually a male in his late twenties; he retained his language, customs and dress, and planned to return to China once he made his fortune.

The Chinese were attracted to the Comstock Lode because of the prosperity and the opportunities there, and because there was a developing larger Asian community into which the Chinatown, a community within a community, could exist symbiotically attached to the economic, social and political base of the larger community.[4] It was in Chinatown that individual Chinese could "find fellowship, companions, social familiarity and solace. Chinatown acted as a partial buffer against prejudices, hatreds and depredations of hostile whites."[5]

Chinatown was located on the only naturally level area within the limits of Virginia City, east of C Street, the main thoroughfare. Union Street ran through its center and was bisected by side streets (G through K) and numerous alleys. The quarter was described as a crowded, "narrow-laned shacktown" composed of unpainted dilapidated shanties. This is confirmed by the few photographs which exist of it. Some Chinese rented dwellings from white landlords, but many relied upon their own integrity in constructing dwellings. Since the price of brick and wood was high, the Chinese used a variety of building materials. Pieces of stone from the immediate vicinity were gathered along with empty coal oil cans which were used as building materials. The cans were filled with earth and piled one upon another, creating a fireproof and bulletproof structure. Other Chinese simply dug holes into the hillsides, covered them with sticks, straw and occasionally with planks, and fitted a door facing east. Wealthy merchants were able to purchase lots and they constructed substantial brick buildings whose windows were protected with iron shutters. As an added precaution against fire damage, they constructed special storage cellars. The opening was covered with a piece of iron and then covered with two inches of earth, which successfully kept out the fire, water and smoke.[6]

Fire was always a serious and constant threat to frontier mining towns and Virginia City's Chinatown was no exception. The quarter possessed all of the ingredients for disastrous fires: crowded conditions, flimsy wooden shacks, open fires and unsafe chimneys, fireworks, and arson on the part of rival factions. During the twenty years under consideration, numerous fires destroyed substantial portions of Chinatown, and the great fire of October, 1875, completely leveled it. Since a fire in Chinatown could easily spread to the rest of the community, by 1877 a six inch water pipe had been laid under Union Street with a hydrant located at the intersection of I Street. The city fathers hoped that the excellent water pressure in the pipe would be enough to control Chinatown's fires.[7]

Besides living within their own community, the Chinese remained distinctive from the rest of the community through the wearing of traditional clothes. Both men and women wore wide-legged, blue cotton breeches, black smocks and slippers. The women tied their hair in red and blue gingham handkerchiefs while the men wore their hair in queues either hanging down the back or coiled up under their umbrella-like bamboo hats, "greasy and sooty in color." The trademark of the cooks was the blue frock and rimless cap. Wealthy merchants wore rich silks at festival time when they visited friends. Although it was not common, a few Chinese dressed in the "American-style."[8]

Many Chinese who moved to Virginia City sought to find employment; others started their own businesses. They were handicapped by white prejudice, and by traditions which viewed them as a threat to white organized labor. As a result of these attitudes and fears the Chinese often were forced into those economic corners of the community ignored by whites. The Chinese were employed either outside their community, or within to provide services for their countrymen.

Large numbers of Chinese were employed by whites who regarded them as cheap labor, and as especially dependable workers; the Chinese were often kept on in the face of opposition from anti-Chinese organizations. In 1880 there were over one hundred Chinese employed as cooks in boardinghouses, restaurants, hotels, mining companies and private homes. The Chinese cooks were taught how to prepare American cuisine, and did not present their employers nor their employers' customers with Chinese delicacies. Other Chinese found employment as servants in the homes of the wealthy. Saloons and other businesses hired Chinese to clean up, while the management of the six-story International Hotel employed Chinese to wash the exterior windows. Although it was not common, Chinese were hired by the municipal government on a number of occasions. In December, 1871, they were hired to sweep mud off the streets because, as the prejudiced Irish foreman pointed out, they could be hired cheaper than using mules.[9] In 1878 and 1879 Ah Kee, San Sing and Camp Sing were paid various fees ranging from $4.50 to $10.00 on a monthly basis by the county commissioners for undisclosed services.[10]

The remainder of the Chinese population was either self-employed or worked for other Chinese. The majority of people in this category were involved in the laundry trade, which became synonymous with the Chinese. Although Chinese laundries probably appeared as soon as Virginia City was settled, little is known of their origin. The first reference made to Chinese laundries appeared in the first *Directory of Nevada Territory* of 1862 which listed Lee Ching and Sam Kee as owners.[11] Laundries were not confined to Chinatown but were located throughout the city, providing ready and convenient service to customers. The laundries averaged six workers to a wash house and operated quite efficiently. A typical wash house consisted of several large barrel tubs through which water constantly passed. The soiled clothes were wadded and then hit with a board until the dirt was removed. The clothes were then dried on the roof of the laundry after which they were ironed and packaged.[12]

During the winter months a common figure on the streets of Virginia City was the Chinese wood peddler. The Chinese displaced the Paiute Indians as wood retailers because the latter could not compete with them. Prior to the completion of the Virginia and Truckee Railroad in 1870, the Chinese dominated the retailed wood market; when the roads were bad, or the snow too deep and the regular wood supply could not get through, everyone was happy to buy small quantities at their doorsteps from the Chinese.[13]

As was the case in other economic activities, the Chinese wood gatherers were at the mercy of white competitors. The white wood cutters first worked an area and removed the large trees; when they were finished, the Chinese were allowed to take the roots, stumps, and brush. At first the Chinese were able to find wood conveniently located on Cedar Hill and other locations close to town, but that rapidly changed. By the summer of 1864 their donkey trains were seen in lengthy lines coming from the Palmyra District and El Dorado Canyon. Fifteen years later they were forced to travel sixteen to eighteen miles north of the Geiger Grade and ten miles down Six Mile Canyon in order to find wood; in many cases they dealt with sagebrush.[14]

Even with the restrictions and dwindling supply, the wood business proved to be extremely profitable for many Chinese. During the summer of 1869 Kwong Toa gathered over seven hundred cords of wood; in 1877 a group of Chinese operating in Six Mile Canyon used fifteen donkeys in their operation. In warm weather wood sold for $1 per donkey load and the price could double when the weather got cold. One donkey load which cost $1.50 in 1868 gave the purchaser six fires in a common parlor stove. During the winter of 1866–1867 when there was six feet of snow on the ground and all transportation was halted, the Chinese sold firewood at $40 and even $60 per cord. With prices so high they even burrowed into the snow in search of roots. At this time there was a group of Chinese wood peddlers in Virginia City who were realizing a fabulous $300 per day with 50% profit. The Chinese themselves purchased sagebrush faggots since they utilized little fuel except for cooking and sold the larger pieces for higher prices to whites.[15]

The decline in the Chinese wood business came with the completion of the Virginia and Truckee Railroad, which brought in a steady and reliable supply of cheaper firewood and longer-burning Rocky Mountain coal. As a result the number of Chinese engaged in the trade dropped from a record high in 1868 of about 150, to only 66 listed in the 1870 census. Ten years later there were only eight sawyers and four peddlers in business. Some Chinese began peddling coal and charcoal or sold their services as sawyers. In the hard economic times of the late 1870s whites further cut into their activities, but during their heyday the Chinese wood peddlers provided residents of Virginia City with an extremely important service.[16]

Another good example of a successful economic activity engaged in by the Chinese on the Comstock Lode is to be found in their development of agriculture. Due to crowded conditions in China, farmers there had a long tradition of intensive farming with an emphasis on high yields per acre. The Chinese approach to agriculture appeared in Virginia City where they constituted one of the few groups to successfully attempt to garden on the barren slopes of Mount Davidson. As early as the summer of 1863 the efforts of a single Chinese gardener on a small piece of land to the east of town proved to be productive. Soon other Chinese followed his example and a new business activity developed: the gardener and the vegetable peddler.

Many gardens were developed along the outskirts of Virginia City, although the largest were located at the foot of Union Street close to Chinatown. These gardens were fenced in with a variety of materials ranging from scrap wood to flattened coal oil cans. Water—a most necessary and precious commodity in the desert—was expensive, and the Chinese solved the problem by diverting some of the run-off which went down Union Street and by tapping sewer water. In 1877 they contemplated using the hot water pumped from the Norcross & Savage Mine for additional gardens to the south.[17]

Planting began after the last frost, perhaps as early as Mid-March, and continued into late October. The Chinese cultivated a variety of vegetables to be sold in local markets, and Chinese vegetables used in their own cuisine. Their gardens received high praise from the community. A *Territorial Enterprise* reporter wrote in the summer of 1877 that "every patch of ground cultivated by them is a model of neatness, and they pay such strict attention to the rotation of crops that something is constructively growing in every bed and plot." Their vegetables were considered fresher and of better quality than those from California, and the term "Chinese garden" came to denote freshness and quality throughout the community.[18] After the harvest, with the aid of a polebasket or a donkey, they sold the produce to hotels, restaurants, saloons, and private homes.

Mining, the life blood of the Comstock Lode, was an activity which the Chinese entered with great difficulty. From the time of the first settlements Chinese were legally prohibited from mining. However, by 1878 a number of them had moved into abandoned mine sites in Gold Canyon and by 1880 Seven Mile Canyon was the location of a Chinese mining operation which included six laborers and a cook. The Chinese miners were only allowed to work dumps and tailing sites not wanted by whites. They constructed special sluices to combat the blue sand, pebbles and stones. Although they were plagued by summer drought and winter floods some of the miners realized between $1.50 and $2.00 per day for their efforts. However, mining never did prove to be an important economic endeavor among the Chinese.[19]

Chinese were also occupied in a variety of jobs and tasks throughout Virginia City. Some would visit homes and seek jobs repairing chairs, or chopping and sawing wood. Cigars produces in Chinatown were sold throughout the Comstock, although this endeavor was the object of an attack by the Anti-Chinese League. Chinese ragpickers scoured the town for rags, baled them and created immense piles at the Virginia & Truckee Railroad depot where they were shipped to be processed into paper and shoddy. Besides peddling firewood and home-grown vegetables, Chinese sold watercress gathered from the surrounding hillsides and even fresh fish. A one-eyed Chinese fellow made the rounds between 9:00 a.m. and midnight selling hot tamales for a Mexican woman and became a town character.[20]

In areas distant from Virginia City, Chinese found employment in activities otherwise barred them on the Comstock. After the completion of the Central Pacific Railroad in May 1869, there were thousands of unemployed Chinese, some of whom found employment in the construction of the Virginia & Truckee Railroad. Although Chinese were not employed by the V & T Railroad in Storey County, they were used elsewhere along the right-of-way; when the railroad was extended from Carson City to Reno, between 400 and 500 Chinese were employed. Chinese were hired as wood cutters in the mountains above Carson City and Genoa, although their presence angered many whites. Along the Carson River, Chinese were employed at the Union Mill.[21]

Many Chinese living within Chinatown found employment by providing services to their fellow countrymen. There were Chinese physicians and pharmacists who maintained health services for Chinese and also white clients. In 1870 there were two pharmacists, Quing Quong and Chung Ching, who operated stores in Chinatown; in addition, there were four physicians: Hop Lock, Wing Song, Al Leong, and Loonsing Tong. Eight years later there were six Chinese physicians and of this number three were located outside of Chinatown in order to cater to white clients. Hop Lock is the best known Chinese physician and was respected in both the Chinese and white communities. He arrived on the Comstock in the early 1860s and treated ailments with herbs and roots. An 1864 newspaper advertisement boasted that he "professes to cure all diseases on this coast" and in subsequent ads, pleased white patients testified to his successful treatment of their ailments without the use of poisonous medicines. Lock's office in 1867 was located on South C Street, and this assured white patients. His reputation attracted two rivals who rented space on either side of him in order to confuse prospective clients. Three years later he moved closer to Chinatown and located at the northeast corner of D and Union Streets. Dr. Lock had a number of legal problems to face. He did not pay a special federal tax and was convicted and fined $75. Early in 1871, together with Chung Chow he was arrested on a murder charge. A two month long trial found Lock not guilty and he then passed from the Comstock scene.[22]

Chinese merchants operated stores which provided the population essential native foods and general goods. In 1878–79 there were six Chinese merchants in Virginia City. At this time Kong Tai Chong & Company (located at 7 North H Street) advertised in the *Virginia Chronicle* that they were "dealers in groceries, fresh fruits, etc., at San Francisco prices, freight added." Sam Sing and Hop Sing, two leading merchants of Chinatown, filled their stores with Chinese delicacies and attracted white patrons who sought their pork products. At New Year's these shops were filled with a special assortment of fancy goods.[23]

In addition to these grocery markets, there were sausage shops, restaurants, barbershops, cobblers, jewelers, and tailors. Many Chinese used their skills to produce toys, festival candles and kits. Most of the kites flown by white children were purchased form the Chinese who were recognized as "experts in their manufacture." The kites ranged from ordinary ones to elaborate affairs shaped like birds, eagles or butterflies with lanterns attached; some were capable of discharging fireworks.[24]

Some Chinese, including wealthy merchants like Hop Sing, joined the whites affected by the stock mania and speculated in the hope of instant wealth. They waited on the fringes of white crowds anxiously seeking the latest news of their investments; in many cases the results were adverse.[25]

Prostitution, gambling, and the sale and use of opium were carried on by the Chinese and often flourished because of white patronage. The traditional family structure was deficient in Chinese communities in the United States because Chinese males planned on residing in the United States on a temporary basis and then returning to their families in China. Also, there were traditional prohibitions against Chinese leaving their homes. As a result, the Chinese prostitute was important for services she provided the community and as a prospective wife. Various companies imported Chinese women for $200 and resold them on the Comstock for between $800 and $1000. The Chinese prostitutes were considered to be close to the bottom of the social structure. They were kept in tiny rooms and furnished with old clothes on which to sleep. There is no record of the fees charged to customers, but Asian brothels in San Francisco at the same time charged as little as $1.00. In 1870 there were seventy Chinese prostitutes in Virginia City, comprising most of the females in the Chinese community. Many of them were married and yet continued to ply their trade. For some, such an existence was intolerable and overdoses of opium provided means of escape.[26]

Gambling flourished throughout the West and the Comstock was no exception. The Chinese gambler was an important figure in Chinese society in America. In 1870 there were forty-two Chinese who listed themselves in the census as "gamblers," and ten years later this figure had declined to thirty-two. They tended to amass large sums of money and gems in a relatively short period of time. A wealthy gambler in 1871 possessed the following personal estate: over a dozen cans of opium worth $200, $1250 in gold and silver coins, jewelry valued at $300, and silks and fine clothing valued at $200. One lucky gambler won $1600 in ten days and continued with his good fortune.[27]

Gambling halls were scattered throughout Chinatown and did a brisk business catering to Chinese and whites interested in trying their luck at lotteries, diana, fan-tan and a variety of poker games. Although the Chinese dominated gambling in Chinatown, some whites unsuccessfully tried to compete.

By the latter half of the 1870s the gambling parlors began to experience a serious decline. In response to a municipal ordinance which taxed them, most of the operators closed down by March, 1875. Eventually some of them reopened after paying the tax, but at about the same time the Chinese population began to decline as the Chinese left Virginia City seeking their fortunes elsewhere. It became difficult to operate at a profit, and by 1879 there were only two fan-tan games in operation.[28]

The smoking of opium, a habit-forming narcotic, had developed among the Chinese in the seventeenth century. Foreign traders introduced vast quantities in the 1830s and 1840s. By 1838 nine out of ten Chinese in Kwangtung Province were addicts.[29] The importation of opium in the United States was legal in the nineteenth century, and in 1870 2,413,073 pounds of opium worth $13,824,535 were legally imported into the United States.[30]

The Chinese who arrived on the Comstock carried on this tradition of opium smoking. Opium dens were a feature of Chinatown and the smell of opium wafted through the quarter. The Chinese were firmly entrenched as operators of the dens and their clients were both Chinese and whites. The exteriors of the dens were similar to surrounding structures, but the interiors consisted of a labyrinth of tiny rooms and numerous doors to be used as exits in case of a police raid. The dens were scattered throughout Chinatown and beyond, although a large number of them were concentrated on G Street.[31]

Opium smoking became extremely popular among whites by the mid-1870s. Both males and females as young as twelve years of age, young adults and older people made the trip to the dens. As a result of this white demand for opium, the Chinese opened new dens and expanded smaller, older, inadequate ones. In some cases they added special rooms for women. By 1875 some fifty young men were identified as addicts and after the great fire of that year, opium dens were some of the first structures to be constructed in Chinatown. Sing Woh, an operator of a den at the corner of Union and H Streets, observed that between 1871 and 1876 his annual purchases of opium had jumped from 5 1/2 pounds to over thirty-five pounds.[32]

A trip to an opium den usually began at dusk, although some whites arrived at various hours of the day and night. Once in the den, having paid the police man to look the other way, the scenario would develop as described in the *Virginia Chronicle* in 1875:

> I paid the Chinaman who fixed the pipe twenty-five cents, and he gave me a bunk. It was not elegantly fitted up. I lay on a piece of matting and had a small soap box for a pillow. The pipe, which was an eight-sided stone knob, with a small hole in the center just large enough to admit the end of a dangling needle, was placed in my hands. He gave me a small lamp, about a thimbleful of opium and a darning needle. I knew nothing about how to manage the pipe, but the old fellow was attentive, and I was soon as able as he. First he dipped the end of the darning needle into the little pot of opium, then held the end upon which the opium adhered above the flame of the lamp. The opium sputtered and finally swelled up into a little round ball. This was then forced into the little hole in the pipe and the flame again applied to the opium. I was told to inhale, and did so. That was the whole operation, and I repeated it until I felt that I could stand no more.[33]

As long as opium was smoked exclusively by the Chinese, whites were not concerned. The *Virginia Chronicle* in 1879 saw opium smoking among "loafers, roughs and desperadoes" as a social benefit since it calmed them down and saved the state money. However, when large numbers of whites took to smoking opium that was another matter. During the mid-1870s most of the city newspapers ran lengthy exposés of the horrible practice of opium smoking. The *Virginia Chronicle* summed up one of its articles on the subject: "There is no city on the coast where the Oriental custom of smoking opium is more thoroughly established than here [Virginia City], or in which it is calculated to produce more destructive effects."[34]

In response to these exposés the city, and eventually the state of Nevada, passed anti-opium laws. The Board of Aldermen passed an ordinance in September,

1876, which abolished opium dens and levied a $50 to $500 fine and/or a ten day to six month jail sentence on convicted operators. The state legislature passed a bill on February 9, 1877, which made it illegal to smoke opium or possess an opium pipe or a part of it. The guilty party could receive a $500 fine and/or six months in the state prison. Two years later the "opium law" was amended to increase the fine to $1000 and the prison sentence to two years. It also made it mandatory that only pharmacists could dispense opium with medical prescriptions and landlords became liable for opium smoking among their tenants.[35]

Despite all of these ordinances and laws, opium smoking continued. The operators were arrested and charged with violations of the law, but not the smokers. In many cases the smokers were asked to act as witnesses against the operators. A major obstacle to enforcement was the fact that both regular and special policemen assigned to Chinatown accepted bribes and looked away when smokers arrived. White informers, in Chinese pay, gave advance warning of an impending raid and operators usually destroyed incriminating evidence before police could arrive, making a conviction extremely difficult to obtain. Despite all of these obstacles, the police did make successful raids and were given strong encouragement by the Special Board of Police Commissioners in 1879, which called for more frequent and irregular raids[36]

Both the smokers and operators reacted to these laws and their enforcement in a variety of ways to circumvent the law. At first large numbers of smokers traveled to Gold Hill and Sutro because enforcement of the law was temporarily lax. Some Chinese smoked tobacco heavily saturated with opium or 14%-16% morphine in regular pipes to avoid detection. As the regular dens were raided and closed, operators moved into the numerous abandoned tunnels in the vicinity and into cellars and backrooms of restaurants and stores.[37]

In retrospect Virginia City's anti-opium campaign proved to be a failure. Even after police reform and many successful raids, both Chinese and whites continued to smoke. In 1881 the *Territorial Enterprise* had a report that there were a dozen or more dens patronized "quite openly and in broad daylight" by a variety of people.[38]

It is unfortunately true that nineteenth-century analysis of, and commentary upon, Chinese culture and amusements often began and ended with the opium den; furthermore, the white use of various drugs, including opium, was too often passed over fairly lightly. A closer look at the sources reveals a variety of amusements, a dedication to the rich, traditional forms of Chinese religion and culture, and a complex set of social and protective organizations.

The Chinese relied on amusements that were both American and Chinese in origin. Youngsters played marbles and ball games, and spun tops. One white reporter wrote that they were more proficient at these games than the white boys. Both males and females attended performances at Piper's Opera House and the circuses that frequently visited Virginia City.[39]

Among the traditional forms of amusement, kite flying predominated. On windy days the sky above Virginia City might be filled with beautiful and elaborate kites shaped as eagles, serpents, birds, and some with special chimes that could be heard a mile or more away, while others were mounted with lanterns and fireworks for evening flying. They played a form of shuttlecock during the progress of which the participants had to remain in a twenty foot circle while the shuttlecock was kicked and hit and at times kept in the air for a solid ten minutes. These games usually attracted large numbers of Chinese and white spectators. Orchestras composed of gongs, drums, cymbals and horns played for festivals, in music halls or to advertise gambling parlors.[40]

Numerous traditional festivals held throughout the year provided some respite from the drudgery of daily life. The chief holiday for the community was the two week celebration in late January and early February (depending on the lunar calendar) leading into Chinese New Year. The pop and sputter of firecrackers was mixed with the sounds from numerous orchestras. Dressed in their finest attire, men and women visited friends, exchanged gifts, and partook of elaborate feasts. In the early autumn there was another important festival which was celebrated in a similar fashion, and throughout the year there were other minor festivals.[41]

At the other end of the spectrum of life in Chinatown were the elaborate funeral ceremonies and colorful processions to the cemetery. The Chinese had two cemeteries in Virginia City: one was located on a hillside to the east of town beyond the county hospital, and the other beyond the Sierra Nevada Mine dump to the north of town. The burial grounds are totally barren, and the headstones were made of unpainted boards with the name of the deceased written in pencil. These cemeteries were of a temporary nature since the bones were eventually disinterred, packed and shipped to China for reburial.[42]

Prominent and influential members of the Chinese community were accorded elaborate funerals, which included lengthy processions involving numerous individuals. If the individual were known to the white community the procession would travel along C Street through the heart of the white areas of the city. On November 30, 1878, a typical large funeral took place. An American brass band led the procession, followed by men wearing special badges, then a large vehicle followed by the hearse, a number of female musicians, a regular Chinese band, and a wagon loaded with food for the graveside ceremonies.

Although completely surrounded by an alien culture, the Chinese did not abandon their religion. A number of temples or joss houses were constructed by the companies. One of the earliest temples was completed and dedicated in June, 1864. It was a pagoda-style structure with an intricate entrance gate which led into a courtyard; the main building, with a wooden statue, was located on the east side of the courtyard.[43]

In 1872 the Yeong Wo Company planned to construct a new temple. The members purchased the necessary land from George Downey, but the house in which a celebratory dinner was being held was stoned by the rival Sze Yup Company. Still, by September 2 the new temple, which was located on the corner of H and Union Streets, was ready to be formally dedicated. Its front was decorated with Chinese asters, and for eight days musicians played, firecrackers and fireworks exploded and members prayed. The rivalry between the companies did not end; temples had to be rebuilt on a number of occasions after fires set by rival arsonists destroyed them.[44]

The temples were presided over by two priests dressed in long blue robes. They were kept in neat condition, and the aroma of sandalwood incense filled the area where worshipers could go daily and pray. During the New Year festivities the temples were illuminated with thousands of colored candles and paper lanterns.[45]

Although Chinese culture and religion predominated, there were a number of attempts to develop schools and Christian churches so that assimilation would be accelerated. One of the more successful of these was sponsored by the Episcopal Bishop, Ozi William Whitaker. In June, 1875, an extremely enthusiastic Chinese convert, Ah For, arrived in Virginia City and persuaded Bishop Whitaker to back his plan for the construction of a chapel in Chinatown. Within two months Ah For had collected pledges totaling over $200 from the Chinese community, while white residents and eastern friends of the Bishop provided an additional $300. A neat, comfortable chapel was built on the northwest corner of Taylor and I Streets, just below St. Paul's church. The dedication ceremonies were held the evening of August 14 with 150 Chinese and whites attending. Bishop Whitaker gave a sermon which was translated into Chinese by Ah For, who also preached a sermon of his own.[46]

The chapel was used for religious and educational purposes for the next two months. Two Sunday services were conducted in Chinese and English and were regularly attended although the St. Paul Parish Register shows no evidence of Chinese being baptized. However, on September 28, Wow Heo and Ah Wo were married there by Reverend R. S. Eastman. On September 2, evening classes were commenced where the English language was taught to a number of Chinese.[47] This experiment in assimilation ended on October 26, 1875, when a terrible fire destroyed the chapel along with the entire northern section of Virginia City. There was some talk of rebuilding the chapel and continuing the work, but this was never done. Ah For left the Comstock and eventually went to China where he worked as a missionary.

Crime prevention and the implementation of justice in Chinatown were unique. The Chinese were barred from white courts because they could not testify. In general, the white community was not concerned with justice within the Chinese community as long as white citizens were not threatened. As a result, law enforcement resided with both the Chinese social and political organizations known as companies, and the courts, depending on who acted first. Crimes committed by the Chinese varied greatly all the way from tong wars and murders to burglaries, and various minor offenses.[48]

The Chinese quarter was patrolled by regular city police and at times by special police appropriately called "specials" who were hired by the city. For many years the Chinese has a great friend in George Downey, who was an impartial officer of the law. He first became acquainted with the Chinese in the 1860s when he acquired property in Chinatown; he maintained a close relationship with them until his death. As an officer on the beat and chief of police he attempted to understand the Chinese and their culture and was greatly respected by the people because of his impartiality. In return, the Chinese presented him with gifts as in January 1964, when several wealthy merchants gave him a magnificent diamond ring. Earlier he had been given a solid gold badge. The Chinese also feted him at banquets during their festivals. It was sometimes stated that Downey knew every Chinese in the quarter, which was close to the truth. His death, caused by an overdose of laudanum on August 14, 1872, caused a serious gap between the police and the Chinese.[49]

After Downey's death, relations between the Chinese and the police deteriorated. Some of the "specials" were retained by various companies and tended to provoke trouble rather than stop it. The Board of Aldermen sought to end this problem by eliminating the "specials" and replacing them with regular police.

Even the regular police were not beyond taking bribes. Police sent to control opium smoking would "look the other way" for a dollar or two. In 1876 the *Virginia Evening Chronicle* carried a story about Chief of Police Charles White who allegedly was collecting money on a weekly basis from the Chinese at the following rates: 25¢ per household, $1.00 per store, and $2.00 per gambling parlor. The chief denied these charges, but the paper recommended that "specials" be rehired to deal with Chinese problems.[50]

During the 1870s, true family life was non-existent although the population was relatively young. Few Chinese women came to the United States during the period of unrestricted immigration (1850–1882) because custom forbade them to leave their homes, and very few males expected to remain permanently in the United States. This situation was clearly reflected in Storey County where in 1875 there were 1,254 Chinese males and only 87 females.[51]

The women who did come to the United States were introduced in most instances by the companies and forced into prostitution. When a Chinese sought a wife he was forced to purchase her for a price which varied between $400 and $800. Once the woman had been purchased, her husband faced the problem of protecting her from kidnappers. Some Chinese tried to make their marriages more secure by taking their vows before a judge or clergyman.[52]

There were few powerful and wealthy Chinese in Virginia City. The thirteen laundrymen who listed their personal worth in the 1870 census averaged $411, while the four physicians averaged $1,000 and the two pharmacists had personal estates of $2,000 and $3,000. Merchants had the greatest wealth, power and influence within the community, and they were usually connected with the companies. In 1870 the four merchants listed in the census averaged $2,500 in their personal estates.[53]

When discussing Chinese activity in the Far West the term "company" is used. The company was a social organization which promoted solidarity and mutual aid in order to cope with the hostile social environment. The first companies were established in California and spread to Virginia City; they included the Sam Yup or Three Districts Company (1851); Sze Yup or Four Districts Company (1851); Yeong Wo or Masculine Harmony Company (1852); Ning Yung Company or Association of Masculine Tranquility (1854); and Hop Wo Company or the Company of the United Harmony (1862). There is no evidence that the Yun Wo (Human Harmony) Association founded in 1852 or the Kong Chow (Ridge Region) Association founded in 1867 were active in the Comstock.[54] These companies offered a variety of services to their members and insulated them from white society. For example, in 1866 when sixteen Chinese migrating to the Idaho mines were dumped off in the Nevada desert, they wired Ah Kee, agent for the Sze Yup Company, for assistance in returning to Virginia City. Companies owned and operated stores, brothels, gambling halls, and opium dens, all of which brought them considerable profit. They controlled the labor force, the payments of debts, and one even sold licenses at $30 per month for laundries.[55] Among their members, the companies maintained their own law and system of justice. When Ng Tong Low and Ah Moo, officials of the Ning Yeong Company, were involved in a stabbing during a dominoes game, the company attempted to keep the police from being involved. At other times when white justice interfered, the companies hired lawyers and backed their respective members by filling the court room.[56]

Rivalry among the companies predated their arrival and establishment on the Comstock. Officer Downey stopped trouble before it started on June 30, 1864, when he arrested fifteen Chinese, after bitter feelings led to written challenges appearing on the streets. By 1871, due to sporadic fighting, shootings, and killings, Chinatown had gained a reputation as a center of crime and violence among whites.[57]

Two of the most prominent leaders in Chinatown were Sam Sing and Hop Sing. Sam Sing got his start as a sagacious businessman and labor contractor for the railroads. He eventually moved to Virginia City and opened his store-headquarters (valued at $1,200) on the southeast corner of H and Union Streets.[58] Whites considered him a reliable businessman with excellent credit, and he was so influential among the Chinese that he virtually controlled Chinatown. At times he courted influential members of the white power structure. On February 1, 1875, for example, he invited Charles De Long, former minister to Japan, Colonel R. H. Taylor, Major R. M. Daggett and a number of police officials to a forty course dinner served on solid gold ware by waiters dressed in white linen.[59] His chief rival was Hop Sing, a merchant whose power was nearly equal. In 1879 Hop Sing contracted 260 Chinese laborers to complete work on an irrigation project in Truckee Meadows. Hop Sing had his headquarters in three structures valued at $2,161 located on the northwest corner of K and Union Streets. When he died in 1887, at 62 he was accorded an elaborate funeral as a distinguished member of the Chinese community.[60]

A brief study of the war which developed between these two men and their respective companies during 1875–1876 gives an excellent picture of the nature of these struggles and the various forces in action. The cause of the trouble, which developed early in 1875, is unclear although economic rivalry was probably an important factor. Throughout most of 1875 Chinese went about armed with six-shooters, and periods of violence were followed by periods of calm. Then in December, large-scale fighting broke out and fighters form Carson City were imported. In an attempt to ward off further violence Mayor John C. Currie met with the Chinese leaders and warned them that unless peace was restored there was the possibility of action by white vigilante groups.

The mayor's warning was ignored by the Chinese, and they prepared for increased hostilities. Sam Sing had 6 × 10 inch loopholes cut into his building and stationed his fighters at the rear of the building. These fighters included local Chinese, a few whites, and Chinese imported from Carson City, Reno, and Sacramento. Hop Sing's store was fortified with an old box-stove filled with earth and flanked by numerous coal oil cans filled with dirt. Sheet iron shutters protected the windows and guns and knives were ready for action. One of the groups even constructed a reflector at Union and G Streets which kept the street illuminated at night to counter the possibility of a sneak attack.

After two weeks of preparation, fighting broke out in earnest and continued until February, Sam Sing went through the streets with body guards and there were rewards posted for the leaders of both groups. Other Chinese merchants were equally cautious and only ventured out of doors heavily armed.[62]

These hostilities had a negative effect on Chinese businessmen. They lost business because individuals feared to enter Chinatown under the circumstances. Whites who lived in the vicinity of Chinatown feared that they would become the victims of stray bullets. A *Territorial Enterprise* editorial warned that the death of an innocent white would bring the entire white population down against the Chinese. To impress upon the Chinese the level of the white community's concern, the grand jury met with both Sam Sing and Hop Sing and warned them of possible interracial violence. The fighting formally ended with the signing of a peace treaty under the mediation of Charles De Long. If one of the two parties to the treaty violated the agreement it would lose the support of the Chinese community. It looked as if the peace would be permanent.[63]

Soon after this development a number of white people living in the vicinity of Chinatown formed the Home Protection Society in an attempt to maintain law and order among the Chinese. At the first meeting held on February 29, 1876, over four hundred people applied for membership. The Society met regularly Saturday evenings. Its members divided themselves into twelve lodges and were always ready for action at the sound of exploding giant powder cartridges.[64]

A hatchet attack on a Chinese resident soon after brought the Protectors out and they began their own investigation. The Hop Wo Company was considered the guilty organization; it was given a date by which the guilty party would have to be produced. When the March 28th deadline passed and a culprit was not presented, members marched on Chinatown and searched all of the houses without warrants while the police watched passively. This action caused some Chinese to flee Gold Hill and it greatly concerned many innocent Chinese. The Society also issued a warning to special policeman Bamfield to leave Chinatown. He was residing at Sam Sing's establishment, and was considered a source of trouble.[65]

Trouble continued sporadically through 1877; both sides used the courts and newspapers to protect themselves and influence the public against their rivals. In February of 1877 the Board of Police Commissioners met to discuss the trouble and how it might be terminated. The Board came to the conclusion that the special police, who were paid by the Chinese, were extremely lax in enforcing the law. It was recommended that the specials be removed and replaced with regular police. All of this white-sponsored activity helped the violence to subside, although the fear of renewed hostility lingered.[66] There was a great deal of white racial prejudice directed against the Chinese of Virginia City. On September 20, 1877, *The Footlight* best summed up this attitude:

> They refuse to adopt our language, dress, customs, and the manner of living. By means of their strange language they attain a secrecy, unenjoyable by even the most secret societies in our midst. They have their own courts, tribunals, and though in every respect they are a race entirely alien to us, yet they enjoy the protection of our laws, as well as the meanest white man.

The newspaper further stated that it held "the whole Chinese Companies responsible for aggression against white life and property."

White prejudice was based on ignorance, fear and misunderstanding. Whites generally ignored Chinatown and the Chinese and never attempted to understand their culture. Chinatown itself was an island surrounded by Virginia City, and appeared to be filled with strange people, exotic foods, and sights that had nothing to do with the average citizen. The white conception of Chinatown was that it was filthy and a breeding ground for disease. Mary M. Mathews, who only visited a number of washhouses, a store and a temple, recorded her impression:

> Chinatown, of Virginia City, like Chinatown of every other city of the coast—a loathsome, filthy den—it is enough to breed cholera or any other pestilential disease.[67]

She further recommended that visitors to Chinatown saturate themselves from head to toe with bay rum and camphor to ward off disease. The newspapers constantly referred to Chinatown as that "odiferous suburb" or that "savory suburb."

The quarter did attract whites seeking the special services Chinatown had to offer, or the exotic sights and sounds, especially at festival time. Whites seeking opium, gambling, or prostitutes kept many of these businesses in operation and allowed them to expand. The sounds and sights of Chinese New Year attracted large numbers of whites of all ages. They visited the gaily-decorated stores and temples and witnessed the "strange carryings-on of the Celestials." The Chinese gave the women and children candies and nuts while the men drank gin or whiskey.[68] The staff of the *Territorial Enterprise* (usually led by Dan De Quille) would make the rounds of China town for liquid refreshments after a hard day. Alfred Doten, editor of the *Gold Hill News,* had close friends in Chinatown and visited often. On the evening of June 28, 1865, he led a distinguished group of men including Schuyler Colfax (soon to be Grant's vice-president), Lieutenant-Governor Bross of Illinois, a Mr. Bowles (editor of the *Springfield Republican*), the *Enterprise* staff, and police officials through Chinatown.[69]

Most whites found traditional Chinese food "loathsome to look at and taste." *The Virginia Daily Union* printed a racist description of Chinese cuisine: "The long tailed brutes are delighting themselves with worm soup, stewed kitten, roasted puppies, young entrails fried with batter and bird's nest dressing, opium, whiskey, and other favorite viands and drinks." Some, like Doten, tried the food but found it to be "queer looking messes," while others detested what they regarded as gruesome smells of doubtful meats. For many the food looked good, but they would not eat it unless they were starving. Whites usually avoided the food offered by a Chinese host but enjoyed his brandy and cigars.[70]

The Chinese found little justice in the legal system since they could not testify in court, and many whites took advantage of that situation. When an old Chinese sawyer demanded his promised wages he was viciously attacked with a ten pound rock and severely injured. I. Arnold of Gold Hill passed around bogus $20 pieces to the Chinese knowing that he would never get convicted. Chinese were beaten and shot at when they sought to collect their bills or wages or were totally ignored by unconcerned whites. Spurred by parental attitudes and encouraged onlookers, young boys often attacked the Chinese. Washhouses were set ablaze or had their windows broken. Chinese laborers innocently pursuing their tasks were tripped, stoned, pelted with snowballs, rocks and broken bottles, much to the amusement of white bystanders. The violence often knew no bounds: an armed youth coasting down icy Union Street shot a Chinese worker when he did not promptly get out of the youth's way.[71]

Whites showed a lack of compassion toward the Chinese following the great fire of October 26, 1875, which destroyed the north end of Virginia City including Chinatown. Large quantities of food and clothing were sent to Virginia City by the citizens of California and Nevada, and San Francisco's Chinese community generously contributed cash and provisions to be distributed without any restrictions. But at first, while whites enjoyed the comfort of the warm basement of the Third Ward School well supplied with hot food and drink, over two hundred Chinese waited outside in a freezing mist for scraps tossed to them. Officer Thomas Jackson finally intervened with the Distribution Committee, and had large quantities of rice, oil, flour, sugar, and red woolen shirts divided among the representatives of the five companies for distribution. The *Territorial Enterprise* admitted that "the neglect of these people was not entirely Christian," but later justified this behavior as being caused by tradition rather than the fault of individual whites.[72]

Throughout this period white laborers feared that cheap Chinese labor would displace them and took appropriate action to see that this would not happen. On October 30, 1866, a "Grand Democratic and Anti-Chinese Torchlight Procession" made its way through Virginia City in a show of strength. In the following months an anti-coolie frenzy developed in California; the *Territorial Enterprise* pointed out that such agitation was limited in Nevada, and to calm white fears noted that Chinese could not become naturalized citizens and thus could never gain the power of the ballot box. French-Canadian wood choppers organized in 1867–1868 against the Chinese who were hired to cut wood above Carson City. They had a brief skirmish with the Chinese which led to a stalemate.[73]

The greatest reactions against Chinese laborers was directed against their use on the construction of the Virginia and Truckee Railroad between Carson City and Virginia City. Soon after grading began on February 18, 1869, railroad officials led by William Sharon found it difficult to get laborers to work on the railroad. As a result they began to hire unemployed Chinese who had formerly worked on the Central Pacific Railroad as it was being hacked through the Sierra Nevada. By April 4 there were two hundred whites and three hundred Chinese scattered in some fifteen camps along the railroad. Plans called for increasing the number of Chinese workers to one thousand because of their desire to work and willingness to accept cheap wages, which were half those paid to whites.[74]

White opposition to the influx of Chinese laborers grew steadily. On August 3 a Workingman's Convention consisting of leaders from the Miner's Unions of Virginia City, Gold Hill, Humboldt, and White Pine, the Washoe Typographical Union, and the Brewer's Association was convened in the Storey County Courthouse. At the end of their meeting they issued a statement of solidarity:

> We call upon all men who favor our views to join with us in the endeavor to save our State from the pollution of Asiatic serfdom now threatening its social and material prosperity.[75]

They further condemned "short-sighted capitalists and unthinking men" who favored the use of coolie labor, planned on the use of legal action and thus to avoid violence in their efforts to drive the Chinese from Nevada. The miners further rationalized that if the Chinese remained they would destroy the prosperity of Nevada by driving out the white population because of their cheap labor. Some 1500 handbills were distributed condemning the "foul body of conspirators" headed by Sharon.

As the opposition grew, words gave way to action. On Wednesday, September 29, a mob of between 350 and 400 miners from the Gold Hill and Virginia City Miners' Unions, led by a fife and drum and followed by a large body of spectators marched on the Chinese who were grading the railbed south of Gold Hill just outside of Storey County. Sheriff W. J. Cummings and his deputy sheriff tried to stop the crowd, but they were pushed aside by the president of the Gold Hill union who said they would cease their activity only after they had gotten rid of the Chinese. Even before the miners reached the site some 60 Chinese had fled into the hills; the remainder were given thirty minutes to pack and leave. The miners then proceeded to level their shanties and threatened their employers with reprisals if the Chinese were returned to work.[76]

On the following day editorials in the *Territorial Enterprise* and *Gold Hill Daily News* thoroughly condemned the entire affair, the first of its kind in Storey County. The newspapers called for the arrest and conviction of those involved, but lamented it would be impossible to find a jury in the area that would convict the men. The *Territorial Enterprise* further indicated the real nature of the problem: "There are many persons who are very anxious to take the place of the Chinese, but we have not seen any of them as yet, except as such wished to act as bosses."[77]

During the first week of October the Chinese who had been laying a half mile or more of track per day were idle while Sharon tried to allay the miners' fears. He met with them and explained that by using white laborers it would cost the railroad $3 million to construct the line between Carson City and Virginia City, while by employing Chinese laborers, costs would be reduced by half. The miners also heard him explain that allowing construction to continue would eventually mean low grade ore could be shipped out, thus giving the miners more work and reducing the price of lumber and fuel. Eventually both parties signed a mutual agreement whereby Sharon would not employ Chinese on the railroad, or in the mines and mills within Storey County, and the miners would not bother the Chinese workers. With these conflicts resolved, construction of the railroad returned to normal on October 21.[78]

Organized resistance against Chinese labor developed again in May 1876, when the Virginia Anti-Chinese Union was formed. The organization passed a series of resolutions which stated that the presence of the Chinese in Nevada "was injurious to the welfare of the State and a danger to the Republic," and that the Chinese caused white unemployment which led to unrest among the jobless. Since it was impossible to "civilize" the Chinese, the union proposed to use legal means to remove them and keep other Chinese out; the leaders could not predict future developments if legal means did not work.[79]

In August the original union was incorporated as the Order of Caucasians with branches in Virginia City and Gold Hill. It was the seventh such branch on the Pacific Coast and the second in Nevada, following Reno. The new organization demanded that whites stop hiring Chinese and give whites an opportunity to work. "Watty" Hall of Hall's Pioneer Laundry planned to discharge his numerous Chinese employees in July, but to be on the safe side traveled to the Bay Area to seek white replacements. After searching San Francisco and Oakland and offering prospective workers high wages, he returned to Virginia City alone. The Ashland House on The Divide took more direct action and fired all of its Chinese employees.[80]

Many businesses advertised in the newspapers that they did not use Chinese labor nor did they sell products made by Chinese. In January 1867 Kingsbury's

Chop House announced: "None of your Hongkong John fixings" here, while Barnum Restaurant explained: "The establishment is kept by Mrs. Hancock, a French lady who has her own views on the China question. She bars all Celestial chefs de cuisine from her restaurant. White cooks alone are employed." The International Cigar Stone let it be known: "No Chinese Cigars kept in this Establishment."[81]

The Order promoted its anti-Chinese position through meetings, lectures and street rallies. Lectures like the one given by P. S. Downey, Supreme Chief of the Order of Caucasians, entitled: "Labors of the Late Congressional Committee of Investigation on the Mongolian Question" stressed moderation and called for Federal action to rid the Pacific Coast of the Chinese.[82]

In response to this activity the *Territorial Enterprise* editorialized that it was a good intention to displace the Chinese labor, but whites must prove themselves as good or better than the Chinese. The paper continued:

> The fact that Chinese domestics are so generally employed on this coast is because . . . they have proven themselves to be better servants than white men and women. John is a heathen, but he is not in the habit of getting drunk; he is a Pagan, but he is patient, industrious and faithful: he may steal sugar from the pantry, but he never makes the kitchen howl with the presence of a big cousin; he is a worshipper of Joss, but he is punctual in his duties and never carries slander between his own and the next kitchen.[83]

In a challenge to white workers the newspapers stated that opportunity was available and the whites should live up to its demands.

Official discrimination against the Chinese is to be found in the ordinances of both Gold Hill and Virginia City and in laws passed by the state legislature. The earliest dates from June, 1859 when the miners of Gold Hill sought to bring law and order to the community. In a series of rules and regulations governing them one read: "No Chinaman shall hold a claim in this district," which extended on a meridian from Dayton to Steamboat Valley.[84] In 1864 Gold Hill passed an ordinance which made it illegal for a Chinese resident to live within four hundred feet of a white person unless permission was granted. The reasons given for this ordinance were that the Chinese were considered unhealthy, created fire hazards, and caused property values to drop. The fines for violations ran from $100 to $500.[85] The territorial legislature of Nevada passed a law in 1861 which discriminated against the Chinese and others. It was a misdemeanor punishable from one to two years in prison if a white person married any black, mulatoo, Indian or Chinese. The person who performed the ceremony could get a one to three year sentence. The penalty for a white cohabiting with a Chinese person was a $100–$500 fine and/or one to six months in jail. The fine was to be placed into the county treasury and set apart for the common school fund of the territory.[86] Virginia City passed an ordinance in June, 1875 whereby any citizen residing within the city limits west of H Street could petition for removal of Chinese residents. If an inhabited structure were declared a nuisance by the Board of Aldermen, the chief of police was to have the individual removed within ten days. Fear of fire caused Chinese firecrackers and fireworks to be declared illegal in 1877, with $100 fines and/or fifty days in jail.[87] When the State of Nevada took a census in 1875, the census takers did not bother to list the individual Chinese by name and occupation but merely listed "Chinaman" or "Chinawoman."[88] The extent of the anti-Chinese feeling in Nevada perhaps is best seen in the outcome of a vote taken in 1880: 17,259 voted against Chinese immigration and 183 in favor.[89] This anti-Chinese sentiment was not a local phenomenon; during the latter half of the nineteenth century there was a strong upsurge of nativism throughout the United States and it often found expression in legislative enactments.[90]

Anti-Chinese feeling also prevailed among the Paiutes who lived in the vicinity of Virginia City. From the beginning of their encounters, the Indians despised the Chinese for their aggressive work ethic, their tendency to use even the scraps of the environment such as the roots of pine nut trees, and their proclivity to take Indian jobs. As whites initially moved into the area, Paiute males found employment as wood choppers, and females as servants and launderers. The Chinese cut into this activity by selling precut wood and returning finished laundry.[91] On the streets it was a question of survival, with both races fighting over scraps of wood, coal and charcoal and sometimes attracting crowds of 200 to 300 amused whites who watched the struggles of desperate groups.[92]

The Paiutes seized many opportunities to ridicule and to physically attack the Chinese; and they often bragged to newspaper reporters there would be a massacre if the whites would not interfere. A frequent complaint was that the Chinese worked hard and then refused to spend their money in town, sending it instead to China, while the Indians spent theirs locally. Paiutes also took great pleasure in tracking Chinese suspects, attempting to catch them quickly and collect rewards.[93] For their part, unhindered by white laws against selling Paiutes intoxicating liquors, the Chinese sold them horrible concoctions called "China gin" which they passed off as expensive whiskey. They tried to control unruly and threatening Indians by simply cutting off the supply if they got too violent.[94]

The Chinese of Virginia City constantly migrated to new gold and silver strikes seeking their fortunes. The only criterion was that enough whites had preceded them to offer protection against the Indians. Beginning in the spring of 1865 numerous Chinese left the Comstock for the mining camps of Idaho and Montana. Both Virginia City and Dayton became important stops for California Chinese who were making the trip. In May, 1867 there were over four hundred Chinese resting at Dayton and three hundred and fifty more were anticipated.[95] Pioche's boom in the early 1870s drew many of Virginia City's Chinese, and the depressed economic conditions of the late 1870s caused half of Chinatown's population to leave for Belmont, Bodie and Tuscarora. The Chinese who remained usually were too poor to leave and as a result the few Chinese businesses that remained were adversely affected.[96]

By 1880 the Big Bonanza on the Comstock was over. The price of stocks was down, and many people were unemployed. Both whites and Chinese left the area. In 1880 there were 642 Chinese in Storey County. By 1890, the figure had declined by nearly 50%, and in 1900 there were only sixty-one Chinese remaining.[97] There were a few who remained in Virginia City after the turn of the century, like Charlie Ching and Chung Kee, both of whom operated small shops. By 1940 all were gone. The collection of shanties called Chinatown had slowly succumbed to fire and the elements.[98] Today nothing remains of the original Chinatown and its people except sagebrush-covered lots and the bitter memory of their struggle to survive.

NOTES

1. Studies dealing with Chinese on the mining frontier: Effie Mona Mack, *Nevada: A History of the State from Earliest Times through the Civil War* (Glendale, Calif.: Arthur H. Clark, 1936): *Nevada State Journal*, November 16, 1958; Gary P. BeDunnah, *History of the Chinese in Nevada, 1855–1904* (San Francisco: R & E Research Associates, 1973); Grant K. Anderson, "Deadwood's Chinatown," *South Dakota History* 5 (Summer, 1975), 266–285; Duane A. Smith, *Rocky Mountain Mining Camps: The Urban Frontier:* (Lincoln: University of Nebraska Press, 1974), pp. 29–30; William S. Greever, *The Bonanza West: The Story of the Western Mining Rushes, 1848–1900* (Norman: University of Oklahoma Press, 1963); Patricia K. Ourada, "The Chinese in Colorado," *Colorado Magazine* 29 (1952), 273–284; Dana E. Balibrera, "Virginia City and the Immigrant," M.A. thesis, University of Nevada, Reno, 1965, pp. 60–67; Rodman W. Paul, "The Origin of the Chinese Issue in California," *Mississippi Valley Historical Review* 25 (1938–1939), 181–196; Thomas W. Chim, ed. *A History of the Chinese in California: A Syllabus* (San Francisco: Chinese Historical Society of America, 1969); Rose Hum Lee, "The Chinese Communities in the Rocky Mountain States," Ph.D. dissertation, University of Chicago, 1947; Gregg Lee Carter, "Social Demography of the Chinese in Nevada, 1870–1880," *Nevada Historical Society Quarterly* 18 (Summer 1975), 72–89; George M. Blackburn and Sherman L. Ricards, "The Chinese in Virginia City, Nevada: 1870," *Amerasia* 7 (1980), 51–71.

2. Myron Angel, ed., *History of Nevada* (Oakland: Thompson & West, 1881), p. 51; Hubert H. Bancroft, *History of Nevada, Colorado and Wyoming, 1540–1888* (San Francisco: The History Company, 1890), pp. 77, 95, 292; Dan De Quille, *A History of the Comstock Silver Lode and Mines* (Virginia City: F. Boegle, 1889, 1973 reprint), p. 102.

3. San Francisco *Daily Alta California*, March 27 and 31, 1860; J. Ross Browne, "A Peep at Washoe," *Harper's New Monthly Magazine* 22 (December, 1860), 1–17; (January, 1861), 145–162; (February, 1861), 289–305.

4. Rose Hum Lee, "The Chinese Communities in the Rocky Mountain States," p. 5.

5. Stanford M. Lyman, *The Asian in the West* (Reno: University of Nevada Social Science and Humanities Publication No. 4, 1970), pp. 9, 11.

6. *Virginia City Territorial Enterprise* (hereafter cited: TE), January 25, 1876; *Virginia Evening Chronicle* (hereafter cited VEC), December 20, 23, 1875; Deeds, Recorder and Auditor, Storey County Court House, Virginia City, Nevada, Vol. 26, p. 424; Vol. 27, p. 657; Vol. 28, p. 174; Vol. 30, p. 81; Vol. 31, p. 630; Vol. 32, p. 403; Vol. 33, p. 35.

7. TE August 31, 1869; March 5, 1870; June 25, 1872; July 17, 1872; July 19, 1872; August 22, 1872; July 13, 1877; 1877 Map of Virginia City, Bancroft Library, University of California, Berkeley; Thomas H. Kinnersley, "Virginia, Nevada, 1859–1890: A Study of Police, Water, and Fire Problems," Ph.D. dissertation, University of California, Los Angeles, 1974.

8. TE August 22, 1868; July 22, 1871; April 14, 1878.

9. *Gold Hill Evening News* (hereafter cited: GHEN) July 15, 1864; TE September 20, 1867; November 12, 1871; December 17, 1871; July 2, 1879.

10. Minute Book, County Commissioners, Storey County, Nevada, December 7, 1877–September 5, 1881, Clerk's Office, Storey County Court House, pp. 14 and 175.

11. *First Directory of Nevada Territory of 1862* (Los Gatos, Calif.: Talisman Press, 1962), pp. 134, 161; Gregg Lee Carter, "Social Demography of the Chinese in Nevada, 1870–1880," pp. 72–89.

12. Mrs. Mary M. Mathews, *Ten Years in Nevada* (Buffalo, N.Y.: Baker, Jones & Co., 1880), p. 252.

13. TE March 8, 1868; October 23, 1870; February 14, 1878.

14. Eliot Lord, *Comstock Mining and Miners* (Berkeley: Howell-North, 1959, reprint of 1883 edition), p. 204; TE August 19, 1877; February 15, 1878, January 22, 1881.

15. TE August 28, 1869; August 19, 1877; January 16, 1868; GHEN April 5, 1866; TE January 22, 1881.

16. TE November 22, 1877; December 31, 1879; January 26, 1881.

17. VEC June 14, 1875; TE September 21, 1877; February 1, 1877. The Chinese were not the only gardners using sewer water. On September 9, 1873, for instance, John Dohle was granted the use of water flowing through Mill Street. The only stipulation was that he must keep the sewer in good repair (Record [Board of Aldermen, Virginia City, Nevada], January 1, 1867–March 28, 1876, Clerk's Office, Storey County Court House); VEC June 19, 1875; TE June 18, 1871; August 18, 1878; *Virginia Chronicle* (hereafter cited: VC) July 30, 1879; TE April 10, 1880; May 7, 1880.

18. VEC January 14, 1875; June 19, 1875; September 2, 1875; TE June 18, 1871; July 10, 1877; Wilbur S. Shepperson, *Restless Strangers: Nevada's Immigrants and Their Interpreters* (Reno: University of Nevada Press, 1970), p. 111.

19. TE July 17, 1878; August 24, 1881; July 28, 1889; January 22, 1881; March 31, 1881; June 19, 1881; October 15, 1881; November 4, 1881.

20. TE July 23, 1880; March 28–29, 1869; May 12, 1878; June 2, 1875; September 20, 1878; March 17, 1877; June 8, 1879; November 29, 1876; *Gold Hill News* (hereafter cited GHN) May 25, 1864; TE September 9, 1876; May 4, 1878; May 10, 1878.

21. Daniel W. Strong to George Strong, Dutch Flat, Calif., February 22, 1869, Nevada Historical Society, Reno, #2125; TE July 20, 1871; July 26, 1871; October 30, 1872; October 7, 1871; VEC January 19, 1875.

22. *The Daily Safeguard*, October 19, 1868; TE May 27, 1868; December 15, 1870; February 21, 1871; April 5, 1871; April 9, 1871; Wells Fargo Express, *Directory of Chinese Business Houses* (San Francisco: Britton & Rey Litho, 1878), p. 84; Record Group 21, U.S. District Court, District of Nevada, Carson City-Reno, Criminal Case Files, 1865–1949, Series 1, Box 5, Federal Archives and Records Center, San Bruno, CA #519.

23. VC September 23, 1879; February 11, 1880; VEC December 11, 1875; D. M. Bishop & Co. (compilers) *Directory of Virginia City, 1878–1879* (San Francisco: B. C. Vandall, 1878), p. 574.

24. Mathews, *Ten Years in Nevada*, p. 251; GHEN February 14, 1866; VC July 29, 1879; VEC July 16, 1875.

25. TE March 14, 1871; August 9, 1878; September 5, 1878; January 7, 1880.

26. VEC September 11, 1875; October 25, 1875; TE February 18, 1871; November 13, 1875; Marion Goldman, "Sexual Commerce on the Comstock Lode," *Nevada Historical Society Quarterly* 21 (Summer, 1978), 110, 118.

27. TE February 5, 1871; November 14, 1873.

28. TE October 4, 1872; VC December 3, 1870; November 28, 1879; January 26, 1880.

29. John K. Fairbank, Edwin O. Reischauer, and Albert M. Craig, *East Asia: Tradition and Transformation* (Boston: Houghton Mifflin Co., 1973), p. 450; Immanuel C. Y. Hsu, *The Rise of Modern China* (New York: Oxford University Press, 1970), p. 217.

30. Gregory Lee Mark, "Racial, Economic and Political Factors in the Development of America's First Drug Laws," *Issues in Criminology* 10 (Spring, 1975), 61.

31. VEC June 8, 1875; VC September 13, 1879; VEC January 19, 1876.

32. VEC March 31, 1875; February 10, 1876; VC September 30, 1879; VEC February 15, 1876.

33. VEC March 31, 1875.

34. VEC June 8, 1875.

35. J. H. Graham, *Revised Ordinances of the City of Virginia* (Virginia City: Enterprise Steam Printing House, 1878), p. 116; TE March 39, 1879; February 18, 1880; March 9, 1881; April 1, 1881. Henry C. Cutting (compiler) *The Compiled Laws of Nevada in Force from 1861 to 1900 (Inclusive).* (Carson City: Andrew Maute, 1900), p. 937.

36. TE April 3, 1879; *The Footlight* (hereafter cited: TF) November 1, 1877; TE August 27, 1877; November 1, 1877; November 3, 1877; November 24, 1877; April 2, 1877; July 23, 1879; September 3, 1879; September 11, 1879; September 30, 1879; VC July 21, 1879.

37. TE April 10, 1877; April 22, 1877; VC March 20, 1880; February 24, 1880; July 2, 1879; March 13, 1881; April 1, 1881.

38. TE March 8, 1881.

39. TE April 17, 1878; VC May 16, 1879.

40. TE July 22, 1871; VEC June 2, 1875; TE May 24, 1877; April 5, 1878; May 7, 1878; VC May 16, 1879; TE March 24, 1869.

41. TE February 19, 1871; GHEN February 14, 1866; February 15, 1866; V. R. Burkhardt, *Chinese Creeds and Customs* (Hong Kong: The South China Morning Post, Ltd., 1953); Walter Van Tilberg Clark, ed., *The Journals of Alfred Doten* (Reno: University of Nevada Press, 1973), 2:877. (Cited as Doten, *Journals.*)

42. TE July 24, 1877; John Taylor, *A Kid on the Comstock: Reminiscences of a Virginia City Childhood,* Dolores Bryant Waldorf (ed.) (Palo Alto: American West Publishing Company, 1970), pp. 84, 86.

43. GHEN June 8, 1864; TE June 10, 1871.

44. TE September 3, 1872; June 19, 1872; March 13, 1878; VC December 4, 1879. One temple was located 61.2 feet north of Union Street on the west side of I Street. The other was located approximately 150 feet north of Union Street on the west side of K Street. (Map Book, 1875, Assessor's Office, Storey County Court House, p. 89.)

45. Mathews, *Ten Years in Nevada,* p. 251. In 1928 one of the temples was still standing in Virginia City but was exposed to the elements. It measured approximately 30 − 60 feet. William Marks, Jr. to the author; Virginia City; Nevada, March 8, 1976; C. Grant Loomis, "Chinese Lore from Nevada, 1867–1878," *California Folklore Quarterly* 5 (January–April, 1946), 185–196.

46. "Inventory of the Church Archives: Protestant Episcopal Church," The Nevada Historical Records Survey Project (WPA), Reno, 1941, p. 12; TE July 3, 1875; July 14,

1875; August 15, 1875; March 28, 1876; VEC August 14, 1875; August 16, 1875; September 2, 1875.

47. "St. Paul's Parish Register" Vol. I, 1862–September 1868; Vol. 2, 1868–1883; Nevada State Historical Society, Reno: Record, Marriages A, Recorder and Auditor, Storey County Courthouse, p. 323.

48. TE January 19, 1878; January 27, 1878; February 19, 1878; February 21, 1878.

49. *Gold Hill News* June 10, 1864; GHEN February 8, 1866; February 14, 1866; TE February 24, 1868; May 5, 1868; GHEN April 19, 1865; TE May 19, 1869; Doten, *Journals*, II:839, 866–867, 877, 1171. For an in-depth study of Virginia City's police force see Thomas H. Kinnersley, "Virginia, Nevada, 1859–1890: A Study of Police, Water, and Fire Problems," Ph.D. Dissertation, University of California, Los Angeles, 1974, pp. 57–98; *The Daily Union* January 6, 1864 (Bancroft Library).

50. VEC February 15, 1876; February 17, 1876.

51. Sandmeyer, *The Anti-Chinese Movement*, pp. 17, 34; Lyman, *The Asian in the West*, pp. 18–19. *Appendix to Journals of Senate and Assembly of the English Session of the Legislature of the State of Nevada* (Carson City: John J. Hill, State Printer, 1877), III, 615.

52. TE May 25, 1866; October 23, 1866; October 9, 1866; December 17, 1867; November 2, 1870; October 3, 1872; June 7, 1878; January 11, 1876; April 11, 1875; May 28, 1875; January 12, 1878; Record, Marriages A, Recorder and Auditor, Storey County Court House [1865 and 1879], pp. 66, 108, 195, 301, 323, 340, 441, and 462.

53. Population Schedules of the 9th Census of the United States, 1870. Roll 835. Nevada, Volume 1 (313–592A). National Archives Microscopy No. 593.

54. William Hoy, *The Chinese Six Companies* (San Francisco: Chinese Consolidated Benevolent Association, 1942); Lyman, *The Asian in the West*, p. 227; Gunther Barth, *Bitter Struggle: A History of the Chinese in the United States, 1850–1870* (Cambridge: Harvard University Press, 1964), pp. 76–99; William Speer, "Democracy of the Chinese," *Harper's Monthly Magazine*, XXXVII (November, 1868), 839–848; Stanford M. Lyman, "Conflict and the Web of Group Affiliation in San Francisco's Chinatown, 1850–1910," *Pacific Historical Review* 43 (November, 1974), 473–499.

55. TE May 16, 1866; VEC April 27, 1875; TE November 16, 1878.

56. TE November 16, 1878.

57. TE July 14, 1871; November 11, 1871.

58. Deeds, Vol. 28. Recorder and Auditor, p. 174; Plat Book, 1871 and Map Book, 1875, p. 75; Assessor's Office, Storey County Court House.

59. VEC December 11, 1875; February 14, 1876; TE February 1, 1876; Record of Births and Deaths, "A"; November 10, 1887, Recorder and Auditor Office, Storey County Court House, p. 25. Identification of the leadership of the various companies is lost due to a lack of white understanding of the companies.

60. TE December 13, 1879; Doten, *Journals*, 3: 1686; Deeds, Recorder and Auditor, Storey County Court House; Vol. 26, pp. 424 and Vol. 27, p. 657. Plat Book, 1872, Assessor's Office, Storey County Court House.

61. VEC December 11, 15, 23, 1875; TE February 15, 1876; VEC January 15, 1876.

62. TE February 6, 15, 1876.

63. TE February 16, 24 and 27, 1876; VEC February 28, 1876; Lyman, *Chinese Americans* (New York: Random House, 1974).

64. VEC March 1, 13, 1876; TE, March 19, 1876.

65. TE March 21–22, 1876; March 28, 1876; April 11, 1876; May 3, 1876; March 3, 1876; July 20, 1876.

66. TE, February 1, 3, 1877; May 22–23, 1877; October 18–19, 1877.

67. Mathews, *Ten Years in Nevada*, p. 249. GHDN January 7, 1870; TE January 9, 1873; April 27, 1871.

68. GHEN, February 15, 1866; Doten, *Journals*, II: 877.

69. Doten, *Journals*, II: 817, 839.

70. Ibid., II, 866–857; Mathews, *Ten Years in Nevada*, p. 250; Lord, *Comstock Mining*, p. 199; GHN, November 26, 1864; GHEN, February 14, 1866; *The Virginia Daily Union*, February 4, 1867.

71. GHEN January 9, 1865; VEC January 6, 25, 1875; May 8, 1877; February 8, 1868; September 24, 1868; GHEN September 2, 1865; TE March 17, 1876; August 29, 1880; February 11, 1873; October 28, 1870; October 18, 1870; GHEN July 18, 1854; TE May 27, 1880; Waldorf, *A Kid on the Comstock*, pp. 42, 44.

72. For an eyewitness account of the fire see Lewis Atherton, ed. "Fire on the Comstock," *American West* 2 (Winter, 1965), 24–34; TE, November 4, 27, 30, December 2, 3, 1875.

73. GHEN October 29, 1866; TE May 3, 1867; January 9, 1868, *Carson Daily Appeal*, May 1, 3, 5, 1868; Shepperson, *Restless Strangers*.

74. TE February 20, March 11, 23, April 9, May 6, 1869; Lucius Beebee and Charles Clegg, *Virginia and Truckee: A Story of Virginia City and Comstock Times* (Stanford: Stanford University Press, 1949). p. 15.

75. TE August 3, 1869.

76. TE September 29, 1869.

77. TE September 30, 1869; October 1, 1869; GHDN September 30, 1869. Conrad Wiegand, editor of *The People's Tribune*, theorized that (January 1870, Nevada Newspaper Miscellany, 1862–1905, [broken], Reel 1, Bancroft Library, Vol. 1) Sharon's spies in the labor unions orchestrated the affair so that the financial backers of the Virginia and Truckee Railroad would return their support. Wiegand proposed that the state investigate the matter. [Gold Hill] *The People's Tribune*.

78. TE October 3, 5–9, 13, 21, 1869. The agreement between Sharon and the miners to not allow Chinese railroad workers to work in Storey County was violated in April, 1875 when the Chinese started to work on a siding into the Caledonia and Overman mines. Two hundred miners from the Gold Hill Miners' Union marched to the site and drove 25 to 30 Chinese away. The Chinese were paid and discharged and white workers took their place. VEC April 28, 29, 1875.

79. TE May 17, 1876; *The Daily Mining Reporter* (Silver City) May 6, 18, and 23, 1876.

80. TE June 8, 18, 29, August 25, September 3, 5, 1876; July 2, 1876; July 11, 1876.

81. TE January 13, 1872, January 5, 1876; December 27, 1878.

82. TE July 14, 1876; March 28, 1877; January 6, 1877.

83. TE June 24, 1876.

84. Lord, *Comstock Mining*, p. 44; U.S. Bureau of the Census, *Tenth Census of the United States: 1880. Mining Laws*, XIV, 509–510.

85. GHN September 10, 1864.

86. *Laws of the Territory of Nevada* (San Francisco: Valentine & Co., 1862), pp. 93–94.

87. Graham, *Revised Ordinances*, p. 114.

88. Appendix . . . 8th Session of the Legislature . . . Nevada, III, 1–615.

89. TE February 3, 1881; John Koontz (ed.), *Political History of Nevada* (Carson City: State Printers Office, 1960), p. 60; for an in-depth study of Nevada newspaper reaction to the Chinese, see: Be Dunnah, *History of the Chinese in Nevada*.

90. Robert H. Wiebe, *The Search for Order, 1877–1920* (New York: Hill and Wang, 1967), pp. 54–58.

91. TE January 5, 1877; September 21, 1877; Waldorf, *A Kid on the Comstock*, p. 79.

92. TE May 19, 1872; November 30, 1872; GHN October 31, 1864.

93. TE September 3, 1876; June 17, 1871; Waldorf, *A Kid on the Comstock*, pp. 85–86; VEC April 1875; September 1, 1875. Novelist Frank Norris observed the same type of behavior being practiced by Caucasian women in San Francisco during the late nineteenth century.

94. Fred H. Hart, *The Sazerac Lying Club: A Nevada Book* (San Francisco: Henry Keller & Co., 1878), p. 208.

95. GHDN May 15, 1865; May 20, 23, 1876; April 20, 25–28, May 16–18, 1866; TE May 23, 24, 1867.

96. TE February 9, 1871; December 19, 1877.

97. U.S. Department of the Interior, Census Office, *The Compendium of the Eleventh Census: 1890. Population, Part I.* (Washington, D.C.: U.S. Government Printing Office, 1894), p. 560; U.S. Department of the Interior, Census Office, *Twelfth Census of the United States, Taken in the Year 1990. Population*, Vol. 1, Part I (Washington, D.C.: U.S. Government Printing Office, 1901), p. 627.

98. *Carson News*, October 19, 1913; Rose Zannini, "Charlie Ching," (1932), manuscript at the Nevada State Historical Society, Reno; Dorothy Young Nichols, *Virginia City . . . in My Day: A Memory Album*, Halmar F. Moser, ed. (Placerville: privately printed, 1973), p. 17.

7

Chapter 13 from *Roughing It*

Mark Twain

Of course there was a large Chinese population in Virginia—it is the case with every town and city on the Pacific coast. They are a harmless race when white men either let them alone or treat them no worse than dogs; in fact, they are almost entirely harmless anyhow, for they seldom think of resenting the vilest insults or the cruelest injuries. They are quiet, peaceable, tractable, free from drunkenness, and they are as industrious as the day is long. A disorderly Chinaman is rare, and a lazy one does not exist. So long as a Chinaman has strength to use his hands he needs no support from anybody; white men often complain of want of work, but a Chinaman offers no such complaint; he always manages to find something to do. He is a great convenience to everybody—even to the worst class of white men, for he bears the most of their sins, suffering fines for their petty thefts, imprisonment for their robberies, and death for their murders. Any white man can swear a Chinaman's life away in the courts, but no Chinaman can testify against a white man. Ours is the "land of the free"—nobody denies that—nobody challenges it. [Maybe it is because we won't let other people testify.] As I write, news comes that in board daylight in San Francisco, some boys have stoned an inoffensive Chinaman to death, and that although a large crowd witnessed the shameful deed, no one interfered.

There are seventy thousand (and possibly one hundred thousand) Chinamen on the Pacific coast. There were about a thousand in Virginia. They were penned into a "Chinese quarter"—a thing which they do not particularly object to, as they are fond of herding together. Their buildings were of wood; usually only one story high, and set thickly together along streets scarcely wide enough for a wagon to pass through. Their quarter was a little removed from the rest of the town. The chief employment of Chinamen in towns is to wash clothing. They always send a bill pinned to the clothes. It is mere ceremony, for it does not enlighten the customer much. Their price for washing was $2.50 per dozen—rather cheaper than white people could afford to wash for at that time. A very common sign on the Chinese houses was: "See Yup, Washer and Ironer"; "Hong Wo, Washer"; "Sam

Sing & Ah Hop, Washing." The house-servants, cooks, etc., in California and
Nevada, were chiefly Chinamen. There were few white servants and no China-
women so employed. Chinamen make good house-servants, being quick, obedi-
ent, patient, quick to learn, and tirelessly industrious. They do not need to be
taught a thing twice, as a general thing. They are imitative. If a Chinaman were
to see his master break up a center-table, in a passion, and kindle a fire with it,
that Chinaman would be likely to resort to the furniture for fuel forever afterward.

All Chinamen can read, write, and cipher with easy facility—pity but all our
petted *voters* could. In California they rent little patches of ground and do a deal
of gardening. They will raise surprising crops of vegetables on a sand-pile. They
waste nothing. What is rubbish to a Christian, a Chinaman carefully preserves
and makes useful in one way or another. He gathers up all the old oyster and sardine cans that white people throw away, and procures marketable tin and solder
from them by melting. He gathers up old bones and turns them into manure. In
California he gets a living out of old mining claims that white men have abandoned as exhausted and worthless—and then the officers come down on him
once a month with an exorbitant swindle to which the legislature has given the
broad, general name of "foreign" mining tax, but it is usually inflicted on no foreigners but Chinamen. This swindle has in some cases been repeated once or
twice on the same victim in the course of the same month—but the public treasury was not additionally enriched by it, probably.

Chinamen hold their dead in great reverence—they worship their departed an-
cestors, in fact. Hence, in China, a man's front yard, back yard, or any other part
of his premises, is made his family burying-ground, in order that he may visit the
graves at any and all times. Therefore that huge empire is one mighty cemetery;
it is ridged and wrinkled from its center to its circumference with graves—and
inasmuch as every foot of ground must be made to do its utmost, in China, lest
the swarming population suffer for food, the very graves are cultivated and yield
a harvest, custom holding this to be no dishonor to the dead. Since the departed
are held in such worshipful reverence, a Chinaman cannot bear that any indig-
nity be offered the places where they sleep. Mr. Burlingame said that herein lay
China's bitter opposition to railroads; a road could not be built anywhere in the
empire without disturbing the graves of their ancestors or friends.

A Chinaman hardly believes he could enjoy the hereafter except his body lay
in his beloved China; also, he desires to receive, himself, after death, that worship
with which he has honored his dead that preceded him. Therefore, if he visits a
foreign country, he makes arrangements to have his bones returned to China in
case he dies; if he hires to go to a foreign country on a labor contract, there is always a stipulation that his body shall be taken back to China if he dies; if the government sells a gang of coolies to a foreigner for the usual five-year term, it is specified in the contract that their bodies shall be restored to China in case of death.
On the Pacific coast the Chinamen all belong to one or another of several great
companies or organizations, and these companies keep track of their members,
register their names, and ship their bodies home when they die. The See Yup

Company is held to be the largest of these. The Ning Yeong Company is next, and numbers eighteen thousand members on the coast. Its headquarters are at San Francisco, where it has a costly temple, several great officers (one of whom keeps regal state in seclusion and cannot be approached by common humanity), and a numerous priesthood. In it I was shown a register of its members, with the dead and the date of their shipment to China duly marked. Every ship that sails from San Francisco carries away a heavy freight of Chinese corpses—or did, at least, until the legislature, with an ingenious refinement of Christian cruelty, forbade the shipments, as a neat underhanded way of deterring Chinese immigration. The bill was offered, whether it passed or not. It is my impression that it passed. There was another bill—it became a law—compelling every incoming Chinaman to be vaccinated on the wharf and pay a duly-appointed quack (no decent doctor would defile himself with such legalized robbery) ten dollars for it. As few importers of Chinese would want to go to an expense like that, the lawmakers thought this would be another heavy blow to Chinese immigration.

What the Chinese quarter of Virginia was like—or, indeed, what the Chinese quarter of any Pacific coast town was and is like—may be gathered from this item which I printed in the *Enterprise* while reporting for that paper:

CHINATOWN.—Accompanied by a fellow-reporter, we made a trip through our Chinese quarter the other night. The Chinese have built their portion of the city to suit themselves; and as they keep neither carriages nor wagons, their streets are not wide enough, as a general thing, to admit of the passage of vehicles. At ten o'clock at night the Chinaman may be seen in all his glory. In every little cooped-up, dingy cavern of a hut, faint with the odor of burning Josh-lights and with nothing to see the gloom by save the sickly, guttering tallow candle, were two or three yellow, long-tailed vagabonds, coiled up on a sort of short truckle-bed, smoking opium, motionless and with their lusterless eyes turned inward from excess of satisfaction—or rather the recent smoker looks thus, immediately after having passed the pipe to his neighbor—for opium-smoking is a comfortless operation, and requires constant attention. A lamp sits on the bed, the length of the long pipe-stem from the smoker's mouth; he puts a pellet of opium on the end of a wire, sets it on fire, and plasters it into the pipe much as a Christian would fill a hole with putty; then he applied the bowl to the lamp and proceeds to smoke—and the stewing and frying of the drug and the gurgling of the juices in the stem would well-nigh turn the stomach of a statue. John likes it, though; it soothes him; he takes about two dozen whiffs, and then rolls over to dream. Heaven only knows what, for we could not imagine by looking at the soggy creature. Possibly in his visions he travels far away from the gross world and his regular washing, and feasts on succulent rats and birds'-nests in Paradise.

Mr. Ah Sing keeps a general grocery and provision store at No. 13 Wang Street. He lavished his hospitality upon our party in the friendliest way. He had various kinds of colored and colorless wines and brandies, with unprounounceable names, imported from China in little crockery jugs, and which he offered to us in dainty little miniature wash-basins of porcelain. He offered us a mess of birds'-nests; also, small, neat sausages, of which we could have swallowed several yards if we had chosen to try, but we suspected that each link contained the corpse of a mouse, and therefore refrained. Mr. Sing had in his store a thousand articles of merchandise, curious to behold, impossible to imagine the uses of, and beyond our ability to describe.

His ducks, however, and his eggs, we could understand, the former were split open and flattened out like codfish, and came from China in that shape, and the latter were plastered over with some kind of paste which kept them fresh and palatable through the long voyage.

We found Mr. Hong Wo, No. 23 Chow-chow Street, making up a lottery scheme—in fact, we found a dozen others occupied in the same way in various parts of the quarter, for about every third Chinaman runs a lottery, and the balance of the tribe "buck" at it. "Tom," who speaks faultless English, and used to be chief and cook only to the *Territorial Enterprise,* when the establishment kept bachelor's hall two years ago; said that "Sometimes Chinaman buy ticket one dollar hap, ketch um two tree hundred, sometime no ketch um anything; lottery like one man fight um seventy—maybe be whip, maybe he get whip heself, welly good." However, the percentage being sixty-nine against him, the chances are, as a general thing, the "he get whip heself." We could not see that these lotteries differed in any respect from our own, save that the figures being Chinese, no ignorant white man might ever hope to succeed in telling "t'other from which"; the manner of drawing is similar to ours.

Mr. See Yup keeps a fancy store on Live Fox Street. He sold us fans of white feathers, gorgeously ornamented; perfumery that smelled like Limburger cheese, Chinese pens, and watch-charms made of a stone unscratchable with steel instruments, yet polished and tinted like the inner coat of a sea-shell.[1] As tokens of his esteem, See Yup presented the party with gaudy plumes made of gold tinsel and trimmed with peacocks' feathers. We ate chow-chow with chop-sticks in the celestial restaurants; our comrade chided the moon-eyed damsels in front of the houses for their want of feminine reserve; we received protecting Josh-lights from our hosts and "dickered" for a pagan god or two. Finally, we were impressed with the genius of a Chinese bookkeeper; he figured up his accounts on a machine like a gridiron with buttons strung on its bars; the different rows represented units, tens, hundreds, and thousands. He fingered them with incredible rapidity—in fact, he pushed them from place to place as fast as a musical professor's fingers travel over the keys of a piano.

They are a kindly-disposed, well-meaning race, and are respected and well treated by the upper classes, all over the Pacific coast. No Californian *gentleman or lady* abuses or oppresses a Chinaman, under any circumstances, an explanation that seems to be much needed in the East. Only the scum of the population do it—they and their children; they, and, naturally and consistently, the policemen and politicians, likewise, for these are the dust-licking pimps and slaves of the scum, there as well as elsewhere in America.

NOTE

1. A peculiar species of the "jade-stone"—to a Chinaman peculiarly precious.

8

Territory of New Mexico v. Yee Shun (1882): A Turning Point in Chinese Legal Relationships in the Trans-Mississippi West

John R. Wunder

The legal relationships of the Chinese in the American West during the post–Civil War era included numerous complex issues to be resolved. These issues went to the heart of basic human rights—the right to own property, the right to work in certain jobs, and the right to participate in the American constitutional system. One of these latter rights—the ability of the Chinese to testify in court—was resolved eventually in part by a landmark case: *Territory of New Mexico v. Yee Shun* (1882).[1]

The *Yee Shun* precedent, articulated by the New Mexico Territory Supreme Court, decided whether non-Christian Chinese could take an oath to testify in court. The court held that Chinese were allowed to testify but only after they were subjected to racial, cultural, and religious probing. Nevertheless, a legal breakthrough had occurred. Throughout the trans-Mississippi West religious belief could no longer prevent Chinese witnesses from testifying in most jurisdictions.[2]

Before the *Yee Shun* precedent, only Colorado, Iowa, Nebraska, Nevada, Oregon, and Texas had protected the Chinese right to take an oath before a court. These protections occurred in state constitutions but had not been tested in court. Special oath ceremonies were required in California and in Arkansas, but Chinese testimony was not allowed if the litigant denied the being of a God.[3] After *Yee Shun*, most states and territories accepted the New Mexico decision as law.[4]

Given the importance of this case to the developing relationship of law and race in the nineteenth-century American West, it is crucial to understand the forces that led to this particular decision. In short, what follows is a legal biographical essay designed to trace the "lifespan" of *Territory of New Mexico v. Yee Shun*.[5]

On February 24, 1882, Yee Shun got off a train at the depot in Las Vegas, New Mexico Territory, and walked to John Lee's laundry. New Mexico Territory in the 1880s was in its formative years. Twelve counties were divided into three judicial districts for administrative law purposes. Las Vegas, in San Miguel County, and Santa Fe comprised one of the judicial districts. The first railroad to enter New Mexico, the Atchison, Topeka and Santa Fe, reached Las Vegas along the Old Santa Fe Trail through Raton Pass. More than 1,000 miles of railroad track already had been laid in the territory connecting it to Colorado, Texas, and Arizona Territory. Santa Fe was the largest city in the territory with 6,185 residents in 1890. The population of Las Vegas was nearly 2,000, making it one of the ten largest towns in the territory.[6]

Las Vegas grew as a city of dualities. Old Town constituted the more established, affluent section; New town included East Las Vegas and a merchant area around the depot. By 1882 Chinese residents had begun to concentrate in New Town. The first Chinese had arrived in Las Vegas five years earlier to work on the railroad and conduct service businesses such as laundries and restaurants. By 1890 a Chinatown had developed in the 300 and 400 blocks of Grand Avenue. Six Chinese laundries separated by restaurants and boarding houses dotted the street. John Lee's laundry was located at 411 ½ Grand Avenue. To the east was an upholstery shop and to the west was a large building of furnished rooms. Across the street was an intersection with Sixth Street. One block north was Railroad Avenue and the Atchison, Topeka and Santa Fe Railroad depot.[7] On the evening of February 24, 1882, a murder occurred in John Lee's laundry for which Yee Shun would be charged.

The Chinese constituted 1 percent of all persons living in the Southwest by 1880. Mining, railroad, and service business opportunities attracted most Chinese to the region. Chinese communities developed in numerous New Mexican towns, most notably in Silver City, Albuquerque, Raton, and Las Vegas. Although the Chinese tended to contribute economically to the betterment of most communities, their reception had not been pleasant. In Deming, when two Chinese tried to claim a lot, E. A. Kidder prevented it with violence. According to the *Deming Headlight*, "when on Monday last two hop joint Celestials attempted to make a location, he [Kidder] enforced with a club a vigorous protest." The Chinese opted not to locate on the lot, and the paper called for a more desirable citizen to buy the property so the incident would not be repeated.[8]

Rumored Silver City and Raton disturbances caused the governor of New Mexico Territory to request federal troops. None were forthcoming although anti-Chinese cells were active in Silver City. At the Blackhawk mine, violence broke out. Thirty-two white miners threatened bodily harm to mine manager Platt McDonald's Chinese cook. Only the intervention of McDonald's wife reportedly prevented bloodshed. The men were fired, the company woodyard was set afire, and the cook left. In the mid-1880s the West seemed consumed with anti-Chinese hysteria, and New Mexico was not immune.[9]

Into this racially tense arena came Yee Shun. Born in China, he emigrated to the United States shortly before 1882. Like most young Chinese, Yee Shun was a laborer. Prison records described him as five feet three and one-half inches tall, with black hair, black eyes, and a light yellow-brown complexion. Yee Shun was twenty years old when he arrived in Las Vegas on the evening of February 24, 1882, the night of the murder.[10]

The killing occurred at John Lee's laundry on Grand Avenue. Inside the two-part building were two Chinese—the owner, who was laying down in a corner smoking opium, and his ironer, known as Jo Chinaman. Coming to visit around 7:00 p.m. were Ah Locke and Sam Lee. They had come to buy out John Lee, offering to purchase his laundry, house, and lot. John Lee set $1,700 as the asking price. They said that was too much, so Lee came down to $1,400.[11]

Yee Shun arrived about a half hour later. He said he was looking for a friend, Gum Ting. Yee Shun had been working in Silver Cliff, Colorado, but was in the process of relocating. He thought he would come to Las Vegas to work in a hotel laundry, but he had decided to go on to Albuquerque instead. Thus, he wanted to ask his friend to forward any mail he might receive. Yee Shun asked the four men if anyone knew Gum Ting. John Lee said he did, and that after he finished smoking, he would take Yee Shun to Gum Ting's home. He offered Yee Shun a seat.[12]

At this point Jim Lee (also known as Sam Ling Wing and as Frank) came into the room from a back room and sat on a soap box near the stove. Suddenly two shots rang out from a .44 caliber Bulldog pistol. Jim Lee slumped to the floor in the middle doorway. In the midst of the smoke and fire, the four Chinese capable of fleeing did so. Yee Shun was first out the front door followed closely by Ah Locke and Sam Lee. Jo Chinaman ran out the back door. John Lee, dead or dying, was in no condition to escape.[13]

Jo Chinaman went to tell the butcher—a Mr. Baker—next-door to the incident, then he informed Jim Lee's brother, before returning to the scene of the murder. Ah Locke and Sam Lee ran to Sam Lee's laundry on Eighth Street, where they stayed the night. In testimony, Ah Locke said they were all extremely frightened. When asked: "Ever hear pistol shots before?" Ah Locke replied, "In this town I saw lots of pistol shooting before."[14]

Having only just arrived in Las Vegas, Yee Shun ran toward the railroad tracks and livery stables before walking on to Sixth Street toward the scene of the murder. D. B. Borden, who had been strolling with his wife Jennie and saw the commotion, demanded that Yee Shun stop and explain his behavior. Yee Shun told him he was afraid and had panicked. Borden then turned Yee Shun over to Marshal H. J. Franklin, who put him under arrest. After spending a half hour at the jail, Franklin and Yee Shun returned to John Lee's laundry, where Dr. Russell Bailey was conducting an inquest. Jim Lee was Dr. Bailey's laundryman. Bailey cut the bullet out of the body and gave it to Franklin. Jo Chinaman was then asked under oath to identify Yee Shun as the killer, but he refused.[15]

Nevertheless, Yee Shun was arraigned on March 10, 1883, before LeBaron Bradford Prince, chief justice of the New Mexico Territory Supreme Court, and charged with murder. John Lee was later added to the indictment. Both pleaded not guilty, and Sidney Barnes, attorney for John Lee, successfully moved for two separate trials. Change of venue requests were denied, but a postponement was granted for the fall term. Yee Shun's attorney, T. A. Green, would have time to prepare a defense.[16]

The murder trial of Yee Shun began on August 16, 1882, with a new judge, Chief Justice Samuel B. Axtell, presiding. A jury of twelve was chosen. They included Blas Martinez, Manual Tagaija, Runaldo Archibeque, Alsolinario Almanzar, Jose Leon Martinez, Hijinio Garcia, Marcos Tagoya, Ysidro Torres, Manuel Jimenes, Manuel Urioste, Juan Chavez, and Juan E. Sena. All were Mexican-American residents of Las Vegas. Attorneys present included T. A. Green for the defendant and Attorney General William Breeden for the territory. When actual testimony began on August 17, the prosecution sought to place Yee Shun in John Lee's laundry at the time of the murder with the murder weapon and to identify him as the killer. Breeden called six witnesses to establish his case.[17]

The first witness sworn was D. B. Borden. He and his wife had been out for an evening walk and were heading for their residence on Lincoln Avenue when they heard two shots and saw a man with a pistol run out of John Lee's laundry. Borden followed the man across the street and through a vacant lot, then lost him only to see the man again walking toward him near Dr. Bailey's office on Sixth Avenue in front of the Martinez Dry Goods Store. Borden stopped the man and had him arrested by Marshal Franklin. Borden admitted the man he stopped had no weapon on him, but Borden looked around Dr. Bailey's lot and found a pistol that had been fired recently. The man arrested was Yee Shun, but Borden could not swear that the defendant was the man he had seen leaving the laundry.[18]

San Miguel deputy sheriff Marshal H. J. Franklin then identified Yee Shun as the man arrested. Franklin also testified that Borden had found the .44 caliber Bulldog pistol with two chambers discharged and given it to him. Franklin had given the gun to Justice of the Peace William Steele at the coroner's inquest. When Franklin head the shots, he ran to the laundry and then turned up Sixth Avenue to make the arrest. According to Franklin, Yee Shun had understood English and he had spoken in English. William Steele was called to testify next and presented the pistol as well as the bullet Dr. Bailey had taken from Jim Lee's body.[19]

The prosecution then turned to R. P. Hesser, who claimed to be an eyewitness. Hesser had arrived in Las Vegas from Kansas City on February 22. He said he was going to Kate Nelson's restaurant when he heard a shot, then saw Yee Shun with a pistol. Under cross-examination Hesser seemed rather vague.[20]

> *Green:* Can you name, or did you know any of the men you saw there at the wash-house?
> *Hesser:* I cannot name them.

Green: Did you know any of them?

Hesser: No, sir, not by name.

Green: State whether they were Americans, Chinamen, or what kind of men they were?

Hesser: They were Americans.

Green: How many Chinamen did you see?

Hesser: At the time of the shooting, or [in the laundry] afterwards?

Green: I am asking you, at the time you got there.

Hesser: I saw one or two.

Green: State whether or not you were the first man that got there?

Hesser: I don't know.

Judge Axtell intervened to get Hesser to clarify his statements identifying the defendant. Green took exception to the court's interruption, arguing that Hesser was a drifter—a sign painter and a coal miner from Pennsylvania and Iowa. Green asked Hesser why he needed to be subpoenaed to testify. Hesser said he did not like trials. Pressing further, Green finally asked: "Have you a special prejudice against Chinamen?" Hesser tried to deny the accusation, "No sir, not a bit. Notice they get my washing when it is dirty." After another series of sharp exchanges, Green submitted a question in writing to Judge Axtell. "I want to ask this witness whether or not he is not a fancy house runner or pimp as they are called. I am told he is." Judge Axtell disallowed the question. Nevertheless, Hesser's testimony was littered with inaccuracies and had not proven persuasive.[21]

The key witness for the prosecution, Jo Chinaman, came next. Chinaman was a twenty-six-year-old ironer employed by John Lee, who had been present when the murder was committed. Chinaman had been in Las Vegas for one year, having migrated from Shasta, California, where he had been a gold miner. Jo Chinaman was sworn at the beginning of his testimony, and it was this portion of the trial that proved to make new law. Through an interpreter, the attorneys quizzed Chinaman.[22]

Green: I will ask you if you believe in Chinese worship: their Chinese Joss houses, do you believe in Chinese Joss?

Jo: I live in a Chinese house.

Green: I will ask you if you believe in the Chinese joss house where they worship, where they have their religious services? Do you ever go with Chinamen in this country where they worship? Do you understand what a God is?

Jo: I don't know what it is? Yes, I believe the Chinese religion.

Green: Have you ever changed from Chinese to Christian religion since you came to this country?

Jo: I am a Chinaman, and believe in the Chinese religion.

Green: Was you ever a witness in court before?

Jo: Yes.

Green: Do you know anything about the obligations of an oath under the Christian religions?

Jo: I don't know.

Breeden then sought to soften the blow to allow Jo Chinaman to testify.

> *Breeden:* Ask him what he is to do, or what his duty is in telling his story as a
> witness? If he knows what his duty is as to telling the truth?
> *Jo:* I can tell the truth in this case.
> Breeden: Do you know that you are sworn here so that you are to tell the truth?
> *Jo:* Yes.

Judge Axtell allowed Jo Chinaman to be sworn for testimony. Green offered a strong objection.

Attorney General Breeden proceeded to take Chinaman through the events leading toward the murder. In the process Chinaman identified Yee Shun specifically as the killer. But Chinaman also laid the groundwork for what an alert attorney might have used for perjury. Green did not recognize the inconsistencies. At one point Chinaman testified that Yee Shun said nothing at all and shot Jim Lee when he came in the door. Later, under cross-examination, Chinaman said Yee Shun "just went in, and just talk with one person; put his hand in his pants pocket, drew a pistol and shot." Chinaman also testified that only four persons were in the laundry at the time of the murder, instead of six. Two others had come by earlier to try to force John Lee to sell out. Chinaman said they argued that there were too many laundries in town. He suggested a shakedown was happening.[23]

Under severe cross-examination the defense began to build its case for a Tong murder. Green established that Jo Chinaman left town after the murder. He was given $30 to go to Pueblo, Colorado. If he stayed there, Green suggested Chinaman would have been killed. Chinaman was a member of the Hip Wo Company, the same as Jim Lee and one of the two trial interpreters, it was later discovered. Green also noted how Tam Kay Tung, owner of two laundries, was assisting the prosecution, and that he had helped Jo Chinaman. Chinaman then became uncooperative as a witness.[24]

The prosecution next called Dr. Russell Bailey, who verified the gunshot wounds to the deceased, and recalled Borden and Franklin to go over the discovery of the pistol.[25] The prosecution then rested. Jo Chinaman's testimony was crucial. Only Chinaman had identified Yee Shun as the murderer.

T. A. Green pinned Yee Shun's defense on the testimony of the defendant and two other eyewitnesses, Ah Locke and Sam Lee. Locke stated Yee Shun was unarmed, that the defendant had not fired a shot, and that the shots came from the back. Lee verified Locke's testimony. On cross-examination, Lee admitted he belonged to the Kong Chow Company, and that Yee Shun was a member of the Sam Yup Company.[26] Breeden tried to establish an unsavory motive in Locke's testimony by forcing him to admit that he used the name John Lee. Breeden then asked Locke:[27]

> *Breeden:* What is your religion?
> *Ah Locke:* American, and Chinese too.

Breeden: Have a mixed religion, do you?

Ah Locke: Yes, sir.

Breeden: When did you get American religion?

Ah Locke: In Denver.

Breeden: Didn't you learn it for this case so as to come in and testify about it?

Ah Locke: At the church in Denver.

Breeden: In the church you went to in Denver, did you hear the American religion?

Ah Locke: Yes, sir.

Breeden: What is the American religion?

Ah Locke: American believes that good men are sent to Heaven and badmen to Hell.

Breeden: What is the Chinese religion?

Ah Locke: The Chinese religion is to always do good.

Breeden: Haven't you been going to Sunday school here a little, getting ready for this trial? Haven't you been to Sunday school at all?

Ah Locke: No, sir.

Clearly, the attorney general was worried about an appeal based upon oath-taking objections.

Yee Shun took the stand next, but before he testified for very long, the court interrupted and allowed the prosecution to call Jennie Borden to tell her account. Evidently, she had been unavailable at the beginning of the trial. This tactic upset the momentum for the defense, and then the defendant's attorney may have made a crucial error in his cross-examination of Mrs. Borden.[28]

Green: I will get you to state whether or not you were present with your husband when he pursued someone that ran from the washhouse?

J. Borden: Yes, sir.

Green: I will get you to state whether or not it was light enough to distinguish a man as to whether it was a Mexican or American?

J. Borden: Not unless I met them face to face.

The all-Hispanic jury no doubt listened intently to this new racial element interjected into the trial. Yee Shun returned to the stand and denied shooting Jim Lee, but the damage had been done and the defense never recovered. Green called J. C. Minner, whom he mistakenly believed could impeach the previous testimony of Hesser. This tactic backfired when Minner could not verify that Hesser ran a "fancy house," although Franklin said Hesser had a bad reputation. The defense rested.[29]

The jury could not help but be confused. A murder had occurred, but there was conflicting testimony over who had weapons, who was present, who had seen the murder, and who had fired the shots. Identity of the witnesses and accuracy of the interpreters also was doubtful. There also was question whether the fundamental legal basis upon which testimony could be heard was satisfied, and it was this latter issue that proved to be the basis of Yee Shun's appeal. Despite the uncertainties, the jury found Yee Shun guilty of second degree murder, and Judge Axtell sentenced him to life in prison. Yee Shun was removed from the courtroom and transported to the Kansas State Penitentiary where he awaited his appeal.[30]

Yee Shun's attorney filed an appeal with the New Mexico Territory Supreme Court upon conclusion of the trial. Green argued that oath-taking in an American court required the belief in Judeo-Christian traditions or in a life hereafter. Because Chinaman admitted he was "of the Chinese religion," judicial error occurred when Judge Axtell allowed his testimony. The court, composed of justices Axtell, Joseph Bell, and Warren Bristol, met, heard arguments, and in January 1884, decided against Yee Shun. Chief Justice Axtell did not participate in the opinion, which was authored by Bell, a former New York attorney who handled the judicial business of the Second District headquartered in Albuquerque. Judge Bristol, originally from Minnesota, assigned to the Third District centered in Taos, and who would die unexpectedly later that year in Deming, concurred. Knowledge of anti-Chinese activities in Silver City and Raton no doubt had reached both Bell and Bristol by the time they heard the *Yee Shun* case.[31]

The primary basis for appeal concerned the examination of Chinaman's fitness to take an oath. After reciting his testimony and the questions Green and Breeden had asked, Bell concluded that no reversible error had been committed in the trial and that the record did not show the witness to be incompetent.[32]

Bell went further, however. He noted that Chinaman had not been quizzed on his specific religious beliefs. Bell adopted the maxims found in *Greenleaf on Evidence* suggesting a twofold test: 1) if the witness is not a Christian, then the court can inquire into the custom used in oath-taking in the witness' home country; 2) if the witness takes an oath, then attorneys may ask if the witness believes the oath to be binding on his conscience. "The defect of religious belief is never presumed," Bell declared. "It is, therefore, incumbent on the party objecting to the competency of a witness on this ground to *show want of religious belief as to render him incompetent. . . .*" Moreover, Bell ruled, such evidence must be evidence aliunde. In other words, outside sources must be used to impeach the witness.[33] It was not enough for Green to prove Chinaman did not believe in Judeo-Christian principles. Green should have called witnesses establishing Chinese oath-taking customs and Chinese religious beliefs. Not doing so allowed Chinaman's testimony to stand.

Twenty-two-year-old Yee Shun was in Leavenworth, Kansas, when he heard the results of his appeal. Life imprisonment awaited him without recourse. The prospect may have proved to be too much for him for on September 11, 1884, sometime during the morning, Yee Shun committed suicide, hanging himself with a small cord taken from his bed.[34]

Territory of New Mexico v. Yee Shun proved to be an important legal hallmark in the relationship between the Chinese and American law and a significant social and political development among Chinese in the American West. These generalizations were as much a product of historical circumstance, however, as of substantive legal change.

The early 1880s were not easy times for Chinese living in the American West. Anti-Chinese violence and cultural attacks already had begun in the rural West and were spreading to the cities. Moreover, violence within Chinese communities was escalating. Early Chinese communities, especially in California, sought to maintain cultural identities and order from within. Based upon blood and region, social organizations such as the Six Companies evolved and sought to protect Chinese culture, religion, economic freedoms, and legal rights.[35] Three of the Six Companies—Kong Chow (through Sam Lee), Hip Wo (through Jo Chinaman), and Sam Yup (through Yee Shun) were represented at the trial.[36]

Chinese also were members of other social organizations, such as benevolent societies, trade groups, and lodges. Such groups concentrated in parlors or halls called "tongs." Much misunderstanding by nineteenth-century non-Chinese Americans occurred over the role of tongs. Writes Shih-Shan Henry Tsai:

> it was difficult for outsiders to distinguish a militant tong from a pacific one. This difficulty was compounded by overlapping membership, since many people belonged to more than one tong. A respectable merchant, for instance, had automatic membership in one of the Six Companies; he probably held membership in one or two benevolent tongs. He might also join a secret society tong for protection against fighting tongs. Economic motives and the preservation of clan prestige were the most important causes of tong violence.[37]

Tong wars arose throughout the West in the 1880s. At first the Six Companies tried to prevent the violence. The trial record of the *Yee Shun* case suggests tong economic violence in Las Vegas over the control of the laundry business and an early attempt by the Six Companies to stop it. Most of the witnesses immediately left Las Vegas after the murder of Jim Lee, and yet they were encouraged to return for the trial. There is evidence of payments, free lodging, coercion, and influence from Denver and San Francisco Chinese. Even Jo Chinaman came forward to testify after refusing to participate initially.[38]

A fundamental question remains: Why would the Six Companies wish to have the John Lee laundry incident tried openly in court? Perhaps the situation was out of hand in New Mexico, and leaders could not control the violence through informal pressures. Perhaps no agreement could be reached among the three companies involved, and neutral parties forced a public hearing. Whatever the reason, the Yee Shun trial marked an early attempt by the Six Companies to quell intra-Chinese violence. This early example of Chinese cooperation to prevent further incidents proved futile as tong violence increased, eventually culminating in a major San Francisco feud in 1886 that caused heavy loss of property and lives.[39]

Although the Six Companies did not prevent future violence through the Yee Shun trial, the court action did result in a significant legal precedent. Prior to *Yee*

Shun, the legal right of Chinese to testify in American courts was unclear. The stumbling block was the oath. After *Yee Shun,* Chinese clearly could testify in open court, but the cost was high. Chinese cultural and religious practices could be scrutinized by attorneys before non-Chinese juries, and racial and cultural discrimination was deemed appropriate. Non-Chinese did not have to submit to such treatment when they used American court systems.[40]

The *Yee Shun* precedent held sway throughout most of the trans-Mississippi West for Chinese litigants, and it was even used to apply to other Asian-American minorities. In 1909 the Nebraska Supreme Court invoked *Territory of New Mexico v. Yee Shun* to determine if a Japanese witness, Jack Naoi, could be disqualified "for the alleged reason that Japan is a heathen country." Because counsel did not determine whether the witness practiced Buddhism or Shintoism or establish Japanese customs on oath-taking, Justice Jesse L. Root ruled that Naoi was presumed competent to testify. The *Yee Shun* rule prevailed.[41]

Thus, when Yee Shun got off the train in Las Vegas that fateful night and walked to John Lee's laundry, he unknowingly became an important participant in developing Chinese legal relationships. Race and law collided in the courtroom, and the compromised outcome, although adopted as the law of the West, would prove unsettling, particularly to the Chinese. Western America's legal precedents were no more colorblind than those made by other nineteenth- and early-twentieth-century judiciaries and legislatures in the United States.

NOTES

1. See Milton R. Konvitz, *The Alien and the Asiatic in American Law* (Ithaca: Cornell University Press, 1946) and John R. Wunder, "The Chinese and the Courts in the Pacific Northwest: Justice Denied?" *Pacific Historical Review,* 52 (May 1983), 191–211; John R. Wunder, "Law and Chinese in Frontier Montana," *Montana, The Magazine of Western History,* 30 (Summer 1980), 18–30; and John R. Wunder, "The Courts and the Chinese in Frontier Idaho," *Idaho Yesterdays,* 25 (Spring 1981), 23–32; 3 New Mexico Reports (record of court proceedings), 100 (1884). See also 2 Pacific Reporter 80 (1884).

2. For an introduction of the *Yee Shun* case, see John R. Wunder, "Chinese in Trouble: Criminal Law and Race on the Trans-Mississippi West Frontier," *Western Historical Quarterly,* 17 (January 1986), 25–41.

3. Colorado, *Colorado Constitution,* Article II, Section 4 (1876); Iowa, *Iowa Constitution,* Article I, Section 4 (1857); Nebraska, *Nebraska Constitution,* Article I, Section IV (1875); Nevada, *Nevada Constitution,* Article I, Section 4 (1864); Oregon, *Oregon Constitution,* Article I, Section 67 (1859); Texas, *Texas Constitution,* Article I, Section 5 (1876); California, *California Code of Civil Procedure,* Section 2096 (1872); Arkansas, *Arkansas Constitution,* Article XIX, Section 1 (1874).

4. See Arizona, *Arizona Revised Statues,* Section 1866 and 2037 (1887); Colorado, *Colorado Annotated Statutes,* Section 4821 (1891); Idaho, *Idaho Constitution,* Article I, Section 4 (1899); Montana, *Montana Constitution,* Article III, Section 4 (1889); Nebraska, *Nebraska Compiled Statutes,* Section 5939 (1899); New Mexico Territory, *New*

Mexico Compiled Laws, Section 3015 (1897); North Dakota, *North Dakota Constitution*, Article I, Section 4 (1889); Oklahoma Territory, *Oklahoma Statutes*, Section 4229 (1893); Texas, *Texas Penal Code*, Section 776 (1895); Utah, *Utah Constitution*, Article I, Section 4 (1895); Wyoming, *Wyoming Constitution*, Article I, Section 18 (1889). States attempting to restrict the *Yee Shun* decision included Arkansas, *Arkansas Statues*, Section 2924 (1894); Kansas, *Kansas General Statutes*, Chapter 95, Section 351 (1897); Minnesota, *Minnesota General Statutes*, Section 5665 (1894); Missouri, *Missouri Revised Statutes*, Section 8842 (1899); Washington, *Washington Code and Statutes*, Section 6057 (1897). Only Louisiana continued to bar Chinese testimony if a Chinese witness refused to certify belief in God, Louisiana, *Louisiana Criminal Proceedings*, Section 478 (1894).

    5. This essay follows a legal biographical approach tracing the "lifespan" of a legal dispute. For other models, see James R. McGovern, *Anatomy of a Lynching: The Killing of Claude Neal* (Baton Rouge: Louisiana State University Press, 1982); Marc A. Franklin, *The Biography of a Legal Dispute: An Introduction to American Civil Procedure* (Mineola, New York: Foundation Press, 1968); and Anthony Lewis, *Gideon's Trumpet* (New York: Alfred A. Knopf, 1964); and John R. Wunder, "Constitutional Oversight: *Clark v. Bazadone* and the Territorial Court as the Court of Last Resort," *The Old Northwest*, 4 (September 1978), 259–84.

    6. Warren Beck and Ynez D. Haase, *Historical Atlas of New Mexico* (Norman: University of Oklahoma Press, 1969), 45–46, 53, 58, 62.

    7. F. Stanley, *The Las Vegas Story* (Denver: World Press, 1951), 179; *Sanborn Maps of New Mexico*, Las Vegas, San Miguel County, 1890, Section 4. Laundries were located at 311, 411 ½, 419 ½, and 421 on Grand Avenue and 10 Lincoln Avenue. The laundry located at 411-1/2 Grand was the site of the murder.

    8. Francis A. Walker, *Tenth Census of the United States, 1880: Population* (Washington, D.C.: 1880), 38–39; *Deming Headlight*, September 28, 1888.

    9. *Silver City Enterprise*, November 27, 1885, December 11 and 25, 1885, January 1, 15, and 22, 1886. See also Roger Daniels, ed., *Anti-Chinese Violence in North America* (New York: Arno Press, 1978) and Elmer Clarence Sandmeyer, *The Anti-Chinese Movement in California* (Urbana: University of Illinois Press, 1939).

    10. Prisoner Ledgers A & E, Number 2763, Kansas State Penitentiary Records, Kansas State Archives, Topeka, Kansas.

    11. *Territory of New Mexico v. Yee Shun* (1882); trial transcript, 49–55, 111–33, San Miguel County District Court Records, New Mexico State Archives, Santa Fe.

    12. *Ibid.*, 59–60, 113–36.

    13. *Ibid.*, 49–76, 86–111.

    14. *Ibid.*, 59–60, 107, 133–36.

    15. *Ibid.*, 1–14, 16–20, 77–80, 136–43.

    16. Criminal Record Book A, United States District Court of New Mexico Territory, San Miguel County, New Mexico State Archives, Santa Fe, 88; Criminal Record Book A, 90–91, 95, 99, 101, 115. See also Walter J. Donlon, "LeBaron Bradford Prince, Chief Justice and Governor of New Mexico Territory, 1879-1893" (doctoral dissertation, University of New Mexico, 1967).

    17. Criminal Record Book A, 115–16, 160–61.

    18. *Yee Shun* trial transcript, 1–14.

    19. *Ibid.*, 14–24, 24–26.

    20. *Ibid.*, 26–28.

21. *Ibid.*, 34–36, 38, 47.

22. *Ibid.*, 49, 50–51.

23. *Ibid.*, 54, 55–63, 75.

24. *Ibid.*, 65–71, 80–81.

25. *Ibid.*, 77, 85.

26. *Ibid.*, 86–133.

27. *Ibid.*, 109–10.

28. *Ibid.*, 137.

29. *Ibid.*, 168–75.

30. Prisoner Ledgers, Kansas State Penitentiary Records. New Mexico sent its felony prisoners to Kansas because New Mexico did not have a secure prison facility.

31. 3 New Mexico Reports 100 (1884); 2 Pacific Reports iv (1884).

32. 3 New Mexico Reports 100 (1884).

33. Italics added, 3 NM 100 at 103 (1884). See also Henry Campbell Black, *Black's Law Dictionary* (St. Paul: West Publishing, 1968), 97–98.

34. Leavenworth *Times*, September 12, 1884, p. 4.

35. Alexander Saxton, *The Indispensable Enemy: Labor and the Anti-Chinese Movement in California* (Berkeley: University of California Press, 1971), 7–9; Shih-Shan Henry Tsai, *The Chinese Experience in America* (Bloomington: Indiana University Press, 1986), 45–51; Shih-Shan Henry Tsai, *China and the Overseas Chinese in the United States, 1868–1911* (Fayetteville: University of Arkansas Press, 1983), 31–42. See also Sucheng Chan, "Chinese Livelihood in Rural California: The Impact of Economic Change, 1860–1880," *Pacific Historical Review*, 53 (August 1984), 272–307.

36. *Yee Shun* trial transcript, 49–76, 80–81, 86–136, 143–68.

37. Tsai, *Chinese Experience*, 51, 54.

38. *Yee Shun*, trial transcript, 49–76.

39. Tsai, *Chinese Experience*, 54–55.

40. John Henry Wigmore, A *Treatise on the System of Evidence in Trials at Common Law* (4 vols., Boston: Little, Brown, 1904), III: 2365–71. See also Edward W. Cleary, ed., *McCormick on Evidence* (St. Paul: West Publishing, 1972), 141–42.

41. *Pumphrey v. State* 122 Northwest Reporter 19 at 20 (1909), 122 Northwest Reporter 19 at 21 (1909). The former case also is found at 84 Nebraska Report 36 (1909).

9

The Chinese in Texas

Edward J. M. Rhoads

Since their arrival in this country more than a century ago, the Chinese have, despite their inconsequential numbers, attracted an extraordinary amount of attention from their fellow Americans, often as targets of nativist hostility or as picturesque objects of curiosity. Much of what has been written about the Chinese in America has hitherto focused on their tribulations in the late nineteenth century in the western states. Relatively little is known about their experiences in other places, such as Texas. The Chinese in Texas were only a small minority, never more than 2 percent, of the Chinese in America; nevertheless, their history closely paralleled that of the Chinese elsewhere. This study traces their development from 1870 to 1970 through four periods, during each of which they were, by coincidence, concentrated in a different county of the state.[1]

The Chinese first came to Texas as part of their initial mass exodus out of the west coast made possible by the completion of the transcontinental railroad in May, 1869 (see table 9.1). Those who headed for Texas came in particular to take advantage of the critical labor shortage that prevailed throughout much of the South after the Civil War. Many white southerners were then convinced that their recently emancipated slaves could no longer be depended upon and were seeking an alternative source of cheap labor. One solution, developed and publicized at a convention of southern planters and railroad financiers in Memphis in July, 1869, was to import the needed workers from China, whose entry into the United States at that time was not yet hindered by immigration restrictions. In the wake of the Memphis convention, Chinese labor contractors from San Francisco, such as Cornelius Koopmanschap and Kim Wing, toured the South to explain the arrangements and to take orders. In Texas, Koopmanschap offered to supply any number of Chinese for five-year terms at a rate of eight to ten dollars gold a month for field hands and fifteen dollars for railroad workers, both with board.[2]

Opinion in Texas generally, though not universally, favored the Memphis proposal. While the Dallas *Herald* bitterly warned against "filling our fields and work shops and railroad lines with the offal of China and other idolatrous lands beyond

Table 9.1 The Chinese in the United States and in Texas, 1860–1970

	Total Chinese population in United States	Chinese in Texas as percentage of Chinese in U.S.	Chinese population in Texas	Total Population in Texas	Chinese as percentage of total population in Texas	Males per 100 females among Chinese in Texas	Urban-rural ratio among Chinese in Texas	Foreign born as percentage of Chinese in Texas
1860	34,933	—	—	604,215	—	—	—	—
1870	63,199	0.04%	25	818,579	0.003%	n.a.	n.a.	n.a.
1880	105,465	0.1%	136	1,591,749	0.01%	6,700.0	n.a.	n.a.
1880	107,488	0.7%	710	2,235,527	0.03%	5,816.7	n.a.	n.a.
1900	89,863	0.9%	836	3,048,710	0.03%	6,330.8	n.a.	n.a.
1910	71,531	0.8%	595	3,896,542	0.02%	4,476.9	88.1%	82.4%
1920	61,639	1.3%	773	4,663,228	0.02%	1,256.1	75.7%	70.5%
1930	74,954	0.9%	703	5,824,715	0.01%	347.8	95.3%	58.7%
1940	77,504	1.3%	1,031	6,414,824	0.02%	274.9	96.0%	50.9%
1950	117,629	2.0%	2,435	7,711,194	0.03%	167.9	87.2%	n.a.
1960	237,292[a]	1.8%	4,172	9,579,677	0.04%	132.7	97.5%	46.0%
1970	435,062[a]	1.8%	7,635	11,196,730	0.07%	114.3	97.0%	49.9%

n.a. = not available.

[a]Includes Hawaii.

Source: U.S. Department of the Interior, Census Office, *Ninth Census—Volume I: The Statistics of the Population of the United States . . .* (Washington, D.C., 1872), Table 1, 8; ibid., *Statistics of the Population of the United States at the Tenth Census (June 1, 1880) . . .* (Washington, D.C., 1883), Table V, 408–411; U.S., Department of Commerce, Bureau of the Census, *Thirteenth Census of the United States, Taken in the Year 1910: Volume III: Population, 1910 . . .* (Washington, D.C., 1913), Texas, Table 15, p. 803; ibid., *Sixteenth Census of the United States: 1940: Population: Volume II: Characteristics of the Population . . .: Part 6: Pennsylvania-Texas* (Washington, D.C., 1943), Texas, Table 6, p. 764; ibid., *A Report of the Seventeenth Decennial Census of the United States: Census of Population: 1950: Volume II: Characteristics of the Population . . .: Part 43: Texas* (Washington, D.C., 1952), Table 14, p. 63; ibid., *The Eighteenth Decennial Census of the United States: Census of the Population: 1960: Volume I: Characteristics of the Population . . .: Part I: United States Summary* (Washington, D.C., 1964), Table 44, pp. 144–145; ibid., *Part 45: Texas* (Washington, D.C., 1963), Table 1, p. 19, Table 15, p. 64, Table 99, p. 680; U.S., Department of Commerce, Bureau of the Census, *1970 Census of Population: Volume I: Characteristics of the Population: Part I: United States Summary, Section I* (Washington, D.C., 1973), Table 48, p. 262; ibid.; *Part 45: Texas, Section I* (Washington, D.C., 1973), Table 17, p. 103, Table 18, p. 104; ibid., *Section 2*, Table 139, pp. 1269–1270.

the Western ocean" and vilified the Chinese as "miserable yellow imbecile dwarfs," the Galveston *News*, the state's leading paper, expressed the more representative view. It carried an endorsement of the Chinese as "the best, cheapest and most reliable laborers ever known." The *News* argued, moreover, that they would have a salutary effect upon the emancipated slaves: "When the negro once finds out it is work or starve he will not hesitate long between the two. Welcome then, John Chinaman.[3]

In Texas, the initial demand for Chinese laborers came from the railroad companies, anxious to resume construction after the Civil War. Late in 1869, the Memphis, El Paso and Pacific Railroad arranged with Koopmanschap for a gang of five hundred Chinese rail hands to be employed on its line in northeast Texas near Jefferson. By the end of the year, newspapers in the state were announcing the imminent arrival of the Chinese. However, evidently because of last minute financial difficulties on the part of the railroad, they never appeared.[4]

The first Chinese actually to reach Texas—they were also the first large contingent to arrive in the entire South—came instead to work on the Houston and Texas Central, then the biggest railroad company in the state. On November 10, 1869, the company, through its agent John G. Walker, signed a contract with the San Francisco labor contractor Chew Ah Heang for three hundred workers. Two months later they were in Texas. They had come from California via Council Bluffs, St. Louis, and New Orleans, arriving by train in Houston around January 10, 1870. From Houston they proceeded directly to the H.&T.C. railroad at Calvert, in Robertson County, and began work at once extending the line toward Corsicana and ultimately Dallas. Their first project was the eighteen-mile stretch from Bremond to Thornton.[5]

The Chinese work gang on the H.&T.C. numbered between 247 and 267. It was, with but one exception, an all male crew, composed mostly of young men in their late twenties. According to the contract, the workers were paid twenty dollars silver a month; additionally, they were furnished at the company's expense a specified daily ration as well as lodging in tents and huts. In return, they worked twenty-six days a month, probably mostly as graders preparing the right of way.[6]

On the job and off, the Chinese generally kept to themselves. They had their own Chinese foremen, each responsible for one hundred workers. They lived at their own camps and ate their own kind of food, consisting of rice, pork, dried fish, vegetables, and tea. Though at least one of the foremen was fluent in English, most of the laborers evidently spoke only Chinese. They dressed, even in winter, in light cotton blouses and loose pants, wore straw hats shaped like "inverted washbowls," and plaited their hair in the customary queue. Finally, they observed their own holidays, such as the Lunar New York celebrated at Bremond at the end of January, 1870, when "In full Chinese costume, including large umbrellas, they promenaded the streets, 'to the delight of the juveniles without distinction of race or color.' "[7]

This, however, was one of the few occasions on which the Chinese literally went to town. They seldom appeared in Calvert, and when they did they rarely patronised the local merchants. Their obvious indifference to acculturation and, more particularly, their all male composition suggest that they, like the other Chinese in America at the time, were only "sojourners," who did not intend to settle down and become permanent residents. Instead, their aim was primarily economic: to earn enough money to pay off the debt they had incurred in securing passage to the United States in the first place and then to save for their eventual return, hopefully in wealth, to China and to the families they had left behind.[8]

The Chinese on the Houston and Texas Central were, as advertised, good workers, industrious and docile. Theodore Kosse, chief engineer of the railroad, commented a month after their arrival that the Chinese "have, so far, proved themselves fully equal to any other class of laborers in the work of construction." According to the Calvert *Enterprise*, "They remain at camps during resting hours, are not addicted to drunkenness, and for this reason will doubtless count more full time than the Irish or negro laborers employed on the road."[9]

Yet, despite such initial comments, the Chinese actually worked on the line for only six months rather than the three years for which they had been hired. In July, 1870, the *Enterprise*, reversing its previous assessment, reported that "The Chinese at work on the Central Railroad are said to be very lazy and trifling, requiring constant watching. They do not average more than half as much as a hard working white man, and 'play off,' 'shirk,' 'soldier,' or whatever you may call it, to perfection." A month later, the paper claimed that "the company would like to get rid of them." The Bremond correspondent for the Waco *Register* similarly described "the Chinese laborers on the Central Railroad a failure."[10]

How the industrious workers of February had become "worthless" by July is a mystery. One reason for the company's change of attitude may have been that their mere presence upset some of the other laborers, such as the 150 Irishmen who reportedly left their jobs rather than work alongside the "pig-tailed Chinese." Another reason may have been financial. In mid-1870 the company encountered certain difficulties leading to a slowdown in construction and so may have been anxious to cut expenditures by reneging on its Chinese labor contract. Whatever the reason, by the beginning of September, according to the Bryan *Appeal*, the Chinese "have all quit work, and have entered suit against their employers for wages and for a failure of compliance with contract." It is unclear what happened to this suit, but the road was afterwards completed to Dallas in July, 1872, without the further use of Chinese labor.[11]

Because the railroad company is not likely to have shipped them back to San Francisco as their contract had stipulated, it appears that many of the 250-odd Chinese workers discharged by the H.&T.C. at first simply remained where they were. By November, 1870, only a few months later, some Chinese had found employment on James Scott Hanna's cotton farm in the rich Brazos River bottom land just west of Calvert. From then until at least 1882 a number of Chinese worked on the Hanna property as sharecroppers and field hands. Several of Hanna's contracts with the Chinese farmers are extant. One contract, dated December 13, 1872, provided for Sin Yong and John See to farm thirty acres of his land, twenty in cotton and ten in corn, with half of both crops going to Hanna and the other half going to the two Chinese. Another contract a year later provided for a group of seventeen Chinese to work as field hands and cotton pickers at a monthly wage of between fifteen and eighteen dollars, board included. Others in the Calvert area, such as John H. Drennan, likewise employed Chinese on their farms.[12]

Not all of the Chinese cotton farmers in Calvert, however, were former H.&T.C. laborers. As some of the original field hands moved away, the plantation owners began replenishing their work force with Chinese brought directly from China or perhaps, what was more likely, from Cuba. The J. H. Hanna family, for example, imported an additional fifty-nine Chinese laborers through the port of Galveston in September, 1874. By 1880, judging by the median age (thirty) of the Chinese in Robertson County at that time, most of the displaced railroad workers, who by then would have been almost ten years older than this, were gone and had been replaced by these new arrivals.[13]

Thus, for the first ten years of their presence in Texas, the Chinese were heavily concentrated in Robertson County. In 1880, when Texas reported a total of 136 Chinese, over half of them (72) were located in that one county. The rest were thinly scattered across the northeastern quadrant of the state, as only two other counties, Galveston and Travis, had a population of ten or more Chinese (see table 9.2). Whereas the Chinese elsewhere in the state generally lived in urban areas and operated laundries, those in Robertson County were, with but one exception (a "huckster"), all farmers or farm laborers. As such, of course, they were a rural population, living mostly on the outskirts of Calvert and Hearne. They were all males, as were all but one of the Chinese elsewhere in the state. Despite their median age, only four of the Chinese in Robertson County were married and living with their wives, none of whom, of course, was Chinese. This highly abnormal situation developed and was perpetuated partly because of the antipathy of the local populace, particularly the whites, toward interracial marriages. Thus, of the four Chinese who were married, three were married to blacks and only one to a white. But probably a more important reason was the "sojourner" attitude that persisted among the Chinese themselves.[14]

With the Chinese "bachelors" gradually dying off or drifting away either to return to China or simply to go elsewhere, but also because the end of Reconstruction eliminated the demand for Chinese as substitutes for blacks, who were again coming under white control, the Chinese population in Robertson County steadily declined after 1880 until it disappeared from the census enumeration around 1940 (see Table 9.2). Since the few who had settled down had had no alternative but to intermarry with local residents, their offspring were not classified in the census as Chinese but, depending on the mother, as either "mulatto" or "white." Consequently, when the Chinese progenitors of such mixed families died off, so apparently did the Chinese of the county. But some of their descendants, such as the Yepp

Table 9.2 The Chinese in Selected Counties in Texas, 1870–1970

	Robertson	El Paso	Bexar	Harris	Dallas	Travis	Tarrant	Galveston	Jefferson	McLennan
1870 (2)[a]	3	0	0	0	0	0	0	0	0	0
1880 (3)	72	0	0	7	6	10	3	15	0	3
1890 (14)	38	225	46	8	63	8	40	42	0	11
1900 (11)	26	336	54	43	24	22	23	68	4	22
1910 (11)	5	253	63	11	16	14	59	46	12	17
1920 (9)	5	137	283	49	11	26	86	36	36	12
1930 (9)	1	181	321	31	10	29	40	16	15	3
1940 (12)	n.a.	213	488	121	22	34	28	16	12	12
1950 (21)	n.a.	245	656	620	227	86	69	46	18	26
1960 (25)	0	285	938	1,874	236	94	117	49	27	49
1970 (40)	0	332	1,052	3,677	711	332	245	56	40	66

n.a. = not available

[a]Number of counties with ten or more Chinese given in parentheses.

Sources: U.S., Department of the Interior, Census Office, *Statistics of the Population of the United States at the Tenth Census (June 1, 1881)* . . . (Washington, D.C., 1883), Table V, 408–411; U.S., Department of Commerce, Bureau of the Census, *Thirteenth Census of the United States Taken in the Year 1910: Volume III: Population, 1910* . . . (Washington, D.C., 1913), Texas, Table 15, p. 803; ibid., *Fifteenth Census of the United States: 1930: Population: Volume III, Part 2* . . . *Montana-Wyoming* (Washington, D.C., 1932), Texas, Table 17, pp. 1014–1015; ibid., *Sixteen Census of the United States: 1940: Population. Volume II: Characteristics of the Population* . . . : *Part 6: Pennsylvania-Texas* (Washington, D.C., 1943), Texas, Table 25, p. 904; ibid., *A Report of the Seventeenth Decennial Census of the United States: Census of Population: 1950: Volume II: Characteristics of the Population* . . . : *Part 43: Texas* (Washington, D.C., 1952), Table 47, p. 280; ibid., *The Eighteenth Decennial Census of the United States: Census of Population: 1960: Volume I: Characteristics of the Population* . . . : *Part 45: Texas* (Washington, D.C., 1963), Table 28, pp. 245–263; ibid, *1970 Census of Population: Volume I: Characteristics of the Population: Part 45: Texas, Section I* (Washington, D.C., 1973), Table 34, pp. 264–271.

family of Calvert, did in fact remain, even though they had been largely absorbed into the local population. Therefore, the decline of the Chinese in Robertson County was not quite so complete as the census would suggest.[15]

In 1881, as the first group of Chinese immigrants to Texas began to pass from the scene, a second contingent of several thousand entered the state. Like the first

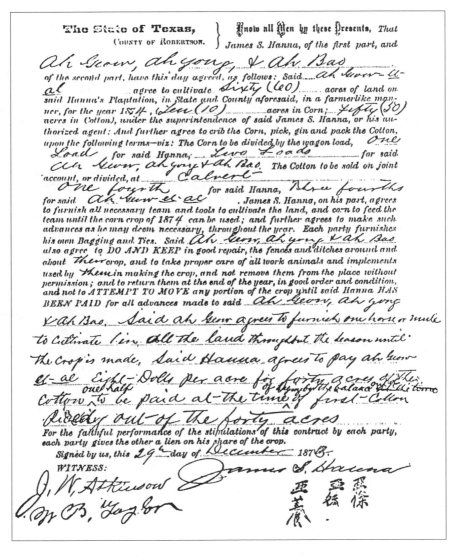

Figure 9.1   An 1874 contract between sharecroppers Ah Geow, Ah Yong, and Ah Bao and plantation owner James Scott Hanna. Courtesy of the Alamo Library and Institute of Texan Cultures.

group, they arrived as railroad builders from the west. This time they came with the Southern Pacific Railroad, which, threading its way from Los Angeles, reached El Paso in May, 1881. From El Paso, the road continued eastward for another 460 miles to the Pecos River, where on January 12, 1883, it joined tracks with the Galveston, Harrisburg and San Antonio Railway to become the nation's second transcontinental line. The vast majority of the Southern Pacific work force were Chinese. As they neared the end of the line, the Chinese accounted for some 2,600 of approximately 3,000 laborers; moreover, they did "all [the] work except to drive the big teams. . . ."[16]

For the Chinese rail hands, life was difficult in the desolate and rugged trans-Pecos region of West Texas. Their supervisor was "burly, domineering" J. H. Strobridge, who fifteen years earlier had spurred their fellow countrymen on the first transcontinental road to their legendary feats in the Sierra Nevada. Under Strobridge, the San Antonio *Light* reported, "The Chinese are treated more like slaves than anything else, they are drove [sic] round and sometimes used severely, if they don't work to suit the bosses." In addition, the Chinese again had to contend with the hostility of other railroad workers. On one occasion, Mexican section hands outside El Paso beat up a group of them and ran them off. On another, an Irish laborer near the Pecos murdered one of them, giving rise to Judge Roy Bean's notorious finding that there was no law in Texas against "killing a Chinaman." Yet other hazards confronted them. On December 31, 1881, a band of Apache Indians swept down upon a surveying gang of eleven Chinese at Eagle Pass and killed them all.[17]

When the railroad was completed in 1883, most of the Southern Pacific work force was withdrawn to Arizona and California. Some of the workers, however, remained behind in the state. They were soon joined by other Chinese, many of whom were fleeing eastward by rail from the virulent anti-Chinese agitation then current throughout the Far West. In either case, the new railroad brought about a large increase in the Chinese population in Texas, from 136 in 1880 to 710 in 1890. The number of counties with ten or more Chinese also jumped from three to fourteen (see Table 9.2). In the meantime, however, as part of the anti-Chinese movement, Congress in 1882 had passed the first of the Chinese exclusion acts. Thereafter, in a sharp departure from the traditional American policy of unrestricted immigration for every nationality, all Chinese, excepting only merchants, teachers, students, and travelers, were barred from entering the country. Because of the exclusion laws, the Chinese population in Texas began to decline around 1900; it was down to 595 in 1910 (see Table 9.1). It also contracted spatially, as the number of counties with ten or more Chinese dropped from fourteen in 1890 to eleven in 1900 and 1910 (see Table 9.2).[18]

The Chinese during this period congregated mostly in railroad centers, ranging from the large established cities in East and Central Texas to the small boom towns out west. Indeed, because the new rail connections with California ran through the region, West Texas attracted a disproportionate number of the new arrivals, with most of the immigrants flocking especially to El Paso. Located at the gateway to the West and served by both the Southern Pacific and the Texas and Pacific (as well as by the Mexican Central), El Paso from 1881 on replaced Robertson as the county with the largest Chinese population in the state. It remained so until 1917, during which time its share of the Chinese in Texas ranged from 32 percent in 1890 to 43 percent in 1910 (see Table 9.2).[19]

The Chinese in El Paso engaged in a variety of occupations, some of which, such as laundries and cafes, were characteristic of their compatriots all over the state. Throughout most of this thirty-seven-year period the Chinese practically monopolized the clothes washing business in El Paso, owning thirteen out of fifteen laundries in 1886 and twelve out of sixteen in 1907. The Chinese elsewhere were similarly dominant. Twenty or more Chinese hand laundries existed in each of the state's biggest cities in the 1880s and 1890s; in Galveston in 1893, for example, thirty-two out of thirty-six laundries were Chinese. At the same time, Chinese laundries in twos and threes were also located in many of the state's smaller cities, such as Corsicana, Denison, Cleburne, San Angelo, and Amarillo. The Chinese went into the laundry business because it was generally considered woman's work and did not compete with male wage earners and also because it did not require a large capital investment from the Chinese. In the 1890s, however, the hand laundry began losing out to the steam laundry, to which the Chinese, in Texas at least, were never able to adjust, probably on account of the expensive equipment. In Galveston, the number of Chinese laundries dropped from thirty-two in 1893 to nineteen in 1901 and then to eight in 1911. Only in El Paso did Chinese domination of the laundry business persist well beyond the 1890s.[20]

The Chinese also owned a sizable share of the restaurants in El Paso: three out of twelve in 1886; five out of eleven in 1892; and thirteen out of sixty-six in 1907. These were essentially chop houses serving meat-and-potato dishes, as American tastes did not yet take to Chinese cooking. Chinese-run cafes were a familiar feature of other Texas cities too. They were usually located near the railroad station, catering to those who either worked on or traveled by trains. Sam Mar Dock's Cotton Belt Restaurant in Tyler, for example, was situated directly opposite the depot and was a favorite eating place for the railwaymen.[21]

Finally, apart from some who worked as train wipers and the like for the railroad companies, the Chinese in El Paso were involved in a substantial way with truck farming also. They grew the vegetables in the outskirts, then peddled them from wagons in the city streets. Indeed, in 1893 the "garden vegetable business" along with the laundries were the two lines of trade in which the Chinese were said to have a virtual monopoly.[22]

Despite their involvement with truck farming, the Chinese of El Paso County were, unlike those of Robertson County earlier, overwhelmingly an urban population, as 90 percent—228 out of 253 in 1910—lived within the city limits of El Paso. This urban concentration was characteristic of the Chinese statewide as well and stood in marked contrast with the general population of the state, which was then 76 percent rural. Numerically, in the 1890s, when the city was still rather small, they amounted to 2 to 4 percent of the city's population. They were at that time sufficiently numerous and concentrated to form a Chinatown.[23]

El Paso's Chinatown centered on South Oregon Street between Overland and Second Street (now Paisano), not far from the Southern Pacific depot. Here in this two-block-long area were located the boarding houses where many of the Chinese lived and the Chinese merchandise stores—seven in 1892, eight in 1907—where they bought their special provisions. Here too was the lodge hall of the Chee Kung Tong (Zhigong tang), the overseas branch of the notorious Triad Society, which seems to have been the central institution of the community; in 1892 nearly half of the city's Chinese belonged to it. In this small area the Chinese pursued their own way of life, separated from the rest of El Paso. They consulted their herbalist doctors and celebrated their distinctive festivals, with the Lunar New Year never failing to attract the attention of the city's newspapers. They even had their own unofficial but universally recognized "mayor," who in the period around 1910 was the cafe-owner Mar Wing Kee.[24] Finally, they had their own burial ground. Located within Concordia Cemetery, some distance from the old Chinatown and enclosed by a separate set of walls, the Chinese Cemetery in 1973 had about a hundred marked graves, the oldest of which dated from 1915. (There may be others, perhaps older, graves that are unmarked.) It is the only Chinese cemetery in Texas.

The grave markers are an invaluable source on the makeup of Chinatown. They show that almost all of the Chinese in El Paso, as in America then, were Cantonese from the "four counties" (Siyi, Sze Yap) region of Kwangtung in South China. Specifically, over half were from Taishan (Toishan; formerly Xinning [Sunning]) County. Another 30 percent were from neighboring Kaiping (Hoiping) County, with most of the remainder split between Enping (Yanping) and Xinhui (Sunwui) counties. They also show that among the Chinese in El Paso the most common surnames were Yu (Yee), Ma (Mar) and Huang (Wong).[25]

Finally, the grave stones indicate that the El Paso Chinatown was composed almost entirely of men, as only a handful of the graves are for women. Indeed, according to a special census take in 1916, over 98 percent of the Chinese in the city—239 out of 243—were males. This condition, which had prevailed in Robertson County also, was similarly characteristic of the Chinese in the entire state; out of a statewide total of 595 Chinese in 1910, only 13 were women. Moreover, the Chinese in El Paso were practically all *adult* males, since all but 8 of the 239 men were 21 years or older.[26]

Although such a society of "bachelors" had originated largely because of the "sojourner" attitude of the pioneering Chinese themselves, it was not greatly reinforced by the new American immigration laws. Under the exclusion laws, even if they now wanted to, most of the Chinese living in the United States were forever barred from bringing their wives to join them in this country. The only exceptions were those women whose husbands belonged to one of the four categories specifically exempted from exclusion. Among the dozen or so women to settle in Texas in this period was the wife of the cafe proprietor Sam Mar Dock, who, after one of her husband's visits to Taishan County, accompanied him back to Tyler in 1910. With so few other Chinese women around, however, those who thus uprooted themselves from their familiar surroundings in China to come to America often faced a lonely, unhappy existence. As for the men who were not prosperous enough to return periodically to their families in China or who, like the laundrymen, did not belong to the exempt categories, they were cut off from normal family life for the duration of their stay in America, because, as in Robertson County earlier, intermarriage was possible but rare.[27]

During this period of anti-Chinese feelings, the rest of El Paso did not look kindly upon the Chinese in their midst. First of all, they resented the commercial success of the Chinese. The *Daily Herald,* for example, complained in 1889 that "An indulgent public has permitted the pig tails to corner the laundry business of the city," while a year later the *Times,* claiming that the Chinese were depriving white washerwomen of employment, applauded the efforts of the steam laundries to drive the hand laundries out of business. On occasion, official harassment reinforced editorial indignation, such as in September, 1893, when the police charged sixteen out of eighteen Chinese laundries with lacking the safety furnaces required by city ordinance. The Chinese share of the restaurant business also came in for criticism. Some competitors made it a part of their advertising: "the best 35¢ meals in the city—no Chinese employed." When the Chinese sent their savings back to their families in China, this too was denounced, as an unacceptable drain on the American economy.[28]

The rest of El Paso also objected to the opium dens and gambling halls that dotted Chinatown. Such establishments were characteristic of all Chinatowns, inhabited as they were by unattached males with time on their hands. But probably it was because they were patronised by many non-Chinese as well as Chinese that they drew the wrath of the press and clergy. Between 1882 and 1886 the El Paso city council passed at least three anti-opium ordinances, all of which seem to have been no more than momentarily effective. In 1893 the *Evening Tribune* once again raised the alarm: "Opium joints on South Oregon are a disgrace to our city. Is it possible that the powers that be cannot close them up?" Responding to such demands, the police repeatedly raided Chinatown, each time causing much consternation among its residents.[29]

A final reason for the popular antipathy toward Chinatown was its alleged involvement in the smuggling of Chinese into the United States in disregard of the exclusion laws. Because of its excellent rail connections on either side of the border, El Paso was throughout this period a major point of entry for Chinese attempting to sneak in by way of Mexico. Toward the end of this period, the anti-Chinese violence unleashed by the Mexican Revolution generated an additional flood of Chinese desperate to cross the border. Aided by professional smuggling rings, which reportedly charged $200 a head, the Chinese would wade across the Rio Grande from Juárez, then hide out in El Paso until they could be sent on to the north and west in sealed freight cars. Many of course were caught and deported, but many also escaped detection.[30]

The American immigration service in El Paso was convinced that the entire Chinese community was "banded together as one man" in support of these illegal activities. The chief immigration inspector, for example, charged in 1905 that "In certain alleys in El Paso houses occupied by Chinese have been constructed so that illegally resident Chinese can be concealed in chambers under the ground or spaces between the roof and ceiling." Indeed, it was commonly believed that "Chinese buildings were linked by a honeycomb of underground passages in the area of South Oregon Street, in the heart of Chinatown, which made it possible for Chinese to enter one house and exit through another house several doors or blocks away." A few underground rooms have, in fact, been excavated underneath El Paso's Chinatown, but as yet no network of subterranean passages.[31]

To cope with this alleged smuggling operation, the immigration authorities resorted to making "domiciliary visits" among the resident Chinese. These were unannounced raids and searches, including, it appears, dragnet searches. On at least one occasion, in July, 1895, federal agents rounded up the entire Chinese population in El Paso, to discover only two Chinese out of five hundred lacking the certificate of residence required by the exclusion laws. Similar searches were carried out in other towns near the border, such as in Sanderson in 1905.[32]

The Chinese, however, did not, either in El Paso or in the United States as a whole, meekly accept the harsh treatment dealt out to them, though their efforts were necessarily limited because they were, by yet another of the exclusion laws, denied the right of citizenship. In 1892, after Congress had passed the Geary Act extending for ten more years the exclusion policy and requiring the Chinese to register with the government, the Chinese Consolidated Benevolent Association in San Francisco, better known as the Six Companies, spearheaded a campaign to test the constitutionality of the act by urging the Chinese across the country not to file for the certificate of residence. The Chinese in El Paso agreed initially to go along with the campaign but in the end, for some unknown reason, failed to follow through. In Galveston, however, about half of the local Chinese, twenty-three out of fifty-six, complied with the campaign by not registering. Unfortunately, the Supreme Court eventually ruled in favor of the act. Ten years later, in 1902, the Six Companies once again opposed, with no more success, the indefinite extension of the exclusion laws. Toward the expenses of this new campaign the Chinese in El Paso contributed the not inconsiderable sum of $1,500.[33]

Meanwhile, the Chinese in American began for the first time to take an active interest in the affairs of their homeland. They came to realize that without a stronger regime in China, they could not expect any better treatment from the American government. This was the message of the various Chinese leaders who, during the decade preceding the republican revolution in 1911, crisscrossed America in search of funds and support among the scattered émigré communities. With a small Chinese population, El Paso and the rest of Texas did not figure prominently in their travels. Nevertheless, in November, 1905, the constitutional monarchist Kang You-wei visited the Chinese in San Antonio for about a week while on his way from New Orleans to Mexico.[34] The republican revolutionary leader, Sun Yat-sen, apparently never came through Texas.

The heyday of the Chinese community in El Paso was around the turn of the century. Since then the size of the Chinese population at best remained stationary, while the rest of the city grew tremendously (see Table 9.2). Whereas in 1900 the Chinese had amounted to 1.9 percent of the city's population, by 1916 they were already down to 0.4 percent. In 1970 they were an even more insignificant portion (0.09 percent) of the population. As the relative number of the Chinese in El Paso declined, so inevitably did its Chinatown. It disappeared when the Chinese "bachelors" on South Oregon Street began dying off in the late 1930s and early 1940s. As recently as 1937 or 1938 Chinatown was still essentially intact; ten years later most of it was gone. In 1947–1948, for example, the local Chee Kung Tong faded from existence. By 1970 no trace of the original Chinatown remained, though the Chinese Cemetery still existed and was still in use.[35]

In 1917, long before the El Paso Chinatown disappeared, a third wave of Chinese hit the state with the arrival of the "Pershing Chinese." These originally were among the 30,000 Chinese living in Mexico, where, as incidents like the massacre of 303 Chinese at Torreón in May, 1911, revealed, they may have fared even worse than they did north of the border. When General John J. Pershing invaded Chihuahua in March, 1916, in pursuit of Pancho Villa, most Mexicans refused, of course, to cooperate with him. Only the Chinese, embittered perhaps by their treatment in Mexico, were willing to deal with the Americans. They followed Pershing's army wherever it went and eventually gained the provost marshal's approval to set up shops, cafes, and laundries catering to the 6,000 American troops. When the time came eleven months later to withdraw the expeditionary force, its mission unaccomplished, Pershing asked for and received permission from the American immigration service to set aside the exclusion laws and bring his 527 Chinese followers, all of them men, into the United States. In June, 1917, the army moved most of the Chinese to Fort Sam Houston in San Antonio. There they remained as wards of the army until 1921, when a special act of Congress, passed at the urging of Pershing, granted the right of residence to the 365 men who were still there. Upon their release from the army, many of the refugees chose initially to stay in San Antonio.[36]

If Pershing's refugees had not entered the state, the Chinese population in Texas during the interwar years would have continued the numerical decline that went back to 1900. Even with the refugees, it continued to contract spatially, as the Chinese quietly withdrew from one after another of the state's smaller cities, from Denison to San Angelo to Sanderson, leaving behind them, as the only reminders of their former presence in such places, a few laconic entries in the old city directories and an occasional grave marker in the cemeteries. In both 1920 and 1930, only nine counties reported a population of ten or more Chinese (see Table 9.2). The demographic trends in Texas began to reverse themselves in the 1930s, during the depression, when Chinese in other parts of the country drifted to the South, reportedly in search of work. As a result, in 1940 the number of Chinese in the state was up to 1,031. Then, the repeal of the exclusion law in 1943 permitted the first substantial influx of new immigrants from China in over sixty years. The Chinese population in Texas rose again. By 1950 it was more than double what it had been in 1940, and the number of counties with ten or more Chinese residents had climbed to twenty-one (see Tables 9.1 and 9.2).[37]

With the arrival of Pershing's refugees in 1917, Bexar replaced El Paso as the county having the most Chinese; in 1940 it contained 47 percent of the state's total Chinese population. Even more so than in El Paso previously, the Chinese in Bexar County were an overwhelmingly urban community. In 1940, all but 17 of the 488 Chinese inhabitants in the county were to be found in the city of San Antonio. Elsewhere in the state at this time the Chinese were to an identical extent (96 percent) living in urban areas (see Table 9.1). San Antonio remained the center of Chinese life in Texas until the early 1950s.[38]

NOTES

1. On the Chinese in America, see Betty Lee Sung, *Mountain of Gold: The Story of the Chinese in America* (New York, 1971); Rose Hum Lee, *The Chinese in the United States of America* (Hong Kong, 1960); H. Mark Lai and Philip P. Choy, *Outlines History of the Chinese in America* (San Francisco, 1973); and Victor G. Nee and Brett de Bary Nee, *Longtime Californ': A Documentary Study of an American Chinatown* (New York, 1973). For two very brief overall accounts of the Chinese in Texas, see Houston *Chronicle*, July 14, 1968; and *People*, Newsletter of the University of Texas, Institute of Texan Cultures, II (January–February, 1972), 2, 7.

2. Gunther Barth, *Bitter Strength: A History of the Chinese in the United States 1850–1870* (Cambridge, 1964), 188–197; Etta B. Peabody, "Effort of the South to Import Chinese Coolies, 1865-1870" (M. A. thesis, Baylor University, 1967); Galveston *Tri-weekly News*, May 9, 20, 25, July 11, 25, 1870.

3. Dallas *Herald*, July 30, 1870 (first and second quotations); Galveston *Tri-weekly News*, June 9, 1869 (third quotation), January 10, 1870 (fourth quotations).

4. Koopmanschap & Co. to B. H. Epperson, November 1, 1869. B. H. Epperson Papers (Archives, University of Texas Library, Austin); Galveston *Tri-weekly News*, September 29, November 24, 1869; Dallas *Herald*, January 27, 1870.

5. Peabody, "Effort of the South to Import Chinese," 57–65; Barth, *Bitter Strength*, 196; Galveston *Tri-weekly News*, January 14, 1870; Houston *Chronicle*, January 11, 1942.

6. Memorandum of an agreement between John G. Walker and Chew-Ah-Heang, November 10, 1869, Houston and Texas Central Railway Co. (Southern Pacific Co., Houston), Record Book No. 55, pp. 20–22. (I wish to thank L. Tuilly Ellis for bringing this document to my attention). See also Peabody, "Effort of the South to Import Chinese," 57–60; Houston *Telegraph*, January 13, 1870; Galveston *Tri-weekly News*, January 19, 1870.

7. Galveston, *Tri-weekly News*, February 18 (second quotation), March 9, 1870; Houston *Telegraph*, January 13, 1870 (first quotation).

8. Galveston *Tri-weekly News*, January 19, February 16, 1870. On the Chinese as "so-journers," see Barth, *Bitter Strength*.

9. Galveston *Tri-weekly News*, February 2 (second quotation), 4, 16 (first quotation), March 9, 1870.

10. Galveston *Tri-weekly News*, July 4, 1870 (first quotation); Dallas *Herald*, July 12, (third quotation), August 20, 1870 (second quotation); Houston *Telegraph*, August 2, 1870. For a dissenting view, see Houston *Telegraph*, August 10, 1870.

11. Dallas *Herald*, February 3, 1870 (second quotation); Galveston *Daily News*, March 10, 1870; James V. Reese, "The Early History of Labor Organizations in Texas 1828–1876," *Southwestern Historical Quarterly*, LXXII (July, 1968), 14–15; Galveston *Tri-weekly News*, September 2, 1870 (third quotation).

12. Pauline Doremus and Pauline Burnitt to E. J. M. R., February 22, 1974, interview. See also the file, "Robertson county; Chinese farmers of 1870's" (Texas Historical Commission, Austin); Rufe O'Keefe, *Cowboy Life: Reminiscences of an Early Life, Early Boyhood and Experiences as a Cowboy on the Range, on the Trail, as Manager of a Ranch and then Owner and Operator in Cattle* (San Antonio, 1936), 10. For the labor contracts and related documents, see China file (Institute of Texas Cultures, San Antonio); this file will hereafter be cited as China file (ITC).

13. Texas, Bureau of Immigration, *Annual Report of the Superintendent of Immigration of the State of Texas, for the Year 1874* (Houston, 1874), 14–15 (I wish to thank Arthur Mayer for drawing this source to my attention); U.S. Department of the Interior, Census Office, Tenth Census of the United States, 1880, Population Schedule, Robertson County (microfilm; Archives, University of Texas Library, Austin). This microfilm document is hereafter cited as Tenth Census, 1880, Population Schedule (microfilm).

14. Tenth Census, 1880, Population Schedules, Anderson, Bosque, Cooke, Dallas, Galveston, Grayson, Harris, Kaufman, Tarrant, Tom Green, Travis, and Washington counties (microfilm).

15. Dallas *Morning News*, June 25, 1972; Mr. and Mrs. Johnnie Yepp to E. J. M. R., February 22, 1974, interview. See also the file, "Robertson county: Chinese farmers of 1870's"; Doris Black, "The Black Chinese," *Sepia*, XXIV (January, 1975), 18–24.

16. San Antonio *Evening Light*, August 15, 1882 (quotation): J. Morgan Broaddus, Jr., *The Legal Heritage of El Paso*, ed. Samuel D). Myers (El Paso, 1963), 134; S. G. Reed, *A History of the Texas Railroads and of Transportation Conditions under Spain and Mexico and the Republic and the State* (Houston, 1941), 197–198. Although it is frequently said that the Chinese also helped to build the Texas and Pacific Railroad, there is no hard evidence that this was in fact so. See Velma Barrett and Hazel Oliver, *Odessa: City of Dreams, a Miracle of the Texas Prairies* (San Antonio, 1952), 18; Brutus Clay Chrisman, *Early Days in Callahan County* (Abilene, 1966), 166; Betty Orbeck (ed.), "Moving West with the Texas and Pacific: From the Pages of The Dallas Weekly Herald," *The Permian Historical Annual XIII* (December, 1973), unpaginated note 12 (following p. 51).

17. On Strobridge, see Oscar Lewis, *The Big Four: The Story of Huntington, Stanford, Hopkins, and Crocker, and of the Building of the Central Pacific* (New York, 1955), 62 (first quotation), 69–101; San Antonio *Evening Light*, October 10, 1882 (second quotation): Dallas *Weekly Herald*, January 5, August 10, 1882; C. L. Sonnichsen, *Roy Bean: Law West of the Pecos* (New York, 1958); 119–123; Everett Lloyd, *Law West of the Pecos: The Story of Roy Bean* (San Antonio, 1967), 73 (third quotation).

18. San Antonio *Evening Light*, October 10, 1882; San Antonio *Daily Express*, October 13, 15, 1882. On the exclusion laws and their subsequent history, see *Sung, Mountain of Gold*, 49–47, 74–94.

19. On the Chinese in West Texas towns, see Myrtle R. Dove, "A History of Toyah, Texas" (M.A. thesis, Sul Ross State College, 1949), 27, 65–69; San Angelo *Standard-Times*, March 8, 1970. For a somewhat different account of the El Paso Chinese community than what follows, see Nancy Farrar, *The Chinese in El Paso* (El Paso, 1972).

20. See the El Paso and other city directories for this period.

21. El Paso city directories for 1886–1887, 1892–1893, and 1907; Julian MarDock, "The Levee: A Nostalgic Look at Tyler's Railside Business District," *Chronicles of Smith County, Texas*, X (Spring 1971), 44; Julian MarDock to E. J. M., May 30, 1974, interview; V. H. Whitlock, *Cowboy Life on the Llano Estacado* (Norman, 1970), 49–50.

22. *El Paso Herald*, April 5, 1893 (quotation); Chew Din to E. J. M. R., September 27, 1973, interview. See also the El Paso city directory for 1900.

23. U.S., Department of Commerce, Bureau of the Census, *Special Census of the Population of El Paso, Tex., January 15, 1916 (Washington, D.C.*, 1916), 6; ibid, *Thirteenth Census of the United States, Taken in the Year 1910: Volume III: Population, 1910. . .* (Washington, D.C. 1913), Texas, 772.

24. City of El Paso, Department of Planning, *A Short History of South El Paso* (1967), 9–11; El Paso *Daily Herald*, November 14, 1892; El Paso *Herald*, December 26, 1910; January 7, 1913; El Paso *Times*, October 18, 1927. See also the street listings in this area of town in the El Paso city directories for this period. On the Chee Kung Tong, see Lee, *Chinese in the United States*, 168–173. On the location of Chinatowns near transport terminals, see Rhoads Murphey, "Boston's Chinatown," *Economic Geography*, XXVIII (July, 1952), 247.

25. This information was collected by the author during a visit to the cemetery in September, 1973.

26. U.S., Department of Commerce, Bureau of the Census, *Special Census of the Population of El Paso, Tex., January 15, 1916*, p. 6.

27. Julian MarDock to E. J. M. R., May 30, 1974; interview; Stanford M. Lyman, *Chinese Americans* (New York, 1974), 86–89. For two instances of intermarriage in Texas, see *Austin Statesman*, November 16, 1881; Dallas *Morning News*, July 18, 19, 21, 23, 1893.

28. El Paso *Daily Herald*, February 6, 1889; El Paso *Times*, March 25, 1890; Farrar, *Chinese in El Paso*, 9 (second quotation); El Paso *Evening Tribune*, September 26, 1893, as recorded in the Newspaper Index, El Paso Public Library (I was unable to locate the original source): Broaddus, *The Legal Heritage of El Paso*, 149–150.

29. Lyman, *Chinese Americans*, 42, 96–105; Farrar, *Chinese in El Paso*, 16–19 (quotation); El Paso *Herald*, May 21, 1901. Prostitution, another vice said to be typical of Chinatowns, was not mentioned in the El Paso press.

30 Farrar, *Chinese in El Paso*, 19–22; U.S., Congress House, *Compilation from the Records of the Bureau of Immigration of Facts Concerning the Enforcement of the Chinese Exclusion Laws*, H. Doc. 847, 59th Cong., 1st Sess. (Serial 4990), 13–15, 61 (cited hereafter as *Facts Concerning the Enforcement of the Chinese Exclusion Laws*). On the anti-Chinese violence in Mexico, see Charles C. Cumberland, "The Sonora Chinese and the Mexican Revolution," *Hispanic American Historical Review*, XL (May, 1960), 191–211.

31. *Facts Concerning the Enforcement of the Chinese Exclusion Laws*, 14 (first and second quotations); Farrar, *Chinese in El Paso*, 20 (third quotation): El Paso *Herald*, January 17, 1907; W. W. Bridgers, "Just Chatting" (a scrapbook of his newspaper columns in the El Paso Public Library), I, 64–65.

32. *Facts Concerning the Enforcement of the Chinese Exclusion Laws,* 61 (quotation); El Paso *Daily Herald,* July 30, 1895; San Angelo *Standard-Times,* March 8, 1970.

33. San Antonio *Express,* September 20, 1892; El Paso *Daily Herald,* May 9, 1893; Dallas *Morning News,* May 21, 1893; Farrar, *Chinese in El Paso,* 21–22; Lyman, *Chinese Americans,* 66–67.

34. Jung-pang Lo (ed. and trans.), *K'ang Yu-wei: A Biography and a Symposium* (Tucson, 1967), 201; San Antonio *Express,* November 24, 1905.

35. Chew Din to E. J. M. R., September 27, 1973; interview. See also the city directories and the occasional obituaries of long-time Chinese residents in the El Paso newspapers.

36. See Edward Eugene Briscoe, "Pershing's Chinese Refugees in Texas," *Southwestern Historical Quarterly,* LXII (April, 1959), 467–488, and his earlier "Pershing's Chinese Refugees: An Odyssey of the Southwest" (M.A. thesis, Saint Mary's University, San Antonio, 1947). On the Chinese in Mexico, see Cumberland, "Sonora Chinese," 191–192.

37. Denison *Herald,* April 7, 1968; San Angelo *Standard-Times,* August 29, 1954; March 8, 1970; Lee, *Chinese in the United States,* 38–39; Sung, *Mountain of Gold,* 77–82.

38. U.S., Department of Commerce, Bureau of the Census, *Sixteenth Census of the United States.*

Part III

Chinese in the Northwest
(Oregon, Washington, Idaho)

10

Excerpts from *The Chinese in Eastern Oregon, 1860–1890*

Christopher Howard Edson

CHAPTER 6: CENSUS INFORMATION

Although reminiscences, local histories, and newspapers contain casual references to the presence of Chinese and their occupations, only census records of the various counties indicate their actual numbers, ages, and occupations. Before using the census records, however, one must consider certain factors which, if disregarded, would result in an incorrect assessment. First, as stated in the introduction, the original schedules of the census for 1890 have been destroyed; consequently, an individual enumeration of the Chinese for that census year is impossible. Second, as the focus of this study is the Blue Mountain region of Eastern Oregon, eastern counties outside of the placer-mining areas have been omitted from consideration. These other eastern counties reflected an insignificant Chinese population and, with the exception of Lake County, were not organized until after 1880.[1] Wasco County, however, has been included for the entire period from 1860 to 1890, due both to its large Chinese population and to the fact that the placer-mining counties of Baker, Grant, Umatilla, and Union, were originally organized from its territory.[2] Finally, county boundaries and census precincts changed frequently between 1860 and 1890. While no attempt has been made to correlate the census precincts for the thirty year period, a recent study has made it possible to trace the development of county lines[3] (see figures 10.1–10.4).

In 1860, only five of the 425 Chinese listed in Oregon resided east of the Cascades. All were residents of The Dalles, four of them laundrymen and the other a cook.[4] By 1870 there were 1,762 Chinese in Eastern Oregon, comprising 13.5 per cent of the total population. From 1870 to 1880 the Chinese population nearly doubled, but the 3,223 Chinese now comprised only 8.9 per cent of the population. By 1890, the Chinese population had diminished to 1,315, a mere

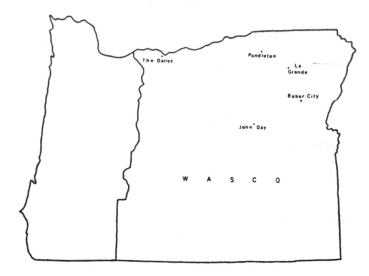

Figure 10.1   Eastern Oregon County boundaries, 1860.

2.8 per cent of the total (table 10.1). Despite their relatively small numbers in the total area, the Chinese were of a greater importance to the society and its economy than their numbers indicated. This was due to their almost total identification with the two most important activities in the development of Eastern Oregon: mining and

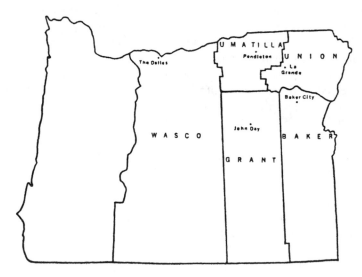

Figure 10.2   Eastern Oregon County boundaries, 1870.

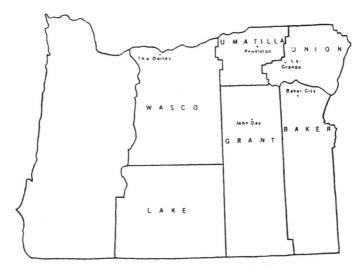

Figure 10.3   Eastern Oregon County boundaries, 1880.

railroad construction. Finally, while the total population of Eastern Oregon continued to increase during the decades from 1860 to 1890, the Chinese population, after rising during the 1860's and 1870's, eventually decreased, suggesting the relative decline of both placer mining and railroad construction in the 1880's.

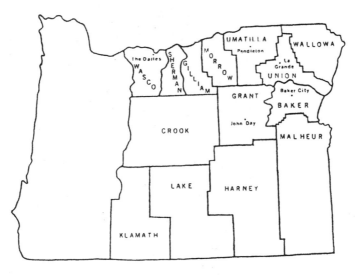

Figure 10.4   Eastern Oregon County boundaries, 1890.

Table 10.1 Comparative Figures of Chinese to Total Population in Oregon and the Eastern Counties, 1860–1890

County	1860		1870		1880		1890	
	Chinese	Total	Chinese	Total	Chinese	Total	Chinese	Total
The State	425	52,465	3,330	90,923	9,510	174,768	9,540	313,767
Baker[a]	—	—	680	2,804	787	4,616	398	6,764
Grant[b]	—	—	940	2,251	905	4,303	326	5,080
Umatilla[a]	—	—	70	2,916	138	9,607	261	13,381
Union[b]	—	—	45	2,552	235	6,650	125	12,044
Wasco	5	1,689	27	2,509	1,158	11,120	205	9,183
County Total	5	1,689	1,762	13,032	3,223	36,296	1,315	46,452

[a]1862 Baker and Umatilla organized from Wasco.
[b]1864 Grant and Union organized from Wasco.

Source: U.S. Census Office, *Eighth Census of the United States, 1860, Vol. I, Population*, p. 404; *Eleventh Census of the United States, 1890, Vol. I, Population, pt. 1*, pp. 36, 521.

The Chinese miners in 1870 were concentrated around Auburn, Clarksville, and Humboldt in Baker County, and Granite, Union, and Canyon City in Grant County. Smaller groups, however, were found throughout the rest of Grant and Baker Counties, as well as in the southern parts of Umatilla and Union Counties. In many precincts the Chinese miners outnumbered white miners, sometimes by considerable numbers. In the entire placer-mining area of Eastern Oregon, the Chinese miners outnumbered their white counterparts by 1,516 to 960. Of the 2,476 miners reported in 1870, 61.2 per cent were Chinese (table 10.2).

A comparison of the population statistics of 1870 with those of 1880 indicates the instability and transitory nature of the mining communities. Some districts, most notably Auburn in Baker County, and Granite in Grant County, experienced sharp declines as the placer tailings yielded their last few ounces of gold. On the other hand, new placer areas were developed, such as Sumpter in Baker County, and Sparta in Union County. By this time the Chinese mining community of Eastern Oregon had increased to 1,605, as compared to only 566 white miners. Of the 2,171 miners reported in 1880, 73.9 per cent were Chinese (table 10.3).

The decline of the total number of miners in Eastern Oregon between 1870 and 1880 is representative of the decline in mining throughout the state. The census reports for all Oregon show 1,793 miners in 1860, 3,965 in 1870, 3,699 in 1880, and only 2,165 in 1890.[5] Meanwhile, during the same three decades, the state's total population increased from 52,465 to 313,767 (*supra*, table 10.1). The special nature of the Chinese mining operations, however, resulted in an increase in the number of Chinese miners between 1870 and 1880. Most of the readily accessible gold had been mined before 1880, and only the persistent Chinese continued, on a large scale, to rework the old placer tailings. Although quartz mining, a more efficient method of gold extraction, had been introduced near Baker City as early as 1864,[6] the capital required for its equipment was so great that few such operations were established. Only large mining companies, through the public sale of stock, were able to raise the needed capital and make the operation profitable.[7]

Auburn was a town that experienced the usual pattern of mining decline in the 1860's. As the white miners found the area unprofitable and moved to richer diggings, "the city of Auburn was inherited by the meek, pig-tailed orientals."[8] As it passed into a "ghost-town" in the 1880's it was recorded: "When the Chinese miners had gleaned the last meager cleanup of dust from the gulches, the story of Auburn was ended."[9]

CHAPTER 8: THE NATURE OF THE CHINESE COMMUNITY

We have observed the Chinese thus far in their primary environment of mining; however, not all Chinese in Eastern Oregon were miners, nor did the Chinese miners always remain in the mines. Many of the larger towns, such as Canyon City and John Day in Grant County, and Baker City and Auburn in Baker

Table 10.2 Proportion of Chinese and Chinese Miners to White Miners in the Eastern Counties of Oregon, 1870

County and District	White Miners	Chinese Miners	Other Chinese	Total Chinese
Baker County				
Shasta	75	24	5	29
Amelia	19	14	0	14
Clarksville	65	160	42	202
Auburn	86	212	21	233
Baker City	21	12	17	29
Powder River	127	37	0	37
Humboldt	82	132	3	135
Other	53	0	1	1
Total	528	591	89	680
Grant County				
Granite	48	337	28	365
Olive Creek	75	38	0	38
Union	49	187	12	199
Marysville	37	24	1	25
Canyon City	53	130	32	162
John Day	20	81	4	85
Elk Precinct	19	56	4	60
Other	85	2	4	6
Total	386	855	85	940
Umatilla County				
Pendleton-Willow Cr.	2	0	9	9
Umatilla	0	36	22	58
Other	0	0	3	3
Total	2	36	34	70
Union County				
La Grande & District	10	34	6	40
Union	30	0	1	1
Other	4	0	4	4
Total	44	34	11	45
Grand Total	960	1,516	219	1,735

Source: U.S. Census Office, *Original Schedules of the Ninth Census of Population, 1870, for Oregon.* (Microfilm).

County, had separate Chinese communities or "chinatowns." As the illiterate or poorly educated Chinese immigrant left little or no written record of his life or his environment,[10] our knowledge of these settlements must come entirely from reports by whites, who were not usually well-acquainted with the Chinese. To the

Table 10.3 Proportion of Chinese and Chinese Miners to White Miners in the Eastern Counties of Oregon, 1880

County and District	White Miners	Chinese Miners	Other Chinese	Total Chinese
Baker County				
Baker City	29	2	73	75
Sumpter	26	184	13	197
Clarks Creek	26	83	4	87
Auburn	26	87	6	93
Burnt River	48	30	3	33
Conner Creek	17	37	8	45
Humboldt Basin	12	85	16	101
Other	169	130	26	156
Total	353	638	149	787
Grant County				
Marysville	22	64	1	65
Union	16	41	3	44
Olive Creek	20	59	3	62
Elk Creek	11	122	6	128
Granite	35	119	4	123
Canyon City	25	49	37	86
John Day	0	315	43	358
Other	50	21	18	39
Total	179	790	115	905
Umatilla County				
Umatilla	0	0	92	92
Other	0	0	46	46
Total	0	0	138	138
Union County				
La Grande-Union	3	0	14	14
Sparta-Eagle Precinct	25	170	37	207
Other	6	7	7	14
Total	34	177	58	235
Grand Total	566	1,605	460	2,065

Source: U.S. Census Office, *Original Schedules of the Tenth Census of Population, 1880, for Oregon.* (Microfilm).

Chinese, who were sometimes forced apart from the white community,[11] these "chinatowns" provided "a release for emotions checked by restraint and oppression, and provided a brief retreat from work in an alien environment into a world resembling home."[12]

Due to the transient nature of most mining communities, it is difficult to determine the actual numbers of any group in a mining town at any particular time. The local census of Baker City, for example, listed 166 Chinese in 1879,[13] while the United States Census of the following year listed only seventy-five.[14] Although it is difficult to generalize about a specific Chinese community for any length of time, original census reports, newspapers, and reminiscences give some general indication as to the lives and customs of the Chinese in Eastern Oregon.

Although in 1870 mining was listed as the occupation of 1,516 (87.4 per cent) of the Chinese in Blue Mountain region of Eastern Oregon, 219 (12.5 per cent) reported other occupations. Similarly, in 1880, 1,605 (77.7 per cent) were recorded as miners, while 460 (22.3 per cent) listed other employment. These non-mining Chinese had a variety of occupations: Hop Kee was a "merchant" and Wo Ke was a "loafer," Hong Chang was a "doctor" and Ti Pon was a "whore," Ah Kim was a "gentleman" and Ah Soo simply listed "work hard."[15] In descending order of frequency, the non-mining Chinese of Eastern Oregon were railroad workers, cooks, laundrymen, laborers, prostitutes, merchants, clerks, gamblers, et cetera.

Just as the Chinese miners avoided unpleasant contact and competition with the white miners, the non-mining Chinese rarely competed with the white labor force. The high incidence of Chinese employment in the tasks of a menial or domestic nature suggests that they performed the chores of everyday living which the whites wished to avoid. The mining communities, primarily comprised of unmarried males, required cooks, laundrymen, and domestics, consequently, the non-mining Chinese complemented rather than competed with the whites for employment. The Chinese were also employed for such objectionable chores as scrubbing tobacco-spit from the floor of the Baker City post office.[16] Finally, the Chinese filled the demand for hard physical labor such as the clearing of farm-land (primarily in Western Oregon). "This work is of a kind which white men will not pursue for any length of time"; the white laborer usually "hunts for a softer job."[17]

Over a thousand Chinese east of the Cascades were employed as railroad workers, as many white laborers had "quit work in consequence of the hot weather, while others have quit because they could get, temporarily, greater wages at harvesting.[18] In the 1880's the Oregon Railway and Navigation Company was constructing a line eastward from The Dalles along the south bank of the Columbia River to Wallula on the border of the Washington Territory. Much of the labor on this line, and on another line extending west towards Portland, was done by Chinese. An English visitor to The Dalles in 1882 observed about 500 Chinese at work, "spread in a long line on the face of a terrible rock, which looked as if five thousand Chinamen might work at it in vain for a year to make a fit passage for the train."[19]

Throughout the placer-mining era the Chinese community remained almost completely male, because of the usually male nature of mining towns and the male character of Chinese immigration. In the area under study in 1870, there were only forty-three females, or 2 percent of the total Chinese population, and in 1880, forty-seven females, or 1 percent of the total number of Chinese (table 10.4).

Table 10.4 Chinese Population in the Eastern Counties of Oregon by Sex, 1870 and 1880

County	1870					1880				
	Total	Male	Percent	Female	Percent	Total	Male	Percent	Female	Percent
The State	3,330	3,232	97	98	3	9,510	9,346	98	164	2
Baker	680	662	97	18	3	787	756	96	31	4
Grant	940	928	99	12	1	905	897	99	8	1
Umatilla	70	69	99	1	1	138	135	98	3	2
Union	45	37	82	8	18	235	234	99	1	—
Wasco	27	23	85	4	15	1,158	1,154	99	4	—
County Total	1,762	1,719	98	43	2	3,223	3,176	99	47	1

Source: U.S. Census Office, *Ninth Census of the United States, 1870, Vol. I, Population and Social Statistics,* pp. 608–609; *Tenth Census of the United States, 1880, Vol. I, Population,* p. 545; *Original Schedules, 1870, 1880.*

Table 10.5 Average Age of the Chinese Population in Eastern Oregon, by Sex, 1860–1880[a]

Sex	1860	1870	1880
Male	27	33	38
Female	20	26	30
Total	27	33	37

[a]Figures for 1860 based on a fifty percent sample of the state of Oregon; figures for 1870 and 1880 based on a twenty-five percent sample of the Eastern Oregon counties.

Source: U.S. Census Office, *Original Schedules, 1860, 1870, 1880.*

Approximately half of these females in both 1870 and 1880 were variously listed as prostitutes, whores, courtesans, or workers in the bawdy houses—depending on the census taker's terminological preferences. The remainder were listed as house-keepers, servants, hotel workers, and wives of Chinese miners or merchants.

The marital status of both male and female Chinese in Eastern Oregon can only be speculative, as census takers, when enumerating the Chinese, generally did not record information concerning literacy, marital status, and personal wealth. In some cases, indeed, the only entry other than occupation which appeared on the census originals was the word "chinaman."[20] The only married Chinese females appear in the Baker County census records for 1880: eight were listed as wives of Chinese, and one as the wife of a white miner on Conner Creek. Similarly, the only record of married Chinese males appears in the Baker and Wasco County census records for 1880: Baker reporting fifty-nine married males, and Wasco twenty-nine. Due to the lack of consistency on the part of the census takers, it is doubtful whether the census originals give a true picture of the marital status of the Chinese. It has been estimated that at least one-half of the Chinese immigrants had wives in China, "... for no man in China over twenty remains unmarried unless he is a wanderer or very poor."[21]

The average age of the Chinese population in Eastern Oregon increased from twenty-seven to thirty-seven during the two decades from 1860 to 1880 (Table 10.5). This general increase suggests that many of the sojourners were unable to achieve their goal of returning to China and thus had remained in North America. Extremes of age were rare: however, two miners, Ah Goon and Ah Gim, were eighty-two and seventy-three years respectively. Children were also rare, only two being reported in Eastern Oregon in 1870, and three in 1880.

Although ethnically and physically isolated from the white settlements, the Chinese communities became tolerated and functional parts of the society. An Auburn store account in 1868 illustrates the interaction which took place on the commercial level. The account reads: "Hop Lee, Dr. [debit] to 1 sack rice, 7.50 . . . Ah Kee, Dr. to 1 sack flour, 2.50 . . . Ah Foo, Dr. to 1 quart Brandy, 1.25, 1 bean stick, .50 . . . Ah Hee, Dr. to 1 hatchet, 1.50. . . ."[22]

The Chinese also set up their own business ventures, such as the Kam Wah Chung Company in John Day, which was established in 1871. It was purchased in 1887 by Lung On who, in association with a blind doctor named Ing Hay, operated it as a flourishing medical and importing business. From gold-miner, to merchant, to real estate investor, Lung On built an estate worth $89,000 upon his death in 1940.[23]

Reminiscences and local histories have recorded other examples of the Chinese presence in Eastern Oregon. A Chinese Joss House (a religious and social gathering place) was completed in Baker City in 1883. This impressive two-story brick structure, finished inside with hardwood, was reported to have cost $10,000.[24] The Chinese were also remembered in Baker City for having introduced the grapefruit, although for a long time they were the only ones to eat them.[25] An early rancher of the John Day region, Herman Oliver recalled that after the mines ran out in the 1880's, the Chinese made possible a good business in raising hogs. "They were all fond of pork—they seemed to prefer it to all other meat. They often bought our weaners and fattened them with waste vegetables and garbage."[26]

The Chinese, however, were principally remembered for, what seemed to the whites, their strange customs and habits. The John Day rancher, Herman Oliver, declared: "We didn't look at them the way we did at other people. They were strange and foreign. It is somewhat the same way with a new boy in school."[27] Wearing of queues,[28] smoking opium until "the smoke could be cut with a case-knife,"[29] gambling incessantly,[30] and sending the remains of the deceased to China,[31] elicited a response of curiosity and wonderment from the white population. While some whites marveled at the use of chopsticks, which "moved at a terrible rate" in the hands of Chinese,[32] others noticed strange medical practices, such as the use of herbs, worms, and bugs to cure "all manner of diseases."[33] Chinese New Year's celebrations brought much comment from the whites in Eastern Oregon. In addition to feasting and exploding firecrackers, the Chinese were remembered for drinking moderately and extending their hospitality to all, regardless of "race or color."[34] Herman Oliver described in detail one particular custom, the funeral procession:

> Some Chinese would go in front and scatter all along the road pieces of thin paper resembling tissue. These were about four by six inches and had many small holes in them, much as though a pencil had been shoved through as often as possible without making the holes join. They told us that the devil had to go back and forth through all these holes before he could overtake the corpse.[35]

The Chinese, on the other hand, were often amazed at the strange customs and institutions in the United States. As reported by the *Bedrock Democrat*, the Chinese saw our law courts in the following manner: "One man is quite silent, another talks all the time, and twelve wise men condemn the man who has not said a word."[36]

Through the preservation of familiar patterns and customs, the Chinese settlements offered the immigrant a brief respite from the toil and drudgery of labor in an alien environment. Whether creating a bit of China in America through the celebration of Chinese holidays, or escaping the rigors of life through the use of opium, the Chinese immigrant maintained his ties with the past and compromised with the present. Although there were numerous expressions of hostility by the white community in Eastern Oregon, the alien ways of the Chinese were generally tolerated. According to an account of the John Day settlement in 1885:

> The inhabitants of this quaint settlement are orderly and apparently contented, and while, as is their way, they do not mingle with the Americans nor do they adopt American manners and customs, they are not considered a detriment to the town.[37]

The Chinese in Eastern Oregon were often considered "good people, hard working and honest"[38]—yet they remained a people apart from white society.

NOTES

1. These other eastern counties, dates of organization, and numbers of Chinese in 1890, were as follows: Crook (1882), 9; Klamath (1882), 3; Morrow (1885), 25; Gilliam (1885), 41; Wallowa (1887), none; Malheur (1887), 82; Sherman (1889), 25; and Harney (1889), 16. Lake County, organized in 1875, reported 7 Chinese in 1880 and 19 in 1890. U.S. Census Office, *Eleventh Census of the United States, 1890.* Vol. 1, *Population,* pt. 1, pp. 36, 440; *Tenth Census of the United States, 1880,* Vol. I, *Population,* p. 405.

2. Baker, 1862; Grant, 1864; Umatilla, 1862; Union, 1864. U.S. Census Office, *Ninth Census of the United States, 1870,* Vol. 1, *Population and Social Statistics,* p. 57.

3. Edward G. Stephan, "Intra-State Boundaries: A Set of Historical Maps Showing the Development of County Government in Oregon" (Unpublished Study, University of Oregon, 1968). (Mimeographed).

4. U.S. Census Office, *Original Schedules of the Eighth Census of Population, 1860, For Oregon.* (Microfilm). Of the remaining 420 Chinese in Western Oregon, 370 were listed as miners.

5. U.S. Census Office, *Eighth Census of the United States, 1860,* Vol. 1, *Population,* p. 405; *Ninth Census of the United States, 1870,* Vol. 1. *Population and Social Statistics,* pp. 682–683; *Tenth Census of the United States, 1880,* Vol. 1, *Population,* p. 735; *Eleventh Census of the United States, 1890,* Vol. 1, *Population,* pt. 2, p. 331.

6. Bancroft, *Oregon,* p. 739.

7. Hiatt, *Thirty One Years,* p. 143; *Bedrock Democrat,* February 14, 1872, p. 2, March 6, 1872, p. 3, October 9, 1872, p. 3.

8. Jim Hayes, "Auburn—A Ghostly Gold City of Oregon," *Daily Oregonian,* November 5, 1933, magazine section, p. 3.

9. Verne Bright, "Blue Mountain Eldorados: Auburn, 1861," *Oregon Historical Quarterly,* LXII (September, 1961), p. 236.

10. Barth, *Bitter Strength,* p. 7.

11. *Bedrock Democraft,* March 13, 1872, p. 3; Western Historical Publishing Company, *History,* p. 436.

12. Barth, *Bitter Strength,* p. 109.

13. Western Historical Publishing Company, *History,* p. 210.

14. U.S. Census Office, *Original Schedules, 1880.*

15. *Ibid., Original Schedules, 1870, 1880.*

16. *Bedrock Democrat,* April 17, 1873, p. 3.

17. *Daily Oregonian,* March 4, 1886, p. 4.

18. *Ibid.,* July 16, 1870, p. 3.

19. Nash, *Two Years in Oregon,* p. 204.

20. Other than occupation, the word "Chinaman" was the only entry to appear for over 200 of the 245 Chinese miners in Jackson County in 1860. Likewise, over 900 of the 981 railroad laborers in Wasco County in 1880 were listed as "Chinaman." Other general terms such as "China Charley" and "John Chinaman" were frequently used from 1860 to 1880. U.S. Census Office, *Original Schedules, 1860, 1870, 1880.* (Microfilm).

21. Coolidge, *Chinese Immigration,* p. 18.

22. Bright, "Blue Mountain Eldorados," p. 236, quoted in, "Daily Sales of an Auburn Store in 1858," no. 4, Mimeo-Bulletins of the Historical Records Survey of Oregon, W.P.A., pp. 1, 4, 8.

23. Gordon F. Glass, private interviews conducted in John Day, Oregon, September, 1969. Lung On's estate is currently being managed by the city of John Day.

24. Wesley Andrews, "Baker City in the Eighties: Boyhood Memories," *Oregon Historical Quarterly*, L (June, 1949), p. 87: Western Historical Publishing Company, *History*, p. 211.

25. Andrews, "Baker City," p. 88.

26. Oliver, *Gold and Cattle Country*, p. 58.

27. *Ibid.*, p. 159.

28. *Ibid.*, p. 160; *Bedrock Democrat*, March 13, 1872, p. 3, April 17, 1872, p. 3.

29. *Bedrock Democrat*, February 14, 1872, p. 3; Nash, *Oregon: There and Back*, p. 62; Oliver, *Gold and Cattle Country*, p. 158; Andrews, "Baker City," p. 87.

30. *Bedrock Democrat*, March 13, 1872, p. 4; Hayes, "Auburn—A Ghostly Gold City of Oregon," p. 3; Oliver, *God and Cattle Country*, p. 158.

31. *Bedrock Democrat*, May 18, 1870, p. 4, October 2, 1872, p. 1.

32. Nash, *Two Years in Oregon*, p. 203.

33. *Bedrock Democrat*, February 7, 1872, p. 1.

34. *Ibid.*, February 12, 1873, p. 2, February 14, 1872, p. 3; Nash, *Two Years in Oregon*, p. 207.

35. Oliver, *Gold and Cattle Country*, p. 159.

36. March 20, 1872, p. 1.

37. Western Historical Publishing Company, *History*, p. 443.

38. *Blue Mountain Eagle* (Canyon City), May 31, 1962, centennial edition, section 4, p. 4.

11

Chinese Culture in the Inland Empire

Nancy K. Feichter

Won Chung, who presided over a laundry in Spokane, was considered to be a man of remarkable insight, and his wisdom was reported in terms of derision for his race and respect for his genius. One day Wee Gee came into the laundry and the subsequent conversation ensued:

> "What for ladee alle timee lear plants and lidee blicycle?"
> Won Chung slowly and deliberately squirted the water in his mouth over the clothes before him and turning toward his partner gave him a look of deep sympathy.
> "You no sabee what for? You heap blig fool. Ladee likee be allee samee man. She likee lear plants, vest, necktlye and lawkee with her hands in plants plockets. Bimeby man he no goee dlown tolown, dlinkee bleer, getee dlunk, makee fun and klickee Chinaman; ladee she goee dlown tlown, dlinkee bleer, gette dlunk and glabbee Chinaman by clue say, 'Hey, John, what for you no goee black and lickee Jap?'. . ."[1]

The conversation continued liberally sprinkled with the tendency to substitute "1" for any letter they found difficult to pronounce. When one of the "new women" came in with some shirts and collars to be washed, the conversation was closed. Nonetheless, the dialogue proved to be a "capsule comment" of at least one Chinaman's assessment of the society in which he found himself. The society with which the Inland Empire Chinese had to cope was not only a white one undergoing change but also a Chinese one also undergoing a metamorphosis due to the interaction of one culture upon the other. To understand the nature of this interaction, it is necessary to look within the transplanted Chinese communities and at some of their customs, cultural pursuits, and everyday habits.

Perhaps the most significant feature of the perpetuation of any culture lies in the educational traditions of that culture. The American Chinese were concerned with this aspect particularly in so far as it became necessary for them to learn English. There was practical value involved for not only did knowledge of English make it easier to adjust to white society, but if one returned to China with some knowledge of English, he might be able to obtain a better position. Thus it was claimed that "a desire to learn the language of his adopted country seems to be one of the highest ambitions of the Chinese immigrant," and it was generalized that the Chinese immigrant "studies his native text-books, attends Sunday-schools, and tries to glean a word or two from every foreigner [American] with whom he comes in contact."[2]

One of these "Sunday-schools" available in Inland Empire Chinese in Spokane was located in a storeroom on Post street, south of the Northern Pacific tracks. It was not exclusively devoted to the Chinese, although it was called the Chinese Mission. In the class there were — besides the forty Chinese — five Germans, three Scandinavians, two Negroes, five Japanese, and half a dozen of various nationalities. Of the thirty volunteer teachers under the direction of the missionary in charge, Mrs. Rosencrans, there were two from the Presbyterian church and two from the Methodist church, and the rest were from the Baptist churches. The teachers each took turns with three or four at the mission each evening. Each evening, except Wednesday, there was a class with attendance more or less regular. Saturday evenings were devoted to prayer meetings. General teachings were subjects of the other evenings.

Of the Chinese students only a half dozen were described as good Christians with the remainder being more anxious to learn to read and write English. They ranged in age from twenty-four to forty-five, were devoted students, and all "registered" as the missionary in charge made it an entrance requirement that they be able to show their registration papers. "I have never seen a Chinaman, no matter how humble his station," stated Mrs. Rosencrans, "who could not read and write in Chinese."[3]

Also in Spokane was a Chinese mission school connected with the Christian Alliance under the superintendency of Mrs. J. E. Cusick. This school was conducted solely, it was maintained, "in the interest of the conversion of the Chinese to the Christian religion."[4] However, a program put on by the school in the spring of 1895 for an audience of over 500 people indicated that some of the twenty-two persons enrolled in the school were able to give recitations in English as well as songs in Chinese, and a secondary purpose of teaching English to the Chinese was perhaps implied at that time. The "novel" entertainment which drew considerable interest was concluded by the Chinese students repeating the Lord's prayer in English and indulging with their guests in refreshments of ice cream, cake, and coffee.[5]

Several months later this Christian Alliance hall on North Riverside was the scene of a ceremony welcoming three Chinese into Christianity. They were accepted as members of the Christian Alliance with all benefits and privileges when the Rev. B. F. Morse baptized them in a large tank. The Christian Alliance had at that time over seventy members and their Chinese mission school had thirty-one registered Chinese, "all anxious to learn the English language, and more of Christianity."[6]

There are illustrations of attempts to "Americanize" either through learning English or adopting Christianity. "Americanization," however, need not have been the sole motive of Gue Owen, for instance, a Grangeville, Idaho, Christian who had cut off his queue, gone to school, and joined the Methodist church.[7] One Chinaman, Lee Wing Tong, "gleaned" his knowledge of English not from attending church or school particularly but by subscribing to the Lewiston *Teller*.[8] Other "educated" Chinese became ordained ministers; one named Jo Hawk helped the Christian ladies of Pendleton, Oregon, celebrate the twenty-first anniversary of their board of missions,[9] and another preached to his people in their native language.[10] The "heathen Chinee" could also be touched by the spirit of the Salvation Army. During an Army visit to the county jail at Missoula, Montana, Ah Wing No.1, waiting for deportation, was seen kneeling in prayer by the side of an Indian.[11]

Chinese religious sentiments were expressed not only through Christian churches but also in Masonic temples and Chinese churches. These Chinese "churches" were called *joss houses* and were in the nature of "chapels." Lewiston, Idaho, was the religious headquarters for the Chinese miners of central Idaho, and the church there was the scene of unique ceremonies. It was there that the miners shook the joss sticks, studied the ancient codes, and sought advice from their gods in an effort to ascertain the best direction to go seek gold. The ninety joss sticks also served to tell at which side of the table to sit if playing cards or whether to sit down and play at all. These same sticks helped Jim Ye Ott, an east Lewiston vegetable gardner, tell the town's fortune each New Year's Eve.[12]

At the Lewiston "joss house" there was an altar carved from hardwood and supported by two pillars. Hanging from this altar were banners with Chinese inscriptions, and behind the altar resided the "presence" of five gods: Wah Hoo, medicine; Toy Bock Hung Gwan, riches; Bock I, god of the North, Guan Han Suing, god of heaven; and Gong Gung, general assistant to all the gods. A Chinese Masonic temple in Lewiston also had a silkened altar, gongs, and cowskin drums, but no joss sticks nor lanterns with trailing silk tassels.[13] There was a Chinese Masonic Lodge, moreover, in Spokane[14] and in Walla Walla.[15]

The religious and educational activities described above were significant in sustaining their dignity and emotional security as human beings and in retaining their identity to traditional Chinese culture. The more colorful and public aspects of this identity, however, brought them closer to the white society in which they lived. The rituals, ceremonies, and festivities were matters of curiosity to the rest of the community, and most particularly were the Chinese funerals and New Year celebrations a matter of interest to the whites.

One ritual eliciting such interest was Mon Hop's funeral in Spokane in 1886 which attracted such an immense crowd that the deceased was overlooked. In the middle of Front street, two tables were spread with food. Candles and punk sticks were burned while a white-gowned Chinese with a red sash and others with red and white bits of rag orated and performed rites. When the body was buried, the property of the deceased was heaped and burned over his grave. Because only a few Chinese took an *active* part in the ceremonies, it was supposed that Mon Hop was a member of a secret organization.[16]

When Chew Peit was buried at Fairmont cemetery in Spokane in 1892, each of the white persons present was given a silver dime and pieces of Chinese candy after paper, sandal wood, and incense were burned over the grave. However, one of the most elaborate funerals which took place in Spokane was that of Wong How, a Chinese gambler. It was reportedly the "grandest" event that had occurred in Spokane's Chinese community. Other Chinese had subscribed money for the funeral expenses to give the "most gorgeous rites that have ever been accorded any Chinaman in the state of Washington."[17] The funeral began at about two o'-clock with at least 200 Chinese meeting and forming a procession to escort the body to Wong How's former home. The procession and subsequent proceedings were described as follows:

> First came three men on black horses, followed by two more in a spring wagon, who scattered bits of red paper all along the way. This was the spirit money, and was scattered freely, so the greedy bad spirits would be too busy picking it up to bother themselves about Won How. They appeared to be negligent, however, and most of the red paper fell in the hands of small boys. Beside the wagon walked an ear-splitting flute player, hard at work.
>
> Behind the spring wagon came the hearses, closely followed by a gayly dressed Chinaman who carried a long pole from which bright banners streamed in every direction. Another bore a tablet mounted on a pole and inscribed with sacred texts. A third man carried a huge umbrella of colored paper which he kept turning rapidly round and round. . . .
>
> Won How's house is opposite the First avenue fire station. They halted in front of it, and the coffin was taken from the hearse and placed on trestles. A table was quickly spread at its foot loaded with preserves, chickens, roast pig and other dainties. The flute-player executed another awful solo, and the mourners advanced singly to the foot of the table. Each poured a little tea and rice upon the ground, waived [*sic*] a blazing punk stick solemnly, and after thus offering the dead spirit food, water and fire, they bowed to the corpse three times and withdrew.
>
> Then the high priest in gay robes stepped forward and occupied a half hour in singing, praying and preaching in the most solemn manner possible . . .
>
> The ceremonies ended by covering the coffin with a rich red blanket and the body was replaced in the hearse. A Chinaman mounted the box . . . to scatter red paper on the way and they journeyed to the cemetery. On arriving at the grave the tables were again prepared and the mourners enjoyed a hearty feast. The clothes and bedding of the dead man were all burned at the grave, rice sprinkled over the coffin and Won How's funeral was ended.[18]

One Chinese funeral in Lewiston was conducted by the Chinese Masons. It was the funeral of Tu Guong, a merchant at Elk City, Idaho, who had died in a Chinese gambling den in Lewiston. The funeral, in 1887, was attended by approximately one hundred Chinese who partook of a feast consisting of roast hogs, sheep, chickens, ducks as well as candy, nuts, and cigars. Those conducting the ceremonies wore white and red ribbons or rags in the buttonholes of their coats.[19]

At Elk City, Idaho, the Chinese when burying their dead would distribute bits of punched paper along the roadside on the way to the cemetery. It was believed that the devil would have to crawl through each of the holes in order to reach the burial ground which in Elk City was located on a hillside. The graves were shallow and with any heavy rain or a wet season the coffins were exposed. The body would then decay more quickly and when but the bones remained, they were burned and ashes sent back to China.[20]

The Chinese were, by and large, quite concerned about death and the desirability of having their bones rest eventually in the soil of China. Representatives of the Chinese government or of the Chinese Six Companies would make trips throughout the country to gather up the bones of the dead and return them for burial to China. Some "Celestials," paying 2½ per cent of their earnings to the company having them in charge, were assured that if taken ill they would be taken care of at the expense of the company. Moreover, these Chinese were assured that if they were to die their bones would be shipped back to China if so requested.[21] In central Idaho the Six Companies were said to have gone around collecting bones every ten years with the Chinese seemingly knowing where each and every deceased fellow-countryman lay buried.[22]

In 1893, the bones of forty Chinese were disinterred from the Walla Walla cemetery for return to China. They were put into small square boxes which were labeled with the address to which they were to be sent.[23]

Fear of evil spirits or devils caused the Chinese to treat the sick and dying in not altogether kind ways. Often, when one lay dying, he was moved out of the house because if he should die in the house it would thereupon be "contaminated."[24] Nonetheless, kindness or devotion to the sick and honor to the dead were existent. In 1884, a Chinaman died and was buried in the cemetery of Colville. Another one who lived at Sixteen-mile Bar made regular pilgrimages to his friend's grave every three months. There he would burn punk and colored paper, place upon the grave roast chicken and Chinese whisky, and after making the proper incantations to ward off the devil, he would depart.[25]

But funerals were not the only occasions for festivities within the Inland Empire Chinese communities. Chinese New Year, occurring in February, was a time of fireworks and feasting and constituted their chief celebration. They were known to have fired off a hundred dollar's worth of crackers, bombs, and rockets in one display, and the whites who visited their communities at this time were some times entertained and given handsome presents.[26] Sometimes their celebrations came into conflict with the white community. One year the Chinese in Spokane began to set off their fireworks and were preparing to have a good time generally. They were, thereupon, notified by the police that the observance of the Christian Sabbath took precedence over their "heathen festivals."[27]

The 1896 New Year was celebrated in typical fashion by the Chinese in Spokane where the noise around Front street attracted a large crowd. After this celebration, they were expected to go back to "their regular occupations, contract debts and with them enemies, know that when the next New Year rolls around they will be able to call everything off."[28] Starbuck, Washington, having a large number of "Celestials" in its community, noted with interest the 24-hour welcome to the New Year.[29]

Other occasions were used by the Chinese to have a "glorious time." When a new lodge of Chinese Free Masons was instituted by Grand Master Tue Chuck, of Portland, in Walla Walla, the twelve candidates given the degree were treated to a night of feasting with about 100 present.[30]

The Chinese, however, did not always need an "occasion" to celebrate. They were able to entertain themselves simply and spontaneously. Many, being good natured and fun-loving,[31] enjoyed life. A Chinese flag raising could elicit a noisy demonstration and a fair evening breeze could give birth to a sky full of kites.[32]

The celebrations, festivals, and feasts which they indulged in at the appropriate times contrasted, moreover, to their every day living habits. Their menu, for instance, was generally simple. For breakfast a typical diet of dried fish, rice, and tea sufficed. Noon luncheon also featured rice. Those who worked on the railroads were known to consume a great amount of weak, cold tea between meals. This between-meals tea was carried about in two cans on a pole balanced across the shoulders of the younger, smaller Chinese who were really yet boys.[33]

The dinner habits of "John Chinaman" were described in condescending tones by a Spokane newsman in 1892:

> It is every man for himself to secure the most of the nearest food. As the whistle of the cannery sounds the dinner horn, there is a general shuffling of sandals along the floor, and the Chinamen were hurrying to their boarding house. On entering the door each seizes a china bowl and makes for the huge caldron of rice. With one scoop of a ladle the bowl is filled with steaming rice . . . On each of these tables has been placed bowls containing pork, fish, Chinese cabbage, a sait sauce, each article of food being dipped in the latter before eaten. Armed with chop-sticks the contents of the different bowls are turned over and over by the eaters, in an endeavor to find some piece more tender than the other.
>
> The dishes were rinsed out with tea which is drunk after having performed the duty as dishwater, the Chinese pipe is produced and passed from one to another . . . It is a superstition among Chinese that anything eaten in the presence of an uninvited white man will certainly disagree with them.[34]

The after-supper or dinner pipes of either tobacco or opium appeared to be a usual pleasure.[35] After-supper entertainment, moreover, could consist also of reading, writing, or playing cards.[36]

The dinner habits were but part of those living habits which could give rise to comments and, at times, considerable concern on the part of the white community. By and large, the larger community gave recognition to the generally prover-bial personal cleanliness of the individual Chinese. However, this often con-trasted with the crowded, sometimes filthy living conditions of some of their "Chi-natowns." Dirty and dilapidated though the Chinese quarters may have been, there is one evidence that an effort was made by them in Spokane at least to clear away trash. That they continued to dump it into the river above the falls prompted a concise comment: "They need watching."[37]

Lewiston, Idaho, in early 1872, was decrying the great scarcity of tenements suitable for the residence of families. It was stated that there were many old di-lapidated buildings, some occupied by the Chinese, but which were entirely "un-suited to the wants of neat and tidy tenants."[38] A couple of decades later, in 1894, Walla Walla was scandalized by the condition of its Chinese quarter—the extent of its filth and squalor. But particularly sad for the interested white community was the fact that in one of the worst places, "infested with vermin, decaying ani-mal and vegetable matter, sat a white woman, at home and contented with her opium pipe and depraved companions."[39]

At times the white population could be moved to feel pity, contempt, or fear at the supposed depravity, moral degeneration, and disease sometimes exhibited by the Chinese. In Lewiston one was known to live with a white man. His feet and hands had been frozen, and mortification which set in caused all his fingers to drop off and a portion of one of his feet. He was said to have been guilty of sell-ing liquor to the Indians, and was generally filthy and diseased, but the *Idaho Sig-nal* maintained that he "surely ought not to be allowed to remain in such a state of suffering without some medical treatment, even if he is a Chinaman, and some-thing ought done [*sic*] for him; he is helpless."[40]

Whenever a report of leprosy was circulated, the Chinese community was likely to become suspect. This suspicion occasioned a visit of the Health Officer and the City Marshal to a Chinaman in Walla Walla. They found that he did not have leprosy, but they decided that Wall Walla's Chinatown needed a cleanup and or-dered one.[41]

Another leprosy scare occurred in Spokane when a druggist had three Chinese visit his store. They wanted something for the sores of one, but the druggist, be-ing suspicious of leprosy, ordered them from his store and notified city officials. A search party was sent out to find the supposed leper in his supposed hideout—a laundry. He was finally found in the attic, but the suspected case of leprosy turned out to be only a case of acne which was not even contagious. The unfortunate Chinese had attempted to doctor himself with argentic nitrate and hence his skin suffered from hideous black spots. It seemed that the poor fellow was afraid of be-ing shipped to China. Someone had told him the officers were looking for him for that reason. When found this not to be so, he "grinned and fawned around the health officer like a pet poodle."[42]

One of the most interesting "crusades" against the "evil" practices of the "Ce-lestials" by the reform-minded white populace was directed against Ah Yen , a proprietor of a fancy goods store in Spokane, for binding the feet of his oldest child. The local ladies of the Humane Society called upon the parents, found them obdurate, and thereupon asked the police to interfere.

> Like a mandarin with a commission from a viceroy Officer Bringold entered the abode and requested the woman to unloosen the bandages. In the name of Confucius she refused, pointed to her own feet and asked the officer to depart.[43]

The interest engendered in the case brought forth the curiosity of the local journalists and a visit to the home of Ah Yen resulted in an article which reveals the following subtle assessment of Chinese culture:

> There wee many quaint articles of furniture in the room, betokening that far Mongolian country where the roses have no fragrance, and the women no petticoats; where the laborer has no Sabbath and the magistrate no sense of honor; where the needle points to the south, and the sign of being puzzled is to scratch the feet; where the seat of the intellect is the stomach, and to take off your hat an insolent gesture; where writing runs from right to left, and people wear white when in mourning; where people when out for a social walk go behind one another, and where the feet of the female children of aristocratic birth are bandaged from infancy until they stop growing.
>
> On one side of the room was a bamboo cradle with a canopy of pongee silk and in the cradle an infant, crying in Chinese.
>
> Near-by was the girl with the bandaged feet. The mother cannot speak English, but her husband can talk "Melican" like an auctioneer. He said that Chinese girls' feet were made small as a mark of membership of the "four hundled." The feet of the females of common Chinese people could grow like gondolas, but his family was descended from the Wei dynasty, and he defied anybody to compel him to let his daughter's feet grow as large as the feet of American girls.
>
> The thought was enough to make a Chinaman hit the pipe.[44]

The suggestion was made that somebody should be induced to make a thorough investigation of the situation. However, the Humane Society decided that there did not appear to be any great evidence of cruelty and suffering, and there the matter rested. Ah Yen and his family had originally lived in Rathdrum, Idaho, and his second child was the first Chinese baby born in Spokane.[45]

Chinese babies were a decided rarity, and the birth of what was considered the first born to Chinese parents in central Idaho at Mt. Idaho, on July 2, 1866, brought forth a great deal of curiosity and kind attention from both the Chinese and white residents. The baby, a girl, had her hair shaved on the 30th and 60th days after her birth,[46] and a small pocket suspended around her neck was filled with gold dust and other presents.[47]

The "kind attention" of white residents could be directed to other than Chinese babies. When a white girl was discovered living with a Chinaman for several months, the ladies of Colfax, Washington, members of the W.C.T.U., found themselves involved in a small scale reform campaign. Apparently the girl had "sunk" to her present living arrangement because she used morphine excessively. The ladies supplied her and her little girl with clothing and sent them to the poor farm. Neither the girl nor her "landlord" welcomed the departure to the farm, but the "charitable" ladies threatened that the child would be taken from her if she did not go.[48]

How much miscegenation there was on such personal levels remains but a guess. But a full-blooded Mongolian with a full-blooded Caucasian for a wife was considered a "strange anomaly" when they registered one evening at a Spokane hotel. They, of course, attracted comments of all sorts as they seemed to be happy and had plenty of money. But when she dropped a remark that he was merely her Chinese cook, the hotel proprietor decided to investigate. The true nature of their relationship was never discovered, however, because they had disappeared.[49]

One mixed marriage which has provided considerable copy for romanticists and journalists alike concerns that of Polly Bemis. Sister Alfreda Elsensohn sums up the several accounts of Polly by backing up the consensus that, although Polly may not have been won in a poker game, at least poker had something to do with it.[50] Polly came into the central Idaho mining area supposedly with her "owner" who was a wealthy Chinaman, Hong King. He was either not as clever or as lucky as Bemis in a poker game. The end result was his loss of Polly. But, in this instance, the old adage that one man's loss is another man's gain proved true, for Bemis gained a wife — Polly and he being married August 13, 1894, and moving to a camp on the Salmon River where they lived out their lives.[51] Their memories live on in the geography of the Salmon River country—Polly Creek and Bemis mountain.[52]

Another mixed marriage involved an Indian woman who had married a Canadian born man who was one-half Chinese and one-half Indian. Mrs. Lum lived in British Columbia and wanted to move to her allotment in the Colville reservation. John Webster, Indian agent, had sought to help her arrange for her husband's admission into the United States to live and work on the allotment. In 1905 he informed her that he was unable to do anything because her husband was not regarded as being within any of the classes excepted from the operation of the exclusion act, and no exception would be made for his "peculiar case."[53]

An estimate of the number who married Indians for the benefit of their allotments or for other reasons cannot be made. However, it is apparent that although early victims of Indian depredations, not all the Chinese translated this into hatred for them. One story is told of a garden worker in the Chinese village which was situated at the foot of the Chelan River. Described as a "moon-eyed" young man with a voice as gentle "as a muffled bell,"[54] he was in love with an Indian maiden who lived on the banks of Lake Chelan. He vowed never to declare his love. Thus he remained in his garden dreaming, sighing, and gazing at the stars. One day he was found dead, presumed to have died of a broken heart. He had so evoked the sympathy and sense of the romantic in the minds of his fellow countrymen that when the village was deserted, not one vandal touched the garden.[55]

Just as love and marriage call for universal recognition among the races of mankind, so also do a sense of humor, loyalty, and the compulsion for self-preservation. From this pot-pourri of human characteristics arise the clowns, the fools, and the heroes, and both great and humble men. The Inland Empire Chinese evidenced all of these characteristics.

Some of these characteristics are illustrated in the person of Lee Hong, the sheepherder who worked for Frank Lyongs in the Klickitat Valley of Washington. When Lyons became financially involved about 1893, he turned over his sheep to an Arlington, Oregon, bank which agreed to pay off all his employees. As for Lee Hong, the bank told him that he had to collect his money from Lyons himself. Lee agreed to work for his boss on an IOU basis, but at the same time, he wrote to his Tong affiliate in San Francisco to inquire concerning the rights in the form of a labor lien.

When the bank demanded possession of Lee Hong's flock of sheep, he produced a letter in English from his Tong which stated that they would back him up in any legal action provided he followed instructions about remaining in possession of the sheep over which he had charge. The bank gave him a check for the amount of his claim, $1200. Suspecting there might be a "catch," Lee Hong made inquiry into the value of the check and was told that it was no good. Galloping back to his sheep, he found that one of the bank officials was trying to "steal" his sheep. John Sinclair, with whom he had boarded the sheep, ordered the men off his premises and indicated his indignation at their trying to beat a man—even if just a Chinaman—out of hard earned wages. The subsequent rebounding of the rubber check constituted a written acknowledgment of Lee Hong's claim. The court trial at Goldendale concerning it attracted every flock master and herder from the countryside.[56]

A Chinaman who showed equal determination and pride was Lee Man (Mann) who first arrived in San Francisco in 1869 as a youth of fifteen. After accumulating several thousand dollars from gold mining and buying and selling beef cattle in California, he returned to China, married his sweetheart, and returned again to America. In 1885 he reached Elk City, Idaho, where he conducted a general merchandise store. When the first school was established in Elk City in 1895 with Judge Carney as the first teacher, the forty-year-old Lee Man was included among the pupils. Lee was interested in mining properties as well, and a general expulsion of Chinese from the mines caused him to lose $30,000 in credit accounts held for his countrymen. He went to Wenatchee, Washington, in 1906 to engage in fruit growing. He returned to Elk City in 1931. All through the years, he corresponded with his wife and sent money for the support of her and his son. But he never again returned to China, having died at Grangeville, Idaho, at the age of 87.[57]

A supposed "glimpse into Chinese life" was provided when Lee Man went to Spokane to spend the winter of 1895–96. He seems to have incurred the displeasure of the Spokane Chinese by associating with the white populace in preference to the Chinese. Moreover, he readily voiced disapproval when two of his countrymen attempted to slash one another with knives. He was on friendly terms with Ah Yen, the Spokane merchant who incurred the wrath of the local Humane Society for binding the feet of his daughter. The two went out one evening for amusement. Although disapproving of gambling, Lee Man lent Yen $10 to play faro. Yen lost, wanted more money to play, and Man lent $5 more with the understanding that the winnings, if any, should be divided. Yen won $50, gave his partner $20, went back to play and lost again. Thereupon he hunted up his friend asking for the $20 he had recently given him. This the exasperated Lee Man refused to give with the result that Yen threatened him. Man's response to this was to go to the courts. Ah Yen gave a bond of $300 as a guaranty that he would keep the peace toward his friend. The quarrel, however, brought out the fact that Man had no certificate of registration and, moreover, had once been suspected of helping someone steal the wife of one of Ah Yen's cousins.[58]

The game of faro which caused the trouble between Lee Man and Ah Yen was a favorite of the Chinese who indulged in gambling, and gambling for some Chinese was a business enterprise. As early as 1865 there was an established "Chinese Gambling Company" which owed Marcus Oppenheimer $34.38.[59] Those "companies" who managed a typical lottery did not need to indulge in any fraud or manipulation to make money, since the possibility of the customer winning was very slight. One usual way of playing a lottery was to play for prizes of 20 cents, $20, $100, $200, or $400. As much as ten percent of the prize money would be held out by the management, and thus a ticket holder would not get all the money his ticket might win. The lottery ticket contained eighty Chinese characters in a square. The player would mark out with an ink brush ten of these. He would keep one ticket and the "company" would keep two duplicates.

The "drawing" the player never saw. The eighty characters would be printed on large, separate squares, distributed in four numbered bowls—twenty characters to each bowl. Then there were four Chinese numbers in another bowl from which a blindfolded Chinese would draw one. The numbered bowl corresponding to the number drawn was then taken and the twenty Chinese characters it contained were called off and marked out with an ink brush on a slip similar to that given the players. The player had to have five characters on his slip corresponding to those marked off by the company. He had to have six to get $2, seven to get $20, nine to get $200, and all he had marked out to get $400. To get five characters to correspond was relatively easy, but after that the chances were small.[60]

The Chinese, however, were not the sole customers of their own gambling houses. In a raid upon the Chinese gambling institutions of Butte, Montana, three whites as well as twelve Chinese and $531 in cash were rounded up.[61]

"Shoo Fly" was another notable Chinaman. Having been born in Walla Walla he was entitled to vote and along with another eligible Chinese voter, Andy Lee (Andrew Johnson), voted a mixed ticket in the 1888 election.[62] "Shoo Fly" served as interpreter and helped his fellow countrymen when in trouble.[63]

The town of Chesaw in the state of Washington was named after a "remarkable" Chinaman who prospected for gold in the Okanogan country before the Civil War. Later he owned a store on the Columbia River near the mouth of the Okanogan and employed miners to wash gold on the bars along the banks of the Columbia. He was known as a daring horseman who could rope a steer as ably as any western cowboy.[64] Most Chinese, however, did not have reputations as equestrians. They were considered more at home flat-footed. Thus an account of a Sunday morning horseback ride by several of them in Spokane is told with colorful metaphors:

> As the timid celestials mounted the animals some one gave a yell, and the horses dashed off perfectly unmanageable. The Chinamen shrieked lustily and hung on to the saddle like grim death, their knees drawn up to their chin. It was one of the most ludicrous exhibitions ever witnessed. The horses struck out in different directions. One of the Chinamen was thrown off, while the others hung on until the animals grew weary. It was an experience that the indulgers are not liable to try again for some time.[65]

The white people were not the only ones who found amusement in the discomforts and misfortunes of the Chinese. Some were lodged in jail at Dayton, Washington, and Indian Jim, awaiting trial for horse stealing, was greatly amused. Lying back in his cell, laughing until tears came to his eyes, he shouted at the top of his voice, "Hiyu Ketchum John."[66]

One instance which illustrates another way by which the Chinese were used by the whites for their amusement occurred in Spokane. A Mr. Simpson, with several of his buddies, found entertainment by taking one to a saloon, getting him drunk, and then having him dance and sing for them. The unfortunate Chinaman was thereupon hauled into court on the charge of drunkenness. The judge, however, suspended the sentence upon learning how he had become drunk.[67] There is some evidence within the Inland Empire, therefore, to support the general opinion that the "Chinese were a constant source of amusement, if not of dislike or contempt, to the frontier."[68]

Many instances could be cited of the white men enjoying bedeviling the Chinese. About the turn of the century, Prosser, Washington, had several Chinese restaurants and one proprietor named Charley was the favorite brunt of the jokes, practical and verbal, of one Ed Bean. One day he stuffed Charley's chimney with a gunny sack and waited to see him get mad. Charley, smelling the proverbial "rat," was able to laugh at the joke.[69] D. E. Tower of Pullman, Washington, recalls that for teenage fun in Walla Walla during the Eighties, the boys would pelt the Chinese with rocks and ask for handouts.[70]

The white community although finding amusement in a Chinaman's discomfiture could also find amusement in the Chinese sense of humor. A story was told of one who went up to the depot at Hailey, Idaho, to see about buying a ticket for

San Francisco. He was heard to have made the following remark: "Me go horse-back get there plitty quick; go on cars get there heap quicker; go by telegraph, Gee Klise, get there before 'um start!"[71]

The Chinese could be heroic and generous and was sometimes given due credit for these qualities. When the fire bug visited Colfax in April 1893, the efforts of a Chinese employee of the Baldwin Hotel helped save the lives of the guests.[72] Chinese generosity was recognized but not always appreciated. They often gave candy to the white children or handkerchiefs at New Years.[73] A Mrs. Young who resided at Elk City, Idaho, did not always like the melted sticky mass she would find in her boy's pockets.[74]

Chinese ingenuity was supposedly at its best when some of the miners prepared nuggets for sale by tossing bits of lead into a pan filled with amalgam. Amalgam coated lead was a fair imitation of gold.[75] There were some whites who firmly believed that the Chinese exercised their ingenuity most in being bad. "Of course," maintained one Inland Empire reporter, "this does not apply to every one of them, but it fits a great majority."[76] But this journalist stoutly insisted that the Chinese were apt pupils in the school of naughtiness and that no better illustration of their shrewdness could be found than in the Chinaman who had removed the figures fifty from a revenue stamp and pasted them on a dollar in such a way as to make it appear to be a $50 note. He passed it, promised to make it good, but failing to do so, landed in court.[77] The reporter did not explain how this paragon of ingenuity was not shrewd enough to stay out of court.

Ingenuity, generosity, dignity, and courage, then, were all personal characteristics attributed to the Chinese in the Inland Empire. The instances of these characteristics recorded above were surely repeated with various modifications by many unknown Chinese throughout the area. These traits as well as certain social and cultural features of the Chinese communities were not always adequately understood by the whites. For example, the habit of confusing the Chinese "tongs" and their functions with the Six Companies was perhaps understandable, for many conceptions of the Chinese harbored by the general public were no doubt colored by ignorance, fear, distrust, and mixed feelings both of apathy and curiosity.

The following assessment of the Chinese community in Spokane illustrated also a subtle assumption by the white community that the Six Companies was close to being omnipotent within the Chinese community:

> The Chinese have peculiar ways of settling affairs. What they cannot adjust under the very stringent rules of their peculiar secret order they refer to the Six Companies, and the decision is final, no matter what it may be. A few days before I left Spokane a Chinaman and a woman purporting to be his wife arrived from San Francisco. The next day the husband of the woman came and demanded his wife. The eloping couple declined to be separated, and the injured husband appealed to the Masons, who called upon the wife to return to her lawful spouse. This she refused to do, and the entire matter was referred to the Six Companies. Pending a decision from that arbiter

in all moral, financial, personal and domestic troubles, the husband patiently smokes his pipe within a block of where his wife is living with her paramour. No thought of revenge before the Six Companies has acted enters his head, but if the decision should be against the despoiler of his home, when it is announced, every Chinaman in Spokane will assist in carrying out the decree and punishing the offender.[78]

The Colfax *Commoner* estimated that the Six Companies held a mortgage on the lives of 80 percent of all the Chinese in the United States and Canada.[79] The Six Companies would lend money, in other ways act as bankers, give advice, care for those who were sick, furnish lawyers and interpreters, and guarantee to return to China the body, "dead or alive," of every Chinaman who arrived on the American shore. In return, each Chinese under the auspices of the Six Companies was bound to pay back all the money loaned to him and through agreement with steamship lines, the Six Companies were able to prevent his return to China unless no longer indebted to the companies.[80]

The tongs, on the other hand, grew out of the efforts of the smaller family groups to combat the oppression of the large families which ruled the Six Companies. The first tong was in a sense a Chinese Vigilance Committee. But the fraternal, relatively non-political tongs as they spread out across the land and developed inter-state organizations gradually evolved an intense rivalry.[81] Nonetheless, the tongs did function as mutual aid societies and centers for social and personal activities.[82] That the tongs functioned within the Inland Empire before 1900 has been demonstrated, but the extent of their activities and the magnitude of any rivalries cannot be determined clearly from the evidence available.

But one available bit of evidence concerning the Inland Empire Chinese tended to exemplify the old saying that the world moves. Walking down an Ellensburg street during the early '90's one day was a Chinaman whistling "Annie Rooney," followed closely by a blanketed Indian playing "Home Sweet Home" on a harmonica.[83]

NOTES

1. *Spokesman-Review*, July 14, 1895, p. 7., c. 2.
2. Culin, *Journal of American Folklore*, III, No. 10, p. 192.
3. *Spokesman-Review*, March 3, 1895, p. 7., c. 5.
4. *Spokesman-Review*, May 28, 1895, p. 5., c. 3.
5. *Ibid.*
6. *Spokesman-Review*, January 20, 1896, p. 3., c. 4.
7. Elsensohn, I, 136.
8. Lewiston *Teller*, September 15, 1887, p. 3., c. 2.
9. *Oregonian*, October 24, 1895, p. 3., c. 2.
10. *Spokesman-Review*, March 15, 1897, p. 6., c. 1.
11. *Spokesman-Review*, July 28, 1895, p. 4., c. 2.
12. Lewiston *Tribune*, April 25, 1948, Sec. 2., p. 1., c. 1.

13. *Ibid.*

14. *Northwest Tribune*, September 16, 1892, p. 8, c. 1.

15. *Oregonian*, October 10, 1893, p. 4., c. 7.

16. Spokane *Review*, October 28, 1886, p. 2., c. 4.

17. *Spokesman*, January 24, 1893, p. 3., c. 2.

18. *Ibid.*

19. Lewiston *Teller*, February 21, 1887, p. 3., c. 2.

20. Colfax *Commoner*, May 26, 1893, p. 2., c. 2.; Lewiston *Tribune*, April 25, 1948, Sec. 2., p. 1., c. 1.

21. Elsensohn, II, 115.

22. Elsensohn, II, 115.

23. *Oregonian*, August 31, 1893, p. 4., c. 7.

24. Elsensohn, I, 165.

25. From the Colville *Reporter* as quoted in the Spokane Falls *Review*, July 29, 1886, p. 3., c. 1.

26. Lewiston *Teller*, February 3, 1887, p. 3., c. 2.; Idaho *Free Press*, February 24, 1888, as quoted in Elsensohn, I, 136.

27. Spokane *Review*, February 27, 1893, p. 3., c. 2.

28. *Spokesman-Review*, February 20, 1896, p. 3., c. 2.

29. *Spokesman-Review*, February 13, 1896, p. 8, c. 4.

30. Colfax *Commoner*, October 13, 1893, p. 5., c. 4.; *Oregonian*, October 10, 1893, p. 4., c. 7.

31. Elsensohn, I, 165.

32. Spokane Falls *Review*, June 20, 1884, p. 3., c. 1.; September 13, 1884, p. 2., c. 6.

33. Ingersoll, *Among the Rockies*, p. 28.

34. Spokane *Review*, June 10, 1892, p. 7., c. 1.

35. Elsensohn, I, 165; Ingersoll, *Among the Rockies*, p. 28.

36. *Ibid.*, p. 29.

37. Spokane Falls *Evening Review*, June 17, 1884, p. 3., c. 1.

38. *Idaho Signal*, March 30, 1872, p. 3., c. 1.

39. *Oregonian*, May 20, 1894, p. 4., c. 7.

40. *Idaho Signal*, May 25, 1872, p. 3., c. 1.

41. Spokane *Review*, March 2, 1893, p. 8., c. 2.

42. Spokane *Review*, April 16, 1892, p. 4., c. 2.

43. *Spokesman*, June 23, 1892, p. 3., c. 1.

44. *Ibid.*

45. *Spokesman-Review*, March 3, 1895, p. 7., c. 5.

46. Idaho County *Free Press*, August 13, 1886.

47. Elsensohn, I, 121–122.

48. *Spokesman-Review*, February 7, 1896, p. 8., c. 2.; February 15, 1896, p. 8., c. 3.

49. Spokane *Review*, January 13, 1892, p. 5., c. 2.

50. Elsensohn, I, 94.

51. *Ibid.*; Bailey, p. 675.

52. Barrette, *Inland Empire Magazine*, October 12, 1952, p. 2.

53. Letter of John MacAdam Webster to Mrs. Julia Lum, July 22, 1905, in the Webster Collection (State College of Washington Archives, Pullman, Washington), No. 17, p. 73.

54. *Spokesman*, May 19, 1892, p. 2., c. 1.

55. *Ibid.*

56. Ballou, pp. 138–139.

57. Elsensohn, I, 167.

58. *Spokesman-Review*, February 1, 1896, p. 7., c. 1.; February 2, 1896, p. 3., c. 4.

59. Oppenheimer, Bills Receivable to June, 1865.

60. *Spokesman-Review*, March 27, 1896, p. 6., c. 1.

61. *Spokesman-Review*, February 9, 1896, p. 12., c. 2.

62. *Northwest Tribune*, September 12, 1884, p. 4., c. 1.; *Stevens County Miner*, December 20, 1888, p. 3., c. 3.

63. *Oregonian*, October 1, 1893, p. 4., c. 7.

64. Dan Drumheller, *"Uncle Dan" Drumheller Tells Thrills of Western Trails in 1854* (Spokane, Washington: Inland American Printing Co., 1925), pp. 123–124.

65. Spokane *Review*, April 27, 1886, p. 2., c. 2.

66. Dayton *Chronicle*, October 20, 1883, p. 3., c. 1.

67. *Spokesman*, August 5, 1891, p. 5., c. 2.

68. Housman, *Washington Historical Quarterly*, XXVI, No. 4., p. 269.

69. Helga A. Travis, *The Umatilla Trail* (New York: Exposition Press, 1951), p. 151.

70. Interview with D. E. Tower, April 29, 1958.

71. Lewiston *Teller*, August 16, 1888, p. 3., c. 2.

72. W. L. Lever, *An Illustrated History of Whitman County* (Spokane: W. L. Lever, 1901), p. 155.

73. Elsensohn, II, 113, 114.

74. Elsensohn, I, 164.

75. Donaldson, p. 35.

76. Spokane *Review*, May 8, 1886, p. 2., c. 1.

77. *Ibid.*

78. *Spokesman-Review*, January 23, 1896, p. 5., c. 2.

79. Colfax *Commoner*, May 26, 1893, p. 2., c. 2.

80. *Ibid.*

81. Eng Ying Gong and Bruce Grant, *Tong War!* (New York: Nicholas Brown, 1930), p. 25–28. Chapter XXI of this book concerns the activities of the author in the tongs of the Pacific Northwest during 1917. He traveled between Seattle, Portland, Spokane, Pendleton, and La Grande. Particular mention was made of La Grande's 100 Chinese who were equally divided into two tongs, the Hip Sings and the Hop Sings, and who indulged in considerable and profound rivalry. The six month's bloodshed prevalent throughout the West in 1917 was worse in the Northwest than elsewhere and was the bitterest of tong war outside of those of 1924 in the East. The 1917 tong wars did much, according to Eng Gong, toward populating the East with Chinese. Other accounts of tongs in Mears, McLeod, and Charles R. Shepard, *The Ways of Ah Sin* (New York: Fleming H. Revell Company, 1923).

82. Mears, p. 373.

83. *Spokesman*, October 3, 1891, p. 5., c. 3.

12

The Snake River Massacre of Chinese Miners, 1887

David H. Stratton

No account of early gold-seekers in the inland Pacific Northwest should be considered complete without a discussion of the Snake River massacre of 1887. In this atrocity thirty-one Chinese miners were brutally slain by a gang of "cowboys," with robbery being the principal motive. The tragic event stands as one of the worst, yet least-known, instances of violence against Chinese nationals in America. Because of the remoteness and rugged terrain of Hells Canyon, where the massacre took place, the details were never fully understood, even in adjacent parts of the Pacific Northwest.

Hells Canyon in the middle Snake River, which provides a boundary between Idaho and Oregon, has long inspired wonder and fear in the hearts of observers. In 1813 Robert Stuart of the Astorian fur-trading venture attempted to describe the awesome depths of this chasm. He asked those who might read his journal to imagine that the treacherous river had first carved a subterranean tunnel deep under the lofty mountains, and that huge slabs of rock had then started falling from the cavern's vaulted ceiling until in time a monstrous cleft had opened to the sky and created "the bed of this tumultuous water course." Later, in 1895, crew members of the *Norma*, one of the two steamboats ever to descend the Snake through Hells Canyon, reportedly "saw stars through the gloom" at the canyon's depths even though the sun was shining brightly in the sky high above.[1]

Quite simply, the Snake defile is the deepest gorge anywhere in North America; and comparisons naturally arise with the better known Grand Canyon of the Colorado River. Like a mysterious inner sanctum—inhospitable, isolated, and austere—Hells Canyon averages 5,510 feet in depth for forty miles, as it cuts through a basaltic plateau between the Blue Mountains on the west and the Salmon Mountains of Idaho and threads its way through intervening tall peaks, rough ravines, and steep ridges. But since the towering Seven Devils Mountains

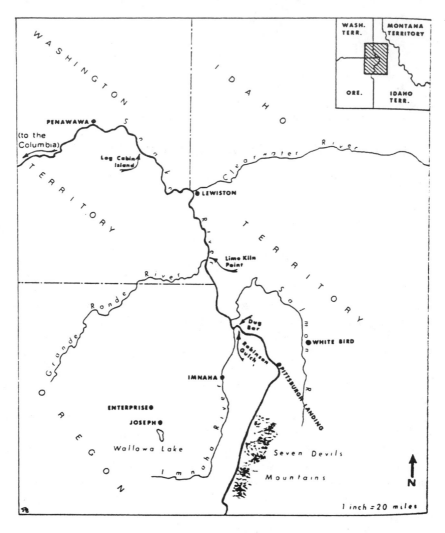

Figure 12.1   Snake River area of Chinese massacre of 1887.

form a part of the eastern wall on the Idaho side, the vertical extremity there is 7,900 feet, or a mile and half from the rim to the river below. The Grand Canyon's greatest depth is 6,100 feet, or over a third of a mile less than its challenger in the Pacific Northwest. Hells Canyon is not only deeper and in some places narrower than the more famous gorge in Arizona, but it carries twice the volume of water, which was, before modern dambuilding, sometimes constricted between solid rock faces to a width of only one hundred feet. Elsewhere along the river, where at its top the canyon may measure from five to ten miles across, sandbars and fertile earthen benches have been formed in the shadow of the harsh, foreboding roughness of dark basaltic walls.[2]

Beginning with the California gold rush, successive tidal waves of frontier mining excitement swept across the trans-Mississippi West in the years 1848–80. In 1861 placer mining quickly arose near both ends of Hells Canyon and soon spread in several directions. It was only a matter of time until the relentless prospectors would try their luck in the deepest gorge of North America, only to encounter one of their severest tests.[3] The diggings here were not nearly as rich as those in the adjoining districts along the Clearwater, Salmon, and Powder rivers. Not only was the gold in these sandbars usually flour fine, but it occurred in thin, widely scattered alluvial deposits. In such circumstances, prospecting with the washing pan, rocker, or other primitive methods which had proved successful elsewhere was like "looking for a needle in a haystack." Often the minuscule gold flakes floated away instead of settling to the bottom of the pan; and the occasional "nugget" might be no larger than half a kernel of wheat. Although some persistent miners experimented with more sophisticated techniques, their efforts were never rewarded with satisfying results.

Since Hells Canyon itself never experienced a gold rush, it is difficult to determine when individual prospectors or small groups of them started penetrating its recesses. A relatively few miners did enter the canyon area and discover a mineralized belt near the head of the gorge and in the southern Wallowa and Seven Devils Mountains. Most of these finds were made during the 1870s and 1880s. Significant development began later, in the 1890s, not with placer mining but in quartz modes of the industrialized era, and not in gold but in copper. Thus the first permanent white inhabitants in the canyon combined prospecting with stock raising, mainly because neither pursuit alone—nor both together, for that matter—offered more than a scant subsistence.

During the placer mining period in the Far West, thousands of Chinese left their homeland for the gold fields of America. Later, thousands more came to the construction camps of the Western railroads. They spread out into all the mining areas of the inland Pacific Northwest. In the gold camps they at first operated laundries or restaurants, worked as domestic servants, and served as manual laborers. Then, as the placers ran out, the Chinese usually were permitted to buy the exhausted diggings at a steep price, whereupon the whites departed. The older the district, the more likely it was that the Orientals would outnumber the whites. In short, the appearance of large numbers of Chinese in a district almost always signaled its decline, for white miners customarily restricted the influx of the Orientals until the readily accessible mineral wealth was gone.[4]

People of many nationalities and races from all over the world came to the Western mining camps, but the "Celestials" or "Tartars" from China were the only ones always regarded as foreigners and intruders by the white prospectors. The whites complained about the strange customs and dress of the Chinese, and that the Orientals were only sojourners, who sent good American money back to

China and would soon return there themselves, that they were prone to unlawful conduct, that they smoked opium until "the smoke could be cut with a caseknife," that they gambled incessantly, that they were obsessed with returning the remains of the dead to their homeland instead of opting for burials in American soil, that they practiced a heathen religion, and so on. As a result, the Chinese were subjected to general hostility and forced to pay special taxes and fees in nearly every camp. They experienced atrocities in the form of robberies, beatings, lynchings, and mass murders. Thus everyone on the mining frontier, whether in the Pacific Northwest or elsewhere, knew the odds against a person who had no more than a "Chinaman's chance."[5]

Even the Indians seemed to despise their distant kinsmen and often attacked the Chinese. For instance, in 1866 Egan and a band of his Paiutes encountered a large traveling party of Chinese miners along the headwaters of the Owyhee River in southeastern Oregon. After receiving assurances of mercy, the Orientals voluntarily gave up. Between forty and fifty of the unarmed Chinese were promptly slaughtered and scalped, with only one boy surviving the massacre. When an army detachment arrived on the scene, it found the mutilated bodies scattered for miles on the lonely trail. Later, in 1875, Indians along the Columbia River near Chelan Falls in Washington Territory practically declared war on Chinese miners in the area, and in one particularly fierce attacked killed every last one of a large group of unprotected Chinese miners who were at work on high benches three hundred feet above the Columbia.[6] Probably the old miners' ballad, "John Chinaman's Appeal," accurately portrayed the animosity many Indians had for the Chinese:

> I met a big stout Indian once,
>   He stopped me by the trail, Sir.
> He drew an awful scalping knife,
>   And I trembled for my tail, Sir.
> He caught me by my hair, it's true,
>   In a manner quite uncivil,
> But when he saw my awful queue,
>   He thought I was the devil.[7]

Nor did the Chinese who went to work on cattle ranches get jobs as cowhands, but instead worked at the menial tasks of cooks and household servants. The common contemptuous belief among ranchers and cowboys was that the Chinese, despite their traditional skills as mounted soldiers, could not ride a horse.

By the 1880s significant numbers of Chinese had moved from the mining districts and railroad construction camps to the coastal cities of California and the Pacific Northwest. Widespread resentment against the Orientals, which was embodied in the terms "Yellow Peril" and "The Chinese Must Go," caused Congress to pass the Chinese Exclusion Act of 1882. This measure, which was strengthened by additional legislation in 1884, banned the immigration of Chinese laborers for ten years and prohibited the naturalization of all Chinese. Such restrictions failed to stop the rising storm of protest. In 1885 and 1886 anti-Chinese agitation and riots swept across the West, with major outbreaks of violence occurring in such widely separated places as Redding and Eureka, California; Tacoma and Seattle, Washington; and Rock Springs, Wyoming. At Rock Springs, an industrialized mining town, twenty-eight Chinese were killed and fifteen seriously wounded in a labor dispute.[8] Nor did the remote mining districts of the inland Pacific Northwest escape these troubles. For instance, the wanton killing of Chinese had started in Idaho as early as 1866 and 1867. Then, in 1885, the murder of a white merchant at Pierce, in the Clearwater River mining country, resulted in the trumped-up arrest of five Orientals, who were subsequently lynched by a band of masked men.[9]

In the midst of this turmoil Oregon remained comparatively peaceful. True, the state constitution of 1859 legally, but not in actuality, prohibited most Chinese from owning real estate or working mining claims, and the legislature authorized some restrictive measures and discriminatory taxes against them. Nor was the Beaver State free of extralegal prejudice, hostility, and violence. Even in the rough-and-ready mining camps of eastern Oregon, however, there were relatively few major instances of anti-Chinese bloodshed—except for the appalling Snake River massacre of 1887.[10]

Chinese prospectors apparently did not appear in appreciable numbers in Hells Canyon until the 1880s, just at the time the widespread anti-Oriental agitation was reaching its height. Other Chinese undoubtedly had arrived earlier in that decade, and some even in the 1860s, but from October 1886 through the spring of 1887 several parties of about ten or twelve men went up the Snake River above Lewiston, Idaho Territory, to search for gold. Two such groups, led by Chea Po and Lee She, made the trip upriver in October 1886, straining at ropes as they trudged along the shore and pulled two boats loaded with supplies through the surging rapids. Perhaps these two parties tried their luck at several different places, but by the next spring they had divided into separate contingents, with the Lee She detachment going up to the mouth of Salt Creek and the Chea Po group staying downriver in the vicinity of Deep Creek and Robinson Gulch near the mouth of the Imnaha River, all on the Oregon side of the Snake.[11]

Robinson Gulch was only a short distance upriver from Dug Bar, a favorite Snake River fording place of the Nez Perce Indians, who by this time had been removed from the Hells Canyon country. In fact, only ten years before Chief Joseph and his Wallowa band had crossed the river at Dug Bar in the dramatic exodus from their homeland preceding the Nez Perce war of 1877. So Chea Po's party at the downriver camp apparently had selected a lonely, isolated spot where they could run their hand-operated fluvial rockers without being molested.[12]

As it happened, though, the epidemic of anti-Chinese violence swept even into this remote canyon. A few cattlemen now wintered their herds in the general area and an occasional white miner passed by; but the real danger was posed by the outlaws and fugitives who frequented the vicinity. For years this inaccessible canyon country had been "the general rendezvous of all the horse and cattle thieves of Oregon, Idaho, and Washington," many of whom used the Dug Bar ford in their two-way trafficking of stolen animals across the Snake between Oregon and Idaho. Several bodies had been found there, some of which bore "marks of brutal treatment," and a man might well risk his life "to hunt his lost or stolen stock unless accompanied by well-armed friends."[13] Dug Bar itself was named for Thomas J. Douglas, who in about 1880 started ranging his horses there after reportedly robbing a Montana stage of a shipment of gold bars. Douglas was shot and killed from ambush in 1883. He supposedly had buried the stolen gold nearby, but repeated digging by many persons has never uncovered it.[14]

On Dug Creek about a half mile down the Snake from the lower Chinese camp stood the old Douglas cabin. In the spring of 1887 a gang of six men and a boy met at the cabin and made it their temporary headquarters. Bruce Evans, a locally celebrated outlaw known as "Old Blue," was the ringleader. He was wanted for robbery as well as horse stealing. J. T. ("Tigh") Canfield was also a notorious horse thief and cattle rustler, and C. O. LaRue had an equally unsavory reputation. At least two of the others, Frank Vaughn and Carl (or Hezekiah) Hughes, operated more-or-less legitimate ranches in the lower Wallowa Valley vicinity, and another, Hiram Maynard, probably had local ranching connections. Robert McMillan was a fifteen-year-old youth who apparently had fallen into bad company. Those of the gang who were accomplished horse thieves had often stopped at Dug Bar to swim stolen stock across the Snake to hideouts in Idaho, and they became convinced that the Chinese miners at nearby Robinson Gulch had found a large amount of gold.[15]

On or about May 25, 1887, some or all of the gang formulated a plan to murder the Orientals. While Vaughn stayed behind at the cabin and prepared dinner, the other six rode their horses to the steep slopes overlooking the Snake River. Hughes and Maynard were posted along the river as lookouts, one upstream and the other downstream from the massacre site, while young McMillan was left in charge of the horses. Canfield and LaRue, who stood above on the rim of Robinson Gulch, and Evans, who was stationed below, began shooting down at the unsuspecting miners on the gravel bar. As the shots of the long-range rifles echoed up the canyon walls above the roar of the river, the trapped Chinese scrambled helplessly about trying to escape. Despite their best efforts, they were killed one by one, and some were horribly mutilated in the process or soon afterwards. The murderers, having exhausted their ammunition, broke one arm of the last Oriental, perhaps as torture in trying to obtain information about hidden gold. When the injured man ran to the river and tried to escape in a boat, the killers caught him and beat out his brains with a rock.[16] In short order ten men lay brutally murdered in what had been a peaceful mining camp.

That evening the killers returned to the Douglas camp, obtained more ammunition, and the next morning the three principal culprits, Evans, Canfield, and

LaRue, went back to the massacre site at Robinson Gulch. Eight more Chinese came to the camp in a boat during the day, and they also were quickly slain. The three white men then traveled by boat to another Chinese camp about four miles away where thirteen Chinese were mining on a river bar. These unfortunate Orientals suffered the same fate as their slaughtered countrymen.[17] In two days of bloody violence thirty-one hapless Chinese miners had died, or three more than the twenty-eight Orientals who had lost their lives in the much-publicized mob action at Rock Springs, Wyoming. Only the death count in the legendary slaughter by Paiute Indians of forty to sixty Chinese miners in 1866 exceeded the toll of the Snake River massacre.

The brutality of the Snake River atrocity was probably unexcelled, whether by whites or Indians, in all the anti-Chinese violence of the American West. After the first day's onslaught at Robins Gulch, the killers wrecked and burned the camp and then threw the mutilated corpses into the Snake River. The bodies of the other Chinese received similar treatment. Since it was the high-water stage of the spring runoff, the dead Chinese were found for months (some accounts say for years)[18] afterwards along the lower river. One body was soon discovered above Lewiston, Idaho, near the Lime Kiln Point with a bullet hole in its back and two ax wounds on the back of the head. Another corpse became lodged in driftwood at Log Cabin Island, the present site of Lower Granite Dam. It had two gunshot wounds in the back, the head and left arm chopped off by an ax, and the severed head and limb wrapped in a coat which was bound to the waist by a belt. A third body was found at Penawawa, Washington, some forty miles below Lewiston and one hundred miles from the massacre site. The dead man had been shot in the chest just below the heart and his head was "very much cut and chopped."[19] A federal official who investigated the slaughter later reported, "It was the most Cold Blooded Cowardly tre[a]chery I have ever heard tell of on this Coast, and I am a [California] '49er'[;] every one was shot, cut up and stripped and thrown in the River."[20]

It was never determined for sure whether the murderers obtained a substantial amount of gold at the Chinese camps, although rumors circulated that the robberies netted as much as $20,000 or $55,500 or as little as $1,000 or $2,000. According to one story, the loot amounted to between $4,000 and $5,000, which was entrusted to one of the ringleaders to exchange for coined money. But he supposedly absconded with the gold and the other killers received nothing for their bloody deeds.[21]

George S. Craig, the cattleman who owned the old Douglas cabin and wintered his stock in the area, later said that when he and his son returned the next fall they found numerous human skeletons lodged along the river in rocks and on bars. "The coyotes or buzzards had cleaned most of the flesh off of them, so we did not know they were Chinamen. We couldn't imagine how so many men had been killed without our hearing about it." Craig also said that the Orientals did not have much gold dust. They had been working in the Robinson Gulch vicinity for only six weeks, having arrived there about April 10, 1887, and this portion of the Snake was not known for its mineral wealth, even by paltry Hells Canyon standards. Also, these diggings, which remained clearly visible for years, indicated that relatively little mining had been done. Craig did claim that his son found a nugget "as big as a ten dollar gold piece" in the ashes of the lower Chinese camp. Although hardly a creditable theory, Craig suggested that the outlaws had not killed the Chinese for gold, but to remove them from the Dug Bar vicinity as witnesses of the stolen stock operations.[22] An eastern Oregon newspaper concluded that it made little difference whether the murderers "acted for love of gold, or merely to satisfy their evil inclinations," the guilty persons must suffer the full penalty of the law for their "atrocious deeds." More to the point, stated another forthright editor, "No community is safe where such men go unpunished."[23]

Whatever the rewards and motives, the legend persisted that a cache of gold lay hidden along the Snake River which the killers had either overlooked or had secreted away for retrieval later. In the early 1890s a local rancher reported finding $450 in retorted gold and a long strand of braided human hair buried in a round tea can near the massacre site. He also said that he found an additional $200 in gold scattered among the boulders. With part of this newfound wealth he promptly bought himself a good pair of field glasses. In 1902 two young prospectors appeared in Joseph, Oregon, with a flask containing $700 in gold dust which they said had been unearthed at an old Chinese camp. It was assumed in the Hells Canyon country that the killers had hidden the flask and overlooked it when they came back for their loot.[24] Grace Jordan, who lived in the Hells Canyon area during the 1930s, has commented that ever since the atrocity, "someone was always returning secretly to renew the search" for Oriental gold.[25] As a more grisly reminder of the tragedy, a Chinese skull fashioned into a sugar bowl graced the kitchen table of one ranch house for many years.

In the first part of June 1887 Lee She and the Chinese miners from the upper diggings of Salt Creek came by boat to pay a visit to their countrymen at Robinson Gulch. Upon reaching the downriver bar, the new arrivals beheld a scene of horror and destruction. They found the deserted camp "in a broken up condition," with tools, blankets, and cooking utensils scattered about on the bar, and the boat belonging to Chea Po stranded on some rocks with holes chopped in the bottom. Three bodies still remained in or near the river. It seemed that the murderers had wanted "to destroy every vestige of evidence of the existence of a camp."[26]

The Chinese fled from the scene in terror, their boat speeding along downstream on the swollen river, and reported the crime to the authorities at Lewiston.[27] Learning of the slaughter from newspaper accounts, the Chinese consul general in San Francisco requested the Sam Yup Company, one of the controversial Chinese Six Companies in California which controlled these Oriental nationals, to take charge of the case. The company immediately dispatched Lee Loi to Lewiston, where he hired United States Commissioner, J. K. Vincent as a special investigator. As a representative of the powerful Sam Yup Company, the English-speaking Lee Loi also offered a reward of $1,000 for the apprehension of the murderers, and the consul general in San Francisco posted an additional amount.[28]

The investigation conducted by Vincent, previously a forty-niner in California, assumed the aspects of a Western movie thriller. High water in the middle Snake River made it impossible for him to reach the massacre site and discover the full details. But he worked at "ferreting out the matter" by questioning the Chinese miners who had discovered the atrocity and by maintaining surveillance of white encampments in the upriver mountain country. As a result, he traced some of the murdered miners' provisions, especially their particular kind of flour, to certain white men. For six days Vincent trailed a suspect who was the last person known to have visited the ill-fated Oriental diggings and who had been telling "some very curious stories about the matter." In that vicinity, he reported, there were twenty or thirty badmen, and he had been watched very closely for several days. In time Vincent's investigation petered out, however, and repeated letters to him from the Chinese consul general asking for information went unanswered. The consular official ordered Lee Loi and another Chinese at Lewiston, Chea Tsze-ke, to continue their inquiries, but they had no success in discovering the names of the guilty persons.[29]

Finally, in February 1888, the Chinese minister to the United States, Chang Yen Hoon (more correctly Chang Yin-huan), sent a detailed report of the crime to Secretary of State Thomas F. Bayard. The minister did so, he wrote, with the hope that local authorities would be encouraged to do their duty in administering justice and punishing the killers. He pointed out that this case, in which ten men (the full number was not yet known) "were murdered and their bodies mutilated in a most shocking manner and thrown away," differed greatly from the usual homicide. He then lectured the secretary of state on the moral implications involved. If the killers remained at large, the Chinese minister said, "other wicked persons may from their hatred of the Chinese, follow ... [this example,] which will affect the interest and safety of the Chinese resident there and elsewhere in the United States."[30]

Secretary Bayard received the news with dismay. At that time he was negotiating a new treaty with China which would practically exclude Chinese laborers from the United States for twenty years; but Minister Chang kept insisting that no settlement was possible until the United States agreed to pay indemnities for earlier losses of Chinese property and lives. On March 12, 1888, about a month after the Chinese minister notified Secretary Bayard of the Snake River massacre, the two diplomatic representatives signed the new treaty. As a part of the agreement, the United States consented to pay $276,619.75 "for all losses and injuries" suffered by specified groups of Chinese nationals in this country.[31] But full information about the Snake River tragedy was not available when these negotiations took place, and the amount of indemnities did not include payment for the lives and property lost in Hells Canyon. Minister Chang stated in his list detailing the Chinese deaths, "If the Snake River murders are omitted[,] of which no accurate information is yet received, there remain 40 lives of Chinese by riots and violence for which no compensation has yet been made."[32] Furthermore, the diplomatic climate soon changed, thereby removing the necessity for the United States to offer additional indemnities as an inducement for Chinese cooperation in treaty-making.

When the Chinese government stalled on giving its final approval to the proposed treaty, President Grover Cleveland arranged for Congress to pass the Scott Act of 1888, which prohibited the reentry of some 20,000 Chinese laborers who had left the United States temporarily. This measure was commonly regarded as a political sop to the Western states, which Cleveland regarded as crucial in the impending presidential election. The treaty negotiated by Secretary Bayard and Minister Chang was never reviewed. Thus the relatives of the murdered Snake River miners never received any indemnities, although the amount of $276,619.75 for earlier atrocities was paid by the United States to China.[33]

Meanwhile the wheels of justice were moving slowly in the Pacific Northwest. When Secretary Bayard had learned of the Snake River massacre, he had assured Minister Chang that steps would be taken to apprehend the guilty persons. Subsequent correspondence between the State Department and officials in the Territory of Idaho and the State of Oregon revealed both disinterest and an inability to cope with the case. It also showed the division of authority among various government units, so much revered by Americans but nevertheless always confusing to foreigners. For instance, Governor Edward A. Stevenson of Idaho declared that although one of the bodies had been found in his territory, the murders had actually been committed in Oregon, and therefore Idaho had no jurisdiction in the matter.[34] J. K. Vincent of Lewiston, that old crime fighter who earlier had been employed by the Sam Yup Company, already had issued a "John Doe" warrant for the arrest of the unknown murderers. He now reported to Governor Stevenson that he possessed new evidence about the identity of the killers, but could not follow this promising lead without additional compensation because "most of us here are too poor to work for glory, [even] in tracing up such brutal murders." The sheriff at Lewiston, in Idaho, was ready and willing to arrest the guilty persons, Vincent claimed, but had no authority to do so in Oregon.[35]

Three months after Minister Chang had apprised Secretary Bayard of the massacre, and almost eleven months after the event itself, the State Department notified the Chinese minister of the first real break in the case. Former United States Senator James H. Slater, now living in Joseph, Oregon, had written federal authorities in Portland that six gang members were under indictment in Wallowa County for the murder and robbery of the Chinese miners. Of the six, however, only three were being held in jail, while a seventh member had turned state's evidence. The three ringleaders, Bruce Evans, J. T. Canfield, and Homer LaRue, who actually did the killing, had skipped out of the state and their whereabouts were unknown. Senator Slater stated that local sentiment was "quite intense" about bringing all the murderers to justice, but observed that Wallowa County could not afford to hire detectives to track down the fugitives, and that the Oregon governor could use extradition only if he knew their location. Under these circumstances, Slater declared, the federal government must find a way to apprehend the three fugitive killers.[36] Federal authorities showed little interest in this suggestion. According to one State Department official, the best means of helping the local court bring the accused killers to justice was by calling Minister Chang's attention to the latest information. Then the Chinese government could employ detectives or special agents to pursue this matter "in which Chinese interests are so deeply concerned."[37]

In the end no one was ever convicted and punished by law for the Snake River massacre, although there were many stories in the Hells Canyon country about "the wrecked lives that followed the murderers."[38] Originally, before the facts of the massacre became known, two of the ringleaders, Bruce Evans and J. T. Canfield, had been arrested in Joseph for stealing livestock and changing brands. The other principal murderer, Homer LaRue, had already left the country, probably sometime in July 1887. Joseph, although the country seat of Wallowa County, was only a rough mountain village with a "chicken coop" of a jail. During his first night of imprisonment, Evans hoodwinked Sheriff Thomas Humphreys into taking him to the outhouse where someone had hidden a six-shooter for the outlaw. Evans disarmed the sheriff and fled to parts unknown, leaving a wife and family behind. Canfield either shot his way out of jail or was released on bail—the accounts differ—and promptly disappeared.[39] Later it was rumored in Wallowa County that LaRue was killed in a poker game in California; and that Canfield went to Kansas, served a term in the state penitentiary, and then operated a blacksmith shop at Glenns Ferry, Idaho. As for Evans, otherwise known as "Old Blue," he reportedly lost himself in the Big Hole country of Montana, but not without leaving his mark on Hells Canyon folklore.[40] One local ballad entitled "Old Blue," which recounts the various exploits of the three ringleaders, alludes to the Chinese massacre in the last stanza:

It was late in the evening, when they brained the last man,
And in fear, bid farewell to their Snake River Land.
For the Officers were coming, not for the men they slew,
And they took into custody, their Captain Old Blue.[41]

The sudden departure of Evans and Canfield apparently loosened the consciences and tongues of the remaining gang members, who had been threatened with death if they "talked." Perhaps under pressure from his family, Frank Vaughn turned state's evidence, testified before the grand jury, and "gave the whole matter away." In March 1888 the Wallowa County circuit court at Joseph issued an indictment against all the gang members except Vaughn. Upon being jailed, the others on hand—Carl Hughes, Hiram Maynard, and young Robert McMillan—also became extremely cooperative and tried to outdo each other in exonerating themselves and laying all the blame on the three absent ringleaders, as they did in their subsequent trial.[42] On August 28, 1888, Hughes, Maynard, and McMillan were arraigned for murder, and the next day entered a plea of not guilty. The trial ended on September 1 with a verdict of not guilty for all three defendants. Vaughn was absolved of any further liability, and the case was continued against the departed ringleaders.[43] Ironically, young McMillan, who had just turned sixteen, died of diphtheria shortly after the trial, but managed to cleanse his soul once more by making a deathbed confession to his father.[44]

At first glance the Snake River murders might appear to have had little or nothing in common with the wave of anti-Chinese violence characterized by the well-known episodes in Western urban and industrialized areas such as Rock Springs, Wyoming, and Tacoma and Seattle, Washington. After all, the basic sin of human greed—the love of money as the root of all evil—seemingly explained this atrocity. Upon closer examination, however, it is obvious that a similar strain of racism constituted the fundamental cause of all these outbreaks. In the first place, those responsible for the Snake River massacre thought the Chinese miners had found a large amount of gold, despite the common knowledge that Hells Canyon placer diggings were notoriously unrewarding. Why, then, did the killers believe that the Chinese had acquired appreciable mineral wealth? Western tradition held that the Chinese as a race worked longer and harder, lived more frugally, and by their meticulous efforts usually extracted significant amounts of gold from worked-over cliams and relatively worthless prospects. Thus the Snake River Orientals died because their race had a well-deserved reputation for diligence. Secondly, they were murdered because whites customarily held Chinese in low esteem. To put it another way, the killers might have robbed a small group of white miners, and might possibly have shot some of them, but would they have casually slaughtered thirty-one of their fellow Caucasians? Probably not. As a contemporary white rancher commented about the acquittal of the three gang members who stood trial, "I guess if they had killed 31 white men something would have been done about it, but none of the jury knew the Chinamen or cared much about it, so they turned the men loose."[45]

NOTES

1. Philip A. Rollins, ed., *The Discovery of the Oregon Trail* (New York: Charles Scribner's Sons, 1935), p. 81; Captain W. P. Gray to Director, U.S. Geological Survey, December 2, 1920, in " 'She will strike about there. . . .': Steamboating in Hell's Canyon," *Idaho Yesterdays* 1, no. 2 (Summer 1957): 6–9.

2. General geographical and geological information was obtained from Ewart M. Baldwin, *Geology of Oregon* (Eugene: University of Oregon Cooperative Book Store, 1959), pp. 87, 92, 95; Leonard C. Ekman, *Scenic Geology of the Pacific Northwest*, ed. L. K. Phillips (Portland: Binfords and Mort, 1862), pp. 198–202, 211; William Ashworth, *Hells Canyon: The Deepest Gorge on Earth* (New York: Hawthorn Books, 1977), pp. xiii–xvi; Gerald J. Tucker, *The Story of Hells Canyon* (n.p., 1977), pp. 1–6). Hells Canyon as a name for this long stretch of the Snake River did not come into general use until the twentieth century.

3. For general information on the Inland Empire gold rush, see William J. Trimble, *The Mining Advance into the Inland Empire*, Bulletin of the University of Wisconsin No. 638 (Madison, 1914, reprint ed., New York: Johnson Reprint Corp., 1972); Rodman W. Paul, *Mining Frontiers of the Far West, 1848–1880* (New York: Holt, Rinehart and Winston, 1963), pp. 40–41, 135–53; William S. Greever, *The Bonanza West: The Story of the Western Mining Rushes* (Norman, Okla.: University of Oklahoma Press, 1963), chap. 11; Isaac Hiatt, *Thirty-one Years in Baker County: A History of the County from 1861 to 1893* (Baker, Ore.: Abbott & Foster, 1893), pp. 6–25. For detailed information on mining activity in the Hells Canyon area, see David H. Stratton and Glen W. Lindeman, *A Study of Historical Resources of the Hells Canyon National Recreation Area*, 2 vols. (Baker, Ore.: Hells Canyon National Recreation Area Planning Team, United States Forest Service, 1978), 1:24–51.

4. These works provide information on the Chinese in the Inland Empire mining districts: Trimble, *Mining Advance into the Inland Empire*, pp. 144–46; Paul, *Mining Frontiers of the Far West*, pp. 143–44; Helen B. Rand, *Gold, Jade and Elegance* (Baker, Ore.: Record-Courier, Printers, 1974), pp. 41–52.

5. See Gunther Barth, *Bitter Strength: A History of the Chinese in the United States, 1850–1870* (Cambridge, Mass.: Harvard University Press, 1964); Mary Roberts Coolidge, *Chinese Immigration* (New York: Henry Holt and Co., 1909); Stuart C. Miller, *The Unwelcome Immigrant: The American Image of the Chinese* (Berkeley: University of California Press, 1969); Betty Lee Sung, *Mountain of Gold: The Story of the Chinese in America* (New York: Macmillan Co., 1967); Christopher H. Edson, *The Chinese in Eastern Oregon, 1860–1890* (San Francisco: R and E Research Associates, 1974); Nancy K. Feichter, "The Chinese in the Inland Empire During the Nineteenth Century" (M.A. thesis, Washington State University, 1959).

6. *History of the Pacific Northwest: Oregon and Washington*, 2 vols. (Portland: North Pacific History Co., 1889), 2:23; Hubert Howe Bancroft, *Works*, vol. 30: *Oregon, 1848–1888* (San Francisco: History Company, 1888), pp. 521–22; *History of Baker, Grant, Malheur and Harney Counties—State of Oregon* (n.p.: Western Historical Publishing Co., 1902), pp. 520–21; *History of the Big Bend Country Embracing Lincoln, Douglas, Adams and Franklin Counties—State of Washington* (n.p.: Western Historical Publishing Co., 1904), pp. 522–23. See also Robert E. Wynne, "Reaction to the Chinese in the Pacific Northwest and British Columbia, 1850 to 1910" (Ph.D. dissertation, University of Washington, 1964), pp. 59–60; Lorraine B. Hildebrand, *Straw Hats, Sandals and Steel: The Chinese in Washington State* (Tacoma: Washington State American Revolution Bicentennial Commission, 1977), pp. 16–17. For the massacre on the Owyhee River the death toll has been variously estimated at 40 to 150 killed. See Bancroft, *Oregon*, fn. 9, p. 521.

7. From *Gold Diggers Song Book of 1856*, quoted in Stan Steiner, *Fusang: The Chinese Who Built America* (New York: Harper Colophon Books, 1980), p. 155. Steiner's view of relations between the Indians and Chinese is quite different from the one presented here.

8. Jules A. Karlin, "The Anti-Chinese Outbreak in Tacoma, 1885," *Pacific Historical Review* 23 (August 1954): 271–83, and "The Anti-Chinese Outbreaks in Seattle, 1885–1886," *Pacific Northwest Quarterly* 39 (April 1948): 103–30; Coolidge, *Chinese Immigration*, p. 188; W. P. Wilcox, "Anti-Chinese Riots in Washington," *Washington Historical Quarterly* 20 (July 1929): 204–12; James A. Halseth and Bruce A. Glasrud, "Anti-Chinese Movements in Washington, 1885–1886: A Reconsideration," in *The Northwest Mosaic: Minority Conflicts in Pacific Northwest History*, ed. James A. Halseth and Bruce A.

Glasrud (Boulder: Pruett Publishing Co., 1977), pp. 116–39; Paul Crane and Alfred Larson, "The Chinese Massacre," *Annals of Wyoming 12* (January 1940): 47–55, 153–61.

9. Merrill D. Beal and Merle W. Wells, *History of Idaho,* 3 vols. (New York: Lewis Historical Publishing Co., 1959), 1:313–15, 577–80.

10. F. G. Young, "Why Oregon Has Never Had An Oriental Problem," *Annals of American Academy of Political and Social Science 34* (1909):306–10; Wynne, "Reaction to Chinese in Pacific Northwest," pp. 43–46, 66–73, 102–04; Edson, *Chinese in Eastern Oregon,* pp. 9–10, 21, 42–52.

11. Chang Yen Hoon, Chinese Minister to the United States, to Thomas F. Bayard, Secretary of State, February 16, 1888, Microfilm M98. Notes from the Chinese Legation in the U.S. to the Department of State, 1868–1906, Record Group 59, National Archives and Records Service (hereafter cited as Notes from Chinese Legation, RG 59, NARS).

12. See Tucker, *Story of Hells Canyon,* pp. 106–10.

13. *Walla Walla Statesman,* September 30, 1891.

14. J. H. Horner, "Origin of Wallowa County Place Names," ed. Grace Butterfield Bartlett, pp. 98–99, mimeographed manuscript, Historical Files, Wallowa-Whitman National Forest, Baker, Oregon.

15. Notes from a stenographic report taken during an interview with George S. Craig, March 2, 1936, Enterprise, Oregon (hereafter cited as Craig interview), in a handwritten manuscript, "Wallowa County History: Chinese Massacre—1887—Eureka," Works Progress Administration, Historical Records Survey, Oregon Records, BX 66–30, in Special Collections, University of Oregon Library, Eugene (hereafter cited as WPA Historical Records Survey, BX No., UO); Verle Bechtel, "The Chinese Massacre in the Snake River Canyon," seminar paper, Department of History, University of Oregon, May 26, 1961. The author of this seminar paper, which contains personal sources of information no longer available, was kind enough to send me a copy of it.

16. Craig interview; *Wallowa Signal,* April 13, 1888; quoted in *History of Union and Wallowa Counties—State of Oregon* (n.p.: Western Historical Publishing Co., 1902), p. 486, also quoted in more detail in *Walla Walla Weekly Union,* April 28, 1888, and in *Lewiston Teller,* April 26,May 3, 1888; *Portland Morning Oregonian,* April 27, 1888; *Walla Walla Statesman,* September 30, 1891; *Spokane Spokesman,* October 1, 1891. Good summaries of the events involved in the massacre are given in Bob Sincock, " 'Case Is Closed': Fifty Years Ago Snake River Flowed Blood and International Complications Lingered Long," *Portland Oregon Journal,* September 18, 1938, newspaper clipping in WPA Historical Records Survey, BX 66–29, UO; Gerald J. Tucker, "Massacre for Gold," *Old West,* Fall 1967, pp. 26–28, 48; Bill Gulick, "Murder in Hells Canyon: Dam Is Reminder of Brutal Episode," *Seattle Times Magazine,* July 1, 1973, pp. 8–9.

17. Handwritten manuscript, "Wallowa County History: Chinese Massacre—1887—Eureka," WPA Historical Records Survey, BX 66–29, UO; *Wallowa Chieftain,* April 19, 1888, as cited in *Portland Morning Oregonian,* April 27, 1888; *Walla Walla Statesman,* September 30, 1891; *Spokane Spokesman,* October 1, 1891. A spirited controversy still exists in the Hells Canyon country over the exact site of the Snake River massacre, with Robinson Gulch and nearby Deep Creek being the main contenders. Part of the confusion may have arisen because the killings took place at two, and perhaps three, different locations.

18. Craig interview.

19. Copies of the People of the United States for the Territory of Idaho v. John Doe, Richard Doe *et al.,*"John Doe" Warrant of Arrest—both in Justice or U.S. Commissioner

Court of Lewiston Precinct, Nez Perce County, Idaho Territory, June 18, 1887—, and sworn statement, July 8, 1887, by J. K. Vincent, U.S. Commissioner and Justice of the Peace, Lewiston, Nez Perce County, Idaho Territory, enclosed in Chang Yen Hoon to Thomas F. Bayard, February 16, 1888, Notes from Chinese Legation, RG 59, NARS.

20. Copy of J. K. Vincent to Liung Ting-tsan, Chinese Consul General, and F. A. Bee, Chinese Consul, San Francisco, enclosed in *ibid.* See also *Lewiston Teller*, June 30, 1888.

21. *Lewiston Teller*, June 16, 1887; *Wallowa Signal*, April 13, 1888, quoted in *History of Union and Wallowa Counties*, p. 486; Tucker, *Story of Hells Canyon*, p. 110; *Walla Walla Statesman*, September 30, 1891.

22. Craig interview; Fred Lockley, "Observations and Impressions of the Journal Man," *Portland Oregon Journal*, undated newspaper interview with George S. Craig, Wallowa County Museum, Joseph, Oregon. In support of Craig's theory about the killing, a Chinese miner reported that a cowboy had told him of seeing eight other cowboys forcibly expel a party of Chinese prospectors from a sandbar in that vicinity shortly before the massacre and throw their provisions and bedding into the Snake River. Although none of the Chinese was killed, the entire party fled from the scene by boat. After the massacre the Chinese miner assumed that the eight cowboys were the same ones responsible for the killings. Chang Yen Hoon to Thomas F. Bayard, February 16, 1888, Notes from Chinese Legation, RG 59, NARS.

23. *Portland Morning Oregonian*, April 27, 1888; *Pendleton East Oregonian*, updated newspaper article, Wallowa County Museum, Joseph, Oregon.

24. Horner, "Origin of Wallowa County Place Names," p. 31; *Lewiston Morning Tribune*, November 1, 1902.

25. Grace Jordan, *Home Below Hell's Canyon* (New York: Thomas Y. Crowell Co., 1954), p. 9.

26. *Lewiston Teller*, June 16 and 23, 1887.

27. *Ibid.*, June 16, 1887.

28. Chang Yen Hoon to Thomas F. Bayard, February 16, 1888, Notes from Chinese Legation, RG 59, NARS; copy of Liung Ting-tsan and F. A. Bee to J. K. Vincent, enclosed in *ibid.*

29. Copy of J. K. Vincent to Liung Ting-tsan and F. A. Bee, July 19, 1887, enclosed in *ibid.* See also *Lewiston Teller*, August 11, 1887.

30. Chang Yen Hoon to Thomas F. Bayard, February 16, 1888, Notes from Chinese Legation, RG 59, NARS.

31. Charles C. Tansill, *The Foreign Policy of Thomas F. Bayard, 1885–1897* (New York: Fordham University Press, 1940), chap. 5; Jack Chen, *The Chinese of America* (San Francisco: Harper & Row, 1980), pp. 125–80.

32. Chang Yen Hoon to Thomas F. Bayard, March 3, 1888, with enclosed lists of Chinese property losses and deaths, Notes from Chinese Legation, RG 59, NARS.

33. Tansill, *Foreign Policy of Bayard*, pp. 161–81; G. L. Rives, Acting Secretary of State, to Chang Yen Hoon, October 19, 1888, Microfilm M99, Notes to Foreign Legations in the United States from the Department of State, 1834–1906—China, June 3, 1868–January 4, 1899, Record Group 59, National Archives and Records Service (hereafter cited as Notes to Foreign Legations—China, RG 59, NARS); statement of receipt signed by Chang Yen Hoon, January 11, 1889, Notes from Chinese Legations, RG 59, NARS. In March 1887 the United States had paid the Chinese government $147,748.74 for Chinese losses in the Rock Springs, Wyoming, mob violence, so the amount of $276,619.75 was in compensation for losses since that event. Tansill, *Foreign Policy of Bayard*, p. 149. As late as 1891 the

Chinese government considered reviving the case for indemnities in the Snake River massacre. *Spokane Spokesman*, October 1 and 2, 1891.

34. Edward A. Stevenson to Thomas F. Bayard, April 19, 1888, Microfilm M179, Miscellaneous Letters of the Department of State, 1789–1906, Record Group 59, National Archives and Records Service (hereafter cited as Miscellaneous Letters of State Department, RG 59, NARS).

35. Copy of J. K. Vincent to Edward A. Stevenson, April 14, 1888, enclosed in *ibid.*

36. Copy of James H. Slater to L. L. McArthur, U.S. Attorney for the District of Oregon, Portland, April 25, 1888, enclosed in McArthur to Secretary of State Thomas F. Bayard, April 28, 1888, Miscellaneous Letters of State Department, RG 59, NARS. See also G. L. Rives, Acting Secretary of State, to Chang Yen Hoon, May 15, 1888, Notes to Foreign Legations—China, RG 59, NARS.

37. G. L. Rives, Acting Secretary of State, to L. L. McArthur, May 10, 1888, Miscellaneous Letters of State Department, RG 59, NARS.

38. *Lewiston Morning Tribune*, November 1, 1902.

39. Craig interview; *Wallowa Chieftain*, April 19, 1888, as cited in *Portland Morning Oregonian*, April 27, 1888. See also Bechtel, "Chinese Massacre," pp. 11–12; Gulick, "Murder in Hells Canyon," p. 9; Sincock, " 'Case Is Closed' "; Tucker, "Massacre for Gold," pp. 28, 48.

40. Craig interview.

41. Horner, "Origin of Wallowa County Place Names," p. 21.

42. Copy of James H. Slater to L. L. McArthur, April 25, 1888, enclosed in McArthur to Thomas F. Bayard, April 28, 1888, Miscellaneous Letter of State Department, RG 59, NARS.

43. The Wallowa County circuit court record of the trial, which is quite brief, is quoted in Tucker, "Massacre for Gold," p. 28. Craig interview provides additional information, as do the notes from court papers dated May 1, 1887, to March 27, 1888, WPA Historical Records Survey, BX 66–30, UO.

44. *Walla Walla Statesman*, September 30, 1891.

45. George S. Craig in undated newspaper interview by Fred Lockley, "Observations and Impressions of the Journal Man," *Portland Oregon Journal*, in Wallowa County Museum, Joseph, Oregon. This remark is also quoted in Tucker, "Massacre for Gold," p. 48. For a general assessment of white perceptions of the Chinese, see Roger Daniels, "Majority Images—Minority Realities: A Perspective on Anti-Orientalism in the United States," in Jack Salzman, ed., *An Annual of American Cultural Studies: Prospects*, vol. 2 (Hempstead, N.Y.: Burt Franklin & Co., 1976), pp. 209–62.

13

"A Chinaman's Chance" on the Rocky Mountain Mining Frontier

Liping Zhu

In 1927, twenty-one years after her family migrated back to Canton, China, from Idaho City, Idaho, American-born For Cue Di Sang, a native of the Boise Basin, wrote to Charley Jones, editor of the *Idaho World,* expressing her regrets about leaving the United States. "China is really a very difficult country," For Cue told her longtime friend."I knew it before by hearing the Chinese talking of it. These Chinese are the one went from here out to America. How foolish my father is to bring such a crowd of native-born children back to China. Now what's the good to them. Of course, they haven't starve, but either of them are a bit happy, nor satisfied being here."[1] Like all of her siblings, For Cue hoped to return to America, the country of her birth and of numerous happy memories.

The experience of For Cue's family on the Rocky Mountain mining frontier was largely a story of success. As a poor Chinese peasant, Loke Kee, For Cue's maternal grandfather, came to southwestern Idaho's Boise Basin in 1863 in search of the "American dream." Loke Kee first mined gold and then ran a general store. After decades of hard work, this Chinese immigrant was able to accumulate a fortune of some sixty thousand to ninety thousand dollars. He became a local celebrity, a Chinese "Horatio Alger" who rose from rags to riches. While many people, including whites, may have envied his life-style and personal wealth, Loke Kee could never forget his homeland. In 1906 he returned to China to retire. Despite protests from his offspring, Loke Kee willfully took the entire family—three generations and more than thirty members, including For Cue—back to China.[2]

As soon as they landed in Hong Kong, octogenarian Loke Kee died of exhaustion from the long trip. The rest of the family eventually reached the mainland. Most of the younger generations had been born in Idaho but now were forced to live in a foreign land. As transplanted Chinese Americans, their new life was not easy. Chinese society was turbulent, stricken by constant civil wars, and For Cue's family eventually lost its grandfather's fortune. For solace and assistance, For Cue reached back to her roots and called on her American friends for financial help.[3] The sharp contrast between the two worlds rekindled her affection for the United States, for in her mind there was no doubt that the American West had been a golden land of opportunity for her family.

For Cue's perceptions of the Chinese experience in the nineteenth-century American West were quite different from that of commentators of our generation and before. Since the era of Mark Twain, Mary Hallock Foote, and Charles M. Russell, when thousands of Chinese immigrated to the American West Coast annually, writers and historians have portrayed Chinese immigrants as "victims." For them, the American frontier was a place that offered no more than "a Chinaman's chance." This fictional personification of "John Chinaman" stereotyped the Chinese as either indigent coolies destined for economic exploitation or passive victims of racial violence. By examining only a part of the Chinese experience in the West, ethnicity scholars have generally preferred to tell a dark story of oppression. As one immigration historian noted, the Chinese "have been more celebrated for what has happened to them than for what they have accomplished."[4]

Current popular and scholarly portrayals similarly tend to present a negative view of Chinese life in the western United States. From the very beginning, western historians had problems incorporating the Chinese into their frontier "drama." If the frontier, as Frederick Jackson Turner stated, was "the meeting point between savagery and civilization," on which side did the Chinese belong? The dilemma prompted most early western historians to treat the Chinese as irrelevant to frontier history by simply ignoring them.[5]

Recently, a new group of western historians has consciously included such long-neglected ethnic minorities as Asian-Americans into the mainstream of western historiography. To these western historians, the unbroken past of the American West represents a conquest of all unprivileged minorities by Anglo-Americans. As one historian put it, on the nineteenth-century American frontier, "there was not equal opportunity for Indians, blacks, Chinese, and Hispanics." Another new western historian adds: "there were at least eight oppressed races in the West: Indians, Hispanics, Chinese, Japanese, blacks, Mormons, strikers, and radicals." In such views, the Chinese were "victims" on the American frontier. Despite their good intention of reclaiming this sub-field from ethnic scholars, the new western historians are still writing "negative history" about the early Chinese experience and telling only partial truth.[6]

It is true that many Chinese immigrants in nineteenth-century American encountered exploitation, injustice, violence, and discrimination on a daily basis. No place was immune from these viruses. The collective story of the Chinese in the Boise Basin of Idaho, however, suggests positive experiences as well. For Cue Di Sang's saga was just one of them. Like many other immigrants, the Chinese on this unique Rocky Mountain mining frontier had remarkable access to economic upward mobility and, in the end, tasted more success than failure in their search for better lives.

The Boise Basin in an area of about four hundred square miles whose geographic center lies about forty miles north of present-day Boise, Idaho. Gold discoveries in southern Idaho introduced an influx of prospectors, miners, and settlers in the basin in 1862.[7] Although the Chinese missed the initial rush, they came soon after and throughout the next decade from California, Nevada, and Oregon in small but repeated waves. After completion of the first transcontinental railroad in 1869, thousands of former railroad laborers, including Chinese from Central Pacific construction crews from northern Utah and Nevada, resettled in Idaho in search of economic independence. They came into the territory as the renowned "Sixty-Niners." Their large numbers created a unique population ratio: By 1870 Idaho contained the largest percentage of Chinese population per capita in the nation. The Chinese (4,274 in total) comprised nearly 30 percent of Idaho Territory's entire population (14,999). In the Boise Basin, where placer mining was the principal occupation, the Chinese community boasted an even larger percentage (46 percent), with 1,754 members in a total population of 3,834. In the mining camps of Idaho City, Placerville, Centerville, and Pioneerville, Chinese immigrants often comprised a majority. Unlike many other boom-and-bust mining areas in the West, the Chinese miners and their families worked and lived in the basis for more than half a century.[8]

Despite the Boise Basin's isolation and underdevelopment, the Chinese established a decent standard of living for themselves. The argument that all of the "Chinamen," like the antebellum slaves, perpetually struggled between poverty and misery has little support in this region.[9] Judged by both contemporary and comparative standards, most Chinese lived well, enjoying a salubrious climate, a nutritious diet, spacious living accommodations, and effective medical care.

Like Idaho Territory overall, the Boise Basin possessed a healthy climate, which in those days determined the intrinsic worth of a country for habitation. The dry, rarified atmosphere, steady temperature, and cool nights produced a vigorous yet entirely bearable climate that reduced illnesses. Residents could endure both summers and winters without excessive discomfort or suffering. Sunstroke, for example, was unheard of in the basin. Many residents afflicted with respiratory diseases found relief and often a permanent cure. In contrast to Guangdong Province, China, the home of many immigrants, where torrid heat and high humidity created fertile conditions for tropical diseases and epidemics such as leprosy, malaria, cholera, and typhoid, the Boise Basin provided Chinese immigrants with a much healthier place to live. The basin also proved to be one of the healthiest regions in the United States. According to the national census of 1870, Idaho Territory had the nation's lowest mortality rate of 0.33 percent, while Arizona had the highest with 2.61 percent. Idaho thus earned the nickname "the great sanitarium of the Pacific Slope."[10]

An abundance of timber in the Boise Basin was another natural gift the Chinese were not accustomed to enjoying. To those who came from the Pearl River Delta, China, where timber was a precious commodity for an exploding population, log

cabins and wooden houses were considered luxuries. When the Chinese first arrived in the basin, they either rented or bought houses from white miners. If a Chinese miner purchased a mining claim, the deal usually included the existing buildings. Because the Chinese integrated into all the mining camps, they lived in
housing comparable in quality to that of other residents. Chinese immigrants most
often adopted log cabins and saltboxes, simple board-and-batten structures, as their
dwellings, homes far superior to those they had left behind in China.[11]

The space rather than the style of the residences often decided their quality.
Most mining towns consisted of an overwhelming majority of single males. As a
result, several miners often shared a single house. On many occasions Chinese
miners shared rooms with whites. In 1870 a dwelling housed an average of 3.67
Chinese. A decade later the number had increased to 3.77, and in 1900 it had
dropped to 3.21.[12] If four persons lived in a twelve-by-thirty-foot house, which was
not considered spacious, each dweller occupied ninety square feet. Comparatively, this spatial arrangement gave the Chinese more room than they would have
had on average in China and more space than other workers in the United States,
especially urban wage earners. In 1893, for example, a New York survey revealed
that an urban worker had only thirty-five square feet of sleeping space.[13] Thus, the
Chinese in the Boise Basin generally lived more comfortably than city laborers,
who often crowded into filthy eastern tenements.

Likewise, Idaho Chinese eating habits contributed to a better material life. Their
diet consisted of a healthy combination of rice, beef, pork, chicken, cabbage, potatoes, beans, onions, squash, carrots, beets, turnips, tomatoes, melons, cucumbers,
sugar, and tea. Almost from the beginning, moreover, the Chinese imported a number of native delicacies. The people of the Boise Basin could buy everything available in San Francisco, such as bamboo shoots, mushrooms, dry bean curd, cuttle-
fish, dried oysters, Chinese ham, salt ginger, orange skins, and dry duck. The
seemingly remote western frontier, tied to the international trade network of the
West Coast, gave the Boise Basin Chinese a remarkably diverse selection of food.[14]

An index of meat consumption also points to a hearty diet among Idaho's Chinese residents. Because of limited meat supplies in Canton, like elsewhere in
China, Chinese people for centuries had had to rely on beans to obtain sufficient
protein. Soon after mining camps were established in southern Idaho, herds of
cattle were driven in regularly, and beef became one of the cheapest foods. The
Chinese also raised pigs. Although Chinese settlers consumed a large quantity of
beef, chicken and pork were the preferred meats. As a contemporary letter from
Idaho City noted, "the principal meat diet of the Chinese is pork and chicken; of
the former, the average daily consumption, purchased at the various meat markets, is 500 pounds and of hogs slaughtered by themselves about 500 pounds
more." At that time, about one thousand Chinese people were living in Idaho City
and the surrounding areas. In other words, the average daily consumption of pork
alone was one pound per person. This high consumption of meat per capita sur-
passed that in China, even in the late twentieth century.[15]

Combined with the high protein in their diets, the Chinese consumed large quantities of vitamin-rich vegetables. This balanced diet contrasted significantly with the eating habits of most white miners, who ate a monotonous diet of bread, bacon, butter, beans, beef, sugar, coffee, and dried fruits. Lacking the vitamin nutrition of vegetables, early white miners frequently suffered from scurvy. Consequently, they tried to avoid vitamin deficiencies by taking green onions and potatoes soaked in vinegar. In contrast, the Chinese maintained a regular supply of vegetables from backyard and garden production. They were reported raising up to six crops from the same ground in a three-month growing season, although Chinese cabbage was their main crop. In general, the Chinese diet, rich with vegetables, proved to be a superior and more balanced diet than that of the average Anglo-American miner.[16]

In addition to a nutritious and balanced diet, proper medical care helped maintain a high quality of life among Boise Basin Chinese. While seeking American doctors in emergency situations, Chinese miners depended heavily on their own physicians for general medical care. Traditional Chinese medical practices revolved around herbal medicine. Based on plant, mineral, and animal substances, Chinese herbal medicine was far more effective in dealing with chronic diseases. Prior to the scientific and pharmaceutical revolution of the twentieth century, Euramerican medicine shared a strong similarity with Chinese medicine in its use of herbal materials (such as inorganic salts and tinctures) in the formulation of drugs. But Chinese medicine was a more complex science than its western counterpart.[17] In the Boise Basin Chinese physicians traveled from camp to camp to practice their native medicine, and their success with herbal medicines and acupuncture convinced many whites to visit Chinese "medicine men."

A moderate climate, adequate housing, balanced diet, and advanced medical care all contributed not only to better health for the Boise Basin Chinese but also to a low mortality rate. Frontier Idaho in 1870 had the lowest death rate in the nation at 0.33 percent. That same year, of a total of 4,274, only 7 Chinese individuals died. In other words their mortality rate was only 0.16 percent, or about half that of whites. Ten years later the territorial death rate increased to 0.99 percent, but the Chinese mortality rate rose to only 0.41 percent. At the time, the death of infants under the age of five years comprised one-third of all deaths. Because so few Chinese women and children lived in Idaho, infant mortality was rare in the Chinese community. Likewise, there were few elderly Chinese. Thus, special circumstances combined to keep the Chinese mortality rate down, but Chinese pioneers were more apt to survive on the Rocky Mountain mining frontier than their white counterparts.[18]

As a part of the American frontier, the Boise Basin provided the Chinese with not only a healthy place to live but also ample opportunity for financial success. Gold was king, and an overwhelming majority of the Chinese immigrants were engaged in placer mining. In 1870, 92 percent of this ethnic group in Boise County worked on mining claims, as opposed to about 60 percent of the white populace.[19] Because they missed the initial 1862–1863 rush, early Chinese pioneers encountered little "free ground." As they often did in western mining, the Chinese purchased mining claims from Anglo owners, who had worked out the initial gold, sold the claim, and left for new discoveries. According to existing mining records, Chinese themselves staked only thirteen claims in the basin during the entire nineteenth century.[20] Economic hardship brought about by fires in Idaho City and drought throughout the region in the 1860s encouraged white owners to liquidate their holdings. Often presenting themselves at the right place at the right time, Chinese miners took advantage of low prices and became an economic force in the local placering business.

Hoping to strike it rich, both individuals with limited savings and companies with large capital resources participated in the mining frenzy. Everyone tried to grab a piece of ground with mineral potential. Depending on size and quality, a claim could bring as little as $50 and as much as $10,000. Most claims sold for several hundred dollars.[21] In 1873 the Chinese-owned Man See & Company bought two claims consisting of 4,172 feet of ground along Ophir Creek from Conners & Co. for $8,200. The deal included water rights, a blacksmith shop, and mining tools. Payment was made immediately in cash. Another large acquisition took place in 1867 when Ah Heing paid Patrick Henry $4,700 for a claim on Mores Creek.[22] As recorded in the deed books, these high-priced transactions demonstrated Chinese willingness and ability to invest in an Anglo-dominated market.

On a smaller scale, many individuals who could not afford to buy large claims cooperated as mining groups. Forming a "company" these individuals became partners, contributed the necessary capital, and performed all the labor. Most deeds contained one or two Anglo and numerous Chinese signatures, which meant that all the persons working for the company had a share in the claim. Multiple-partner purchases allowed individual Chinese to invest an affordable dollar amount in the company. In an 1869 case, for example, twelve Chinese bought a claim on Mores Creek for $700 from A. D. Sanders & Co. If the investment was divided equally, each investor needed to provide only $58 to complete the deal. The number of shareholders sometimes ran higher. In 1871 twenty-two Chinese sold George W. Grafts a claim for $300, resulting in a profit of only $13.60 per seller. Regardless, Chinese cooperative ventures significantly increased individual purchasing power and strengthened the Chinese competitive position in the basin.[23]

Even Chinese miners with very limited means could purchase claims on the installment plan. The buying group made what down payment it could, and then the partners worked the mine under contract, making weekly or monthly payments in gold dust. Until the balance was paid off, the seller supervised the daily operation. Sometimes the payment schedules lasted for more than a year. On October 8, 1867, Ah Go & Co. contracted with A. F. Hart for the purchase of a mining property near Warm Springs for $1,500. Ah Go put $250 cash down and agreed to pay $100 per week, providing the weather allowed steady work on the claim. When working conditions were prohibitive in winter, Ah Go was free from payments. As a result, he was able to sit on the property until May 1868, when he resumed production. He fulfilled the agreement by making final payment on November 18, 1868, thus earning ownership of the site. In 1866 Abram Harvey & Co. sold a claim on Mores Creek to a group of Chinese organized as Jakey & Co. for $2,500. The Chinese had little cash, so Abram Harvey let them pay "from the proceeds of claim from the processes of each day's work except the sum of $6 per week to each and every hand that may be employed." Thus, the Chinese miners could support themselves with toiling toward ownership of their claims.[24]

Those Chinese miners unable to afford mine investments often became wage earners, an arrangement that provided an opportunity for economic advancement for even the poorest immigrants. The Chinese worked cheaply to be competitive with the other impoverished immigrants in the labor pool. Added to this advantage was the ability of Chinese miners to live on a cheaper yet healthier diet. If a Chinese miner consumed one pound of beef daily at twenty-five cents, two pounds of rice at forty cents, and some vegetables for another ten cents, and paid twenty-five cents for rent, he could live easily on a dollar a day. On the other hand, the average white miner, staying at a boarding house and being charged about fifteen dollars per week for room and board, needed more than two dollars a day to survive. In the late 1860s the Chinese spent five hundred dollars annually per capita, in contrast to one thousand dollars spent by white men.[25] Consequently, the Chinese, able to work for lower wages, could force whites out of the job market, which sometimes caused tensions. To Chinese pioneers, however, a lower wage was better than no wage at all.

The mining frontier not only welcomed "free" laborers, it helped to *create* "free" laborers. Although a majority of the Chinese immigrants who came to American in the nineteenth century were "free man," a number of peasants arrived "under contract," which required them to work for their sponsor for a certain period in exchange for their ocean fare. Many of them, however, ran away as soon as they got off the boat. An English captain once lamented, "the fifteen coolies I brought from China, and who were under a bond for two years with the party who engaged them, were no sooner ashore than they resisted their contract, and each turned his separate way. Nor would the authorities interfere." Runaways were so common that in 1852 California state senator George B. Tingley introduced a bill in the state legislature to enforce all contracts made in China, but public outrage against slavery and coolie labor alike killed the measure.[26]

Runaways quickly branched out from the West Coast to the interior, many making it to the Idaho frontier. If a person were too poor to go to Idaho, he could join a Chinese company in California or Nevada, which would often pay his travel expenses. On arrival in the Boise Basin, he simply broke the contract by running away. Another kind of runaway was more feared, however. In 1883 two Chinese miners, Chow Kung Lein and Loo Hue, of Sing Hop & Co., slipped away with fourteen hundred dollars worth of supplies. These runaways angered company officials, who could no nothing except place a notice in the local newspapers smearing their names and proclaiming them "opium addicts and swindlers."[27]

In the Boise Basin a few of the Chinese did extremely well in their search for upward economic mobility. Admittedly, many Chinese miners never made fortunes on the frontier, but neither did many white pioneers. Some lucky ones achieved the American dream. In 1876 an Idaho City newspaper reported that "a party of Chinamen, mining on North Elk, a short distance above town, the other day cleaned up six thousand dollars; after a run of only twenty-four days." The same year, the *Idaho Statesman* reported that on Ophir Creek, "a large Chinese company [Man See & Co.] own a claim for which they paid $8,000 three years ago. The same property could not now be bought for $20,000." It is difficult to estimate how much an individual Chinese miner made in his seasonal mining operation because he frequently carried most of his gold out of the territory and sent it back to China without reporting it.[28] In one instance when a stagecoach running between Idaho City and Quartzburg was held up by highwaymen, a Chinese miner on board lost $7,000.[29] Few individuals were probably more successful, however, than Pon Yam and Loke Kee, who started as poor immigrants but were eventually numbered among the region's "rich and famous." Pon Yam once possessed the largest diamond ring in the basin, about two carats, and Loke Kee, as noted, accumulated a fortune of $60,000 to $90,000. To these Chinese, at least, the myth of the American dream became reality.[30]

While in search of the American dream, the Chinese constantly fought for racial equality and social justice when and where they could. One of the battlegrounds was the American legal system. Like other ethnic groups elsewhere in the United States, the Chinese suffered under a racist legal system. In 1854 the California Supreme Court, in *People v. Hall*, denied the Chinese the right to testify. The immediate consequence was an increase of crimes against Chinese in the mining districts because the perpetrators realized their victims could not testify against them. Without the victim's testimony, conviction was virtually impossible. Even if whites witnessed the crime, they often ignored it. Understanding the importance of their own testimony, therefore, the Chinese pressed hard for reform in Idaho's courts. In 1866, during Radical Reconstruction, Congress passed the Civil Rights Act to give the freedmen "full and equal benefit of all laws." This principle was soon added to the Constitution as the Fourteenth Amendment. With the hope of gaining equal rights, Idaho's Chinese immediately held camp meetings and passed resolutions to endorse the new legislation. Demanding certain legal privileges, the Chinese soon won the right to testify in Idaho's courts.[31]

After securing their right to bear witness, Idaho's Chinese quickly confronted another contentious issue—that of courtroom oath-taking. In early cases, especially, the Chinese commonly demanded that their witnesses be sworn in by the native method, which, they believed, was the only way to guarantee veracity, and their insistence on the matter led to open conflict. The confrontations usually ended with a frontier judge agreeing to a Chinese oath-taking ceremony in the courtroom. In front of the judge each Chinese witness cut off a live chicken's head to draw the blood on a platter. The witness, who had written his oath on a piece of paper, dipped it in the blood. The paper then was properly burned with a candle. Once, in neighboring Owyhee County, Sheriff Rube Springer volunteered to administer the oath. During the proceedings, a fascinated judge named Lewis leaned across the bench and asked the interpreter, "what does that all mean?" Obviously, the judge did not understand the whole meaning, and neither did Sheriff Springer. A few days later, local Chinese were upset when they learned that Springer had taken the dead chicken, which was to have been buried, and eaten it for dinner.[32]

Almost from the start, Idaho's courts allowed the Chinese to file complaints against both Chinese and whites in civil disputes. Various factors helped nurture Idaho's liberal legal system. In the early years some Chinese took the law into their own hands and administered justice in traditional ways. In 1869 a poor Chinese man in Centerville was imprisoned by some of his countrymen for not paying a debt. After being informed of this by inquisitive whites, Sheriff Frank Britten went on a door-to-door search for the private jail. Eventually, he discovered a cellar with no light or fresh air, in the corner of which sat the shivering debt prisoner, who had been severely tortured. The officer compelled the jailer to take the starving man to a restaurant for a good breakfast. After restoring the prisoner's liberty, the sheriff told the jailer that self-appointed justice and "such summary remedies were not allowed in this country." The incident drew public attention and prompted the *Idaho Statesman* to comment: "such occurrence[s] show that a system of heathen punishment by secret tribunals exist among our Chinese population." The newspaper suggested that "the best remedy is to impartially enforce the law, and particularly impress them [the Chinese] with their duty to submit to the proper authorities." Whites, it would seem, were willing to give the Chinese more rights in the regular courts than what "heathen justice" provided.[33]

The sheer size of the Chinese population in Boise Basin as well as in Idaho at large was probably an even greater factor in the Chinese acquiring equal access to American courts. Concerned with government revenues, local courts often encouraged the Chinese to file more suits. In each case the government charged the loser about twenty dollars to cover court costs and sheriff's fees. With the Chinese constituting half the county's and almost one-third of the territory's population, Idaho could not afford to lose this revenue base by blocking their suits. Enterprising white lawyers also favored equal access to justice because they were able to solicit more clients. Court documents indicate, for example, that Charles S. Kingsley, a former Methodist minister and leader of the basin's vigilantes, did a lucrative business with local Chinese and became a powerful lawyer after winning their trust.[34]

In addition, a few influential whites in the region pushed for Chinese equal rights. With their own moral consciousness, such leading citizens as a governor, a legislator, a judge, and a newspaper editor gave sympathy to the unprivileged, including Chinese, and dared to speak up for fairness. In 1868 Republican Governor George L. Woods of Oregon vetoed a bill imposing a tax upon the Chinese.

As an independent thinker, Matthew Deady, a United States district judge in Oregon, defended Chinese rights in many influential decisions, which had a great impact on judicial development in the Pacific Northwest.[35] In Idaho Territory the voices of equal justice came mainly from new appointees by President Ulysses S. Grant. Most outspoken were United States Marshal Henry W. Moulton and United States Attorney Joseph W. Houston. Both men thought a special tax on the Chinese "was contrary to the American tradition of human equality." Calling himself the leader of "a great movement to ameliorate the condition of the Chinamen in Idaho," Moulton urged local Republicans to fight discrimination.[36] A combination of economic interest and moral obligation thus forced a frontier legal system to act more fairly toward the Chinese.

Adapting to the unique legal situation in Boise Country as well as in Idaho, Chinese residents used the courts frequently and skillfully to redress grievances, willfully pursuing justice and protecting their self-interests. Sometimes, disputes seemed too insignificant for legal action, but Chinese litigants were known to punish their opponents by taking them to court. In 1870, for example, several Chinese laborers who worked for Robinson, Taylor & Co. took their white employers to court. For unknown reasons, the firm refused to pay the Chinese. Intending to punish Robinson and Taylor, each laborer filed a separate civil suit; Ah Lung demanded $15.00, Ah Tung $30.00, and Ah Hee and Ah Why $7.50 each. If Robinson and Taylor lost the case, they would have to pay four separate court fees, which would cost them dearly. Intimidated by these Chinese legal actions, the firm agreed to give the money to the laborers without delay. The court then dismissed the case at the plaintiffs' request. Similar cases appear in existing court records.[37]

With the right to initiate litigation, the Chinese not only challenged individual opponents but used every opportunity to pursue constitutional and civil rights issues as well. The most famous case was *Ah Bow v. Britten* (1869). In 1864 the Idaho Territorial Legislation passed a law requiring a head tax of $4.00 per month on all Chinese who lived in mining areas. Later the head tax was raised to $5.00. Passively resisting the discriminatory legislation, a majority of Chinese in the territory refused to pay the head tax. The deputy sheriff of Shoshone County lamented that only 20 percent of the nine hundred Chinese miners paid it.[38] Boise Basin Chinese took even more direct action and challenged the law's constitutionality in Idaho's courts.

National and local politics played a vital role in provoking such legal battles. Although Idaho Territory had a Democratic majority, Boise City, with some federal appointees, was a Republican stronghold. Political tension between the two sides often ran high. Republicans, seeking a political issue to use against the Democrats, found that the Chinese head tax had violated the Civil Rights Act of 1866. Motivated by both moral idealism and partisan politics, Joseph W. Houston, the newly appointed United States attorney, led the fight to rescind the tax. If the Chinese community agreed to pay a "liberal fee," he and other so-called "Rocky Mountain Carpetbaggers" promised to seek an injunction against Boise County Sheriff Frank Britten to prevent further collection of all taxes on Chinese laborers until the court ruling. The Chinese community immediately raised $600 in greenbacks and $1,000 in gold coin and hired Joseph W. Houston, Henry W. Prickett, and former territorial supreme court justice John R. McBride as legal counsel.[39]

On July 14, 1869, the case of *Ah Bow v. Britten* opened in the district court in Boise City. Because the tax issue had become the basis for a partisan fray, many leading figures in the region took part in the proceedings and attended the trial. In what became a highly publicized case, attorneys for the plaintiff presented a strong argument, and Judge David Noggle, a Grant appointee, sided with the Chinese in his decision. Noggle stopped short of striking down the head tax, however, and his lengthy, ambiguous decision alienated everyone, Republicans, Democrats and Chinese alike. The Republicans gained no political capital; the Democrats felt insulted; and the Chinese lost their money.[40] Still, the Chinese had the satisfaction of employing one group of whites against another by playing China's traditional game of "using one barbarian against another."

Although evidence suggests that Chinese immigrants never served on an Idaho jury, the Chinese did enjoy a monopoly on the influential position of courtroom interpreter. Such men held greater power than today's court interpreters, for the scope of the job went far beyond strict translation. In addition to interpretation, these Chinese legal representatives served as quasi-lawyers, giving their own opinions, manipulating witnesses, and striking deals with their opponents. As a result, white judges and attorneys willingly recognized the interpreters as legal stand-ins.[41]

The Boise Basin's most famous "quasi-lawyer" was Billy Wy. Coming from California in 1865 with the first group of Chinese miners to migrate to Idaho City, Wy, then thirty-four, spoke English fluently. He immediately perceived the prospects of "courtroom mining." He read law and, until his death in 1883, made a good living interpreting for the courts and for Idaho businessmen. As the *Idaho World* reported, Wy "understood and could quote law phrases like a disciple of Blackstone." His enthusiasm and effectiveness for compromise made him a legal liaison between whites and Chinese. Both sides trusted and liked him. When Wy died, Judge W. B. Moore delivered a noble eulogy in praise of both Wy's talent and contribution to the community, saying: "There was one good trait, among many others, about Billy . . . his enthusiasm for compromises." Whenever there were legal differences between Chinese or between Chinese and whites, Moore said, Wy "was most always successful in effecting a compromise when he started in for that purpose." A great number of the whites went to Idaho City's "Chinatown" to view Wy's body and say farewell to their beloved interpreter.[42]

Although enjoying a great many legal privileges and protection in Idaho's courts, Chinese people of the Boise Basin found other ways to settle disputes and sometimes resorted to a different kind of frontier justice. Violence was the chief alternative to litigation. Chinese laborers have commonly been viewed as "innocent victims" of western violence, and in truth they often suffered from arson, assault, murder, and massacre. What did not occur in the Boise Basin, however, were disturbances anything like the anti-Chinese riots in Denver in 1880 and in Rock Springs, Wyoming, in 1885, or the riots and expulsions of Seattle and Tacoma in 1885–1886. To be sure, Idaho was not immune from anti-Chinese violence. From 1863 to 1900 eleven anti-Chinese riots killed 25 Idaho Chinese and displaced 528 others. Most of these incidents took place in central and northern Idaho, however, and none occurred in the Boise Basin.[43]

More likely, Chinese settlers in the Boise Basin suffered violence at the hands of other Chinese.[44] Indeed, Chinese played all the frontier roles—"victor," "victim," and "villain." Some Chinese immigrants themselves, with evil minds and ferocious personalities, were arsonists, assailants, robbers, and killers, but even righteous people did not hesitate to exercise the right of self-defense in a fierce manner. As the *Idaho World* put it, "A Chinaman is slow to deeds of desperation but when he starts in he generally means business." Like other westerners, most Chinese were peaceful but they could be provoked to violence, and some went about well-armed. According to contemporary accounts and subsequent archaeological excavations, at least some Chinese in the Boise Basin possessed an awesome arsenal of firearms, ranging from an 1857 Smith & Wesson revolver to an 1873 Springfield army rifle. Similar to other nineteenth-century westerners, many young Chinese males carried bowie knives and Colt revolvers on their hips in public. To some, six-shooters seemed to provide a sense of security and equality, lending aptness to historian Walter Prescott Webb's observation that "God made some men large and some small, but Colonel Colt made them all equal."[45]

The basin's Chinese were most likely to use fire, fists, or firearms to terrorize or punish their enemies. Unlike other forms of violence, fire acquired little direct confrontation. At night it was easy for a person to slip by a night watchman and set fire to a store or house. A successful arsonist could destroy his enemy's entire fortune with one blow. With a lower risk for the perpetrator of being caught, arson seems to have been the crime of choice, judging from court documents involving Chinese. In a murderous twist on arson, someone decided to get rid of Lee Pow, a leading Idaho City merchant, by secreting a "bomb" made of gunpowder under Pow's house. At two o'clock in the morning when Pow was sleeping the device went off and set part of his residence afire. The powder had been slightly misplaced and Pow, although scared "out of his wits," escaped the explosion. In settling more modest disputes, Chinese individuals resorted to fists to punish opponents on the streets. In China fistfighting was generally accepted as a means of dealing with personal conflicts, and battery violated no law unless one person severely injured another. Boise Basin Chinese therefore frequently resorted to fists, and the practice drew public scrutiny. Arrests of Chinese most commonly were for battery and assault, for "showing deadly weapons," and for "disturbing the peace."[46]

In taking up violent actions the Chinese did not discriminate. Their knives and bullets were used against both Chinese and whites. In 1870, for example, Edward Cahill was mining next to a Chinese company on Mores Creek, about six miles from Idaho City. When the two sides quarreled over use of water, a verbal argument escalated into serious violence. Waiting until Cahill was alone, three Chinese men, Hen Lee, Ah Teung, and San Sing, overtook Cahill and killed him with a shot through the neck execution style. Justice Thomas Bowen, a Civil War general and a Grant appointee, discharged all the suspects, however, when he found insufficient evidence to convict them. Upon acquittal, the three Chinese went to Loon Creek in Lemhi County (today, Custer County) and robbed the cellar of H. Wolfson & Co. A local vigilance committee ordered the three to leave town within twenty-four hours, but the Chinese men refused, threatening to kill the white leaders. Local citizens finally quelled the problem by ambushing and killing the Asian desperados in a shoot-out. On the street in a mining camp, a hot-tempered Chinese with his weapons in view sometimes scared peaceful citizens, and even white hoodlums thought twice about harassing armed Chinese.[47]

Aside from isolated incidents of violence, Chinese immigrants experienced the Boise Basin as an economic battlefield, especially early on. An initial stage of contention, mainly the first decade of their arrival in Idaho, characterized the Chinese experience. The initial influx of Chinese miners into the basin drew Chinese into a series of conflicts with Euramericans, and each side showed little tolerance for the other. The Chinese traditionally lumped other nationalities and ethnic groups together as "barbarians," distrusting them and despising their values and customs. For their part, Euramericans generally viewed the Cantonese as "an uncivilized race" with strange costume, diet, and religion. Shared ignorance fueled antagonism and discrimination, but with time everyday contact worked if not cultural melding then a certain egalitarianism, and the two groups came to appreciate each other's customs.

Daily activities, such as mining transactions, merchandising, social gatherings, cooperative ventures—and certain special events like Chinese funerals, New Year's, and the Fourth of July—encouraged tolerant, even respectful coexistence. When a Chinese funeral procession marched from the center of a town to the nearby cemetery, it created a striking scene. Firecrackers and music alerted the entire town to the solemn event. In the early years, before they had formed their own band with native instruments, the Chinese might hire a brass band to accompany the mourners. On one occasion, the Irish brass band of Idaho City led the procession across town to the burial site. Although an unusual mixture of two cultures, nobody at the time thought it improper. In February 1870, when merchant Lee Pow's bookkeeper died, the Idaho City band was called "to discourse the Dead March from Saul, Mozart's Twelfth Mass, or some other doleful requiem."[48] At another funeral, mischievous band members are said to have played a joke on the "gullible Celestials." As Chinese pallbearers slowly lowered the coffin into the grave, the band broke into an Irish drinking song, "Down went McGinty."[49]

Chinese funerals brought the two cultures together in other ways as well. Whenever an individual Chinese died in the camp, his friends or clan members would arrange a sumptuous funeral. According to tradition, a huge amount of food was left at the gravesite so that the deceased would not starve in the other world. In at least one instance, white children followed the burial party and took advantage of the custom by engaging in "a big feed" after the Chinese left the cemetery. At the end of the funeral, family and friends generously gave everyone in attendance a small pouch of gold dust "to buy some little token in remembrance of the deceased." With the promise of such gifts, Chinese funerals attracted large numbers of whites, who both observed and participated in the Far Eastern rituals.[50]

Another exciting occasion for all concerned was the Chinese New Year. Firecrackers always pleased and delighted white children, who loitered around Chinese stores or houses to watch the celebration. During the holiday season, Chinese merchants and their families generously offered neighboring children litchi nuts, coconut candy, and cookies. In the mining camps, children anxiously awaited the Chinese New Year, which occurred a few weeks after Christmas. Upon receiving calls from "their American friends," Chinese merchants kept their stores open on New Year's Day and treated special guests to cigars, champagne, wine, and other refreshments. Instead of receiving gifts on the holiday, the Chinese took pleasure in presenting gifts, such as tea, cigars, silk handkerchiefs, and baskets, to their white friends. As the *Idaho World* once commented, the Chinese "are very liberal in their gifts to those with whom they have business relations, and in whom they have confidence." Such demonstrations of friendly Chinese-white relations reveal that the Chinese merchants were often closer to their white counterparts, who were in the same class, than to working class Chinese. Class often superseded race.[51]

Just as Americans attended the Chinese New Year's jubilation, the Chinese celebrated American Independence Day. Beginning in the 1870s the Chinese were formally invited to the festival on the Fourth of July. In the afternoon of July 4, 1875, for example, the local Chinese band proudly led the Idaho City parade. To many Americans, the six-piece band with drum, gong, horn, cymbal, and other instruments "made the most hideous noise." Immediately behind the band was the "Goddess of Liberty" mounted on a cart decorated with evergreens and ribbons. To celebrate the holiday each year, the Chinese not only participated in celebratory competitions, such as sprints, bicycle races, and tugs-of-war but they made financial contributions. On the Fourth of July in 1902, for example, Chen Yuen Lee, a Chinese firm in Centerville, presented the town with a string of firecrackers valued at twenty-five dollars. By participating in each other's festivals, the Americans and the Chinese in these mining camps were sharing features of their cultures through social interaction. The result was cultural appreciation and a sharing of common experiences.[52]

Integration of Chinese children into public schools represented another egalitarian feature of Boise Basin society. Admission of Chinese students varied from place to place in the American West. In California the Chinese, like African-Americans and Mexican-Americans, attended separate schools. Yet in Idaho the

Chinese did not suffer such treatment. As early as 1869 the Chinese in Boise City of neighboring Ada County argued that they paid property taxes and therefore applied for admission of their children to the public schools, and a year later, the schools began to admit Chinese children. In part, the city could not afford a separate school for the small number of Chinese students, but good relations with the dominant Anglo society must have contributed to their winning equal access to education, else they would not have been admitted. Similar integration came to Idaho City schools with admittance of four Chinese students in 1882.[53]

Racial and cultural mixing in Idaho's schools, moreover, was gender blind. For the first time, female Chinese children enjoyed equality in education. In China parents sent only boys to private teachers for education; traditionally, girls were denied this right. In America, however, both Chinese boys and girls attended public school and received their education free. Among the first four Chinese pupils to enter public school in Idaho City was a girl named Ti Ti, Loke Kee's daughter and For Cue's mother. According to the *Idaho World*, Ti Ti was "an extraordinary smart Chinese girl. . . . She astonished some visitors from Boise by her proficiency in writing, reading and arithmetic." Because of equal education, Ti Ti studied American democracy and later participated in the process. As a contemporary reported: "she is familiar with all bills before the legislature, is well informed on political parties and public men of the country." In the late 1890s she began to vote, joining the first generation of American women to exercise this political right.[54]

Beginning in the 1890s when members of the first generation of Boise Basin Chinese born in America reached their adulthood, they began to participate more fully in the democratic process. While blacks in the South were losing the franchise, the Chinese in the Boise Basin were lining up at ballot boxes for the first time. Although no Chinese ever applied for citizenship, they did acquire voting rights. According to Boise County records, the Chinese started paying a nine-dollar poll tax to cast their votes. Some Chinese waived the privilege to save their money for other purposes, but in certain elections, the Chinese vote proved critical. In 1899, for example, E. W. Jones of the Boise Basin reportedly was sent to the state legislature by three decisive votes from "young Mongols." Chinese acquisition of voting rights marked an important step toward political equality.[55]

Although Chinese legal rights varied from place to place, equitable economic opportunities for Chinese people existed everywhere in the American West, from the Boise Basin mining camps to San Francisco's Chinatown to California's agricultural regions. Less than half of the Chinese in San Francisco and Sacramento from 1870 to 1900, for example, were working class—40 percent or more earned a living as entrepreneurs, and 5 to 12 percent were professionals and artisans. In rural California, success stories among Chinese gardeners and farmers were frequent as well. For them, as one historian put it, "the nuggets they found turned out to be green."[56]

Despite hardship and discrimination, moreover, the Chinese in Idaho, and elsewhere in America, lived better than did their counterparts in contemporary China. Wars and famines ravaged China constantly during the nineteenth century. Twenty million people died during the Taiping Rebellion (1851–1864) alone. Because of poverty at home more than three hundred thousand Chinese immigrated to America in search of better lives. Many achieved their dreams. As one historian noted, their continued immigration to the United States, even after the Chinese Exclusion Act of 1882 forced them to resort to desperate measures to gain entry, showed that many Chinese envisioned far superior lives in the United States.[57]

Thus, the story of the Boise Basin Chinese would seem just one of many positive episodes for Chinese people in the nineteenth-century American West. To be sure, further studies are needed to arrive at more accurate generalizations, but in the Boise Basin at least, victimization, unhappiness, and oppression were not predominant themes. On the contrary, the brighter aspects of free soil, free labor, and free gold overshadowed the darker side of exploitation, injustice, and discrimination. The experience of the Chinese people who settled in the Boise Basin indicates that as a "land of opportunity," the Rocky Mountain mining frontier, although hardly perfect, offered Chinese immigrants opportunities far beyond the proverbial "Chinaman's chance" either in the American West or in China.

The difference between the way things were in the Boise Basin and the way things could have been in China was not lost on For Due Di Sang and her family. Indeed, the contrast became all too clear when Loke Kee returned to China with his family in 1906. During the 1920s, For Cue suffered through continuous civil wars and famines in China. The family treasures accumulated by her grandfather Loke Kee were depleted, and the family struggled just to survive. Looking for help, For Cue reached across the Pacific for financial and moral support from her American friends in the Boise Basin, and Idahoans Charles Jones, Amelia Garrecht, and Emma Day always responded, generously sending For Cue money to assist her family. For Cue, meanwhile, longed to return to America. To keep up-to-date with the culture in which she had grown up, she asked her friends to send her copies of the *Idaho World* and the Sears Roebuck and the Montgomery Ward catalogs. In the late 1930s, when the Japanese invaded southern China, her family fled their home to a safer place. Before leaving, For Cue buried her last fifty dollars in the backyard, money sent to her by her friends in the Boise Basin. Invading Japanese soldiers discovered the money and confiscated it, however, rendering For Cue penniless. Her American friends nonetheless continued assisting her family until Japan attacked Pearl Harbor in December 1941, after which communications were cut off for the remainder of the Second World War.[58]

After the war For Cue, then living in the British colony of Hong Kong, resumed correspondence with her American friends. She still hoped to return to the United States but was too old to meet the immigration requirement that she prove she could earn her own living. Never giving up hope, For Cue Di Sang, an eighty-year-old Chinese-American, died in Hong Kong in 1968—a year after the ferment of the Cultural Revolution spread from mainland China to her home city. Her death ended the long-lived communications between her family and the people of the Boise Basin.

A year later, Florence McClaren, a Boise resident and descendent of Idaho pioneers, went to Hong Kong on a tour. On a crowded bus in a city of millions, she entered a fateful conversation with a tour guide named Paul Chan. Chan was proud to tell McClaren that his mother, For Cue Di Sang (Florence Chan), was an American. Upon learning that McClaren was from Idaho, Chan asked her if she knew of Idaho City. When McClaren answered "yes," Chan grew excited and said" "Oh, Idaho City a great city with a bank." McClaren immediately corrected him. "No, Idaho City is almost a ghost town."[59] Undoubtedly, Paul Chan had heard many stories from his mother about the glorious days of the Boise Basin. Despite her death and her beloved American town having nearly been abandoned to the ghost, the legend of Chinese success and golden opportunities in the Rocky Mountain West lived on with a new generation, even on the other side of the world.

NOTES

1. For Cue Di Sang to Charles Jones, March 12, 1927, Alfred Day Collection, 1006 E. State Street, Boise, Idaho (hereafter Day Collection). For Cue's English name is Florence. Her grammatical errors have not been corrected.

2. Stephen Frank Smith, interview by Anabelle Alexander, June 15, 1970, OH 74, transcript, Oral History Collection, Idaho State Historical Society (hereafter OH-ISHS); *Idaho Statesman*, June 6, 1943.

3. *Idaho World*, February 21, 1907; For Cue Di Sang to Amelia Garrecht, February 7, 1923, Day Collection.

4. Roger Daniels, *Asian American: Chinese and Japanese in the United States since 1850* (Seattle: University of Washington Press, 1988), 4. Negative images of the nineteenth-century Chinese experience in the West have become deeply rooted. See Elmer Clarence Sandmeyer, *The Anti-Chinese Movement in California* (Urbana: University of Illinois Press, 1939); Gunther Paul Barth, *Bitter Strength: A History of the Chinese in the United States, 1850–1870* (Cambridge: Harvard University Press, 1964); and Alexander Saxton *The Indispensable Enemy: Labor and the Anti-Chinese Movement in California* (Berkeley: University of California Press, 1971). For recent, more balanced studies, see Sucheng Chan, *This Bitter Sweet Soil: The Chinese in California Agriculture, 1860–1910* (Berkeley: University of California Press, 1986); Benson Tong, *Unsubmissive Women: Chinese Prostitutes in Nineteenth-Century San Francisco* (Norman: University of Oklahoma Press, 1994); Charles J. McClain, *In Search of Equality: The Chinese Struggle against Discrimination in Nineteenth-Century America* (Berkeley: University of California Press, 1994); and Ronald Takaki, *Strangers from a Different Shore: A History of Asian Americans* (New York: Penguin Books, 1989).

5. See for example Frederic Logan Paxson, *History of the American Frontier, 1763–1893* (Boston: Houghton Mifflin Company, 1924), 498; and Ray Allen Billington and Martin Ridge, *Westward Expansion: A History of the American Frontier*, 5th ed. (New York: Macmillan Publishing Co., 1982), 583.

6. Richard White, *"It's Your Misfortune and None of My Own": A History of the American West* (Norman: University of Oklahoma Press, 1991), 285. Although discriminated against, Mormons, strikers, and radicals do not constitute racial groups. Patricia Nelson

Limerick, *The Legacy of Conquest: The Unbroken Past of the American West* (New York: W. W. Norton & Company, 1987), 289. By contrast Randall E. Rohe has advised historians to "move away from the over-worked theme of anti-Chinese discrimination." Randall E. Rohe, "After the Gold Rush: Chinese Mining in the Far West, 1850–1890," *Montana The Magazine of Western History*, 32 (Autumn 1982), 19.

7. The Boise Basin encompasses four hundred square miles. Its geographical center is about forty miles northeast of Boise City. The main Boise Basin mining area covered two hundred square miles and included Idaho City, Placerville, Centerville, and Pioneerville. The Boise Basin is in Boise County; Boise City is in Ada County. This study focuses on the Boise Basin.

8. Bureau of the Census, *The Ninth Census*, Population, vol. I (Washington, D.C.: Government Printing Office, 1872), 23, 107 (hereafter *Ninth Census*).

9. See Shih-shan Henry Tsai, *The Chinese Experience in America* (Bloomington: Indiana University Press, 1896), 33; and Sandmeyer, *Anti-Chinese Movement in California*, 110.

10. Wallace W. Elliott, *History of Idaho Territory* (San Francisco: Wallace W. Elliott & Co., Publishers, 1884), 102–8.

11. The saltbox originated in colonial New England and prevailed in primitive environments such as the western mining frontier. In Guangdong province, China, timber was a precious commodity, and a wooden structure symbolized wealth and power. More affluent Chinese lived in brick houses, whereas peasants used rice stalks to build shanties.

12. Bureau of the Census, *Ms Census* (Washington, D.C.: Government Printing Office, 1870, 1880, 1900), (hereafter *MS Census* and date).

13. Robert William Fogel and Stanley L. Engerman, *Time on the Cross: The Economics of American Negro Slavery* (Boston: Little, Brown and Company, 1974), 116.

14. Chinese Business Ledger, St. Gertrude Museum, Cottonwood, Idaho; Robert F. G. Spier, "Food Habits of Nineteenth-Century California Chinese," *California Historical Society Quarterly*, 37 (June 1858), 80; Joseph R. Conlin, *Bacon, Beans and Galantines: Food and Foodways on the Western Mining Frontier* (Reno: University of Nevada Press, 1986), 186–95.

15. *Capital Chronicle*, September 11, 1869. Chinese in northern Idaho apparently had similar patterns of meat consumption. See Julia G. Longenecker and Darby C. Stapp, "The Study of Faunal Remains from an Overseas Chinese Mining Camp in Northern Idaho," in Priscilla Wegars, ed. *Hidden Heritage: Historical Archaeology of the Overseas Chinese* (Amityville, N.Y.: Baywood Publishing Company, 1993), 103–4.

16. Conlin, *Bacon, Beans and Galantines*, 186–95; C. J. Brosnan, *History of the State of Idaho* (New York: Charles Scribner's Sons, 1918), 104–5; *Idaho Tri-Weekly Statesman*, June 5, 1869; *Idaho World*, August 18, 1885.

17. Paul D. Buell and Christopher Muench, "A Chinese Apothecary in Frontier Idaho," *The Annals of the Chinese Historical Society of the Pacific Northwest 1* (1983), 42–46; Christopher Muench, "One Hundred Years of Medicine: The Ah-Fong Physicians of Idaho," in Henry G. Schwarz, ed., *Chinese Medicine on the Golden Mountain: An Interpretive Guide* (Seattle: Chinese Historical Society of the Pacific Northwest, 1984), 51–78; *Idaho World*, November 3, 1891.

18. *Ninth Census*, Vital Statistics, vol. 2, p. 323; *Tenth Census*, Mortality and Vital Statistics, vol. 11, part 1, pp. 18–19.

19. *MS Census*, 1870; Elliott West, "Five Idaho Mining Towns: A Computer Profile," *Pacific Northwest Quarterly*, 72 (July 1982), 112.

20. Survey of existing records at Boise County Auditor and Recorder's Office, Idaho

City (hereafter Boise County Auditor and Recorder); and at Idaho State Historical Society, Boise (hereafter ISHS). Some early mining claim records have been lost.

21. The information comes from a survey of deeds, mining sale books, records of transfer of mining claims, and mortgage records, Boise County Auditor and Recorder.

22. Deed Book, vol. 13, pp. 536–37, vol. 9, pp. 786–87, ibid.

23. Ibid., vol. 12, p. 100, vol. 13, p. 42, ibid.

24. Miscellaneous Records, pp. 292–93, and Deed Book, vol. 8, pp. 766–68, ibid.

25. *Capital Chronicle*, December 1, 1869.

26. Edward Lucatt, *Rovings in the Pacific from 1837 to 1849* (2 vols., London: Longman, Brown, Green, and Longmans, 1857), 2:363; Thomas W. Chinn, *A History of the Chinese in California: A Syllabus* (San Francisco: Chinese Historical Society of America, 1969), 13–15.

27. *Idaho World*, July 24, 1883.

28. *Idaho World*, June 6, 1876; *Idaho Statesman*, August 10, 1876; *Report of the Governor of Idaho to the Secretary of the Interior* (Washington, D.C.: Government Printing Office, 1886), 6.

29. *Idaho Daily Statesman*, January 3, 1909.

30. Upward economic mobility for Boise Basin Chinese was similar to that of Chinese immigrants in Pierce City, a northern Idaho mining center. Pierce City Chinese also engaged in high-priced mining purchases and acquired valuable real estate properties. Darby C. Stapp, "The Documentary Record of an Overseas Chinse Mining Camp," in Wegards, ed., *Hidden Heritage,*, 18–29.

31. Charles J. McClain, Jr., "The Chinese Struggle for Civil Rights in Nineteenth Century America: The First Phase, 1850–1870" *California Law Review*, 72 (July 1984), 548–50; *Idaho Statesman*, August 28, 1869; *Owyhee Avalanche*, November 3, 1866; *Idaho World*, June 9, 1866.

32. *Owyhee Avalanche*, June 26, 1869; Thomas Donaldson, *Idaho of Yesterday* (Caldwell: Caxton Printers, 1941), 52–53. According to old Chinese culture, blood means seriousness. When smoke of the burning paper on which the oath is written swirls upwards, the Lord of heaven is witnessing the oath. If a person tells a lie, God will kill him like a chicken and separate his spirit from his body like the chicken's head from hers.

33. *Idaho Statesman*, October 21, 1869.

34. Judgment Record, no. 2, 1871–1898, p. 161, and other records, Boise County Auditor and Recorder.

35. Hubert Howe Bancroft, *History of Oregon* (2 vols., San Francisco: History Company, Publishers, 1883), 2:663–66; *Washington Standard*, November 21, 1868; Ralph James Mooney, "Matthew Deady and the Federal Judicial Response to Racism in the Early West," *Oregon Law Review*, 63 (December 1984), 584–627; Charles H. Carey, *History of Oregon* (Chicago: Pioneer Historical Publishing Company, 1922), 821–22.

36. Donaldson, *Idaho of Yesterdays*, 186; Ronald H. Limbaugh, *Rocky Mountain Carpetbaggers: Idaho's Territorial Governors, 1863–1890* (Moscow: University Press of Idaho, 1982), 83–85; *Idaho Statesman*, January 29, 1870.

37. Court Records 1867–1884, pp. 416–19, Boise County Court House, Idaho City, Idaho (hereafter Boise County Court House). See, for example, *Yip Kee vs. Wolf & Burson Company* (1872), Judgment Records, vol. 2, 1871–1898, Boise County Auditor and Recorder; *Ah Yan vs. Pat Gallaghan* (1868), Court Records, 1867–1884, and *Kum Kee vs. S. Dempsey* (1869), Court Records, 1867–1884, Boise County Court House.

38. Limbaugh, *Rocky Mountain Carpetbaggers*, 84; John Wunder, "The Courts and the Chinese in Frontier Idaho," *Idaho Yesterdays*, 25 (Spring 1981), 25.

39 Limbaugh, *Rocky Mountain Carpetbaggers*, 55, 77, 83–85; Wunder, "Courts and the Chinese in Frontier Idaho," 25–26; *Boise Democrat*, March 3, 1869; Civil and Criminal Register, United States District Courts for the District of Idaho, pp. 140–41, Record Group 21, National Archives, Seattle.

40. *Idaho Statesman,* August 28, 1869; *Capital Chronicle*, September 1, 1869.

41. *Idaho World*, January 23, 1877, Noember 27, 1883.

42. *Idaho World*, November 27, 1883.

43. Richard Maxwell Brown, "Western Violence: Structure, Values, Myth," *Western Historical Quarterly*, 24 (February 1993), 7; John Wunder, "Anti-Chinese Violence in the American West, 1850–1910," in John McLaren, Hamar Foster, and Chet Orloff, eds., *Law for the Elephant, Law for the Beaver: Essays in the Legal History of the North American West* (Pasadena: Nineth Judicial Circuit Historical Society, 1992), 214, 219–20, 231.

44. A survey of the so-called "Chinese Files" at Boise County Court House, Idaho City, shows that the most common crimes committed by the Chinese were battery, murder, larceny, and arson, from 1865 to 1885 (hereafter Chinese Files). The Chinese Files, organized by year from 1865 to 1912, contain various legal documents, including warrants, affidavits, letters, subpoenas, and statements. They are not indexed or cataloged and are incomplete. Legal documents related to Chinese people nonetheless were better preserved than those related to whites. The area's large Chinese population may have forced the court to create a separate file for them.

45. *Idaho World*, October 30, 1891; William P. Geer, "Salvage Excavation of BS-780: An Early Boise Basin Chinese Placer Mining Site," prepared for the United States Forest Service, Boise National Forest office, Boise, Idaho; Walter Prescott Webb, *The Great Plains* (Boston: Ginn and Company, 1931), 494.

46. *Idaho World*, July 18, 1872; Chinese Files. Assessment of most common arrests is based on warrants and subpoenas. Not all the cases ended with conviction.

47. *Idaho Statesman*, October 22, November 5, 1870, June 20, 1871; *Idaho World*, June 22, 1871.

48. *Idaho World*, February 3, 1870.

49. Boise Basin oral tradition. The author heard this story from local residents during his research trip in summer 1992.

50. *Idaho World*, June 30, July 4, 1876; Rupert Thorne, interview by Michelle Harley, March 10, 1981, interview 387-B, transcript, Oral History Collection, Boise Basin Library, Idaho City, Idaho (hereafter OH-Boise Basin Library).

51. Chester Andrew Calderwood, interview by Kris Hoffman and Nancy Stringfellow, March 21, 1981, 387-C, transcript, OH-Boise Basin Library; Walter T. Berry, interview by Blaine Holden, November 5, 1969, OH 9, transcript, OH-ISHS; *Idaho World*, February 15, 1872, Janaury 30, 1873.

52. *Owyhee Weekly Avalanche*, July 10, 1875; *Idaho World*, July7, 1899; July 6, 1900, July 21, 1902.

53. R. Guy McClellan, *The Golden State: A History of the Region West of the Rocky Mountains* (Philadelphia: William Flint & Co., 1872), 385–388; *Washington Standard*, July 31, 1869; *Idaho World*, April 25, 1882.

54. *Idaho World*, April 25, 1882; *Payette Independent*, n.d., newspaper clips, Day Collection.

55. Citizenship Records, Boise County Auditor and Recorder; Assessment Books, 1898, 1899, 1900, 1901, 1902, Boise County Treasurer's Office, Idaho City, Idaho; Undated newspaper clips, Day Collection.

56. Chan, *This Bitter-Sweet Soil*, 155–57, 404.

57. Daniels, *Asian America*, 20.

58. For Cue Di Sang to Amelia Garrecht, November 21, 1926, Day Collection; *Capital News*, March 1939, in vertical files, ISHS. Boise Basin citizens maintained a close relationship with For Cue Di Sang's family. In 1921, for example, they also helped For cue's younger brother, Dye Get Song, return to the United States. He settled in Seattle.

59. *Idaho Statesman*, November 11, 1974.

14

Polly Bemis, Legendary Heroine

Sister M. Alfreda Elsensohn

Perhaps no one person in Idaho County has evoked more interest than the Chinese woman, Polly Bemis. She seems to have attained national fame. Requests for pictures or information about her have come from New York City, Denver, Tacoma, Spokane, Ashley Falls, Massachusetts; from Oregon, from Pocatello.

In 1953 the author received a letter from J. C. Safley, then editor of the *San Diego Union* and a former editor, between 1917 and 1924, of the *Idaho County Free Press*. Among comments on Volume I, *Pioneer Days in Idaho County*, which he had just read, was the following: "I interviewed Polly Bemis when she like a modern Rip Van Winkle, emerged from half a century's slumber beneath the shadow of majestic Buffalo Hump."

Polly was born September 11, 1853, in China on the frontier near one of the upper rivers of China. Her parents were poor and suffered from drought to their crops and from the ravages of brigands. One year these outlaws raided the country and took all the crops. To prevent starvation for the rest of the family in that year of famine her father sold her to one of the leaders of the plundering band in exchange for seed to plant another crop.

In 1921 she told the Countess Gizyeka (Eleanor Patterson), "Day sellee me . . . slave girl. Old woman she shmuggle me into Portland [probably from San Francisco]. I cost $2500. . . . Old Chinese man he took me along to Warrens in a pack train."

There are many variations in accounts of Polly but it is certain that she was not a poker bride. Her Chinese name was Lalu Nathoy but when she first came to Warren she was introduced as Polly and the name stayed with her. She came to Warren as a girl of nineteen on July 8, 1872, on a saddle horse. At first she worked in a saloon owned by her Chinese master, Hong King. One night Charlie Bemis, the gambler, was playing cards with the Chinaman. For Charlie his money was at stake and his saloon and for the Chinaman it was his slave girl and a little bit of gold. Charlie won.

Who was Charlie Bemis? According to Peter Klinkhammer, Charles A. Bemis was born in 1848 in Connecticut. He came to Warren in 1863 or 1864 with his

father, who worked a claim. Since he was not inclined to hard work, Bemis took
to the saloon business early in life.

Since there was no dance music in the mining camp Bemis played the tunes
he knew on the violin and Peter Bemer put down the notes. The author has seen
this book. It had the date 1864 written on one page and in another place "Camp
Washington, Warrens diggins." Once written, the book was used for dance music.
It was given to the late Taylor Smith of New Meadows by Charlie Bemis when
Taylor was fourteen years old. Information about it was sent to H. J. Swinney at
the State Museum. Mr. Swinney borrowed the book long enough to have a re-
production made. During the centennial year the music was used for a new
record, "We Sing of Idaho."

Polly was a friend to lonely Idaho miners, first as a dancehall hostess and later
as a homesteader down on the Salmon River. When things got too rough in the
dancehall Polly used to fly out the back door and into Bemis's back door or if unable to do this she used to call Bemis and he never failed her. His quiet, sober,
stern personality together with his reputation for being able to keep a can rolling
with his six-shooter, saved Polly from several threatening situations.

In 1890 an incident occurred between Johnny Cox, a half-breed Lapwai Indian
and Bemis, over a poker game. The following day, Bemis was reclining full length
on a bench when Cox appeared suddenly. He demanded one hundred and fifty
dollars of Bemis and told Bemis he would give him time to roll a cigarette to get
the money for him. Bemis tarried and Cox suddenly shot Bemis through the left
cheek. It missed his eye however. A doctor was called but he did not do much for
the injured man. Polly is credited with cleaning out the wound with her crochet
hook, and caring for the injury in her own way until he recovered.

When school came to Warren, Polly remarked, "I can't go to school, I got to
make money. God gave me that much," she said, pointing to her head. "I learn
right along." She knew the name of every child born in Warren and the date of
its birth. She also remembered every death and when it occurred.

Polly had been taught the art of goldsmithing and she used to beg nuggets from
her friends. These she fashioned into hammers and picks and other trinkets which
she sold.

Bemis finally decided that since Polly had really saved his life he owed it to her
to marry her. They were married on August 13, 1894. The original marriage certificate is in St. Gertrude's Museum. It reads as follows:

> This is to certify that on this 13th day of August, 1894, I have joined in the holy
> bonds of matrimony Chas. A. Bemis and Miss Polly Nathoy at the residence of C.
> A. Bemis.
>
> August 13th 1894
Warrens, Idaho Co.
>
> *Witness*
> W. J. Kelly, A. D. Smead, Justice of the Peace
> George L. Patterson

Two years after the marriage Polly received her certificate of residence under the provisions of the Act of Congress approved November 3, 1893. In this certificate she is described as 47 years old, 5 feet tall and dark. The date of the certificate issued from Helena, Montana, by the Collector of Internal Revenue, is August 10, 1896.[1]

After the marriage Bemis bought a ranch on the Salmon. The Canyon where they settled is 285 miles long and about 6,000 feet deep. The Bemis farm contained only fifteen acres of tillable land, but it would, and under Polly's care it did, raise plums, pears, grapes, cherries, strawberries, blackberries, corn, clover, watermelons and all kinds of garden truck. She had some chickens, ducks and a cow. She became an adept fisherwoman.

The historic Shepp ranch is located at the confluence of Crooked Creek and the main Salmon and across the river is the Bemis place or Polly place as it is sometimes called. Charles Shepp was a Klondike argonaut and had been Rex Beach's partner in Nome. Shepp gravitated from Buffalo Hump to the Salmon River as early as 1899. His friendship with Charles Bemis and his Chinese wife, Polly, began at that time. In 1903 Shepp brought his friend Peter Klinkhammer from Buffalo Hump to the river. They purchased the ranch from Smith and Williams, later homesteading its 137 acres.

A phone line was strung from Shepp ranch to Polly place in 1919. Diary entries indicate that Bemis was already an invalid. Since Polly could neither read nor write, Shepp took care of her secretarial needs as indicated by some diary entries: "Over river. Ordered garden seeds for Polly. . . ." "Over river. Measured Polly for dress and ordered specs for her from Montgomery Ward."

One day in August, 1922, the phone rang urgently and repeatedly but Polly failed to answer Shepp's responses. His diary reads: "Peter went to Dixie a.m. Bemis house burned. . . . Got the old man out by the skin of my teeth. Lost Teddy (Polly's dog). He got burned. Polly and I got the old man over about 4. Had hard time. Didn't save a single thing. The whole place was on fire when I got over. Everybody's feet burned."

Another entry reads: "Pete back last night after dark. Brought jars and flours. Over river this eve. Got all Polly's chickens—30."

"Oct. 29, 1922. Bemis passed in at 3 a.m. I went up to War Eagle camp at 5 a.m. to get Schultz and Holmes. We buried the old man right after dinner. Fine day." The men who gathered for the funeral first made a box coffin. Then they buried Bemis on the river bank.

"Nov. 1, 1922. Polly going to Warrens. Took her stuff over river. Pete went to Warrens with Polly. Took 4 horses."

The following spring, 1923, Shepp and Klinkhammer started getting logs ready for another house on the Bemis ranch site.

Another quote from Shepp's diary is identified only as 1924. It says: "Cut grass along ditch. Pete back from Warrens with Polly. Got all her stuff down. Cloudy."[2]

Charlie set about making a bed, chairs, and table. The two men continued to do the heavy gardening and provided Polly with wood, game, and her few necessities.

She had entered into an agreement with Shepp and Klinkhammer by which her property was deeded to them and in return they would care for her. The half mile of thin telephone wire had always fascinated Polly and the day was not complete unless she used it once. If Shepp did not call her she would call him.

"How many eggs you get today? Six! I get 10." Then there was a peal of merry girlish laughter from a throat old enough to know nothing but a cackle. "How many fish you catch? None! You no good! You fella come over Sunday. I cook a great big one I catch today."

When Polly first heard the radio at Shepp and Klinkhammer's place, she thought it was evil spirits chattering out of the box and wanted to run away.

It seems that often after their marriage Polly would find Bemis playing cribbage with friends. She would approach him and count one, two, three, up to fifteen and then say, "You go home and put wood in the woodbox. Yes um, there's no wood in my woodbox." And Bemis would go.

On another occasion Bemis was one day attentively watching a nest of ants and called Polly. "Bemis," she said, "if you'd work um like these ants we wouldn't be poor folks."

There were not many visitors at the Bemis ranch but there were occasional prospectors in summer, or a boatload of adventurers with Captain Guleke of Salmon City, who three or four times a year would shoot down the "River of No Return," and always stop at the Bemis ranch. On one occasion when a party was planned Polly wanted a new dress but had only outing flannel on hand so she made a dress of that material and decorated it with her gold coin buttons. Nine of these coins are on exhibition in St. Gertrude's Museum.

It was in August, 1923, that Polly was brought out to Grangeville in an automobile. While visiting Mrs. Bertha Long, whose acquaintance she had made long ago in Warren, the parrot began to chatter, "What does Polly want for breakfast? Polly wants something for breakfast." The Chinese woman was puzzled and wanted to know how the bird knew her name. Mrs. Long explained that the bird's name was Polly too.

The parrot was a large green bird with gold and green wings and Polly called it a "talkee bird." She said, "This is the first talkee bird me see um since I leave um Shanghai. Most birds in Shanghai talkee hi-yu bad; this talkee bird talkee nice."

In Grangeville Polly saw her first motion-picture show and her first train. Some pioneers say that she rode on the train as far as Fenn and others say that she was only taken to the depot to witness the arrival of the evening train.

When Polly left Grangeville in 1923 she was dressed in a new outfit which included a new dress, a gay hat and white shoes, and a grip filled with new clothing, all gifts of white friends. "Maybe I come back next year," Polly declared, "it take hiyu money, but maybe I come back."

In 1924 Polly made a trip to Boise with Mr. and Mrs. Jay Czizek who once lived at Warren. They took her to the Idanha Hotel after she had seen her streetcar, her first high building, her second movie show and had ridden in her first elevator, all in one day. Commenting on her trip she said, "My husband say we will never see railroad and then he die, then I go to dentist. Now I see Boise, big city stores, streetcars run middle of street. Lots of people. I like it but it makes me tired to look so much."

Of Czizek she said, reminiscing, "Czizek ate in my boarding house thirty-two years ago. I know him long time."

The two friends, Shepp and Klinkhammer, continued to look after Polly. When she became ill in 1933 the two men took her on horseback to the War Eagle Mine and there an ambulance sent by the county sheriff was waiting to take her to Grangeville, where she was placed in a nursing home.

In 1942 Mr. Frank McGrane, Sr., recalled a visit with Polly when she was ill in Grangeville. Polly said to him, "Charlie wouldn't have died so soon if he hadn't been lazy. He just sat around till he was no account." Mrs. Bertha Long also visited her and said, "You'll soon get well." She answered, "No, me too old to get well, me have to go to other world to get well."

Polly died November 6, 1933. She had expressed a wish to be buried down by the roaring Salmon but since neither Shepp nor Klinkhammer could be located at the time of her death she was buried in Prairie View cemetery in Grangeville. Shepp died in 1936 and was laid to rest on the Salmon beside Bemis.

In August, 1933, when the press first announced the illness of Polly, Lamont Johnson, living in Twin Falls at the time, wrote to Polly in Grangeville. A letter soon came back from Mrs. Eva Weaver of the Weaver Nursing Home who was nursing Polly. Mrs. Weaver wrote Mr. Johnson that she would write the story of Polly as she told it. The story was published in the Portland *Oregonian* on November 4, 1933, and two days later Polly died. Various newspapers of the Northwest, in her obituary, quoted the *Oregonian* article which stated clearly that Polly was not a poker bride.

It was in 1943 that the first items in the so-called Bemis collection in St. Gertrude's Museum at Cottonwood were received from Mr. Klinkhammer. This was during the course of the research involved in the production of *Pioneer Days in Idaho County*, Volumes I and II, by this author. Besides the buttons made of gold coins already mentioned and the original marriage certificate there are three dresses which belonged to Polly, a sunbonnet, a brown shawl, numerous pieces of crocheted work, silverware given to Polly by friends, a few pieces of jewelry, and photos. The last of the items was brought to St. Gertrude's on January 15, 1964.

NOTES

1. Other source materials give her age as 43 in 1896.
2. Article by Marybelle Filer in *Idaho County Free Press*, June 16, 1966.

15

Pierce City Incident, 1885–1886

Kenneth Owens

Informal justice meted out by miners' courts and vigilante committees in the frontier mining camps carried a reputation for efficiency, crude and occasionally over-hasty. With the organization of Idaho's territorial government, the pioneer legislators took pains to institute at once a more even-handed system of law and order.[1] But the understaffed territorial judiciary, handicapped by the difficulties of travel within their vast jurisdiction, could not always bring the benefits of legal due process to Idaho's more remote areas.[2]

Long after the mining frontier's disorderly first years, recourse to direct community action remained a recognized part of the local legal machinery in the isolated gold camps of northern Idaho, as was proved by a dramatic case which begins with a hatchet murder at Pierce City in the fall of 1885. A certain degree of racial intolerance blended with the sense of outraged justice that impelled the white men of the region to action, and an irregular trial by vigilantes led to the lynching of five Chinese.

This case gained significance when the federal government pressured the governor of Idaho Territory into initiating a unique investigation of the affair. The Pierce City incident thus became far more than just another hanging, for it had given rise to international complications which caused considerable concern in Washington, if not in Idaho. With the growing demand in the federal territories for home rule, the Idaho governor's handling of the situation, his sympathy with the vigilantes and his obvious bias against all Idaho Chinese, provides a choice illustration of prevailing tendencies within the administration of the territories. In the ambivalent relationship between the territories and the central government, regional interests were coming to dominate as the central authorities finally gave power to the developing class of western political leaders in the closing years of Idaho's territorial period.

The peculiar situation at Pierce City in the mid-1880's largely explains the origin of the case. Located high up in the Bitterroot range on Oro Fino Creek, a tributary of the Clearwater River, the town had faded greatly from its days of prosperity at the center of northern Idaho's first gold mining district.[3] The richer diggings had long since played out, and only a handful of white men remained in the district. But there had grown up a large population of Chinese miners who worked the placer claims abandoned by the whites. Pierce City remained also something of a commercial center; local merchants packed in goods and conducted a considerable provisioning and merchandising business for the surrounding region, increasing their profits by trade with the Indians on the nearby Nez Perce reservation.[4]

In all such mercantile enterprises there existed a brisk competition between the leading Chinese firm of Lee Kee Nam and Company and D. M. Fraser, an old resident who had established his business during Pierce City's gold rush period. Fraser was very well respected throughout the area. Thus his friends were deeply shocked to find his body the morning of September 10, 1885, shot and "terribly chopped to pieces in his own store," with a blood-stained hatchet and knife lying on the floor amid bloody tracks.[5]

News of Fraser's brutal murder spread quickly, and white men rushed to Pierce City from all the surrounding country to insure that justice was done. Immediately a special messenger from Pierce City carried a plea for help downriver to Lewiston, the nearest sizeable town. In response, according to a Lewiston newspaper editor, some twenty or twenty-five townsmen started back upriver to lend force to the prosecution. As if by common agreement, the men of the region seemed determined from the first to seek vengeance for Fraser's death according to the procedures more typical of the earliest frontier days.[6]

Meanwhile Pierce City's citizens had begun a search for the murderers. Their suspicions not unnaturally fell upon Lee Kee Nam, the Chinese merchant, and his partner. As reinforcement rode in, the white men constituted themselves a vigilance committee and started action without the encumbrance of formal rules of evidence or a regard for the niceties of criminal procedure. They placed a noose around Lee Kee Nam's neck, hoisted him into the air, and dropped him unconscious. Then the vigilantes brought Lee's partner to view the apparently dead merchant. Threatened with the same fate, the terrified partner babbled that Lee Kee Nam had been solely responsible for Fraser's violent death. When the luckless merchant revived and heard the story, he placed all blame upon the partner, and the two orientals began a bitter round of counter-incrimination which completely satisfied the listening vigilantes that both were guilty.[7] Along with the two storekeepers, the vigilantes took into custody three other Chinese, one a hard-featured barber, the second a gambler, and the third "a parasite of one of the Chinese prostitutes of the camp." On the heads of these unsavory characters the vigilantes placed the blame for actually committing the murder allegedly plotted by Lee Kee Nam and his partner.[8]

At this point the leaders of the Pierce City vigilantes apparently felt their task had been completed. Like the miners' courts of earlier days, they carried out their investigation while memories of the crime remained fresh. Almost before the properly constituted officials could receive any notice of the incident, the men of the region had determined the guilt of the five Chinese by their own rough methods. But now the responsible vigilante captains seemed agreed to turn the evildoers over to the territorial authorities, though there must have been some in the camp who protested such a turn of events. The local deputy sheriff, who had previously refrained from any exercise of authority, took custody of the prisoners for safe delivery to the county seat, where the Chinese would await formal trial and the sentence of law. Since Pierce City was included in Shoshone County and the county seat was then at Murray, the deputy swore in a half dozen men as a posse to assist him on the arduous journey of five days or more over the mountains to the north.[9]

After making their preparations, the deputy and his small posse rode out of town on the morning of September eighteenth, with the prisoners tied together and jouncing along in a wagon. But they did not travel far. Just a few miles outside of Pierce City, at a spot where the road passed through a dense growth of timber and underbrush, the procession was halted by a large group of men, masked and armed, who took the posse's weapons and ordered them to head back, leaving the prisoners behind.[10] Then the lynching party hastily improvised a gallows, fixed the ropes in place, and swung the struggling Chinese out of the wagon. According to one newspaper report, the hangmen failed to make a clean job of it: "When the sheriff's posse returned later in the day, they found the five Chinamen hanging by the necks on a pole lashed to two pine trees. The pole had been broken and lashed to a center post, so that the victims must have been hoisted twice."[11] Whether intentionally or not, the Chinese had suffered a death nearly as horrible as the hatchet murder for which they had been summarily convicted and executed.

Almost certainly the hanging of five Chinese would have ended the case in the early frontier days, the whole episode becoming another tale to be recounted by old timers. But orientals in the western United States were becoming alarmed by an increasing bitterness entering racial relations during the mid-1880's. Demagogic politicians, opportunistic labor leaders, and fanatical reformers were taking up the cry that the Chinaman must go, giving new malice to old prejudices.[12] Only two weeks before the Pierce City incident, white miners on strike at the Union Pacific's Rock Springs coal mines had invaded a settlement of Chinese laborers, shooting all who were slow to flee and in addition burning company property. While the stern action of Wyoming's territorial governor and federal troops prevented an even bloodier outcome at Rock Springs, Chinese residents were being threatened with violence in a score of other towns.[13] The editor of the *Idaho World* summed up the views of many of his fellow citizens: the Chinese must be refused all employment and totally ostracized; otherwise, "The Mongolian will become a fixture on this coast and remain a menace to labor and a nightmare to civilization."[14]

In this atmosphere of rising racial tension, it seemed plausible to concerned Chinese that their countrymen hanged at Pierce City had been innocent scapegoats. As soon as news of the hanging reached Portland, the Chinese merchant community in that city sent agents upriver to Lewiston and into northern Idaho, both to safeguard the property of their people and to check the facts in the case.[15] When these agents returned to Lewiston from Pierce City, they reported themselves satisfied that the dead men had indeed been guilty, and richly deserved their fate.[16] But a contrary account reached the Chinese Consul at San Francisco who forwarded a note of protest to the Chinese Minister in Washington, D.C., and the Minister in turn applied to the Secretary of State for an investigation.[17] Thus the federal government, in keeping with treaty obligations, was forced to take notice of the entire affair, although the people of the Pierce City district considered it strictly their own concern.

In dealing with the territories, the officials at the national capital had to rely primarily upon the federally appointed territorial governors.[18] Just after the events at Pierce City reached their violent climax, Edward A. Stevenson received appointment as Governor of Idaho Territory, and to this new man there fell the responsibility of investigating the incident. Governor Stevenson was a person whom the majority of Idahoans could trust, for he knew the interests of the territory and the feelings of its people. He had come to Idaho from the California gold fields in 1863, and over the years built up a sizeable fortune in mining and farming. A man of enterprise, Stevenson had also achieved a prominent position in the territorial Democratic Party organization. His appointment as territorial governor came in recognition of his generous financial contributions to the party and his many years of service as chairman of the Idaho Democratic Central Committee.[19] Since he was the first resident of the territory to be so honored, Stevenson's appointment in a larger sense marked the great change in territorial appointive practices which President Cleveland was attempting to carry through, giving fuller recognition and voice to western party leaders in the management of territorial affairs.[20] One of the results of this change, as Governor Stevenson's handling of the investigation at Pierce City illustrates so well, was that western viewpoints and western standards of public policy increasingly came to override the policy aims of the national authorities in territorial affairs.

With the delay normal in diplomatic exchanges, Governor Stevenson did not learn of the Chinese government's interest in the Pierce City incident until the latter part of April, 1886. Though Fraser's murder and the hanging of the Chinese had been reported fully in the territorial newspapers, the new Governor obviously considered it none of his business until the Secretary of State wrote him, requesting a full investigation.[21] Stevenson then replied immediately to the Secretary of State, promising that he would take "the earliest opportunity" to visit northern Idaho "and try to obtain the facts connected with that disgraceful outrage. . . ."[22] For another three months he did nothing in the matter, except to report that the impassable condition of the roads in the district still prevented the trip.[23]

Meanwhile the Governor did take a firm stand in quelling the general threat of violence to the Chinese throughout Idaho. When the Boise Anti-Chinese League set May 1, 1886, as a deadline date for the Chinese to leave the territory peaceably, and allied groups in various other towns followed suit, Stevenson issued a strong proclamation directing the anti-Chinese leagues to preserve order and instructing law officers "to use every precaution to prevent all riotous demonstrations. . . ."[24] This act, courageous for an Idaho political figure in that day, helped prevent armed demonstrations against the Chinese, although opponents of the administration employed the continuing anti-Chinese agitation as a partisan device. When he finally began a trip north to inquire into the lynching incident the Governor adopted a far more politic approach.

Stevenson stopped first at Lewiston, in order to smooth the way for his delicate mission, and consulted one of the town's prominent attorneys. For the Governor's benefit, this attorney wrote a remarkable letter of introduction to the Justice of the Peace at Pierce City, carefully explaining the circumstances which brought the territorial executive into this remote region. Governor Stevenson, the attorney made clear, came only at the request of the State Department; the federal authorities were acting upon the complaint of the Chinese government that the men had been put to death merely because they were Chinamen. The attorney asked the Justice of the Peace and his friends to extend the Governor and his party every facility so they "may arrive at the real cause of the Execution." It was strongly emphasized that "The Governor does not want names as to parties who took part in the hanging; but the cause which lead [sic] to it." The Lewiston attorney took pains to leave nothing to the imagination of the Pierce City gentry. "Therefore," he directed, "have a full investigation, and let it Clearly appear that the Chinamen who were hung were the real Murders [sic] of Mr. Fraser, and that they were hung for committing the Act, and for that only." Finally, the attorney named specifically the trustworthy Chinese who should be permitted also to give evidence to the Governor.[25] If there was an element of wry humor in these directions for "a full investigation" which would "let it Clearly appear" that only the single foregone conclusion was possible—that the five men lynched had been unquestionably guilty—it escaped the officials who were intent upon the correct handling of a difficult situation.

With such careful preparation, the actual inquiry at Pierce City proved uneventful. Governor Stevenson found for his report to the Secretary of State only the information deemed appropriate by the local citizens. The deputy and his posse, Stevenson wrote to Washington, "were so badly frightened on being suddenly surrounded by a large number of blackened, disguised, masked, armed men . . . they were unable to recognize any of the party." The hanging itself had been a rash act, the Governor allowed, but the various charges of the Chinese government were entirely without foundation. While he regretted that the men of the region had taken justice into their own hands, Stevenson had "no doubt that the Chinese hanged, were the identical parties, who so cruelly, shockingly and brutally murdered, without the least provocation (except jealousy) one of the best citizens of Idaho."[26]

The Governor was not content to prove merely that the facts of the case justified the course pursued by the Pierce City vigilantes. He concluded his report with a lecture to the Secretary of State on the Chinese problem in the far west.

There was no use trying to hide the fact, Stevenson declared, "that many such devilish acts have been perpetrated by Chinese; and their low filthy habits; their highbinder piratical societies, together with their low dens of infamy, prostitution and opium smoking, have disgusted our people. . . ." On behalf of the territory, the Governor guaranteed that the Chinese would receive the protection of the laws while they remained, but he also spoke the hope of his fellow citizens that "the day is not far distant when Congress will relieve us of their presence."[27] As other troubled men of an earlier generation hoped to end the Negro problem by colonizing all American colored persons in Africa, Governor Stevenson believed that a policy of Chinese exclusion and deportation could substitute for tolerance.

In his administration of Idaho Territory, Governor Stevenson proved a preeminent representative of that class of western men, with large economic interests as well as prominent political positions, who were assuming the direction of territorial affairs. Stevenson, like the Idaho leaders in both major political parties, sought to consolidate his position behind the appealing popular demand for "Home Rule" in the territories.[28] Though he would not countenance wholesale violence against the Chinese because of his conservative predilections and his concern for the territory's reputation, obviously the Governor did not sympathize with the Secretary of State's attempt to uphold a more impartial standard of justice in the Pierce City affair. The national authorities and the Chinese government, lacking other official channels for investigation, had to accept Governor Stevenson's report as the full story of the incident. In this case "Home Rule" meant in effect the privilege of Idaho citizens to enforce their own concept of justice, supported by virulent regional prejudices, without the interference of responsible federal officials. Thus both racial intolerance and the violation of basic legal rights were sustained in this particular instance by the democratic creed of local self-government as it applied to the far west.

NOTES

1. *Idaho Session Laws*, 1863–1864, 234–235, 435–75; *1864*, 213–97, 298–383. For the history of irregular popular justice in Idaho during the mining rush period see Hubert Howe Bancroft, *Popular Tribunals* [volumes 31 and 32 in H . H. Bancroft, *History of the Pacific States of North America*] (San Francisco, 1887), I:664–73; Hiram T. French, *History of Idaho; A Narrative Account of Its Historical Progress, Its People and Its Principal Interests* (Chicago, 1914), I:555–63.

2. For a perceptive contemporary analysis of the territorial legal system as administered in Idaho see *Report of The Governor of Idaho*, October 8, 1879, 46 Cong., 2 Sess., House Executive Document 1, part 5, vol. 2 (serial 1911), 425–26.

3. For the beginnings of mining in the Pierce City Region see William J. Trimble, *The Mining Advance into the Inland Empire* . . . [Bulletin of the University of Wisconsin, No. 638] (Madison, 1914), 63–67; Hubert Howe Bancroft, *History of Washington, Idaho, and Montana* [volume 26 in H. H. Bancroft, *History of the Pacific States of North America*] (San

Francisco, 1890), 234–45; W. A. Goulder, *Reminiscences; Incidents in the Life of a Pioneer in Oregon and Idaho* (Boise, 1909), 203–223.

4. Report of Governor Stevenson to Secretary of State Bayard, August 2, 1886, Idaho Territorial Papers, General Records of the Department of the Interior, RG 48, National Archives. Varying estimates place Pierce City's white population in 1885 somewhere between six and thirty, while a Lewiston editor states that approximately 350 Chinese resided in the town: *Lewiston Teller*, quoted in *Idaho World* (Idaho City), September 235, 1885.

5. *Lewiston Teller*, quoted in *Idaho World*, September 25, 1885; Report of Governor Stevenson to Secretary Bayard, August 2, 1886, Idaho Territorial Papers, Interior Department.

6. *Lewiston Teller*, quoted in *Idaho World*, September 26, 1885. This enthusiastic response by the Lewiston men seems more significant since the initial report carefully avoided placing suspicion upon any particular group, stating that nothing made it certain "whether his murderers were Americans or Chinese, whether the murder was committed by persons in town or out of it."

7. This account of the vigilante proceedings was given by the editor of the *Nez Perce News* (Lewiston), reportedly from an eye witness account, and reprinted by the *Idaho World* (Idaho City), October 9, 1885.

8. *Ibid.*, Report of Governor Stevenson to Secretary of State Bayard, August 1, 1886, Idaho Territorial Papers, Interior Department.

9. Report of Governor Stevenson to Secretary of State Bayard, August 2, 1886, Idaho Territorial Papers, Interior Department.

10. Report of Governor Stevenson to Secretary of State Bayard, August 2, 1886, Idaho Territorial Papers, Interior Department; *Nez Perce News*, quoted in *Idaho World*, October 9, 1885.

11. *Nez Perce News*, quoted in *Idaho World*, October 9, 1885.

12. Some of the materials for a study of the anti-Chinese movement in Idaho have been gathered in Fern C. Trull, *The History of the Chinese in Idaho from 1864 to 1910* (unpublished master's thesis, University of Oregon, 1946), which is written from an overly romantic pro-Chinese viewpoint. There is no general account of the anti-Chinese movement in the Rocky Mountain and Pacific Coast territories and states, though the movement erupted violently in 1885 and 1886 after a long period of agitation, and remained a potent political issue years after the violence had run its course. For an introductory background study see Mary R. Coolidge, *Chinese Immigration* (New York, 1909), and Jules Alexander Karlin, "Anti-Chinese Outbreaks in Seattle, 1885–1886," *Pacific Northwest Quarterly* (April, 1948), 39:103–130.

13. Primary sources for the "Rock Springs Massacre" are contained in the *Report of The Governor of Wyoming*, November 25, 1885, 49 Cong., 1 Sess., House Executive Document 12, No. 1, part 5, vol. 1 (serial 2379), 1121 *et seq.*, and Francis E. Warren Executive Letterbooks, Wyoming State Archives and Historical Department.

14. *Idaho World*, October 23, 1885.

15. *Morning Oregonian* (Portland), September 24, 30, 1885.

16. *Lewiston Teller*, quoted in *Idaho World*, October 16, 1885.

17. Secretary of State Bayard to Governor Stevenson, April 21, 1886, Domestic Letters, CLX, General Records of the Department of State, RG 49, National Archives.

18. While the territorial service was always subject to a considerable degree of confusion regarding lines of authority, the territorial governors occupied the position of most direct and responsible administrative leadership. On this point see Kenneth N. Owens, *Frontier Governors; A Study of the Territorial Executives in the History of Washington, Idaho,*

Montana, Wyoming, and Dakota Territories (unpublished doctoral dissertation, University of Minnesota, 1959), 1–7 and *passim.* For a scholarly general survey of the administrative framework of territorial government see Earl S. Pomerov, *The Territories and the United States, 1861–1890; Studies in Colonial Administration* (Philadelphia, 1947).

19. Edward A. Stevenson to President Cleveland, September 16, 1885, Appointment File 236. Appointment Papers of Territorial Governors and Secretaries, Appointments Division, General Records of the Department of the Interior, RG 48, National Archives; Governor Stevenson to President Cleveland, September 10, 1885, Grover Cleveland Papers, Division of Manuscripts, Library of Congress.

20. See Owens, 269 *et seq.*; Pomeroy, 73–79.

21. Secretary of State Bayard to Governor Stevenson, April 21, 1886, Domestic Letters, CLX, State Department.

22. Governor Stevenson to Secretary of State Bayard, April 29, 1886, Idaho Territorial Papers, Interior Department.

23. Governor Stevenson to Secretary of State Bayard, June 8, 1886, and Report of Governor Stevenson to Secretary of State Bayard, August 2, 1886, Idaho Territorial Papers, Interior Department.

24. Proclamation of April 27, 1886, Idaho Territorial Papers, Interior Department; Trull, 203–19.

25. Jasper Rand to I. B. Cowan, July 15, 1886, Israel Burr Cowan Papers, Idaho State Historical Society. I am indebted to Dr. Merle Wells for calling this amazing letter to my attention.

26. Report of Governor Stevenson to Secretary of State Bayard, August 2, 1886, Idaho Territorial Papers, Interior Department.

27. Report of Governor Stevenson to Secretary of State Bayard, August 2, 1886, Idaho Territorial Papers, Interior Department. Stevenson's political astuteness was demonstrated further when he had copies of this report prepared for widespread distribution and saw that it was reprinted in the territory's Democratic newspapers; see copy filed August 23, 1886, Territorial Executive Papers, Idaho Historical Society; *Idaho World,* August 20, 1886.

28. For a fuller treatment of Stevenson's administration see Owens 307–15.

Part IV

Chinese in the Rocky Mountains (Utah, Colorado, Wyoming, Montana, South Dakota)

16

Utah's Chinatowns: The Development and Decline of Extinct Ethnic Enclaves

Daniel Liestman

The labors of the Chinese in constructing the transcontinental railroad are legendary. Too often, though, this is the only context in which the Chinese are mentioned as a component of Utah's history.[1] In fact, the driving of the golden spike marks the beginning of a distinctive element in Utah's history. Following events at Promontory in 1869, most Chinese began congregating in Chinatowns that coexisted within a number of Zion's towns and cities. The largest such enclave was in Salt Lake City with others in Ogden, Corinne, Park City, Silver Reef, and elsewhere.

The Chinese added an interesting element to Utah's ethnic mix which otherwise consisted largely of those of European descent. Reactions to the Chinese varied. Some Euro-American groups took particular exception to the presence of the Chinese while others remained less interested. In particular those who found themselves in the lower echelons of the social-economic hierarchy seemed particularly interested in distancing themselves from the Chinese whom they perceived as rivals. The antipathy of the Irish for the Chinese is well known and underscored by the violence that occurred between the two groups during the construction of the transcontinental railroad. Other groups, such as Italians and Slavs, often came to Utah as unskilled laborers and sought to be portrayed as superior to and distinct from the Chinese. This did not always occur. Miners at one camp banned both Chinese and Italians from their diggings.[2] In spite of their own diversity, most white residents of Utah tended to view the Chinese as a faceless, if not nameless, seemingly indistinguishable group of people who tended to cluster in predominantly white communities. Members of many minority cultures engaged in such behavior. As a result, Salt Lake City not only had a Chinatown but a Little Denmark in its Second Ward.[3] Across Utah there were Greek Towns, Bohunk Towns for Serbs, Croats, and Slovenes, and Little Italys among others. Due to obvious racial and cultural differences Chinese enclaves formed a readily identifiable but unassimilable and short-lived presence. Although some 5,000 Chinese currently live in the state, no Chinatowns remain.[4] This paper expands on existing research by examining the development of Utah's Chinatowns, the response to these settlements, and their demise. Implicit in this thesis is an obvious deficiency—the lack of a Chinese perspective. Such an admittedly unbalanced approach, however, reflects the nature of extant primary source materials rather than a deliberate oversight or agenda.

Initially, Chinese in the territory avoided white settlements as they lived in dugouts or tents along rail lines, working as section crews or station cooks. A few entrepreneurial ones operated laundries that followed work crews.[5] Only gradually did they begin to move into predominantly white settlements. Although Utah's white residents could not help but be aware of the anti-Chinese attitudes reaching across the nation, local opinion leaders nevertheless did not initially object to the Chinese living among them. James H. Beadle of Corinne's *Utah Reporter* declared the so called "Chinese problem" to be nothing but "baseless political humbug," declaring, "We need large numbers in this Territory." In the *Salt Lake Herald*, William C. Dunbar viewed the threat of Chinese labor as "overrated," while the Mormon *Deseret Evening News* lauded the Chinese as hard working, skillful, and intelligent, adding, "There is probably no people on the continent who are likely to be less disturbed or affected by the introduction . . . of this element [the Chinese] than the people of Utah." Franklin Richard's *Ogden Junction* was less effusive. He considered the Chinese to be "heathens and barbarians" but cheerfully added that they were no worse so than many European immigrants or Americans for that matter.[6]

With the completion of the transcontinental line the Chinese and other railroad laborers began settling in Bear River Valley towns such as Corinne and in other railroad towns before moving on to places like Salt Lake City. Not until 1882 did the *Deseret Evening News* first mention a "Chinese quarter" in that city. Prior to that the *Salt Lake Tribune* had observed that the Chinese were "rather backward about entering Mormondom." Available census information confirms the gradual clustering of Chinese in specific cities. Admittedly, such data are fallible. Nonetheless, by using Box Elder, Salt Lake, Weber, Washington, and Summit counties as examples some general trends can be seen. The 1870 census reported a total of 455 Chinese in Utah with more than 90 percent of them located in Box Elder County and most of the rest in Summit County. Over the ensuing decades Box Elder showed a steady decline in its Chinese population through 1920 when the census found none living there. As one might expect, the Chinese population in Washington County peaked in 1880 with 53. By 1890 there were only 2 and after that none, reflecting the end of the mining boom in Silver Reef. The number of Chinese recorded for Utah as a whole (806) and for the counties of Weber (106), and Summit (121) peaked in 1890. For Salt Lake County 1890 and 1900 were the high points with 269 and 271 Chinese listed, respectively. These figures show the movement of many Chinese to the state's urban centers. By 1920 only 342 Chinese were enumerated by the census, with most of them living in Salt Lake or Weber counties.[7]

The arrival of the Chinese into urban areas affected both white residents and the Chinese. At first contact, residents reflected their Anglo-American values by commenting on the "peculiar" attire of the Chinese and their exotic appearances. Gradually, however, hints of anti-Chinese sentiments surfaced.[8] The Chinese came together in the Chinatowns not only because they sought to be among their own people but also because many of them shared common family names and traditionally lived near one another. Since most Chinese did not plan to settle permanently in America they wanted to retain their culture by maintaining close contact with one another. The overwhelming number of Chinese were bachelor males or married men whose families had remained in China. Lonely and homesick in a strange land, they sought one another's company. Consequently, they organized Chinatowns on an extended kinship basis to meet their affiliative needs.[9] In addition, such living arrangements contributed in some measure to the preservation and continuation of their familiar way of life, particularly through associations like the Bing Kong Tong in Salt Lake City. Thus, Chinatowns offered their residents both physical and psychological security.

These enclaves did not, however, meet all the psychosocial needs of the Chinese. The shortage of females, for example, largely precluded the establishment of nuclear families.[10] The few Chinese women had come usually as either spouses or prostitutes. Respectable wives traditionally remained at home and had little contact with whites. When they did emerge publicly their appearance was cause for considerable comment such as occurred when three Chinese women attended a Salt Lake fair in 1873 where their presence caused much comment among the rest of the fairgoers. As there were few eligible Chinese women, weddings were rare. The first occurred in 1870 when John Tip married Ma Coy in a civil ceremony performed at the bride's Corinne restaurant. Only a handful of other marriages occurred, and few produced children. Utah's miscegenation law forbade Chinese men from marrying Caucasian women, and virtually no other alternatives existed. There were anomalous cases such as a Chinese man and a white woman from Scofield who married.[11] Few Chinese children lived in Utah's Chinatowns, and those that did kept to themselves. On rare occasions they would be seen by whites, as in the case of a young Chinese boy who lived as a beggar on Salt Lake City's streets. This, too, was an anomaly since children usually belonged to well-to-do Chinese merchants who could afford to bring their families over to America.[12]

Another factor precluding stable Chinatowns was their transient populations. Chinese often moved wherever they thought they could obtain the best economic opportunities. On the heels of the Black Hills gold rush, for example, a number of Chinese merchants left Salt Lake City for Deadwood, Dakota Territory, to open new businesses. Other Chinese engaged in seasonal labor and left Salt Lake City during the winter. This seemingly opportunistic attitude contributed to white citizen's prejudice against these overseas Chinese workers whom they perceived to be nothing but sojourners and uninterested in building a stable community.[13] In spite of such issues, Chinatowns offered the Chinese security and cultural familiarity as

well as economic potential—a factor that largely determined where these enclaves developed.

In Utah, Chinatowns occupied an older section of their host city near the central business district and close to available transportation networks. In Salt Lake
City, Chinatown centered around Plum Alley which ran north from Second South
to First South between Main and State streets. Corinne's first Chinatown centered
near the intersection of Fourth Avenue and Montana Street. Following a major fire
on September 25, 1871, the city fathers zoned a new area for the enclave. Chinatown then bordered North Front Street and the Bear River between First and Second near the steamboat wharf. Ogden's Chinatown was less centralized but was situated along Fifth Avenue north of Main. Silver Reef's Chinese lived on the east end
of Centre Street. The most unusual Chinatown site was in Park City where Chinese lived in approximately twenty buildings along Silver Creek. The site sat so low
along the flood plain that a bright red foot bridge crossed over the Chinese buildings from Marsac Avenue on Rossie Hill down toward Main.[14]

Morphologically, Chinatowns tended to develop in linear patterns. In some
measure this reflected site topography. The ravine created by Silver Creek, for example, confined growth in much of Park City. Similarly, Corinne's was restricted
by the Bear River. In Salt Lake City, however, the nascent Chinatown along Plum
Alley developed and grew into more of a reticulated pattern incorporating parts
of Third South, Commercial Avenue, and East Temple (Main Street).[15]

Residents of Chinatowns often found employment within the enclave through local Chinese labor brokers.[16] Inhabitants saved money by living frugally in the back
of stores or in adjacent shared housing. Such arrangements removed the Chinese
from residential competition with the dominant society. Chinese usually rented the
property they occupied. In part, this reflected their economic and social status. It also
underscored their transient lifestyle. Few, save established merchants, sought long-
term locational commitment. Perhaps the Chinese also feared the loss of real estate
should they be expelled as occurred in nearby Rock Springs, Wyoming, in 1885.
Most Chinatowns remained fixed until their extinction and did not usually relocate
even though their residents maintained a high degree of mobility.

Although Chinatowns remained segregated from the communities within
which they existed, they did not live in isolation from one another. They formed
distinct settlement nodes linked by rail and other overland routes with other Chinatowns across the region, including those in Montana and Idaho. The larger
Chinatowns also acted as hubs. Salt Lake City's gained ascendancy over others.
Chinese from across Utah as well as the western United States considered it a regional center for many activities. Utah's Chinese retained strong links with Chinese officials in the U.S. due to their location on the major east-west axis across
the country from San Francisco to Washington, D.C.[17]

Chinatowns and other ethnic enclaves did not blend into the local environment. Sunnywide's Ragtown where many poor Italians lived in squalid tents was
one example of the conspicuously impoverished conditions faced by many im-

Interior view of a Chinese barber shop in Denver, Colorado [circa 1910]. Courtesy, Colorado Historical Society, negative CHS X3408.

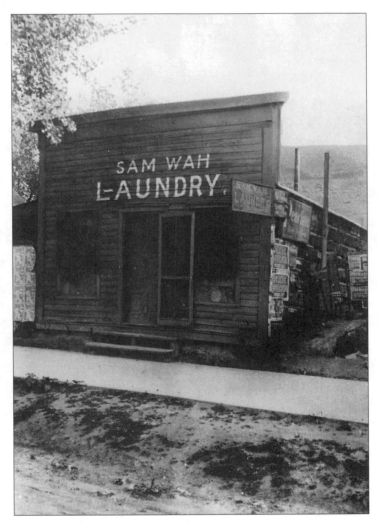

Façade of Sam Wah's Laundry, Colorado Avenue, Colorado City, (capital of Colorado Territory in 1861) [circa 1890]. Courtesy of the Denver Public Library.

A Chinese-owned tobacco store in Denver, Colorado [circa 1910]. Courtesy, Colorado Historical Society, negative CHS X3537.

A man poses on a wooden sidewalk near a Chinese laundry (location unknown) [circa 1880]. Courtesy of the Denver Public Library.

Railroad workers—Chinese and Anglo—pose on a Union Pacific Railroad Company light car [circa 1880]. Courtesy of the Denver Public Library.

A stereoscopic view of Central Pacific Railroad construction at Promontory, Utah [circa 1869]. Courtesy of the Denver Public Library.

Chinese Miners work at a sluice [circa 1881]. Courtesy of the Denver Public Library.

Dr. James Underhill, a professor at the Colorado School of Mines, poses with Chinese miners in the school's Edgar Experimental Mine near Idaho Springs [circa 1920]. Courtesy of the Denver Public Library.

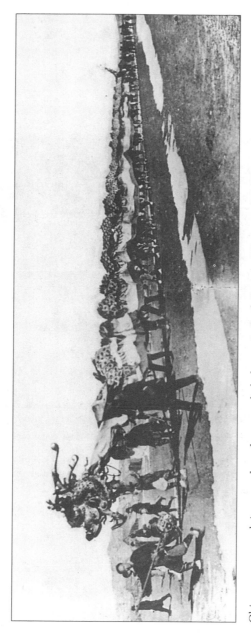

Chinese men march in a parade and carry a cloth dragon in Rock Springs, Wyoming [1899]. Courtesy of the Denver Public Library.

Handwritten on back of print; "Denver street scenes: Hop Alley, a Denver Chinaman getting ready for the New Year festivities while his brother Celestial smokes his pipe while waiting for the celebration to begin. Probably taken before 1912." Courtesy of the Denver Public Library.

Two unidentified Chinese actors in a Portland, Oregon, theater. Courtesy of the Denver Public Library.

A Chinese fishing village near the Pacific Ocean. The buildings are surrounded by bamboo shoot fences [circa 1380]. Courtesy of the Denver Public Library.

A family at dinner in Denver, Colorado, November 1914. Courtesy, Colorado Historical Society, CHS X3534.

A group including one Chinese man stands near a sturdy building in Denver, Colorado, housing a Chinese business, Yee Lee & Co. [circa 1920]. Courtesy of the Denver Public Library.

Men, women, and children stand outdoors near a Chinese masonic lodge [June 3, 1928]. Courtesy of the Denver Public Library.

A vegetable peddler on a street in Idaho City, Idaho [circa 1890]. Courtesy of the Denver Public Library.

migrants.[18] However, as Chinatowns grew they seemed to be singled out for special attention, and nativists perceived them in darkest terms. The local press often exploited and reinforced the negative views of Chinatowns as unhealthy havens of immoral and illegal activities. Little opportunity existed to alter such misconceptions. Civic leaders thought Chinatowns to be unhealthy due to population congestion, unsanitary conditions, and rare diseases carried by Chinese. Complaints frequently centered around malodorous pig sties or pools of stagnant water near wash houses, particularly during the summer months. Reports of some Chinese with Hansen's disease, or leprosy, further fostered this perception, even though such accounts were often without foundation.[19]

Whites also saw Chinatowns as centers of immorality. This perception stemmed in large measure from cultural dissonance. Local moral and religious leaders considered opium and gambling nefarious illegal activities, while for the Chinese they were a cultural component of their traditional lifestyle. The Chinese usually gambled among themselves often placing bets with brass coins valued at about $\frac{1}{10}$ of a penny in games of fan tan. For higher stakes, Silver Reef's Chinese residents played a lottery which reportedly could pay out up to $10,000. Even though gambling was one of the few recreational activities available to the Chinese, authorities arrested those involved with such games. In September 1873 Salt Lake City Police began raiding Chinese gambling "dens." Ogden Police launched their largest gambling crackdown on Chinese in 1887, arresting seventeen in one night's raid. In response to enhanced police activity Chinese began posting lookouts. Police in turn resorted to stealth and speed in conducting raids, albeit with limited success.[20]

Most whites saw opium as a much greater evil. In China use of the drug had increased dramatically under British-fostered trade. Many Chinese, consequently, brought their addiction to the U.S. Possession and use of the drug was not illegal until 1914 with passage of the federal Harrison Act, but it was unlawful to smuggle the black tar-like substance into the country without paying federal duties or taxes. In 1879 the Salt Lake City Council passed an ordinance outlawing opium dens. Police, however, confessed to the difficulty of obtaining evidence because the Chinese tended to be wary of selling to those they did not know. Park City saw a similar law overturned by its municipal court which ruled that the city had no right to pass an ordinance under its charter. Beyond this, most considered the effects of the drug to be debilitating and immoral. Contemporary accounts frequently describe in vivid terms the dismal conditions of these "dens of infamy" and the "pernicious" effect of the drug. Nonetheless, a number of men and women from all social strata and races smoked opium with the Chinese, leaving some to decry the "Saintly Salt Lakers" who "Hit the Pipe."[21]

Chinese prostitution, "the meanest of moral ulcers," as one observer saw it, occurred largely because the Chinese lived in "reproductive isolation" with prostitution as the only available outlet. Convicted prostitutes, nonetheless, faced stiff sentences. A Corinne court fined seven Chinese women $100 each. When they could not pay the judge ordered them incarcerated. Even when the court reduced the fine the women remained jailed. Two Salt Lake Chinese women arrested twice in one week each received fines of $500. Prostitutes who escaped their "owners" were often pursued since they cost their "owners" between $150 and $600. A Chinese in Silver Reef even advertised a $50 reward for the return of one of his missing women. This reinforced the belief among Euro-Americans that the Chinese women were little more than slaves.[22] In spite of public opposition little was done to curtail prostitution, and few arrests occurred.

To a lesser degree Chinatowns were also perceived as sequestering illegal immigrants. Beginning in 1882 a series of federal laws severely restricted Chinese immigration. Many Chinese opposed this racist legislation and sought to circumvent it by continuing to enter the country. The *Deseret Evening News* decried the number of "wily and cunning" Chinese who entered the country illegally, while the *Salt Lake Herald* maintained that it was "very common" among the city's Chinese to have entered the country with fraudulent documents. In 1895 a federal investigator came to Salt Lake City searching for illegal immigrants. His assignment proved difficult as the Chinese remained reticent; many "suddenly developed an ignorance of English that was surprising" when queried on such matters. One Chinese informant, however, made a startling revelation. He said an unnamed government official in Ogden sold illegal documentation. These fraudulent papers, he said, were supposedly cheaper in Ogden than those available in San Francisco.[23]

Beyond this level of Chinese and white rancor there existed a history of competition and conflict among the Chinese themselves. In 1873 a gang of Chinese on the Utah Railroad hanged one of their own for reasons not revealed to any whites. Theft and violence occurred between Chinese individuals more often than groups, although in 1883 a war between the Hoo Sing and Bing Kong tongs broke out across the United States. In Salt Lake a Hoo Sing member shot his own uncle who belonged to the rival tong. The Bing Kong eventually gained supremacy.[24] Most of the time, however, conflict and violence occurred among individual Chinese over scarce resources.[25]

There are numerous reports of Chinese stealing and fighting among themselves. Usually such disputes involved minor stolen household items or gambling losses. In some instances the disagreement centered around more significant matters. In 1897 Yee Yen, a Chinese financial agent, absconded with $8,000 in savings from the Chinese of Salt Lake. Territorial officials captured, tried, and convicted him. The case dew so much attention that the Chinese consul traveled to Utah to attend the trial.[26] In some instances, violence occurred. For example, in Ogden, Ching Yu received three deep hatchet wounds to his head when he attempted to collect a business debt.[27] Since women were few, competition for their attention could be intense. In one case a Chinese man from Ogden paid a trio of Euro-Americans $300 to abscond with a Chinese woman living with her husband in Sandy. The kidnappers made off with her, but her husband intercepted them and retrieved his wife.[28] The most sensational Chinese murder occurred in Alta where two Chinese men stabbed and robbed a woman known as China Mary. The dramatic nature of the case attracted considerable attention across the territory and the lurid details received considerable coverage in the local press which depicted the Chinese as wanton and immoral.[29]

In spite of discrimination, danger, and difficulties, Chinatowns still offered the Chinese the best circumstances for economic betterment. Initially, employment in Chinatowns centered around what might be considered traditional primary-level occupations. After the driving of the golden spike both the Central Pacific and the Union Pacific as well as smaller lines employed Chinese primarily on section crews.[30] In spite of their reputation as being docile and manageable the Chinese proved militant at times. In an extreme case a section crew near Corinne rebelled over the firing of one of their own and attacked Frank Donsure, the section boss, with the iron rods used to repair the track. Donsure escaped and the railroad fired the Chinese. Chinese also worked for mining companies in different capacities. Response to them varied. At the Mud Creek Coal Mines eighteen armed guards protected forty Chinese workers from the other disgruntled miners—probably Italians. The Samson Mine near Park City, however, fired all of its Chinese after two engaged in a bloody fight.[31]

Eventually Utah law forbade Chinese and other aliens from working in the mines; however, a loophole allowed those of European ancestry to continue working. In lieu of citizenship, the law stipulated that an alien could declare his intention of becoming a naturalized citizen. As most Chinese had no intention of becoming Americans they remained excluded from the mines. Chinese continued to work for mining companies near Park City and Alta in support services such as cooking and serving in the miners' boarding houses. In these roles they interacted successfully with other ethnic groups. At Bingham Canyon, for example, a Chinese laundry served the Slavic miners of the Highland Boy Gold Mine.[32]

Chinese railroad and mine workers frequently found themselves in direct economic competition with whites. What fostered particular resentment was the fact that Chinese accepted a much lower standard of living and worked for less than the average laborer. The seeming economic success of the Chinese led whites to fear loss of employment or potential income. Beyond these perceptions, influences outside Utah reinforced growing anti-Chinese attitudes.

Dennis Kearney, the nation's foremost anti-Chinese agitator from San Francisco, stopped at Salt Lake City in 1883 long enough to criticize employers of Chinese. Five years later, in an interview with the *Salt Lake Herald*, Kearney again lashed out at the continued efforts of the white "Chinese slave-dealers" to allow more Chinese to enter the country and undermine the labor market. In 1884 Dr. Charles Carroll O'Donnell, president of San Francisco's Workingman's Anti-Coolie League, expressed such views much more emphatically. In Salt Lake he vigorously lectured on the evils of Chinese labor. O'Donnell had a particular fixation with Chinese lepers and expended considerable effort expounding on this issue. He had reportedly brought two lepers with him to display on his nationwide tour with the intent of abandoning the unfortunate pair in Washington, D.C., for the federal government to care for.

Although many regarded O'Donnell as a "crank," Utahns by the early 1880s had become increasingly antagonistic toward the Chinese. The *Park Mining Record* termed "Chinese cheap labor" to be the "foundation for crime and destitution" and claimed their "presence tends to increase vice and immorality," while the *Corinne Daily Mail* decried the ongoing "inhuman traffic" of Chinese.[33] As anti-Chinese views became increasingly persistent it is not surprising that random acts of violence ranging from vandalism to physical assaults occurred. Although Utah experienced less intense anti-Chinese agitation than most places in the West it was by no means exempt from such activities.[34] Youths frequently perpetrated vandalism against the Chinese, leading one Salt Lake observer to comment, "The boys who run the streets seem to think they are licensed to abuse Chinamen in every conceivable way," adding, "they break the windows of the Heathens, throw rocks at their doors, take advantage of a solitary Chinaman and pull his que [*sic*], and attempt violence against him; and always make a liberal use of the vilest, filthiest and most brutal expressions towards them."[35] Such actions, though, were not restricted to young offenders; adults also occasionally assaulted Chinese with little or no provocation. Robbers often singled out Chinese victims, believing that they carried considerable amounts of cash. At Corinne an extreme example of anti-Chinese activity occurred when a Chinese accused of murder was lynched from a rail trestle by a mob.[36]

In Ogden the Knights of Labor mounted a systematic effort in the summer of 1885. They and the *Ogden Herald* advocated a boycott of Chinese vegetable vendors with the call, "Let all unite in a vigorous effort to withdraw support from the creatures who destroy the dignity of labor and who bring upon honest toilers the curse of want and degradation." Not all whites responded favorably. As the scope of the boycott expanded, attorney P. J. Barrett dismissed it, noting that the Chinese did work no one else was willing to do. A letter to the *Herald* cryptically signed by "Vindex" also condemned the Knights' tactics. Tensions escalated, and at least one labor faction openly spoke of resorting to "explosives and the rope" to remove the Chinese. In an effort to bolster support for the boycott the Knights published a litany of familiar charges against the Chinese and called on Ogdenites to "expel the vile leper . . . preying upon our country." In an outdoor mass meeting, newly appointed Judge A. Heed told those assembled, "There is nothing that can be said in favor of the Chinese. We must get rid of them." Gen. Nathan Kimball also addressed the boisterous crowd but said the Chinese must be protected, adding, "they have as much right here as Irishmen." He urged the Knights to "stick to their avocations and work for themselves and not against another class." Kimball stood his ground in the face of the hostile assembly until finished. Judge Heed returned to give what one observer called "a forcible and somewhat profane speech depreciating in strong terms the classing of Irishmen with Chinamen." Afterwards the "noisy and incongruous multitude" dispersed. The Chinese remained unconcerned about all the activity. Ty Kee of Ogden reported that during the boycott the Chinese sold more vegetables than ever, and laundries maintained the same amount of business. The Chinese met among themselves, Ty said, and decided to stay in Ogden rather than be run off.[37]

The boycott continued into fall. In October the Troy Laundry in Ogden guaranteed that Chinese laundries would be out of business within sixty days if no one patronized the Chinese wash houses and instead took their laundry to the larger, white-owned establishment. The Knights meanwhile sought to intensify the boycott by publishing the names of firms and individuals continuing to do business and sympathizing with the Chinese. The union recommended that these businesses be boycotted too. The plan backfired when several of the thirty-two names appearing on the list, including the Troy Laundry, turned out to be solidly anti-Chinese. Many in Ogden strongly denounced the Knights' ineptness, and the labor organization seemed unable to decide if it should call off the whole boycott and lose face or go through their list and decide whom to exempt. Complicating the issue was a report in the *Salt Lake Tribune* claiming that the Mormon church was behind the boycott since most of the businesses on the list belonged to gentiles. The *Ogden Herald* quickly denounced the *Tribune* report, calling it "consummate bosh." The Knights issued a statement saying that many of the names on the infamous list appeared there by mistake and withdrew many of them. They added that the Mormons were not behind the boycott. Some Ogdenites, still indignant at the action of the Knights, publicly denounced the boycott while urging that more constructive approaches be considered. By the end of October the *Ogden Herald* declared the boycott to have been "a total failure in every respect" and reported the Knights to be bitterly divided among themselves.[38]

Events in Ogden caught the attention of the rest of the territory. The *Park Mining Record* tried unsuccessfully to garner similar support against Park City's Chinese. The *Deseret Evening News* credited the Knights for not resorting to violence but said the boycott would not be effective. The *Salt Lake Herald*, however, thought the boycott "proper" to the point of reprinting the infamous list and predicting success for the Knights. The abortive Ogden boycott did not end organized labor's antipathy toward the Chinese. In 1893 the Federated Trades and Labor Council of Utah passed a resolution supporting the rigorous enforcement of the Geary law which continued the 1882 Exclusion Act.[39]

Even in the face of violence and recrimination, the Chinese did not respond in kind. Though there are occasional reports of Chinese taking on or even shooting at assailants, overall they realized the futility of retaliating in a concerted effort as they were too weak to possibly succeed.[40] Economically dependent upon white employers and customers, they did not want to do anything that might endanger their economic status, lead to deportation, or escalate into further violence. In essence, they resorted to the traditional wisdom of their culture which counseled, "recompence injury with kindness" and "lack of forbearance in small matters upsets great plans."[41]

Given their experience in competing directly with Euro-American labor at the primary and secondary levels of economic activity, the Chinese defined for themselves new economic niches at the tertiary level with minimal direct competition. Chinatowns saw laundries become the most common business enterprise. By 1886 there were at least fifteen Chinese laundries in Salt Lake City alone. Even as late as 1911 Chinese laundries existed in the smaller communities of Mercur, Eureka, and Milford. Such work was labor intensive, but it represented an attractive business opportunity for the Chinese. Most operations were modest, employing no more than a handful of Chinese, often in small, two-room buildings, although in Salt Lake City some Chinese converted a large home on West Temple into a wash house. The laundry industry was also open to the Chinese due in no small part to the relative lack of non-Mormon women. Gentiles patronized the laundry services offered by the Chinese as most preferred not to conduct business with the Mormons. As a result, Mormon women who took in laundry lost business, leaving one Saint to complain, "Gentiles prefer taking their soiled linen to confucian [*sic*] Mongolians" rather than to "Christian Caucasians." At least one Mormon elder patronized a Chinese establishment and complained that his endowment garment was returned with the openings sewed up![42]

Even though laundries were the most frequent enterprise in Utah Chinatowns, the dominant business was the Chinese merchant house or store, which exerted considerable influence among the Chinese. In 1880 Salt Lake had just three such stores. By the turn of the century that number had increased only to seven. But by locating within Chinatown, these merchants effectively controlled the market to the Chinese. Some of the larger stores also attracted white customers since they sold American goods as well as novelty items from China and Japan. Beyond their economic status Chinese merchants exercised considerable influence and control over the residents of Chinatown.

Merchants often assumed positions of leadership within the local Chinese community. In 1874 Sam Lee was regarded as the chief spokesperson for the Salt Lake Chinese. It was unclear to white observers if he was a political boss or a clan leader. As the local society grew and developed, Chin Quan Chan, or Chin Chin as he was commonly called by whites, became recognized as the "mayor" of Salt Lake City's Chinatown, and Dave Hing was noted as "deputy mayor." Little is known of Hing, but he is described as being well educated and able to speak English fluently. Chin moved to Salt Lake from Ogden and as "mayor" assumed positions of community leadership and social responsibility. He owned much of the Chinese-occupied property in Salt Lake City and had extensive business interests among the Chinese, including a labor brokerage. In 1912 he announced plans to return to Hong Kong permanently but estimated it would take him a year to close out his business affairs in Utah. He often adjudicated disputes among the Chinese. Whites, too, held him in special esteem, and his opinions on a variety of topics appeared in the local papers. He also acted as an intermediary between his people and local authorities. In 1912 he complained that police harassed Chinese for playing games that did not involve gambling but were simply unfamiliar to whites. He said officers broke down the doors to his home and entered with revolvers drawn to arrest fifteen Chinese playing there. Chin reported that not only were the charges false, but such action was bad for business and projected a negative image of the Chinese. Evidently his words had some effect for the court dismissed all but two of the cases.

Chin's tenure as "mayor" was not always smooth. After visiting China and remarrying following the death of his first wife, he discovered that some of Salt Lake's Chinese sought to keep him from returning to the U.S. Then customs officials in Port Townsend, Washington, received word that Chin was smuggling prostitutes. False affidavits also said he had sold his business interests and therefore could not legally return as a merchant under federal law. Only after an extended legal struggle did Chin and his family secure entrance. Upon returning to Utah he regained his lost prestige and authority. Possibly the effort to usurp him was part of a larger struggle between rival tongs.[43]

Chinese engaged in other occupations that did not compete directly with whites. To enumerate all of these would go beyond the scope of this essay; however, a few are worthy of particular mention. Chinese cooks received praise for being both economical and skillful. Most Chinatowns had at least one Chinese restaurant that catered to both whites and Chinese, and some were quite elaborate. Charley Ong Lung's in Park City, for example, was described as "first class" and served "choice meals." Others were less polished, and, of some, whites complained that cooks spat on both food and utensils. For the Chinese, restaurants were more than a place to eat: they served as a meeting and lodging place where they could share and maintain their culture and heritage among their fellow countrymen.

In particular, restaurants that were service points for both whites and Chinese prospered. By 1902 two Ogden establishments had moved into newly refurbished buildings. The city's four restaurants were so successful that some whites speculated that a Chinese restaurant syndicate existed to drive white-owned establishments out of business. Although the charge was unsubstantiated, members of the local labor federation talked of boycotting the restaurants. Two years later the city passed an ordinance banning booths, a common seating arrangement in Chinese restaurants. A municipal court convicted Tom Sing and "Jim" under the new law. They appealed and the ordinance was overturned after a district court ruled the law "arbitrary" and acquitted the pair.

Groups of Chinese made a livelihood as greengrocers. A number tilled a garden in Salt Lake's Eighth Ward. Their spread included ditches that led to collection pools, fruit trees, and means for spreading manure. The farmers watched their crops with hand-held sprinklers filled at the collection pools. The Chinese replanted their land two to three times per season and consequently had larger annual yields per acre than their white counterparts. These farmers also lived on their land in small shanties shared with pigs and chickens. As early as April, gardeners began peddling their produce in the city's streets to white customers. Some

carried their goods in baskets suspended from a yoke, while those with more prosperous operations used horse-drawn wagons. Some whites objected to the stench
of the manure the Chinese used on the soil. In Ogden the odor became so offensive to some citizens that the city banned the use of the fertilizer.[44]

Chinese filled other occupational positions. Some worked in white households
as domestic servants where they received particular praise for being neat and
clean. They also earned high praise as babysitters. Others operated or worked on
ranches.[45] Chinese herbalists or physicians lived in a number of Chinatowns and
saw patients of all races suffering from illness or injury. A Chinese living in Terrace, Box Elder County, for example, used dried rattlesnake verom as a poultice
to draw a steel fragment out of a white man's hand. Sometimes treating whites
caused problems as in the case of Soo Lung Kee who was arrested for prescribing
opium. It is unclear how many Chinese health practitioners there were, but a report in the *Ogden Standard* indicated that there was a Chinese hospital in that
city. Chinese physicians apparently had some standing in their communities, too,
as a "Dr. Sam" was regarded as a leader among the Chinese in Mercur.[46] Other
Chinese occupations operated outside the law. In the mid 1870s a number of Chinese engaged in making cigars. The practice was not illegal per se; however, they
failed to pay a special tax on the manufacture and sale of tobacco products. The
courts considered such infractions seriously. Moushu, Ah Tong, and Wah Hing
each received one-year prison sentences for making cigars.[47]

Overall, the Chinese moved successfully to tertiary level economic activity. The
Chinese and Euro-Americans interacted primarily at the economic level, and only
moderate social interaction occurred. Occasionally, whites commented on Chinese social activities, celebrations, and other festivals or funerals. A few visited open
houses hosted by Chinese to celebrate the New York, for example.[48] Other forms of
social interaction, such as gambling and opium smoking, violated the social con-
ventions of the dominant society but included members of both races. Beyond such
activities, little social interaction occurred, with one notable exception.

Some Protestant churches in Utah initiated contact with Chinese as a means
of converting them. The standard approach was to offer English classes and once
the Chinese grasped the language teach them the gospel. The Congregational
church in Salt Lake City began classes in September 1881 with just five students
under the direction of Lena Wakefield of Reading, Massachusetts, who was affil-
iated with the American Home Missionary Society (AHMS). Before taking on the
Chinese mission she taught at the Salt Lake Academy. The mission grew rapidly
under Annie F. Chapman who started as a tutor and became director in 1883 after Wakefield left on account of her health. One of Chapman's first actions was
to start an evening school where English was taught. By 1895 over one hundred
were enrolled in the classes and sixty-two were in the Sunday School program.
The school's Chinese hosted a number of interracial banquets and concerts that
were quite popular. Several Chinese Christians became active in the missionary
work. Jung O. Loy, a Chinese convert from Sacramento, proved a particularly

adept student and often volunteered to serve as a translator and teacher. He was a close friend of Wakefield, and she continued to pay him his full salary of twenty dollars a month until the AHMS assumed half of the obligation. Even then she continued to support him with ten dollars a month out of her own pocket. Jung served for many years as an assistant in the evening school. Other Chinese became active in the mission. The AHMS commissioned Wong Gee Lee, a local convert to assist in reaching his countrymen. Another Chinese wrote to the society that he conducted Bible studies and taught evening language classes and that demand was increasing. Evening classes usually opened with hymns, prayer, and scripture reading. Students then paired off with a tutor to study their lessons. The Chinese used *Lippincott's First Reader* or *Loomis's English and Chinese Lessons*, which had biblical selections in it, as well as the Bible for text. Closing exercises consisted of singing and recitation of the Lord's Prayer. Attendance in 1886 ranged from seventeen to thirty students. The Methodists held their own services for the Chinese and found music to be particularly effective in increasing attendance. An observer noted that as soon as the organ began the Chinese started singing enthusiastically.

Some Mormons and gentiles complained the schools were a poor vehicle for converting Chinese. The *Deseret Evening News* said it was nearly impossible to obtain a genuine conversion from a Chinese person. The *Ogden Standard* maintained that Chinese converts were "neither Christians nor heathens" and that missionary efforts would be better spent on the needy in large cities.[49]

The Protestants countered with arguments of their own. Chapman reported the school to be an effective means of reaching the Chinese whom she described as attentive students coming from as far away as Rock Springs, Wyoming, to study. a Chinese leader in the mission reported that several men had expressed interest in uniting with the local Congregational church but their application for membership was put on hold because he and other church leaders did not want them to rush into a decision "until they understand just what they were doing, and have knowledge of the way to remain faithful."[50] Some Chinese did join; in 1884 nine Chinese united with the local church. The Salt Lake Methodists reported that Chinese Christians remained true to their new faith and sought to evangelize other Chinese. The Ogden Baptist church, which also operated a Chinese Sunday School, had thirty-five in attendance in 1892 and reported two converts. Such programs assisted the Chinese in other ways, too, as kidnapped Chinese women or prostitutes who escaped sometimes found refuge in church missions. In a 1900 case a woman left "her supposed husband" and ultimately went to a Christian mission home in California. The *Deseret Evening News*, while dubious of the couple's marriage, nevertheless complained of Protestant work that "enters families and severs ties that should be sacred."[51]

The Church of Jesus Christ of Latter-day Saints, in spite of its active missionary program, had virtually nothing to do with the Chinese in Utah even though Mormon missionaries worked among the Chinese in California and Hong Kong.

The *Deseret Evening News* dismissed gentile efforts by intimating that the Chinese were not sincere in their conversion testimonies. A California Mormon, Locke Melone, reported a conversation with Brigham Young in which the prophet stated that if one Chinese Mormon could be obtained others would follow. That did not occur. Ah Sin, the second wife of a Salt Lake merchant, and some of her children became Mormons, but there was no conversion movement even though Plum Alley was less than two blocks from Temple Square. Overall, the Chinese seemed uninterested in Mormonism. Chen Lanbin, the Chinese government's first minister to the U.S., traveled through Utah on his way to Washington, D.C. He commented on the practice of polygamy, noting, "this religion permits the taking of concubines," but saw little else worth mentioning regarding Mormonism.[52] Beyond such impressionistic encounters little contact of a religious nature occurred between the Chinese and the Saints.

Traditional Chinese belief practices centered around the Joss House as a locus of worship. One such tabernacle is said to have accompanied the Chinese working on the Central Pacific. Another reportedly existed in Corinne. In Salt Lake there was one above Ah Woo's store on the corner of Commercial and Plum Alley which opened in 1895. It contained a likeness of Quon Kong, a god of war. The Chinese made food offerings, particularly during holidays such as the New Year. The offering table before the god's image was illuminated with candles and scented with incense. The walls along the table contained characters in gilded frames describing the god's virtues.[53]

Despite varied economic and social roles, Utah's Chinatowns were short lived. A combination of factors led to their extinction. Fires wreaked particular havoc. Several fires in Salt Lake destroyed some Chinese homes and businesses but never threatened the enclave as a whole. More severe conflagrations occurred elsewhere. At Corinne in September 1871 a fire destroyed most of Chinatown and killed a Chinese woman. Authorities charged two Chinese men with arson. The Chinese residents remained, but the city forced them to rebuild in a less desirable part of town near the Bear River.[54] In May 1879 a fire destroyed part of Silver Reef, leaving Chinatown untouched—but only temporarily. Six weeks later much of Chinatown went up in flames. The second blaze began in a Chinese-occupied building and quickly spread. Firefighters tore down a number of small Chinese buildings to create a fire break to save "the property of white citizens." The Chinese, nevertheless, set out to rebuild. In 1898 a fire destroyed much of Park City, including its Chinatown. Although the Chinese rebuilt some of the structures, including the famous bridge, the losses destroyed much of the city's Chinatown.[55] The other enclaves survived their fires and continued. However, the cost of rebuilding doubtless put a drag on further economic growth.

Other factors contributed even more to the demise of the Chinatowns. Anti-Chinese laws and ordinances at the national and local levels sought either to discourage the prosperity of the Chinese or to simply harass them. Beginning in

1882 a series of federal exclusion laws severely curtailed the number of Chinese allowed to enter the country. Support for the legislation was not universal. The *Salt Lake Herald* called the bill "wicked" and "un-American." Nevertheless, ten years later the Geary Act continued the exclusion period for another ten years and sought to register all Chinese in the country with a photo-identification system. The *Deseret Evening News* saw this bill as a better alternative to expulsion and hypothesized that it would have the same effect since "the race would in course of time dwindle away." All across the country the Chinese refused to register. The *Deseret Evening News* even feared the Chinese would resort to reprisals. None occurred and after the U.S. Supreme Court ruled the law constitutional most of Utah's Chinese complied with the law.[56]

Local laws also sought to restrict the Chinese. In 1874 Salt Lake City declared Chinese laundries to be public nuisances and fined several Chinese for operating them. Later that year the council passed a statute aimed at the Chinese to keep them from butchering pigs within the city limits. Another ordinance forbade the Chinese to let off fireworks to celebrate their New Year. They also had to pay the poll tax even though they were not citizens.[57]

Both Ogden and Salt Lake City considered zoning to restrict the Chinese. The Ogden City Council received a petition to forbid the establishment of any Chinese laundries along major thoroughfares but did not enact such a law. In 1874 the Salt Lake City Council received a petition to create a Chinese ghetto by requiring Chinese wash houses to relocate in a particular zone. The council passed the matter on to the city marshal who presumably found it unenforceable since he did not follow through on it. Eight years later support again grew to have the city declare the Chinese to be a "common nuisance" and restricted to a certain area. In 1883 Jim Lung asked the city to designate an area where wash houses could locate and drain off their wash water. The council debated an ordinance to place all Chinese wash houses outside the city limits. Other Salt Lake Chinese soon made it quite clear that Jim Lung did not speak for them and protested any effort to move them out of the city, fearing it would drive them out of business. Jack Fong told authorities that an unidentified white man had paid him to submit the petition and that some Chinese were so incensed they wanted to kill him. Given that information the city dropped the idea.[58]

The federal laws proved particularly effective in contributing to the demise of Utah's Chinatowns by placing restrictions on continued Chinese immigration. Local statutes, on the other hand, did little to directly impede the movements of Chinese. Equally, important though, they did nothing to encourage growth of the Chinese enclaves. Rather, they articulated an anti-Chinese attitude that continued to remind the Chinese they were not welcome. A 1901 article in the *Deseret Evening News* maintained that the Chinese contributed very little to the American economy either as producers or consumers. A second article, a year later, urged continued exclusion of the Chinese as there was "no reason why the United States should be opened to them."[59]

The population of the Chinese enclaves diminished for several reasons: The Chinese came as sojourners—as did many immigrants from southern France, seeking financial opportunities in the United States and returning home to live out their years in an improved economic and social position. As many of the Chinese who came in the late nineteenth century advanced in years they did return to China. This voluntary out-migration depleted the population of Utah's Chinatowns. Occasionally, forced migration occurred. According to one source, a vigilante committee in 1886 forced the Chinese in Corinne aboard a Central Pacific train and warned them that if they returned they would be killed. Bingham, with a population of largely Slavic miners, reportedly ran its Chinese out in 1880 due to a rumored case of leprosy in that city's Chinatown. At other times migration was voluntary. As early as the 1870s Chinese began leaving Utah for the gold fields of Montana and Idaho.

The Chinese continued to come and go as opportunities became available. By the turn of the century, the remaining Chinese consisted mostly of older men. Surprisingly, the Sino-Japanese War of 1894–96 did little to draw Chinese home to support their country's occupation of Korea. A white observer noted that Salt Lake Chinese showed little interest in the course of the war and no interest in fighting the Japanese. In 1906 the Jing Dynasty, in an apparent attempt to regain the popular support of the people, assumed the responsibility of transporting all Chinese laborers back to China without charge provided they had some form of disability or were elderly. Many Chinese left, but some like Ding Ling Ho of Park City remained in Utah to live out their lives. Ding died in 1926 at the age of seventy-two.[60]

Chinese communities were also vulnerable to the changing socioeconomic patterns of the host society. Although Salt Lake City and Ogden grew and continue to prosper, Park City and Silver Reef failed when their boom economics foundered during periods of economic retrenchment. Corinne lost its viability after the railroad bypassed the town. Chinese in all of these locations experienced occupational succession. For example, the demand for traditional Chinese enterprises like laundries gradually diminished with the arrival of more white women and the establishment of family life in mining towns. By creating and developing their own niches and continuing to interact with the host society largely at the economic level only, the Chinese soon found themselves identified with certain roles and unable to find different occupational opportunities. Other ethnic groups also displaced the Chinese. In particular, Japanese immigrants assumed many of the positions formerly held by the Chinese railroad workers who quit following the Rock Springs massacre. Later, Japanese laborers worked for mining firms and became farm laborers, further displacing the Chinese.[61]

Encroachment also affected the Chinatowns as the host society gradually moved within the boundaries of the Chinese enclaves. As early as 1883 Salt Lake City began tearing down Chinese-occupied buildings. By the late 1880s a number of Chinese structures in both Salt Lake City and Ogden had been demolished to make way for new buildings. So extensive was this destruction that some Salt Lake residents declared, "China-town is doomed." Its reported death was premature. The Chinese enclaves continued into the twentieth century; however, by 1914 the population had begun to decline dramatically. The Great Depression forced most of the remaining Chinese stores to close, and many Utah Chinese moved to California in search of better economic opportunities. In 1940 Chinese vacated the last large tenement in Plum Alley as crews prepared to demolish it. Many of the displaced Chinese left Utah. The last remnants of Plum Alley came down in 1952 when workers razed the area to make way for a parking lot. A social vestige of the period remains in the form of the Bing Kong Tong. This benevolent association continues as a social organization for Chinese people, but it is no longer located at the site of the city's historic Chinatown.[62]

Unlike some ethnic enclaves that have tended to decay over several generations, Utah's Chinatowns became virtually extinct within one generation. Although the Chinese suffered many deprivations and much discrimination as a result of their clustering in Chinatowns, they lived in these enclaves because of the value they placed on economic opportunities, familial relations, and culture. The Chinatowns lost population to attrition rather than assimilation, for these enclaves did not serve as transition points for Chinese seeking to acculturate themselves into the host society. Nor did whites seek to secure the social participation of the Chinese. Indeed, some even sought to remove the Chinese from participating economically in the community. Despite their early demise, it is important to remember that Chinatowns nevertheless contributed a unique element to Utah's colorful past.

NOTES

1. Exceptions include "The Early Chinese of Western United States" in Kate B. Carter, ed., *Our Pioneer Heritage*, 20 vols. (Salt Lake City: Daughters of the Utah Pioneers, 1857–77), 10:129–81; Don C. Conley, "The Pioneer Chinese in Utah" in *The Peoples of Utah*, ed Helen Z. Papanikolas (Salt Lake City: Utah State Historical Society, 1976), pp. 251–77; Don C. Conley, "The Pioneer Chinese in Utah" (M.A. thesis, Brigham Young University, 1976)—all subsequent references to Conley's work are to this thesis; Lester A. Hubbard, "John Chinaman in the West," *Western Humanities Review* 4 (1950): 311–21; Dean L. May, *Utah: A People's History* (Salt Lake City: University of Utah Press, 1987), pp. 141–55; Leslie G. Kelen and Sandra T. Fuller, eds., *The Other Utahns: A Photographic Portfolio* (Salt Lake City: University of Utah Press, 1988), pp. 48–61.

2. *Salt Lake Tribune*, May 11, 1882; *Ogden Standard*, January 19, 1902, September 1, 1891.

3. William Mulder, "Scandinavian Sage" in *The Peoples of Utah*, p. 172.

4. U.S. Bureau of the Census, *1990 Census of Population and Housing*, Summary Tape File 2A, Utah.

5. John Simpson Ross, *Crossing the Continent by Rail in 1869* (Fort Bragg, Calif.: Mendocino County Historical Society, 1969), p. 17; Adolph Reeder, "This Is Promontory as I Remember It," MS at Golden Spike National Historic Site, Promontory, Utah, n.p.; Bernice Gibbs Anderson, Oral History Project at University of Utah, interviewed by Phil Notarianni and Greg Thompson, August 15, 1975, at Corinne, Utah, transcript in Special

Collections, Marriott Library, University of Utah; Mr. and Mrs. William W. Bowe, Ethnic Oral History Collections, interviewed by Ellis LeFevere, August 19, 1974, transcript at Golden Spike National Historic Site; *Cincinnati Excursion to California* (Indianapolis: Cincinnati and Lafayette Railroad, 1870), p. 39; *Ogden Daily Herald,* June 4, 1881; *Utah Tri-Weekly Reporters,* January 4, 1870; "Across the Continent, 1877–78," *Bulletin of the British Association for American Studies* new series 9 (1964):60–61; *Utah Reporter,* December 16, 1869, May 28, 1870; *Deseret Evening News,* May 30, 1870, July 7, 1870.

6. *Daily Utah Reporter,* April 9, August 1, 1870; *Salt Lake Herald,* September 11, 1870; *Deseret Evening News,* July 9, May 20, 1869; Journal History of the Church, LDS Church Archives, Salt Lake City, May 26, 1869, pp. 5–6; *Ogden Junction,* August 6, 1870, May 24, 1873, December 19, 1874.

7. "Utah's Chinese Heritage," typescript, Golden Spike National Historic Site; *Deseret Evening News,* January 29, 1873; *Silver Reef Miner,* May 24, 1879; Golden Spike Oral History Project, Bernice Gibbs Anderson manuscript material, MS-85, p. 70.

8. *Salt Lake Tribune,* May 4, 1871, January 29, 1874, June 2, 1878; *Corinne Daily Mail,* September 25, 1875; *Salt Lake Herald,* September 11, 1870; *Utah Reporter,* November 14, 1870; *Ogden Junction,* January 29, 1879.

9. "Ching Chao Wu, "Chinatowns: A Study of Symbiosis and Assimilation" (Ph.D. diss., University of Chicago, 1928), pp. 157–58; D. Y. Yuan, "Voluntary Segregation: A Study of New Chinatowns," *Phylon* 24 (1963):255–65; Melford S. Weiss, *Valley City: A Chinese Community in America* (Cambridge, Mass.: Schenkman Publishing Company, 1974), pp. 33–34; *Salt Lake Tribune,* January 22, 1898.

10. Angela Chan Conley, "The Social Problems of the Chinese in Salt Lake City" (M.S. thesis, University of Utah, 1973), pp. 5–6, 25–27.

11. *Corinne Daily Miner,* January 7, 1875; *Our Pioneer Heritage,* 10:454; Milton Knovitz, *The Alien and the Asiatic in American Law* (Ithaca: Cornell University Press, 1946), p. 232; Frances Cunningham to author, undated; *Deseret Evening News,* October 8, 1873.

12. *Salt Lake Tribune,* December 21, 1883; *Ogden Standard,* December 22, 1904.

13. *Deseret Evening News,* December 8, 1879; Payul C. P. Sin, "The Sojourner," *American Journal of Sociology* 8 (1952):34–44; Franklin Ng, "The Sojourner, Return Migration, and Immigration History," *Chinese America: History and Perspectives* (1987):53–71; Annie E. Chapman, "Work among the Chinese," *The Home Missionary* 80 (1886):284.

14. Conley, "Pioneer Chinese," p. 68; Conrad Eliott, "Chinatown," *The Lodestar* (1978); 9; "List of Laundries for 1911," Immigration and Statistics Letter Books, Utah State Archives, Salt Lake City; pp. 59–60; *Sanborn Fire Map for Ogden* (New York: Sanborn, 1884); Alfred Bleack Stucki, "A Historical Record of Silver Reef: Southern Utah Mining Town" (M.A. thesis, Brigham Young University, 1966), p. 44; *Sanborn Fire Map for Park City* (New York: Sanborn, 1889); Raye Carlson Price, *Diggings and Doings in Park City,* 2d ed. (Salt Lake City: University of Utah Press, 1972); *Daily Corinne Reporter,* September 25, 26, October 19, 1871.

15. *Sanborn Fire Map for Salt Lake City* (New York; Sanborn Map and Publishing, 1882); *Polk's Salt Lake City Directory,* 1896; Richard C. Roberts and Richard W. Sadler, *Ogden: Junction City* (Northridge, Calif.: Windsor Publications, 1985), pp. 94–95; Chuen-yan David Lai, *Chinatowns: Towns within Cities in Canada* (Vancouver: University of British Columbia Press, 1988), pp. 5–7.

16. *Utah Record,* September 7, 1870.

17. *Salt Lake Tribune,* March 9, 1884; *Deseret Evening News,* February 8, 1902.

18. Philip F. Notarianni, "Italianta in Utah" in *The Peoples of Utah*, pp. 307–8.

19. *Salt Lake Herald*, August 21, 1874, September 29, 1888, June 23, 1886, June 19, 1891, April 14, 1891.

20. John Eldredge to "Denny," March 18, 1985, Golden Spike National Historical Site; Record of Arrests No. 2, 1896-97, Utah State Archives; *Silver Reef Miner*, January 17, 1880; *Salt Lake Herald*, September 2, 4, 1873, December 14, 1875, May 23, 1882, October 21, 1885; *Ogden Morning Herald*, August 7, 9, 25, 1887; *Park Mining Record*, April 6, 1895; *Deseret Evening News*, October 20, 1885.

21. Chinese were not the only ones arrested for keeping opium dens. In 1892 U.S. Marshal Elias H. Parsons was tried for renting a den on Plum Alley to some Chinese. *Salt Lake Tribune*, December 4, 1880, April 4, 1886, January 10, 1886; *Salt Lake Herald*, October 15, 1875, October 16, 1878, November 20, 1879, June 14, 1883, September 16, 1881, November 10, 1883, July 17, 1885, June 13, 1880, March 9, April 28, 1892; *Deseret Evening News*, April 23, September 18, November 20, 21, 22, 1879; *Park Mining Record*, April 4, 1885; *Ogden Herald*, October 27, 1887.

22. *Utah Reporter*, November 14, 1870; *Deseret Evening News*, January 29, 1873, May 28, 1872; *Corinne Daily Journal*, May 9, 10, 1871; November 14, 1870; *Silver Reef Miner*, June 14, 1874; *Cottonwood Observer*, July 19, 1873; *Deseret Evening News*, March 19, 1879.

23. *Deseret Evening News*, June 20, 1890; *Salt Lake Herald*, July 17–20, 1895.

24. *Deseret Evening News*, September 13, 1873; Florence C. Lister and Robert H. Lister, "Chinese Sojourners in Territorial Prescott," *Journal of the Southwest* 31 (1989): 25; *Salt Lake Telegram*, February 8, 1884; *Deseret Evening News*, January 5, 1872.

25. Stanford Lyman, *Chinatown and Little Tokyo: Power, Conflict, and Community among Chinese and Japanese Immigrants in America* (Millwood, N.Y.: Associated Faculty Press, 1986), pp. 69–219.

26. *Salt Lake Herald*, March 19, 1897.

27. *Deseret Evening News*, May 21, 1875; *Ogden Standard*, March 28, 1900, January 7, 1888; *Salt Lake Herald*, May 15, 1889; *Corinne Daily Mail*, January 5, 1875; *Park Mining Record*, June 10, 1882.

28. *Salt Lake Herald*, December 1, 2, 1890, April 18, 1884; *Corinne Daily Miner*, January 5, 1875; *Ogden Junction*, May 6, 1874; *Salt Lake Tribune*, May 6, 9, 1899.

29. *Deseret Evening News*, October 11, 1887; *Salt Lake Herald*, May 5, 1888.

30. *Salt Lake Herald*, April 20, 1883, October 6, 1885; *Silver Reef Miner*, June 10, 1882.

31. *Ogden Daily Herald*, July 30, 1881; *Ogden Junction*, December 15, 1875; *Corinne Daily Miner*, September 6, 1875; *Deseret Evening News*, September 13, 1873.

32. *Corinne Daily Mail*, July 12, 1875; *Park Mining Record*, September 18, 1886, October 27, 1883, September 13, 1884; *Deseret Evening News*, September 13, 1873; *Salt Lake Herald*, June 7, 1871, March 11, 1885, April 20, 1883; October 6, 1885; *Salt Lake Tribune*, December 12, 1883; James Bonwick, *Mormons and the Silver Mines* (London: Hodder Stoughton, 1872), pp. 370–85; Conley, "Pioneer Chinese," 84, 144; Konvitz, *The Alien and Asiatic in American Law*, p. 199; Pauli Murray, *States' Laws on Race and Color* (Nashville: Woman's Division of Christian Service, Board of Missions and Church Extension, Methodist Church, 1859), p. 458; Joseph Stipanovich, "South Slav Settlements in Utah, 1890–1935," *Utah Historical Quarterly* 43 (1975):463.

33. *Park Mining Record*, March 11, 1882; *Ogden Daily Herald*, November 22, 1884; *Corinne Daily Mail*, September 12, 1874; *Silver Reef Miner*, June 14, 1879; *Salt Lake Herald*, April 11, 1882.

34. Govenor of Utah, "Report to the Secretary of the Interior," 50th Cong., 1st sess. (1877–88), *House Ex. Doc.*, vol. 10, no. 1, pt. 5, serial #2541, October 10, 1887.

35. *Salt Lake Herald*, May 24, 1873, January 22, 1891, May 4, 1890, July 7, 1873, April 15, 1874, August 20, 1885, May 9, 1883, August 20, 1885.

36. *Utah Mining Gazette*, April 18, 1874; *Ogden Herald*, October 30, 1887, November 22, 1887, April 26, 1882; *Vernal Express*, April 28, 1898; Carter, *Our Pioneer Heritage*, 10:431.

37. *Ogden Herald,* August 11, 13, 14, 15, 17, 19, 23, 1885.

38. *Ogden Herald*, October 15, 19, 21, 1885.

39. *Park Mining Record*, August 15, 1885; *Deseret Evening News*, October 20, 1885, June 10, 1893; *Salt Lake Herald*, October 20, 1885.

40. *Salt Lake Herald*, February 4, 1895, May 9, 1893, May 24, 1873, October 2, 1888; *Park Mining Record*, August 7, 1880.

41. Chia-Lin, "Gold Dreams in Blue Mountains" (M.A. thesis, Portland State University, 1967), pp. 112–13; Conley, "Pioneer Chinese," p. 64.

42. Kate Carter, ed., *Heart Throbs of the West*, 12 vols. (Salt Lake City: Daughters of the Utah Pioneers, 1939–51), 5:368–70; Carter, *Our Pioneer Heritage*, 10:446–17; "List of Laundries for 1911"; *Salt Lake Herald*, July 2, 1873, December 4, 1880; *Salt Lake Tribune*, December 3, 1880, April 19, 1891, December 18, 1881, October 15, 1883; *Deseret Evening News*, July 19, 1873, August 21, 1874, August 14, 1874, June 21, 1882; *Utah Reporter*, August 11, 12, 1870; *St. George Union*, February 1881; *Ogden Herald*, June 18, 1881; *Ogden Standard*, October 18, 1889.

43. *Polks's Salt Lake City Directory*, 1900, 804; Conley, "Pioner Chinese," pp. 42, 66; *Silver Reef Miner*, May 6, 1882; Conley, "Pioneer Chinese," p.62; *Salt Lake Tribune*, June 26, 1898; *Port Townsend Weekly Leader* (Washington), October 14, 1903; *Deseret Evening News*, July 13, 1907, June 25, 1912, January 3, 1903, February 8, 1902.

44. *Salt Lake Herald*, April 28, 1878, June 18, 1893; *Salt Lake Tribune*, May 18, 1882, April 2, 1881, November 14, 1954; *Ogden Standard*, April 14, 1892.

45. *Millard County Blade*, April 25, 1896; "About the Chinese," *Juvenile Instructor* 17 (1882):209; *Park Mining Record*, June 5, August 7, 1880, September 12, 1893; Li Li, "Toward a Cultural Interpretation of the Chinese Restaurant in the Mountain West" (M.A. thesis, Utah State University, 1990); Conley, "Pioneer Chinese," pp. 41–42, 59, 97, 99; *Salt Lake Tribune*, January 22, June 12, 1891, March 11, 1880, April 2, 1899; *Deseret Evening News*, July 12, 1872, *Ogden Daily Herald*, May 14, 1885; *Ogden Standard*, April 4, 1902, March 4, 1904; *Brigham Bugler*, May 30, 1891; *Silver Reef Miner*, May 17, 1879.

46. *Salt Lake Herald*, July 22, 1885; K. E. Covington, "Two Years on the Desert," *True West* 14 (January–February 1967); 68; *Ogden Standard*, July 28, 1897; Lillian Wood, "Lucy Lee: A Family History," graduate seminar paper, University of Utah, 1977, copy at Utah State Historical Society; *Ogden Daily Herald*, May 14, 1885.

47. *Deseret Evening News*, April 13, 1877.

48. *Ogden Standard*, January 13, 1888; *Ogden Daily Herald*, August 17, 1886, September 1, 1884; *Salt Lake Tribune*, September 27, 1889; January 21, 1880, January 22, 1898; *Salt Lake Herald*, February 8, 1872; *Deseret Evening News*, October 22, 1875, February 8, 1902; *Corinne Daily Mail*, April 5, 1875.

49. *Deseret Evening News*, April 14, 1882; *Ogden Standard*, February 15, 1896.

50. "Chinese Missionary, Utah," *The Home Missionary* 58 (June 1885):51.

51. "Congregational Chinese Sunday School and Evening School," *The Church Review* 4 (December 29, 1895):5; Mrs. Marcus Jones, "The Congregational Chinese Mis-

sion, Salt Lake City, Utah," *American Missionary* 51 (1857):238–39; Chapman, "Work among the Chinese," pp. 281–85; *Salt Lake Herald*, February 19, 1888; *Salt Lake Tribune*, February 6, 1886, February 12, 1892, March 26, June 12, August 8, December 27, 1883; "Utah Letter," *Pacific Baptist*, October 1892, p. 12; Annie E. Chapman, "O Loy and Gee, *The Home Missionary* 65 (1887):227; Ambrose B. Carlton, *The Wonderlands of the Wild West* (n.p.: Author, 1891), pp. 95–97; *Deseret Evening News*, April 24, 1900.

52. *Deseret Evening News*, May 20, July 16, 1869, March 16, 1879, October 15, 1892; Journal History, September 25, 1894, June 3, 1854, January 12, March 14, 1855, March 26, 1910; Hosea M. Stout, *On the Mormon Frontier: The Diary of Hosea M. Stout* (Salt Lake City: University of Utah Press and Utah State Historical Society, 1964), pp. 156–57, 164–65; *Salt Lake Tribune*, July 11, 1876; Xi Feng, "The Chinese through the Utah Press," seminar paper in author's possession, April 1990, pp. 13–14, 17–18; Carter, *Our Pioneer Heritage*, 10:136–40, 448; Conley, "Pioneer Chinese," pp. 75–76; Chen Lanbin, "Travel in the Interior" in *Land without Ghosts*, ed. and trans. R. David Arkush and Leo O. Lee (Berkeley: University of California Press, 1989), p. 51.

53. Dennis Bingham, "The Chinese in the Building of the Transcontinental Railroad," May 18, 1969, p. 11, MS, LDS Church Archives; *Utah Reporter*, September 27, 1870; *Deseret Evening News*, February 8, 1902, July 13, 1907, December 14, 1895; Conley, "Pioneer Chinese," p. 106.

54. *Salt Lake Herald*, February 12, 1890, June 4, 1889, September 27, 1871; *Salt Lake Tribune*, October 30, 1879, August 14, 1883; *Daily Corinne Reporter*, September 25, 1871, October 13, 19, 1871, September 27, 1875.

55. *Silver Reef Miner*, May 31, 1879, July 12, 1879; *Park Mining Record*, June 25, 1898; Katherine Reynolds, *Park City* (Los Angeles: Weller Institute, 1984); Elliot, "Chinatown," p. 9.

56. *Park Mining Record*, March 3, 1894; *Deseret Evening News*, April 22, September 12, 1892; *Salt Lake Herald*, April 19, 1882, April 11, 1893.

57. *Deseret Evening News*, August 21, 1874; *Salt Lake Herald*, November 25, August 17, 1874, January 28, 1887; *Salt Lake Tribune*, January 25, 1899.

58. *Ogden Junction*, February 1, 1879; *Salt Lake Herald*, August 21, 1874, September 8, 1882, November 11, 1883; Salt Lake City Council Minutes, August 18, 1874; *Deseret Evening News*, June 21, 1882; *Salt Lake Tribune*, September 19, October 14, 1883.

59. *Deseret Evening News*, December 31, 1901, January 17, 1902.

60. Lucius Beebe, *The Central Pacific and the Southern Pacific Railroads* (Berkeley, Calif.: Howell-North, 1963), pp. 152–53; *Salt Lake Tribune*, April 27, 1880; *Utah Reporter*, April 16, 1870; *Corinne Daily Reporter*, July 22, 1871; *Corinne Daily Journal*, July 14, 1871; *Deseret Evening News*, August 6, 1894; Chen, "Gold Dream." p. 118; Elliott, "Chinatown," p. 9.

61. Covington, "Two Years in the Desert," p. 68; Anderson interview, pp. 3–4; Journal History, July 26, 1901; R. D. McKenzie, "The Oriental Finds a Job: Changing Roles of Chinese and Japanese Workers," *The Survey* 56 (1926):151; Helen Z. Papanikolas and Alice Kasai, "Japanese Life in Utah" in *The Peoples of Utah*, pp. 336–39; *Ogden Standard*, February 28, 1902; Richard O. Ulibarri, "Utah's Ethnic Minorities: A Survey," *Utah Historical Quarterly* 40 (1973):222; Allan Kent Powell, "The 'Foreign Element' and the 1903-4 Carbon County Coal Miner's Strike," *Utah Historical Quarterly* 43 (1975):145.

62. *Salt Lake Tribune*, April 25, 1883, September 6, 1888, September 28, 1889; *Salt Lake Herald*, September 12, 1889, October 2, 1889; *Ogden Standard*, May 11, 1888; Conley, "Pioneer Chinese," *Salt Lake Telegram*, March 21, 1938, February 8, 1940; *Deseret Evening News*, March 1, 1952; Elliott "Chinatown," p. 9; Ulibarri, "Utah Ethnic Minorities," p. 227.

17

The Pioneer Chinese of Utah

Don C. Conley

The distance from the subtropical rice paddies of China's southernmost province to the mountainous desert of the Great Basin spans one-third of the earth's circumference. Along this tumultuous course of Pacific Ocean waves and Sierra Nevada mountain peaks came Chinese men to forge an integral but mostly forgotten link in Utah's frontier life.

The construction of the Central Pacific from Sacramento to Promontory brought the first Chinese into what is now the state of Utah. At one point there were more than twelve thousand Chinese employed in the building of the Central Pacific.[1] E. B. Crocker, brother of Charles Crocker, Central Pacific general superintendent, was among the first to suggest using Chinese laborers.[2] Charles Crocker tried to persuade his Irish construction superintendent, J. H. Strobridge, to employ Chinese, but he resisted until labor became scarce and then consented to experiment with fifty Chinese. These fifty did so well that no limit was placed on Chinese employment.[3]

After moving across Nevada into Utah, the Central Pacific met the Union Pacific at Promontory. Chinese participated at the joining of the rails. In preparation for driving the Golden Spike

> a slicked-up team of the Union Pacific's best Irish track-layers had already swung the west rail across the gap in the track and spiked it down, except on the missing tie. Now a gang of Chinese, in clean blue jackets, moved out to put the final, east rail in place.[4]

In all the talk that took place at Promontory on that occasion, no mention was made of the Chinese contribution; but the Chinese were not altogether forgotten. At a Sacramento celebration, Charles Crocker "in his brief, proud speech was the only one of the day that recognized the role of the Chinese." "In the midst of our rejoicing," he said, "I wish to call to mind that the early completion of this railroad we have built has been in great measure due to the poor, destitute class of laborers called the Chinese—to the fidelity and industry they have shown."[5]

On the centennial of that memorable event at Promontory, May 10, 1969, in a speech given by Secretary of the Treasury John Volpe the gargantuan task, the sweat, lifeblood, and genius of the Chinese railroad man was left unmentioned.[6]

Promontory became the gateway for most Chinese coming into Utah in frontier times. Between 1870 and 1880 the greatest population of Chinese in the state lived within the boundaries of Box Elder County, employed almost entirely as section hands on the railroad.[7]

In the late 1880s and early nineties, when W. A. "Pappy" Clay was just a boy, he was allowed entrance into a world unknown to most, excepting the Chinese who possessed it. Wallace Clay was born March 11, 1884, three hundred feet from that historic spot where "the golden spike" joined the Union Pacific and the Central Pacific. From 1884 to 1893 his father was the telegraph operator and Central Pacific agent at Blue Creek where Wallace Clay's childhood was surrounded by the objects and people of the railroad in its day of glory. The precocious observations of the child were still present in the man of ninety years when he was interviewed:

> After they used them [the Chinese] in the construction of the Central Pacific roadbed, then about every twelve or fourteen miles they had a section house along to keep the track up after it was built, and at each one of these section houses they had a section boss and he was usually a big, burly Irishman, and then he usually had about thirty Chinese coolies working under him as section hands, and that was the set up all the way from Ogden to Roseberg, California.[8]
>
> My name being Wallace Clay, was changed by those Orientals to "Wah Lee, Melicum Boy," and I more or less lived with them from 1889 to 1892, and only slept with my parents and had breakfast at home mostly at Blue Creek Water Tank Station during one-half of each twenty-four hours.[9]

Because he was inquisitive, bright, and just a child, Wallace Clay was allowed to see and experience first hand what was only conjecture and mystery to most Caucasian Americans of that era. He explained in fascinating detail the intricate and well-camouflaged construction of an opium den and of the dream world in which the opium smoker moves—a process Clay observed rather than actually experienced. He spoke of moments of sharing, of an interchange of knowledge and friendship:

> When not "raising taps and tapping ties" those good Chinamen, among whom were "my very best friends" were many who probably got homesick for their wives and children in China, so they took me as a sort of pet and they gave me much Chinese candy and firecrackers and Chinese money and they asked many questions about American life and I asked them many questions about life in China. . . .
>
> I will now describe how my "Chinese friends" lived at old Blue Creek Station in 1891. The antiquated box-car they lived in had been remodeled into a "work-car," in one end of which a series of small bunk beds had been built as a vertical column of three bunks one above the other on both sides of the car-end from floor to ceiling so

that around eighteen Chinamen could sleep in the bedroom end of the car, while
the other end of the car served as a kitchen and dining room wherein there was a cast
iron cook stove with its stove pipe going up through the roof of the car and with all
kinds of pots and pans and skillets hanging around the walls, plus cubby holes for tea
cups and big and little blue china bowls and chop sticks and wooden table and
benches—about like we now find in forest service camp grounds—occupying the
middle of the car.

After twelve-hour shifts on the railroad roadbed, these men who conquered
some of the most rugged terrain in the West let their thoughts turn toward loved
ones. Clay often saw them "writing long letters back home to China wherein they
used little paint brushes to make their Chinese hieroglyphics or picture writing.
. . ." The Chinese also indulged in the age-old remedy for aching muscles, taking
"time to prepare a nice hot evening bath" in a big wooden tub of steaming water.

Since even the sound of music in the West was alien to the Chinese, with their
own traditions of sacred, dramatic, and popular music—written in an entirely different scale from western music—the men Clay knew played two common instruments, the *lo* (large gong) and, possibly, the *nu k'in* (two-stringed fiddle.) The
familiar sounds may have eased their loneliness.

The men also took pride in preparing and sharing delicious-sounding meals.
As heirs of one of the world's great classic cuisines, these Chinese obtained the
necessary ingredients and combined and ate them with gusto. While the meal was
a single course and not so elegant as Peking duck, it was surely satisfying to hungry workers.

The cooks built their own type of outdoor ovens in the dirt banks along side of the
sidetrack, and their stake pot spits along side their bunk cars, where they did most of
their cooking when the weather permitted. Each cook would have the use of a very
big iron kettle hung over an open fire and into it they would dump a couple of measures of Chinese unhulled brown rice, Chinese noodles, bamboo sprouts and dried
seaweed, different Chinese seasonings, and American chickens cut up into small
pieces. . . . When the cook stirred up the fire and the concoction began to swell until finally the kettle would be nearly full of steaming, nearly dry brown rice with the
cut-up chicken all through it.

Each Chinaman would take his big blue bowl and ladle it full of the mixture and
deftly entwine his chopsticks between his fingers and string the mixture into his
mouth in one continuous operation, while in the meantime he would be drinking
his cup of tea and still more tea. I was the curious, watching kid so the cook would
ladle up a little blue bowlful for me (Little Wah Lee) and hand me a pair of chopsticks and with them I would try to eat like the rest of my buddies, but I never could
get the "knack" so I would end up eating with my fingers which would make the Chinese laugh and I would get no tea.[10]

Besides Wallace Clay, there were other earlier (but none so excellent) eyewitnesses of Chinese life in Box Elder County. Among the earliest recorded obser-

vations were those by a group of excursionists from Cincinnati experimenting with the new-found luxury of railroad travel. Here is their report written September 7, 1869:

"Eighth Letter" Promontory

It was there that the excursionists saw the Chinamen. Sam Hing and Ah Lee have little huts adorned with signs, vouching for "good washing and ironing done here." A gang of Chinese laborers, in loose blue muslin garments and peaked parasol hats of straw, were grading a new switch at the station. Their slow, measured way of plying their shovels explosive cackle of conversation, and frugal midday meal, and manner of eating, amused those who watched them.[11]

Corinne, the once-booming railroad center, had a Chinese community in its heyday. The artifacts of an old Chinese laundry are among the memorabilia housed in the railroad museum there. An editorial from the *Utah Reporter* provides a vivid, although ethnocentric, impression of its international atmosphere:

Corinne is just now a fine place for the study of ethnology. We have in and around the city some five hundred Indians, *two or three hundred Chinese*, and quite a number of citizens of African descent. Our streets are gay with red blankets, paint and feathers, with Mongolian blue and purple, and with all the varieties of costume affected by hunters, miners, merchants, ranchmen and freighters of the "superior race".[12]

The same newspaper reported the first known Chinese wedding, attesting to the presence of Chinese women in the territory.

[O]n the evening of Saturday, the twenty-third, by Justice Sewell, Mr. John Tip ["John" was a nickname applied to all Chinese males in frontier times.] to Miss Ma Choy both of the Flowery Kingdom, but now residents of Corinne. The affair took place at the restaurant of Mrs. Clemmens and the happy bridegroom indulged in quite a handsome "set out" of cake, wine and other delicacies. Several ladies and gentlemen of the Anglo-Saxon "Persuasian" were present by invitation and the novel affair was by them pronounced a very pleasant occasion. We understand that the history of the lovers has been a romantic one, and that John secured his fair one by a regular American runaway. The surroundings were well worthy of the first Mongolian wedding in Utah.[13]

Terrace, like Kelton and many other legendary Utah ghost towns, boasted a large Chinese community in frontier days. Terrace was located about one hundred miles west of Promontory; little remains of it since a fire drove out its few remaining inhabitants in 1900. According to the 1880 Census there were fifty-four Chinese in Terrace, only one of whom was a woman. Most of the men were railroad employees, but others were independent small businessmen. One man named Hong Lee "kept a store," another, Wah Hing, ran a laundry. Ching Moon was a grocer, and the only woman, true to frontier expectations, was a twenty-eight-year-old prostitute. One Won Tz Chong performed the handiwork of a tailor, and another, Ah Lei, raised vegetables in his own garden. Apparently there were two Chinese laundries in Terrace, because Wa Hop was a laundry proprietor also.

How valuable are the census records? Regarding the history of the pioneer Chinese in the West, census records are perhaps more informative than the few other records available. Such simple statistics as names, ages, occupations, and literacy, in the dearth of written history about the Chinese in the state, help clarify certain misconceptions: many of these first Chinese could read and write, which puts to rest the faulty notion that they were all *coolies*. Far from being unskilled, a number of the Chinese took advantage of the economic potential of the new towns to leave the ranks of labor and open their own businesses.

In recent times, Frank Tinker told of souvenir-seekers in Terrace discovering evidence of the lives of those persons listed on the census rolls: Chinese pottery, coins, and assorted artifacts.[14]

Tinker has also recorded the familiar experiences of a few oldtimers, George Grose and the Hersheys, who observed the attempts to keep cultural customs alive even while enduring the isolation imposed upon so many Chinese men in mining and railroad towns throughout the old West.

> Once a year, on their New Years Day, the Chinese made long strips of white coconut candy which the youngsters of the village came to beg. There were no wives here and no children. When the men died they were taken to a cemetery west of town which defies location today. Later some of the remains were shipped back to China.[15]

The practice of burying the body for a period of five to ten years, exhuming it, and shipping the bones back to the homeland to be placed in the ancestral tomb may be compared in part to the desire of many people for burial in native soil. Ancestor reverence, a significant aspect of religion in China (Buddhism, Taoism, and Ancestor Reverence), apparently motivated this custom among Chinese.

As the railroad center for Utah, Ogden witnessed the development of a Chinatown with census figures rising from 33 Chinese in 1880 to 106 in 1890.[16] The Chinese section was characterized by "many rows of low wooden structures . . . built along Twenty-fifth Street from the Broom Hotel to the railroad station, four city blocks west of Washington Boulevard, and many of these establishments were operated by the Chinese."[17]

Among laundries operated by Chinese in Ogden were: Ching Wah, 2438 Grant Avenue, Hang Yei, 2222 Grant Avenue, Sam Wah, 271 Twenty-fifth Street, Sue Wah, 123 Twenty-fifth Street, and Wong Lee at 229 Twenty-fifth Street.[18]

Wong Leung Ka was one of the earliest established Chinese merchants in Ogden. He arrived around 1880 but did not come with the influx of railroad workers.

However, like many other Chinese of that period, he came to this country with-out wife or family. Unlike settlers from northern Europe, most Chinese had not left their homeland permanently, and most intended to return. What little is known about Wong Leung Ka was revealed by his son, Wong Siu Pang of Salt Lake City. Wong Siu Pang, who had never known his father, learned of him from family members, mostly from an older brother, the only other child in the family, who lives in Wyoming and has been in the United States for over fifty years. Wong Leung Ka resided in Ogden for forty-six years. During those years, he returned to his family in China twice. Each visit lasted less than a year because he traveled with a business visa that did not allow him to remain away longer.

"Sing Lung Store" was the name of Wong Leung Ka's shop in Ogden. The store carried groceries, canned goods, and Chinese imported items. Above the store, in the upper level of the building, were sleeping rooms. Wong Leung Ka was known for his compassion and generosity. When times were hard and men were unem-ployed, Chinese in the area sought Leung Ka's store as a place of refuge. Sleep-ing rooms and meals were provided. When, and if, employment was found, the men would pay back what they could.

In 1927, while waiting to embark to China for a third time, he died suddenly at the age of sixty-nine. His dream of returning to see his youngest son and enjoy a reunion with his family was unfulfilled.[19] The basic pattern of the sojourn of Wong Leung Ka was repeated thousands of times by other Chinese.

> Because some Chinese had such difficulties living in America, so he hoped his chil-dren would not come here to live.[20]

This was the message of Wong Leung Ka to his sons. But like their father, a spirit of adventure and faith brought them to this country where they have made their homes. Sometime after the youngest son Wong Siu Pang emigrated with his wife, three sons, and daughter in 1964, he and his older brother drove to Ogden and stood on the site of "Sing Lung Store." It was no longer there, and everything all around was changed. The old proprietor's grandchildren were being educated at the University of Utah and other institutions of higher learning. Among them are two promising artists, a scientist, and an inventor, children of Wong Siu Pang.

In the 1870s a controversial theory that Chinese immigration to the United States should be suspended because of high unemployment and job shortage was initiated in California, rapidly filtered into all states and territories of the United States, and was especially defended by those areas with Chinese popu-lations. It was also argued that unemployment was high and jobs were scarce because the Chinese, willing to work for lower wages, were usurping jobs right-fully meant for white Americans. Newspapers in Utah shared the attitude of ed-itors throughout the western region: the Chinese must go. The uproar culmi-nated in the passage of the Chinese exclusion laws beginning in 1882. An editorial in the *Ogden Junction* said:

But when every argument in favor of the Chinese is exhausted, the case of today is not covered; for times are hard, work in places is difficult if not impossible to get and the wages of white men, as a consequence, have dwindled to such an extent that there is at least but a trifling difference between the prices paid for work performed by the white man and that done by the copper-colored incubus. The first care of the nation should be the welfare of its subjects, and when we are brought into competition for day's labor, something must be done. There are unquestionably more workmen than there is work to be performed; and to divide what little there is with the inferior and alien race, is not a good nor a just policy.[21]

The editorial made no note of Chinese-owned businesses that contributed to the economic health of the area by creating jobs and markets for goods and services. Also ignored was the employment of Chinese on the Central Pacific Railroad out of desperation because not enough local citizens were willing to hazard such work.[22]

Since 1900 the largest Chinese population in Utah has been consistently in Salt Lake City. After railroad employment diminished for the Chinese in Box Elder County, the greatest number of Chinese remaining in Utah gravitated to the capital city. The 1890 Census counted 271 Chinese in Salt Lake City, whereas Box Elder County had only 147 for the same period.

Plum Alley ran north and south dividing the city block between Main and State streets, the cross streets being First and Second souths. Within and around Plum Alley the Chinese developed a microcommunity with grocery and merchandise stores, laundries and restaurants. Henry Ju, as a child in the 1930s, recalled accompanying his father Joy to Plum Alley on special occasions:

> They used to have those little shops where you could go and buy Chinese groceries that they sent from Frisco to here . . . then you'd look in the back and see a bunch a guys settin' around tables gambling; and how some of 'em used to sit there an smoke their water pipes.
>
> On New Year's Day [Chinese Lunar New Year] they had a big New Year's celebration sponsored by the tong in Plum Alley and they'd invite the police chief and mayor and all the dignitaries and they'd set around there and eat all the goodies and some of them old guys [the old Chinese men] would come over and give us the red envelopes with money in them [A Chinese tradition: the older married people give money to the young people, mostly children, in red decorated envelopes, the contents known as "lucky money"]; that's all us kids looked forward to . . . That was quite a haul, when you'd get up there you might get twenty bucks—they used to give silver dollars.[23]

Salt Lake City architect William Louie, grandson of a pioneer Chinese railroad worker, said that according to ancient custom the men probably paid all their debts before the dawning of the Lunar New Year, and in camp the cook would have plenty of hot water ready for the required bath. After a midnight feast of abalone and other special foods not eaten every day, the first day of the new year was a fast from all meat. Coming from a family-oriented culture where children are prized, the men were noted for their generosity toward American youngsters, especially on Lunar New Year. Mr. Louis recalled that they always seemed to put lots of money in the traditional red packets for the children in Ogden.[24]

Holidays provided occasion for greater merging between the Chinese community and the majority populace. A New Year's parade during the 1890s in Salt Lake City is recalled by Ivy C. Towler:

> A prominent feature of nearly all New Year parades was a huge Chinese dragon two hundred feet long which progressed along the street like a gigantic centipede. The dragon itself, which swayed from side to side, had a head six feet tall spitting fire from its vicious red mouth. The back of the creature of red, yellow and green painted canvas was suspended on arched staves, supported by poles from within, placed at regular intervals, giving its body a muscular appearance. The curtained sides hung down within two feet of the ground showing the legs and sandled [sic] feet of many Chinese marching in regular rhythm.[25]

Jimmy Wong, a Salt Lake restaurant owner, told of the history of the Bing Kung Tong, the Salt Lake chapter of the Chinese Benevolent Society with headquarters in San Francisco. He said, "There are chapters in Los Angeles, Denver, Sacramento, Oakland, Fresno, Portland, Seattle, and other major cities with large Chinese contingencies throughout the West." The first quarters for the tong were located in Plum Alley before the turn of the century, but Wong could not pinpoint the exact year it was first organized in Utah.[26] William J. Christiansen's research into the objectives and functioning of the old tong concluded:

> As in other larger western cities, the Salt Lake City Bing Kung Tong's main function was economic. It provided jobs and job counseling, transportation, translating services, lawyers, and letter writing services. Meetings were held often and economic matters were discussed. Another function was the provision of social activities such as gambling.[27]

Another major Utah Chinatown existed in Park City, the once-famous mining town, from its earliest days. According to the 1890 Census, 131 Chinese resided there. The first railroads into Park City were constructed in part by Chinese labor.

> All the men working on the Echo and Park City Railroad have been discharged and Chinese labor substituted in their place. The former class were being paid 1.75 per day; the latter required only 1.10. Some day when we are looking through a very powerful microscope we would like to examine the soul of a corporation like the Echo and Park City Railroad Company.[28]

This project, in addition to mining, which always attracted Chinese to provide community services, was probably what encouraged the development of the Park

City Chinatown. Fraser Buck, an oldtime Park City resident, had the following to say about the Chinese in the mining settlement:

> The Chinese moved into an area back of Main Street about a block above the post office; they had about fourteen or so houses there. They were very nice, they didn't cause the people in town a lot of trouble. There are still two or three houses standing left from the old Chinatown sector.
>
> There was a Chinaman came here called, "Old Grover" [nicknamed for Grover Cleveland] and he passed away just a few years back, but he was an old, old-timer. He was quite progressive—he acquired a house or two and rented until he built himself quite a thing. He had a son, "Joe Grover" come from China who lived with him and he inherited the houses that he had. Sometimes we used to say that he had eighty houses, but I don't think that's possible.
>
> There were a few women—and there was China Mary—she lived down here on Main Street and was well received by the town.
>
> The mines all had Chinese, one or two, and when they got going, they had up to five Chinese, most of them. They took care of the cleaning [in the mines and for the miners] and all that kind of work, and the cooking.[29]

A landmark in old Park City was the "China Bridge" that stretched across Chinatown from Rossie Hill, the residential section of Park City.

> They built the "China Bridge"—people in Rossie Hill—they didn't like to come down through Chinatown.
>
> Chinese laundries and restaurants were scattered in different parts of the town. Wash houses were not allowed on Main Street.[30]

An advertisement in the *Park Record* tells of a Chinese restaurant in old Park City:

> Charley Ong Lung has lately opened up a first class restaurant, opposite the Marsarc Mill, where can be had choice meals at all hours. Oysters in every style. Meal tickets—twenty one meals for $7.[31]

Fraser Buck's impression was that most of the town did not resent the Chinese. However, this was not always true:

> Yesterday a smart aleck thought to exhibit his smartness in front of Greenwald's by attacking an inoffensive Chinaman, who was passing along the street molesting no one. He grasped the Celestial and threw him down and pulled his queue rather too severely for John's liking. The Chinaman hastened to his feet and gathered up an armful of rocks and started for the S.A., who threw his hand back to his hip pocket under the pretense of drawing a pistol. This movement had not the effect of checking the Chinaman, who pressed him so closely and hurled stones so rapidly that the S.A. was forced to take to his heels for safety.[32]

The Chinese continued to be victims of sporadic, racially inspired difficulties into the first decade of the 1900s. During 1902 and 1903 the miners union campaigned to boycott Chinese restaurants and laundries, to end employment of Chinese, and to prohibit the selling and buying a Chinese goods. The acting consul general in San Francisco sent a petition of redress from See Lee and others in Park City, with a sample of articles published in the *Park Record* and a handbill, to the Chinese chargé d'affaires in Washington, D.C. The articles, entitled "White or Chinese" and signed "Saltair," complained that ninety-eight widows were forced to compete with Chinese restaurants and laundries.

> Shall the widows famish while the heathen Chinese feast? . . . All members of organized labor are in duty bound to patronize only white labor, and such establishments as employ only white labor. . . . The unorganized laborers of the camp who patronize the Oriental competitors of our race . . . are a greater menace . . . than an equal number of "scabs." Either the widows or the Chinese must go.

The handbill was also anonymous:

Patronize Home Industry

> By spending your money with your own race, or braid your hair in a pig tail and move to Hongkong. . . . Benedict Arnold was a traitor to his country but he never stooped so low as to patronize Chinese.[33]

Of the early Chinese in Tooele County, none was more famous than Sam Wing, known as "Doc Chinaman" to his fellow townspeople in Mercur. Besides practicing medicine [Chinese herbal], he was the proprietor of a laundry that employed four Chinese men.

In the early years of her marriage (1904–5), Evalee McBride Fackrell was the next door neighbor of the doctor and his wife Molly, both of whom, she said, spoke English well. Mrs. Frackrell expressed great faith in Sam Wing as a physician:

> When the doctors out there [Mercur] had a case that they didn't know how to cure, and got so bad—they sent for him and that man pulled many a case through that the doctors would have lost. Everybody thought if they just had the "Doc" to take care of them, they'd be all right.[34]

On one occasion when Mrs. Fackrell's baby was crying during the early morning hours, the "Doc," recognizing symptoms of colic, came into the Fackrell home and rubbed a "Chinese peppermint oil" around the baby's mouth and navel. The baby ceased crying immediately and his mother thought the "Doc" had drugged him. Sam Wing assured her that the baby would be all right, and his words proved true.

Mrs. Fackrell described Molly's home:

> Just a beautiful little home, just a little home. . . . with two rooms, and the men that run the laundry lived back further—I never went into their apartment at all. They had their laundry in the back part of the home.

Molly often came to visit Mrs. Fackrell, particularly to admire her baby boy. She would hold him on her knee and bounce him saying, "A pretty baby, a nica baby." Mrs. Fackrell said, "She [Molly] had children, and they were in China, and they couldn't bring them over here, and she was lonesome." Molly pined for her children and the "Doc" finally insisted she return to China. In later years Mrs. Fackrell remembered seeing Sam Wing often at the New York Cafe in downtown Salt Lake. After leaving Mercur he ran the Chinese Herbal Medicine Store near the Salt Lake railroad terminal. Whether he ever returned to China is not known.

In Carbon County during the 1880s, the Chinese worked in Pleasant Valley as coal miners. No one seemed to care if they ran laundries, sold vegetables, repaired cane-bottom chairs, or cooked their ancient cuisine. But the free enterprise system could only tolerate so much freedom in the 1880s.

> At the reopening of Utah mine, Chinese were sent in. On their behalf I will say that there is still standing a portion of the mine entry that was driven by them and it is as beautiful a piece of work as one could wish to see in a coal mine. Evidently no powder was used for blasting. Entry was driven exclusively with pick work. The sides are perfectly straight to a certain height and the roof is semi-arched. Due to the method of working this entry will stand indefinitely.

> A short time after the Chinese were imported into Pleasant Valley, white labor started to come in and naturally resented the presence of the yellow men. When white labor was strong enough they brought the situation to a climax and took the law into their own hands. One day they herded the Chinese into a box car, fastened the doors and started the car down grade. Fortunately, the car kept the track until it reached a place near Hales where there is an adverse grade. It stopped there and evidently the "Chinks" traveled the rest of the way on foot. At least they have not been seen in Pleasant Valley from that day to this.[35]

In the Uinta Basin during the late 1880s and the early part of this century, few personalities stand out with such prominence as Wong Sing. He had a humble beginning as a laundryman at Fort Duchesne in 1889, but during the twenties he owned and operated a merchandise store which boasted an inventory of between sixty and seventy thousand dollars.[36]

Phoebe Litster remembered as a girl in Vernal that:

> Wong Sing and two other Chinese set up a washing and cleaning shop. I was about ten or twelve. . . . [1891] and then I got married and we were transferred to Fort Duchesne,

he had that store there all the time. . . . Everybody traded with him, and always, before the depression, he put a sack of candy in people's groceries before they went
home. When my boy Robert was born, he came to see the baby and put a dollar in
the baby's hand. He was thoughtful, he was good; he was good to all the people.[37]

Besides general merchandise, the store handled furniture, ready-to-wear, meat,
and groceries and acted as general agent for machinery companies and other
firms.[38] Phoebe Litster's son-in-law, Oliver Bradley Cloward, joined Wong Sing
as an order boy in 1921. Mr. Cloward was impressed by his benefactor.

He was a stocky built man (about five feet six inches, five feet seven), he wasn't a
flashy man, he was just a common, everyday man. He just wore kinda pants, and he
usually had a yellow shirt on. . .

The remarkable thing about him was he had very much patience—that didn't seem
to matter to him as long as you was honest. . . . He'd try to train you in his way, and
he did. He taught me to figure, and he taught me to write better, and how to treat
people and how to meet 'em. . . .

He had an old pair of overshoes sitting around that'd been on the shelves you know,
for a long while—and some poor family come in there—they got those overshoes
free; or if anybody had a fire in the neighborhood, Wong Sing was there, and usually
contributed the most to help those people out. . . .

People respected him; they came from Vernal to trade with him, they came from La-
point—all over the Basin—I've known cattlemen to come from around Vernal there
and spent two hundred dollars at once with him.

I never heard of him being dishonest with any man in all of my life.

I was kinda backward—and he brought that out of me—he really made something
out of me. He really taught me. He never taught me anything bad. He'd always say,
"Let's do it this way," and if I ever made a mistake—I don't known of him ever bawl-
ing me out.

He trusted people so, I guess he lost lots of money by trusting, but he just seemed like
he couldn't see a family in need.[39]

Wong Sing spoke the Ute language and displayed a knowledgeable interest and
respect for Indian culture. His annual calendars were always designed with an Indian motif.[40]

The Indians would trust him—I never seen anything like it the way they trusted him.
He [Wong Sing] could speak it [the Ute language] fluently. He could tell you from

memory the different things that'd happened [Uinta Basin Indian history]. When I worked there, there was still some of the old chiefs, that'd come there, and he'd tell me about them. He knew, I believe, every Indian on that reservation, their character, and what they'd do, better than any man (I think) that'd ever lived out there.[41]

When Wong Sing died in a 1934 auto accident, sixty Ute men assembled at the office of the Indian agency to mourn his passing.[42]

Other Chinese lived throughout Utah in the nineteenth century. In Washington County, the boom town of Silver Reef had a total Chinese population of fifty-one in 1880. Of these, ten were women.[43] Prominent Utah author Juanita L. Brooks recalled hearing that

some of the white men knew that the leader of the Chinese had a white mistress — they tried to burn him out, I think they lit the fire — he didn't leave.[44]

During her father-in-law's declining years, Eva L. Miles wrote down his memories of life in Silver Reef:

When a Chinese man or woman died they were buried in a grave yard east and a little south of Bonanza Flat. . . .

When they would take a person (corpse) to the grave yard, they would carry them on a littler and one or two Chinamen would go ahead of them, carrying a lot of small pieces of paper about two inches square. They would throw these in every direction in front and to the sides.[45]

This paper was "spirit money," used to detract and appease the evil spirits who would otherwise deter the soul's successful journey heavenward.

They thought that if the man or woman who was buried was going to heaven, they'd need to have time to eat or drink while they went. So they'd have a lot of nice aromatic roast pork and other delicacies to take down for this person to eat and a bottle of liquor.

Well, they'd put it on the grave and go away. When evening came, the Indians would come and eat the pork and drink the liquor.[46]

Juanita L. Brooks also recalled that:

One of the men [a scholarly Chinese] tried to teach him [George F. Miles] Chinese. . . . He was young, inquisitive, and a brilliant, little chap. So he was friendly enough, that they took time with him, for him to learn to read.[47]

Silver Reef's Chinese community advertised a variety of services in the *Silver Reef Miner*:

> Call around to Hop Lee's establishment and be convinced that there is no better repairer of chairs in the Reef.[48]

Other items and advertisements in the *Silver Reef Miner* were:

SAM WING
First Wash-house
Bonanza
(lower Main Street)
Washing, ironing and fluting. Work done
promptly and in best of style.[49]

(It is possible that this Sam Wing is the same Sam Wing [Doc Chinaman] who later had a laundry in Mercur along with his Chinese medical practice.)

> Charley Legget, the well-known Oriental caterer, has established a baker in upper Chinatown, next to Hop Lee's store, where can be found at all times a supply of bread and table pastry. The more poetical name of the dealer in baked dough is Ah Fung.[50]
>
> The Chinese New Year was appropriately celebrated here this week. Firecrackers, Celestial music, lots of fun and forgiving of past grievances were the orders of the day.[51]

During pioneer times, the number of Chinese converted to Christianity in Utah was minimal. But this is not to say that various denominations did not show an interest in the Chinese and a sympathy for their problems. Mormon leader James E. Talmage was one.

> Talmage, at Brooklyn tabernacle, last night, denounced the anti-Chinese law, said come the Chinese had, come they would, come they should. God liked the Chinese physiognomy so well that he had made four hundred millions of them, while he had only made one Kearney [the instigator of the anti-Chinese movement]. Talmage liked the paganism which endured insult uncomplainingly better than the Christianity which mauls and stones them. The Nation that got the inside track with them would be the richest nation of the globe.[52]

Among members of the Congregational church of Salt Lake City were some Chinese. An 1897 newspaper article described "a Chinese Christmas entertainment" that took place at the church "in a hall ornamented with diverse kinds of Oriental creations until it presented a very pretty and picturesque scene. The entire program was carried out by the Chinese (Sunday School scholars) themselves.[53]

The decades between 1900 and 1930 were the years of growing Chinese activity around Plum Alley. In Ogden, Chinese businesses dotted Twenty-fifth Street and spread to Grant and Lincoln avenues north. As in most Chinese communities, there were few families. In Ogden, four or five families provided the rare presence of women and children. However, during the depression years a declining population took its toll of laundries, stores, and restaurants, and by 1940 the number of Chinese in the two principal cities reached a low of fewer than five hundred. It was in this setting that the second-generation Chinese grew up.[54]

NOTES

1. George Kraus, "Chinese Laborers and the Construction of the Central Pacific," *Utah Historical Quarterly* 37 (1969): 42–44.

2. Alexander Saxton, "The Army of Canton in the High Sierra," *Pacific Historical Review* 35 (1966): 141–52.

3. Wesley S. Griswold, *A Work of Giants: Building the First Transcontinental Railroad* (New York, 1962), p. 111.

4. Griswold, *A Work of Giants*, p. 326.

5. Robert West Howard, *The Great Iron Trail: The Story of the First Transcontinental Railroad* (New York, 1962), pp. 336–37.

6. Francis L. K. Hau, *The Challenge of the American Dream: The Chinese in the United States* (Belmont, Calif., 1971), p. 104.

7. 1870 Census.

8. Interview with Wallace E. Clay, Hot Springs, Utah, December 2, 1974.

9. Wallace E. Clay, "Personal Life of a Chinese Coolie 1869–1899." Unpublished paper written January 2, 1969.

10. *Ibid.*

11. *Cincinnati Excursion to California*, Indianapolis, Cincinnati and Lafayette Railroad, 1870, pp. 38–39.

12. *Utah Reporter* (Corinne), April 26, 1870. Emphasis added.

13. *Ibid.*

14. Frank Tinker, *Salt Lake Tribune*, January 26, 1964.

15. *Ibid.*

16. 1880, 1890 Censuses.

17. Kate B. Carter, comp., "The Early Chinese of Western United States," in *Our Pioneer Heritage*, 17 vols. (Salt Lake City, 1958–), 10:478.

18. *Ibid.*, 10:475.

19. Interview with Wong Siu Pang, Salt Lake City, November 27, 1974.

20. *Ibid.*

21. *Ogden Junction*, January 29, 1879.

22. Griswold, *A Work of Giants*, p. 11.

23. Interview with Henry Ju, December 3, 1974, Magna, Utah.

24. *Salt Lake Tribune*, February 15, 1972.

25. Carter, "The Early Chinese of Western United States," 10:456.

26. Interview with Jimmy Wong, December 3, 1974, Salt Lake City.

27. William J. Christiansen, "Chinese Ethnicity and Network Relationships in Salt Lake City" (Spring 1972), University of Utah, paper for Dr. Tom Collins, p. 8.

28. *Silver Reef Miner*, June 10, 1882.

29. Interview with Fraser Buck, November 29, 1974, Park City, Utah.

30. *Ibid.*

31. *Park City Mining Record*, June 5, 1880.

32. *Park City Mining Record*, August 7, 1880.

33. Governor's Correspondence, Utah State Archives, State Capitol, Salt Lake City.

34. Interview with Evalee McBride Fackrell, December 5, 1974, Holladay, Utah.

35. Thursey Jessen Reynolds, et al., eds., *Centennial Echoes from Carbon County*, (Price[?], 1948), p. 37.

36. Carter, "The Early Chinese of Western United States," 10:464–69.

37. Interview with Phoebe Litster, December 5, 1974, Salt Lake City.

38. Carter, "The Early Chinese of Western United States," 10:464–69.

39. Interview with Oliver Bradley Cloward, December 6, 1974, Orem, Utah.

40. Carter, "The Early Chinese of Western United States," 10:464–69.

41. Cloward interview.

42. Carter, "The Early Chinese of Western United States," 10:464–69.

43. 1880 Census.

44. Interview with Juanita Brooks, December 5, 1974, Salt Lake City.

45. A handwritten memoir by Eva L. Miles, sister of Juanita Brooks, sent to the author in a letter dated June 1, 1975, from St. George, Utah.

46. *Ibid.*

47. Juanita Brooks interview.

48. *Silver Reef Miner*, December 2, 1882.

49. *Ibid.*

50. *Ibid.*

51. *Ibid.*, February 10, 1883.

52. *Ogden Junction*, February 5, 1879.

53. *Deseret News*, December 20, 1897.

54. Typescript by William Wong Louie.

18

The Chinese in Gilpin County

Gerald E. Rudolph

Central City was the first mining town to attract large numbers of Chinese. In 1873 Alexander and Robert Cameron contracted for forty-five Chinese laborers to work the placer diggings in a section of the north Clear Creek Valley below Central City. The men were to be paid thirty-five dollars per month and were to provide their own board. Previously the workers had been employed on the Texas Pacific Railroad as graders. They came from Texas to Central City, arriving June 7, 1873, and started to work two days later.[1]

The local newspaper reported the new arrivals with mixed emotions. Comments such as "They appear to prefer the 'Melican chicken' to Chinese rats," alternated with such statements as "They work steadily and faithfully, yet talk almost incessantly. But they have learned the trick of working and talking at the same time."[2] The Cameron brothers were apparently pleased with their bargain for they went ahead with arrangements to bring more Chinese into the area.

Forty Chinese from Evanston, Wyoming, who had been employed by the Union Pacific, composed the second contingent. They arrived in July, 1873, and arranged to go into business for themselves. They purchased the necessary equipment in Denver and leased several hundred feet of ground from the Camerons. A third group of "seventeen celestials, including one of the female persuasion, arrived from Utah yesterday [September 27, 1873] and went up via the Colorado Central to Blackhawk. They are to be employed at Cameron's diggings, on Clear Creek. . . ."[3] Twenty-eight more from Cheyenne and other points on the Union Pacific arrived in January, 1874. In February of that year the *News* reported that:

> About a dozen Chinamen came in on the Kansas Pacific train last evening. They are ticketed for Central City from St. Louis, and it is supposed they have been engaged for mining purposes.[4]

More were to follow. The *Rocky Mountain News* of May 21, 1874, announced that twenty-five Chinese had arrived in Denver from California en route to Black

Hawk. There were twenty-two men, two women, and one baby. The next day the *News* stated that forty-three Chinese had come in on the Kansas Pacific from New Orleans. They, too, were bound for Black Hawk.

A large colony soon developed by the placer mining site on North Clear Creek. At the first most of the Chinese lived in small huts in an area which became known as Cameron's Camp or Camerontown, but later they acquired an unused railroad section house near the base of Cottonwood Gulch. From the very beginning a few lived in Black Hawk and some of the nearby settlements. On July 13, 1873, the Central City *Daily Register* remarked, "One of Cameron's Chinamen has bought a house in Black Hawk."

Opposition to the Chinese soon developed. To begin with, ready-made prejudices had been imported from California. Antagonism to the Chinese had reached a serious point in California before any of them had ever entered Colorado. In mining camps throughout the West many Chinese were badly treated, beaten up, and sometimes killed. Since most of the Chinese in the United States were not and could not become citizens, they could not press charges against an alleged offender in an American court. Neither could they testify in their own defense; this made them easy targets for anyone who had inclined to rob or harm them. The term "not a Chinaman's chance" developed as a result. Individuals or small groups, such as those who operated placer mines in remote mountainous regions, were especially easy prey for antagonistic whites.

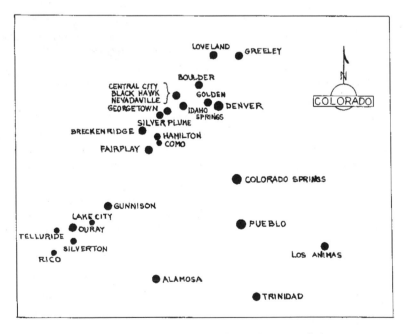

Figure 18.1   Areas in which the Chinese settled.

Some of the complaints against the Chinese perhaps were justified, but most were not. They were simply different in so many ways that it was easy to suspect and dislike them. The color of their skin, their facial features, type of dress, religion, language, and customs were different. The only Americans whom the Chinese resembled were the Indians. With the exception of the nose, the facial characteristics of the Chinese and Indians are very similar. They both have straight black hair, dark brown eyes, high cheekbones, and scant body hair and beard. Existing prejudices against the Indians were directed toward the Chinese.

The clothing for Chinese men and women alike consisted of pantaloons, blouses, soft-soled cloth slippers, and either black skull caps or basket bats.

> The Chinese usually wore side cotton pantaloons of a blackish color, barely reaching to his ankles. His equally wide and shapeless blouse of the same material fell to his knees and fitted close up to his neck. It overlapped down the front and was fastened with loops or brass buttons. In cold weather he wore a sleeveless coat of quilted material. The laborers in the mines and fields wore a wide-umbrella-shaped hat made of split bamboo or grass. . . . The Chinese women wore blouses and trousers similar to those worn by the men, only they were of a fine material and usually girdled with a brightly colored sash.[5]

The same apparel was worn, no matter what the temperature, both summer and winter.

Most Americans considered the Chinese to be heathen, i.e., non-Christian. Some were Christians upon their arrival in the United States; nearly all of these were students who had been exposed to Christian missions in China. Others became Christian after having lived here a while, but many retained their native beliefs. "The Chinese brought with them no organized religious system per se, but they imported a complex blend of traits selected from two ethical systems—Confucianism and Taoism—as well as some religious practices identified with Buddhism."[6]

The average Chinese immigrant knew no language other than his own. Those who worked on the railroads in the mines acquired very little English because they did not associate with English-speaking workers, mingling instead almost entirely with their own kind. In addition, the tone of their voice often seemed shrill and bird-like to Americans.

The native customs and mannerisms also tended to alienate them from the dominant society in which they lived. Their very industry and frugality seemed to set them apart. The chief goal of most Chinese immigrants to the United States was to make their fortunes and return to their homes in China. Most of them came without their families and attempted to live as inexpensively as possible.

One of the most damaging criticisms against them was that they obtained many of their supplies directly from China. In spite of the transportation expense, the low cost of goods in China enabled them to do so. Food, clothing, and even a few items of furniture were brought over by the Chinese commercial organizations located on the Pacific Coast known as the "Six Companies."[7]

It was easy, therefore, to become prejudiced against the Chinese. They were different, they were assumed to be serious competitors of white labor, and they invested very little of their earnings in the communities in which they lived. However, the work of agitators, both amateur and professional, appears to have been the main cause for the development of antagonistic attitudes toward the Chinese. They proved themselves quite adept at remembering latent antipathies. The role of the agitator and demagogue was described in the Central City *Register.*

> According to the prophecy of not a few political economists, there is danger of our having a superabundance of them [Chinese] in Colorado. They would have us believe that . . . the continent is to experience a regular human tidal wave, that will strand intelligent white labor in its course, revolutionizing our whole industrial system, and reducing the working classes to a condition of comparative degradation.
>
> This has been a pet idea, not with the laboring classes themselves, but rather with the demagogues, the blatant, self-constituted champions of the poor man, who have sounded an alarm abroad through the land, thinking they saw political capital in the distance.[8]

In the spring of 1874, an incident occurred which revealed the anti-Chinese feeling of many of the white miners. The *Rocky Mountain News* on March 6, 1874, reported that the chief agent of the Nederland Mining Company, P. H. Van Diest, had arranged with a certain Mr. Thayer to furnish enough Chinese laborers to work the very profitable Caribou Mine.[9] Although the *News* said, "They are to take the place of the laborers now employed," the company contended that they were going to work around the shaft house, not underground.

The night of their arrival, March 29, a group of approximately forty masked men, most of whom were armed, forced the twenty-five Chinese out of the area. The citizens of Nederland promptly drew up a petition vowing to apprehend those involved and bring them to justice.[10] The Central City *Register* editorially disapproved of the act but expressed contempt for Chinese labor in general.

> We had hoped that no part of our territory would be disgraced by the persecution of Chinamen. . . . Our own opinion is that the men engaged in this affair, have not only acted unlawfully, but very foolishly. We believe that one month's trial of Chinese cheap labor about a mine or mill would have settled the question forever, and the company would be glad at the end of that time to replace them with men of any other nationality.[11]

Another event occurred that spring which damaged relations between the whites and Chinese. The town of Central City was almost completely destroyed by fire. At mid-morning on May 21, 1874, flames burst out of a shack in Dostal Alley near Spring Street. The shanty was occupied by two or three Chinese who had been using it as a laundry and as living quarters. There is conflicting evidence as to the cause of the fire. Several accounts say the Chinese had been holding a religious ceremony. Joss sticks were burned and incense spread on live coals. Somehow they got out of control and flames sprang up, rapidly igniting the sun-parched building. This explanation seems to have arisen from rumors which started shortly after the fire. Another explanation is that the fire had started in a defective chimney flue, spreading swiftly to adjacent frame houses which were built quite close to one another. A bucket brigade was immediately available to fight the fire, but there was no water in the Gulch. Soon the business section was engulfed. All but a few buildings had been consumed before the flames were finally subdued. The Chinese were blamed for the conflagration and at least one of them narrowly averted being lynched.[12]

The Chinese engaged in gulch or placer mining almost exclusively. Anti-Chinese sentiment would undoubtedly have been greater had they attempted to gain employment as lode miners. Few could begrudge their working the placer mines because most of the areas in which they sluiced had already been worked once and sometimes twice by white miners. It was considered quite remarkable that they were able to make the gulches pay at all. The *Register* commented favorably on this fact: "To be sure they do not spend very freely with us the money the make here, nevertheless, they are a benefit to the county in that by means of their steady, laborious efforts, as well as their simple and cheap mode of living, they are able to make profitably productive many of our placer claims that most of our white men would be unable to make 'grub' from and which must otherwise remain unworked."[13]

The Chinese labor crews usually had a leader or boss referred to as the "head man." Five head men known to have been in the Gilpin County area were Ah Say, Ah Chee Leung, Ah Moon, Bong Young, and Lin Sou Shin. Ah Say was the head man who brought the second group of Chinese into Gilpin County; he probably did not remain, however, as he was employed by the Union Pacific and was reported as being only temporarily in charge of the men on their trip from Evanston.[14] Ah Chee Leung worked with Lin Sou Chin, but seems to have been of lesser importance. Ah Moon was an active Chinese leader in both Gilpin County and the South Park area. Bong Young, who was listed in the 1880 census as a "Captain of Chinamen," was widely known and respected by Chinese and whites alike. The *Rocky Mountain News*, which was usually reluctant to print anything favorable about the Chinese, had this to say about him:

> The doctor [Bong Young] is a finely educated gentleman, speaking and writing English quite as well as the best educated citizen in Colorado. . . . he came to this country as a common laborer eight years ago, six of which he has spent in Colorado, principally in the vicinity of Central City, During the time he has acquired his knowledge of the English language without the aid of an instructor. On all questions of the day Mr. Bong is as well posted as is any other citizen of Central.[15]

In addition to his business in Central City, Bong Young was the owner of a Chinese store on Sixteenth Street in Denver. He helped effect a settlement of the 1880 Denver riot claims.[16]

The most outstanding and colorful head man in Colorado was Lin Sou Chin. Tall (6 feet, 2 inches), blue eyed, energetic, and highly intelligent, Lin Sou was the "head man" for Chinese labor crews in Gilpin and Boulder Counties and much of the South Park area. Lin Sou had been in charge of the first gang of Chinese laborers to work on the Central Pacific Railroad in 1859. He remained with the railroad throughout its construction. Like many others, Lin Sou found himself unemployed after the Central Pacific and Union Pacific had met at Promontory Point near Ogden, Utah, in May, 1869. He soon came to Colorado and became a boss of Chinese placer miners. A short while later, he brought his wife from China to Gilpin County. A daughter, Lily Chin, who was born in 1873, was the first Chinese known to have been born in Colorado.

According to one account, Lin Sou created quite a stir upon his arrival:

> John T. Pursell had every confidence in the man and extended the warm hand of welcome to him. . . . Pursell took him to Joe Thatcher's First National establishment at Central City. The eyes of the clerks bulged out when Lin Sou laid down sixty thousand dollars as his initial deposit and from that minute the Chinese Credit Mobilier was set up as one of the fixtures of the camp.[17]

Lin Sou spoke English well. He procured work and arranged the contracts for his people within a large area which included South Park. In return, they purchased their supplies, many of which were obtained in China, from him. He is reported to have bossed 300 Chinese placer miners in the early 1870's for Warren Thomas, pioneer real estate man in Gregory Gulch, a mile and half below Black Hawk.[18] In 1874, Lin Sou had men hired out to William Queen in the Lake District of Lower Russell Gulch, to Blake and Company two and half miles below the mouth of Russell Gulch on North Clear Creek, and to the Camerons' on North Clear Creek. The men were paid forty dollars a month, which was five dollars a month more than the first contingent of Chinese laborers in Gilpin County had received.[19] After August, 1874, Lin Sou leased the Cameron claims. He paid the owners between twenty-five and thirty-three and a third percent of the gross profit, the amount depending upon the location. In the fall of 1874 he employed thirty-five men along North Clear Creek in the vicinity of the Central City Railroad's Smith Hill Station. Portions of these claims were sub-leased to three different groups. The placer diggings in all of these areas had recently been worked by white labor and abandoned because of their failure to yield a profit.[20] The *Register* had earlier observed: "Chin Lin Sou exercises a sort of supervisory care over everything and his authority is absolute."[21]

Lin Sou appears in the records under a variety of names. His last name was Chin; but like the names of many other Chinese in the United States, it was frequently turned around. He is listed in various newspapers and records as Chin Lin Sou, Chan Lin Sou, Sou Chin Lin, Sou Lin, Soy Lin, Lin Soy, Lin Saw, Lin Sow, and Lin Sue. The activities listed and the physical descriptions given with these names (his extraordinary height and unusual blue eyes) leave no doubt that all of the names refer to the same person. Today his name can be found on the back of seat number six in row "A" behind the dress circle, center section, in the Central City Opera House. It is printed in inverse order, as he was most commonly known. The inscription reads, "Chin Lin Sou, 1871."

NOTES

1. Boulder *News*, June 13, 1873; Central City *Daily Register*, July 19, 1873.
2. Central City *Daily Register*, July 19, 1873.
3. *Rocky Mountain News*, September 28, 1873.
4. *Ibid.*, February 20, 1874.
5. Patricia K. Ourada, "The Chinese in Colorado," *The Colorado Magazine*, XXIX (October, 1952), p. 275.
6. Rose Hum Lee, *The Chinese in the United States of America* (Hong Kong: University of Hong Kong Press, 1960), p. 278.
7. Ourada, *The Colorado Magazine*, XXIX (1952), p. 280.
8. Central City *Daily Register*, July 19, 1873.
9. Approximately $350,000 worth of bullion was taken out of the Caribou in 1874 and 1875. See Duane A. Smith, "The Caribou—A Forgotten Mine," *The Colorado Magazine*, XXXIX (January, 1962), p. 50.
10. Boulder *News*, April 3, 1874; *Rocky Mountain News*, April 4, 1874.
11. Central City *Weekly Register*, April 8, 1874.
12. Caroline Bancroft, *Gulch of Gold* (Denver: Sage Books, 1958), pp. 260–61. It is somewhat ironical that today the inner walls of the Central City fire house building are papered with orange Chinese newspapers.
13. Central City *Daily Register*, October 30, 1874.
14. *Ibid.*, July 19, 1873.
15. *Rocky Mountain News*, January 1, 1881.
16. Nearly two years after the riot Bong Young and Ah Moon were co-defendants in a legal suit filed by W. C. Fullerton and Ed Hurlburt in November, 1882. See *Register of Actions*, Gilpin County Court, p. 126, number 1239.
17. "Frontier Sketches" from the Denver *Field and Farm* in the Dawson Scrapbook, IX, Library, State Historical Society of Colorado.
18. Denver *Post*, June 25, 1937.
19. The monthly wage for Chinese laborers on the Central Pacific Railroad was twenty-six dollars a month from 1865 until 1868 when it was raised to thirty-five dollars. See Irving Stone, *Men to Match My Mountains* (Garden City, New York: Doubleday and Company, 1956), pp. 235 and 289.
20. Central City *Daily Register*, October 30, 1874.
21. *Ibid.*, July 19, 1873.

19

The Chinese in Denver: Their Location and Occupations

Gerald E. Rudolph

The first Chinese to settle in Denver arrived in 1870. By October, twenty-nine men and thirteen women were living in a few small houses on Wazee Street between "F" (Fifteenth) and "G" (Sixteenth).[1] The following spring the colony had expanded to Blake Street. Most of the dwellings in which the Chinese lived were small frame buildings, but in 1874 a one-story brick residence was built on the corner of Sixteenth and Wazee.[2]

Chinatown soon extended along Wazee Street to a point midway between Sixteenth and Seventeenth. "Hop Alley" was another term for this Chinese colony. "Hop" referred to the opium which was sometimes used by the Chinese, and "Alley" referred to rear entrances to many of the Chinese buildings in the alley between Wazee and Blake. Another derogatory name applied to the area was "Chinktown." An important part of "Hop Alley" was directly behind the prosperous American House Hotel.

Friction had developed between two factions or tongs by the mid-1880's. Partly at the suggestion of Mayor Wolfe Londoner, the faction led by Chin Poo moved across Cherry Creek to Thirteenth and Blake, an area which was known as the "West Side." Chin Poo had become more westernized than many of his countrymen. He and his followers attempted to establish a Chinese colony that would be acceptable to all or most of the city's population. The *News*, usually critical of the Chinese stated:

> The quarters occupied by Chin Poo [are] remarkable. In his place in West Denver there are no alleys, no passages or dark hallways, the floors are kept clean, are scrubbed daily, and all the houses are well lighted and ventilated. No such things as double bunks are seen there. . . . Chin Poo has fitted up a restaurant for the whites . . . a Chinese cook prepares anything in session. Their opium rooms are also clean and well aired.[3]

315

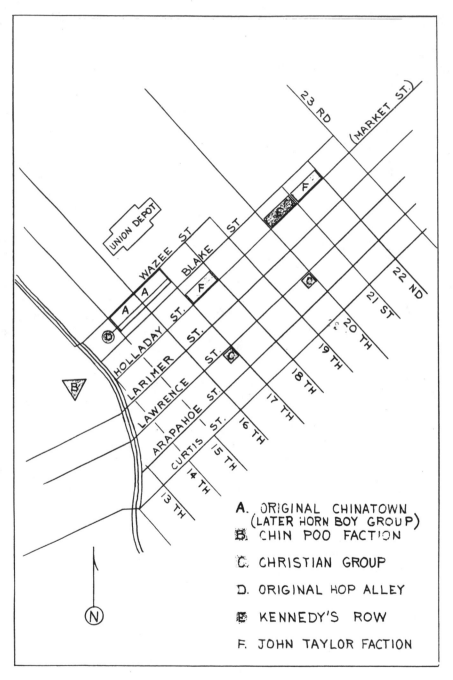

Figure 19.1 Chinese in Denver, 1869–1940.

The original Chinatown on Wazee Street was further divided when many of its inhabitants moved "uptown" to an area called Kennedy's Row on Holladay Street (the name was later changed to Market Street) between Twentieth and Twenty-first. New quarters were established during 1889 and 1890 in a compact area. The *News* presented an interesting commentary on the structural composition of the new Chinatown and, incidentally, on Chinese customs and type of urban social organization.

> The new quarters consist of four lots, the front of which is closely built up and a number of little brick shanties, which face on the alley, and are about twenty feet in depth, and in a space between a courtyard about fifty feet square is formed from which point every window can be seen in the new joss house [place of worship] up a flight of stairs, and even the plank walk across the rickety roof. By a narrow passage on the extreme left the alley can be reached, and on the opposite side is another house, divided into at least twenty compartments. In here the barber shops, a small restaurant and two opium joints are located. Off from the courtyard there are about thirty houses, which are cut up into probably 200 rooms, all of which are about twelve feet in height, and in many of which, a second floor has been built of thin boards.[4]

It is not surprising that the "Hop Alley" label was applied to this settlement also. It eventually extended along Market Street to Twenty-second. The Chinese who lived there became known as the John Taylor faction, named after their leader. A dozen years later the *News*, stated, ". . . there are shops right out on Market and Blake Streets where gaudy Chinese goods and wonderful embroideries . . . are sold . . . [but] the back courts are the favorite living places of the Chinese. . . ."[5] Most of the Chinese who had become Christians settled even farther uptown. Their houses were located on Lawrence Street at Seventeenth and at Twentieth.[6]

Each group was augmented by new arrivals, increasing Denver's Chinese population from 238 in 1880 to 461 by 1885; in 1890, it stood at 980. After the latter date it began to decline. The original Chinatown was almost deserted when the West Side and the Market Street sections were being developed.

> In the old place on Wazee Street remains only the joss house . . . and 'for rent' signs only ornament the exterior of the squatty buildings in which they once lived.[7]

It was not long, though, before Wazee Street was again the site of a living Chinatown. Many of the Chinese who had settled on the West Side with Chin Poo drifted back. Their numbers were increased by some of the Chinese who had just come to Denver. For some time the members of this revitalized Chinatown were referred to as the "Horn Boy faction."

On July 16, 1901, a permit was issued for the opening of a Chinese hotel. The old Central Theater on Market Street between Twentieth and Twenty-first was remodeled and converted into a hotel with a store in front. It was reported to be the first Chinese hotel in Denver and the only one between San Francisco and "the East."[8] The Market Street settlement grew until there was no more room, and another section was established on the same street between Seventeenth and Eighteenth.[9]

The Chinese frequently found it difficult to make a living. They were excluded from many occupations and professions by law. Some employers would not hire them simply because they were Chinese and organized labor kept them out of the unions. They were welcomed only in jobs that were considered women's work.

The first Chinese to live in Denver were railway employees who worked on the new roadbeds and as firemen. There were not many, and much of the time they were not in town; Denver was merely their headquarters. Railways employing some Chinese labor were the Denver and Rio Grande, the Kansas and Pacific, and the Union Pacific.[10]

Most of the Chinese in Denver worked as laundrymen. A few were employed as cooks; several operated stores or shops and eventually restaurants. Three or four styled themselves physicians and sold various types of remedies. Some sold opium and provided rooms where the drug could be smoked while others earned their living by gambling and a few operated houses of prostitution.

Prior to 1902, Denver was in Arapahoe County. The 1880 census showed that there were 238 Chinese in the county at that time. One hundred twenty-six were laundry workers; six others were listed as laundry owners or keepers. Entries in the enumeration districts varied. For instance the following terms were used to designate occupation: Launderer, laundry, laundryman, washeeman, washer, washerman, washing, washman, works in laundry. Entries which indicate laundry ownership or proprietorship are listed as "Laundry owner" and "keeps Laundry." Another term, "wash house," could be interpreted as meaning either ownership or employee. If it is understood to refer to ownership, there were 12 owners or keepers and 120 employees.

Six of the Arapahoe County Chinese were listed as cooks; two as miners; two as saddle tree makers; one as a barkeeper; and four as servants, i.e., a coachman, a chamber maid, a laundress, and a butler. These servants plus one of the six cooks were all employed by Colonel James and Mrs. Catherine Archer. There was no occupation named for 86 Chinese persons although some of them were undoubtedly engaged in some type of work. Thirteen of those listed with no occupation were married females. The only females shown to have occupations were the chambermaid and the laundress, servants of the Archers. The small number of females is one reason why the Chinese population in the state did not become very large. Census reports show that there were only 15 in the entire state in 1880. Five years later there were 26, while in 1890 there were just 34; by 1900 the number had declined to 24.

The business *Directory of the City of Denver* listed Chinese laundries under the heading of "Laundries" from 1873 to 1875. After that no Chinese laundries were listed under that heading. One might surmise that this was a form of discrimination against the Chinese, especially when other laundries continued to be listed in the business section. Under the alphabetical listing of names, however, those Chinese who did laundry were indicated by terms such as "washing" or "laundry" after their name and address.

In 1873 four laundries were advertised in the Directory; three, with Chinese names. In 1874 there were fifteen laundries listed, thirteen of which were Chinese. Four out of the seven laundries shown in 1875 were Chinese. By 1886 twenty individual Chinese had the word "laundry" after their names. Some of the laundries were operated by one man, but most employed others. In 1887 only twelve Chinese laundrymen were listed. Ten years later there were seventeen. There were, however, thirty-two laundries (all non-Chinese) advertised under the regular laundry section. In 1898 there were twenty Chinese laundrymen listed. There were nineteen in 1899, one of whom was labeled an "ironer." Seventeen were listed for 1900. By 1905 there were only nine, although forty-eight non-Chinese laundries were shown. In 1910 there were five Chinese laundrymen listed and sixty-four non-Chinese laundries advertised.

The *Directory of the City of Denver* also revealed other Chinese endeavors. The Dibble and Thayer Chinese merchandise store was listed in 1875 and 1876. Another merchandise store, the Yok Hion, was advertised in 1877 and 1878. Five stores were listed for 1886 and six for 1887. In 1897 and 1898, there were twelve listings for Chinese goods. The number dropped to ten in 1899 and to eight in 1900. There were only four listed for 1905 and none for 1910.

Other listings showed a physician for 1886 and 1887; a doctor, a grocer, and a seller of Chinese remedies for 1897; an interpreter and two dealers in Chinese remedies for 1898; just one salesman of remedies for 1899 and 1900; one porter for 1900; and one grocer for 1910.[11]

Chinese stores were patronized by both Chinese and whites. The latter frequently made more purchases than the Chinese. This is not difficult to understand in light of Patricia Ourada's statement:

> Nowhere else in America could one find such exquisite material as the silken bolts in the Chinese merchant shops. Many a miner recklessly laid golden nuggets on the counter in return for a silk sash or a dainty fan for the hard working frontier woman who had given up the frills of the East.[12]

The *Rocky Mountain News* on August 24, 1881, carried the following advertisement:

Chinese Notion Store
Teas, Fans, Silk Handkerchiefs, Dishes, and all Kinds of Chinese Fancy Goods at
283 Twentieth Street   Lee Chung Long

Most of the goods in the shops were imported directly from China. There were a wide variety of items which included such things as herbs, lichee nuts, Chinese ginger, tea, canned fruits, sugar cane, pickled bamboo shoots, birds' nests, various kinds of sauces and relishes, incense sticks; jewelry, silks, and clothing.[13]

One of the stores on Market Street was kept by Lily Look and her husband. Lily, the daughter of Lin Sou Shin, was the first Chinese born in Colorado. After her father's death in 1894, she was called the "Queen of Chinatown."

The most pretentious general merchandise store in 1921, according to the *News*, was that of Q. Louie.[14] The Denver *Telephone Directory* listed a Chinese shop, The Wah Fung Curio Company, from 1905 to 1924 and Woo Quong Hung's grocery store from 1908 to 1928. Mr. Hung was also the owner of several Denver restaurants. He was the mayor of Chinatown for a number of years until his death in 1927.

The Colorado Bureau of Labor Statistics was established in 1887 to provide statistics on thirteen different subjects, one of which was the Chinese in the state. Information was to be given about the "number and condition . . . their social and sanitary habits; number of married and single; the number employed and the nature of their employment . . .; the amount expended by them in rent, food and clothing, and in what proportion such amounts are expended for foreign and home productions respectively; [and] to what extent their labor comes in competition with the other industrial classes of the state."[15] From the beginning the *Labor Statistics Reports* revealed animosity toward the Chinese. Some of them degenerated into little more than diatribes, naming all the reasons why the "Chinese should go." Little faith can be placed in many of the figures which are cited in the *Reports*. Nevertheless, they do reveal some pertinent information.

One major complaint was that Chinese laundrymen were depriving large numbers of white people from earning a decent living. It was stated that "no less than 1,200 more white persons would find employment at washing in the city of Denver were there no Chinamen here."[16] A number of white laundry proprietors and employees testified to the undesirability of the Chinese.[17] The report for 1889–1890 said that in Denver there were 300 Chinese laundrymen, 142 gambler's, 50 merchants, 50 employed as cooks, porters, and waiters, 20 farmers, 10 doctors, 10 barbers, and 17 women whose occupations were not listed.[18]

The 1891–1892 report listed 589 male Chinese. There were 405 laundrymen, 60 storekeepers and clerks, 33 in fantan houses and 17 lottery agents (gambling), 15 janitors and servants, 12 opium house employees, 8 joss house (places or worship) employees, 8 barbers, 8 restaurant keepers, 6 physicians, 2 interpreters, 1 fruit dealer, 1 butcher, 1 druggist, and 12 in miscellaneous occupations.[19]

Another complaint about the Chinese was that very little of their earnings went back into the economy of the area. Instead their money was spent on merchandise shipped in from China. Savings were usually sent back to relatives in China or were taken there when the sojourner returned. This complaint seems to have been valid. It was reiterated in the 1907–1908 report. It is interesting to note, however, that the same report showed China as an important market for mining machinery which was manufactured in Denver.[20]

Lengthy accounts were written about the Chinese in the biennial reports for 1891–1892 and 1901–1902. Calumnious remarks were made about their table etiquette, their personal attire and appearance, their customs and their religion. More deserved comments, perhaps, were made about the opium and gambling places. The 1901–1902 report said, "If the secrets of Chinatown were published, while the exposure would no doubt involve many who occupy good positions in society, it would expose to the public gaze a condition of immorality, vice, crime, and indecency that would cause the masses of the people to rise up in righteous indignation and remove this plague spot from their midst.[21]

Denver's Chinese population dropped from 980 in 1890 to 306 in 1900. After that the population continued to decline. By 1940 there were only 110 in the city. The Chinese were gradually crowded out of the laundry business. As that happened, they turned more and more to restaurants and catered primarily to non-Chinese.

NOTES

1. Wazee is a Chinese name.
2. *Rocky Mountain News,* June 3, 1874.
3. *Ibid.,* January 6, 1890.
4. *Ibid.*
5. *Ibid.,* August 10, 1902.
6. Denver *Republican,* February 16, 1893.
7. *Rocky Mountain News,* January 6, 1890.
8. Denver *Republican,* July 17, 1901.
9. Denver *Times,* February 18, 1901.
10. LeRoy R. Hafen (ed.), *Colorado and Its People A Narrative and Topical History of the Centennial State* (New York: Lewis Historical Publishing Company, 1948), II, 115; and *Rocky Mountain News,* March 27, 1880.
11. Corbett, Hoye and Company's *Directory of the City of Denver, 1873–1875;* and Corbett and Ballinger, *Directory of the City of Denver, 1886–1887, 1897–1900, 1905, and 1910.*
12. Ourada, *The Colorado Magazine,* XXIX (1952), 280.
13. Forbes Parkhill, *The Wildest of the West* (Denver: Sage Books, 1957), p. 109.
14. *Rocky Mountain News,* August 14, 1921.
15. *Colorado Bureau of Labor Statistics, Twelfth Biennial Report, 1909–1910* (Denver: Smith-Brooks Printing Company, 1911), p. 7.
16. *Colorado Bureau of Labor Statistics, Second Biennial Report, 1889–1890* (Denver: Collier and Cleveland Lithography Company, 1890), p. 57.
17. *Ibid.,* pp. 57–58.
18. *Ibid.,* p. 59.
19. *Labor Statistics, Third Biennial Report, 1891–1892,* p. 136.
20. *Colorado Bureau of Labor Statistics, Eleventh Biennial Report, 1907–1908* (Denver: Smith-Brooks Printing Company, 1908), p. 40.
21. *Labor Statistics, Eighth Biennial Report, 1901–1902,* p. 299.

20

Denver's Anti-Chinese Riot, 1880

Roy T. Wortman

The year 1848 marked the discovery of gold in California and an embryonic Chinese migration to the United States. Chinese immigration was stimulated by the Taiping Rebellion (1850–1864) and the Burlingame Treaty of 1868, which allowed Chinese laborers to enter the United States and which recognized "the inherent and inalienable right of man to change his home and allegiance."[1] Most of the Chinese settled in California, but a few ventured eastward.

In 1869, the first Chinese settled in Colorado. "He's come," said the *Colorado Tribune*, "the first John China man in Denver. He came in yesterday, a short, fat, round-faced, almond-eyed beauty. . . . He appeared quite happy to get among civilized people."[2] With the completion of the transcontinental railroad a small number of Chinese settled in Denver.[3] A territorial house joint resolution of February 11, 1870, encouraged Chinese immigration because "immigration of Chinese later is eminently calculated to hasten the development and early prosperity of the Territory, by supplying the demands of cheap labor."[4]

By the latter part of 1870 there were forty-two Chinese in Denver.[5] Most of them came from the Pacific coast, but a few were imported from Louisiana in 1874 to work in the Cameron mines.[6] Because the Orientals were willing to work for cheaper wages, and because of their strange language and customs, they were the victims of xenophobia. Of all the anti-Chinese nativists, the most infamous was California's Irish-born, naturalized American citizen, Denis Kearney. Most vocal in the late 1870's, he feared that cheap Chinese labor would displace unskilled white labor. Kearney maintained that "the Chinaman must leave our shores." His supporters backed him not only with shouts of "Immericky for Immerikens, bejabers!" but with actual acts of violence as well.[7]

Nativist sentiments were not confined to California. Colorado's Chinese population also suffered from mistreatment at the hands of the whites. In 1871 the first anti-Chinese incident in Colorado occurred when vandals set fire to a Chinese house.[8] In March, 1874, one hundred and sixty Chinese laborers at Nederland were threatened with harm, and in that same year anti-Chinese sentiment was exacerbated when Italian coal miners in Caribou were replaced with cheaper Chinese laborers.[9] Leadville, in 1879, did not have to proclaim the nativist slogan of "the Chinese must go," for they didn't have any Chinese; rather, they raised banners stating that "the Chinese must not come!"[10]

A Colorado newspaper in 1880 described the state's population and dealt with the lower orders: "Then there were the Indians, the Chinese, and the Mexicans. Of these it would be difficult to say which is the worst class. We have quite a number of Celestial heathens in this state."[11] The census of 1880 listed 612 Chinese in the state,[12] with 238 of them living in Denver.[13] F. A. Bee, the Chinese consul who visited Denver after the riot of October 31, 1880, perhaps gave a more accurate estimate of 450 Chinese in Denver, out of a total population of about 40,000.[14] Most of Denver's Chinese were laundrymen. A Colorado visitor from Illinois noted in her diary in July, 1880: "Laundry—Lee Whang and Whang Lee, or something similar are to be seen at almost every turn."[15] Since most of Denver's Chinese were laundrymen, they did not pose a serious threat to unskilled white labor; the nativists, however, thought differently, as events of the 1880 Garfield-Hancock presidential campaign would show.

Denver's *Rocky Mountain News*, owned by W. A. H. Loveland, a prominent Democrat, made its campaign position clear in August, 1880, when it supported Hancock:

> Indeed, "Garfieldism" already means jobbery cloaked in pious hypocrisy and glittering eloquence, while "Hancockism" means gallantry in the hour of danger, magnanimity to a brave but crushed foe, and strict enforcement of the law in time of peace.[16]

With its Democratic sympathies for the laboring class, the *News* launched a campaign against the Republicans and the Chinese. The campaign was intensified in October, 1880, the month before elections. On October 20, the New York *Truth*, a Democratic newspaper, published the "Morey letter," which was purportedly written by Garfield. Dated January 23, 1880, and addressed to H. S. Morey of the Employer's Union of Lynn, Massachusetts, it read:

> I take it that the question of employers is only a question of private and corporate economy, and individuals or companies have the right to buy labor where they can get it cheapest.
>   We have a treaty with the Chinese government, which should be religiously kept until its provisions are abrogated by the actions of the general government, and I am not prepared to say that it should be abrogated until our great manufacturing interests are concerned in the matter of labor.[17]

The *News* took up the cry on October 21, when it printed the letter under a headline reading: "Political Death Warrant of the Radical Candidate."[18] The Republicans contended that the letter was a forgery; even Democratic newspapers

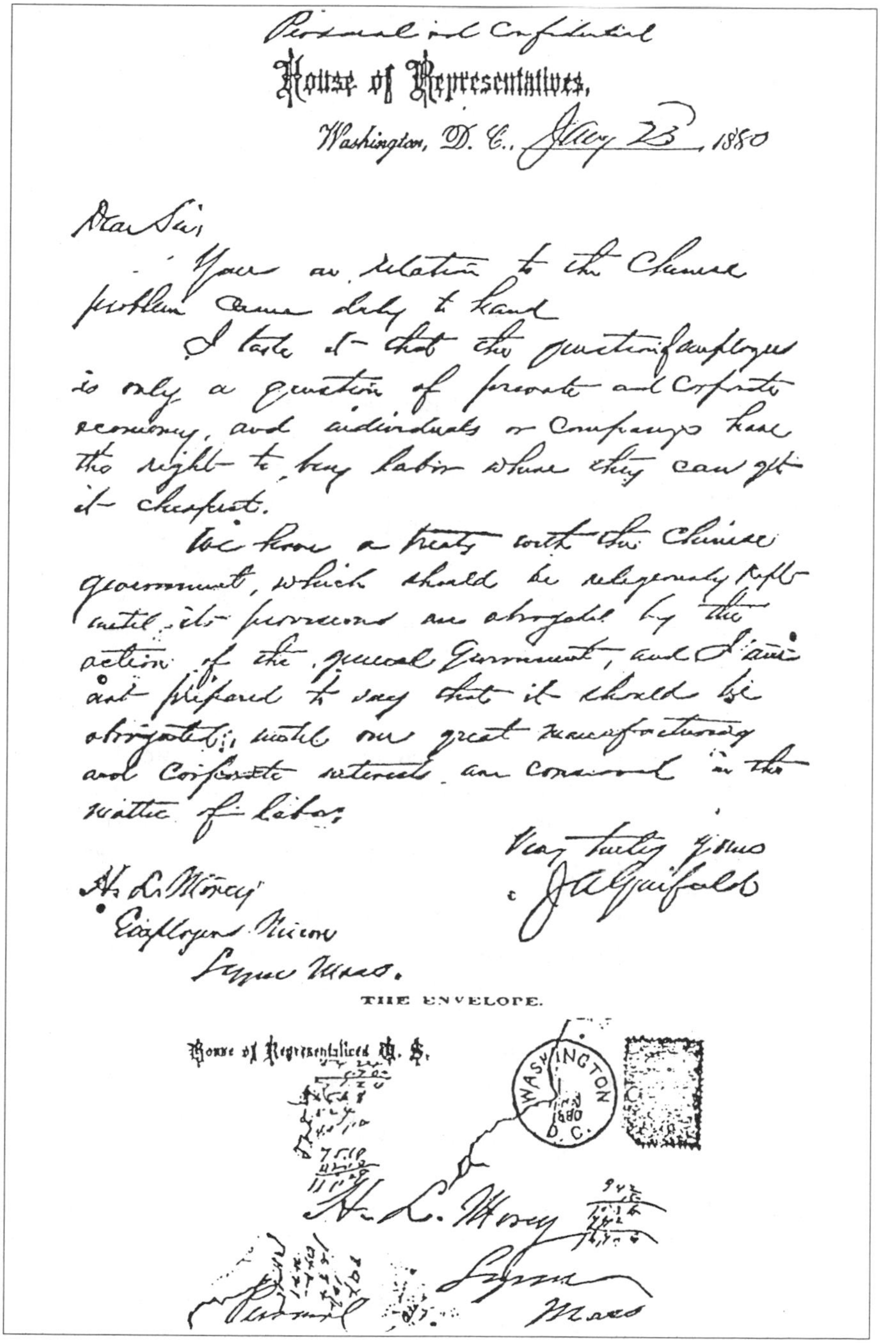

Figure 20.1   Garfield's famous cheap labor letter.

such as the *Philadelphia Times*, the *New York World*, and the *Chicago Times* denounced the letter as a fraud.[19] The *News*, however, stood firm, and used the Morey letter as a campaign issue. A rival newspaper, the *Denver Republican*, caustically commented that "in Siam the penalty for lying is to have the mouth sewed up. That would not work here since the Democrats got hold of that forged letter. There is not enough thread in this nation to go around."[20] Even the *News* would later report that the letter was a forgery, but this came after the elections.[21]

Invectives against Garfield and the Chinese increased as the election grew closer. The wiley heathen, the "Pest of the Pacific Coast," lamented the *News* on October 23, is invading the state, forcing men into starvation and women into prostitution. "California is already ruined through Chinese labor and Nevada is seriously injured, and now Colorado is threatened with the same disaster."[22] Opium smoking was attacked, because the dens on Arapahoe Street catered to Caucasian women as well as to Chinese. But the opium business was not a serious threat to white labor, the *News* said, because it "is only monopolized by a few Chinamen. It takes capital to run opium joints, and John is coming now in such large numbers that he has to occupy other fields of labor, which he does very successfully."[23] The issue of October 27, which attacked the opium dens, was also concerned with morality in other spheres. An anonymous person, signing himself as "For Hancock," thanked the *News* for exposing the dens. In his letter to the editor he continued his moralizing by stating that "Chinese harlots have diseased small boys of ten years of age and upwards, of some of the most respected citizens."[24]

Next day, on October 28, the *News* noted that the Chinese, instead of the tariff question, would be the chief campaign issue in Colorado.[25] The newspaper also hinted at violence: "There has been considerable talk about town the past few days about running out the Chinese. The flock is increasing every week, and they are not wanted."[26] Garfield was attacked because "he voted to 'conserve' the interests of the capitalists. He voted to starve our laboring men."[27] Facsimiles of the Morey letter were featured in the *News* issues of October 29, 30, and 31.

Colorado's Democratic party was charged with importing illegal voters to swell its ranks in the election on Tuesday, November 2.[28] Many of the alleged illegal voters marched in a Democratic parade in downtown Denver on Saturday evening, October 30, the night before the riot. Transparencies with anti-Chinese slogans were carried by various members of the parade, leading the *Denver Daily Times* to make a perceptive observation on nativism:

> The happiest man in the procession on Saturday night was an old, gray headed veteran who had seen a dozen presidential campaigns. The anti-Chinese transparencies, he said, reminded him of the know nothing days of a quarter of a century ago. True, he stated, the weather vane had shifted around a little; then it was anti-Paddy, it is now anti-Chinese and pagan, but as the latter had a smattering of native Americanism about it, he felt as though his younger days were coming back.[29]

The background for the riot was set. The anti-Chinese campaign issue, the inflammatory writings of the *Rocky Mountain News,* and the hostile feelings of the crowd in Saturday night's parade merely needed a spark. It came on Sunday afternoon, October 31.

Although there are several versions for the immediate cause of the riot,[30] possibly the most accurate is the statement of John Asmussén, in whose saloon at Wazee and Sixteenth Streets the riot started. According to Asmussén, a white man and two Chinese were playing pool, when three or four inebriated whites entered and quarreled with them.

> One of the Chinamen asked them to quit; the men then commenced abusing the Chinamen, and I remonstrated with them, and they said they were as good as Chinamen, and they came up to the bar and got some beer. While they were drinking I advised the Chinamen to go out of the house to prevent a row, and they went out at the back door. After a few minutes one of the white men went out at the back door and struck one of the Chinamen without any provocation. Another one of the crowd called to one of the gang inside to "come on Charley, he has got him," and he picked up a piece of board and struck at the Chinese. . . . This was the beginning of the riot.[31]

By two o'clock a crowd of approximately three thousand people gathered at the scene of the fight in Denver's Chinatown at Blake and Wazee Streets, between Sixteenth and Seventeenth Streets.[32] The milling mob, composed of the alleged illegal voters, Irishmen, and some Negroes,[33] called for the death of the Chinese and shouted: "Garfield's Chinaman," and "Hurrah for Hancock," "I have not seen," said the London *Times* correspondent, "so dastardly a set of rascals gathered together since the days when the Communards of Paris declared war against the persons who were both peaceable and respectable."[34]

In 1880 Denver's police department numbered between twenty-five and thirty men.[35] They were without competent leadership, for their chief had been removed because of dereliction of duty earlier in October.[36] According to Mayor Richard Sopris only eight men were on duty at the outbreak of the riot,[37] and they were unable to handle the crowd.

Early in the afternoon Mayor Sopris arrived on the scene with reel and hose carts from the Denver Fire Department. Before using the hoses, Sopris sought to pacify the crowd with a speech:

> *Gentlemen*—the people of this city do not desire mob violence. I do not think that the majority of you desire it. I see before me men who are apparently intelligent and honest gentlemen, and I know you cannot desire such a thing.[38]

His speech was jeered with cheers for Hancock. Some peaceful spectators urged the fire department to disperse the crowed with water. The crowd, angered by this, answered with yells of "wash the damn Chinamen out—drown the sons of b———s."[39] William Roberts, foreman of Hook Number Two and Hose Number Four, feared that the mob's anger would increase if the hoses were used. Roberts pleaded with Mayor Sopris, but the latter was adamant; the crowd would be hosed down. The Woodie Fishers, a Denver fire company, laid out a hundred and fifty feet of hose backed up with a one hundred pound hydrant pressure. Jets of water were directed at the mob, who retreated out of range. The mob's violence was intensified by the soaking; picking up bricks from a construction site, some of the mob—Civil War veterans, according to Roberts—began hurling them at the firemen. The mob halted momentarily when it saw that one of the firemen, Dick Brooks, was bleeding,[40] but the crowd was once again aroused when some-one cried: "Hurrah for Hancock."[41] The fire department was ineffective; the mob vented its fury on Chinatown and looted the saloons which were shut by order of Sopris.[42] At 4:30 P.M. J. F. Welborn of the Democratic State Central Committee attempted to pacify the mob.

> In behalf of the Democratic party . . . I beg you to disperse and go to your homes. This course is not calculated to serve the Democracy; it will—it may—injure the cause of Hancock. I beg of you to cease and go home.[43]

Welborn's speech subdued some of the mob's anger, but by dusk cries of "burn them out" were raised. The mob raided washhouses, looted Chinese homes, and injured many Chinese. When the rioters moved from Blake Street to Arapahoe they attempted to destroy a Chinese laundry patronized by Him Moon, a gam-bler. An anonymous London *Times* correspondent who witnessed the riot de-scribed the encounter between Moon and the mob.[44]

> Happily . . . some of the least reputable citizens distinguished themselves by showing a humane and courageous spirit. One of them, Jim Moon, is a gamester who recently had a fight with the police, and who bears a character which is not to be envied. I learn that he opposed single-handed a portion of the mob. . . . Facing the crowed, he demanded in very strong language[45] what they wanted. No response being made, he added, "This Chinaman is an inoffensive man, and you shant touch him, not a — — one of you." This speech being enforced by the mute elegance of a levelled revolver, the crowd turned abruptly away, being afraid, according to the slang phase common in this country, "to face the music."[46]

The rioters also had a skirmish with some of the city's prostitutes. At Seventeenth and Holladay Streets, Liz Preston, a madam of a local brothel, was protecting four cowering Chinese with a shotgun. According to fireman William Roberts, a force of "ten Amazonian beauties" armed with champagne bottles, stove pokers, and high-heeled shoes, backed up Miss Preston. The crowd finally retreated when Roberts—who was by this time in the riot made a deputy sheriff—and his men arrived. The four Chinese were placed for protection in the side parlor of Miss

Preston's brothel. By the end of the riot the madam and her colleagues had sheltered thirty-four Chinese. Recalling the role of the prostitutes on the riot, Roberts said: "That day the pariahs, the outcasts of society, the denizens of Holladay Street, the center of the red light district, put themselves in the hall of fame. . . . And perhaps the recording angel gave them one white mark."[47]

The recording angel might have approved of the actions of "the denizens of Holladay Street," but the actions of the rioters would have surely merited a different rating. By six o'clock the crowd had destroyed every washhouse in Chinatown. During the course of the riot Mayor Sopris notified the city councilmen of an emergency meeting; by six o'clock a sufficient number had arrived to approve his appointment of Dave Cook as acting police chief.[48] Cook appointed one hundred and twenty-five special policemen.[49] Coordinating the efforts of the special police and Sheriff Spangler's newly appointed deputies, Cook began to quell the riot. Although later sources[50] suggest that the National Guard was used in suppressing the mob, an examination of the Guard papers reveals that this was not the case.[51] Three of Denver's Guard units—two infantry companies and the Chaffee Light Artillery—voluntarily assembled at their armories in case they were needed.[52] Under arms, the Governor's Guard later moved into an alley near the riot where their presence (but not their participation) posed a threat to the rioters.[53] Cook felt that municipal and county forces could adequately handle the mob and did not, therefore, request National Guard aid.

Cook's police and Spangler's deputies were unable to act in time to save the life of Sing Lee, a laundryman. The mob attacked Sing at Nineteenth and Lawrence Streets. George Hickey, a printer, gave this account:

> I saw Sing Lee on his knees, and when he saw me he came and dropped down in front of me for protection, and I endeavored [*sic*] to shield him and prevent them from putting the rope around his neck. The crowd then commenced kicking him, and said I was a damned Chinaman, and they would hang me if I did not get away, and attempted to put the rope over my neck.[54]

Sing was dragged down Nineteenth Street by the mob. Dr. C. C. Bradbury saw Sing on the pavement. "Blood splattered all over my clothes as I knelt down beside him, placing my own body between him and the vengeful throng, and I received several severe blows."[55] When one of the crowd yelled: "God d———n you, I'll kill you if you don't clear out," Bradbury was forced to leave.[56] After the mob had finished with Sing at Nineteenth and Arapahoe he was taken to Dr. O. G. Cranston's office in the Moffat and Rassler Block. Medical efforts failed to save him; he died at 8:30 P.M. "from compression of the brain, caused by being beaten and kicked."[57]

After Sing's death the mob lost much of its momentum. Under pressure from the forces of Cook and Spangler the mob diminished in size at nine o'clock. At eleven o'clock General Cook made an inspection of the streets and reported that all was quiet. By midnight the immediate danger had passed.[58] By the time the riot had ended, between 134 and 400 Chinese were placed in the county jail for safekeeping.[59] On November 4, they were released to face the ruins. Every Chinese house, with perhaps one or two exceptions, had been destroyed. The *Rocky Mountain News* described the Chinese quarters as being "gutted as completely as though a cyclone had come in one door and passed . . . out the rear. There was nothing left . . . whole, and the rooms, so recently the abode of ignorance, vice, and shame, contained nothing beyond the horrid stench emitted by the little wads of opium."[60]

Of the rioters arrested, most were dismissed on the grounds of insufficient evidence.[61] In February, 1881, the alleged murderers of Sing Lee were tried and found not guilty.[62]

The police maintained patrols until election day, watching for a renewed outbreak of hostility. Speaking of Denver's law enforcement, the *Georgetown Courier* noted that "the policemen did their duty like men. They stood up manfully in their efforts for the preservation of peace, life, and property."[63] A coroner's jury investigation, however, did not believe that the law enforcement resources were adequate. After ten days of investigation a report was released stating that the mob

> could have been suppressed by the regular police force had they fearlessly arrested the ringleaders; but which owing to the disorganized condition of the police force of the city, and the incompetency and inefficiency of its government by the proper authority, and the failing of the county authorities to render the necessary aid . . . required in such emergencies, the mob assumed such portions [sic] as culminated in the destruction of human life and the disgrace of the city in not affording protection to life and property.[64]

A prominent citizen of Denver, M. M. Pomeroy, also felt that the riot could have been suppressed in its incipient stage. "Had there been a prompt meeting of the mob with lead instead of streams of water at two o'clock in the afternoon," said Pomeroy, "the riot would have died a-borning."[65]

On Monday, the day after the riot, the *Rocky Mountain News* maintained in a headline that "The Outrageous Throwing of Water Caused it All."[66] A few days later the *News* proclaimed that more was gained for the anti-opium crusade through mob rule than through all the words of preachers.[67] Showing no remorse at all, the *News* referred to "the alleged Denver riot"[68] and still retained its motto, "The Chinese must go."[69] Other Denver newspapers reacted in a different manner, using the riot to condemn the *News* and to gain Republican votes on Tuesday. The *Denver Daily Times* commented: "The *News* charges the riot of Sunday upon the Firemen as a result of throwing water upon the mob, from which we suppose that the *News* wishes to be understood as asserting that cold water will effect an average Democratic crowd as a red flag will a bull."[70] The *Denver Republican* also blamed the *News* for the riot and stated:

> Till last Sunday we thought the Democratic party possessed of a liberal spark of human sympathy. The Chinamen of Denver never violated any law. John Brown was hung for violating the laws of Virginia. John Hus, and Wickcliffe [sic] and George Washington broke the laws of their time, and we raise them as heroes because they

broke bad laws. . . But these poor creatures who were murdered by Denver Democrats had faithfully kept every law. Their only offense was that they . . . washed the linen of their white oppressors better and cheaper. . . . The blue-eyed, light haired men who murdered these Chinamen were serfs and slaves for centuries and waited till Christianity and humanity broke their fetters.[71]

In an address to Denver Republicans, Judge J. B. Belford capitalized on the riot and used it as an election issue. The rioters, he said, could merely be added on to a long list of Democratic mobs—the whisky rebels of Pennsylvania, the South Carolina nullifiers, and the Confederate States of America.[72] Reaction to the riot also came from Denver's churches. The Congregational Association entered an "earnest protest against the unreasoning prejudice cherished by some portion of our citizens,"[73] while the Rev. Dr. Westwood of the Central Presbyterian Church pleaded that Christians should stand up for the Chinese.[74] Denver feminists could not resist combining the temperance crusade with their gentle chastisement. In their paper, "Devoted to the Interests of Humanity, Woman's Political Equality, and Individuality," they remarked:

As regards the mob violence of our own lovely city . . . let us not believe that our Democratic editors anticipated the wicked outcome of their inciting editorials. If the consequences could have been foreseen, these gentlemen would have drawn milder similes and not have exasperated the ever reckless Irishman with the fermenting sour mash which he is so prone to carry in his manly bosom.[75]

Newspapers in other parts of the state were also critical of the riot. The Colorado Springs *Weekly Gazette* blamed the riot on the Democratic procession with its "transparencies covered with the communistic utterances of the News."[76] The *Leadville Daily Herald* contended that "the worst of Chinese are angels of light" when compared to the rioters,[77] while the Central City *Daily Register-Call* succinctly expressed its opinion in five words: "The democratic party should die."[78] *The Express,* Fort Collins' Republican newspaper, angrily commented that only "the party that hung negroes to lamp posts and burned colored orphans in New York would torture . . . Chinamen in Denver."[79] On the other hand the *Fort Collins Courier,* a Democratic newspaper, blamed the riot on misgovernment in Denver and audaciously stated that "the democracy of Colorado has reason to be proud of the Rocky Mountain News, and the Leadville Democrat, its two leading organs. Neither has contained a particle of filth during the whole campaign."[80]

Eastern newspapers expressed their indignation. The *New York Times* referred to the incident as a "disgraceful riot."[81] Connecticut's *Hartford Courant* blamed the riot on the publication of the Morey letter and editorialized: "Can any decent, respectable citizen give his aid to a cause which depends on such methods for success?"[82] On the West coast the *San Francisco Chronicle,* a Republican and violent anti-Chinese newspaper, sanctimoniously headlined the telegraphic dispatch of the riot: "The Democratic Forgery Bears Bloody Fruit."[83] The San Francisco *Daily*

Alta California considered the Democratic party as an unholy alliance of rebels who hated national authority, enemies of New York's public schools, Communists, stubborn hereditary Democrats, and demagogues.[84] The paper capitalized on Denver's riot by stating: "If San Francisco wants security against such a demonstration which . . . might be a thousandfold more disastrous than in Denver, she should elect a Republican majority."[85] Of all the comments made on the riot the most appropriate one came from a Chinese lecturer in Chicago, Wong Chin Foo. He declared that "if a single American was treated in China as were the victims of the anti-Chinese riots at Denver, the United States would send 100,000 missionaries to civilize the heathen."[86]

The riot also had diplomatic ramifications. Although the *Rocky Mountain News* estimated "the damage done through the negligence of republican officials: at not over a thousand dollars,[87] Denver attorney E. B. Sleeth had on file one hundred and fifty claims totalling $30,000.[88] Consul F. A. Bee, after investigating the riot, estimated Chinese losses at $53,655.69.[89] Although at least one historian has concluded that the matter of indemnities was settled, an examination of the diplomatic correspondence between the Chinese legation at Washington and Secretaries of State William Evarts and James G. Blaine reveals that the United States refused to pay for losses sustained by Denver's Chinese.[90] On March 25, 1881, Blaine replied to the Chinese legation's inquiry on indemnities. By quoting his predecessor Evarts, Blaine gave the United States government's final point of view on indemnities:

> Under circumstances of this nature, when the government has put forth every legitimate effort to suppress a mob that threatens or attacks alike the safety and security of its own citizens and the foreign residents within its borders, *I know of no principle of national obligation, and there certainly is none arising from treaty stipulation, which renders it incumbent on the Government of the United States to make indemnity to the Chinese residents of Denver, who, in common with citizens of the United States at that time resident in that city, suffered loses from the operations of the mob.* Whatever remedies may be afforded to the citizens of Colorado, or to the citizens of the United States from the other States of the Union resident in Colorado, for losses resulting from that occurrence [*sic*], are equally open to the Chinese residents of Denver who may have suffered from the lawlessness of that mob. This is all that the principles of international law and the usages of national comity demand.[91]

In conclusion it is suggested that the campaign of 1880 and the *Rocky Mountain News*'s stand on the Chinese question magnified a xenophobia which already existed in Colorado because of the issue of cheap Chinese labor. The anti-Chinese articles in the October issues of the *News*, the Democratic procession the evening before the riot, and the hostility of the laboring class exploded on Sunday, October 31. Denver's police department was unable to handle the mob, and although Cook and Spangler eventually dispersed the rioters, their efforts came too late in the day to protect Chinese life and property. Of Denver's riot, the correspondent of the London *Times* rightly said: "With the scenes which I witnessed yesterday still vivid before my eyes, I cannot help thinking how bitter a sarcasm does the conduct of the riotous citizens of Denver pass upon the immortal Declaration of Independence."[92] The riot ended; anti-Chinese hostility did not. In his 1881 inauguration speech Governor Pitkin deplored the riot but nevertheless feared that the Chinese posed a threat to the American laborer and his family.[93] Arguing for the Chinese Exclusion Act of 1882, the speech of Senator Henry M. Teller, Republican from Colorado, was a classical example of Social Darwinism.[94] Congress voted for the act, but this did not placate nativist sentiment in Colorado. Sporadic actions against the Chinese continued, and as late as 1898 Chinese were not allowed to settle in Leadville.[95] Given the situation of the Chinese in the United States, it was with reason that Mark Twain noted that

> a Chinaman had no rights that any man was bound to respect; that he had no sorrows that any man was bound to pity, that neither his life nor his liberty was worth the purchase of a penny when a white man needed a scapegoat; that . . . nobody befriended them, nobody spared them suffering when it was convenient to inflict it; everybody, individuals, communities, the majesty of the State itself, joined in hating, abusing, and persecuting these humble strangers.[96]

NOTES

1. S. W. Kung, *Chinese in American Life: Some Aspects of Their History, Status, Problems, and Contributions* (Seattle: University of Washington Press, 1962), p. 75.

2. *Colorado Tribune* (Denver), June 29, 1869, p. 5, typewritten copy in the library of the State Historical Society of Colorado, hereinafter cited as SHSC.

3. Patricia Ourada, "The Chinese in Colorado," *The Colorado Magazine*, XXIX (October, 1952), 276. For an excellent account of the state's Chinese, see Gerald E. Rudolph, "The Chinese in Colorado, 1869–1911" (unpublished Master's thesis, University of Denver, 1964). Rudolph's chapter on the anti-Chinese riot is based mainly on two sources: the *Rocky Mountain News* (Denver), and U.S. Congress, House of Representatives, *Foreign Relations, 1881–82*, 47th Cong., 1st Sess., 1882.

4. Colorado Territory, Legislative Assembly, House, *Joint Resolution for the Encouragement of Chinese Immigration into Colorado Territory*, 8th Sess., 1870, p. 134.

5. *Daily Register* (Central City), October 30, 1870, p. 4; Ourada, *The Colorado Magazine*, XXIX (1952), 275.

6. Ourada, *The Colorado Magazine*, XXIX (1952), 277.

7. Lawrence H. Battistini, *The Rise of American Influence in Asia and the Pacific* (East Lansing: Michigan State University Press, 1960), p. 105.

8. *Rocky Mountain News*, April 19, 1871, p. 1.

9. Ourada, *The Colorado Magazine*, XXIX (1952), 278–79.

10. *Denver Tribune*, May 8, 1879, typewritten copy in SHSC.

11. Unidentified clipping dated 1880. Dawson Scrapbook, XXIX, 147, in SHSC.

12. U.S. Bureau of the Census, *Tenth Census of the United States: 1880. Population*, I, 379.

13. *Ibid.*, p. 416.

14. F. A. Bee, December 8, 1880, to Consul-General Chen Shu Tang, San Francisco, *Foreign Relations, 1881–82*, p. 323.

15. Rezin H. Constant, "Colorado as Seen by a Visitor of 1880," *The Colorado Magazine*, XII (May, 1935), 107. A correspondent who witnessed the riot estimated that there were 200 Chinese laundrymen in Denver. *The Times* (London), November. 19, 1880, p.3.

16. *Rocky Mountain News*, August 11, 1880, p. 4.

17. *Ibid.*, October 21, 1880, p. 1.

18. *Ibid.*

19. *Daily Register Call* (Central City) November 1, 1880, p. 2.

20. *Denver Republican*, November 1, 1880, p. 2.

21. *Rocky Mountain News*, January 6, 1881, p. 6.

22. *Ibid.*, October 23, 1880, p. 8.

23. *Ibid.*, October 27, 1880, p. 5.

24. *Ibid.*, p. 2.

25. *Ibid.*, October 28, 1880, p. 6.

26. *Ibid.*, p. 3.

27. *Ibid.*, p. 6.

28. *Denver Daily Times*, November 1, 1880, p. 2, and November 2, 1880, p. 2; *Denver Republican, November 1, 1880*, p. 3; *Denver Tribune*, November 1, 1880, p. 1. The *Daily Alta California* (San Francisco), November 1, 1880, p. 1, estimated that 8,000 people were illegally registered in Denver.

29. *Denver Daily Times*, November 1, 1880, p. 2.

30. Battistini, *Rise of American Influence in Asia*, p. 105; Robert Perkin, *The First Hundred Years: An Informal History of Denver and the Rocky Mountain News* (New York: Doubleday & Co., 1959), p. 353; Jerome C. Smiley, *History of Denver, With Outlines of the Earlier History of the Rocky Mountain West* (Denver: Times-Sun Publ. Co., 1901), pp. 471–72; and William Roberts, "The Chinese Riot, October 31st, 1880," p. 1, unpublished MS in the Denver Veteran Volunteer Firemen's Association Papers, No. 5 in Western History Department, Denver Public Library. Hereinafter cited as Roberts MS.

31. *Foreign Relations, 1881–82*, pp. 332–33.

32. Mayor Sopris' estimate to the city council, *Rocky Mountain News*, November 10, 1880, p. 8.

33. *The Colorado Antelope* (Denver), December, 1880, p. 4; *Denver Republican*, November 1, 1880, p. 4; *The Times* (London), November 19, 1880, p. 3; *Rocky Mountain News*, November 1, 1880, p. 8.

34. *The Times* (London), November 19, 1880, p. 3.

35. Smiley, *History of Denver*, p. 472.

36. See the *Rocky Mountain News*, November 19, 1880, p. 3, for an account of the problems of the police department.

37. *Denver Daily Times*, November 10, 1880, p. 2.

38. *Denver Tribune*, November 1, 1880, p. 1.

39. *Ibid.*

40. Roberts MS, pp. 4–5.

41. *Denver Tribune*, November 1, 1880, p. 1.

42. Roberts MS, p. 6.

43. *Denver Tribune*, November 1, 1880, p. 1.

44. Because the "strict rule of anonymity, we are unable to reveal . . . who wrote the dispatch in which you are interested." Letter from W. R. A. Easthope, editor of the London *Times* Archives, March 29, 1965.

45. Moon's "very strong language," not described by the *Times* correspondent, was: "What in hell do you fellows want?" *Denver Tribune*, November 1, 1880, p. 1.

46. *The Times* (London), November 19, 1880, p. 3. Moon was killed by Clay Wilson in Denver, June 17, 1881. The *Ouray Times* apparently neglected to remember Moon's service to the Chinese when it stated that "Wilson has done the city of Denver a great favor by putting this desperate man out of the way." *Ouray Times*, June 18, 1881, p. 1.

47. Roberts MS, p. 11.

48. *Denver Daily Times*, November 1, 1880, p. 2.

49. *Rocky Mountain News*, November 10, 1880, p. 8.

50. See for example, Forbes Parkhill, *The Wildest of the West* (New York: Henry Holt & Co., 1951), p. 112. Ourada, *The Colorado Magazine*, XXIX (1952), 293, states that the National Guard was sent to the riot.

51. An examination of the *Biennial Report of the Adjutant General* [1880], of the *General Orders, 1879–1883*, and of the *Records of the Office of Governor Frederick W. Pitkin, 1879–1883: Executive Orders*, in the Colorado State Archives. Denver, revealed that the National Guard was not officially called up for riot duty by state authority. Denver newspapers the day after the riot made no mention of National Guard participation in quelling the mob. John Nankivell, *History of the Military Organization of the State of Colorado, 1860–1935* (Denver: W. H. Whistler Co., 1935), and [Eugene K. Stimson] *Chaffee Light Artillery, First Brigade, C.N.G.* (Denver: Press of Carson, Hurst, & Harper [1892] do not mention Guard participation in suppressing the mob.

52. *Denver Republican*, November 1, 1880, p. 4.

53. Testimony of M. M. Pomeroy, *Foreign Relations, 1881–82*, p. 334.

54. Testimony of George Hickey, *ibid.*, p. 330.

55. *Rocky Mountain News*, February 17, 1881, p. 8.

56. *Ibid.*

57. Coroner's report in *Denver Daily Times*, November 16, 1880, p. 4; also in *Foreign Relations, 1881–82*, p. 326.

58. *Denver Daily Times*, November 1, 1880, p. 2.

59. Figures for the number of Chinese jailed for protection vary with the source: *Denver Daily Times*, November 1, 1880, p. 2–134 jailed: *Georgetown Courier*, November 4, 1880, p. 2–145 jailed; *Denver Tribune*, November 1, 1880. p. 1–158 jailed; *Rocky Mountain News*, November 1, 1880, p. 4–185; *Denver Republican*, November 1, 1880, p. 4–225 Chinese jailed, including 11 women and one boy; *Colorado Miner* (Georgetown), November 6, 1880, p. 3—"upwards of 300"; F. A. Bee to Chen Shu Tang, December 8, 1880, *Foreign Relations, 1881–82*, p. 324, estimated the number at over 400.

60. *Rocky Mountain News*, November 1, 1880, p. 8.

61. *Ibid.*, November 12, 1880, p. 2.

62. *Ibid.*, February 19, 1881, p. 5. The actual transcript of the trial is not available.

63. *Georgetown Courier*, November 4, 1880, p. 2.

64. *Denver Daily Times*, November 16, 1880, p. 4; *Foreign Relations, 1881–82*, p. 326.

65. Testimony of M. M. Pomeroy, *Foreign Relations, 1881–82*, p. 334.

66. *Rocky Mountain News*, November 1, 1880, p. 4.

67. *Ibid.*, November 5, 1880, p. 4.

68. *Ibid.*, November 11, 1880, p. 4.

69. *Ibid.*, December 12, 1880, p. 4.

70. *Denver Daily Times*, November 2, 1880, p. 2.

71. *Denver Republican*, November 2, 1880, p. 2.

72. *Leadville Daily Herald*, November 2, 1880, p. 1.

73. *Denver Tribune*, November 7, 1880, p. 8.

74. *Denver Republican*, November 2, 1880, p. 4.

75. *The Colorado Antelope* (Denver), December, 1880, p. 4.

76. *Weekly Gazette* (Colorado Springs), quoted in *Denver Daily Times*, November 6, 1880, p. 3.

77. *Leadville Daily Herald*, November 2, 1880, p. 2.

78. *Daily Register-Call* (Central City), November 4, 1880, p. 2.

79. *The Express* (Fort Collins), November 4, 1880, p. 2.

80. *Fort Collins Courier*, November 4, 1880, p. 5.

81. *New York Times*, November 1, 1880, p. 5.

82. *Hartford Courant*, November 1, 1880, p. 2.

83. *San Francisco Chronicle*, November 1, 1880, p. 3.

84. *Daily Alta California* (San Francisco), October 31, 1880, p. 2.

85. *Ibid.*, November 2, 1880, p. 2.

86. *Denver Daily Times*, December 13, 1880, p. 2.

87. *Rocky Mountain News*, November 2, 1880, p. 2.

88. *Denver Daily Times*, November 30, 1880, p. 4.

89. *Foreign Relations, 1881–82*, p. 325.

90. Ourada, *The Colorado Magazine*, XXIX (1952), p. 283, states: "With the passing of the international negotiations and the final payment of the indemnity by Denver, the Chinese, instead of being terrified into leaving the city, began to rebuild Hop Alley [Chinatown]." The author based her conclusion on a *Denver Tribune* article of November 30, 1880. The *Tribune's* Issue of November 30 is not included in the bound *Tribune* collection in the SHSC. A typewritten copy of a *Tribune* article dated November 30, 1880, in a reference file, SHSC, deals with Consul Bee's visit to Denver and mentions attempts made to secure indemnity for the Chinese, but makes no mention of a "final payment." The *Denver Daily Times*, November 30, 1880, p. 4, states that claims were still in the process of adjudication. Payment could not have been final because the *Denver Daily Times* for November 30 reports that the claims were being forwarded to Washington for settlement. Furthermore, the *Denver Daily Times*, December 2, 1880, p. 4, states that Consul Bee returned to San Francisco with 121 claims totalling $43,000 against Denver. The claims were still in the process of being examined. In view of this, as well as the diplomatic correspondence between the Chinese Legation and Secretaries of State Evaris and Blaine, Ourada's statement about "final payments" is probably in error.

91. Blaine to Chen Lau Pin, Washington, February 25, 1881, *Foreign Relations, 1881–82*, p. 335. Emphasis added.

92. *The Times* (London), November 19, 1880, p. 3.

93. The complete text of Pitkin's inaugural address may be found in the *Denver Tribune*, January 12, 1881, p. 8.

94. U.S., *Congressional Record*, 47th Cong., 1st Sess, 1882, XIII, Part 2, 1645–46.

95. *Denver Times*, January 9, 1902, p. 1.

96. Mark Twain, "Disgraceful Persecution of a Boy," Janet Smith (ed.), *Mark Twain on the Damned Human Race* (New York: Hill & Wang, 1962), p. 80.

21

A Chinese Romance: A Story of Canton, San Francisco, and Denver

Daily Denver Tribune

Escape of the Hok-Yop Girls, and Their Marriage with Two of the Sing-Ye Boys. Arrest, Trial and Acquittal of one of the Brides.

Two years and five months ago,—according to the interpreted statements of Ah Fee, the Hok Yop company's agent in Denver, and the two girls themselves,—one So Frane, a worthless loafer in Canton, and to the Hop Yop Tea and Coffee Importing Company of San Francisco, two orphan girls, names respectively Miss Ging Yow and her sister, Miss King Yok. The Hok Yop Company were to pay the expenses of these two girls to Denver, Colorado, in consideration that they become inmates of Ah Fee's and his brother, Wah Kee's house of prostitution on Wazee Street, Denver, Here the girls were to remain as slaves for two years, to work out their passage money, which was charged against them at $80. King Uok and Ging Yow, both of them small and rather good looking Chinese girls, at the end of their loathsome term of slavery demanded their freedom. Ah Fee not only refused to let them leave his vile den, but on their persistent application to be let go.

Tied a cat to the girls' leg, and beat the girl about the room, causing the cat to scratch and bite the girls' legs in a manner fearful to behold. Somewhat more than a month a go, two of the Sam Sing Company's men,—an opposition establishment of the Hok Yop Company, of which Ah Fee is the Denver agent,—commenced to pay frequent visits to Ah Fee's gambling house and bagnio. One of these pig-tailed lovers was named Loo Quong, the other Fong Lea. They had known and loved Miss King Yok and Miss Ging Yow when boys and girls together, in the streets of Canton. The old love again re-kindled, and a double wedding agreed upon. But the Yok Yop men were too vigilans for the two Sam Sing lovers, and drove them away. The Sam Sing men sent word if the girls were not permitted to leave, they would burn down the house. This threat was put into execution about two weeks ago, and

A Chinese cremation took place on Wazee street, and Ah Fee lost two houses. But this only made Ah Fee more stubborn. He watched his fifteen female slaves with redoubted vigilance, while the Sam Sing men watched their opportunity. They sent to Fairplay for one Sam Lee-Moking, a chinaman who speaks English well, and who by nine years experience in an American family in San Francisco has acquired an insight into American manners. The lovers of Sam Lee held a council of war, and this is what resulted therefrom: A Chinese marriage under difficulties.

A license was first obtained for the marriage of Mr. Loo Quong to Miss Ging Yow, both of Canton, and Mr. Fong Len to Miss King Yok, of the same place. The police were notified to be on hand. A reporter for THE TRIBUNE was sent for. Judge Sayer was prepared and City Attorney Patterson appeared as sponsor for the blushing brides. About seven o'clock in the morning, while the unsuspecting Ah Fee was gone to the post office, Loo Quong and Fong Len, drove suddenly up before Ah Fee's front door in a carriage. The expedient brides were on the alert and unlocked the doors and rushed forth to their lovers, who held out their arms to receive them in the carriage.

SHADES OF CONFUCIUS!

This sudden attack of the Sam King men upon the Hok Yop stronghold of Ah Fee, was a complete surprise. The alarm was given and a sortie was made in force by at least twenty yelling and shrieking Chinese men and women, to prevent the escape of the girls, who in their terror, turned complete somersaults over the carriage doors landing flat upon their backs in the arms of their tallow faced shaved headed lovers. The carriage drove off amid a perfect babel of confusion, and closely pursued by the discomforted Hok Yop tribe.

The wedding was nothing very remarkable. The court room was densely crowded. The Sam Sing men rallied in force to protect the escaped damsels and their husbands from the infuriated Hok Yop men. Lee Moking interpreted the ceremony in Chinese to the two happy pairs, and in a few minutes the two abducted Canton girls were free from Ah Fee's slavery. Judge Sayer very generously declined to enact his legal perquisites of the first kisses upon the brides; both of whom stood patiently waiting and blushing with red banana handkerchiefs to their faces. Under the escort of City Attorney Patterson, their authorized attorney they returned to their carriage and were driven home, but not before they had all been to a photograph gallery and had their pictures taken—to guard against kidnapping it is said.

THE BRIDE ARRESTED

Ah Fee on his return from the post office was astonished to find his two hand-somest girls (for whom he claims to have paid $1,600) gone, taken away by the hated Sam Sing clan. He rushed out at once and swore out a warrant, charging Ging Yow, the oldest of the sisters, with a theft of $400, and shortly afterwards the happy bride became a weeping prisoner in the county jail. The same afternoon the examination came off before Judge Walker, at which the Hok Yops and the Sam Songs rallied in force, and feeling ran very high. Justice Whittier opened a counsel for Ah Fee, and Wah Kee as interpreter. City Attorney Patterson appeared for Ging Yow, and Lee Moking as interpreter.

The prosecution failed to sustain the charges made of the larceny of $400, and the bridal party went home free, but far from happy. The Hop Yop clan, to the number of at least twenty, skirmished on their flank, and threatened the worst kind of Chinese vengences. This so alarmed the bridal party that a detachment of police were called upon to protect them.

The end of this romance is not yet. The newly married quartette start for Fairplay tomorrow to join a party of forty Sam Sing Chinamen, who are at work in the mines. Meantime, Ah Fee, who publishes a card in another column, has telegraphed to the powerful Hop Yops Company for assistance and support to a fight against the Sam Sing men, who threaten to rob him of all his slaves in marrying them. There will be some Celestial blood spilled here before long, as the Sam Sing men threaten to marry all of the Hok Yop women.

22

Chinese Emigrants in Southwest Wyoming, 1868–1885

A. Dudley Gardner

The central focus of articles and books written about Chinese history in Wyoming has been the Chinese Massacre that took place on September 2, 1885. As a result of this tragedy, twenty-eight Chinese died in Rock Springs, and most of the north side of town was burned to the ground. This tragedy was preceded by seventeen years of Chinese immigration into Wyoming Territory. However, it has been the Chinese Massacre, not the emigration, that has most often been discussed and written about by historians.[1] Asians rarely receive recognition as important players in the development of Wyoming.

The fact that Asian history in Wyoming receives little attention is not due to a conscious policy by historians to avoid ethnic groups from the Pacific Rim, but is more the result of not being able to find readily primary source material about Chinese emigrants in Wyoming. Currently, the amount of available primary materials is increasing and a broad view of the Chinese role in Wyoming is beginning to merge. It is now possible to discuss briefly the Chinese contribution to Wyoming during the territorial period. Here we will briefly review the role the Chinese played in Wyoming prior to 1885.

In the years between 1868 and 1886, the Chinese contributed much to the development of southern Wyoming. They were also the victims of racial prejudice. While contributing to the growth of the territory, the Chinese were viewed as a problem. Prejudice was a fact rarely hidden or apologized for in the territorial newspapers.

The first newspaper to print "anti-Chinese" articles was the *Frontier Index*. In 1868, Legh Freeman, the editor of the *Frontier Index*, called his newspaper an anti-Black, anti-Indian, and anti-Chinese newspaper. Freeman headed his editorial column with the words, "The Motto of this Column: Only White Men to be naturalized in the United States. The RACES and SEXES in their respective spheres as God Almighty created them."[2] The Cheyenne newspapers were no kinder to emigrants. By the late 1870s, when anti-Chinese sentiment was at a fevered pitch throughout the West, the *Cheyenne Daily Leader* led off one of their stories by saying ". . . We are being ruined by Chinese thieving."[3] Throughout the West, there was widespread prejudice aimed at Chinese emigrants. For example, in 1866, the *Montana Radiator* reported that the "Mongolian hordes" were preventing "Helena women from making a living washing clothes."[4] People in Wyoming Territory viewed the Chinese much like other "Westerners" and perceived them as a threat to their jobs and economic well-being.

In Wyoming the first Chinese emigrated to become railroad workers. The 1870 United States census records show that in southwest Wyoming, specifically Uinta and Sweetwater counties, all the Chinese listed were employed as laborers at either railroad stations or section camps. At the time, both Uinta and Sweetwater counties ran from the Utah and Colorado borders to the Montana border. Within these two counties, there were ninety-six Chinese "laborers." No other occupation is listed nor were there any Chinese females living in these two counties.[5] As laborers in railroad camps, the Chinese all worked for the Union Pacific Railroad.

The Union Pacific Railroad initially recruited Chinese laborers to work on their mainline. After 1874, when labor unrest developed in their coal mines, Union Pacific Railroad also began hiring Chinese workers to extract coal at their various mines throughout southern Wyoming. Employing Chinese miners or railroad workers was a matter of both convenience and economics. In 1870, Union Pacific's auditor, J. W. Gannet, wrote to Oliver Ames, the president of Union Pacific, that "The difference between Irish and Chinese as to expense appears small. Utah having as many Chinese on a 5 miles section as Platte [division] has of Irish on a 6 mile section. This, however, may be unnecessary as I am told that an irishman performs no more labor than a Chinese. . . ."[6] Grenville M. Dodge, after the completion of the Transcontinental Railroad in 1869, planned to discharge the "Irishmen" and replace them with Chinese workers, "a move he thought would cut labor costs in half."[7]

Employing Chinese railroad workers was a profitable venture for Union Pacific. At remote section camps, such as Red Desert in Sweetwater County, the majority of the residents were Chinese. In 1870 there were twenty inhabitants at Red Desert. Of this number, twelve were Chinese. Of course, the Chinese at Red Desert were all laborers. The section foreman at the camp was an American.[8] Red Desert's counterpart, located to the east, was called Washakie. At Washakie there were twenty-three residents. The section foreman was an American and the crew foreman was Irish, but the thirteen laborers were all Chinese.[9]

In the various section camps along the Union Pacific mainline in southwest Wyoming, Chinese workers outnumbered all other nationalities. In 1870 Sweetwater County had seventy-nine Chinese residents. This figure represents roughly 4 percent of the county's entire population. However, this population was concentrated into isolated areas with no Chinese residents reported at Green River or Rock Springs, the largest towns along the Union Pacific mainline in Sweetwater County.[10]

Throughout the decade of the 1870s the number of Chinese living in southwestern Wyoming steadily increased. What is more important is that while the population increased, so did the diversity. At Rock Springs, where most of the Chinese residents of Sweetwater County lived in 1880, there were Chinese miners, laborers, and cooks, along with a barber, gambler, and a priest. The fact that Rock Springs had a resident priest is of some interest, as he is seemingly the only one in the territory and possibly served a wider community.[11] The person employed as a professional gambler probably helped provide recreation for more than just the Chinese residents of Rock Springs.

Throughout Sweetwater County in 1880, the majority of the Chinese residents either worked on the railroad or in the coal mines, but some were also involved in a variety of occupations. At Green River, there was a Chinese doctor. At Miners Delight, Atlantic City, and Red Canyon, Chinese gold miners were employed. At Fort Washakie and Green River there were Chinese servants and waiters. A number of places had Chinese wash houses. A few communities also had Chinese cooks. However, throughout Sweetwater County there were only thirteen cooks and two wash house attendants employed. The majority of the 193 Chinese residents living in Sweetwater County in 1880 were either working in the mines or for the railroad.[12]

Both Rock Springs and Green River had Chinese women living in their towns in 1880. Although small in number, all of the female residents were employed outside the home. In Green River two women worked as servants, whereas the only woman in Rock Springs was a cook.[13] While the female population was a relatively small proportion of the total Chinese population, it is significant because folklore surrounding the Chinese Massacre often puts forth the idea that there were no Chinese women living in Rock Springs in the years prior to 1885. Overall, there were only three Chinese females in Sweetwater County and the Chinese emigrants only represent 7.5 percent of the county's entire population. Yet what is worth noting is the fact that this small percentage of the population was concentrated in areas where their numbers were extremely visible. In Rock Springs, for example, the Chinese represented 16 percent of the town's population. At railroad camps, such as Washakie Station, they represented 58 percent of the 1880 population.[14]

As the number of Chinese living in Wyoming began to increase, the states' newspapers devoted more and more time discussing whether Asians should be allowed into the United States. The newspapers also published articles describing the day to day activities of Chinese in Wyoming. While most newspapers published the recurring theme "the Chinese must GO," they provided information about the Chinese living in Wyoming. (In the newspapers of the nineteenth century, emphasis was always given on the verb go, and it was often capitalized in the newspaper print).

In 1882, "a newly appointed attache to the Chinese embassy at Washington [D.C.]" visited Wyoming. Chang Tsung Liang took the opportunity to criticize the press for not portraying the Chinese in a favorable light. He accused the newspapers of creating the nationwide anti-Chinese sentiment that existed at the time. Chang also reported about conditions he had encountered in Wyoming. The attache, according to the *Cheyenne Daily Leader,*

> [E]xpressed his pleasure at the prosperous appearance of Cheyenne as compared with other towns he had passed along the route, inquired after his countrymen here and if they were "comfortable" and mentioned, evidently with hurt feelings, the very rude manner in which some loafers had behaved at Rock Springs as he passed through there, in calling him "bad names" "not like gentlemen and very rude."[15]

In another article, the *Leader* interviewed a Chinese merchant, who was passing through Cheyenne on business. The merchant, named Ah Lun, was a prosperous businessman. Often even the positive articles about Chinese immigrants were written somewhat "tongue in cheek," but these articles at least provided a different viewpoint. For example, the Chinese merchant Ah Lun, was described as follows:

> This celestial gentleman speaks good English and is quite social, freely imparting the course of his journey in a business, offhand way, and taking part in general conversation. He was attired in the conventional Chinese garments, but of very fine material, largely black silk and satin. Someone wondered (audibly) how he could keep his white stockings so clean, and a German friend suggested that he "put on a clean pair efry day aind dat so?" And Ah smiled assent.[16]

Chinese merchants and attaches, while both holding respected positions, were not shown the respect extended to Americans or Europeans who held the same positions.

Throughout the West the Chinese were viewed as second class citizens. Companies in Wyoming Territory, like those in neighboring territories, often viewed the Chinese as if they were property or chattel, rather than employees. A contract dated December 24, 1875, between "Beckwith, Quinn, & Co. and Union Pacific Railroad Co.," illustrates the fact that Beckwith and Quinn, not the Chinese miner or railroad workers, decided the conditions under which they were to be employed. The contract for "Chinese labor and etc. Sale of Supplies, Rent of Warehouse Rock S." reads as follows:

> *Agreement* made and entered into, this 24th day of December A.D. 1875, between *Beckwith, Quinn & Co.,* of Evanston Wyoming Territory of the first part, and the *Union Pacific Railroad Co., of the second part, — Witnesseth:*
> *The parties of the first part,* hereby agree to furnish to the party of the Second part, all the Chinese laborers requisite for the complete working of their several coal mines on the line of the Union Pacific Railroad, at the same prices and on the same terms and conditions as stated in a certain Contract for similar service made by Sisson Wallace & Co., for and in behalf of Chinese laborers, with the Rocky Mountain Coal & Mining Co., a copy of which is hereto attached, and made a part of this agreement.

The said parties of the first part further agree to furnish to the said party of the Second part, upon a reasonable notice from their Gen'l. Superintendent, a sufficient number of Chinese laborers for the repairs of the track of the Union Pacific Railroad, or such portion thereof, in addition to that which is now being worked by Chinamen, as the party of the Second part may require. . . .[17]

The attached service contract stated:

Chinamen agree to mine the coal, load it in Pit cars, and deliver it at the mouth of the room free from slack and rock, and assorted, either lump, small or mixed as directed, at Seventy four (74) cents con per ton of Twenty Two Hundred and Forty (2240) pounds, from all places, either rooms, levels or air courses.

All cars or coal sent out of the mine in which there is slack or rock, will be docked half of their weight, and if men disobey their Foreman, or persist in sending out slack or rock, after being docked, they will be discharged.

All men are to commence and stop work by the whistle.

Company are to furnish tools, do the blacksmithing and repairing, furnish mules, harness and pit cars, and supply of water for the men.

Company are to deliver coal at the houses of all the laborers, for which the Chinamen are to pay 50 Cents per man per month.

Company are to furnish houses for the Chinamen to live in at $5, per month for each house.[18]

The Chinese, like their American counterparts, labored in the coal mines under extremely harsh conditions. When the Almy mine first exploded in 1881, thirty-eight miners died. Of this number, thirty-five were Chinese and three were what the newspapers of the time called "white men."[19] This was the first coal mine explosion in Wyoming history. It would not be the last time emigrants would lose their lives mining coal in Wyoming.

The problem of prejudice, added to the problems of working in a hazardous job, made the Chinese emigrants lives all that more difficult. The fact that they were contracted laborers was not much different from what other workers in the nineteenth century experienced, but the contract Wyoming Chinese miners had with Beckwith and Quinn differed from the contract the "white miners" received. While a White miner might be forced to sign a rent contract for company housing, there was no middle man with whom the American miners had to deal. Beckwith and Quinn first received the Chinese workers' wages.[20] Under the 1875 contract, Union Pacific paid Beckwith and Quinn; Beckwith and Quinn, in turn, paid the Chinese miners. With this arrangement there was always the possibility that Beckwith and Quinn would profit from Chinese workers wages.

Faced with seemingly insurmountable challenges and even in the face of prejudice, the Chinese who lived in Wyoming Territory developed a full fledged ethnic community that maintained close ties to their homeland. They maintained traditional dress, as is pointed out in the article about the merchant visiting Cheyenne. The Chinese also practiced their own religions. The 1880 census states that a Chinese priest lived in Rock Springs. Bill Nye, "the humorist," in one of his columns made light of the "celestial Josh." While his article makes light of this "bass wood diety," he pointed out that Chinese religions and traditions were being practiced in Wyoming. Nye's criticism of the diety states:

> I do not wish to be understood as interfering with any man's religious views: but when polygamy is made a divine decree, or a bass wood deity is whittled out and painted red to look up to and to worship, I cannot treat that so called religious belief with courtesy and reverence. I am quite liberal in all religious matters. People have noticed that and remarked it, but the Oriental god of commerce seems to me to be greatly overrated.[21]

Nye, in his much noted satiric wit, provided a glimpse of fact. The Chinese did indeed set up Joss Houses and bring in notions of gods that could help them prosper. The hope of prospering is why they came to Wyoming.

The newspapers of the nineteenth century often commented on the fact "white men" were losing their jobs to Chinese workers.[22] The problem was simple and straightforward. While many blamed the Union Pacific for bringing the Chinese into Wyoming, most workers vented their frustrations against these Asian emigrants. The newspapers of the late nineteenth century recorded this frustration. The newspapers also grasped the basic reason behind why the Chinese chose to work in railroad camps, gold mines, and coal mines, but they failed to perceive the basic economic, social, and cultural reasons behind why the Chinese chose to emigrate to Wyoming. Only recently have historians, such as Henry Tsia, begun to discuss the complexities of why the Chinese came to America.[23] Comprehending why the Chinese came to Wyoming in the late 1800s was of little interest to most newspaper editors. The prejudice of the last century is obvious; with newspapers and state and territorial laws reflecting this fact.[24] The Chinese Massacre tragically revealed the depth of this prejudice. What is sometimes lost in discussing and describing the Chinese experience in Wyoming is that they contributed much to the development of the territory and later the state.

Chinese emigrants contributed to the development of the territory in many ways. The contributions came during Wyoming's early years and continue to the present. During the territorial years the Chinese worked as coal miners, railroad repairmen, cooks, waiters, servants, barbers, doctors, priests, merchants, wash house attendants, and proprietors. They often served in roles traditionally relegated to females in the nineteenth century. This caused a few problems, most notably in Helena, Montana, where there was a protest against Chinese laundries. But in Wyoming, where most of the Chinese lived in remote towns and section camps, Chinese cooks, waiters, laundry men, and servants found ready employment. In towns like Rock Springs where the ratio was almost four men to every one woman, the Chinese filled an important niche. Performing services that were often seen as demeaning, or of lesser status, the Chinese contributed much to the welfare and well-being of miners, railroad workers, and even the people in the surrounding agricultural communities.

Within the mining and railroad industries, the contributions of the Chinese to Wyoming are even more obvious. By 1885 the number of Chinese living in Rock Springs had increased to five hundred residents,[25] most of whom were coal miners. On the average, in 1885, the coal miners at Rock Springs produced "450 cars per week." The coal mines at Rock Springs were "the largest in the west"[26] and the Union Pacific Railroad depended on the Rock Springs coal miners for the bulk of their coal supply. To illustrate how important the Chinese miners were to Union Pacific's ventures at Rock Springs: in October, 1885, one month after the Chinese Massacre, the Rock Springs No. 3 mine produced between 245 and 280 cars per week. *The Cheyenne Daily Leader* stated: "About 200 Chinamen were working in No. 3. . . . There are no white miners . . ." underground.[27] Only two other mines were being operated by Union Pacific in late October 1885. Number 1 mine had 130 Chinese and only twenty-five White miners underground. Union Pacific No. 4 had thirty Chinese and four White coal miners employed.[28] In light of the fact these Chinese miners were working with the charred remains of the once sizeable Chinatown right at their doorstep, their contribution to the continued operation of the Union Pacific Railroad is worth remembering. In spite of great adversity, the Chinese workers of the last century contributed much to the future state of Wyoming. This contribution is yet to be fully understood. As more efforts focus on the various jobs and services the Chinese actually performed in Wyoming, our view of the Asian experience in the state will be more complete.

NOTES

1. Examples of works which have discussed the Chinese Massacre in some detail include: T. A. Larson, *History of Wyoming*, 2nd ed., rev. (Lincoln: University of Nebraska Press, 1978); Dell Isham, *Rock Springs Massacre 1885*(Master's Thesis, University of Wyoming, 1967); Isaac Hill Bromley, *The Chinese Massacre at Rock Springs Wyoming Territory* (Boston: Franklin Press, Rand, Avery and Company, 1886); Robert Rhode, *Booms and Busts on Bitter Creek* (Boulder, Colorado: Pruett Press, 1987). In addition to these books and the thesis, several pamphlets and articles have been published dealing specifically with the Chinese Massacre. Among the articles published are two pieces by Paul Crane and T. A. Larson, "The Chinese Massacre," *Annals of Wyoming* 12 (January 1940):47–55; and 2 (April 1940):153–161. A pamphlet has also been written by Henry F. Chadey, *The Chinese Story and Rock Springs, Wyoming* (Green River, Wyoming: Sweetwater County Historical Museum, n.d.).

2. *Frontier Index* [Green River City, Wyoming], August 11, 1868. The capitalization of the words are as they appear in the original column.

3. *Cheyenne Daily Leader*, May 6, 1879.

4. *Montana Radiator* [Helena, Montana], January 24, 1866; John R. Wunder, "Law and Chinese in Frontier Montana," *Montana the Magazine of Western History* 30 (Summer 1980):18–31.

5. *Ninth Census of the United States, 1870* (Washington, D.C.: Government Printing Office, 1872).

6. J. W. Gannett to Oliver Ames, August 27, 1870, UPRR Collection, Office of the President, MS 3761, SG2, Box 6, Nebraska State Museum and Archives, Lincoln.

7. Maury Klein, *Union Pacific: The Birth of a Railroad, 1862–1893* (Garden City, New York: Doubleday and Company, Inc., 1987), p. 238.

8. *Ninth Census of the United States, 1870.*

9. *Ninth Census of the United States, 1870.*

10. *Ninth Census of the United States, 1870.*

11. *Tenth Census of the United States, 1880* (Washington, D.C.: Government Printing Office, 1883).

12. *Tenth Census of the United States, 1880.*

13. *Tenth Census of the United States, 1880.*

14. *Tenth Census of the United States, 1880.* The point about Chinese women living in the United States is somewhat complex. Stacy A. Flaherty, in his article "Boycott in Butte: Organized Labor and the Chinese Community, 1896–1897," *Montana the Magazine of Western History* 37 (Winter 1987):41, gives the following insight. "Most Chinese men left their wives and families in China while they sojourned in the United States. They sent money to their families or saved money to buy passage for their wives. Traditionally, a respectable Chinese woman did not leave home even with her husband. . . . The U.S. Government excluded wives from coming with immigrant Chinese laborers, but wives of merchants were allowed to enter the country." For more on Chinese families see Stanford M. Lyman, "Marriage and Family Among Chinese Immigrants to America, 1850–1906," in *The Asians in the West* (Reno: University of Nevada Press, 1970), pp 27–31.

15. *Cheyenne Daily Leader*, June 16, 1882.

16. *Cheyenne Daily Leader*, September 6, 1881.

17. "Contract for Chinese Labor & etc., Sale of Supplies, Rent of Warehouse Rock S," December 24, 1875, p. 1, Beckwith, Quinn, and Company and Union Pacific Railroad Co., U.P. Coal Box 3, Union Pacific Archives, Omaha, Nebraska (hereafter cited as UP).

18. "Contract for Chinese Labor & etc., Sale of Supplies, Rent of Warehouse Rock S," December 24, 1875, p. 3, UP.

19. A. Dudley Gardner and Verla R. Flores, *Forgotten Frontier: A History of Wyoming Coal Mining* (Boulder, Colorado: Westview Press, 1989), p. 42.

20. "Contract for Chinese Labor & etc., Sale of Supplies, Rent of Warehouse Rock S," December 24, 1875, p. 1, UP.

21. *Cheyenne Daily Leader*, February 22, 1884.

22. *e.g. Wyoming Tribune* [Cheyenne], May 14, 1870.

23. See Shih-shan Henry Tsai, *China and the Overseas Chinese in the United States, 1868–1911* (Fayetteville: University of Arkansas Press, 1983).

24. *Laws of Wyoming* (Cheyenne: H. Gla[aa]rcke; Leader Steam Book and Job Print, 1876), chapter 64. This law was "An Act to Prevent Intermarriage between White Persons and those of Negro or Mongolian Blood."

25. *Cheyenne Daily Leader*, September 4, 1885, p. 3.

26. *Cheyenne Daily Leader*, September 4, 1885, p. 3.

27. *Cheyenne Daily Leader*, October 15, 1885, p. 3.

28. *Cheyenne Daily Leader*, October 25, 1885, p. 3.

23

David G. Thomas' Memories of the Chinese Riot

As told to his daughter Mrs. J. H. Goodnough

On the second day of September 1885, in Rock Springs, Wyoming, occurred a riot, so brutal in its actuality, so revolting in its execution and so gruesome in its details, that it made the town, since famous for its coal, equally infamous, and left deep scars in the minds and hearts of the citizens. As I questioned my father about the stirring events which led to the actual riot, I could not but be impressed. He sat calmly smoking his friendly pipe and animatedly related events as he saw them. He told of the progress which civilization has brought in its wake to our city as contrasted with the bloody scenes of the eighties. We who live in Rock Springs and love it, are vitally interested in her history and this was the reason I secured the facts herein quoted.

The opinions expressed may or may not be correct, but they are formed by the impressions made at the time and are our own. My father, David G. Thomas, witnessed the riot from No. Five tipple and actually saw what follows in the narrative.

To understand conditions as they existed, one must go back to the year 1869, when the Southern Pacific Railroad was being completed and Chinese coolies had been imported for the work of building the road. Upon its completion, most of the Chinese were out of work and anxious to become engaged in some remunerative labor. There was a feeling of resentment against them, which grew steadily each year as it was fed on propaganda issued by labor agitators.

The situation in the coal mines at Rock Springs in the year 1876, was anything but pleasant. A strike was in progress, whereby the coal mined was limited in degree and quantity and very few miners were hired. Neither the superintendent nor the mine boss had any authority, the power being relegated to a committee of three miners, a triumvirate, who were the dictators of the mines. Finally the situation became intolerable to mining officials and the agitators were fired, boldly and bodily from any further participation in company affairs. However, a few men, loyal in their devotion, were retained.

To a large extent, the mines were now without white labor, so the question was, "Who should mine the coal?" Beekwith and Quinn agreed to furnish a contract to supply Chinese labor for the mines, with Mr. W. H. O'Donnell, the contact man for the deal in the year 1885. It is well to bear this fact in mind, as Mr. O'-Donnell, (or "Grandpa" as he was affectionately known to those of us of a younger generation, who worshipped him with a real affection bordering on adoration), was involved in the brutal workings of what we now call "Mob psychology" but which caused him worry and annoyance for two days, when he was guilty of nothing but the faithful discharge of his duties.

The years passed, from 1878–1885, with the spirit of unrest and dissatisfaction gaining ground against the Chinese, not only in Rock Springs, but in California, Colorado and even in Pittsburgh, Pa. In 1885 my father was a mine boss at No. Five and from this point he will tell his own story as he actually saw it, using the first person.

"One week before the riot Mr. C. P. Wassung and I had occasion to visit Laramie, on lodge business. We met an acquaintance, who had no business connections in Rock Springs at the time, but who remarked that he would visit our town in a few days, and that there would be something doing. The 'something doing' part of the conversation made an indelible impression on our minds, when this same man became one of the leaders in the riot of September 2nd. I have reason to believe that he lived and still lives to be very much ashamed of his participation in the disgraceful events.

"I was mine boss at No. Five, and on the morning of Sept. 2nd, I noticed a visible commotion at No. Three. Rumors had reached me that there was violence at No. Six; wherein Chinese miners had been assigned to places previously promised by the superintendent to the white men. It is an unwritten law in the mines, that miners work in certain assigned places. I felt at the time and have since had no reason to change my views, that the Chinese riot was due to the tactlessness of the Mine Superintendent, Jim Evans. He was efficient in working knowledge, but lacking in the virtue of 'tact,' and one error was the only thing needed to fan the flames of revolt and race hatred to red heat and start the riot which cost the lives of 27 innocent men. I never felt that the men wanted to riot at this time.

"To quote from *The Rock Springs Independent,* dated Sept. 3, 1885: "Today for the first time in a good many years there is not a Chinaman in Rock Springs. The five or six hundred who were working in the mines here have been driven out, and nothing but heaps of smoking ruins mark the spot where Chinatown stood. The feeling against the Chinese has been growing stronger all summer. The fact that the white men had been turned off the sections, and hundreds of white men were seeking in vain for work, while the Chinese were being shipped in by the car load and given work strengthened the feeling against them. It needed but little to incite this feeling into an active crusade, and that came yesterday morning at No. Six. All the entries at No. Six were stopped the first of the month, and Mr.

Evans, Mine Superintendent, marked off a number of rooms in the entries. In No. Five entry eight Chinamen were working and four rooms were marked off for them. In No. Thirteen entry, Mr. Whitehouse and Mr. Jenkins were working and Evans told them they could have rooms in that entry or in No. Eleven or No. Five. They chose No. Five entry and when they went to work Tuesday, Dave Brookman, who was acting as pit boss in Mr. Francis' absence, told them to take the first rooms marked off. He supposed the Chinamen had begun work on their rooms and that Whitehouse and Jenkins would take the next rooms beyond them. But as the first two rooms of the entry had not been commenced, Whitehouse took one, not knowing that they had been given to the Chinamen. He went up town in the afternoon and during his absence the two Chinamen came in and went to work in the room Whitehouse had started. When Whitehouse came to work two Chinamen were in possession of what he considered his room. He ordered them out, but they wouldn't leave what they thought was their room. High words followed, then blows. The Chinese from other rooms came rushing in, as did the whites and a fight ensued, with picks, shovels, drills and tamping needles for weapons. The Chinamen were worsted, four of them being badly wounded, one of whom has since died.'

"To resume my story from this place. I was standing on No. Five tipple when I distinctly saw a commotion at No. Three mine. I hurried over there to transact some business at the blacksmith shop, and upon its completion, made my way through Chinatown, notifying five or six of my Chinese friends to be careful, as it looked like trouble was brewing. I then returned to No. Five tipple, when I saw the mob now formed with rifles, shot guns and revolvers, stop for a moment at the railroad crossing near the present home of M. W. Medill. Here a shot or two was fired at the defenseless Chinese, who came out of their numerous dugouts and shacks like sheep led to the slaughter—taken by surprise, unarmed and unprotected. They fled precipitously to Bitter Creek, eastward to Burning Mountain and now the riot was on.

"May I say at this point, that one of our leading professional men, was on horseback, waving his hat and shouting loudly, and while he appeared to be unarmed, he was inciting a maddened crowd to bloodthirsty deeds.

"Bullets followed the fleeing Chinese and sixteen of them were killed brutally, while the other casualties met an even more horrible fate the same evening, when some of the citizens satisfied their murderous instincts and inhumanly slew the few remaining Chinese for the money which their victims had hidden on their persons, afterwards setting fire to the buildings to hide the crimes.

"I left for home and went up town. Here an old Chinese laundryman Ah Lee lived in a dirt dugout with a roof of boards. He was so frightened that he bolted his door, but the fiends were not to be cheated of their prey, so they came through the poor old man's roof and murdered him ruthlessly. I asked the same man whom I had previously met in Laramie, 'Why did you kill poor old Ah Lee?' His answer was, 'I had to, Dave, he was coming at me with a knife.' The reader can judge for himself the accuracy of the alibi, self defense, after breaking through a man's roof and shooting him in the back of the head. But dead men tell no tales.

"In this connection may be told the story of a Rock Springs woman, who walked over the body of the dead Chinaman and stole packages of laundry which he had neatly laid aside for delivery.

"Understand, too, we were nervous for our own safety as we were in the employ of the Company and knew not what the mob might decide to do as the next order of business.

"However, around seven o'clock, Frank Hamlin, Lloyd Thomas and I walked over to Chinatown, where we saw lying in the dirt the body of an old Chinaman, whom we had known, shot through the chest and dying slowly. One of the men in the group suggested that we shoot him to get him out of his misery but this we decided not to do, so we left him to die.

"The flames from forty burning houses lighted our faces. When we came to Bitter Creek we saw the body of Joe Brown, one of the first Chinamen killed in the one sided battle.

"We returned to the house of Mr. Tisdale, the general Superintendent, which is located on the present site of the postoffice. Mr. and Mrs. Tisdale were out of town, so Frank Hamlin and I prepared to retire, although we slept little, as the section house had been set on fire by this time and shots were rending the air all night long. We wondered, too, if the mob would not visit Mr. Tisdale's house in a spirit of revenge, but our fears were groundless and we were left undisturbed.

"These were things I actually saw and the next day we heard that Mr. Jim Evans, Mine Superintendent, had been requested to leave town at once, which he did on the night train, never appearing here again.

"To quote again from the local paper, dated the 3rd: 'Well, gentlemen, the next thing is to give Mr. O'Donnell notice to leave and then go over to No. Six,' said one of the men in the crowd. But the crowd was slow in departing on this errand. A large number seemed to think that this was going too far, and of the crowd that gathered in front of O'Donnell's store, the majority did not sympathize with this move. But at somebody's order a note ordering O'Donnell to leave was written and given to Gottsche, his teamster.

"One of the men, who objected loudest to this mode of procedure was the same person we have had occasion to mention before, at Laramie, Ah Lee's murder, etc. but he quit the riot at this place, being highly indignant at the treatment meted to Mr. O'Donnell. However, Mr. O'Donnell was told to come back in two days, which he did, much to the general rejoicing.

"A look around Thursday, revealed some gruesome sights, resembling the methods of the modern racketeer. In the smoking cellar of one Chinese house the blackened bodies of three Chinamen were seen. Three others were in the cellar of another and four more bodies were found near by. From the position of some of the bodies it would seem as if they had begun to dig a hole in the cellar to hide themselves, but the fire overtook them when about half way in the hole, burning their lower limbs to a crisp and leaving the upper trunk untouched.

"A the east end of Chinatown another body was found, charred by the flames and mutilated by hogs. For a long time, pork was not tempting to use as an appetite teaser, and we gladly refrained from including it in our diet. The smell that arose from the smoking ruins was horribly suggestive of burning flesh. Farther east the bodies of four more Chinamen, shot down. In their flight one of them had tumbled over the bank and lay in the creek with face upturned. Still further another Chinaman was found shot in the hips but still alive. He had been shot as he came to the bank. He was taken up town and cared for by Dr. Woodruff. Besides this, two others were seriously wounded.

"One Chinawoman fled with her husband, a gambler, who carried her across Bitter Creek, and both appeared to be unusually calm. Neither of them were among the casualties. The wife of Soo Qui, a boss Chinaman, was badly frightened and with tearful eyes and trembling voice said to the mob, 'Soo he go; I go to him.' The assurance of the men that she would be unharmed failed to calm her and gathering a few household goods she fled to the home of a neighbor.

"A few days after the riot, Mrs. Thayer was visited by a woman who carried a fur coat over her arm, making the statement that this coat was made of a 'H'African Lion', and was too large for her, so she would like to sell it. She failed to convince Mrs. Thayer, however, as the latter had seen the coat too often on Ah Coon, one of the missing Chinese.

"Mr. Joe Young, the sheriff, was in Green River the day of the riot, but placed guards to protect the property of citizens in case of a disturbance.

"A Coroner's jury, who with Dr. Woodruff, examined the dead bodies of the Chinamen, returned a verdict that eleven had been burned to death and four shot by parties unknown to the jury. The bodies were put in rough coffins and buried in the Chinese burying grounds.

"A good many indictments followed the arrival of the troops, which were sent by the Government, but the trial was a farce and the cases dismissed. I was told to report for jury service in Green River and when D. O. Clark asked me why I did not wish to serve, I replied that I did not feel that my back was bullet proof. Such was the attitude of the citizens at the time.

"Gov. Warren came with railroad officials on a special train and took a view of the situation and provisions were sent west for the Chinese near Green River. Troops were ordered to be stationed in Rock Springs, and all of the Chinese were picked up and closely guarded by Uncle Sam's men. Some of the officers located here included Major Freeman, and Captain Coolidge, the adopted father of the Rev. Sherman Coolidge, Indian Episcopal rector at Colorado Springs. The troops remained here until the Spanish American war, and it was with considerable regret that the citizens saw the soldiers depart, as they had become an influence for good in the community.

"And now to tell the story of Pung Chung, our loyal and devoted friend. He went to No. Three when he first heard about the riot through the Chinese whom I had notified, and retraced his steps back again through the mine to No. Five, where he had hoped to find me, but I had left for home by that time. Then he fled to the hills, where he stayed for three or four days, without food or water, and when found, was in a half crazed condition, brought on through fright and starvation, together with exhaustion. He was always our loyal friend and years later I can picture him, an old man, seated on the coping of my wife's grave; in his hand, a few fragrant flowers, pitifully eloquent, his token of respect to her memory. His devotion touched us, and we feel it indeed a privilege to place on his grave, each Decoration day a little flower, with a thought similar to the one expressed by Thomas Campbell—" 'To live in hearts we leave behind / Is not to die'."

24

Rock Springs Incident

Yen Tzu-kuei

Ahsay Avenue in Rock Springs, Wyoming, is named after a Chinese.[1] It is a friendly gesture of the people of Rock Springs toward the Chinese, and quite a contrast to the cruel massacre of Chinese which took place on September 2, 1885, at the same place.

This incident involved Chinese immigrants in America. In the nineteenth century, the population of China increased over 300 percent but the amount of arable land only increased slightly less than 7-1/2 percent. This acute shortage of arable land, successive wars, rebellions, and natural disasters deprived hundreds of millions of Chinese of their livelihood.[2] Poverty and starvation drove some Chinese to seek a chance for survival abroad.

Meanwhile, California was having a boom because of the gold strike in the Sacramento Valley. This created a need for labor which California could not meet, so Chinese laborers were brought here. At first they were welcomed for their thrift, docility, and industry. There were, however, also ill feeling among the miners in the mountains who felt that Chinese immigrants would eventually put them out of work. This fear was imagined rather than actual, however, because the mines were not crowded and the Chinese worked only in abandoned areas.[3]

The Chinese had worked on the Transcontinental Railroad which was being built from the Pacific coast in an eastwardly direction toward the Atlantic. The white workers openly admitted that they were not interested in this work because of the dangers along the suggested route. The use of Chinese immigrants alleviated this problem.

At the time of the completion of the Transcontinental Railroad in 1869, many depleted gold mines were also closed. Thousands of white and Chinese workers lost their jobs. In 1876 California was suffering from drought and depression. Twenty-two thousand Chinese immigrated to California, while the white immigration was nine times that number.[4] This sudden increase of population heightened the fears of the jobless white workers and newly arrived Europeans. The European immigrants were reluctant to accept hard labor and menial tasks, and they became desperate and angry. The Chinese were willing to suffer hardship in order to survive. Moreover, from the employer's point of view, they were docile, industrious, and reliable. Many Chinese were hired by farmers. Others were contracted to build roads, dig canals, work other industries, and work as servants. This aroused envy and hatred among the European workers.[5]

The politicians made use of this sentiment and in order to gain the support of the workers blamed the Chinese for depriving the unemployed white workers of gaining a livelihood. The union leaders also found it necessary to divert the attention of the unemployed white laborers with the anti-Chinese sentiment to cover up their failure to solve the serious unemployment problem.[6]

Therefore the politicians and union leaders deliberately intensified the racial prejudice against the Chinese. The Chinese laborers suffered from acute discrimination based upon this prejudice. And they could not obtain much needed protection and assistance from their own government because China was not concerned about the overseas Chinese populations scattered abroad. The Chinese Embassy was not established in the United States until 1877.[7]

Beginning in the 1850s hundreds of Chinese were murdered by hoodlums in California; it became an almost daily occurrence. Such crimes were often not prosecuted, and only a very few of the murderers were punished.[8] The Chinese miners were often driven off and persecuted. This was often followed by violence as in the case of Coal Creek Mine in Kings County, Washington, where the living quarters of Chinese miners were burned to the ground.[9]

The above-mentioned depression, the anti-Chinese sentiment, the desperate need for survival of unemployed white workers, the unpunished crimes against the Chinese, and their defenseless situation all created an atmosphere which led to the massacre that took place in Rock Springs, Wyoming, in 1885—the most shameful atrocity against Chinese immigrants in American history.[10]

In the latter part of the nineteenth century the miner's life in the Western part of the United States was very hard. However, owing to the acute shortage of labor in such isolated places as Rock Springs, the work of miners was steady and their pay was 30 percent higher than that of miners on the east coast. They worked only three days in a week and were able to determine their own working schedule.[11] Some of them worked for one month, drew their pay, and then left abruptly, causing the company serious inconvenience.

In the autumn of 1875 the coal company employed about 500 white miners in their Rock Springs mines. Winter was fast approaching, requiring more tonnage of coal. Subsequently, S. H. H. Clark, then general superintendent, notified and requested the union leaders to increase the output of coal by at least 25 percent. The union leaders refused. They counteracted by demanding the restoration of their original wage to five cents per bushel. Clark was annoyed by the demand and notified the miners that they could resign from the mines and work elsewhere.[12] A miners' strike followed in November 1875, whereupon the coal company hired 150 Chinese laborers to replace the striking white miners. When the Chinese laborers were brought into Rock Springs, the local situation was very tense. The government had to use federal troops to preserve order. Later, the white miners, realizing their defeat, wanted to return to work at the rate of four cents per bushel. The company, however, would only retain 50 white miners. Later, more Chinese laborers were brought in to work in the mines.

The reason the company was willing to hire more Chinese miners than white miners was probably that Chinese workers were less prone to strike.[13] It was not because they received lower wages since the wages for white miners and Chinese miners were the same. The earnings of Chinese miners averaged $3.00 per day; the standard rate was seventy-four cents per ton. Therefore an average Chinese miner would dig out more than four tons of coal each day. The total amount of coal mined by Chinese miners must have exceeded ten million tons between 1870 and 1910.[14] This considerable amount of coal must have played an important role in promoting the prosperity of the western United States because the coal mines in Rock Springs were the largest in the entire Union Pacific system. The mines delivered one-third to one-half of all the coal used by the Union Pacific.[15]

There were more Chinese miners in this area than any other area of the western part of the United States at that time. The concentration of Chinese miners probably attracted the attention of the white workers and indirectly intensified their hatred against the Chinese.

Two years prior to the massacre, the miners' union was organized by the Knights of Labor.[16] The Knights of Labor was well-known for its anti-Chinese attitude. The association was growing rapidly in the 1880s. At the end of 1878 its membership was only 9,287. In 1883 its membership had increased to 51,914. By 1885 the membership had reached 700,000.[17] Its rapid growth made the union tremendously influential. The strength of the conviction of its members added to that influence. "Chinese Must Go" was one of their most popular slogans and one which they constantly advocated and stressed. The stage was set and the conditions were ripe for a riot, but a fresh excuse was still needed for the outburst of violence.

The union leaders approached the Chinese miners and asked them to participate in a strike against the coal company. The Chinese refused.[18]

A little past 7:00 a.m. on September 2, 1885, an argument between Chinese and white miners about assignment of working rooms took place in the No. 6 mine. Half an hour later, white miners left the mines and marched toward the Knights of Labor Hall, shouting, "White men fall in." According to the Chinese miners, a meeting was held at the hall following the march. The meeting was aimed at the expulsion of the Chinese.[19]

Then the white miners dispersed and went to various saloons to have a few drinks. Shortly afterward, they gathered in the streets carrying firearms, knives, hatchets, and clubs. They decided that the Chinese must leave town immediately. The mob was well organized and approached Chinatown in groups from three different directions.

On their way to Chinatown, they robbed Chinese at gunpoint. They searched for watches, gold, silver, and other valuables and beat up the Chinese victims before releasing them. Some of the rioters, when they could not stop a Chinese, would shoot him on the spot and rob him. When the rioters reached Chinatown, they notified the Chinese to leave the town in one hour and to never return. The Chinese hastily gathered their possessions and proceeded to leave. Before the hour was up, the rioters grew impatient; they wanted the Chinese to leave immediately. Some women cheered on their men. Two of the women fired successive shots, killing two Chinese. This took place just after 3:00 p.m.[20]

Then the mob went into Chinatown, shouting and firing their guns. The unarmed Chinese offered no resistance and grabbed whatever belongings were at hand and fled. They scrambled over the steep banks of Bitter Creek and ran through the sagebrush and up into the hills.

Several shacks in Chinatown were set on fire. The Chinese hiding in these shacks were shot down when they had to come out because of the choking smoke. Others were driven back into the shacks and burned to death. Some of the dead Chinese were thrown into the burning shacks. Some Chinese were too frightened or too sick to leave their homes and were burned alive. The stench of burning flesh was in the air. Those Chinese who managed to escape hid in the hills and did not dare to move until it was safe. Twenty-six Chinese tried to cross the mountains to safety, but most of them, without food or sleep, became very weak and were attacked and eaten by wolves. Others died of hunger and exposure. The great majority of those who escaped had stayed close to the railroad and later were picked up by passing trains. By 9:00 p.m. all 79 Chinese shacks in town had been burned down.[21]

Next morning, the scene was terrible. There were smoldering buildings. The air was filled with the stench of burned flesh. Bodies were scattered and found in nearby places. One charred body was being eaten by hogs. Two other Chinese miners were found murdered in mine No. 3. Another three with bullet wounds in their backs and legs were found alive and taken to Dr. Woodruff, a town physician, for treatment.[22] In contrast, another medical doctor in the town had been a part of the mob. He was riding his horse, waving his hat and shouting loudly, inciting the mob to still greater brutality. He shouted: "No quarters! Shoot them down!" This man, Dr. Edward Murray, had been a resident of Rock Springs for about nine months and was anxious for employment as a physician by the coal department. He had made several attempts to obtain signatures from the miners on a petition for that purpose. His participation in the mob action and his obvious enthusiasm might have aided his efforts.

Subsequently this same Edward Murray served as the foreman of the jury for the trial of sixteen white rioters.[23] According to *The Compiled Laws of Wyoming* for that period, he must have been a United States citizen to be a member of the jury. According to the testimony of one of the Chinese to the presiding judge, Judge Savage, another participant in the massacre was Isaiah Whitehouse. The fact that he was a U.S. citizen is clearly shown by his having been nominated for the local legislature. This contradicted Secretary of State Bayard's later statement that no U.S. citizen was involved and that consequently the U.S. government was not liable for the massacre.[24]

Another unusual aspect of the trial was the testimony of Mr. Thirloway, a minister of Green River, and his family. They testified that the Chinese burned all their own houses and were also guilty of taking the lives of their own countrymen. This peculiar testimony was largely responsible for the later acquittal of the rioters. Since Mr. Thirloway was a "minister of the gospel," his testimony was considered highly credible. Even more damaging was the widely held assumption that Rev. Thirloway's family had the confidence of the Chinese. His testimony was commend on by the *Rock Springs Independent*: "We see a large number of papers attaching undue importance to the testimony of Mr. Thirloway at Green River. . . . Anything more absurd than this could not be imagined by those who were actual eyewitnesses of the occurrence."[25]

There were other strikebreakers at the time, such as Scandinavians and Mormons. In Rock Springs, the Mormons refused to participate in the strike initiated by other white miners. However, unlike the Chinese, they were only forced out; they were not molested physically.[26]

Unfortunately, what the local people did not realize was that the Chinese laborers had not threatened their survival as they had imagined. In fact, in the decade of 1870 to 1880, the Chinese in Wyoming were much less than one percent of the entire population.[27] During this period the population in Wyoming increased from 86,786 to 143,966.[28] This rapid growth also brought prosperity, which proves that the means of survival were plentiful. This can be proved by Cary's statement (he was a delegate of the Wyoming Territory to Congress). According to Cary, the building of the new railroads to the inexhaustible coal fields in Wyoming Territory created a need for 10,000 miners.[29] In 1880 the Chinese who lived in the Wyoming Territory reached their greatest number. The statistics show that there were 914, which was far less than the needed 10,000 miners mentioned by Cary. More significantly, it was the railroad company, which refused to hire some of the white miners that it considered unsuitable, that precipitated the violence. The Chinese miners should not have been blamed. Moreover most of the white miners were just as alien as the Chinese; they were not entitled to enjoy more privileges than the Chinese.[30]

After the incident, the local civil authorities were unable to suppress the rioters and to preserve order. Governor Warren had to cable President Cleveland twice, requesting federal troops to protect the Chinese and to maintain local peace and order, especially after the mob prevented some 500 Chinese from reaching food and shelter. The local sheriff was powerless, and Wyoming Territory had mo militia. Later federal troops were brought in to protect the Chinese.[31]

The attitude of the Union Pacific was very firm throughout the crisis. On September 9, only a week after the massacre, 100 Chinese miners were sent back to

work. The company refused to reinstate those white miners who were considered
to have been participants in the riot. On September 17 a strike was called by the
white miners in protest, but it failed to convince the company. By December 1
some 50 more Chinese were hired to work in the mines. Owing to the introduction of new machinery and the additional number of Chinese workers, the original output of coal was soon restored and increased.[32]

After local order was restored, the sheriff of Sweet Water County (in which
Rock Springs was located) arrested 15 men on charges of rioting.

On September 3 the justice of the peace and acting coroner of Rock Springs,
Ludwigsen, ordered an inquest into the Rock Springs incident. A jury was then
summoned, including Dr. E. S. Murray as its foreman. On September 10 the accused were released and placed under bond to appear in the next session of Sweet
Water County Court. A large number of witnesses were examined, but only the
testimony of the Thirloways was made public. Those who were sympathetic toward the Chinese often refused to testify. David Thomas was one of them. He
stated explicitly that he did not feel his back was bulletproof.[33]

As the result of the grand jury's deliberation no one was found guilty because
no criminal was identified. However, O'Donnell's testimony to Colonel Bee, the
Chinese consul in San Francisco, gave a different picture of the situation. He
stated, "I think nearly all the murderers can be identified. As no concealment was
attempted on the part of murderers, but all done in daylight." In spite of this, none
of the criminals involved in the massacre was ever punished.[34]

Public opinion concerning the massacre varied greatly throughout the United
States. Some local newspapers, such as the *Sweet Water Gazette*, praised the mob.
Other newspapers in the West, such as the *Salt Lake Tribune*, reported the event
in a matter of fact manner. The newspapers in the eastern states invariably condemned the murderers and their barbarity. Editorials of the *New York Times* and
the *New York Herald* in September 1885 were typical examples. Perhaps this criticism awakened in the American public the spirit of fairness and sense of justice,
and this in turn convinced President Cleveland and some congressional leaders
that some redemptive measures should be taken.[35]

President Cleveland sent two messages to Congress, in December 1885 and in
March 1886.[36] While admitting the United States' treaty obligation to protect innocent Chinese, the barbarity of the murders, and the ridiculousness of the decision of
the local court, he denied the liability of the United States government on the
grounds that no United States citizens were involved. He insisted that the murderers be punished and an indemnity be paid to the Chinese on humanitarian grounds.

As a result, an indemnity of $147,000 was paid to the Chinese victims, but no
murderer was ever punished as the President had wished. One may doubt the
accuracy of his statement that no United States citizen was involved. The Congress did not approve the indemnity until one year later, five months and twenty-
two days after Chinese Minister Cheng Tsao-ju's first letter to Secretary of State
Bayard, dated November 30, 1885.[37]

The efforts of Chinese diplomats are briefly outlined below:

On September 13, 1885, Minister Cheng Tsao-ju sent a telegram to Colonel

F. A. Bee asking him to go to Wyoming to investigate the massacre in Rock Springs. Later, Minister Cheng sent Huang Sih-chuan, the Chinese consul in New York, on the same mission. The two Chinese consuls and their interpreters arrived in Rock Springs on September 18, 1885, where they made a thorough investigation and submitted their reports to Minister Cheng.[38]

Based on the information provided by the above-mentioned reports, Minister Cheng wrote a letter to Secretary Bayard on November 30, 1885, reminding him of the massacre and demanding that an indemnity be paid to the Chinese victims, that guilty persons be punished, and that measures be taken to protect Chinese from further attacks. Minister Cheng called Bayard's attention to the indemnities the Chinese government had paid to the United States for war damages and mob activities in China in the past, and demanded that the United States government take action based upon the principle of reciprocal justice and international comity. Cheng did not receive a prompt reply from the Secretary. Therefore, he wrote to him again on February 15, 1886, reminding the Secretary that he had informed him by written notes and personal interviews of the incident and also had expressed concern regarding the continued persecution of Chinese in the United States.[39] He stated, "The Chinese are absolutely terrorized and thus are flocking to San Francisco, where great destitution now exists among them." Probably it was the sense of urgency that Cheng had expressed in his second letter which convinced the Secretary to reply three days later. Secretary Bayard refused to agree that the principles of reciprocity and international comity were applicable in the indemnity demanded by China. The Secretary claimed that the incident was strictly between aliens, that it was a local affair and should be handled by the local authorities. According to Secretary Bayard, the Treaty of 1844 provided that only citizens of the United States lawfully engaged in commerce were allowed to enter certain specified ports in China. Therefore, he maintained, United States citizens in China were more restricted than the Chinese who resided in the United States.[40]

Secretary Bayard's argument shows clearly the United States' use of a double standard. It demanded and received an indemnity of $735,258.97 in 1858 from China for damages not covered in the Treaty. But it refused to pay an indemnity to the Chinese victims of the Rock Springs massacre except on humanitarian grounds.

Forty-one out of forty-eight United States claims in 1858 concerned war damages that "resulted from the bombardment of Canton by the British forces, the burning of factories during the military operations (British) in 1856, the movements of the fleets in that vicinity in 1857 (Whampoo) and the indiscriminate pillage which attended these operations."[41] The government of the United States from its foundation has consistently maintained that it cannot be required, either according to the principles of international law or domestic law, either by foreign governments or individuals, to pay indemnities for damages resulting from the war operations of its own troops or those of foreign nations or rebels (inclusive of pillage activity).[42] However, the United States did not apply this principle to the above-mentioned incidents in China, but rather insisted on indemnification.

In another case, A. P. Edwards was mistaken for a British subject, arrested, placed in irons, and cruelly treated, but for less than one day. He was given

$31,600 for indemnity, despite the fact that the eleventh article of the Treaty of 1858 confers no authority to U.S. officials to demand indemnity for damages sustained by American residents.[43] In order to compare these claims with the damages suffered by the Chinese victims in the Rock Springs incident, a part of the statement made by Huang Shi-chuan, then Chinese consul in New York, is revealing: "With reference to the property destroyed by the mob, I find that everyone of the surviving Chinese has been rendered penniless by the cruel attack. . . . Since the riot took place, it has been impossible for them to secure even a torn sheet or any article of clothing to protect them from the cold, or even the crumbs from a table to satisfy their hunger, or even a plank or mat to rest their bodies on. These poor creatures, numbering hundreds, are all hungry and clothed in rags. . . . The total value of the property lost belonging to over seven hundred persons amounted to only $147,000 this being an average of only a little more than $200 for each. . . ."[44] The above stresses the loss of property, but in addition, twenty-eight Chinese were murdered and fifteen wounded. When the indemnity issue for this massacre was debated in Congress, Senators Mitchell and Cockrell, Congressman McKenna, and Wyoming's delegate Carey objected to the Chinese indemnity despite President Cleveland's appeal on humanitarian grounds.[45]

During a riot in Tientsin in 1870, mainly against the French Mission, some property belonging to the American Board of Missions was destroyed. Upon the request of the French minister and the American minister, nineteen Chinese were brought to trial and found guilty, and they were subsequently executed. In addition, indemnities were paid to the French and American authorities. However, the American minister, Mr. Low, considered "the decision arrived at, after three months of delay, as utterly unsatisfactory."[46] In the case of the massacre of the Chinese in Rock Springs, the indemnity was not paid until one year and five months later, and no criminal was ever punished. Even if the Chinese government had sued the murderers, as suggested by Secretary Bayard, in the local court, it would have been useless. The acquittal of the rioters in Rock Springs by the local court was the best proof of the futility of such attempts.

When it received the news of the Rock Springs massacre, the Peking government was outraged, but it did not want to break off its friendly relations with the U.S. Chinese diplomats were instructed to protest and to demand indemnity. At this time, Minister Cheng Tsao-ju was about to be succeeded by Chang Yin-huan, but Cheng received a directive to remain in order to help Chang to settle this indemnity problem.[47] When the Chinese people heard about the cruelty in the massacre, they became very angry and excited. The Tsung-li Yamen had to give Governor Chang Chih-tung explicit orders to prevent any possible reprisals against Americans in China. Sympathetic toward the local people, Chang forwarded their petition to the government urging the government to protest against the United States Government and to demand immediate action to stop the persecution.[48]

In January 1886 the Tsung-li Yamen made a very strong protest to American Minister Denby, reminding him that the Chinese government could not simply accept the total restriction of the immigration of Chinese laborers for twenty years without first solving the indemnity problems.[49] This decision may have expedited the approval of the indemnity for the massacre in Rock Springs by the Congress the following February. In 1888 the Chinese government accepted the U.S. proposal to restrict the immigration of Chinese laborers for twenty years. This acceptance may have contributed to President Cleveland's success in being nominated for a second term.[50]

In retrospect, one may be shocked by the cruel atrocities committed by rioters, who were ignorant and misled by unscrupulous politicians and union leaders. What did those union leaders do to help discharge miners after the massacre? They did not provide any substantial assistance to them at all. On the contrary, they claimed that they were not involved in the incident in any way.[51] The antagonism between the miners and the railroad company resulted in serious troubles. The Chinese laborers were innocent parties to this struggle and continually tragic victims of the situation. It seems a pity that no one has ever mentioned their blood, sweat, and tears which contributed to the prosperity of the area. As time went by, many Chinese laborers returned to China. Only one descendant of the Chinese miners in Rock Springs still lives there.[52] When the imagined Chinese threat disappeared, Ahsay Avenue was named after a Chinese.

Mrs. Wilmot C. McFadden, head Librarian, Carnegie Public Library, wrote to this writer on November 24, 1972[53]:

> Rock Springs has long been known as a "Melting Pot." At one time there were 52 different nationalities living here. Most of the Chinese (moved to Rock Springs from elsewhere) now own their own business and do very well.

> In Rock Springs, we have an acceptance of different nationalities, races and colors the same way we accept different religions.

People at Rock Springs now seem to have forgotten about the incident that took place eighty-nine years ago.

NOTES

1. Henry F. Chadey, director, Sweetwater County Historical Museum. Letter to Yen Tzu-kuei, dated July 18, 1973.

2. Li Shou-kung, *Chung-kuo chin-tai shih* [Modern Chinese History] (Taipei: San Min Book Company, 1964), pp. 146–147.

3. Coolidge, Mary Roberts, *Chinese Immigration* (New York: Arno Press, 1969), p. 35.

4. Chinese Representatives, "Memorial to President Grant," Augustus Layres, San Francisco, September, 1876, pp. 2–3.

5. Wu Shang-ying, *Mei-kuo hua-ch'iao pai-nien chi-shih* [One Hundred Years of Chinese in the United States and Canada] (Hongkong: published by Wu Shang-ying, 1954), pp. 36–37.

6. Herbert Hill, "Anti-Oriental Agitation and the Rise of Working Class Racism" *Society*, Vol 20, No. 2 (January–February 1973), p. 46.

7. Wu Shang-ying, *One Hundred Years of Chinese in the United States and Canada*, p. 116.

8. Ibid.

9. Herbert Hill, "Anti-Oriental Agitation," p. 44.

10. Wu Shang-ying, *One Hundred Years of Chinese in the United States and Canada*, p. 118.

11. Isaac Hill Bromley, *The Chinese Massacre at Rock Springs, Wyoming Territory* (Boston: Franklin Press, Rand, Avery and Company, 1886) pp. 25, 30, 39. The *New York Times*, September 7, 1885, p. 1.

12. Ibid., p. 30.

13. United States Congress. The House. *Providing Indemnity to Certain Chinese Subjects*. H. R. 2044, 49th Congress, 1st Session, 1885–1886, pp. 4, 11–12.

14. Paul Crane and Alfred Larson, "The Chinese Massacre," *Annals of Wyoming*, Vol. 12, Part I, 1940, p. 54; Part II, p. 161.

15. *History of the Union Pacific Coal Mines 1869–1940* (Omaha, Nebraska: The Colonial Press, 1940) back cover.

16. United States Congress, loc. cit., p. 12.

17. Crane and Larson, "Chinese Massacre," p. 51.

18. Ibid., p. 54.

19. United States Congress, loc. cit., pp. 13–14, 28.

20. Ibid., pp. 28–29.

21. Ibid., pp. 29–30.

22. Ibid., p. 22.

23. Bromley and Hill, *Chinese Massacre*, p. 19. Mrs. J. H. Goodnough, interviewed by A. R. Wilson, *University of Wyoming Journal*, October 22, 1966.

24. United States Congress, loc. cit., p. 26; *The Compiled Laws of Wyoming*, 1876, p. 388.

25. Bromley and Hill, Chinese Massacre, pp. 80–81.

26. *Daily Alta California* (San Francisco), September 7, 1885.

27. Nelson Trottmann, *History of the Union Pacific: A Financial and Economic Survey* (New York: Augustus M. Kelley, 1913), p. 102.

28. Ibid.

29. Crane and Larson, "Chinese Massacre," p. 161.

30. United States Congress, loc. cit., p. 10.

31. Crane and Larson, "Chinese Massacre," pp. 49–50.

32. *Union Pacific Coal Mines*, pp. 88, 90; United States Congress, loc. cit., p. 25.

33. United States Congress, loc. cit., p. 16; Bromley and Hill, *Chinese Massacre*, p. 19; *The Wyoming Press*, "David Thomas Story," April 15, 1931.

34. Ibid., pp. 12, 25.

35. *Sweetwater Gazette* (Green River, Wyoming) quoted in the *New York Evening Post*, September 15, 1885; Editorial, the *New York Herald*, September 8, 1885; Editorial, the *New York Times*, September 4, 1885.

36. Crane and Larson, "Chinese Massacre," Part II, pp. 157–158.

37. Ibid., pp. 155, 160.

38. United States Congress, loc. cit., pp. 9, 11.

39. Ibid., p. 56.

40. Ibid., p. 59.

41. Ibid., p. 41.

42. Ibid., p. 46.

43. Ibid.

44. Ibid., p. 27.

45. Crane and Larson, "Chinese Massacre," Part II, pp. 158–159.

46. United States Congress, loc. cit., p. 50.

47. Wang Tai-fu, Wang Liang (ed.), *Ch'ing-chi wai-chiao-shih-liao* [Historical Materials on Foreign Relations in the Late Ch'ing] (Taipei: Wen Hai Publishing Company, n.d.), *chüan 68, p. 8.*

48. Ibid., *chüan 67, pp. 4–10.*

49. Wu Shang-ying, *One Hundred Years of Chinese in the United States and Canada,* pp. 189–190.

50. Ibid., p. 192.

51. *Union Pacific Coal Mine,* p. 90.

52. Henry F. Chadey's letter to tine writer, dated July 18, 1973.

53. Mrs. McFadden's letter to the writer, dated November 24, 1972.

25

Kwangtung to Big Sky: The Chinese in Montana, 1864–1900

Robert R. Swartout, Jr.

Into the early twentieth century, Montana contained a remarkably heterogeneous society with significant numbers of native Americans, Irish, black Americans, Scandinavians, Jews, and Slavs—to name only a few of the many groups living and working in the region. Among the racial and ethnic minorities that contributed to this fascinating mix, the Chinese were certainly one of the most important. Yet, for far too long many of the historical studies about Chinese immigration to the American West have tended to use these Chinese pioneers simply as a backdrop for analyzing the thinking and behavior of non-Chinese groups.[1] It is time that we begin to focus more of our attention on the Chinese themselves.[2]

By focusing more directly on the Chinese experience, we may better appreciate the valuable economic and cultural contributions that these Asian pioneers made to the development of early Montana society. To understand the extent of the Chinese involvement in Montana's history, we must move beyond our retelling of "colorful and humorous" accounts. The Chinese struggle—and it was a struggle—to achieve social and economic security in Montana was demanding, and it deserves serious historical attention.[3]

The Chinese immigrants arriving in America in the mid-nineteenth century overwhelmingly came from the delta region surrounding Canton in Kwangtung Province. The general reasons behind the desire of certain Chinese to emigrate during the nineteenth century are not too difficult to identify. The great population explosion in China between roughly 1700 and 1850 had placed tremendous pressures on China's traditional agrarian production, and in many parts of China the population had outstripped the land's ability to produce adequate foodstuffs. Another factor contributing to emigration was the gradual decline of the Ch'ing dynasty. The dynasty's inability to rule effectively had resulted in a series of rebellions, the largest and most famous of which was the Taiping Rebellion of

1850–1864. In a broader sense, the decline of the dynasty also led to a rise in both government corruption and banditry, problems that created special burdens for the peasantry.[4] Finally, there was the American factor itself. Between the 1840s and the 1890s, the resource-rich, labor-poor American West offered opportunities to foreign workers searching for financial and material security. In many important respects, Montana was a perfect microcosm of these forces at work within the developing American West.[5]

Why the Chinese immigrants would come almost exclusively from Kwangtung Province — in fact, from just three major regions within the province — is more difficult to pinpoint.[6] One factor might have been the influence of the West on and around Canton during the first half of the nineteenth century. The penetration of imperialist powers during this era certainly led to considerable social and economic dislocation for the Chinese.[7] Another factor might have been the maritime traditions of the southeastern China coast. The story of Chinese emigration to America during the nineteenth century is just part of a much larger movement. For decades, people of this area had traveled abroad in search of wealth and adventure. Between 1850 and 1900, roughly five million Chinese from the southern coastal area would leave the country, only a half-million of whom would go to the United States.[8] Perhaps one of the most critical local forces leading to emigration was that many of these people were "have-nots," with only limited ties to the traditional Chinese order. Some were members of an ethnic minority known as the Hakka, while many others were locally oriented rural poor who viewed emigration simply as a "means of survival" for themselves and their families.[9]

Large-scale Chinese immigration to American began in the late 1840s and early 1850s. Spurred on initially by the great gold discoveries in California, first hundreds and then thousands of Chinese headed east across the Pacific Ocean.[10] With the gradual decline in the placer fields, Chinese workers entered other lines of employment and moved on to other regions of the western United States and Canada. By the 1860s and 1870s, important Chinese communities had been established all along the West Coast — in Oregon, Washington, British Columbia, and California — and within the interior West — in places like Nevada, Idaho, Colorado, Wyoming, and Montana.[11] Of all these Chinese, few have received less attention from historians than those found in the isolated Rocky Mountain state of Montana.[12]

By 1870, census surveyors counted 1,949 Chinese in the first official census taken for the territory of Montana. This may not appear to be an impressive figure, but those 1,949 Chinese represented approximately 10 per cent of Montana's official population in 1870. Moreover, because census records were often notorious for underestimating the Chinese population in any given community, the actual Chinese population may have been much higher — by perhaps 50 per cent or more. In 1880, the official figure for the Chinese population in Montana dipped to 1,765; but by 1890 it was back up to 2,532. From that point on, the number of Chinese in the state, and in the United States as a whole, steadily declined.

This decline was due partly to local factors as well as to the passage of various Chinese exclusion acts passed by the U.S. Congress during the 1880s and 1890s. By 1920, there were fewer than 900 Chinese residents left in Montana out of a total state population of 548,889.[13] It is clear, then, that the major period for Chinese influence in Montana was roughly the last third of the nineteenth century. This period not only represented the largest numbers of Chinese immigrants within the region, but it was also a time when those Chinese made up a large percentage of Montana's total population.

As was true in so many other regions of the West, the discovery of major gold deposits during the early 1860s had a profound effect on the history of Montana. The great gold-mining boom in the high mountain valleys of the Northern Rockies would attract thousands of American miners and would-be miners almost overnight and would lead directly to the creation of the Territory of Montana in 1864.[14] And as was the pattern in many other western states and territories, the development of the goldfields also resulted in the arrival of the first Chinese pioneers in Montana.

As placer camps like Bannack, Virginia City, and Last Chance Gulch built up across western Montana, word went out to the older mining districts of the new opportunities in Montana Territory. Chinese miners—many with extensive mining experience in California, Oregon, Idaho, or elsewhere—began moving into Montana. An 1870 federal government study on mining in the American West reported that "some 2,000 to 3,000 Chinese are domiciled in the Territory of Montana. . . . It is reasonable to expect that their numbers will rapidly increase." The same report commented on the techniques of Chinese miners:

> The Chinese work their own placer claims, either taking up abandoned ground or purchasing claims too low in yield to be worked profitably by white labor. The ground thus obtained sometimes turns out to be very valuable, but usually they work or rework only what would otherwise remain untouched. . . . They are frugal, skillful, and extremely industrious. Frequently maltreated by evil-disposed whites, they rarely, if ever, retaliate.

The author of this valuable report had the insight to note that, contrary to much population opinion, the Chinese miners working in Montana "are not coolies or living in a state of slavery. . . . They seem to be their own masters, only associating together for mutual assistance."[15]

By the early 1870s there were dozens of Chinese mining operations in western Montana. The 1880 census listed 149 Chinese in Missoula County, 710 in Deer Lodge County (which included Butte), 265 in Madison County (Alder Gulch), and 359 in Lewis and Clark County (Helena). Many mining camps that are almost forgotten today, such as the small community of Pioneer located southwest of present-day Garrison, were the site of widespread Chinese activities. Unfortunately, the very success of these Chinese miners helped create a backlash among

many members of Montana's white population. For example, in 1872 the territorial
legislature passed a bill prohibiting aliens (that is, Chinese) from holding titles to any
placer mine or claim. Even though this law was later struck down by the territorial
Supreme Court, it was typical of much of the popular sentiment of the day.[16]

Because the passage of such laws was, at least in part, radically motivated, supporters of the legislation consistently overlooked the contributions that Chinese
miners made to the development of Montana. As one outsider commented at the
time, the law concerning Chinese mining titles

> is certainly destructive of the interests of the community, as may be shown in nu-
> merous instances where the Chinese have purchased, for cash, claims which white
> men could no longer afford to work, and have proceeded to make them productive,
> at a smaller profit to themselves than to the Territory. Besides being bad policy, this
> course toward the Chinese is rank dishonesty.[17]

The notion that Chinese miners competed directly against white miners and thus
"stole" badly needed work from them is largely untrue. In fact, Chinese miners
generally complemented the work being done by white miners and played a vital
role in helping to develop the mineral and commercial resources of the territory.[18]

As placer mining began to fade from the scene during the late 1870s and 1880s,
the role of the Chinese immigrants in Montana also began to change.[19] Chinese
railroad workers in America had first been used on a large scale in the construction of the Central Pacific Railroad during the 1860s. In fact, roughly four-fifths
of all the grading done from Sacramento, California, to Ogden, Utah, was completed by Chinese laborers. Of the 13,500 workers on the Central Pacific payroll
at the time of construction, 12,000 were Chinese.[20]

It is not too surprising, then, that Chinese railroad workers found their way to
Montana. During the early 1880s, the first transcontinental railroad to pass
through Montana—the Northern Pacific—was being constructed at a frantic
pace under the leadership of Henry Villard. Because of the critical shortage of
skilled labor at the western end of the project and the reputation of the Chinese
as experienced and dependable workers, Villard and his associates hired fifteen
thousand Chinese to work on the Northern Pacific line through Washington,
Idaho, and Montana.[21]

The press often referred to these Chinese workers, especially those constructing
the Northern Pacific along the Clark Fork River in northern Idaho and western
Montana, as "Hallett's Army" after construction manager J. L. Hallett. This region
of the Clark Fork contained some of the most rugged terrain found anywhere along
the Northern Pacific line. One newspaper reported on October 28, 1882:

> One must ride over the completed track, or watch the thousands of men at work in
> these rock-ribbed hills, see the deep cuttings, the immense fillings, count the bridges
> and miles of trestle-work that carry the trains safely over streams and arms of lakes and

inlets, to fairly realize the expenditure of muscle . . . necessary for such a work as building a great railway route through this mountainous country. At places, for instance, a point near Cabinet Landing, to the men who do the labor, and even to subordinate leaders, the passage seemed closed against them. The mountain towers like a prop to the sky, and from the water's edge it rises like a wall, presenting no break or crevice for a foothold.[22]

The special skills, dedication, and perseverance of the Chinese workers were critical in overcoming these tremendous obstacles. The same reporter took note of this Chinese contribution, although in somewhat condescending terms. To conquer nature's

insurmountable barrier . . . cable ropes holding a plank staging go down the precipitous sides of the mountain. Down rope ladders, to this staging clamber Chinamen armed with drills, and soon the rock sides are filled with Giant powder. Then they clamber up, the blast is fired, and the foothold made by the explosive soon swarms with Celestials; the "can't be done" has been done. . . .[23]

Chinese workmen not only had to overcome great physical obstructions, but they also had to contend with bitter winter weather: "It was terrible work last winter," one source noted, "with deep snow to clear away at every step, the thermometer registering on an average ten and twelve degrees below zero [fahrenheit], abetted by razor-like winds."[24]

The Chinese also played a crucial role in constructing the Mullan Tunnel, which enabled the Northern Pacific to cross over the Continental Divide not far from Helena, Montana. Chinese workers built the critical stretch of line leading to Stampede Pass in Washington Territory's North Cascade Mountains, which allowed the Northern Pacific to reach Puget Sound. For all of these remarkable efforts, the average Chinese worker was paid about one dollar per day, approximately half of what white workers received.[25] This disparity was but another indication of the racial attitudes existing in nineteenth century America, attitudes that permitted white employers to exploit Chinese laborers because of their "inferiority."

Once the Northern Pacific Railroad reached Puget Sound in 1887, the railroad dismissed most of its Chinese workers, retaining only a few Chinese as section hands. The Great Northern Railroad, which also built a transcontinental line across Montana (it was completed in 1893), employed very few Chinese workers. Both railroads turned increasingly to an even cheaper source of labor, the Japanese workers.

The contributions of Chinese railroad workers to the development of Montana are of significant historical importance. Their expertise in grading, drilling, masonry, and demolition was vital to the construction of the Northern Pacific, which opened Montana to settlement, particularly during the homestead era of the early twentieth century. Thousands of pioneer homesteaders would move into the state and transport their bountiful farm products to markets outside the state along tracks laid by the forgotten pioneers of another sort—the Chinese.

The arrival of Chinese miners and railroad workers during the 1860s, 1870s, and 1880s helped to create other economic opportunities for Chinese pioneers. Local Chinese communities began to develop through much of western Montana. For example, the 1890 census listed 602 Chinese living in Lewis and Clark County (Helena) and another 584 living in Silver Bow County (Butte).[26] Throughout the late nineteenth and early twentieth centuries, the state's largest "Chinatowns" were in Helena and Butte.

These urban residents came from a variety of backgrounds. Some were former miners and railroad workers who had been in Montana for some time, while others were recent arrivals from the West Coast who brought with them particular skills and trades. A few came directly from China, enticed to Montana by relatives and friends already living in the state.

Once the Chinese settled in Montana communities, they pursued a variety of occupations. They owned and operated restaurants, grocery stores, tailor shops, mercantile stores, vegetable gardens, and laundries. In 1890, Helena alone had twenty-six Chinese-owned laundries.[27] Laundry businesses were common because some Chinese had experience in this area, but also because it took little capital to start up such a business and, at least for a while, Chinese laundries posed little threat to established white businesses.[28] In addition to commercial activities, many Chinese provided important social and professional services. In 1900, Butte had at least seven Chinese physicians, some of them serving white as well as Chinese patrons.[29] Chinese skills and diligence were such that their movement into new fields of work was limited only by the unwillingness of the larger white community to accept the Chinese as equal members of society.

Despite intermittent white hostility, Chinese entrepreneurs were valuable to the general community. For instance, they operated pharmacies, laundries, restaurants, mercantile stores, and vegetable gardens that might have otherwise been absent in Montana's early frontier towns. Less well known is the contribution that Chinese businessmen made to the community by paying local taxes, which helped to support community growth not commonly associated with the Chinese. In 1870 tax lists for Lewis and Clark County, for instance, reveal a total assessment of Chinese taxpayers of $38,900. By 1890, the figure had climbed to $80,905. Similar statistics can be found for other Montana communities that had significant Chinese populations[30] At the pre-inflation prices of nineteenth century America, these figures represented a sizable amount of taxable property.

These figures also indicate that many Chinese were not "day laborers" simply passing through the state. Nor were they all sojourners planning to return immediately to China. Although large numbers did return to their homeland, still others decided to remain in the United States to establish what they hoped would be permanent livelihoods for themselves and their families. Perhaps most impressive of all, these self-reliant entrepreneurs were often forced to struggle against significant odds in their efforts to create businesses that would become an integral part of their local communities.

The Chinese pioneers in Montana created a vibrant and complex social network. As was true for many other immigrant groups in nineteenth century America, the recent arrivals from China organized themselves to perpetuate many of their traditional social and cultural practices. Such activities were important in helping the immigrants maintain a sense of identity, particularly when they were confronted by a rather hostile social climate in America.

American conditions alone, however, were not the only factors influencing the unique structure of Chinese immigrant society. Because the overwhelming majority of these people came from one part of China, Chinese immigrants were often able to maintain or to create new social organizations based along traditional clan or district lines. This was especially important because local districts in China, even at the village level, had their own distinct lineages and dialects. Place of origin thus played a critical role in the development of Chinese social relationships in America.[31]

Another important feature of Chinese society in America was the general absence of women. The 1870 Montana census listed only 123 females out of a total Chinese population of 1,949. In 1880, the figures were 80 women out of 1,765; in 1890, 59 out of 2,532; and in 1900, 39 out of 1,739. Chinese women made up no more than 7 per cent, and sometimes as little as 2 per cent, of the total Chinese population in Montana during the nineteenth century.[32]

The absence of women in the Chinese community had a clear effect on the nature of Chinese society in America. To begin with, it helps explain the difficulty the Chinese had in producing future generations in America after the passage of the Chinese exclusion acts. Moreover, Chinese men could not depend on a traditional family dwelling to provide all their social and cultural needs. Consequently, Chinese communities in this country worked to establish institutions that would help to bind people together as they attempted to adjust to the difficulties of living in a new and sometimes hostile country.[33]

One of the most important institutions within Montana's Chinese communities was the local temple, or joss house. Sometimes this institution was contained within a store or private dwelling; other times, particularly in Butte, it was a separate structure entirely. The joss house was a focal point for both social and religious activities within the Chinese community. "The great Chinese Joss," a November 1882 Butte newspaper reported,

> arrived last night by express from California, and is being feasted to-day with all the delicacies of the season. . . . The room in which he has taken up his quarters is gaily decorated with flags, roast hogs, chickens, drums, and a thousand and one articles which defy description. [The Chinese] will wind up with a grand free lunch to-night, at which at least three hundred . . . will be present.[34]

Butte's Chinatown had two separate temples, one of which was not torn down until 1945.[35]

Another institution that sometimes played an important role in the lives of early Montana settlers was the Chinese masonic temple. In addition to providing its members with an opportunity for relaxation and entertainment, this institution, with its emphasis on brotherhood, also reinforced Chinese social and cultural values.

In an effort to maintain a sense of order and group identification, members of the Chinese Masonic Temple in Virginia City compiled a list of twenty-one regulations. Some were designed to protect the group from outside interference and threats. For example, members were required to defend the secrecy of their lodge, and if a member were arrested, he "may not compromise any other brother" of the lodge.[36] Members were also prohibited from assisting Chinese who might belong to rival organizations.

Other regulations were guidelines for ethical social behavior. For instance, members were not to "covet the wife or sisters of brethren because of their beauty." They were warned: "do not occupy by force the property of your brethren" nor "deceive your brethren through fast talking." Members were prohibited from quarreling or feuding in public for fear of damaging the reputation of the brotherhood. More powerful members of the lodge were reminded to not "bully your brethren because of your might." Finally, the regulations established rules for the proper handing of such important social occasions as weddings and funerals.[37] To ensure obedience, specific punishments—such as 306 strokes with a cane—were enumerated.

Taken as a whole, these regulations indicate that Chinese pioneers were often concerned about maintaining order within their communities. Moreover, the masonic temple, like other Chinese institutions, provided its members with a sense of belonging and a feeling of comradery in an apparently harsh and frequently intimidating world.

In the case of Butte, a council of elders representing the four-clan associations eventually formed to provide valuable leadership for the Chinese community. The council, generally made up of leading businessmen, also attempted to resolve conflicts that might flair up among the Chinese.[38] One early Chinese resident in Butte recalled:

> When I first came to Butte about fifty years ago [1890s], there were about thirty-two laundries in the city. About twenty belonged to our clan cousins, while the others belonged to the members of the opposite four-clan association. There were then two large four-clan associations, but the members were not friendly toward each other. Many disputes arose between associations.
>
> In case of a dispute within our own association, it would be settled here. The elders—businessmen and those men who have lived in Butte longest—would hear the facts from the parties in dispute. The council of elders would decide who was right and who was wrong.[39]

When a dispute could not be resolved locally, the case was sent to association headquarters in San Francisco for final settlement. The Chinese communities in

Montana, although geographically isolated, were still able to maintain important social, economic, and cultural ties with the outside world.

The celebration of traditional festivals was also an important feature of Chinese social life. Celebrations included the Ching Ming, Dragon Boat, Moon, and Winter Solstice festivals, but most important of all was the New Year festival.[40] The February 15, 1872, *Helena Weekly Herald* began its story on the Chinese New Year by declaring: "One of the most interesting days we have ever spent in the Territory was on yesterday, during a visit which we made to Chinatown. When we went there, we put ourselves under the care of Tong Hing, and Tong, with his usual urbanity and courtesy, put us through the more prominent of the Celestials." The reporter described in detailed, if rather patronizing, terms the local arrangements made to celebrate this most famous of Chinese festivals.[41]

Ancestor worship, a product of China's strong Confucian heritage, was reinforced through funeral rites and special days of commemoration.[42] The *Herald* reported on April 8, 1869, that

> to-day is the [Chinese] annual Josh Day, on which occasion their custom is to visit the burial places—as our China men and women have done, closing their ceremonies about 2 p.m.—burn incense and innumerable small wax candles about the head stones or boards of the graves, deposit a liberal lunch of choice eatables and drinkables, designed for the spirits of the departed; recite propitiatory prayers to their savior (Josh), and otherwise show themselves sacredly mindful of the welfare of their dead.[43]

While reflecting certain religious duties, these activities served another important purpose. They enabled Chinese pioneers in Montana to maintain a cultural and spiritual link with family and clan members in China. It was unfortunate that various Sinophobic groups in the country would use the very strength of these enduring Chinese customs as a weapon against the immigrants. All too often Americans viewed Chinese social and cultural practices as "proof" that these immigrants could never be assimilated into American society. Some critics even claimed that because of their different ways and values, Chinese immigrants posed a direct threat to the traditional social order in America.

White Montana's response to Chinese immigration largely reflected contemporary regional and national attitudes. Although Chinese settlers in Montana were never the victims of the kind of mass violence that erupted in Rock Springs, Wyoming, in 1885 and along the Snake River in 1877, they were physically and mentally abused and politically exploited well into the early twentieth century.[44] It was not unusual to hear about individual Chinese being harassed or beaten in many nineteenth century Montana communities.[45] Moreover, even before Montana became a state in 1889 lawmakers in the territory passed and attempted to pass laws discriminating against Chinese residents, including one aimed at ownership of mining properties.

A typical example of these anti-Chinese sentiments was expressed in an 1872 law that established a special tax, or "license," on Chinese laundries. In one form or another, this law remained on the books well into the twentieth century.[46] Discrimination against the Chinese became even more pronounced once Montana achieved statehood. In the decade or so after 1889, Montana judicial decisions systematically upheld a number of anti-Chinese laws. "By 1902," writes historian John R. Wunder, "the doors to economic opportunity and cultural equality for Chinese Montanans had been closed with appropriate legal fanfare." On March 3, 1909, the final insult was added when the state legislature passed an anti-miscegenation law prohibiting interracial marriage—a law directed against black Americans and Japanese immigrants as well as against the Chinese.[47]

Why was such animosity directed toward the Chinese, especially when they represented one of the most peaceful and diligent groups in Montana? Nineteenth century critics of Chinese immigration often emphasized that the Chinese introduced tremendous social evils into Montana. Yet, as a group the Chinese were much more law-abiding than many whites were. Between 1900 and 1918, only six Chinese residents of Montana were sent to the state penitentiary, four of them for the same crime. This does not necessarily indicate that Montana's Chinese communities were crime-free, but the evidence does argue against the stereotypical view of Chinese communities as places "teeming" with "tong wars" and "hatchetmen."[48] Some Chinese did have an opium habit (partly because of the Western world's role in expanding the opium trading during the early nineteenth century), but "authorities generally agree that the Chinese were able to exercise better control over opium than most white miners could over whiskey and that they seemed no better or worse for the habit."[49]

Opponents of Chinese immigration also cited the "economic" threat posed by Chinese workers. During the city-wide boycott against Chinese merchants and laborers in Butte from 1897 to 1899, union leaders in the mining city frequently referred to unfair labor competition. Such notions, however, were largely fictitious.[50] To begin with, the Chinese often did the kind of work that many white workers refused to do. Moreover, when the two groups did compete for the same type of job, the Chinese, who were usually excluded from most white-controlled labor unions, were often forced to accept lower wages. The few times when Chinese workers did attempt to strike for higher wages, they found themselves caught between a hostile management and an indifferent general public.[51]

Ultimately, the overriding reason behind the anti-Chinese sentiment in Montana and the rest of the American West was racism—a racism based on cultural stereotypes as well as skin color. It was unfortunate for these Chinese pioneers that their migration to America occurred at a time when racism was especially fashionable in the United States. In fact, the animosity directed toward the Chinese coincided with similar attitudes and acts of violence against black Americans. As the country became increasingly industrialized and urbanized, minorities often became convenient scapegoats for other groups who felt "victimized" by rapid economic and social changes.[52]

An 1893 editorial published in a Butte, newspaper gave voice to this racism: "The Chinaman is no more a citizen than a coyote is a citizen, and never can be." After making obligatory references to cheap labor and opium, the scathing editorial continued:

> The Chinaman's life is not our life; his religion is not our religion. His habits, superstitions, and modes of life are disgusting. He is a parasite, floating across the Pacific and thence penetrating into the interior towns and cities, there to settle down for a brief space and absorb the substance of those with whom he comes into competition. His one object in life is to make all the money he can and return again to his native land, dead or alive. His very existence in our midst is an insult to our own intelligence. Pestilence and disease follow in his wake, no matter what sentimentalists say to the contrary. Let him go hence. He belongs not in Butte.[53]

These racist and stereotypical attitudes were not confined to Butte, but were prevalent in many Montana communities during the late nineteenth century.[54] The power and popularity of such racial sentiments help to explain the ease with which the Montana legislature and the federal government could pass so many discriminatory laws aimed at the Chinese. These laws not only limited economic opportunities and cultural equality for Chinese pioneers, but they also effectively shut off the flow of new arrivals from China. Without new, especially female, emigrants, the once-vibrant Chinese communities of the intermountain states were bound to disappear.

Several important observations can be made from this rather brief description of the Chinese experience in nineteenth century Montana. First of all, one is struck by the great diversity of occupations that the Chinese pioneers pursued in Montana. They did not limit themselves to placer mining or railroad building, but were willing to try almost any occupation that might allow them to achieve financial security and independence. Ultimately, the ability of the Chinese to branch out into new lines of work was limited not so much by their own prejudices and cultural habits as by the prejudices of the larger white community.

One of the most important aspects of the Chinese experience was their contribution to the economic development of nineteenth century Montana. Chinese pioneers were an integral part of the infant mining industry in the territory helping to pump thousands of dollars into the local economy while exploiting resources that other miners often ignored. The Chinese role in building the Northern Pacific Railroad was of tremendous value to the future development of the state, as the railroad made possible the greatest growth in the state's history, from 1890 to 1920. In Montana's budding urban communities, Chinese entrepreneurs provided valuable services to non-Chinese as well as Chinese patrons. Taken as a whole, these contributions played a crucial part in transforming Montana from a primitive, isolated patchwork of localities into an increasingly sophisticated, urbanized, and economically prosperous society.

As these Chinese pioneers contributed to Montana's economic development, they also built a complex and semi-permanent subcommunity of their own. This subcommunity often stressed traditional ties of clan and region, which were reinforced through participation in various cultural and religious activities. Unfortunately, the same customs that gave Chinese pioneers a sense of identity and purpose were used by critics to "prove" that Chinese immigrants were "polluting" America's cultural values and social order. Such attacks made it difficult for non-Chinese Americans to comprehend the richness and subtleties of Chinese customs and traditions.

This inability or unwillingness to appreciate the value of Chinese contributions was a direct result of the racial attitudes of the day. In that sense, the reaction of many white Montanans to the presence of Chinese settlers was all too typical of broader national and regional patterns. Montanans generally supported the passage of federal laws prohibiting Chinese immigration to America. At the local level, Montanans passed a series of state laws, which were upheld by the state Supreme Court, that intentionally discriminated against Chinese Montanans. These prejudices were so pervasive that recognition of the Chinese role in the development of modern Montana would come only after most of the Chinese pioneers and their descendants had left the state.

NOTES

1. See Elmer Clarence Sandmeyer, *The Anti-Chinese Movement in California* (Urbana: University of Illinois Press, 1939); Alexander Saxton, *The Indispensable Enemy: Labor and the Anti-Chinese Movement in California*

2. An excellent example is the recent book by Sucheng Chan, *This Bittersweet Soil: The Chinese in California Agriculture, 1860–1910* (Berkeley and Los Angeles: University of California Press, 1986).

3. To see how the Montana experience fits into a broader, international context, see Michael H. Hunt, *The Making of a Special Relationship: The United States and China to 1914* (New York: Columbia University Press, 1983), especially chapters 2, 3, 7; Shih-shan Henry Tsai, *China and the Overseas Chinese in the United States, 1868–1911* (Fayetteville: University of Arkansas Press, 1983).

4. Hunt, *The Making of a Special Relationship*, 63–64; Jack Chen, *The Chinese of America: From the Beginnings to the Present* (San Francisco: Harper & Row, 1981), 6–9; Frederic Wakeman, Jr., *Strangers at the Gate: Social Disorder in South China, 1838–1861* (Berkeley and Los Angeles: University of California Press, 1966).

5. Chen, *The Chinese of America*, 35–124; Gunther Barth, *Bitter Strength: A History of the Chinese in the United States, 1850–1870* (Cambridge, Massachusetts: Harvard University Press, 1964), 32–49; Kil Young Zo, *Chinese Emigration into the United States, 1850–1880* (New York: Arno Press, 1978), 81–92.

6. The three regions were San-i (Sam Yup in Cantonese), Ssu-i (Sze Yup in Cantonese), and Hsiang-shan (Hueng-shan in Cantonese; later renamed Chung-shan). See Hunt, *The Making of a Special Relationship*, 61–62.

7. See June Mei, "Socioeconomic Origins of Emigration: Guangdong to California, 1850–1882," in *Labor Immigration under Capitalism: Asian Workers in the United States before World War II*, ed. Lucie Cheng and Edna Bonacich (Berkeley and Los Angeles: University of California Press, 1984), 219–247.

8. Hunt, *The Making of a Special Relationship*, 61; Chen, *The Chinese of America*, 10–13.

9. Hunt, *The Making of a Special Relationship*, 63.

10. Chen, *The Chinese of America*, 15–29; Barth, *Bitter Strength*, 50–76; Zo, *Chinese Emigration into the United States*, 114-145.

11. See Ping Chiu, *Chinese Labor in California, 1850–1880: An Economic Study* (Madison: University of Wisconsin Press, 1963); Saxton, *The Indispensable Enemy*; Chan, *This Bittersweet Soil*; Wynne, *Reaction to the Chinese in the Pacific Northwest and British Columbia*; James Morton, *In the Sea of Sterile Mountains: The Chinese in British Columbia* (Vancouver: J. J. Douglas Ltd., 1974); Jeffrey Barlow and Christine Richardson, *China Doctor of John Day* (Portland: Binford & Mort, 1979); John R. Wunder, "Chinese in Trouble: Criminal Law and Race on the Trans-Mississippi West Frontier," *Western Historical Quarterly* 17 (January 1986):25–41.

12. To date, only three scholarly articles have been published on the Chinese historical presence in Montana: Larry D. Quinn, " 'Chink Chink Chinaman': The Beginnings of Nativism in Montana," *Pacific Northwest Quarterly* 58 (April 1967):82–89; John R. Wunder, "Law and Chinese in Frontier Montana," *Montana the Magazine of Western History* 30 (Summer 1980):18–30; Stacy A. Flaherty, "Boycott in Butte: Organized Labor and the Chinese Community, 1896–1897," *Montana the Magazine of Western History* 37 (Winter 1987): 34–47. Moreover, these articles deal primarily with the reaction of white Montanans to Chinese rather than with the experiences of the Chinese themselves.

13. U.S., Department of the Interior, Census Office, *Eleventh Census of the United States, 1890: Population, Part I* (Washington, D.C.: Government Printing Office, 1895), 29, 439; U.S., Department of Commerce, Bureau of the Census, *Fourteenth Census of the United States, 1920: Population, Volume II* (Washington, D.C.: Government Printing Office, 1922), 574, 577.

14. Michael P. Malone and Richard B. Roeder, *Montana: A History of Two Centuries* (Seattle: University of Washington Press, 1976), 50–55.

15. Rossiter W. Raymond, "Statistics of Mines and Mining in the States and Territories West of the Rocky Mountains," 41st Cong., 2d sess., 1870, H. Ex. Doc. 207 (Serial 1424), 260.

16. Montana Territory, Legislature Assembly, *Laws, Memorials, and Resolutions of the Territory of Montana, Seventh Session* (Deer Lodge, Montana: James H. Mills, Public Printer, 1972), 593–596; Montana Territory, Legislative Assembly, *Laws, Memorials, and Resolutions of the Territory of Montana, Eighth Session* (Helena: Robert E. Fisk, Public Printer, 1874), 97; Wunder, "Law and Chinese in Frontier Montana," 24–25. The original law stated: "No alien shall be allowed to acquire any title, interest, or possessory or other right to any placer mine or claim, or to the profits or proceeds thereof, in this territory."

17. Rossiter W. Raymond, "Statistics of Mines and Mining in the States and Territories West of the Rocky Mountains," 42d Cong., 2d sess., 1872, H. Ex. Doc. 211 (Serial 1513), 292.

18. See Randall E. Rohe, "After the Gold Rush: Chinese Mining in the Far West, 1850–1890," *Montana the Magazine of Western History* 32 (Autumn 1982):18.

19. Most Chinese miners in Montana worked small placer claims, either individually or with various partners. Generally speaking, the Chinese did not play an important role in

the development of industrial mining in Montana, partly because employers were reluctant to hire them and partly because there were fewer Chinese left in the state by the time industrial mining came into its own around the turn of the century.

20. Chen, *The Chinese of America*, 65–77; Tzu Kuei Yen, "Chinese Workers and the First Transcontinental Railroad of the United States of America" (Ph.D. diss., St. John's University, New York, 1977).

21. "First Across the Northwest—The Northern Pacific," MS 5, President's Subject files, Northern Pacific Railroad Company Records, Box 515, Minnesota Historical Society Archives, St. Paul [NP Records].

22. Newspaper clipping, October 28, 1882, Secretary Scrapbooks, 1866–1896, Box 4, Vol. 25, NP Records.

23. *Ibid.*

24. *Ibid.*

25. Anderson to Harris, August 7, August 31, 1886, Letters Received, Registered: President and Vice President (1882–1893), President's Department, Box 19, NP Records; *Weekly Missoulian*, February 16, 1883.

26. *Eleventh Census of the United States, 1890: Population, Part I*, 439.

27. *Helena City Directory, 1890* (Helena: R.L. Polk & Company, 1890), 465–66.

28. See Paul Ong,"An Ethnic Trade: The Chinese Laundries in Early California," *The Journal of Ethnic Studies* 8 (Winter 1981):95–113. Although laundries were labor-intensive businesses, they did require some capital. In California, "investments ranged from $400 to $1,600, with the average being about $800" (p. 101).

29. *Butte City Directory, 1900* (Butte: R. L. Polk & Company, 1900), 689–690.

30. Lewis and Clark County Tax Lists, 1870, 1890, Montana Historical Society Archives, Helena [MHSA]; Rose Hum Lee, *The Growth and Decline of Chinese Communities in the Rocky Mountain Region* (New York: Arno Press, 1978), 155–165.

31. Hunt, *The Making of a Special Relationship*, 65–73; Zo, *Chinese Emigration into the United States*, 131–139.

32. U.S., Department of the Interior, Census Office, *Ninth Census of the United States, 1870: Population, Volume I* (Washington, D.C.: Government Printing Office, 1872), 609; *Tenth Census of the United States, 1880: Population* (Washington, D.C.: Government Printing Office, 1883), 545; *Eleventh Census of the United States, 1890: Population, Part I*, 488; *Twelfth Census of the United States, 1900: Population, Part I* (Washington, D.C.: Government Printing Office, 1901), 492.

33. Normal male-female relations were skewed even further because an unusually large percentage of the Chinese women in the American West in the nineteenth century were employed as prostitutes. See Lucie Cheng, "Free, Indentured, Enslaved: Chinese Prostitutes in Nineteenth-Century America," in *Labor Immigration under Capitalism*, ed. Cheng and Bonacich, 402–434.

34. (Butte) *Weekly Inter Mountain*, November 23, 1882.

35. Lee, *The Growth and Decline of Chinese Communities*, 263.

36. Chinese Masonic Temple banner, March 3, 1876 (Virginia City), Montana Historical Society Museum, Helena. Regulations translated by Fr. John Wang of Missoula.

37. *Ibid.*

38. Lee, *The Growth and Decline of Chinese Communities*, 226–232.

39. Quoted in *ibid.*, 229.

40. See *ibid.*, 273–280.

41. *Helena Weekly Herald*, February 15, 1872.

42. See *Weekly Missoulian,* June 17, 1881.

43. *Helena Weekly Herald,* April 8, 1869.

44. See Robert R. Swartout, Jr., "In Defense of the West's Chinese," *Oregon Historical Quarterly* 83 (Spring 1982):25–36; David H . Stratton, "The Snake River Massacre of Chinese Miners, 1887," in *A Taste of the West: Essays in Honor of Robert G. Athearn,* ed. Duane E. Smith (Boulder, Colorado: Pruett Publishing Company, 1983), 109–129.

45. See *Helena Weekly Herald,* May 31, 1883, September 24, 1885; *Helena Daily Herald,* January 26, 1870; (Butte) *Tribune Review,* August 4, 1906; *Great Falls Daily Tribune,* December 20, 1903; *Livingston Post,* December 6, 1906; (Miles City) *Yellowstone Journal,* April 5, 1884; (Quigley) *Rock Creek Record,* June 13, 1896; (Deer Lodge) *New North-West,* December 23, 1881; (Butte) *Weekly Miner,* December 27, 1881; August 7, 1891; (Butte) *Semi-Weekly Miner,* October 3, 1885; *Butte Daily Miner,* October 2, October 3, 1893; (Butte) *Daily Inter Mountain,* August 24, 1901; *Anaconda Standard,* January 21, March 8, 1892, January 8, 1893, September 5, 1899.

46. Montana Territory, Legislative Assembly, *Laws, Memorials, and Resolutions of the Territory of Montana, Seventh Session,* 589; State of Montana, *The Codes and Statutes of Montana, 1895, Vol. I* (Butte: Inter Mountain Publishing Company, 1895), 562; State of Montana, *The Revised Codes of Montana, 1907, Vol. I* (Helena: State Publishing Company, 1908), 807. Although Chinese were not specifically named in the law, female-operated laundries and later, steam-type laundries were exempt from paying the tax. These descriptions were synonymous with white-operated laundries. The intent of the law was obviously discriminatory.

47. Wunder, "Law and Chinese in Frontier Montana," 30; William L. Lang, "The Nearly Forgotten Blacks on Last Chance Gulch, 1900–1912," *Pacific Northwest Quarterly* 70 (April 1979):57.

48. Records of the Montana State Board of Prison Commissioners, 1887–1962, RS 197, MHSA.

49. W. Eugene Hollon, *Frontier Violence: Another Look* (New York: Oxford University Press, 1974), 89.

50. Membesr of the Butte Chinese community eventnally took the boycott leaders to court. See *Hum Fay et al. vs. Frank Baldwin et al.* Records, MC 43, MHSA. Local newspapers gave the case extensive coverage, especially the *Anaconda Standard,* the *Inter Mountain,* and the *Butte Miner.* The Chinese won the case in the federal courts in May 1900, but they received no damages to cover their financial losses. See *Butte Miner,* April 4, 1899; *Daily Inter Mountain,* May 19, 1900; and United States District Courts (U.S. Circuit Court—Montana), Final Record, Case #40, RG 21, National Archives—Seattle Branch. For an outstanding study of the entire affair, see Flaherty, "Boycott in Butte." 34–47.

51. See Yen, "Chinese Workers and the First Transcontinental Railroad," 129–131; Chen, *The Chinese of America,* 74–75.

52. See especially Saxton, *The Indispensable Enemy,* and Luther W. Spoehr, "Sambo and the Heathen Chinee: Californians' Racial Stereotypes in the Late 1870s," *Pacific Historical Review* 42 (May 1973):185–204.

53. *Butte Bystander,* February 11, 1893.

54. As early as 1871, a Missoula reporter declared: "The Chinaman lands upon our shores a serf, and remains so. He clings to his idolatry and heathenism with the tenacity of life; lives upon less than the refuse from the table of a civilized man, and devotes his sister to the basest lusts of humanity. . . ." *Missoula Pioneer,* June 22, 1871. For similar comments, see, for example, *Yellowstone Journal,* April 5, 1884; *Livingston Post,* December 6, 1906; *Anaconda Standard,* January 4, 1903.

26

The Heathen Chinee

Larry Barsness

One afternoon a doctor, driving toward Virginia City in his buggy, was startled by shots popping in the diggings across from Nevada City. He looked up just in time to see one Chinese chase another across the tailings. When the pursuer was close enough, he knocked the man down with his shovel. The doctor saw the upright figure belabor the prone figure with shovel blade, until the prone man moved no longer. Then, when more shots sounded and a number of figures scampered across the gulch under a hail of bullets, the doctor drove for Virginia City with the news that the Chinks were embattled just outside town.

When the sheriff arrived, he found a couple of pig-tailed corpses which had been hacked to death, and not another slant-eyed divil in sight. But, picking through the hundred or so Orientals living near by, he somehow chose an Ah Wah and an Ah Yen as the culprits, and carted them off to jail.

The first trial of the two resulted in a hung jury. They had to stay in jail until the next term of court, but they didn't seem to mind their incarceration in the least, or to have any worries about the future. Model prisoners, they were allowed many visitors, who came bearing sweetmeats and hot Chinese dishes to relieve the monotony of Western cooking. Sometimes a number of friends gathered in the cell to help the pair enjoy feast days. These guests were as polite as the prisoners, and always left quietly in a group when the jailer informed them their time was up.

The second trial closed abruptly when it was established that the two prisoners in the dock were not the two men indicted for murder and jailed. These were facsimile prisoners; the genuine articles were bound for China, having walked out of their cells amongst a crowd of their departing guests. The jailer and his white friends had always sworn that all Chinese looked alike to them.

This peculiar blindness toward the yellow man was congenital to the b'hoys in Virginia City. They couldn't see him, because he was a heathen and a slave. To them his food was revolting, his music gold-awful, his women all whores, his scent of musk and opium sinful. Furthermore, they couldn't hear him because his language was an offense to the ears, even names being abominable, so they called each man John and each woman Mary.

They kept their eyes closed and their ears stopped because rumor said John Chinaman was of the dregs of the Chinese Empire, and thus beneath their notice. Rumor said he was pouring toward Montana by the thousands, ready to take every white miner's job from him. Rumor said that he ate mice fried in axle grease, that he lost his strength when his queue was cut off, and that Mary was interesting anatomically. Rumor colored every b'hoy's emotions toward the Chinese, made him blind to their humanity; to him Chinks, niggers, and Injuns were all sub-human, strange offshoots of mankind, whom God had only half-formed. When one of the b'hoys swore he couldn't tell the difference between one Chinese and another, he really meant he was damned if he was going to open his eyes enough to notice any difference.

But the Chinese girls who worked as whores at the lower end of town made the b'hoys blink a little. These women had been sold into bondage by their families and had to serve out their selling price as prostitutes at so much per month. According to the *Post* "... [they] are bought and sold like hogs, the religion of their country pronouncing them to be without souls, and created only for the use of man."[1] Slave sales were not confined to China, these chattels being sold openly in Virginia City. In fact it was reported in the *Post* that one boss Chinaman offered to sell a girl to a "prominent gentleman" about town "at the rather exorbitant figure of $1000." The man declined the purchase as "this property was not the kind . . . [he] wished to pay taxes on."[2] Though slavery had been abolished in the United States, no great fuss was made about the Chinese slave marked by either Union or Confederate sympathizer because the town was "not very intensely interested in the welfare of the heathen Chinee."

On the Virginia City market a young woman in good health could be marketed at $400 to $600; beautiful girls brought more.[3] Among the Chinese they were as valuable as real property in securing a mortgage, and a stray girl was advertised in the paper the same as was any missing property:

Chinese Advertisement

Wang Geu owes Dr. Yee Cheugh Five Hundred and Fifty Dollars. He can not pay it. So, according to Chinese law, he left his woman, Sing Gim, in Dr. Yee Cheugh's possession, as collateral, until the money shall be paid. All right. By and by, all same yesterday, Sing Gim stole Three Hundred Seventy Dollars from Dr. Yee Cheugh, and ran away. Now then, all Chinamen take notice that if you keep Sing Gim, you must pay me Nine Hundred and Twenty Dollars, all same Wang Geu.

Dr. Yee Cheugh[4]

The wonder is that the Chinese-hating editor of this paper had not printed the notice under the heading ESTRAYS. As it was he sardonically hoped something would be done about the affair quickly because he was afraid that the advertisement would bring a fresh batch of missionaries to the Territory.

Many of the Chinese men sent to Virginia City were also slaves. If they were bought and sold on the local market, they made no headlines. Such transactions were not prurient enough to make news.

The men had a good chance to reduce the period of their bondage, for they were in demand about the town as servants and cooks at good wages. A woman's contract sometimes bound her for life by adding a penalty time for the menstrual period which incapacitated her each month.

Something was always astir in Chinatown to upset the residents of the upper part of town. The most frequent of the weird noises that floated up street was the "stentorian roar" which announced the beginning of gambling in the Chinese gambling dens each evening at nine o'clock. "Greenbacks, opium, and joss-gods" were the stakes, and they gambled until the wee hours of the morning, leading one editor to complain, "We don't know and don't care how many years they claim to have been infesting the earth, and only wish they would go to bed like decent people and stop playing their infernal button game of 'Foo-ti-hoo-ti,' so a fellow could get a nap."[5]

Gambling started in Chinatown as soon as enough Chinese had arrived in town to make the games interesting. Naturally, few of the slave-laborers could afford the stakes of the uptown saloons, but they were anxious to bet their pittance against other pittances in a change to better their lot. One good night at the tables could propel a laundryman out of the "washee" business into the position of boss gambolier.

The favorite Chinese gambling game in Virginia City was an uncomplicated guessing game which paid off the lucky guesser. As many could play as could gather around the gambler's table, and each man could bet whatever he pleased, high or low. The gambling master's only equipment was a handful of copper coins, a cup and a pointed stick. When all was ready, the handful of coins went into the cup, the cup turned upside down on the table, and the coins counted out four at a time by means of the pointed stick. The bets were made on odd or even coins remaining, or whether one, two or three coins would remain after all groups of four had been counted out.[6]

White neighbors were welcome at the gambling tables. Those miners who had picked up "a slight acquaintance with the jargon of chow chow" found they could make a little money here without the risks of "bucking the tiger" in the uptown establishments. They soon got used to the thick wreaths of opium smoke which hung over the tables, it having as little effect on the olfactory nerves as tobacco smoke.

Chinese celebrations startled the town several times a year. The Chinese New Year was announced not only by the din of firecrackers, but also by the strange cooking smells, sweet and redolent of sin, which settled in the Gulch and wafted up Wallace Street. Strange concoctions were being made down there, prepared from the weird vegetables those yellow devils grew on the sod roofs of their shanties, and from the chickens, ducks and pigs which they raised for such occasions.

The polite Chinese invited everyone in town to partake of their feasting and celebrating, a hospitality which was never reciprocated. "About half the male population of town" visited Chinatown for one New Year ceremony. Everyone was invited to eat, but only the most hardy attempted the strange food, some claiming the meat came from the carcasses of slaughtered cats, rats and mice; others refusing, as the *Madisonian* editor put it, because the cooking was clean and devoid of the accustomed amount of American dirt.

Most of the visitors to Chinatown on this day were uninterested in eating; they had come to guzzle the good American whisky provided by their hosts. They came early and stayed late and lost all interest in any other proceedings—except that some thought the rumored Chinese custom of canceling all debts on this day would be a fine institution to apply to saloon owners about town.

The Chinese hosts and hostesses, "attired in the latest Pekin fashion," with their queues hanging at full length, the females, "hobbling along in canoes," received their gaping, bearded guests, with formal bows and pleasant smiles, urging them to tables loaded with delicacies. Crackerbox American cabins had been transformed into bits of old China: over the doors of each room were mysterious Chinese inscriptions, placards sprinkled with showers of gold leaf "suggestive of Fortune's shower of wealth." Weird images stood in the corners, incense smoke puffing up in front of them in great dragon-like spirals. Each Chinese, immaculate in holiday blue shirt, cap and trousers, was strangely changed here in his own abode, graciously giving each guest a congratulatory crimson fortune card.

Now, it was the miner who was foreign, but he didn't fell so, for his hosts were so danged courteous and kept urging more whisky and more sweetmeats and more cigars on a man until a fellow almost came to like the yellow cusses. Even the Chinese-baiting newspaper editor had to confess they had their good side on such occasions and grudgingly admitted, "Whatever may be said against them or their peculiar customs, they are at least entitled to the credit of generous hospitality on their festival days. . . ."[7]

The annual "devil driving" exercises also drew crowds of the curious to the lower end of town to witness the "open war declared by Chinamen against his Satanic Majesty" and see the ceremony in which "he is chased around with chin music, one string fiddles, and divil's fire . . . from one China house to another, until he hath not where to lay his head among the celestials, and therefore has to abide, for a time, with his 'heathen' white subjects."[8]

A Chinese funeral smiling its way up Wallace Street, the mourners throughout the ceremony appearing "to be in fine spirits, smiling like the last rose of summer," disturbed the Victorian white more than these other heathenish practices. Such a happy funeral was foreign to Victorian human nature, which had to placate grim Death with a show of grief-stricken mourning. The strange customs of lowering buckets of food into the grave after the corpse, providing the body with a change of underwear and a clean towel, and the like, they could understand, for even the native Indian practiced such superstitions. But at least the Indian had sense enough to wail and mourn a little. This gaiety, this wearing of white mourning bands, this enjoying brandy and cigars at the graveside and this contented smile on the face of a bereaved husband as he provided his dead wife with food, made the Oriental more inscrutable than ever—really put him outside human feeling.

This anti-Chinese sentiment was originally a Californian import. There, where so many households had arrived, much bad feeling had been aroused, most of it based on the rumor that the Chinese were going to take away jobs from American miners, a thing which never did develop. Californians had brought hard tales of the "yellow peril" to Virginia City. Consequently, the town was prepared to hate them. When the original contingent arrived by stagecoach in June of 1865, the *Post*, under Dimsdale's editorship, scornfully listed their names as "Ho-Fie, So-Sli, Lo-Glung, Ku-Long, Whang and Hong" and jibed that, because of their arrival, all the mice in town had declared a retreat.[9]

Through the sixties and seventies this hate campaign was carried on by successive newspapers and editors. They informed their readers that every Chinese in town smoked two dollars' worth of opium every day—forgetting they had previously assessed his wages at a lowly eight to ten dollars per week.[10] The *Montanian*, in referring to the custom of feeding the dead, remarked that "If the living were with the dead, we don't know of any object we would give money for more freely than to buy grub to strew over the mounds that cover their dead carcasses." It further said, "We don't mind hearing of a Chinaman being killed now and then, but it has been coming too thick of late . . . soon there will be a scarcity of Chinese cheap labor in the country. . . . Don't kill them unless they deserve it, but when they do—why kill 'em lots." On another occasion, the editor noted that nine out of ten Chinese had "kleptomania in the worst form, and the prospects for an early Chinese funeral are brightening."[11]

The bitterest of this feeling was expressed in the early 1870's, when the town was almost as much Chinese as it was white, some 272 of the town's 867 residents being Chinese.[12] Actually, the Chinese population had grown by only about one hundred since 1866, when there had been 150 of them in town, including nine women and one baby. At that time only twenty of the men had been miners, the rest being in the "washee business" or working as servants.[13]

Yet violent quarreling between white and Chinese, as reported in the papers, was the exception rather than the rule. One serious altercation between white and yellow miners occurred near Virginia's suburb, Central City, where the Irishmen had been throwing tailings in a Chinese company's ditch. Naturally, the Irish carried the day. Germans and Chinese found themselves sometimes at odds and cursed each other roundly in "fractured English. When they came to the goddle-mighty portion of the debate every window-pane in the street rattled." On one occasion, in a fair fight with a Caucasian, the Chinese had succeeded in blacking the eye of his opponent and was winning the fight, when his queue slipped and provided his opponent with an excellent handhold: finis Chinaman. But these altercations were no more serious than the fisticuffs which were always a part of the Virginia City scene.

The Chinese was something of a fighter. Perhaps his method of fighting, knife in one hand, hatchet in the other, discouraged many white bully b'hoys. Their duels resulted in lopped-off ears and gouged cheeks if not in death.

The antagonism toward the Chinese in Virginia City could not have been directly economic. In the first place, no white mine owner hired any Chinese miners. The Orientals bought and worked only claims that had been worked before — ground the white man did not want. There was little competition in other business. An occasional Chinese operated a store, but it carried mostly Chinese goods. Sometimes the boss Chinese imported silks for local consumption, but they could not have been much competition to local merchants. Nor did the Chinese work for lower wages than the white man in jobs open to both. Those who worked about the town as cooks and servants were paid the prevailing wage for such work, about sixty dollars per month.[14]

Only in the laundry business were the Chinese ever directly charged with economic competition, and that happened in Helena. There a "Committee of Ladies," the laundrywomen, notified sons of Cathay that "they must suspend the washing or laundry business immediately" — an affair that was put into rhyme by the editor of Helena's *Montana Radiator*:

> Chinamen, Chinamen, beware of the day,
> When the women shall meet thee in battle array!
> ....
> Ye hopeless professors of salsoda and soap,
> Beware of the fates that await ye,
> No hangman's committee with ladder and rope,
> But the ladies are coming to bate ye.
> Ye almond eyed leather faced murthering heathens!
> Ye opium and musk stinking varments,
> We will not object to your livin' and breathin'
> But beware of the washing of garments.
> To stay or go ye can do as ye choose,
> To us it don't make any odds
> So long as ye keep your hand off of the clothes,
> And keep out of the lather and suds.[15]

In Virginia City they were accused of charging "four bittee" for "spoiling boiled shirts" but received no threats from the laundresses. The accusation, made by the *Post*, was unwarranted. Bishop Tuttle found their work to be neat and clean. The charge was just a part of the paper's general hate-the-Chinese campaign.

No matter what John Chinaman did, he could not be accepted. If he tried to be Occidental, his efforts were resented even as much as his Oriental ways. If he tried to buy the house a drink in Western manner, he was scorned. When he went on a 'Melican-style party and galloped whooping around the town he very soon found himself thinking things over in the little log jail.

Chinese had no Sundays off, delving from dawn to dark every day, wielding the pick and shovel "with the strength of Sampson and the patience of Job." These miners worked in companies of about fourteen men each, each company with its own cook and living quarters. Most of the time they worked all winter stripping claims, getting ready for the spring sluicing. They worked very primitively, using wheel barrows to trundle the dirt to creek bank, "rewashing old dirt heaps, and making money where anyone else would starve." They were grudgingly admired for their strength:

> Chinamen are heavy on the pack. While the heathen is apparently physically deficient, he can carry a load that would disgust the boss mule of a pack-train. One was noticed going down the gulch with two large rolls of blankets, a sack of rice, a couple of hog's heads, a lot of heavy mining tools, a wheel-barrow and a hand-rocker swinging to his pack-pole. It was a mystery how that Chinaman managed to tote that weary load along so gracefully, and not grunt a groan.[16]

Still, this prowess did nothing to bring them equality with the whites. One could not appear as a witness against a white man, nor could he find justice for himself in the lower courts. Usually little attempt was made by the court to understand the facts if the case concerned only Chinese. In an assault-and-battery trial, in which fifteen Orientals testified, "His Honor, with complacency, singled out the ugliest pig-tail, imposed a one dollar fine and costs and dismissed the outfit. . . . After which Policeman Dan Hammond drove the band downstairs by order of the court."[17]

In another case of one clan against the other, the question of swearing the witnesses by use of the "chicken oath" arose, the prosecuting attorney contending "that unless the chicken was killed it would be no swear for a Chinaman."

The legal nicety in the case, as in all frontier cases involving depositions by Chinese, was whether or not the traditional ". . . and nothing but the Truth, s'help me God" was binding for a heathen. The "Chicken Oath," as used in Chinese courts, was felt to be binding, and hence used occasionally in Virginia City courts when the case involved a white man—or in a murder case, such as this one for which the oath was given:

> Copies of the oaths to be administered to both parties were written in Chinese and handed to them, at the same time each one put a piece of red josh paper into his pocket. Two fowls were then brought in for the purpose of being sacrificed for truth's sake. The head of the first was stretched across a block of wood, behind which were ranged three of the witnesses. A hatchet was handed to the first in the line, who struck the chicken a blow in the neck, the other two Chinamen followed, and the third blow dispatched it. The other fowl was served in the same manner by the two interpreters and the remaining witness. While the fowls were still bleeding, the individuals who were to be sworn stood up before the Clerk and burned the oaths which they had subscribed, at the same time repeating one in their own language, which ended the ceremony.[18]

According to the Chinese, the belief was that if a man so sworn lied, his head would be chopped off in a similar manner.

To go back to the prosecuting attorney, the judge in this case decided that the oath was unnecessary since the case involved only Chinese! Subsequently, the Chinese witnesses answered "yes" to every question, convicting every case—which, the editor remarked, "was a good thing for the school fund."[19]

This lack of justice in the court bothered no one; a Chinese trial was just a good show:

> The scene beggared description. ... Their eyes set at a tangent with their noses; their queues bound round and round their heads, leaving stray locks standing upright or hanging pendant to their shoulders; dressed in every conceivable variety of American and Chinese wearing apparel, from top boots to black bags with arms in them, and all chattering like so many magpies over a carcass; . . .[20]

When the proceedings involved a Chinese "bad girl" who had been robbed while performing an Oriental dance for some white boys, "the full details of which are unfit for . . . a modest newspaper," a real carnival developed, for, during the dance, "Mary became drunk with excitement and stripped off her cotton trousers and nankeen chemisette. Her pantalettes contained a roll of $100 in greenbacks, a gold josh god, and other Chinese valuables, all of which Mary lost." She charged the white boys with stealing her property, and the police court heard testimony for a full two days of fun at the poor girl's expense. At the end of the proceedings, the judge told her, "Mary, from China, stand up! and listen to the majesty of the American law! . . . It now becomes the painful duty of this court to pronounce final sentence upon you! . . . This court decides that you, while in company with white fellers, hereafter (if you want to keep your green backs) do KEEP YOUR BREECHES ON!"[21]

A type of legal heckling was tried by the local legislators who passed various acts to discourage the Chinese. The year following their appearance in town, a bill to tax them appeared in the Territorial Assembly, but failed to pass. Later a license law charging Chinese fifteen dollars per quarter for the privilege of washing and ironing was passed, only to be repealed at the request of Governor Ashley after the signing of the Burlingame Treaty between the United States and China. This treaty, which guaranteed equal rights to citizens of each country residing within the borders of the other, was much resented by some of the miners and legislators. Representative Sample Orr suggested that no foreigner be allowed to work in mines if he had not legally declared his intention to become a citizen, but this was impractical. The Assembly of 1872 passed an act stating that "no subject of the Empire of China known as Chinese, shall acquire, possess or hold in the Territory of Montana any real estate, or mining claims or placer or quartz mines, or any interest in or to real estate, or mines of any kind or nature whatever."[22] The law was on the statute books until 1874, when it was voided by decision of the Supreme Court of the Territory, which said that a Territory cannot interfere with or control public lands within its boundaries. This settled the matter of legislating against them; anyway the scare was over—no hordes of Chinese had descended on the state. Most of the Oriental emigrants had stayed in California where they had landed.

In spite of their many discouragements, the Chinese outstayed most of the placer miners in the gulch. Coming and going from China, one worker being replenished as another left, they worked most of the gulch below Virginia City by hand, taking about forty years to complete the job, finishing about the turn of the century. The other races which had landed fresh from the old country in Alder Gulch had learned American ways and had become assimilated. The Chinese did not; they stayed together, retaining their customs and dressing in Oriental fashion.

They are remembered in 1900, working the lower end of the gulch, a colony of about 200 living in cabins as neat as a pin and still raising their own Chinese vegetables in gardens on the sod roofs. The attitude toward them had changed considerably in the years since their first appearance in the gulch. "They were a fine people," say the septegenarians in town. They remember the strange log temple at the foot of Wallace Street which contained a beautifully decorated altar presided over by a "real priest." It was well worth a visit just to hear the strange music played by a band of stringed instruments.

The last of the two hundred, an old woman, "China Mary" of course, lived in town all alone as late as the twenties, telling of her ribald early-day experiences as a prostitute as matter-of-factly as if she were relating schoolgirl memories.

A lad who grew up in Virginia City may have known a lot about the Vigilantes, but what he was really an authority on, although he didn't know it, was the Chinese, for he had seen queues and padded clothing, had heard the sing-song of the strange heathen language every day of his life. He knew more about the ways of the Chinese than almost any professor in the land: he had watched nimble fingers pluck music out of stringed instruments so often that neither music nor instruments seemed weird any more. He was one of the few white lads in the world who had shot off Chinese firecrackers, who had seen a yellow man smoking opium, who had looked through the holes in Chinese money, tried the brushes and ink which made Chinese writing, or seen the unbelievable chopsticks in action. He was one of the few whites in the world who had eaten Chinese food—most of it stolen from the graves in the Chinese cemetery on the nights following Chinese funerals; free feeds of succulent roast pig and cold rice, washed down with a swig of fiery brands, which the heathen had also left to comfort the departed.[23]

But, even as with their elders, familiarity with the Chinese, instead of leading to understanding, led to contempt. The Chinks were be-deviled in every way the kids could hatch: swipe their laundry, pull their queues, dump their suds, steal and sell their copper boilers, throw rocks at their doors—few b'hoys would say them nay. Pranks played on a laundryman sometimes led to a brief chase down the alley, spluttering Chinese yelling obscenities at departing backs. Most of the kids learned a little Chinese in this way, all of it profane.

NOTES

1. *Montana Post*, Feb. 10, 1866, p. 2.
2. *Montanian*, Dec. 26, 1872, p. 5.
3. *Ibid.*
4. *Ibid.*, Dec. 19, 1872, p. 4.
5. *Ibid.*, Jan. 30, 1873, p. 5.
6. *Montana Post*, Sept. 29, 1866, p. 5.
7. *Ibid.*, Jan. 25, 1868, p. 8.
8. *Montanian*, Nov. 13, 1873, p. 8.
9. *Montana Post*, June 3, 1865, p. 2.
10. *Montanian*, Nov. 7, 1872, p. 5.
11. *Ibid.*, August 31, 1871, p. 5; March 27, 1873, p. 5; June 12, 1873, p. 5.
12. From the 1870 census figures.
13. *Montana Post*, Nov. 3, 1866, p. 5.
14. Tuttle, *op. cit.*, p. 170.
15. *Montana Radiator*, Jan. 27, 1866, p. 3.
16. *Madisonian*, March 8, 1876, p. 3.
17. *Ibid.*, Jan. 8, 1876, p. 3.
18. *Montana Post*, March 21, 1868, p. 8.
19. *Montanian*, April 27, 1871, p. 5.
20. *Montana Post*, Jan. 26, 1867, p. 8.
21. *Madisonian*, Oct. 9, 1875, p. 3.
22. *Montanian*, Dec. 21, 1871, p. 7.
23. *Madisonian*, April 5, 1877, p. 3.

27

Boycott in Butte: Organized Labor and the Chinese Community, 1896–1897

Stacy A. Flaherty

In 1882, the year of the national Chinese Exclusion Act, Butte, Montana, elected its fourth mayor, William Owsley, whose slogan rang, "Down with Chinese Cheap Labor."[1] Like many places in the American West, Butte has been the scene of anti-Chinese hostility, including random violence against Chinese and organized boycotts of Chinese businesses. In 1884, for example, a circular was posted ordering Chinese to leave Butte; and in 1891–1892, organized labor unions unsuccessfully boycotted Chinese businesses with hopes of driving them from the city.[2]

By the end of 1896, several labor leaders had organized another anti-Chinese boycott, determined to win this time. When they officially announced the boycott on January 13, 1897, the unions blamed the Chinese for some economic conditions and condemned their perceived cultural inferiority. Organized labor attacked the Chinese by notifying its members and the general public of a boycott against all Chinese businessmen and workers, including those who employed Chinese. Derisive banners and floats were paraded through the streets informing citizens of the boycott. Union members were stationed near Chinese businesses in order to ward off would-be patrons.

The boycott seriously threatened Butte's Chinese, and many were forced to seek employment in other cities. But one group of Chinese fought back. Unlike many other victims of anti-Chinese hostility in the West, these Chinese did not idly stand by. They responded by filing suit in the district court against the labor unions, requesting damages and an injunction to stop the boycott.

During the mid 1860s, Chinese immigrants came to Montana to mine in the newly discovered goldfields and to work in support services, such as laundries and restaurants. Some historians estimate that eight hundred Chinese had arrived in

BOYCOTT

A General Boycott has been declared upon all CHINESE and JAPANESE Restaurants, Tailor Shops and Wash Houses by the

Silver Bow Trades and Labor Assembly

All Friends and Sympathizers of Organized Labor will assist us in this fight against the lowering Asiatic standards of living and of morals.

AMERICA vs. ASIA

Progress vs. Retrogression

Are the considerations involved.

BY ORDER OF

 Silver Bow Trades and Labor Assembly.

Figure 27.1   Boycott poster.
Source: National Archives—Seattle Branch.

Montana by 1869. An 1870 federal report, however, counted between two thousand and three thousand Chinese in the territory. Chinese concentrated in the urban areas in Montana; by the end of the nineteenth century, the state's largest Chinatowns were found in Lewis and Clark, Silver Bow, and Deer Lodge counties.[3]

Butte, the county seat of Silver Bow County since 1881, had one of the largest Chinese communities in the Rocky Mountains by 1890. Providing the larger community with several services and shops, Butte's Chinatown was located in the central business district, bounded on the east by Main Street, on the west by Montana Street, on the north by Galena Street, and on the south by Mercury Street. But the Chinese businesses spread beyond these boundaries; by the early 1890s, three large restaurants, twenty laundries, four merchandise stores, one tailor, and two doctors made up the majority of Chinese businesses in Butte.[4]

There was popular resentment of the Chinese in Butte. Labor unions, which supported such issues as immigration restrictions, perceived the Chinese as economic competitors and as a threat to community solidarity and family life. The assumption that the Chinese were an inferior and backward people and, therefore, morally, economically, and socially undesirable, served as rationale for exclusion and expulsion. Various actions against the Chinese had failed to force Asians out of Butte. An anti-Chinese boycott in 1891–1892, for example, had ended in failure, which served notice that organized labor would have to put forth a more concerted effort if they wanted to drive the Chinese from Butte.[5]

In late 1896, the Hotel and Restaurant Keepers, proprietors of three leading steam laundries, and a delegation from the Cooks and Waiters' Assembly began another boycott aimed at Chinese businesses and businesses employing Chinese. Three members from each group formed a committee and met "to devise ways and means of boycotting the Chinese element, and also to devise ways and means of collecting the funds necessary to carry on such a boycott."[6] The Cooks and Waiters' Assembly paid one-quarter of the committee's total expenses, and the laundrymen and Hotel and Restaurant Keepers divided the remaining costs. The committee collected money for printing notices and supplies for banners and also for the walking delegates who enforced the boycott in the streets. It met once a week to decide on the action to be taken during the ensuing week.[7] Having a clear memory of the earlier unsuccessful boycott, unions recognized that a more systematic method of boycotting was needed to drive Asians out of Butte.[8]

Union members organized for the fight. By early 1897, a large sum of money had been raised, and a local newspaper reported that "a street committee has had the matter in charge for some time, and several hundred businessmen and politicians will wake up some morning and find their reputations dangling in the air."[9] Other unions in Butte supported the Hotel and Restaurant Keepers, Cooks and Waiters, and laundrymen. Unions representing bakers and hard-rock miners supported the boycott in the name of labor solidarity, even though Chinese did not work in those trades.

The Silver Bow Trades and Labor Assembly, an umbrella organization of Butte's more than thirty labor unions, officially endorsed the boycott on January

13, 1897, with a notice in a local newspaper. They sought to defend "American manhood" and "American womanhood" from the Asians living in Butte by declaring a boycott of all Asian businesses.

> A general boycott has been declared upon all Chinese and Japanese restaurants, tailor shops and wash houses, by the Silver Bow Trades and Labor Assembly. All friends and sympathizers of organized labor will assist in this fight against lowering Asiatic standards of living and of morals.
>   America vs. Asia, progress vs. retrogression, are the considerations now involved. American manhood and American womanhood must be protected from competition with these inferior races and further invasions of industry and further reductions of the wages of native labor by the employment of these people must be strenuously resisted. By order of the Silver Bow Trades and Labor Assembly.
>   P. H. Burns, President
>   G. B. Walters, Secretary[10]

Even though most of the Asians in Butte were Chinese, the unions included Japanese in the boycott. Fitting the Japanese into the same stereotypes imposed on the Chinese, the *Butte Sunday Bystander*, the Silver Bow Trades and Labor's paper, explained that the Japanese posed the same threat as did the Chinese:

> The Japs don't become American citizens any more than the Chinese and their mode of living is not entirely unlike that of the latter class. That they are just as bad as cutting wages and lowly living is demonstrated in Tacoma, Washington. . . . Furthermore, they are as cute as rats, and it is just simply impossible to get rid of them.[11]

The 1896–1897 boycott was spawned by workers growing frustrations with their declining economic positions brought on by the lingering effects of the 1893 depression. As a mining center, Butte was a free-silver town. It had enthusiastically supported the agenda of the rapidly growing Populist part, especially the bimetallism plank of coining money with silver and gold at a ratio of sixteen to one. During the 1896 presidential campaign. Butte and the rest of Montana had fought hard for the free-silver forces of Populist party candidate William Jennings Bryan. Bryan's defeat, however, discouraged his supporters and reinforced the notion held by many workingmen that capitalists controlled the American political system as well as its economic system.[12] It may be that the workingmen vented their frustrations over the lost election on the Chinese.

The boycotters employed a variety of arguments to justify ridding Butte of the Asians, including the competition of cheap labor, the exporting of money to Asia, the claim of cultural and racial inferiority, and the displacement of female workers by Asians. In addition to economic rationales, the labor press contributed deriding comments on Chinese businesses, labeling Chinese laundries "pest houses" and Chinese laundrymen as "leporous [*sic*] and mouth-spraying."[13] These issues fell under the war cry "America vs. Asia." Many of these arguments were similar to those made against the Chinese in other western communities, such as Tacoma, Washington, and Elko, Nevada.[14]

William Hogan, editor of the *Butte Sunday Bystander*, explained the purpose of the boycott: ". . . the primary purpose is to secure living wages for which . . . the Chinese interfered. The Chinese in this matter would be the same as any other person who followed the same policy." According to Hogan, the Chinese stood in the way of labor's goal of securing decent wages for union members.[15]

Michael J. Geiger, a vocal member of the Clerk's Assembly, mixed economic rationales with racism to garner support for the boycott. He argued that the boycott

> would put someone to work that consumes articles that are grown in the United States . . . that is the Chinamen that are here work for half pay and consume little or nothing that is produced in this country . . . while we have our sisters and brothers out of work. . . . We want to call public attention to that fact and I shall do so, and endeavor to get our white sisters and brothers here—Christian people, put to work.[16]

Dan MacDonald, former president of the Silver Bow Trades and Labor Assembly, blamed the Chinese for displacing white workers:

> It simply works an injury on people who are engaged in that particular occupation, and certainly is an injury to the white boys and girls that follow that vocation. I don't consider that white people can maintain their families for the wages that a Chinaman will work for, and for that reason organizations have to exist.[17]

Home Industry, a publication of the Butte Chamber of Commerce, supported the boycott and applauded organized labor for its efforts to employ white men and women and to keep money in Butte by making Chinese "as rare in Butte as a cherry tree."[18]

Another motivation for the boycott was "to better the condition of the female help of Butte City against the Chinese."[19] The Hotel and Restaurant Keepers embraced this issue:

> Owing to the fact that the female portion of our native population were drifting towards Galena street, and that a portion of them were drifting towards Mercury street; in other words, the girls of our town were unable to secure employment of any kind, except prostitution, and that they were drifting towards the hop joints; and so it was brought up to our assembly . . . to confer with and advise some means toward giving employment to the unemployed white girls of Butte.[20]

The *Sunday Bystander* echoed this so-called gallant cause by explaining that there were unemployed women in Butte who were forced into the paths of temptation and shame. Unlike unemployed men, women were not able to travel in boxcars or go to saloons and sleep in chairs. According to the labor paper, the

"American sentiment" endorsed a boycott of those who filled women's places.[21] This rationale played in American society during the late nineteenth century. Labor may have used this reasoning to appeal to the morals of the middle class in Butte, hoping to draw some support for the boycott among that class of society.

The *Bystander* carried updates of and justifications for the boycott. A lengthy editorial on March 27, 1897, argued that the guiding principle of a boycott was that a man enjoys the privilege of patronizing whomever he pleases and can divert patronage by moral suasion. Further, the *Bystander* claimed, the unions were not guilty of any act that was a menace to good public policy and were only doing their duty to their friends.[22]

After obtaining the endorsement of the Silver Bow Trades and Labor Assembly, the boycotters sought to win support in the wider community. They used tactics designed to ridicule and intimidate both Chinese and Japanese residents, employers of Asians, and patrons of Asian businesses. Anti-Chinese banners and wagon floats were displayed throughout Butte. Hired by delegates from the Cooks and Waiters' Assembly, Fred Oram carried a banner from Arizona Street to Broadway Street, through a major Butte business district. The banner advertised the Chinese boycott as well as the boycott of the Will House, a lodging house that employed a Chinese cook.[23]

In addition to the banners, a wagon carried anti-Chinese pictures painted on muslin. A young stockraiser, George Jackson, described the images:

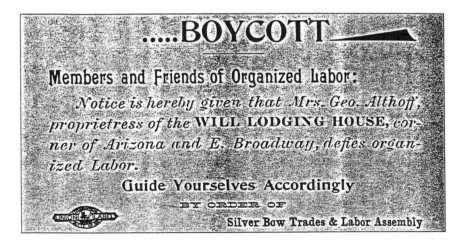

Figure 27.2   The Silver Bow Trades & Labor Assembly handed out this card to encourage the boycott of the Will House, which employed a Chinese cook.
Source: National Archives—Seattle Branch.

One of the representations was a Chinaman making bread, and holding a rat or something over it, as if he intended to drop it into the bread. Another was a Chinaman doing up a white shirt, and he was spitting water or some fluid on the white shirt.[24]

These images held the Chinese up to derision and contempt while soliciting support for the boycott. Quon Loy, a local Chinese merchant, saw the wagon being driven all over Butte, including Chinatown, and found the pictures on the wagon to be insulting and abusive.[25]

Walking delegates from various labor unions enforced a direct boycott of Chinese and Japanese businesses. The delegates were paid to stand in front of Asian businesses and warn patrons of the boycott. Old-timer Andrew Corry was stopped several times by delegates requesting him not to enter Hum Fay's Palace Chop House.[26] The delegates also confronted John A. Leggatt, a mining engineer, as he entered Hum Fay's establishment. He testified about his experience with a walking delegate:

Q) Did you see any evidence of a boycott, other than these banners or dodgers?
A) Yes, men standing around places; one place in front of the Hum Fay's Palace restaurant. . . .
Q) You may tell what you saw there?
A) Well I noticed individuals standing there, and stopping people from going in, and telling them not to go in there that they were boycotting the Chinamen. . . .
Q) Did any of these persons that you say were standing there approach you?
A) They did . . . One man particularly was stepping into the door and he talked to me. . . . They said to me, "don't go in there we have a boycott on the Chinese. Go some place else and eat."
Q) Did you make any reply to that?
A) I replied that it was none of their business, or something like that.
Q) What reply did they make to information of that character?
A) . . . the substance of it was that if I went in there, I would be boycotted myself. . . . I told him to go to Hell.[27]

Walking delegates followed Chinese laundrymen from house to house as they collected or delivered laundry. The laundrymen and those who did business with them were intimidated by these delegates. Delegates also identified white employers and pressured them to discharge their Chinese employees. Forty-year-old laundrymen Chong Jo told of his experience during the boycott:

I have kept a laundry five years. . . . I go up to collect washing, and delegates follow me from house to house. . . . Going to Mrs. Long's house; I go in the house and take the washing, he stand at the door, and give a talk to Mrs. Long. The second time I go to deliver washing she told me they boycotted the Chinese people. . . . Mr. Walters followed me one time. I know he follow me walking along about two hours; I never go into the house. I go inside a fence and stand there about ten minutes; after he gone I come out, and he watch me again, and afterwards in Mrs. Baker's house;

she give the washing to me outside the yard. Mr. George Walters spoke to Mrs. Baker, told her not to give washing to Chinamen.[28]

Thomas Fletcher, a teller at W. A. Clark and Brothers Bank, was told to discharge his Chinese employee and hire a white woman. A walking delegate not only visited Fletcher's home and spoke to his wife, but also visited the bank to press the cause of the boycott.[29]

Many lodging-house keepers were warned to dismiss their Chinese help. Mrs. Margaret Noyes described the boycott of her lodging house. A dodger, or printed handout, declaring Noyes's house boycotted for refusing to fire the Chinese cook, was distributed throughout the neighborhood. With the threat of losing her boarders, many of whom were union members, Noyes discharged her Chinese cook, Sam, and paid a fine of $12.50 to the union to cover the cost of the dodgers. Eventually, Noyes became disgusted with the boycott and sold her business to open another boarding house, but she was plagued by the same threats at the new location as well.[30]

Mrs. Eva Althoff, proprietress of the Will House, another Butte lodging house, was also boycotted for employing Chinese. At first, Althoff resisted the boycott by warning the unions:

> Notice is hereby given that unless the Silver Bow Trades and Labor Assembly and Butte Miner's Union cease boycotting or attempting to boycott the Will House . . . action will be brought against the same for damages, and also to restrain them by law from any further attempts at such boycott, or from continuing such boycotting for any purpose whatever.[31]

Althoff also approached Butte Mayor William Thompson to ask for police protection; her request was denied on the grounds that others would demand the same protection.[32]

The boycotters responded to Althoff's notice by increasing the pressure. Will House boarders were told that if they did not leave Althoff's establishment, their own places of business would be boycotted or they would lose their jobs. According to Mrs. Althoff, Mr. Dorais, the owner of a grocery business on the corner of Arizona and East Park streets, "came to me on a Friday and he said Mrs. Althoff you will have to settle this boycott, or I will have to take every man in your house out, as the union men came to me and told me they would give me till Tuesday to get my men out of the house, and if you don't, we will boycott your store."[33] The *Sunday Bystander* directed an editorial at Althoff, declaring that "anyone who opposes anything that is so American in its nature as the general boycott against the Asiatic races simply put themselves in a ridiculous light, and the sooner they find this out the better they will be."[34] Eventually, Althoff settled the boycott by paying the unions forty-five dollars (the cost of printing and distributing dodgers) and agreeing to hire white help in the future. Labor boasted a "decided victory" over the owner of the Will House.[35]

The situation in Butte was becoming so tense that many citizens feared patronizing the Chinese. Baker John Rudman, a union man, was fearful of being caught trading at Huie Pock's store. He explained, "I was scared when anybody seen me when I go into the store, because they would fine me for it, if anybody seen me from the union."[36]

The boycott claimed a number of casualties in Butte's Chinese community. Hum Jim, a forty-four year-old cook for Miss Nannie Nagle, was discharged and could find no other work.[37] Lock Jim, a vegetable gardner, also fell victim to the boycott. He described how he was followed by a boycott "to a house where I sold vegetables the next day I got there the lady told me she didn't want any more vegetables of me."[38] Before the boycott, Lock Jim sold thirty to forty dollars worth of vegetables a day; during the boycott, he rarely made any sales. Many Chinese laundrymen, laborers, and cooks were discharged after the union threatened their employees.

Chinese merchants and restaurant operators were the main targets of the boycott. These businesses, owned by the wealthiest of the Asians, represented the real potential for economic success among the Chinese and Japanese. Customers of these businesses were pestered and threatened throughout the course of the boycott.

Dr. Huie Pock was a physician and buyer and seller of Chinese and Japanese fancy goods. He moved to Butte in 1889 with his wife, one of the few Chinese women in town.[39] Walking delegates were posted outside his store, warning customers to stay away. Huie Pock's business fell sharply during the boycott, endangering his ability to pay for his city business license.[40]

Restaurant-keeper and merchant Hum Fay had lived in Butte since 1885. His restaurant, the Palace Chop House, sold expensive meals to the workingmen and women of Butte.[41] The boycott severely curtailed Hum Fay's business. Walking delegates kept the Palace under surveillance and prevented customers from entering. Don Len, proprietor of the Wah Chong Tai Company, described how the boycott affected Hum Fay's business:

> Used to be he done a good business before the boycott, but afterwards, as soon as these walking delegates kept there in front of his house, and I believe that his business dropped nine out of ten. There is hardly anybody there at any time I come in there at noon time; used to be a full house at the noon hour before the boycott.[42]

Hum Fay sought to remedy the situation by requesting protection from the mayor and the chief of police. After Hum Fay reminded them that he had paid his taxes and his restaurant license fee and was entitled to help, city officials promised to stop the walking delegates. After several such visits, the officials admitted they could do nothing and suggested he "get a good lawyer, and arrest them."[43]

By the time of the boycott, Quon Loy had lived in Butte for fifteen years. He owned a mercantile store and felt the effects of the boycott on his business. Like Hum Fay, he confronted city officials, claiming that "our people pay licenses and pay taxes and poor taxes just the same as other people, and the walking delegates prevent them from trading, and I think the City ought to do something."[44] But the city did nothing.

The boycott forced approximately three hundred and fifty Chinese out of Butte.[45] Flourishing gardens were abandoned. Many had to leave the city to find work, and those who moved to nearby Anaconda were driven out again. In the spring of 1897, Chinese were reported to be in Billings, Montana, looking for work.[46]

The Silver Bow Trades and Labor Assembly also boycotted Butte's few Japanese businesses. For example, Shikanounsuki Otsuka, a Japanese restaurant owner, was angered enough to appeal to his consul in New York for protection. In his appeal, Otsuka complained of walking delegates in front of his restaurant and of drunkards challenging patrons and breaking windows. The consul referred the matter to Mayor Thompson, who requested instruction from U.S. Secretary of State John Sherman.[47] According to Department of State records, the Japanese consul requested an inquiry into the boycott and protection for his countryman. Mayor Thompson forwarded the letter to the Secretary of State and remarked that all he could do was provide police protection.[48] According to former city detective David Meikeljohn, an officer was put on duty in front of the Japanese restaurant; no similar protection was provided for the Chinese.[49]

In addition to writing his consul in New York, Otsuka wrote his minister in Washington, D.C., asking his advice on how to redress the offenses of the boycotters. The Department of State responded: "There is no statute of the United States which makes the acts you describe a criminal offense against the United States." Redress could only be found through a suit brought by persons injured.[50]

Frustrated by the inability to obtain protection, the Chinese decided to organize a counter movement to halt the boycott. Knowing that their chances were slim, the Chinese collected a legal fund and hired an attorney. The Six Companies in San Francisco, a Chinese benevolent association that spoke for and aided Chinese in America, was leery of fighting the labor union, but the Chinese in Butte went ahead with their plans to seek relief.[51]

On April 15, 1897, Hum Fay, Dear Yick, Hum Tong, and Huie Pock brought suit against several members of Butte labor unions on behalf of themselves and all other Chinese in Silver Bow County. The twenty-two defendants were either active in the boycott and associated with Butte unions or businessmen who would benefit from a successful boycott. The defendants were Frank Baldwin, Griffith E. Taylor, George Morehart, George B. Walters, P. H. Burns, Ed Marchand, H. C. Morgan, M. J. Geiger, Louis Schaffer, Henry LaGalla, Charles Slayton, J. W. Hoffman, George W. Morgan, Frank P. Weldon, Fred Whately, Albin A. Sandahl, Robert E. Taylor, J. H. Free, W. R. Martin, and W. H. Eddy. These men were primarily involved in non-industrial labor and represented a variety of ethnic backgrounds.[52]

Union organizations were also named in the complaint. They were the W. R. Morely Assembly; the Cooks and Waiters' Assembly; the Amalgamated Society of Engineers; the Workingmen's Assembly; the Carpenters' Union; the Plumbers and

Figure 27.3 Some dodgers specified action against particular Chinese businesses. *Source:* National Archives—Seattle Branch.

Gas Fitters' Union; the Tailors' Union; the Bricklayers and Stonemasons' Union; the Bakers' Assembly; the International Brotherhood of Blacksmiths; the Painters, Paper Hangers and Decorators Union; the Butchers' Union; the Musicians' Union; and unions representing moulders, millwrights, and pattern makers, barbers, switchmen, brewers, mill and smeltermen, and tin and sheet-iron workers.

The plaintiffs charged the defendants with unlawful and malicious conspiracy to deprive the Chinese

of the privilege of doing business and of equal protection of the laws, and of equal privileges and immunities under the laws, and to deny them the rights and privileges secured to them by the laws and treaties of the United States.[53]

The complaint detailed the various tactics—banners, dodgers, harassment—that the defendants had used in allegedly violating the rights of the Chinese. Damages requested totaled fifty thousand dollars.

Aware that they were unlike to recover damages from a jury of Silver Bow County citizens, the Chinese filed a complaint in equity, requesting that the court enjoin the defendants from further boycott activities.[54] An equity court administered justice according to fairness as contrasted with the formulated rules of common law. Injunctions were one form of remedy requested in courts of equity. A resort to a remedy in a court of law would have necessitated a multiplicity of lawsuits.

The Chinese community filed a petition joining the prosecution and circulated a petition for redress of the boycott. They collected nearly three hundred signatures from Chinese living in Silver Bow County and delivered it to the court.[55] Hum Jim gathered the names:

> I went around and told them to sign the name on there, and they asked me what it was for and it was all the Chinamen in this town, a white men had boycotted us, and the rest of the Chinamen in this town here is all out of work, and they boycotted us . . . but there is too many Chinamen takes too much time to take them up into court . . . and tell hoe [*sic*] the white man boycotted us, and we all sign our names to them, to that paper, and then we will take it up to court, and those few Chinamen in the court take the whole business.[56]

The lawsuit, which became known as the Chinese boycott case, pitted Butte's Chinese community against the white working community.

The array of legal talent created additional interest in the case. The Chinese community retained Helena lawyer and statesman Wilbur Fisk Sanders.[57] An early pioneer to the state, Sanders had achieved fame in 1863 as the official prosecutor in the Virginia City vigilante trials. Sanders espoused radical Republican philosophies, including the abolition of slavery and a strong federal government. In 1890, he had been elected to the U.S. Senate, where he spoke against Populism, attacking the free-silver position held by the majority of Montanans. After taking this stance, it is likely that Sanders had few friends in the mining center of Butte. He owned no allegiance to labor and seemed to have no qualms about representing the Chinese. Sanders may have been one of the few lawyers willing to defend the Chinese. Fortunately for the Chinese, he was one of the best lawyers in the state.[58] Attorneys James U. Sanders, Wilbur Sander's son, and Francis Brook also counseled the Chinese.

Representing the defendants were Josiah L. and Melvin I. Wines of Butte. Josiah L. Wines had practiced law in Kansas, Nevada, and California before coming to Montana and was a Republican who supported the free-silver issue during the 1896 elections. Melvin I. Wines was a former prosecuting attorney in Butte. They were joined by attorneys John N. Kirk and George A. Clark.[59]

The district judge, Harvard-educated Hiram P. Knowles, was a Republican who had served as a territorial justice and later on the Montana Supreme Court. He was appointed U.S. district judge in 1890.[60] Knowles' career does not lead one to believe that he was a friend of the Chinese. According to legal historian John Wunder, Knowles wrote all the majority opinions of the Montana Supreme Court's decisions against Chinese litigants prior to 1883.[61]

Knowles appointed Henry N. Blake as Master in Chancery of the U.S. District Court. A Master is often appointed when a complicated case is in the court. Such cases were often highly political and demanded much time to gather the facts. The Master would take testimony, make findings of fact, and recommend a decision. Blake, also a Harvard graduate, served as a territorial legislator, territorial justice, and Montana Supreme Court justice. Earlier in his career, Blake had been involved in litigation involving Chinese. He had defended Chinese accused of first-degree murder and had also brought a case against the Chinese over the alien mining law.[62] In his memoirs. Blake recalled the Chinese boycott case as "one of my most important cases."[63] According to Blake, there was a Master in Chancery in Butte who should have taken the case, but he had declined because he feared the Butte unions would boycott him and destroy his legal business.

District Judge Hiram Knowles granted a temporary restraining order halting the boycott on April 16, 1897, and set a hearing for May 10, 1897. But the case was postponed until the court's 1898 term.

The day following the issuance of the temporary restraining order, the *Sunday Bystander* editorialized on "government by injunction." Like labor presses across the United States, Butte's labor newspaper defended the "right" to boycott. The editorial equated the liberty to boycott Asians with the right to free speech and peaceable assemblage. The paper blasted Wilbur Sanders, U.S. Secretary of State Sherman, and the Chinese Six Companies for opposing labor's welfare. The newspaper questioned Sanders's motivation for opposing the boycott, claiming that his law practice was diminishing and his "political anticipations" had not been realized. Sanders was also faulted for accepting a retaining fee from the wealthy Chinese Six Companies, although there is no evidence that the Six Companies was involved in the case.[64]

The Silver Bow Trades and Labor Assembly responded to the injunction by stating that they would obey the order, but they stressed. "We would have it understood that organized labor has never resorted to any force of arms in the prosecution of any boycott and is guilty of no conspiracy."[65] Claiming that the restraining order did not deprive them of the right to withhold patronage, they resolved to do business with their friends and not their enemies.

The unions formed the Chinese Injunction Defense Committee. Frank P. Weldon, a defendant and manager of the Baker Restaurant, represented the Cooks and Waiters' Union on the committee. Its work, as described by Weldon, was of a passive nature — soliciting various organizations to help defray lawyers' expenses in fighting the injunction case.[66]

Hum Fay et al. v. Frank Baldwin et al. began on February 24, 1898, in Butte. Testimony was taken on the application of the plaintiffs to have the temporary in-

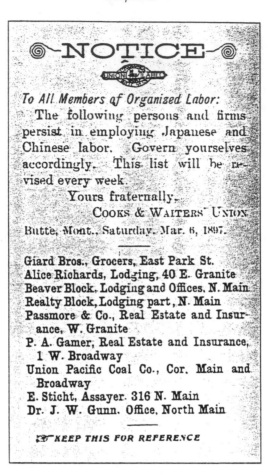

Figure 27.4   Trade unionists extended the boycott to include employers of Chinese. *Source:* National Archives—Seattle Branch.

junction made permanent. During the hearing, approximately one hundred witnesses testified about their knowledge of and their experiences during the boycott of Chinese in Butte from October 1896 to April 1897.

In making the case for the Chinese, Sanders attempted to prove that a boycott existed and that the Chinese were financially injured. He stressed the harmful conspiracy that wreaked havoc on the Chinese community and caused the loss of Chinese jobs and businesses. Since the Chinese were foreigners, they were protected by treaties between the United States and China. As the hearing proceedings got underway, Sanders announced that the matter would be made a question of diplomatic investigation by the U.S. and Chinese governments.[67]

The defendants argued that they were merely patronizing friends' businesses. The defense attorneys brought several union members to the stand to describe the nature of the boycott. Michael J. Geiger described the boycott as a let-alone policy: "to let alone is to do right, to ask our friends to let alone those who are not our friends, not to patronize them, not to do business with them." The boycott, as Geiger defined it, did not include any use of force or threats of intimidation. George W. Morgan, a defendant from the Cooks and Waiters' Assembly, stated that "the term boycott was never used any more than in the capacity of one member withholding his patronage from any outside if he saw fit." "By a boycott I mean," asserted editor Bill Hogan, "that the organizations in Butte were organized for the purpose of promoting the interests in the organized portion of the community." Dan MacDonald described the boycott as an adjustment for grievances to be settled in a peaceable manner and as a withdrawal of patronage from persons antagonistic to union labor. Peaceful means were to be used, not coercion nor intimidation.[68]

After taking testimony, Examiner Henry Blake issued twenty-nine Findings of Fact in March 1899. He determined that some defendants used force to warn customers about boycotted businesses and that the public authorities of Butte and Silver Bow County had not protected the Chinese. Blake also recorded the disappearance of key unions' records books.[69]

The final decision was issued by Judge Knowles on May 18, 1900, three years after the temporary injunction was placed on the defendants and their agents. The injunction was made permanent, and the Chinese were awarded $1,750.05 for legal fees. A local paper announced the final decree as "far reaching" and "sweeping," noting that the decision was "calculated to make the Chinese immune to harm."[70]

What was perceived as a victory for the Chinese proved to be another struggle. Because the defendants were insolvent, the Chinese received no damages. The Chinese argued that public sentiment would not permit a remedy to the situation. Dissatisfied with the court's solution, they turned to the federal government in 1901, requesting the United States to make good its treaty obligations. Chinese minister Wu T'ing-fang appealed to the Department of State to indemnify the Chinese for pecuniary losses and injuries estimated at five hundred thousand dollars.[71] The damages were calculated to cover the years between 1886 and 1901. Secretary of State John Hay replied that none of the allegations warranted diplomatic intervention because of the judicial remedy awarded by the court. Ironically, Hay scolded the Chinese for not appealing to the court sooner:

> If the complainants had promptly availed themselves of their remedial rights, the injuries complained of would have been prevented. Their failure and neglect to so do does not make the United States culpable and responsible for the damages resulting.[72]

The Secretary of State apparently disregarded the history of anti-Chinese actions in Butte and the pressures of public sentiment on the community and the court.

The Chinese had attempted to protect themselves from the boycott by using the only avenues available to them, the courts and the federal government. Yet these avenues were not able to protect the Chinese. The weak position of their homeland, combined with the United States' ineffectiveness in providing protection, left the Chinese vulnerable to the forces of prejudice.

The injunction may have ended some of the overt and highly organized actions against the Chinese and Japanese, but the racism described by many of the residents of Butte did not fade. Racism in Butte obscured and simplified the underlying problems and complex issues of perceived limited employment opportunities for whites, the development of unionism, and the politics of the era. As in other communities, many laborers in Butte argued that Chinese workers took jobs from whites and that they worked for lower wages. These arguments gained credence with workingmen and workingwomen who found themselves without employment during the depressions of the late nineteenth century. For the most part, the Chinese and Japanese held positions that many white workers did not want or ran businesses, such as fancy good stores and laundries, that were not provided by the larger white community. By the late 1890s, however, the steam-laundry business attracted white workers who supplanted or wished to supplant competing Chinese launderers.

In addition to the economic motivations, workingmen used the Chinese issue as a tool for organizing. The 1896–1897 boycott corresponded with the rise of industrial unionism in Butte. The Trades and Labor Assembly enforced the solidarity of white workers by using anti-Chinese rhetoric and encouraging the boycott against not only Chinese, but whites who patronized Asian businesses. In many ways, the boycott was a show of force, a concerted action that demonstrated the resolve of the unions to impress their will on the larger community and to demonstrate the potential of their power and influence. As illustrated by the testimony of witnesses in the Hum Fay case, several white businesses were boycotted for hiring or patronizing Asians. The Trades and Labor Assembly's extension of the boycott to many whites may have caused a backlash within the middle-class community, depriving the unions of support necessary for a successful boycott.

Political conservatives, such as attorney Wilbur Sanders and Examiner Henry Blake, may have used the division between Chinese and other workers to embarrass or deflate labor's efforts. Sanders referred to union members as "worthless characters," and Blake noted a decline in the workers' "spirit of loyalty to their employers."[73]

The 1896–1897 boycott of Asians in Butte was unique in that there was little physical violence against Asians. Even though there is no definitive evidence as to why there was no violence, one could speculate that by the 1890s labor seemed to have learned that the way to garner support among members and the larger community was to peacefully drive out its enemies. This recognition may have also been spurred by the increased use of court injunctions against unions. Peaceful boycotting was a more subtle way to influence community opinion and action than physically harming Chinese, as they had in Denver in 1880 and in Rock Springs, Wyoming, in 1885.[74] Butte's unions may have realized that violence could bring them additional problems, such as federal interference and investigation.

Butte was only one of the many settings for anti-Chinese hostilities. White males joined labor organizations in order to seek economic power, and, in the case of their anti-Chinese actions, to act on their prejudices and dictate social policy. The Chinese were the most vulnerable group in society; they were aliens who were denied the rights afforded other immigrants who settled in the United States. Fundamentally, Butte labor unions waged a campaign based on race; their sentiments and prejudices ran far too deep to be summarily stopped with an injunction.

NOTES

1. Works Progress Administration, *Cooper Camp* (New York: Hastings House, 1943), 109. This was the first election in Butte in which labor issues figured largely in the campaign. *Anaconda Standard*, March 30, 1902.

2. Testimony of David Meikeljohn taken by Henry N. Blake, Esq., Examiner, vol. 3, 149, *Hum Fay et al. v. Frank Baldwin et al.*, Case No. 40, 4 vols. (S. D. Mont 1898), Montana Historical Society Archives, Helena [Hum Fay v. Baldwin]. A discussion of the 1891–1892 boycott can be found in Stacy A. Flaherty, "Asia vs. America: Chinese and Organized Labor in Nineteenth Century Butte, Montana" (M.A. thesis, George Washington University, Washington, D.C., 1986), chapter 4.

3. William S. Greever, *The Bonanza West: The Story of Western Mining Rushes, 1848–1900* (Norman: University of Oklahoma Press, 1963), 235; Rossier W. Raymond, "Statistics of Mines and Mining in the States and Territories West of the Rocky Mountains," 42d Cong., 2d sess., 1872, H. Ex. Doc. 211 (Serial 1513), 272; Bureau of the Census, *Ninth Census of the United States*, Vol. 1: *Statistics of the Population of the United States* (Washington, D.C.: Government Printing Office, 1870), 46; Twelfth Census of the United States, Vol. 1: *Statistics of the Population of the United States* (Washington, D.C.: Government Printing Office, 1900), 567–568.

4. *Butte City Directory, 1891–1892* (St. Paul, Minnesota: R. L. Polk and Company, 1891).

5. Robert McClennan, *The Heathen Chinese: A Study of American Attitudes Toward China, 1890–1905* (Columbus: Ohio State University Press, 1969), 6; Flaherty, "Asia vs. America," chapter 4.

6. Testimony of Frank Baldwin, vol. 3, 273–287, Hum Fay v. Baldwin.

7. Testimony of Frank Baldwin, vol. 3, 277, 281, Hum Fay v. Baldwin.

8. *Butte Sunday Bystander*, January 10, 1897.

9. *Butte Sunday Bystander*, January 17, 1897.

10. (Butte) *Daily Inter Mountain*, January 13, 1897.

11. *Butte Sunday Bystander*, January 17, 1898. See also William Petersen, *Japanese Americans* (New York: Random House, 1971), 31.

12. See Lawrence Goodwyn, *The Populist Moment* (New York: Oxford University Press,

1978); Richard Hofstadter, *The Age of Reform: From Bryan to FDR* (New York: Alfred A. Knopf, 1955); Norman Pollack, *The Populist Response to Industrial America* (Cambridge, Massachusetts: Harvard University Press, 1962); Harold U. Faulkner, *Politics, Reform and Expansion, 1890–1900* (New York: Hastings House, 1959). For Populism in Montana, see Thomas A. Clinch, *Urban Populism and Free Silver in Montana* (Missoula: University of Montana Press, 1970).

13. *Butte Sunday Bystander*, April 10, 1897. This issue also carried an article entitled "The Moral Side of the Chinese Boycott."

14. For Nevada, see Gary P. BeDunnah, *The History of the Chinese in Nevada, 1855–1904* (San Francisco: R & E Research Associates, 1973); for Washington, see James Halseth and Bruce Glasrud, "Anti-Chinese Movements in Washington, 1885–1886: A Reconsideration," in *The Northwest Mosaic*, ed. James A. Halseth and Bruce A. Glasrud (Boulder, Colorado: Pruett Publishing Company, 1977), 116–139; for California, see Ping Chiu, *Chinese Labor in California, 1850–1880: An Economic Study* (Madison: State Historical Society for Wisconsin, 1969).

15. Testimony of William Hogan, vol. 3, 143, Hum Fay v. Baldwin.

16. Testimony of M. J. Geiger, vol. 4, 36–37, Hum Fay v. Baldwin.

17. Testimony of Dan MacDonald, vol. 4, 71, Hum Fay v. Baldwin.

18. *Home Industry* 2 (January 1897): 13.

19. Testimony of George Morehart, vol. 4, 83, Hum Fay v. Baldwin.

20. Testimony of Frank Weldon, vol. 2, 75–76, Hum Fay v. Baldwin.

21. *Butte Sunday Bystander*, January 10, 1897.

22. *Butte Sunday Bystander*, March 27, 1897.

23. Testimony of Fred Oram, vol. 1, 147–154, Hum Fay v. Baldwin.

24. Testimony of George A. Jackson, Vol. 2, 16, Hum Fay v. Baldwin.

25. Testimony of Quon Loy, vol. 3, 188–189, Hum Fay v. Baldwin.

26. Testimony of Andrew V. Corry, vol. 2, 298, Hum Fay v. Baldwin.

27. Testimony of John A. Leggatt, vol. 2, 245–247, Hum Fay v. Baldwin.

28. Testimony of Chong Jo, vol. 3, 225–256, Hum Fay v. Baldwin.

29. Testimony of Thomas Fletcher, vol. 2, 26, Hum Fay v. Baldwin.

30. Testimony of Margaret Noyes, vol. 1, 23–42, Hum Fay v. Baldwin.

31. *Butte Sunday Bystander*, February 28, 1897.

32. Testimony of Eva Athoff, vol. 1, 96, Hum Fay v. Baldwin.

33. Ibid., 80.

34. *Butte Sunday Bystander*, February 28, 1897.

35. *Butte Sunday Bystander*, March 24, 1897.

36. Testimony of John Rudman, vol. 2, 239, Hum Fay v. Baldwin.

37. Testimony of Hum Jim, vol. 2, 179–183, Hum Fay v. Baldwin.

38. Testimony of Lock Jim, vol. 3, 223, Hum Fay v. Baldwin.

39. Most Chinese men left their wives and families in China while they sojourned to the United States. They sent money to their families or saved money to buy passage for their wives. Traditionally, a respectable Chinese woman did not leave home even with her husband. See Shih-shan Henry Tsai, *China and the Overseas Chinese in the United States, 1868–1911* (Fayetteville: University of Arkansas Press, 1983), 17. The U.S. government excluded wives from coming with immigrant Chinese laborers, but wives of merchants were allowed to enter the country. For more on Chinese families, see Stanford M. Lyman, "Mar-

riage and Family Among Chinese Immigrants to America, 1850–1906," in *The Asians in the West* (Reno: University of Nevada Press, 1970), 27–31.

40. Testimony of Huie Pock, vol. 3, 230–235, Hum Fay v. Baldwin.

41. The Palace was located at 37 1/2 West Park Street. Hum Fay was thirty-three years old at the time of the hearing in 1898. He was a registered Chinese alien under the Geary Act of May 5, 1892, which had extended the 1882 Exclusion Act for ten years.

42. Testimony of Don Len, vol. 3, 218, Hum Fay v. Baldwin.

43. Testimony of Hum Fay, vol. 3, 246–248, Hum Fay v. Baldwin.

44. Testimony of Quon Loy, vol. 3, 252, Hum Fay v. Baldwin: *Anaconda Standard*, April 8, 1898. Historian Robert Swartout examined the tax lists for Lewis and Clark County, finding that the Chinese were assessed $38,900 in 1870 and $80,905 in 1890. These figures illustrate that the Chinese did not send all their money to China and that they contributed to the city and county, as well as the state. An examination of the Butte tax records might yield a similar conclusion. Rose Hum Lee examined Chinese real estate holdings in the Silver Bow tax lists. In 1890, the Chinese in the Butte area were assessed $9,340; by 1899, the assessment had increased to $26,200. Rose Hum Lee, *The Growth and Decline of Chinese Communities in the Rocky Mountain Region* (New York: Arno Press, 1979), 155–158.

45. Wu T'ing-fang to David J. Hill, Acting Secretary of State, July 6, 1901, Notes from the Chinese Legation to the Department of State, Records of the Department of State, RG 59, 98, Roll 4, No. 207, National Archives, Washington, D.C. [NA].

46. Several sources describe the impact of the boycott on the Chinese community. See Testimony, vol. 3, Hum Fay v. Baldwin; Lee, *Growth and Decline of Chinese Communities*, 135; *Butte Bystander*, May 22, 1897; *Anaconda Standard*, April 8, 1898.

47. *Daily Inter Mountain*, April 17, 1897.

48. William Thompson to Secretary of State John Sherman, March 6, 1897, Miscellaneous U.S. State Department Letters, RG 59, Micro. 960, frames 350–352. NA. The Department of State acknowledged Thompson's letters on March 13, 1897. The letter from Japanese Consul S. Uchida appears to be a copy of the original sent to Thompson; the copy is on City of Butte stationery.

49. *Anaconda Standard*, April 8, 1898.

50. Tom Hoshi to John Sherman, March 18, 1897, Notes from the Japanese Legation to the U.S. State Department, RG 59, Micro, 163, Roll 6, NA; John Sherman to Hoshi. March 31, 1897, Notes to Foreign Legations in the United States, Japan, RG 59, Micro. 99, Roll 66, No. 27, NA. I could find no additional information indicating any further actions of the Japanese in relation to the 1896–1897 boycott.

51. Lee, *Growth and Decline of Chinese Communities*, 123.

52. Unlike those in the anti-Chinese movement in California, the defendants were not overwhelmingly Irish. Information as to the defendants' ethnic backgrounds and union affiliation was compiled from the *U.S. Manuscript Census, 1900*, Vol. 4; *Silver Bow County, Montana*, NA: *Butte Sunday Bystander*, July 10, 1897; Hearing Testimony, Hum Fay v. Baldwin; Findings of Fact issued by Examiner Henry N. Blake, Hum Fay v. Baldwin; *Butte City Directory, 1895–1898*. See also Flaherty, "Asia vs. America," tables 5 and 6.

53. The *Butte Sunday Bystander*, April 24, 1897, published the full copy of the Bill of Complaint and the restraining order.

54. *Daily Inter Mountain*, April 17, 1897.

55. *Anaconda Standard*, April 8, 1898. The petition was submitted on April 7, 1898, and is on file in RG 21, NA—Seattle Branch.

56. Testimony of Hum Jim, vol. 3, 207, Hum Fay v. Baldwin.

57. In his biographical sketch of Sanders, A. K. McClure portrayed Sanders as voluntarily coming to the aid of the Chinese. A. K. McClure, "Wilbur Fisk Sanders," *Contributions to the Historical Society of Montana*, 10 vols. (1917; reprint, Boston: J. S. Canner, 1966), 8:25–35.

58. See *Dictionary of American Biography*, 20 vols. (New York: Charles Scribner and Sons, 1935), 8:336–337; Michael P. Malone and Richard B. Roeder, *Montana: A History of Two Centuries* (Seattle: University of Washington Press, 1976), chapter 4.

59. For biographical information about the Wineses and Kirk, see Tom Stout, *Montana: Its Story and Biography*, 3 vols. (Chicago: American Historical Society, 1921), 2:538. Also see Joaquin Miller, *An Illustrated History of the State of Montana* (Chicago: Lewis Publishing Company, 1894), 748; Guy X, Piatt, *The Story of Butte* (Butte: Standard Manufacturing and Printing Company, 1897), 28, 94. For Kirk, see *Progressive Men of Montana* (Chicago: A. W. Bowen and Company, 1903), 252.

60. *National Cyclopedia of American Biography*, 63 vols. (New York: James T. White and Company), 4:522; Hubert H. Bancroft, *History of Washington, Idaho and Montana* (San Francisco: History of Company, 1890), 789; Malone and Roeder, *Montana*. 85.

61. John R. Wunder, "Law and Chinese in Frontier Montana," *Montana the Magazine of Western History* 30 (Summer 1980): 25.

62. Wunder, "Law and Chinese," 23–24.

63. Blake's memoirs quoted in Vivian Paladin, ed., "Henry N. Blake: Proper Bostonian, Purposeful Pioneer," *Montana the Magazine of Western History* 14 (October 1964): 55–56. For a sketch of Blake's early Montana experience, see *Contributions to the Montana Historical Society*, 5:253.

64. *Butte Sunday Bystander*, April 17, 1897.

65. *Butte Sunday Bystander*, April 24, 1897.

66. Testimony of Frank Weldon, vol. 2, 67, Hum Fay v. Baldwin.

67. *Daily Inter Mountain*, March 17, 1898. The U.S. government signed several treaties with Peking, most of them favoring the United States and damaging the rights of overseas Chinese in the United States. Under the Burlingame Treaty of 1868 and the 1880 Angell Treaty, the U.S. Government would protect Chinese if they were met with ill treatment. See Tsai, *China and Overseas Chinese*, chapters 3–5.

68. Testimony of M. J. Geiger, vol. 4, 7, Hum Fay v. Baldwin, Geiger was an active union member. The *Butte Sunday Bystander*, November 8, 1896, reported that Geiger spoke in Minnesota and New York for the National Clerks' Union. Testimony of George W. Morgan, vol. 4, 141, Testimony of William Hogan, vol. 3, 140, Testimony of Dan MacDonald, Hum Fay v. Baldwin, Defendant Frank Baldwin also stressed withholding patronage from labor's enemies, vol. 4, 293, Hum Fay v. Baldwin. At the end of the nineteenth century, labor's use of the boycott was a legal issue. See Harry W. Laidler, *Boycotts and the Labor Struggles* (New York: John Lane and Company, 1914), and Leo Wolman, *The Boycott in American Trade Unions* (Baltimore: Johns Hopkins University Press, 1916).

69. Blake sent the Findings of Fact to Judge Knowles in March 1899. A copy of the findings was also sent to the U.S. Department of State. Wu T'ing-fang to Acting Secretary of State David J. Hill, July 6, 1901, Notes from the Chinese Legation, NA.

70. Final Decree, Hum Fay v. Baldwin, NA—Seattle Branch; *Daily Inter Mountain*, May 19, 1900.

71. Wu T'ing-fang to Acting Secretary of State David J. Hill, July 6, 1901. Notes from the Chinese Legation, NA.

72. John Hay to Wu T'ing-fang, December 4, 1901, Notes to Foreign legations from the Department of State, China, RG 59, Micro. 99, Roll 14, No. 188, NA.

73. *Daily Inter Mountain*, May 22, 1897; Paladin, "Henry N. Blake," 56.

74. For Denver, see Roy T. Wortman, "Denver's Anti-Chinese Riot, 1880," *Colorado Magazine* 42 (Fall 1965): 275–291; for Rock Springs, see Paul Crane and Alfred Larson, "The Chinese Massacre," *Annals of Wyoming* 12 (1940): 47–55, and J. H. Bromley, *Chinese Massacre at Rock Springs, Wyoming* (Boston: Franklin Press, Rand Avery and Company, 1886).

28

Deadwood's Chinatown

Grant K. Anderson

In 1874 General George A. Custer's confirmation that gold existed in Dakota's Black Hills touched off the last great gold rush in the continental United States. The region, once reserved for the Sioux Indians, was quickly overrun by prospectors seeking their fortunes in this newest Eldorado.[1] The discovery of gold along Whitewood Creek made Deadwood the metropolis of the Black Hills. Almost overnight, it matured from a hastily constructed mining camp to a permanent center of the gold mining industry. During the mining bonanza of the 1870s and 1880s Deadwood boasted more saloons than churches, claimed Wild Bill Hickok and Calamity Jane as residents, and contained the largest Chinatown of any city east of San Francisco. Although largely ignored by historians, the Chinese were among early Deadwood's most colorful inhabitants.

The Orientals arrived on the trans-Mississippi West mining frontier during the California gold rush of the 1850s. Their unusual customs and traditions, coupled with their low standard of living, caused them to be looked upon as inferior by the white miners. Unable to understand their economic system or clannish ways, white miners developed a prejudice that excluded Orientals from mining in most gold camps until after the boom period passed.[2] This feeling persisted although the number of Chinese was never large—one writer estimates that eight hundred lived in Montana camps in 1869.[3]

The patience and industry of the Chinese miners enabled them to make seemingly worthless claims pay. It has been estimated that white miners, using sluice boxes and cradles, extracted only about 65 percent of the available gold ore before abandoning their claim as worn out. The frugal Chinese, who could live on a quarter's worth of rice, bread, and skunk cabbage daily, then moved in.[4] By reworking the tailings and refuse they were able to profit. This ability to make a profit where others failed led white miners to suspect the Chinese of increasing their income by claim and sluice boxy thievery.[5]

Freight lines operating between Cheyenne, Wyoming Territory, and the Black Hills in late 1875 recorded the transporting of "rice and 'other necessities of life'" for the "so-called 'Celestial chuckleheads from the Flowery Kingdom.'" Late in 1875, Al Hong and Hong Lee were reported as Hills bound passengers, carrying with them full laundry outfits. On 6 January 1876 A. C. Abney left Cheyenne, Deadwood bound. Three Chinese were listed as passengers for the purpose of establishing a "washee house."[6]

Newspaper articles indicate that there was a continual flow of Chinese to the area during 1876–77. The *Cheyenne Daily Leader* commented "John Chinamen still continues to arrive and depart for the Hills as quietly as the Arabs."[7] This observation was borne out several days later when Deadwood's *Black Hills Daily Times* informed its readers that a "party of 50 Chinamen are between Denver and here."[8]

As the number of new arrivals increased, the clannish Orientals banded together, beginning in 1876, to form their own camp between Deadwood and Elizabethtown. Along their one twisting street the Chinese haphazardly constructed frame buildings. A description of Chinatown pictured: "on one side of their principal thoroughfare are their numerous dens and on the opposite side a row of pig pens and between the two the fever of breeding stench is so thick as to be almost visible. Chinatown smells like a bouquet of slaughterhouses."[9]

This peculiar aroma prompted "1 of the Afflicted" to write a letter to the editor. "The male portion of what is known as Chinatown, are in the habit of gathering the intestines of the freshly slaughtered animals from slaughter houses . . . carrying the nasty mess to their homes and cleaning them and scattering the offal promiscuously in that neighborhood." The letter cited the health hazards involved and ended, "We of Elizabethtown pay our taxes and object to placing the health of our wives, children and selves at the mercy of the almond-eyed sons (and daughters) of the Flower Kingdom."[10]

Amid such conditions the Orientals sought their fortunes in Deadwood. A few came to try their luck at placer mining, but it was only a small percentage that were actively engaged in it. Most new arrivals were merchants, laborers, or operators of restaurants and laundries. In such occupations, they found little resentment from Deadwood citizens who considered these jobs beneath their dignity and looked upon the Chinese with curiosity.

Fee Lee Wong, better known as Wing Tsue, was among the first Orientals to arrive in the Black Hills, coming in 1876. "A big, husky Chinese," he opened a shop in Deadwood specializing in goods imported from the Far East. Although "rather forbidding looking" on the outside, the shop contained many beautiful luxury items.[11] Wing Tsue became the most prominent Oriental around Deadwood as his shop was frequented by many whites. He built a fine home that was "heavily draped, thickly carpeted, and filled with teak and enameled goods."[12] When all was ready, he brought his wife directly from China to join him. It is said she was the only Oriental female around Deadwood that was not a resident of the red light district. Mrs. Wing Tsue was described as "painted and mascared . . . the effect was charming. Her black hair was built in a high pyramid with gorgeous pins and combs." Although residing in Deadwood for a number of years, she spoke no English. Their children attended Deadwood public schools and the entire family accepted the western ways and the Christian faith.[13]

Other Chinese merchants, such as Hi Kee, also opened shops along Chinatown's Main Street. Their stores had no windows facing the street, but were lit from windows at the rear of the building. Huge quantities of tea, Oriental silk, embroideries, egg-shell chings, sandals, teak, and carved ivory were sold at these business places.[14]

A handful of Orientals capitalized on the miners' hungry appetites by operating restaurants. Ban Wong, known as Benny, managed the OK Cafe and the Philadelphia Cafe was operated by another Chinese remembered simply as the "Philadelphia Kid." Susie, as the white miners called Wong Kee, owned and operated the Bodega Cafe. When a customer entered the establishment, Susie took the order and filled it personally. He never wrote down any names or asked what a customer ordered. He simply brought the food and set it down. For dessert Wong Kee asked the customer what kind of pie he wanted and then stated that he had apple. In such establishments Deadwood residents could fill themselves with Oriental dishes like chicken rice soup or if they preferred more common fare, roast beef and pie—all for twenty-five cents. Home-brewed rice whiskey was also abundant and flowed freely.[15]

In the midst of the gold rush numerous Oriental women sought riches by engaging in prostitution. The Chinese red light district was portrayed as "plush but for anyone belonging to it." Along that portion of Deadwood's Main Street that ran through Chinatown, a number of cribs were established. Many of these cribs were operated in conjunction with a laundry business.[16] A traveler noted that Gayville contained "about 20 Chinese laundries, each of which has a female partner who sits in the door evenings, and smiles sweetly to the passerby."[17] Miners wishing to partake of their services merely entered one of the booths and pulled a curtain. No attempt at secrecy was made as such operations were condoned in the 1870s and 1880s. An example of this permissiveness was written by editor Porter Warner. "Miss Chinaman, a sister to Heathens, has arrived in this city. She was escorted from the trail by Mr. John, with a brass band, (around his hat). She was attired in corral britches, with a coat cut ranch style, she will locate at the "Washee" between the dump pile and the cider mill."[18] The absence of women on the mining frontier guaranteed the Oriental "soiled doves" a warm reception.

A familiar scene along Chinatown's business district was the laundry or "washee house." Long associated with such operations, Chinese laundries vied with each other in keeping Deadwood citizens in clean clothes. Hop Kees, Yuenwas, Coon Sing, and several other so-called "Knights of the Wash Tub" mined their gold from soiled garments and soap suds. This proved profitable since water was free and wood could be had for the cutting.[19]

With several thousand unwashed miners roaming around the Black Hills, business boomed at the "washee house." From early morning to late evening the Chinese launderer could be found at work in his shop. The dirty garments were washed in tubs filled with water heated in large boilers. This operation could be dangerous and occasionally an accident occurred: "While Hing Gun, a China-man, was removing a boiler of washing from the stove in his washee on Lee Street Monday last, he slipped, and scalded himself fearfully around the thies and knees. Dr. Fing Kee was called, and he used about a rod of plaster to stick the son of a gun together again."[20]

After laundering, the clothes were ironed and returned. When ironing, the Chinese craftsmen sprinkled the clothes by taking a mouthful of water and blow-ing it over the garment. When finished, the laundered garment was returned to its owner by the Oriental bearing a wicker basket on his back. The cost of such services was "25 cents a piece for . . . shirts, drawers and such heavy pieces: boiled shirts, 35 cents."[21]

Such prices led one reporter to moan "people of moderate means are unable to experience the luxuries of a clean shirt even one a week."[22] Anti-Chinese sen-timent prompted Porter Warner of the *Daily Times* to suggest, "would it not be a good investment for some energetic white person to start a laundry here and run it with white labor?"[23] He noted the number of white women seeking work around Deadwood and suggested they employ boys to collect and deliver the laundry. However, miners continued entrusting their washing to Chinatown's mo-nopoly.[24]

So long as they engaged in these menial occupations the Chinese were ac-cepted by Deadwood residents. Changes in mining methods, however, drew the Chinese into mining jobs. By late 1877 and early 1878, the days of placer mining were drawing to a close. The independent prospector, working his individual claim, was being replaced by corporate-owned hard rock lode mining. The prospector now found himself working for wages in someone else's tunnel. Ru-mors began circulating during January 1878 that the California companies own-ing mines around Deadwood were planning to import Chinese coolies as labor-ers. The *Black Hills Daily Times* statement that "500 Chinese are daily expected to arrive at Cheyenne enroute to the Hills"[25] stirred racist sentiments among area residents.

The working men of the gold camp considered the Chinese a direct threat to their livelihood. From past experience the miners knew that Chinese were will-ing to work for a cheaper wage than the $4 to $7 daily being paid experienced miners. Jobs were scarce and any outside competition was resented.[26] Organized resistance to the importation of Chinese laborers began in Lead City during early March 1878. A large gathering, headed by J. O. Reed, formed their first Caucasian League in the Black Hills. Within a week, similar meetings were held in Eliza-bethtown and Central City.[27]

Deadwood's Caucasian League, supported by the Miners Union, went on record as opposing the entrance of any Chinese into the Black Hills. In the words of a reporter, "speeches were made . . . giving our triangle eyed brethren particu-lar fits." Another article summed up the mood of most Black Hills residents by saying, "bills have been presented in Congress to regulate the immigration of Chinese to this country, and for the benefit of our working classes, we hope they will pass."[28]

In an attempt to reassure miners, Kuong Wing explained in the *Daily Times*: "I have undertaking to stop such influx of my people as shall tend to interfere with the labor of white men in the mines of this country, and engage that no immigration of my people shall visit the Hills, except to engage in the lighter occupations of washing, cooking and house servants. I am authorized to make the above statement public by all the Chinese inhabitants of this city who will co-operate with me in this matter."[29] With this, the white residents adopted a wait and see attitude.

However, in August 1878 the miners took more drastic action. Committees were sent to inform Chinese miners and their employers that they must halt operation by ten o'clock on 7 August. This ultimatum was met as the 7 August *Daily Times* reported that Oriental mining labor around Montana City had ceased.[30] However, Chinese were still employed around Crook City on the lower Whitewood and the local press reported, "Nothing is said about it in that neck of the woods."[31] Several bands of Chinese workers did arrive in the Black Hills by mid-1878, but the great migration that was feared failed to materialize. Most new arrivals reworked abandoned claims or sought employment in the "lighter occupations" mentioned by Kuong Wing. By the end of the year racial tension had subsided.

A decade later wood sawyers around Deadwood voiced opposition to the Chinese. About twenty white men were dependent on cutting and supplying cordwood for their livelihood. When residents began having Orientals perform these tasks, the sawyers faced starvation. "They refuse to encroach on the laundry business and, thusly, justly urge that the Chinamen should be prevented from sawing wood," cried a local editor.[32] An agreement to this effect was reached and life returned to normal in and around Chinatown.

Though in a new country, the Chinese did not discard their old-world customs and traditions, which added an interesting flavor to frontier Deadwood and caused suspicion among the whites. As one pioneer observed, "they were really Chinese in those days too, wearing queues wound round their heads and loose dull-blue trousers and long shirts."[33] As the years passed, the Orientals adopted western dress, but clung religiously to wearing their hair braided in the queue. The back hair or tail, as the miners referred to the queue, led to many incidents. Unfortunate Orientals were waylaid and lost their queues to pleasure-seeking miners.[34]

The funeral ritual of the Chinese was one of the most colorful events in their culture. Unlike their white neighbors, the celestials looked upon a funeral as a gay occasion. The death of Yung Set in September 1878 provided the Black Hills with its first of many public Chinese funerals. As one source explained, "curiosity to the peculiar ceremonies ran high."[35] The funeral procession made its way up the Ingleside route to Mount Moriah cemetery. An Oriental, sitting beside the hearse driver, scattered tiny pieces of colored paper along the route. These pieces of paper, each with a hole punched in it, were intended to divert the Devil's attention from the deceased. The Chinese believed Satan must pass through each and every hole before reaching the soul of the dead person. "Following the corpse were four men each bearing a lighted taper about two feet in length, then came two each carrying a staff four feet long and wound with alternate strips of black and white cloth, following these were two white banners with inscriptions in Chinese." Other mourners and curious onlookers followed the banners.[36] During the elaborate gravesite rite incense was burned, sugar cakes passed around, and a small pig sacrificed. The Chinese section of Mount Moriah included a special oven constructed to roast the pig or an occasional Peking duck. The ceremony ended with the placing of some food on the grave.[37]

To the fun-loving Chinese 9 February was the most imported day on the calendar, for this was the beginning of the Chinese New Year. In Deadwood the holiday was observed as in China.[38] The washee houses were closed and no celestial performed any labor during the three-day festival. Oriental flags could be seen flying throughout Chinatown and the sound of exploding fireworks filled the air. All participants donned clean clothes and shoes as open houses were the order of the day. White visitors could frequently be observed helping celebrate what the "followers of Confucius" considered to be everyone's birthday.[39] In addition, the Chinese spent the time taking care of all financial obligations. The *Daily Pioneer* explained that the Orientals must "be at peace with his fellow countrymen, otherwise he is imperatively forbidden any enjoyments of the season. . . . This is a feature to which it would not harm his whiter and more civilized human brother to devote some thought."[40] As one source stated, "the Celestials never do things by halves," and this was certainly true of their New Year's celebration. Great quantities of rice whiskey were consumed and numerous games of chance were played.[41]

The Chinese were extremely fond of gambling and various games could be found in the back rooms of many Oriental businesses. Typical of these sporting events was the daily lottery operated by Wing Tsue. Upon paying a fee, from fifty cents to five dollars, the customer selected a piece of paper bearing several Chinese characters. Since most white residents of Deadwood could not read these characters, they were dependent on the operator's honesty. At night a drawing was held and the winner returned the following morning to collect his prize and pay the next day's fee.[42]

Another popular game was dominoes. Porter Warner observed a game in progress and reported, "it required the handling of at least a dozen of the blocks to make a simple play, and each block is slammed down upon the table with all the might and main of the player. It takes a couple of hours to play a game and the stakes will average one half cent of our money."[43]

Chinatown, like other Black Hills camps, supported a hose team. These teams provided protection against dreaded fires and also provided entertainment on holidays. Chinatown's two teams were similar to those of South Deadwood and the Homestake Mine, but with a dash of color added. The basic unit was a cart, pulled by twelve men, on which several hundred feet of fire hose was wound. Unlike their American counterparts, the Orientals wore elaborate uniforms or running suits consisting of fancy uniforms complete with long stockings.[44]

The Fourth of July offered an opportunity for the teams from the Deadwood region to compete in hose team racing. These contests covered a 300-yard course, the winner being the first team to couple its hose and pump water. The celebration in 1888 provided something unique — "the first hub-and-hub race by exclusively Chinese teams held in the world."[45] Festivities of the day began with a parade down Deadwood's Main Street. Included in the parade were the hose teams captained by Wing Tsue, the Stewart of Chinatown, and Hi Kee. The latter unit was accompanied by a band "capable of discordant sounds to a degree never thought possible — they played from start to finish with determination seemingly born of desperation."[46]

A round of applause greeted the teams as they approached the starting line. Sideline betting made Wing Tsue's team the favorite. A first-hand description of the action stated:

> Like a shot from a gun each team sprang from the start, Tsue's team taking and steadily increasing a lead for the first 150 yards. When one of the tongue men dropped out and his companions, unable to hold the cart, fell to the ground. Thence on, wildest excitement prevailed. Hi Kee's team quickly recovered lost ground and was hub-and-hub with the gyrating cart only a few feet from the outcome, but its apparatus was well in hand and passed over the score mark a winner by 20 feet. Time: 30 1/4 seconds.[47]

Participation in affairs such as hose team racing aided the Chinese in gaining acceptance around Deadwood.

In their business ventures the Orientals found a command of the English language desirable and Congregational and Baptist churches in Deadwood provided such education. In the mid-1880s Reverend Arthur C. Dill of the Congregational Church started evening classes in the church basement. Young women of the parish were urged to spend one evening a week helping an Oriental learn his ABCs. A multitude of Chinese attended, learned their lessons well, and rewarded their teacher's patience with gifts of china, teak, and ivory.[48]

Although the Chinese were generally peaceful citizens, newspaper accounts testify to the fact that they had their scraps with the law. Most cases stemmed from opium smoking, mining claims, or financial matters. A few were of a more humorous nature. The *Daily Times* reported the case of Sam Lee versus Ly Dog in which Ly Dog was accused of assault and battery. Lee was "accompanied by Miss Kie Yie, Wee Lie, and Doctor Dong Gong," according to the *Times*, which portrayed the courtroom as utter chaos.[49] "After considerable pow-wow and confusion among the Celestials, Kie Yie refused to continue to prosecute Ly Dog, it being the day on which the great Kee Wee's feast takes place, and the cost was taxed up to Sam Lee, the complainant, and case discharged."[50]

Less than a month later, a correspondent for the Sioux City Weekly Journal filed a story regarding another Oriental's day in court. Sam Ming, with Coon Sing acting as interpreter, appeared to charge "another heathen Chinese (sic) with larceny of $1,000." Ming claimed to own a woman and considered her valuable property as "the chances for hiring her out was good and frequent and the pay always in advance." The woman had been stolen by another Chinese who took her to Crook City and married her. "The room was soon filled with Chinamen," explained the correspondent, "and a lively time was had of it for awhile." The case was dismissed by the judge because the "theft" was not of cash. The reporter concluded, "so much for justice in Deadwood."[51]

Chinatown was also the scene of one of Deadwood's most mysterious, unsolved crimes. A woman, known simply as "the Yellow Doll," arrived in Deadwood from San Francisco in 1876. She was described as "a beautiful high class girl, of whom the white girls of the Bella Union was extremely jealous of her beauty and lovely clothes." Judge Bennet said she was "of high rank and well-educated." On an October evening in 1877 a group of Orientals were seen running from the home of the Yellow Doll. Investigating authorities discovered that the woman had been brutally murdered with an ax. As the dwelling still contained valuable jewelry, robbery was ruled out as a motive. An extensive investigation was conducted and several suspects arrested. However, it was impossible to gain any information or discover a cause for the crime. One theory, advanced by Postmaster Adams, was that the Yellow Doll was murdered because of the opium question. She had discussed the effects of the drug with him and he contended that she was in Deadwood to close the opium dens.[52]

The earliest Chinese immigrants arriving in the Black Hills brought their drug culture with them. In the 1870s smoking opium was nearly as common as smoking cigarettes today. Opium dens and tong houses were openly operated along Chinatown's Main Street. One reporter explained, "neither judicial nor public opinion was very strong about such things. If a Chinamen wanted to smoke opium, who cared?"[53]

A description of the "smoke house" operated by Lee and Ton pictured it as an underground dive. A committee from the grand jury of Lawrence County reported after visiting an opium den:

> We found a young girl on a pallet with a young man reclining on either side. The cot is a rude structure made of boards covered with an oil cloth or in some instances a gray blanket, at the head, a board six inches wide and elevated about four inches, provided the pillows to rest the head upon, with a lighted lamp in the centre of the cot, a card of opium and a pipe from which each take their opium alternately. A wire is used, on the point of which is rolled a quality of opiate sufficient to make or fill the pipe. This is cooked over the lamp and then ingeniously and dextrously manipulated

preparatory to the smoking. The pipe has a long stem with an oval convex head, and a small tube or hole in the center around which is collected the opium. A vent is made by means of the wire passed through the opium into the tube. The pipe is then placed over the lamp. The smoker sucks or inhales all that can be taken in at one breath and then exhales the smoke. . . . The victims are reduced to a semi-unconscious state where all is placid, calm, serene, and no hilarity.

The visitors concluded, "we visited other dens and found (very unexpectedly) many of whom we meet in the better circles of society. Alas! that human nature should be so frail."[54]

So long as only Chinese frequented such establishments they were tolerated. When white residents began to be listed among joss house customers, racial relations became strained. It was estimated by one newspaper that 90 percent of all opium was consumed by Orientals. "We would not object to them using it . . . it is food to them, but death to young America, and we do not want to see our young men indulge in any such habits."[55] Such opinions prompted concerned miners to blow up opium dens in Lead City and Deadwood.[56] The scope of the problem was discussed by the *Daily Times:* "It is estimated that a thousand dollars a week is taken from circulation here by the Chinese smoke houses. Every dollar which drops into their coffers is salted. Something should be done to root out these institutions. . . . Opium smoking is a greater evil than whiskey drinking."[57] The only action taken, however, during the 1870s was to license opium houses at the same rate as saloons—$300 per year.[58]

By the mid-1880s the drug problem became so acute that action was taken to force the Chinese out of Deadwood. The Club Women were especially instrumental in closing the opium dens. Fearing their men would become addicted, the women requested federal authorities to assist them. However, before the federal agents arrived, a large portion of the Chinese departed from the Black Hills. Most moved on to other mining camps or found employment in such industries as railroad building. Although many Orientals fled to avoid prosecution for opium smoking, those who remained faced little discrimination.[59]

There was not as much prejudice against the Chinese in Deadwood as in other western camps. Except for problems of mining and opium smoking, the Orientals were generally accepted. This was the exception among western mining camps. In Cripple Creek, Colorado, for example, Chinatown was completely destroyed and all the residents driven out by irate miners. But in the Black Hills, those Orientals who remained rose in status and gained the respect of white residents.[60]

Today Deadwood's Chinatown exists only as a memory. Most of the Orientals left the Black Hills after the silver boom of the 1890s collapsed. The remaining few gradually slipped away during the 1920s and 1930s. Many of them, such as Wing Tsue and Ban Wong, returned to China.[61] Few Orientals who came to deadwood had any intentions of settling permanently. Rather, they viewed the Hills as a region of economic opportunity. Profits made here were converted to

Hong Kong currency and sent directly to China. All Chinese longed for the day when they could return to their native land to live their remaining years in comparative ease. For some, like Wing Tsue, Deadwood made the dream come true.[62]

An interesting sidelight to the transitory nature of the Chinese appeared in the *Black Hills Daily Pioneer.* In the article "Why Chinamen Never Naturalize," the *Pioneer* explained that only a handful of Orientals became American citizens. It seemed that the penal code of China made it a capital offense for a person to denounce his citizenship. In addition, all members of the traitor's family would be banished.[63]

Even the Chinese section of Mount Moriah cemetery is empty today. Each Oriental arrived in Deadwood carrying a tine or zinc lined box that was to return his remains to China. When a Chinese died, he was interred in Mount Moriah and his corpse allowed to decompose for a period of years. An undertaker would then disinter the body and place the bones in the various compartments of the lined box. From Deadwood the remains were shipped to San Francisco and then to the Orient for reburial.[64]

Chinatown has vanished but should not be forgotten. An early Deadwood resident reminisced, "the Chinese people did have an influence on our community here in the early years; in the business world and also in our early day culture."[65] The Chinaman, along with the miner and rancher, helped shape the early history of the Black Hills.

NOTES

1. Watson Parker, *Gold in the Black Hills* (Norman: University of Oklahoma Press, 1966), pp. 38–53; Herbert S. Schell, *History of South Dakota* (Lincoln: University of Nebraska Press, 1961), pp. 125–30.

2. Harold E. Briggs, *Frontiers of the Northwest: A History of the Upper Missouri Valley* (New York: D. Appleton Century Co., 1940), p. 73. Other references to racial prejudice may be found in Duane A. Smith, *Rocky Mountain Mining Camps* (Bloomington: Indiana University Press, 1967); and Betty Lee Suey, *Mountain of Gold: The Story of The Chinese in America* (New York: Macmillan Co., 1967).

3. Suey, *Mountain of Gold*, pp. 189–90; Briggs, *Frontiers of the Northwest*, p. 73.

4. Briggs, *Frontiers of the Northwest*, p. 73.

5. Parker, *Gold in the Black Hills*, p. 73; Charles H. Shinn, *Mining Camps: A Study in American Frontier Government* (New York: Harper & Row, 1965), p. 213.

6. Agnes W. Spring, *The Cheyenne and Black Hills Stage and Express Routes* (Glendale, Calif.: Arthur H. Clarke Co., 1949), pp. 77, 79, 159. Other Orientals came to work as laborers. "South Bend boasts the boss Chinaman in the Hills. The other day, on a bet of six dollars, he carried a distance of nearly six hundred feet, twelve five-gallon cans, each of them filled with water, and all of them suspended on a pole, and never came to a halt or spilt any of the water. How is that for high? Sixty gallons of water, 480 pounds" (*Black Hills Daily Times*, 1 Aug. 1878).

7. *Cheyenne Daily Leader*, 23 Apr. 1877, reprinted in Briggs, *Frontiers of the Northwest*, p. 74.

8. *Black Hills Daily Times*, 14 Apr. 1877. The article further stated that "they are coming fully equipped for the mining business."

9. *Black Hills Daily Times*, 21 May 1878. Similar comments were expressed in Parker, *Gold in the Black Hills*, p. 142; Robert J. Casey, *The Black Hills and Their Incredible Characters* (Indianapolis: Bobbs-Merrill Co., 1949), pp. 348–49; Mildred Fielder, ed., *Lawrence County for the Dakota Territory Centennial: 1861–1961* (Lead: Seaton Publishing Co., 1960), p. 28; *Black Hills Daily Times*, 21 Aug. 1877 and 4 May 1878. Concerning a pig raising operation in Chinatown, "This establishment is run on a large scale and the pagens evidently intended to make something of it" (*Black Hills Daily Times*, 13 Feb. 1882).

10. *Black Hills Daily Times*, 9 July 1877. "A Chinaman by any other name would smell as sweet" (*Black Hills Daily Times*, 19 Sept. 1878).

11. William S. Greever, *The Bonanza West: The Story of the Western Mining Rushes, 1848–1900* (Norman: University of Oklahoma, 1963), p. 321; Estelline Bennett, *Old Deadwood Days* (New York: Charles Scribner's Sons, 1935), p. 20; A. H. Shostrom, ed., "The Chinese: Story of Early Days in Deadwood," roundtable discussion held in the Deadwood Public Library, 22 Apr. 1967, p. 1 (hereafter cited as Roundtable); "Field and Stream Magazine," *Denver Post*, 19 Nov. 1912. As business prospered, Wing Tsue expanded his operations by opening stores in Aberdeen and Watertown.

12. Greever, *Bonanza West*, p. 321.

13. Ibid., Bennet, *Old Deadwood Days*, p. 29.

14. Greever, *Bonanza West*, p. 321; Bennett, *Old Deadwood Days*, p. 28. "The numerous bulbs in the stores, offices and residences bought from the Chinamen have at last finished sprouting and are now in bloom. Their flowers look like cheap onion blossom and have a very aesthetic yaller color" (*Black Hills Daily Times*, 14 Feb. 1882). the business sense of the Oriental was typified by the following, "The Chinaman will not trust a citizen, and prefers to weigh the dust (gold) himself before putting it in his bag" (Don C. Clowser, *Deadwood . . . the Historic City* [Deadwood: Fenwyn Press Books, 1969], p. 34).

15. Roundtable, pp. 5, 6, 12–13.

16. Roundtable, p. 5; Bennet, *Old Deadwood Days*, p. 30; *Black Hills Daily Times*, 11 Apr. 1878.

17. *Sioux City Weekly Journal*, 28 June 1877. The *Weekly Journal* maintained a correspondent in the Black Hills who filed numerous reports on happenings around Deadwood.

18. *Black Hills Daily Times*, 20 Apr. 1877.

19. Ibid. 14 July 1877, 28 May 1878; Suey, *Mountain of Gold*, p. 190; *Black Hills Daily Pioneer*, 18 Feb. 1888.

20. *Black Hills Daily Times*, 15 May 1877.

21. *Sioux City Weekly Journal*, 24 May 1877.

22. *Black Hills Daily Times*, 14 July 1877.

23. Ibid., 1 Feb. 1878.

24. Ibid., 30 Sept. 1878.

25. Ibid., 18 Feb. 1878.

26. Parker, *Gold in the Black Hills*, pp. 149, 184–89; *Black Hills Daily Times*, 30 Jan. 1878, 25 Apr. 1878. In a column entitled "It's a Fact" the following appeared, "That the almond-eyed celestials, on the principle of cheap labor and over production, have a corner on the market" (*Black Hills Weekly Times*, 2 Aug. 1879).

27. *Black Hills Daily Times,* 26 Feb. 1878, 3 Mar. 1878, 7 Mar. 1878.

28. *Black Hills Weekly Times,* 1 Feb. 1878, 5 Mar. 1878.

29. "Chinese Not to Engage in Mining," *Black Hills Weekly Times,* 3 Mar. 1878.

30. *Black Hills Daily Times,* 6 Aug. 1878, 7 Aug. 1878.

31. Ibid., 31 Aug. 1878. "It is thought that all the claims in this district will hold out another year and then be good Chinese diggings for a year or two longer" (*Black Hills Daily Times,* 17 Sept. 1878).

32. *Black Hills Daily Pioneer,* 19 Feb. 1888.

33. Bennett, *Old Deadwood Days,* p. 28; Greever, *Bonanza West,* p. 321.

34. *Black Hills Daily Times,* 4 Feb. 1878, 12 July 1878.

35. Ibid., 2 Sept. 1878. Yung Set was a member of the Chinese Free Masons. It was estimated that sixty or seventy Chinese Masons lived at Deadwood during this period. Because Yung Set was poor, the masons paid for his burial. The *Black Hills Daily Pioneer,* 5 Nov. 1879, commenting on the death of E. Chung, stated, "the dead Chinaman will be buried today with all the splendor and pomp usually accorded a Chinese mason, of which organization he was one of the leading officers."

36. *Black Hills Daily Times,* 2 Sept. 1878. Dr. von Wedelstaedt, a physician in Deadwood, always marched in the Chinese funerals. So far as can be determined he was the only white member of the Chinese Masons in Deadwood (Bennett, *Old Deadwood Days,* pp. 30–31).

37. Roundtable, pp. 15–16; Bennett, *Old Deadwood Days,* pp. 30–31. The Chinese believed in the transmigration of the soul and left food for the soul of the deceased to eat on his journey to a new existence (*Black Hills Daily Times,* 2 Sept. 1878).

38. *Black Hills Daily Times,* 3 Feb. 1878.

39. Ibid., 17 Feb. 1881.

40. *Black Hills Daily Pioneer,* 11 Feb. 1888.

41. Ibid., 9 Feb. 1883, 18 Feb. 1883, 17 Feb. 1888.

42. Roundtable, pp. 10–11.

43. *Black Hills Daily Times,* 19 Mar. 1878. A *Daily Times* article of 3 Feb. 1882 claimed the Chinese were also fond of billiards.

44. Roundtable, pp. 3–4; Mildred Fielder, "Wong Family of Deadwood," *Wi-lyohi* 13, no. 11 (1 Feb. 1960): 1.

45. *Black Hills Daily Times,* 6 July 1888.

46. Ibid.

47. Ibid.

48. Roundtable, pp. 2–3; Bennett, *Old Deadwood Days,* pp. 175–76; Briggs, *Frontiers of the Northwest,* p. 105.

49. *Black Hills Daily Times,* 16 June 1877; *Black Hills Daily Pioneer,* 11 Feb. 1888. *Denver Post,* 9 Mar, 1907, tells the story of Chinese assistance in capturing three outlaws by Sheriff Seth Bullock.

50. *Black Hills Daily Times,* 16 June 1877.

51. *Sioux City Weekly Journal,* 12 July 1877. An interesting sidelight to Chinese law cases appeared in the *Black Hills Daily Pioneer,* 11 Oct. 1879. Entitled "Chinese Oaths," this article quoted the *San Francisco Bulletin* as saying if a chicken were killed in their presence and the dead bird held under their arm, the Chinese would tell the truth. If not they would be punished in the next world. The *Pioneer* added, "As we have many cases in our courts when it is necessary to take the testimony of Chinese witnesses, it would be seen

that it will not do to rely upon their statement that they believe in our form of oaths, and in order to get at the exact truth, the superstitious custom may have to be resorted to."

52. Jesse Brown and A. M. Willard, *The Black Hills Trails* (Rapid City: Rapid City Journal Company, 1924), p. 357; Roundtable, p. 13; Mrs. Pontius, Deadwood Public Library, to the author, 19 Apr. 1971. The Yellow Doll has also been the theme for floats appearing in various "Days of '76" parades in Deadwood.

53. Bennett, *Old Deadwood Days*, p. 28.

54. "A Dive into the Opium Dens," *Black Hills Daily Times*, 17 July 1878. Another excellent description of Deadwood's opium houses appeared in the *Black Hills Daily Times*, 8 May 1878, entitled "Our Opium Dens."

55. *Black Hills Daily Times*, 20 Jan. 1882. Other comments regarding whites frequenting opium dens are found in 23 Apr. 1878, and Spring, *Cheyenne and Black Hills Stage and Express Routes*, p. 225. The *Daily Times*, 23 Apr. 1878, suggested that "the best way in the world to shake off one's earth-born turbulence is to go to work, a fact some fail to recognize."

56. *Black Hills Daily Times*, 25 Feb. 1878, 3 Mar. 1878, 2 July 1878, 2 Sept. 1878, 12 Sept. 1878. The *Daily Times* of 2 July 1878 stated "we hope the Chinamen will conclude to move. There is a society in this town who are bent on rooting out these dens."

57. *Black Hills Daily Times*, 6 May 1878.

58. Ibid., 6 July 1878.

59. Roundtable, p. 7; *Black Hills Daily Times*, 9 Feb. 1882.

60. Greever, *The Bonanza West*, p. 321; Casey, *Black Hills and Their Incredible Characters*, pp. 348–49.

61. Roundtable, pp. 2, 5, 6, 9–10, 12.

62. Roundtable, p. 6.

63. "Why Chinamen Never Naturalize," *Black Hills Daily Pioneer*, 4 Feb. 1883. The *Black Hills Daily Times*, 31 Jan. 1882, claimed "Deadwood has perhaps one curiosity that but few other mining towns can boast of, and that is a naturalized Chinaman. This prodigy is none other than Coon Sing." The *Times* also noted Coon Sing always voted straight Republican in elections and complained about discrimination although he was an American citizen.

64. Roundtable, p. 7. "Most of the Chinese came under contract which stipulated that their bodies be sent back to China." The zinc or tin lined boxes used to return decreased Orientals to the Far East measured $10 \times 14 \times 22$ inches (Federal Writers' Project, *South Dakota: A Guide to the State* [Pierre: South Dakota Guide Commission, 1938], p. 106).

65. Roundtable, p. 14.

29

Deadwood Gulch: The Last Chinatown

Joe Sulentic

DEADWOOD
Alias
"Deadwood Gulch"
"The Outlaw Camp"
"Toughest City in the World"
"Biggest Little City in the World"
"Flag City, No. 1 USA"
"Sin City"
"The Last Chinatown"

Chinese immigrants built a Chinatown wherever gold and silver mining or other important work took place. From San Francisco their first Chinatown, they moved east to the Black Hills.

Chinamen left the reworked muddy placer claims in California for work on the railroads. Thousands carried rails and ties for the Union Pacific railroad through Auburn, California, Elko, Nevada and on to Cheyenne. They worked in the copper and coal mines of Montana and Wyoming. At each stop pigtailed men settled in camps and communities were the main reasons for their gregarious living.

The gold strike in Deadwood Gulch and the Black Hills was the last, the largest and most important in their move eastward. Here the Chinese gathered and lived for 50 years, their last Chinatown.

 Silence is a virtue, but undue silence bespeaks a deceitful mind.

JANE—THE SAINT & SINNER

It's easy to remember Martha Jane (Canary) Burke, otherwise known as Calamity Jane, as both a saint and sinner. The pistol packin' mama would steal to help the poor and needy. She was a best friend of the swashbuckling Hickok, an army scout, Indian fighter, mail carrier and bull whacker. She probably was a drunk

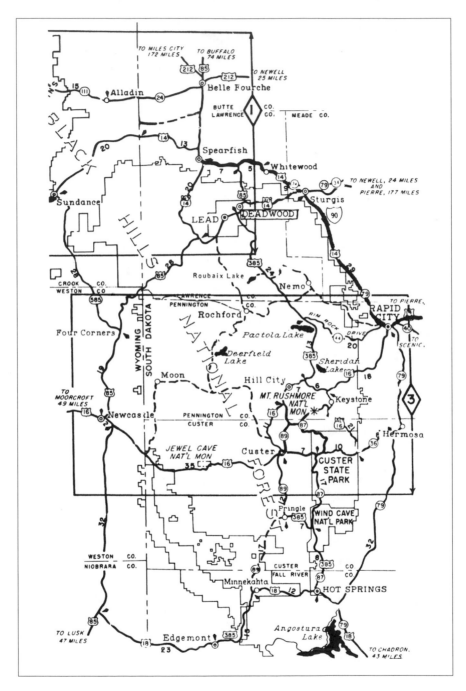

Figure 29.1   Orientation Map of the Black Hills.

and a prostitute too, as many said she was. According to one Deadwood native, a retired postal worker whose parents were pioneers of '76. "Calamity Jane had a mouth so foul she could make the most hardened foul-mouthed soldiers blush."[1]

It might seem surprising under these circumstances to remember Calamity Jane for her big heart. She spent many a night in a miner's cabin ministering to the sick. It was said she'd spend her last cent on someone unable to care for himself.

Calamity Jane lived in a small shack in Deadwood's Chinatown. One confidante of Jane related this story about a prominent businessman who remembers Jane taking a side of bacon from his store. "After she left that evening, I took a quick visual inventory and noticed a slab of bacon missing. I suspected that Calamity had taken it without paying. I walked down Main Street to her shack in Chinatown. The door was partly open and I walked in finding her asleep on a bunk. The slab of bacon was lying on a table nearby. I took the bacon without awakening her and returned it to the store."

Adventure was the hallmark of her life. She was fearless and traveled throughout the West. Her attraction to danger earned for her the name Calamity. Jane could ride the toughest bronc or drive 20 team of oxen over the roughest terrain better than most men. She could often be seen driving such ox teams through Chinatown up Main Street. "As she drove the yokes of oxen along, she would wrap the popper of her bullwhip around the neck or leg of a Chinaman walking along the street."[2]

Calamity Jane was known to carry a whip. She used it on any man who crossed her. She was a crack shot with rifle and sixgun. Jane was offensive to polite society with her loud voice and choice of words.

Few names among the women of those times were more familiar than Calamity Jane. Some writers credit her for spreading first word of Custer's massacre. However, at the time of the battle, she was riding into Deadwood with Hickok and could hardly have known the situation at the Little Big Horn.

Jane shared Hickok's restless nature and ministered to him during his dying moments. Before her death, she asked to be buried alongside him at Mt. Moriah Cemetery.

In spite of her drifter tendencies Calamity Jane always returned to the mining camps and saloons of Deadwood. She was born May 2, 1852, at Princeton, Mo. and died August 2, 1903, at age 51 in Terry, S.D. Mourners lined up from the gate of Mt. Moriah to the lower end of Main Street, a procession of wagons and buggies extended for two miles. To the majority of them she was a generous friend for whom a last farewell was a must.

 Take care of your shop and your shop will take care of you.

DEADWOOD'S CHINATOWN

An essay by a Deadwood fourth grade girl in 1886 gives a word picture of Chinese:

Chinaman have yellow complexion and have moon eyes, black coarse hair. Chinamen are called heathens. They are fond of gambling and painting.

Most Chinamen take in ironing, washing, and chop and saw wood. The money they earn they send back to China. They have small feet. Drink whiskey in their tea, and are fond of sweet meat. They like hog meat, chicken and smoke opium. The women are very fine sewers. They are all very thrifty and cunning. Women take great pains with their hair and dressing. Wear waist coats with wide flowering sleeves and wide pants. Very much educated in Chinese language. They use silk worms. China has a large wall. Joss sticks keep bad men away. . . .

Another revealing fact was printed in the *Deadwood Pioneer* on February 2, 1882: "Deadwood has one curiosity of which no other mining town can boast, and that is a naturalized Chinaman. This prodigy is none other than Coon Sing, who at one time was very wealthy but is now running a wash house."[3]

Two years earlier on January 25, 1880, Coon Sing had been in the news:

There has been trouble brewing for a long time in Chinatown and it has about reached a culmination point. There are several smoke (opium) houses down there in full operation, and some of our officers have been trying to ferret them out and get evidence that would convict them. They have been at work for several days and in passing around amongst them they had Coon Sing with them on several occasions.

Day before yesterday officer Spencer found a complaint against Su Wah and Wat Tong. Judge Clark issued a warrant and they were arrested and brought to court. . . .

In the meantime the whole almond-eyed fraternity was up in arms. They had seen Coon Sing in company of the officers and believed he had informed on them. Friday night they held a meeting and unanimously resolved that the piper who played before Confucius, Coon Sing, should die and a committee was appointed to notify him that within three days he should be killed.

This treatment made to one of Deadwood's rowdies would have no effect what-so-ever, but to Coon Sing it was entirely different, as he well knows the thugging that prevails among his countrymen, even here in the Black Hills. That is, if anyone of them violates one of their laws, in a few days he is found brutally murdered.[4]

Coon Sing asked for and was given legal protection. He lived happily ever after. There were numerous places of prostitution and opium dens in Deadwood. Chinatown was called the "Badlands." Here, at any hour, tough men entertained themselves in the illegal business of opium smoking. Citizens of Deadwood shopped for gifts of Oriental design and patronized laundries and Chinese restaurants.

Chinatown started near 605 Main Street and consisted of mostly unpainted shacks for two and one half blocks along both sides of the street. In addition to homes there were several washhouses, a restaurant, apothecary shop, two stores stocking Oriental gifts, and a church. Some reports indicate saloons were operated in Chinatown. For example: Case No. 74, March 6, 1897, the *State of South Dakota v. Wah Lee* (true name unknown). Wah Lee was charged with selling liquor without a license.

Bordering Chinatown in the area of the rodeo grounds was a large pig barn operated by Chinese. A Chinese firehose building stood in the present location of the Allen Lewis Sheet Metal Shop. Some Chinese operated businesses in other sections of Deadwood and lived on the north edge of the city known as "Slaughter Gulch."

The *Black Hills Times* reported the population of Chinese in Deadwood had reached 500 at one time but no exact figure can be found. Both the national and state census records are incomplete. As a result of the Exclusion Acts and anti-Chinese legislation, Chinese did not keep their own census. They were not anxious to be counted. In Deadwood the disparity between men to women was about 30 to one.

The term joss house, meaning church, is pidgin English (joss is a mispronunciation of the Latin word Deos or God and originated with Portuguese sailors in China). The joss house at 558 Main Street was destroyed by fire in 1879. The second joss house was razed in about 1936 for construction of the present Chevrolet garage.

The joss house was used as a general meeting hall, a storage room for uniforms, musical instruments and for religious services. During the year, 25 to 30 Chinamen used the building for living quarters.[5]

When necessary, the joss house was used as a courtroom. Chinese selected their judge and jury, and also punished Chinese for disobeying laws of the Six Companies and those of Chinatown.

On March 16, 1884, the *Black Hills Times* reported a Chinese style court case.

Charles LaBresche (Deadwood police officer) was waited upon by a Chinaman and was asked that he accompany him to the joss house. Charlie went with him and found a large number of high binders present and seated taking it cool with wine and cigars. He was informed that one of their number, a mason, had become a bad man, a disgrace to the order and had been untrue and inconsistent and always ready for a row. That he had on several occasions used his knife with dangerous assaults. The society of which he was a member had prayerfully and earnestly reasoned with him but the results had been like 'throwing pearl to swine'! The more he was asked the wickeder he had become and they met on this occasion to punish him. They asked the officer to be present to see that good order was preserved.

At a given signal by the Clan Petrix, the offending brother was brought in by the guard with his hands tied behind him and placed in the center of the room. A paper was read to him, supposed by Charlie, to be the indictment. His clothing was removed, with the exception of a light undershirt. He was ordered to kneel at the mat. He did some kicking and to accelerate the movement he was taken by the queue assisted to a kneeling position, his head was brought down to his knees. At another signal from the Clan Petrix, the executioner appeared with a bundle of green birch switches three feet in length. They were tough and graceful. Three of these were selected and one of them given to the ring master. With a few artistic whirls he brought it down on the nude back with all the force that was in him. More blows were given in quick succession making 12 in all. When the bell rang the beating ceased. Charlie was then told the performance was one-third through. There were 24 more lashes to be inflicted. Realizing that he was a conservator of the peace and the rascal had been punished enough for simply cutting a few Chinamen with his knife, the punishment was stopped. The culprit was then taken to another room in the rear of the joss house and tied up.[6]

In rough and tough Deadwood Chinese were treated equally under the law. In one case, 12 Chinese were arrested on charges of using mail to defraud. The case was tried before a grand jury and dismissed.

Occasionally young hoodlums would raid Chinatown. The sport was to catch a Chinaman and cut off his queue. In two such attempts police were called and the hoodlums arrested.

Chinese homes were described as very clean. However, in one news report a resident of Chinatown was ordered by Deadwood officials to "clean up around the premises."

Citizens of Deadwood generally applied Christian principles when dealing with Chinese. They received opportunities in business and were taught English in the homes of whites and their churches. A section of Mr. Moriah Cemetery was set aside for Chinese burial. Chinese responded with a variety of gifts and invitations to their celebrations. Although mystery shrouded most Chinese, they were in most cases generally better treated and accepted in Deadwood than in other parts of the country. Perhaps the people of Deadwood lived by the Chinese proverb: "The broad-minded see the kernal of truth in all faith, the narrow minded see only the differences."

In Chinese, bat and prosperity mean the same thing. Take home a bat meant, take home prosperity.

"GUNG HOY FET TOY"

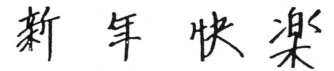

Translated, the above is "Gung Hoy Fet Toy," or "Happy New Year."

The celebration of Chinese New Year was the most impressive festival of the year in Deadwood. Chinese celebrated their New Year to thank heaven for past favors and ask for more.

Some Chinese in Deadwood took a less serious attitude toward the celebration. On one occasion when the ritual was over, a reporter asked a young Chinaman called "Kid" what they did next. Kid replied, "Do like Melican man. Get drunk, got out on street, fight and laisee hellee."[7]

The greeting "Gung hoy fet toy" or "Gung he fa tou," (Happy New Year) was followed by a cheerful and sincere "La Choy" (good-luck). The Chinese Lunar

Year was supposed to have begin in 2397 B.C. New Years Day begins sometime between January 21 and February 19. Each lunar month of each year had its own animal symbol. The Chinese day has only 12 hours. But a Chinese hour consisted of 120 minutes. The hours and years were designated by an animal symbol and repeated annually.

Hours From	Are Called the Hours of the	The Year Will Be
5 a.m. to 7 a.m.	rabbit	1975
7 a.m. to 9 a.m.	dragon	1976
9 a.m. to 11 a.m.	snake	1977
11 a.m. to 1 p.m.	horse	1978
1 p.m. to 3 p.m.	sheep	1979
3 p.m. to 5 p.m.	monkey	1980
5 p.m. to 7 p.m.	cock	1981
7 p.m. to 9 p.m.	dog	1982
9 p.m. to 11 p.m.	boar	1983
11 p.m. to 1 a.m.	rat	1984
1 a.m. to 3 a.m.	ox	1985
3 a.m. to 5 a.m.	tiger	1986

The celebration began just after midnight with a blast from the Chinese band amid the din of firecrackers and small arms fire. Sleep was impossible. The festivities continued for a week or 10 days or as long as finances allowed. Chinese from every mining camp and city in the Hills joined in the observance. All whites were invited and some attended.

Abstaining from eating meat the first day of the New Year and refraining from work for one week or more were customs Chinese observed. Making payment of all obligations was practiced faithfully at this time. Anyone who failed to settle his obligations was everlastingly disgraced, even if he escaped the vengeance of the gods. "Often a Chinaman, unable to settle with his creditors, would take an extra large dose of opium or cut large holes in his jugular vein to escape the punishment of Buddha."[8]

For the occasion, Chinese homes were decorated with paintings of birds, flowers and animals. Portraits of important people of China and gods were displayed. In celebrating the New Year, the Chinese involved nearly all the gods in mythology. The three most important were: the god of the kitchen, the god of wealth, and the god of joy. These gods from mystical regions were welcomed into the homes with rejoicing. This portion of the festivities was called, "offering the rice."

Before the family and friends began the dinner, prayers were offered by the master of the house. He held lighted sticks of incense and while praying he would kneel and bow his head three times before the table.

In closing the New Year, more firecrackers were exploded and mock money was burned. All Chinamen took a hot water bath to purify themselves for the ensuring year. Then the male population started out to call on friends.

粉 Chinese were inveterate gamblers.

CHINESE WORLD CHAMPIONS

Betting was a great pastime in Deadwood. More than $50,000 once was bet on a foot race between two men. Bets were also made on dog and cock fights, firehose teams, horse races, baseball, weather and on the number of children born in a month and many other individual feats.

In one story, John Gorum, a saloon keeper, bet a friend Chet Arkell, that a Chinaman carrying a laundry basket of clothes on his shoulder would fall before he reached his laundry a block away. The bet was called and when the Chinaman was only a few steps from the laundry, he stumbled and fell. Arkell, however, was not aware that his friend and the Chinaman had prearranged the bet the day before.[9]

Dogs fighting on the street was a popular sport in those days. A dog fight was the surest way in the world to draw a quick crowd. In one instance a man, running toward a large crowd, stopped before reaching the scene. He was informed that a man had been murdered. He immediately turned back saying, "O hell! I thought it was a dog fight." To promote business, a saloon keeper on Lee Street purchased a brace of bulldogs. Whenever business was slow he let the dogs fight in front of his saloon.

As mining camps and towns increased in size, the organization of a fire department received first priority. Often the social life of a community centered on its fire department.

Chinatown in Deadwood organized two firehose teams and shared with white men the dangers and thrills of fire fighting throughout the mining camps. Ten of the strongest and fastest men in each community were selected for the firehose team. Speed was the important asset in fire fighting. In order to stress and improve speed, firehose contests between communities were scheduled. Rivalry between opposing teams and spectators was so intense that they would often end in a brawl.

From start to fire hydrant, the race was 300 yards. The teams unwound 300 feet of hose from spindles between two large cart wheels. The ten-man team consisted of a web man, in the lead, whose job was to keep the webbing tight. Following the web man were six men who pulled the cart. Two wheelmen were assigned the job of giving the cart its initial thrust at the sound of the gun then attaching the hose to the hydrant, and turning on the water. The 10th man was the fastest runner on the team. His job was to run with the nozzle and attach it to the hose after the water was turned on. The race required expert timing and cooperation. If the water was turned on too fast, it would beat the nozzleman and result in an amusing spectacle. The team who was first to screw on the nozzle and squirt water was the winner. Every young boy in town wanted to be the nozzleman, because he was always well-known and respected by the community.[10]

Chinese men played a series of games. One game the whites called "catching the devil," (or catching a hat). The men of Chinatown would gather together and wait until a hat was thrown into the group. The man catching the hat was named boss of the joss house for the ensuing year. Generally, the game ended in a brawl. Chinese men organized "tug-of-war" games and entertained the citizens at large with such contests during celebrations.

特 Chinese believed the dragon came from the silk worm.

LITTLE MOON-EYED PINCH FOOT

Chinese prostitutes were called "she-heathens" and "little moon-eyed pinch foots."

"Their heads are stuck out through the holes in their dens and they nod at you as you walk through their quarters, like hideous spavin nightmares" (Spavin, was a disease affecting the hock joint of horses.)[11]

Chinese houses of prostitution in upper Chinatown were washed away in the flood of 1883. They were immediately rebuilt. Prostitution as implied to Christians was something completely different to Chinese women. It was not a part of their moral code.

As in China, detailed biographies of Chinese women in the Black Hills and Deadwood are vague. Prior to 1912, few Chinese women in the United States were known by name. Sue Sing was an exception. She operated a restaurant on lower Main Street. She purchased it form a D. Dandridge for $275 cash. The report said, "She will operate the popular resort in a manner for which she is justly famous."[12]

To Chinese women their glory was in being compatible and devoted to their husbands. The woman planned the family budget and taught frugality in the home. Her most important task was teaching her daughters to cook and sew. She had little to say regarding the rearing of sons.[13]

Today those who remember the Chinese women of Deadwood say they were gracious and charming. They made their own clothes from patterns used in China. During work days they wore simple light blue shirts which fit over darker blue loose fitting pants. They wore handmade cotton sandals. For special occasions their hair was elaborately styled in buns and their dresses made from silk and elegantly embroidered. Chinese women were kind and unassuming. During the epidemic of the late 1800s they helped nurse sick white children and adults.

One Chinese lady remains a legend in Deadwood. She was called "The Yellow Doll." She reportedly performed as a singer and dancer on the stage of a Main Street bar. She was murdered in Chinatown in 1876. Her body was found chopped into pieces. News accounts said expensive jewelry was found on her body, ruling out robbery as the motive. Chinese questioned in the area made no effort to help solve the case. It was said the beautiful Yellow Doll was a favorite to both Chinese and white men in Deadwood, but the dance hall girls called her the "slant-eyed come on."

Chinese women practiced footbinding in Deadwood as they did for centuries in China. Footbinding was an uncivilized custom of wrapping the feet with strips of cloth so tightly that the feet could not grow. As a result, the toes were bent toward the heel and deformed the bones.

It has been argued that this inhuman custom was forced upon the Chinese women by Chinese men to restrict their travel and keep them faithful sexually. The fact that footbinding continued for centuries, and that mothers forced daughters to bind their feet also suggests thoughts of vanity. Like a small waist, tiny feet were rare and difficult to come by and were cherished and desired. It was considered by both sexes as a true mark of beauty.

The tiny shoes worn by the women carried a color code of propriety. Red shoes were worn by young maidens when courting and before retiring at bedtime. Red was a color for good luck. Green was worn for occasions of honor, white for funerals and black for weddings.

A Chinese wedding was another occasion for a celebration. Except for instances when the bride had no choice in selecting her mate. Arrangements for weddings were made by the parents. Generally, a sum of money was paid to the bride's parents by the groom. The younger the girl, the more gifts were expected.

Again the event called for firecrackers, playing the gongs and other musical instruments. The customs in these weddings must have provided a chuckle for many in Deadwood. Sometimes the blood of a chicken was sprinkled around the bride. This was to assure happiness and that children would be born to the couple. In wealthy families, the mother of the bride made a "wedding sword" for the occasion. Chinese coins were sewn together in the shape of a sword about 18 inches long. After the wedding the sword was placed near the entrance of the new home or in a bedroom. The reasons being to bring good luck.

After marriage, the bride's family and ancestry were religiously unimportant. Remarriage was easy for men. Women were required to mourn for three years after the death of a husband. Chinese believed this amount of time was necessary for the spirit (male only) to leave this world.

〖山〗 Mealtime was a peaceful time in Chinese homes. Under no circumstances were arguments permitted.[14]

"GUNG HO!"

> Melican man is all okay—
> Wears stuff hat and big bouquet.
> Melican man no payee wash bill—
> Melican man can go to ———.
> Anon.

The words "Gung ho" meant working together. These words characterized Charlie, Sam and John. No race or group of people could equal the amount of work or the speed at which they accomplished the most adverse and difficult tasks. Large numbers of Chinese were employed in Deadwood in the laundry business. The men, using handmade wicker baskets, picked up and delivered clothes about town.

It was fascinating to watch the Chinese iron clothes. They sprinkled clothing by filling their mouths with water, and blowing it over the garment. Heavy irons, some weighing 24 pounds, were used. Irons were set into a metal ring built especially for this purpose around a pot-bellied stove to hold them while heating.

After washing the clothes, Chinese were careful in draining the water. Small articles of gold dust would cling to the dirty clothes and settle to the bottom of the tub. Chinamen, always methodical, would use tweezers and pick out the specks of gold adding a bonus to the day's work.

From San Francisco to Deadwood they proved themselves experts at placer mining or almost any task. They were careful not to encroach upon placer mining claims belonging to whites and did so only after the claims had been abandoned.

To expedite placer mining, Chinamen designed a unique apparatus that white men called the "Chinese pump." Many placer miners adopted this device. The pump was simply a belt with tin cups attached for lifting water. The belt was approximately 30 feet long. It was placed on an incline into the sump of a placer claim. It was operated by one man turning a windlass on the upper end. The practical function was to remove excess water that would seep into the mining operations.

So industrious were Chinamen at placer mining that they took out "$4 per man," when white miners could barely make the water run. Generally, the claims were not operated during winter when the temperature dropped below zero. Sometimes sluice boxes on Whitewood Creek were dug below the freeze line and operated year-round.

Here, as in other mining camps, Chinamen performed other menial tasks. During the winter they cut wood. The Black Hills were covered with pine trees and belong to anyone willing to cut them. The going price for wood was $4 per cord. Chinese cut the trees into pieces to fit stoves and fireplaces. They loaded wood into carts and sold it in Deadwood.

For a number of years, Chinese used a pair of mules and a wagon that "stunk to high heaven" for collecting garbage in Deadwood. They fed the garbage to their pigs, chickens, ducks and geese which they slaughtered and sold. It was common sight in Chinatown to see the slaughtered poultry with heads still attached hanging from clothesline to dry. Drying preserved the meat in warm weather.

Chinese also operated vegetable gardens. Again they harvested the crops and sold their products to the people of Deadwood. "Chinese cooked the animal, fowl or fish with the head intact. At mealtime, the head was pointed toward the master of the house.

In early China every case ended in conviction. If the party sued was not convicted, the party suing was.

SIN CITY

Yellow man and white man found gambling big in Deadwood. The conversation was simple: "Open" - "pass" - "draw" - "raise" and finally the call. The price — or the prize was rich. In the Green Front and No. 10 Saloon, silver dollars, pokes of gold or mine claims were bet without emotion. The players were deliberate and deadly serious. They were expert gamblers like Poker Alice, Carl Mann and Wild Bill Hickok.

Nearby, a room full of Chinese, gambling and all talking at once, split a treasure at their own games. In the Sacramento and the OK Restaurants men like Hop Wo, Ching Wee, and Big Ears Jack, could gamble at mah-jong, Chinese lottery or draw from a "jar of buttons" in a game of fan-tan.

The lusty souls of Deadwood were given still another vice—opium. The smoke filled dens smelled of sweet incense. The "joints" (opium dens) were in Chinese homes and their places of business. Some were known to exist in under-ground tunnels and in other sections of the city.

From the beginning many in Deadwood found it difficult to abide by the command, "thou shalt not." Outlaws, hobos and prostitutes found the busy camp comfortable.

At the turn of the century Deadwood was known to have 150 dance hall girls. They were directly or indirectly connected with a sporting population numbering about 2,000.

The Gem Theatre and the Green Front were two of the most famous brothels in the West. They were frequently referred to as "dens of iniquity" or "badlands." Some were disguised as rooming houses. Signs, above doorways, read "Ma's Nifty Rooms's," "Brunswick," "The silver Dollar," "The Mansion," "White Front" and the "Three Nickels." The last was located at 555 Main Street.

They were operated by "madams" called: Deaf Nellie, Shasta Babe, Big Hilda, Madam Mustache and Tricksie, among others.

Winerooms with sidedoor entrances were associated with brothels. The sidedoors were called "the doors to hell." Daring young maidens eager to taste wine or beer were escorted through these doors.

The "Green Front" extended from 591 to 601 Main Street. The main floor was divided into a saloon, gambling hall, theatre and dance floor. On the second floor above the dance hall there were about 20 rooms with the names of the girls printed above each door. The building arrangement was typical for brothels in those days. The two story wood structure was razed in 1920.

A problem in Deadwood with "whiskey houses" and brothels resulted in the passing of the Provender Law 40-1-18. It remains on the law books today and reads:

> Fine for exposing animals to elements or depriving of food and water. Every person who shall willfully or negligently maltreat or abuse any domestic animal by exposure to heat or cold, or by deprivation of food or water or by leaving hitched in the open air during cold weather or storm, or in the night time, shall upon conviction be punished by a fine not exceeding $25.[15]

Madams were prepared with feed and water to care for the horses tied in front of their establishments.

Deadwood was so busy with its lusty unrestrained entertainment that laws to restrict opium smoking were used infrequently. The local editor attempted to reverse this trend by calling attention to the dangerous drug. He wrote:

"There ought to be a law passed in every state and territory making the evil in keeping with a penitentiary offense. The Americans, when they commence smoking, seem to become slaves to the habit. It threatens to bring ruin into every household. Coming from China it began its ravages among the American people in San Francisco. As in California and Nevada necessity of repressive laws are apparent."[16]

Ten years later the same Deadwood editor wrote an article entitled: "Poppy Smoking" which reads:

> The attention of city authorities is called to the opium joints now being conducted wide open in that portion of the city known as Chinatown. Where white people, and black ones too, hit the pipes as often as they can raise 50 cents. Owing to the fact that none of the old joints have been molested for some time, several new ones have started up, where can be seen at almost anytime of the day or night, forms of men and women stretched out perfectly unconscious of their surroundings, reveling in the pleasant dreams that the devilish narcotic brings to them for a brief one hour. If the evil cannot be suppressed a restriction can at least be put upon it that will prevent its further spread.[17]

Opium, which comes from the juice of the poppy seed, was continuously smuggled into the United States on ships from the Orient. In order to conceal and transport opium, it was smuggled in packages of food, sewn into clothing, and wrapped with other kinds of merchandise.

After the juice was extracted a cooking process of two or three weeks was required. The smoking process was unique. A metal needle approximately eight inches long (used for loading the pipe), a fire of oil or charcoal and a long stemmed pipe were the materials needed for smoking. After the pipe was loaded it was placed over the fire and heated until the opium fused. The smoker would then take two or three puffs, exhale and fall into a sleep lasting 24 hours or longer.

Opium is known to restrict hunger. In China opium was given to quiet hungry babies. Chinese believed opium smoking was more harmful to whites than to Orientals, but it was known to be deleterious to the entire human organism.

Various rulers in China attempted to stamp out opium smoking. At one time, orders were issued to let addicts more than 40 years of age suffer with the affliction and those under age 40 were shot.

In Deadwood doctors prescribed "ipecac" for an overdose of opium. Ipecac is made from tree roots and was given to induce vomiting. Strong coffee was given as an antidote. A hot bath was ordered and the patient told to keep awake and moving.

Chinese were the first to smoke opium. Other people chewed it or ate it with food. It was usually chocolate brown in color and was delivered to this country ready for roasting. In 1879 opium sold for $4.90 per pound. Chinese called it "yen she."

DEADWOOD THEATRE

H. B. HURST, Manager.

SATURDAY, NOVEMBER 18, 1916

THE CHICAGO ENGLISH OPERA COMPANY PRESENTS

Cavalleria Rusticana

OPERA IN ONE ACT

Libretto by Targioni-Torzetti and Menasci.   Music by Mascagni.

CAST

Santuzza, a village girl.................................Mme. Mercedes Dalmada
Lola, wife of Alfio ....Miss Ruth Marshall-Dye
Turiddu, a young soldier ....Mr. Haigh Jackson
Alfio, a teamster ....Mr. Arthur Deane
Lucia, mother of Turiddu....................................Miss Edna Haseltine

Chorus of peasants and villagers.

Conductor ....Mr. Basil Horsfall

SCENE—A square in a Sicilian Village.

————

FOLLOWED BY

Cleopatra

MUSIC DRAMA IN ONE ACT.

Music by Basil Horsfall.

CAST

Cleopatra, Queen of Egypt ....Mme. Mercedes Dalmada
Charmion, her attendant ....Miss Ruth Dye
Octavious, a Roman General ....Mr. Haigh Jackson

Slaves, Attendants and Soldiers.

Conductor ....Mr. Basil Horsfall

SCENE—The interior of Cleopatra's Palace

(Author's note: Program courtesy Mrs. Dave Hildenbrand, Sturgis, S. D.)

Figure 29.2   Deadwood Theatre program.

Patent medicine No. 1 was sold from wagons. It was a sure cure for nervous debility, vital weakness, depression, weak exhausted feeling and no energy or courage.

DRUGSTORE

Wing Tsue's shop in Deadwood was patterned after apothecary shops of ancient China. A Chinese drugstore could be identified by a metal triangle hanging in front of the building.

The world's oldest drugstores are found in China where sedatives and other drugs were administered as early as 230 B.C. It has been estimated that 314 remedies were taken from the vegetable kingdom, 50 from mineral sources and 78 from the animal world.

This report by a pioneer journalist gives a humorous account of his visit to the drugstore in Deadwood:

While rambling around the "badlands," we have often dropped into the Chinese drugstore and wondered what medicinal virtues could be had. They are healing qualities of root-quackery in good faith.

Tigers bones mixed with harts-horn and the shell of the Terrapin reduced to a tonic jelly is just the thing for debility and rheumatism. The horn of the rhinoceros powdered will knock the spots right off small pox fever. The gall bladder of a cow should be remembered as a cure for insanity and other ailments. It is a sedative tonic and a charm for protection of infants. Glue made of the hide of an ass is a tonic astringent. Cowhide glue is a tonic and a valuable plaster for wounds. Gall bladder of the bear will cure infection of the liver.

Acorns cure epilepsy and dropsy. Should the political speaker become horsey, dried caterpillar is just right to relieve that condition. While the only remedy for a fit of jim-jam fever of dysentery is a dose of dried maggots. The patient is at liberty to decide for himself which is worse, the remedy, or the disease.

Let those who imbibe in whiskey in the dance houses take notice, hedge hog skin from the head has never been sufficiently appreciated by us poor devils. It cures pulmonary troubles and piles. Fish bones are a cure for cancer. Clam shells help deafness, and antelope and deer horns are tonic. Dried rats restore hair.

The profession of a doctor of the Flowery Kingdom has discouragement too. Arsenic should be used with caution. If death is caused from it both the doctor and the druggest are beheaded. If he is made only very sick and recovers they are only strangled. In either case it amounts to about the same thing. Taking all things into consideration, nature had a hard time rescuing a patient from the clutches of a Chinese doctor.[18]

John Coleman, pioneer resident of Buffalo Gap, S.D., remembers that boys in the Black Hills collected acorns for Chinese who used them in the drugstore and shipped them to relatives in China. They received 25 cents per gallon for them.

Wing Tsue's shop sold general merchandise, too. The shelves and counters were lined with silk, tea and various imports from China. Exquisite porcelain jars, jade and ivory birds and animals; crane and tortoise made of brass were displayed and sold. These were considered sacred by the Chinese.[19]

During the reign of Emperor Yaou (2255 B.C.), Chinese believed that the Ye-Chang people delivered a sacred tortoise to the emperor. Inscribed on the tortoise's back was a legend of the events of creation.[20]

In the United States Chinese were amazingly healthy. Their diet was simple, as it was in China. It consisted of rice, fish, fruits and vegetables. They drank small amounts of whiskey in tea and drank wine from thimble-size glasses. A drunk Chinaman was an unusual sight.

 Only watch the flowers bloom and fade, do not say this man is right and that man is wrong.

THE DRAGON TRIP TO PARADISE

"Why do you leave the food around the grave? The dead cannot eat," chided the white man. The Chinese responded.

"They will come up to eat as soon as your dead come up to smell the flowers that you leave on the grave."

The pomp and ceremony of Chinese funerals amazed both young and old in Deadwood. As at weddings, the occasion called for a religious celebration and a feast. A ritual of religious activity prevailed throughout Chinatown for several days.

At times a funeral would be postponed two weeks or more waiting for a favorable day. Sometimes a small fire was built in front of the door of the deceased. Each member of the household jumped over this fire. A proof of sorts, that the deceased, too, could jump over the fire and escape the evil spirits. Joss sticks (sweet smelling wood incense in slender cylinder shapes) were carried. Mourners wore white clothing instead of black. Death to the Chinese was not really a sad occasion.

The celebration was highlighted by a feast. Food was brought in by all the residents of Chinatown and by Chinese from surrounding communities. The feast included a roasted young pig with a large red apple in its mouth. It was placed in a wooden tray approximately four inches deep and was carried in the procession to the cemetery. A half-dozen chickens, ducks and geese were added for good measure. Baskets of oranges, apples, small cakes and candies were special treats. Some of this food was left around the grave. Chinese believed the departed soul would need a three-day supply of food for the "dragon trip" to the land of total bliss. White children, hiding behind trees and rocks, would wait until the ceremony was over and treat themselves to the food.

A wooden coffin bearing the deceased was loaded into an express wagon or buggy at the joss house. The noisy procession then proceeded through China-town and up Main Street. The entire cavalcade was led by one or two men who scattered six-inch square pieces of multicolored paper. The paper, which con-tained many holes, was strewn along the route and burned around the grave. This part of the ritual was performed to confuse the devil who was supposed to pass through each hole in the paper before reaching the soul of the deceased.

The Chinese band performed with large brass gongs, clashing cymbals, tongue-less bells and other odd musical instruments. Chinese loved noise and believed this would scare away the devil.

For a dignitary, the carriage and procession were embellished. Frequently, the Gem Theatre Band would march in the procession playing. "Nearer My God To Thee" and other religious songs.

After the team and wagon reached the base of Mt. Moriah, the men carried the coffin to the gravesite. Here invocations to the many gods took place. Mock money was burned and thrown into the grave. Images of possessions and persons dearest to the departed were drawn on paper and also burned at the grave. These were intended to follow the body and remain with it forever.

Notes taken from the cemetery board meeting July 20, 1908, read:

> A petition came in from the Chinaman through Lee Tang wanting privilege to build a small beehive shaped oven near their Chinaman grounds for the purpose of burn-ing papers in their religious ceremonies. On motion same was granted and an annual rental or so required.

Mt. Moriah, established in 1877, was divided into five sections: Masonic circle, pioneer, fireman, old soldiers and Chinese. Eventually Jewish, mass burial and a children's section were added.

The whirlwinds of life threw out for Charlie, Sam and John on the pine-cov-ered slopes of Mr. Moriah Cemetery. Death, that great equalizer, eradicated lan-guage barriers and cultural differences.

Graves in the Chinese section were once marked with headboards three feet above ground. The boards were inscribed with Chinese writing but have since been destroyed by vandals, weather or souvenir hunters. Today only a sign reading "Chi-nese Section" marks the place where yellow man was buried in Deadwood. A few Chinese graves are mingled with whites in other parts of the cemetery.

Because of the Buddhist teaching of returning the bones back to the place of birth, some Chinese were dug up and returned to China. After perhaps seven years, a Chinese undertaker would disentomb bodies. The bones were wrapped in paper and muslin, and after proper labeling, were placed in a zinc-lined box 10 × 14 × 22 inches. The box was then sealed with lead and returned to San Francisco. From there it was shipped to China and reburied, thus honoring an-cestors and saving the soul from evil.

The Masonic section of the cemetery was established by Lodge No. A.F. & A.M. and is laid out in a perfect circle with the Holy Bible Temple as a centerpiece.

The pioneers, firemen and old soldiers received a special burial section because citizens of Deadwood wished to honor them for their courage and sacrifice. The Jewish section honors several families who contributed to the growth and prosperity of Deadwood. Another division was made for mass burial when 11 miners died in a boarding house fire in 1883. The children's section was the result of an epidemic in 1878–1880.[21]

Seth Bullock, the first sheriff of Lawrence County, is buried here with other well known characters of Deadwood. Bullock held the office of sheriff for one year. In 1900, he was appointed forest supervisor of the Black Hills by President McKinley at the request of Vice President Theodore Roosevelt, a friend of Bullock's.

From the edge of the cliffs, near the flag, is a thrilling panorama of Deadwood and surrounding mountains. Foot trails lead to the chalky pinnacles of White Rocks, a mile above sea level. At this height, Slim Buttes can be seen 100 miles to the north. During the battle of Slim Buttes September 9, 10, 1876, the Sioux and Cheyenne Indians, under the leadership of Chiefs American Horse, Crazy Horse and Roman Nose fought the military forces of General George Crook.

Contrary to popular belief, the bodies of most Chinese buried in Mt. Moriah Cemetery were not "dug up an returned to China." Many of the Chinese brotherhood remain on the rocky slopes of one of our nations most historical and interesting burial grounds.

Another chapter of Deadwood and Chinese may be written in the future. For the gold, that cherished and powerful metal, was not depleted from the Black Hills as Chinese believed. Gold has been mined daily, since the Chinese left the hills, in larger quantities and from greater depths than 100 years ago.

Deadwood is prepared to add to its heritage—the "greatest little city in the world."

NOTES

1. Conversation with Archie Haase, Deadwood, September 1974.

2. Conversation with Paul Marion, former Deadwood resident, July 1974, as told by his mother, an early resident of Deadwood Gulch.

3. *Black Hills Times.*

4. *Black Hills Times.*

5. Conversation July 1973 with Monroe Hattenbach, Sioux City, Iowa, a former businessman in Deadwood.

6. *Black Hills Times,* March 16, 1884.

7. *Black Hills Times.*

8. *Black Hills Times.*

9. Conversation with J. C. (Buzzy) Gorum, Deadwood, 1973.

10. Conversation with J. C. (Buzzy) Gorum, Deadwood, 1973.

11. *Black Hills Times.*

12. *Black Hills Times.*

13. Conversation with Suey (Ying Yee) Pogor, November 1974. Suey operates the CHINA DOLL restaurant with her husband Doug on Sherman Street in Deadwood.

14. Conversation with Suey Pogor, Deadwood, S.D. , November 1974.

15. Information supplied by Clinton Richards. Deadwood attorneys, 1973.

16. *Black Hills Times*, February 11, 1882.

17. *Black Hills Times*, February 11, 1882.

18. *Black Hills Times*, March 17, 1883.

19. Information taken from the unpublished manuscript *The Secret of the Golden Joss,* by the late Lucille Morris Pozansky. Permission to use the story was granted by Mrs. Dave Hildenbrand, Sturgis, South Dakota.

20. *The Secret of the Golden Joss.*

21. Notes taken from Deadwood Chamber of Commerce file.

Appendix

Table A1. Chronology of American History, 1848–1898

1848	American discovery of gold in California.
1860	Abraham Lincoln is elected president.
1861	Civil War begins.
1863	Lincoln issues the Emancipation Proclamation.
1864	Nevada achieves statehood.
1865	Civil War ends.
1868	The United States signs the Burlingame Treaty with China, which allows free immigration between the two countries.
1869	Chinese laborers finish building the Central Pacific Railroad.
1870	U.S. naturalization law excludes Chinese aliens from eligibility for naturalized citizenship.
1873	Banking panic starts an economic depression that lasts for five years.
1877	Crash of the San Francisco stock market. Decline of Comstock silver production. Growth of the anti-Chinese Workingmen's Party in California.
1882	President Chester A. Arthur signs the first Chinese Exclusion Act, which suspends the immigration of Chinese laborers for ten years.
1888	The Scott Act is passed, which prohibits the re-entry of Chinese laborers to the United States from abroad unless such Chinese have families or property valued at $1,000 in the United States.
1892	The Geary Act is passed, which renews the suspension on the immigration of Chinese laborers for another ten years and requires all Chinese laborers in the United States to obtain residence certificates or face deportation.
1893	A financial panic begins a depression that lasts for four years. The United States Supreme Court upholds the Geary Act in the case of *Fong Yue Ting v. U.S.*
1894	In a treaty with China, the United States renews all exclusionary legislation against the Chinese except the Scott Act.
1898	After the Spanish-American War, the United States annexes Hawaii and the Philippines and extends its Chinese exclusion laws to the new possessions. Persons of Chinese descent born in the United States are guaranteed American citizenship by birthright as a result of a court decision in the case of the *U.S. v. Wong Kim Ark.*

Source: Loren B. Chan, "The Chinese in Nevada, An Historical Surgery, 1856–1970," *Nevada Historical Society Quarterly* 25, no. 4 (Winter 1982), table 1.

Table A2. Chronology of American History, 1902–1976

1902	A new U.S. law renews all existing Chinese exclusion legislation.
1904	China refuses to renew its 1894 treaty with the United States. America retaliates by making all of its Chinese exclusion laws permanent. Anti-American trade boycotts are staged in Guangzho (Canton) and Shanghai.
1907	Beginning of a financial panic and depression.
1917	The United States enters World War I.
1918	World War I armistice.
1924	The National Origins Act prohibits American-born Chinese from bringing their foreign-born wives or children to the United States.
1929	The Great Depression begins, and lasts until 1943.
1941	The United States enters World War II as an ally of China.
1943	The United States repeals its Chinese exclusion laws and allows a racial (rather than a national) immigration quota of 105 Chinese per year. Chinese resident aliens were allowed to become naturalized American citizens.
1945	End of World War II.
1950	Beginning of the Korean War.
1952	The McCarran-Walter Act retains a Chinese racial immigration quota of 105 persons per year. It allows Chinese aliens who marry American-born Chinese, other native-born or naturalized Americans to immigrate with nonquota status.
1953	Korean War armistice.
1961	President John F. Kennedy begins direct American military involvement in Vietnam.
1962	Kennedy signs a presidential directive that permits 15,000 Hong Kong refugees to enter the United States between 1962 and 1965.
1965	President Lyndon B. Johnson signs an amendment to the McCarran-Walter Act that abolishes the national origins (or in the case of the Chinese, the racial) quota system. Under this law, aliens of Chinese descent are eligible to immigrate to the United States under their respective national quotas. Maximum national quotas are set at 20,000 persons per year.
1969	President Richard M. Nixon begins American troop withdrawals from Vietnam under his "Vietnamization" policy.
1972	Nixon visits the People's Republic of China.
1974	Nixon resigns as president of the United States.
1975	American and military personnel are evacuated from Vietnam.
1976	The United States celebrates the bicentennial of its political independence.

Source: Loren B. Chan, "The Chinese in Nevada, An Historical Survey, 1856–1970," *Nevada Historical Society Quarterly* 25, no. 4 (Winter 1982), table 2.

Table A3. Chronology of the Chinese Presence in Nevada, 1856–1978

1856	First Chinese moved from California to Nevada to build water ditches on the Carson River.
1859	Discovery of the Comstock Lode.
	White miners in Gold Hill prohibit Chinese from holding claims in the district.
1860	Anti-Chinese movement begins in Carson City.
1868	Unsuccessful attempt of European immigrants to expel all Chinese from Carson City and other parts of the state.
	Central Pacific Railroad enters Nevada with thousands of Chinese laborers.
1869	Completion of the Central Pacific Railroad at Promotory Point, Utah.
	Chinese build the Virginia and Truckee Railroad.
	First Chinese miners arrive in Tuscarora, Elko County.
	White mob expels Chinese inhabitants from the town of Unionville.
1872	Approximately 1,000 Chinese workers in the employ of the Pacific Borax Company work at the salt marshes near Columbus in Esmeralda County.
1873	Chinese workers begin construction of the Eureka and Palisade Railroad.
1874	Chapel of the Good Shepherd, the Protestant Episcopal Chinese Mission, is established in Carson City.
	Charles Wah, a Chinese merchant, is one of the first to settle at Cherry Creek in White Pine County.
1875	Fire destroys Virginia City's Chinese quarter.
	Construction of the Eureka and Palisade Railroad is completed.
	Sum Wah establishes one of the first Chinese businesses in Elko—a laundry.
1876	Two Chinese are killed at Eureka, and others are expelled from town.
	Chinese mine for copper, silver, and gold on a commission basis in the Contact area, northeastern Elko County.
1877	Mann Tonn kills Ah Hoy at Austin and is sentenced to serve 25 years in the Nevada State Prison.
1878	Virginia City has nineteen Chinese-owned businesses.
	Workingmen's Party convention in Reno demands a prohibition on the use of Chinese laborers in the city.
1880	Nevada general election results in the abolition of further Chinese immigration: 17,259 in favor, 193 opposed.
1881	Chinese begin construction of the Nevada-California-Oregon Railway.
1882	Virginia City has only seven Chinese-owned businesses remaining.
1888	Chinese are excluded from the lead, silver, and gold mining operations at Tybo in Nye County.
	Wo Ling, associated with the Ong Cong Lung store in Pioche, has difficulty re-entering the United States because of the Scott Act.
1903	White mob attempts to expel all of the Chinese from Tonopah. As a result, Chong Bing Long, age 66, is murdered there.
1905	Chinese pioneers take part in the founding of Las Vegas. Wong Kee and Ong Loy, restaurant owners; and Ying Lee, a laundryman.
1908	Reno city officials destroy most Chinatown buildings because they are a "public eyesore."
1909	No Chinese are allowed to get off the trains of the Las Vegas and Tonopah Railroad at Goldfield, Esmeralda County.
1912	Most Chinese businesses in Reno are located on the west side of North Virginia Street in buildings with tin roofs.

Table A3.   Chronology of the Chinese Presence in Nevada, 1856–1978

1913	Clark County terminates its contract with Wong Kee to feed jail inmates.
1921	Gee Jon, a member of the Hop Sing Tong, murders Tom Quong Kee, a member of the Bing Kung Tong, at Mina, Mineral County.
1923	Chinese workers build a tramway for the Pacific Portland Cement Company just outside of Empire in northern Washoe County.
1924	Gee Jon is executed at the Nevada State Prison in the nation's first lethal gas execution.
1931	No Chinese are permitted to work in the construction of Hoover Dam.
1937	Reno's branch of the Chinese Consolidated Benevolent Association (the Chinese Six Companies) begins war relief fund-raising activities to aid China's struggle against Japanese aggression.
1938	Reno has four Chinese restaurants in operation.
1952	Bill Fong is elected president of the Nevada Casino Association.
1958	Reno's Chinese temple (joss house) is demolished after flood damage.
1964	Woo Loung Wah, age 105, the sole surviving Chinese worker who helped build the Central Pacific Railroad through the Sierra to Nevada, is honored during the Nevada statehood centennial celebration in Reno.
1966	The Las Vegas Chinese American Benevolent Association is founded.
1973	Dr. Lol Yee-kung demonstrates acupuncture to the Nevada state legislature.
1974	Lilly Fong wins election to the University of Nevada Board of Regents.
1977	The Ying On Merchants and Labor Benevolent Association establishes a branch in Las Vegas.
1978	Lilly Fong is re-elected to a second term on the University of Nevada Board of Regents.

Source: Loren B. Chen, "The Chinese in Nevada, An Historical Survey, 1856–1970," *Nevada Historical Society Quarterly* 25, no. 4 (Winter 1982), table 3.

Table A4.   Nevada's Chinese Population, 1860–1978

Year	Total population, Nevada	Chinese population, Nevada	Chinese percentage of total
1860	6,857	23	0.3
1870	42,491	3,152	7.4
1880	62,266	5,416	8.7
1890	47,355	2,833	6.0
1900	42,335	1,352	3.2
1910	81,875	927	1.1
1920	77,407	689	0.9
1930	91,058	483	0.5
1940	110,247	286	0.3
1950	160,083	281	0.2
1960	285,278	572	0.2
1970	488,738	955	0.2
1978	660,000 (est.)	1,320 (est.)	0.2 (est.)

Source: Loren B. Chan, "The Chinese in Nevada, An Historical Survey, 1856–1970," *Nevada Historical Society Quarterly* 25, no. 4 (Winter 1982), table 4.

Table A5. Chinese Population in Arizona by County, 1870–1900

County	1870	1880	1890	1900
Total	20	1630	1170	1419
Apache	—	62	16	
Cochise	—	—	173	111
Coconino	—	—		86
Gila	—	—	40	49
Graham	—	—	86	140
Maricopa	—	164	234	135
Mohave	—	15	28	50
Navajo	—	—	—	41
Pima	—	1153	299	254
Pinal	—	64	64	54
Santa Cruz	—	—	—	44
Yavapai	12	140	169	394
Yuma	8	32	61	59
San Carlos reservation	—	—	—	2

Source: United States Bureau of the Census, *Twelfth Census of the United States Taken in the Year 1900*, Vol. II: *Population*, Pt. I (Washington D.C.: Government Printing Office), 567–570.

Table A6. Chinese Population in Colorado by County, 1870–1900

County	1870	1880	1890	1900
Total	7	612	1398	599
Arapahoe	4	238	980	310
Bent	—	2	1	2
Boulder	—	18	11	15
Chafee	—	6	14	6
Clear Creek	2	17	7	10
Conejos	—	9	—	3
Custer	—	9	—	1
Delta	—	—	—	2
Dolores	—	—	—	5
Douglas	—	—	1	—
Eagle	—	—	1	—
Elbert	—	1	—	—
El Paso	—	16	69	37
Fremont	—	4	6	14
Gilpin	1	124	49	19
Gunnison	—	—	4	1
Hinsdale	—	3	—	1
Huerfano	—	—	3	5
Jefferson	—	2	9	7
La Plata	—	—	19	—
Larimer	—	3	3	4

Table A6. Continued.

Las Animas	—	6	15	7
Mesa	—	—	3	4
Montrose	—	—	5	—
Morgan	—	—	—	1
Otcro	—	—	6	6
Ouray	—	3	17	20
Park	—	124	62	16
Prowers	—	—	1	1
Pueblo	—	7	82	48
Rio Blanco	—	—	2	1
Rio Grande	—	—	1	—
Saguache	—	—	1	—
San Juan	—	1	8	18
San Miguel	—	—	11	21
Summit	—	19	4	5
Weld	—	—	2	9
Yuma	—	—	1	—

Source: United States Bureau of the Census, *Twelfth Census of the United States Taken in the Year 1900*, Vol. II: *Population*, Pt. I (Washington D.C.: Government Printing Office), 567–570.

Table A7. Chinese Population in Idaho by County, 1870–1900

County	1870	1880	1890	1900
Total	4274	3379	2007	1467
Ada	78	203	131	225
Alturas	314	128	95	v
Bannock	—	—	—	52
Bear Lake	—	—	2	—
Bingham	—	—	67	12
Blaine	—	—	—	78
Boise	1754	1225	421	323
Canyon	—	—	—	45
Cassia	—	22	11	3
Custer	—	—	110	39
Elmore	—	—	76	50
Idaho	425	738	278	114
Kootenai	—	7	144	56
Latah	—	—	28	26
Lemhi	120	262	130	59
Lincoln	—	—	—	15
Logan	—	—	36	—
Nez Perce	747	198	55	76
Oneida	—	61	—	1
Owyhee	368	239	214	171
Shoshone	468	296	201	73
Washington	—	—	8	49

Source: United States Bureau of the Census, *Twelfth Census of the United States Taken in the Year 1900*, Vol. II: *Population*, Pt. I (Washington D.C.: Government Printing Office), 567–570.

Table A8. Chinese Population in Minnesota by County, 1880–1900

County	1880	1890	1900
Total	24	94	166
Anoka	—	1	—
Beltrami	—	—	1
Bigstone	—	1	—
Blue Earth	1	—	1
Carlton	—	2	3
Cass	—	—	4
Clay	—	—	2
Crow Wing	—	2	—
Dakota	2	—	—
Dodge	—	—	2
Douglas	—	1	2
Faribault	—		2
Fillmore	—	1	2
Freeborn	—	—	1
Goodhue	2	—	2
Hennepin	2	17	24
Houston	—	—	1
Itasca	—	—	1
Jackson	—	—	1
Kandiyohi	—	—	5
Lake	—	2	7
Lesueur	—	—	1
Lyon	—	—	4
Martin	—	—	2
Meeker	—	—	2
Morrison	—	1	—
Mower	—	1	1
Nicollet	—	—	2
Nobles	—	—	4
Olmsted	2	—	2
Ottertail	—	1	—
Polk	—	1	10
Ramsey	8	36	28
Redwood	1	—	2
Rice	—	1	
St. Louis	—	24	35
Stearns	—	—	1
Wabasha	—	—	1
Waseca	—	1	2
Washington	2	—	3
Watonwan	—	—	4
Wilkin	—	—	1
Winona	4	1	—

Source: United States Bureau of the Census, *Twelfth Census of the United States Taken in the Year 1900*, Vol. II: *Population*, Pt. I (Washington D.C.: Government Printing Office), 567–570.

Table A9.　Chinese Population in Montana by County, 1870–1900

County	1870	1880	1890	1900
Total	1949	1765	2532	1739
Beaverhead	6	131	92	73
Broadwater	—	—	—	15
Carbon	—	—	—	2
Cascade	—	—	23	5
Choteau	3	18	42	86
Custer	—	2	18	16
Dawson	—	—	4	2
Deerlodge	776	710	438	78
Fergus	—	—	9	14
Flathead	—	—	—	47
Gallatin	4	27	39	55
Granite	—	—	—	71
Jefferson	122	52	46	57
Lewis and Clarke	666	359	602	333
Madison	299	265	155	80
Meagher	29	52	37	9
Missoula	44	149	405	208
Park	—	—	23	42
Ravalli	—	—		30
Silverbow	—	—	584	391
Sweet Grass	—	—	—	18
Teton	—	—	—	17
Yellowstone	—	—	15	90

Source: United States Bureau of the Census, *Twelfth Census of the United States Taken in the Year 1900*, Vol. II: *Population*, Pt. I (Washington D.C.: Government Printing Office), 567–570.

Table A10.　Chinese Population in Nevada by County, 1870–1900

County	1870	1880	1890	1900
Total	3152	5416	2833	1352
Churchill	16	32	30	7
Douglas	23	159	56	19
Elko	439	613	311	191
Esmerelda	56	242	277	115
Eureka	—	633	284	101
Humboldt	220	529	377	225
Lander	218	387	87	71
Lincoln	23	100	34	72
Lyon	116	390	86	39
Nye	6	66	23	7
Ormsby	769	988	760	152
Roop	4	5	—	—
Storey	749	639	245	76
Washoe	221	526	217	246
White Pine	292	107	46	31

Source: United States Bureau of the Census, *Twelfth Census of the United States Taken in the Year 1900*, Vol. II: *Population*, Pt. I (Washington D.C.: Government Printing Office), 567–570.

Table A11. Chinese Population in New Mexico by County, 1880–1900

County	1880	1890	1900
Total	57	361	341
Bernalillo	2	52	49
Chaves	—	—	16
Colfax	—	7	6
Donna Ana	5	1	9
Eddy	—	—	13
Grant	40	180	173
Lincoln	2	23	9
Mora	—	1	—
Otero	—	—	12
San Miguel	6	38	16
Santa Fe	2	7	3
Sierra	—	37	10
Socorro	—	14	16
Taos	—	—	1
Union	—	—	3
Valencia	—	1	5

Source: United States Bureau of the Census, *Twelfth Census of the United States Taken in the Year 1900*, Vol. II: *Population*, Pt. I (Washington D.C.: Government Printing Office), 567–570.

Table A12. Chinese Population in North Dakota by County, 1880–1900

County	1880	1890	1900
Total	8	28	32
Buford	—	1	—
Burleigh	5	2	5
Cass	3	—	2
Dickey	—	2	—
Foster	—	—	1
Grand Forks	—	9	7
Morton	—	2	—
Ramsey	—	1	1
Richland	—	1	—
Sargent	—	1	—
Stark	—	4	7
Traill	—	2	1
Walsh	—	—	2
Williams	—	—	4
Standing Rock reservation	—	3	2

Source: United States Bureau of the Census, *Twelfth Census of the United States Taken in the Year 1900*, Vol. II: *Population*, Pt. I (Washington D.C.: Government Printing Office), 567–570.

Appendix

Table A13. Chinese Population in Oregon by County, 1870–1900

County	1870	1880	1890	1900
Total	3330	9510	9540	10397
Baker	680	787	398	414
Benton	—	53	95	26
Clackamas	50	175	80	66
Clatsop	13	2317	1177	614
Columbia	—	64	23	10
Coos	13	91	90	50
Crook	—	—	9	13
Curry	13	23	58	27
Douglas	76	97	183	26
Gilliam	—	—	41	17
Grant	940	905	326	114
Harney	—	—	16	32
Jackson	634	337	224	43
Josephine	223	291	98	31
Klamath	—	—	3	1
Lake	—	7	19	12
Lane	7	39	51	8
Lincoln	—	—	—	4
Linn	2	99	124	51
Malheur	—	—	82	86
Marion	27	305	367	235
Morrow	—	—	25	13
Multonamah	508	1983	5184	8012
Polk	2	205	59	24
Sherman	—	—	25	15
Umatilla	70	138	261	155
Union	45	235	125	104
Wallowa	—	—	—	1
Wasco	27	1158	205	138
Washington	—	75	171	36
Wheeler	—	—	—	7
Yamhill	1	126	21	12

Source: United States Bureau of the Census, *Twelfth Census of the United States Taken in the Year 1900*, Vol. II: *Population*, Pt. I (Washington D.C.: Government Printing Office), 567–570.

Table A14. Chinese Population in South Dakota by County, 1880–1900

County	1880	1890	1900
Total	230	195	165
Beadle	—	1	—
Brookings	—	1	2
Brown	—	8	—
Butte	—	—	2
Custer	—	2	2
Fall River	—	—	4
Grant	—	1	—
Hughes	—	7	—
Lawrence	220	152	120
Meade	—	4	18
Minnehaha	—	2	1
Pennington	10	14	14
Potter	—	1	—
Todd	—	1	—
Union	—	—	2
Yankton	—	1	—

Source: United States Bureau of the Census, *Twelfth Census of the United States Taken in the Year 1900*, Vol. II: *Population*, Pt. I (Washington D.C.: Government Printing Office), 567–570.

Table A15. Chinese Population in Texas by County, 1870–1900

County	1870	1880	1890	1900
Total	25	136	710	836
Anderson	—	1	1	1
Angelina	—	—	—	1
Aransas	—	—	3	—
Armstrong	—	—	1	—
Austin	—	—	1	—
Bastrop	—	—	—	3
Baylor	—	—	—	1
Bee	—	—	1	—
Bell	—	—	11	10
Bexar	—	—	46	54
Bosque	—	1	—	—
Bowle	—	—	4	—
Brazos	—	—	1	1
Brewster	—	—	2	1
Burleson	—	—	—	2
Caldwell	—	—	—	3
Cameron	—	—	1	—
Cherokee	—	—	1	—
Childress	—	—	2	2
Clay	—	—	1	—
Coleman	—	—	1	1
Collin	—	—	1	2
Colorado	—	—	1	1
Comal	—	—	—	1
Cooke	—	—	11	9
Corryell	—	—	1	—
Dallas	—	—	63	24
Deaf Smith	—	—	—	1
Denton	—	—	1	—
Dewitt	—	—	1	3
Donley	—	—	4	3
Eastland	—	—	—	1
Ellis	—	—	1	2
El Paso	—	—	225	336
Erath	—	—	—	8
Falls	—	—	—	4
Fannin	—	—	6	1
Fayette	—	—	1	—
Galveston	—	15	42	68
Gonzales	—	—	1	4
Grayson	—	2	8	6
Guadalupe	—	—	—	3
Hale	—	—	—	1
Hall	—	—	—	1
Hardeman	—	—	3	1
Harris	—	7	8	43
Harrison	—	—	2	3

Table A15. Continued.

County	1870	1880	1890	1900
Hays	—	—	5	1
Hemphill	—	—	2	1
Hill	—	—	2	1
Hood	11	—	1	—
Hopkins	—	—	1	—
Houston	—	—	—	2
Howard	—	—	11	5
Hunt	—	—	3	6
Jack	1	—	—	1
Jackson	—	—	—	1
Jeff Davis	—	—	3	1
Jefferson	—	—	—	4
Johnson	—	—	2	2
Kaufman	—	3	4	2
Kerr	—	—	1	—
Lamar	—	1	6	1
Lampasas	—	—	2	2
Lavaca	—	—	2	4
Limestone	10	—	—	1
McLennan	—	3	11	22
Marion	—	1	—	1
Maverick	—	—	9	—
Midland	—	—	2	5
Milam	—	—	3	—
Mitchell	—	—	10	3
Montgomery	—	—	1	—
Morris	—	1	—	—
Navarro	—	—	1	6
Nueces	—	—	2	1
Palo Pinto	—	—	—	6
Parker	—	5	2	2
Pecos	—	—	11	8
Potter	—	—	5	3
Presidio	—	—	3	6
Randall	—	—	—	1
Red River	—	—	—	3
Reeves	—	—	16	10
Robertson	3	72	38	26
Rusk	—	—	—	1
Scurry	—	—	—	1
Shackleford	—	—	—	1
Smith	—	—	—	9
Sutton	—	—	1	—
Tarrant	—	3	40	23
Taylor	—	—	14	3
Tom Green	—	2	3	4
Travis	—	10	8	22
Valverde	—	—	6	1

Table A15.   Continued.

County	1870	1880	1890	1900
Van Zandt	—	—	—	1
Victoria	—	—	1	3
Washington	—	1	2	4
Webb	—	—	3	5
Wharton	—	—	—	2
Wheeler	—	—	1	—
Wichita	—	—	2	4
Wilbarger	—	—	9	3
Williamson	—	—	2	4
Wise	—	—	2	1

Source: United States Bureau of the Census, *Twelfth Census of the United States Taken in the Year 1900*, Vol. II: *Population*, Pt. I (Washington D.C.: Government Printing Office), 567–570.

Table A16.   Chinese Population in Utah by County, 1870–1900

County	1870	1880	1890	1900
Total	445	501	806	572
Beaver	—	28	4	4
Boxelder	403	159	147	26
Cache	—	—	2	1
Carbon	—	—	—	4
Davis	—	—	—	6
Emery	—	—	66	1
Grand	—	—	44	—
Iron	—	—	—	3
Juab	—	—	6	29
Millard	—	1	—	—
Morgan	—	17	—	—
Rich	—	—	2	1
Salt Lake	—	131	269	271
Summit	39	67	131	74
Tooele	—	10	8	54
Uinta	—	—	7	5
Utah	—	—	12	3
Wasatch	—	2	—	3
Washington	—	53	2	—
Weber	3	33	106	84

Source: United States Bureau of the Census, *Twelfth Census of the United States Taken in the Year 1900*, Vol. II: *Population*, Pt. I (Washington D.C.: Government Printing Office), 567–570.

Table A17. Chinese Population in Washington by County, 1870–1900

County	1870	1880	1890	1900
Total	234	3186	3260	3629
Adams	—	—	—	2
Asotin	—	—	3	2
Chehalis	—	—	104	24
Chelan	—	—	—	1
Clallam	2	4	53	16
Clarke	—	48	44	51
Columbia	—	38	48	45
Cowlitz	1	28	7	2
Douglas	—	—	14	2
Franklin	—	—	33	25
Garfield	—	—	15	12
Island	7	45	76	53
Jefferson	19	96	453	223
King	33	246	458	459
Kitsap	13	149	60	38
Kittitas	—	—	89	26
Klickitat	—	8	7	5
Lewis	1	13	3	—
Lincoln	—	—	46	22
Mason	1	6	18	32
Okanogan	—	—	1	1
Pacific	6	176	199	81
Pierce	7	155	9	265
San Juan	—	3	—	53
Skagit	—	—	27	183
Skamania	—	3	5	2
Snohomish	3	11	20	8
Spokane	—	219	361	342
Stevens	42	232	35	28
Thurston	19	68	177	58
Wahkiakum	15	559	304	138
Wallawalla	42	512	351	417
Whatcom	21	11	1	839
Whitman	—	530	155	88
Yakima	—	32	84	76

Source: United States Bureau of the Census, *Twelfth Census of the United States Taken in the Year 1900*, Vol. II: *Population*, Pt. I (Washington D.C.: Government Printing Office), 567–570.

Table A18.   Chinese Population in Wyoming by County, 1870–1900

County	1870	1880	1890	1900
Total	143	914	465	461
Albany	2	7	2	8
Bighorn	—	—	—	2
Carbon	1	29	—	—
Converse	—	—	—	4
Crook	—	—	3	2
Fremont	—	—	6	8
Johnson	—	—	3	1
Laramie	13	24	28	34
Natrona	—	—	1	2
Sheridan	—	—	1	9
Sweetwater	95	497	349	318
Uinta	32	357	59	64
Weston	—	—	13	3
Yellowstone National Park	—	—	—	6

Source: United States Bureau of the Census, *Twelfth Census of the United States Taken in the Year 1900*, Vol. II: *Population*, Pt. I (Washington D.C.: Government Printing Office), 567–570.

Table A19.   Percentage Distribution of Chinese Employment in Nevada by Occupation, 1870 and 1880

	1870		1880	
Occupation	% of Chinese Males	% of Chinese Females	% of Chinese Males	% of Chinese Females
Laborer	46	—	32	—
Cook	17	—	18	—
Laundry	12	—	13	—
Miner	8	—	7	—
Woodcutter	4	—	3	—
Gambler	2.5	—	2	—
Peddler	2	—	0.7	—
Merchant[a]	2	—	2	—
Artisan[b]	0.6	—	3	—
Professional[c]	0.7	—	1	—
Prostitute	—	52		24
Housewife	—	30		58
Servant	1	—	4	—
Gardener[d]	0.3	—	2	—
Clerk	0.5	—	1	—
Other	5.2	18	12	18

Calculated from: Population Schedules of the Ninth and Tenth Censuses.
[a]Includes Grocers, general store owners, traders, and tea merchants.
[b]Skilled laborers e.g. carpenters and tailors.
[c]Includes doctors, druggists, and dentists.
[d]Produce growers and sellers.
Source: Greg Lee Carter, "Social Demography of the Chinese in Nevada," *Nevada Historical Society Quarterly* 18, no. 2 (Summer 1975): 84.

Table A20. Occupations of Non-Mining Chinese in the Eastern Counties of Oregon, 1870 and 1880

| | County and Year | | | | | | | | | | | |
| | Baker | | Grant | | Umatilla | | Union | | Wasco | | Totals | |
Occupation	1870	1880	1870	1880	1870	1880	1870	1880	1870	1880	1870	1880
R.R. Labor	—	—	—	—	—	65	—	—	—	1020	—	1085
Cook	20	22	17	36	14	33	6	9	7	46	64	146
Laundry	25	16	8	7	11	26	2	9	11	56	57	114
Laborer	—	13	6	20	—	11	—	1	—	1	6	46
Prostitute	14	17	—	2	8	—	—	3	—	—	22	22
Merchant	1	8	9	9	—	—	—	7	—	2	10	26
Clerk	1	10	4	7	—	—	—	4	—	10	5	31
Gambler	10	4	12	1	—	—	—	6	—	—	22	11
Housekeeper	—	13	9	1	—	—	1	—	3	1	13	15
Servant	1	7	—	1	—	2	1	—	2	7	4	17
Doctor	3	4	3	5	—	1	—	1	1	2	7	13
Gardener	3	4	1	3	1	—	—	2	—	1	5	10
Sawing Wood	—	6	—	4	—	—	—	—	1	4	1	14
Hotel Worker	—	3	1	4	—	—	—	—	1	2	2	9
Farm Labor	1	—	3	—	—	—	1	5	—	—	5	5
Butcher	—	9	1	—	—	—	—	—	—	—	1	9
Shoemaker	1	2	1	1	—	—	—	2	—	—	2	5
Trader	7	—	—	—	—	—	—	—	—	—	7	—
Opium Trader	—	2	—	2	—	—	—	1	—	—	—	5
Tailor	—	1	1	1	—	—	—	1	—	—	1	3
Other	2	8	9	11	—	—	—	7	—	6	11	32
Totals	89	149	85	115	34	138	11	58	26	1158	245	1618

Source: US Census Office, *Original Schedules, 1870, 1880.* Taken from Christopher Edson, *The Chinese in Eastern Oregon, 1860–1890* (San Francisco: R & E Research Associates, 1974), 56.

Table A21. Occupations of Chinese Residing in Territorial Prescott (Arizona)

Occupation	1880	1900	1910
Laundryman	30	61	40
Cook	17	72	53
Domestic servant	14	1	1
Gardener	14	6	9
Laborer	10	37	3
Merchant	2	10	7
Restaurant keeper	2	2	8
Restaurant worker	—	24	—
Waiter	1	6	5
Dishwasher	1	1	1
Clerk	1	—	2
Miner	1	—	3
Brother keeper	1	—	—
Prostitute	5	1	—
Peddler	—	4	—
Hotel proprietor	—	1	1
Contractor	—	1	—
Woodchopper	—	1	—
Shoemaker	—	1	—
Porter	—	—	1
Delivery man	—	—	1
Total	99	229	135

Source: U.S. Federal Census, Arizona Territory Taken from Florence C. Lister and Robert H. Lister, "Chinese Soujourners in Territorial Prescott," *Journal of the Southwest* 31, no. 1 (Spring 1989): 45.

Table A22. Occupations of Chinese Residing in Boise County, Idaho, in 1870, 1880, 1900, and 1910

	1870	*1880*	*1900*	*1910*
Miner	1621	969	202	62
Gardener	2	9	1	—
Prostitute	35	27	—	—
Merchant	6	18	12	—
Clerk	2	6	1	—
Servant	—	14	1	—
Gambling House Owner	5	9	—	—
Gambler	19	30	—	—
Laundryman	17	5	7	—
Restaurant Owner	—	4	—	—
Barker	—	4	1	—
Butcher		2		
Doctor	—	2	—	—
Peddler	—	8	—	—
Porter	1	2	—	—
Interpreter	—	2	—	—
Cook	16	44	25	14
Wood Sawer	—	4	6	—
Carpenter	—	1	—	—
Ditch Tender	—	1	2	1
Laborer	—	20	20	—
Teamster	1	2	1	—
Nurse	—	1	—	—
Cobbler	—	1	—	—
Coffee House Owner	—	1	—	—
Druggist	—	1	—	—
House Wife	4	18	16	2
Child	3	17	9	6
Joss House Worker	—	1	1	—
Blacksmith	1	—	—	—
Stock Raiser	1	—	—	—
Prisoner	10	—	—	—
Hotel Owner	—	—	—	1
No Information	10	1	—	—
Total	1754	1225	305	88

Source: Liping Zhu, "The Chinese on the Rocky Mountain Mining Frontier: The Boise Basin, Idaho, 1863–1910" (Ph.D. Dissertation, University of New Mexico, 1994), 132.

Table A23. Crimes of the Chinese Admitted to Nevada State Prison, 1865–1904

Offenses	Number
Selling whiskey to Indians	72
Burglaries	34
Grand larcenry	29
Assault with intent to kill	13
Violation of opium law	13
Murder–2nd degree	7
House break	5
Selling opium to Indians	4
Jail break	4
Manslaughter	3
Assault with intent to harm	3
Violating revenue law	1
Robbery	1
Attempted rape	1
Murder—1st degree	1

Source: Nevada, "Biennial Report of the Warden of Nevada State Prison," *Appendix to Journals of Senate Assembly*, 1866–1904. Taken from Gary P. BeDunnah, *A History of Chinese in Nevada: 1855–1904* (M.A. Thesis, University of Nevada Reno), 89.

Table A24. Records of Chinese Buried in Mt. Moriah Cemetery (Deadwood)

Date Buried	Name	Age at Death	Address	Doctor	Cause of Death	Lot #	Date Removed
08-22-1886	Chen Yen		Deadwood	Unknown	Unknown	188	10-10-1891
06-27-1888	Chinaman		Deadwood			236	
04-28-1889	Chinaman		Deadwood			240	
03-13-1889	Sam Toy						08-28-1895
03-13-1889	Ching Yon					250	08-28-1896
11-16-1890	Chinaman						
02-01-1891	Wang Chee						
11-05-1879	Chinaman			Chinese Doctor		252	China Gambles (?)
10-26-1880	Chinaman			Chinese Doctor		110	10-10-1889
09-12-1886	Ching Well			Unknown		189	Hip was cousin
03-10-1904	Ching Mong					57	
01-07-1907	Chim Chu	58					
06-23-1907	Die Tmored	83			Old Age		
11-19-1904	Chinaman	60			Unknown		
09-20-1881	Ching Fou					112	Shipped to China
09-28-1901	Gib Mack		Portland[a]	Dr. Allen Corner	Murdered		
08-24-1879	A. H. Hook		Elizabethtown[b]	Chinese Doctor	Fever	244	
07-18-1886	Fuek Jing		Unknown	Unknown	Catarrh	225	
11-26-1883	Jim Wankes	50	Hot Springs		Debility	254	
03-08-1879	Sam Kee		Central City	Dr. H. B. Owens	Fall at South Bend	230	08-28-1885
06-21-1896	Ki You		Buried by Wing Tsue	Unknown	Dropsy		
08-16-1879	Woo Lee		Deadwood	Chinese Doctor	Tuberculosis	243	
08-06-1882	Dan Lung		Deadwood	Chinese Doctor	Fever	159	Shipped to China
05-28-1898	Luke Yen	36	Custer	Unknown	Consumption		(No Date)
08-18-1886	Lee Kow	50	Custer	Unknown	Cancer		

Table A24. Continued.

Date Buried	Name	Age at Death	Address	Doctor	Cause of Death	Lot #	Date Removed
07-14-1899	Lee Wa	48	Deadwood		Died from ache ailments		
04-30-1885	Cse Sun Ming		Deadwood	Chinese Doctor	Consumption		07-1891
02-07-1891	Let Panig		Central City	Unknown	Unknown		08-28-1895
03-04-1901	Lee Tong Young		Deadwood		Dropsy		Moved in 1904
02-22-1880	Yet Beck Sing		Deadwood	Dr. C. W. Meyer	Pneumonia		
08-06-1891	(John) Chin You		Deadwood	Unknown	Unknown		Removed no date
07-02-1882	Young Tny		Deadwood	Wedelstarte	Fever	114	
08-20-1881	Het Wo		Deadwood	Chinese Doctor	Rhumatism	112	
01-30-1895	Wing Tsue	11 mo.	Deadwood	Unknown	Typhoid Fever	264	09-14-1904
08-05-1900	Yse Sing You	55	Deadwood	Ye Ling You	Paralysis		
01-27-1910	Quie Wong			Dr. Allen	Cancer		
06-10-1898	Yee C. Tong	35			Typhoid Fever		09-14-1904
03-16-1900	Sing You (Crazy Man)	55			General Debility		
08-11-1910	Wong Chong	55	Purchased by Wing Tsue	Dr. Moffit	Cancer		
12-02-1914	Wong Tong Bon	66		Dr. Moffit	Cancer	95	
04-06-1910	Chin Yee	41		Dr. Moffit	Pneumonia		
03-23-1911	Chin Hull	55		Dr. Allen	Consumption		
01-21-1896	Ki You		Buried by Wing Tsue in Potter's Field				
04-18-1896	Lee Kow		Buried by Wing Tsue				
01-30-1895	Chinaman		Burial Paid by Wing Tsue $5.00 Potter's Field				

Date	Name		Note
05-15-1898	Chin Guy		
06-13-1898	Yse Tang	03-17-1904	
10-22-1903	Ong Orman	12-10-1903	Pluma
01-07-1907	Chin Chi		Purchased by Burial Paid
01-23-1907	Mot Jan		Purchased by Burial Paid
03-22-1940	Sally Wong		
11-30-1904	Don See		Buried by Wing Tsue
01-13-1898	Die Twoes		Chinawoman
05-07-1894	Chin Yee		Buried by Win Wing Chee (?)

All entries in Deadwood Cemetery were made with pen and ink. A few names were not completely legible.

Source: Joe Sulentic, Deadwood Gulch: The Last Chinatown (Deadwood: Deadwood Gulch Art Gallery), 1975.

aPortland was a mining town near Trojan, South Dakota.

bElizabethtown—subdivision of Deadwood.

Bibliography

PH.D. DISSERTATIONS AND MASTERS THESES

Balibrera, Dana. "Virginia City and the Immigrant." M.A. Thesis, University of Nevada, Reno, 1965.

Baureiss, Gunther A. "The City and the Subcommunity: The Chinese of Calgary." M.A. Thesis, University of Calgary, 1971.

BeDunnah, Gary P. "A History of the Chinese in Nevada: 1855–1904." M.A. Thesis, University of Nevada, Reno, 1966.

Bell, Marie. "The Attitude of Organized Labor toward Immigration." M.A. Thesis, University of Chicago, 1922.

Briscoe, Edward Eugene. "Pershing's Chinese Refugees: An Odyssey of the Southwest." M.A. Thesis, Saint Mary's University, San Antonio, 1947.

Camacho, Beatriz Ramirez. "Los chinos en Mexico. Esbozo de la comunidad de Tampico." M.A. Thesis, Universidad Nacional Autóma de México, 1975.

Chang, Ching-chieh. "The Chinese in Latin America: A Preliminary Geographical Survey with Special Reference to Cuba and Jamaica." Ph.D. Dissertation, University of Maryland, 1956.

Chiang, Wei Vivian. "The Chinese Community in Phoenix, Arizona: A Study of Acculturation and Assimilation." M.A. Thesis, Arizona State University, 1970.

Christian, John Willis. "The Kootenay Gold Rush: The Placer Decade 1862–1872." Ph.D. Dissertation, Washington State University, 1967.

Currier, Viola N. "The Chinese Web in Oregon History." M.A. Thesis, University of Oregon, 1925.

Dawson, J. Brian. "Chinese Urban Communities in Southern Alberta." Ph.D. Dissertation, Saint Louis University, 1957.

Donlon, Walter J. "LeBaron Bradford Prince, Chief Justice and Governor of New Mexico Territory, 1879–1893." Ph.D. Dissertation, University of New Mexico, 1967.

Dove, Myrtle R. "A History of Toyah, Texas." M.A. Thesis, Sul Ross State College, 1949.

Feichter, Nancy Koehler. "The Chinese in the Inland Empire during the Nineteenth Century." M.A. Thesis, State College of Washington, 1959.

Flaherty, Stacy A. "Asia vs. America: Chinese and Organized Labor in Nineteenth Century Butte, Montana." M.A. Thesis, George Washington University, Washington D.C., 1986.

Glich, Clarence. "The Chinese Migrants in Hawaii: A Study in Accomodation." Ph.D. Dissertation, University of Chicago, 1938.

Hoe, Ban Seng. "Structural Changes of Two Chinese Communities in Alberta, Canada." Ph.D. Dissertation, Vanderbilt University, 1974.

Janisch, Hudson N. "The Chinese, the Courts, the Constitution: A Study of the Legal Issues Raised by Chinese Immigration to the United States, 1850–1902." J.S.D. Dissertation, University of Chicago Law School, 1971.

Jaqcues, Leo M. "The Anti-Chinese Campaign in Sonora, Mexico, 1900–1931." Ph.D. Dissertation, University of Arizona, 1974.

Kinnersley, Thomas H. "Virgnia, Nevada, 1859–1890: A Study of Police, Water, and Fire Problems." Ph.D. Dissertation, University of California, Los Angeles, 1974.

Lee, B.Y. "Perpetuation of the Primary Group Patterns among the Chinese in Portland, Oregon." M.A. Thesis, University of Oregon, 1938.

Ling, George Kai Hung. "A Content Analysis of Chinese Crime in Boise and Idaho City between 1865–1895." M.A. Thesis, University of Idaho, 1980.

Loh, Homer C. "Cultural Conflicts of Americans of Chinese Ancestry of Philadelphia." Ph.D. Dissertation. Philadelphia: University of Pennsylvania Libraries, 1945.

Meagher, Arnold J. "The Introduction of Chinese Laborers to Latin America: The 'Coolie Trade,' 1847–1874." Ph.D. Dissertation, University of California at Davis, 1975.

Nims, Amy Elizabeth. "Chinese Life in San Antonio." M.A. Thesis, Southwest Texas State Teachers College, 1941.

Palmer, Howard. "Response to Foreign Immigration: Nativism and Ethnic Tolerance in Alberta, 1880–1920." Ph.D. Dissertation, University of Alberta, 1971.

Peabody, Etta B. "Effort of the South to Import Chinese Coolies, 1865–1870." M.A. Thesis, Baylor University, 1967.

Roberts, William. "The Chinese Riot, October 31st, 1880." M.A. Thesis, Denver Veteran Volunteer Firemen's Association Papers, No. 5, in Western History Department, Denver Public Library.

Rudolph, Gerald E. "The Chinese in Colorado, 1869–1911." M.A. Thesis, University of Colorado, 1964.

Stapp, Darby Campbell. "The Historical Ethnography of a Chinese Mining Community in Idaho." Ph.D. Dissertation, University of Pennsylvania, 1990.

Steeves, Laba Richard. "Chinese Gold Miners of Northeastern Oregon, 1862–1900." M.A. Thesis, University of Oregon, 1984.

Templin, John Alton. "A History of Methodism in Denver, 1876–1912." Ph.D. Dissertation, Iliff School of Theology, Denver, 1956.

Tozier, Warren Wilson. "The History of Gold Mining in the Swank, Pehastian, and Cle-Clum Mining Districts of the Wenatchee Mountains, 1853–1899." M.A. Thesis, Washinton State University, 1965.

Trull, Fern Coble. "The History of the Chinese in Idaho from 1864 to 1910." M.A. Thesis, University of Oregon, 1946.

Tsai, Shih-Shan Henry. "Reaction to Exclusion: Ch'ing Attitudes towards Overseas Chinese in the United States, 1848–1906." Ph.D. Dissertation, University of Oregon, 1970.

Wells, Marianne Kaye. "Chinese Temples in California." M.A. Thesis, University of California Berkeley, 1962.

Wilkoff, Melvin. "Chinese in the Idaho County Gold Fields, 1864–1933." M.A. Thesis, Texas A & M University, 1972.

Williams, Stephen. "The Chinese in California Mines, 1848–1860." M.A. Thesis, Stanford University, 1930.

Wu, Ching-Chao. "Chinatowns: A Study of Symbiosis and Assimilation." Ph.D. Dissertation, University of Chicago, 1926.

———. "Chinese Immigration in the Pacific Area." M.A. Thesis, University of Chicago, 1924.

Wynne, Robert Edward. "Reaction to the Chinese in the Pacific Northwest and British Columbia 1850–1910." Ph.D. Dissertation, University of Washington, 1946.

Yen, Tsu Kuei. "Chinese Workers and the First Transcontinental Railroad of the United States of America." Ph.D. Dissertation, St. John's University, New York, 1977.

Yoder, Phillip D. "The History of Fort Whipple." M.A. Thesis, University of Arizona, Tucson.

Yu, Lihua. "Chinese Immigrants in Idaho." Ph.D. Dissertation, Bowling Green State University, 1991.

BOOKS

Adams, Mildretta. *Historic Silver City*. Nampa, Idaho: Schwartz Printing Company, 1969.

American Association of University Women. *The Drama of Virginia City*. Reno: Nevada State Journal, 1925.

Bailey, R.G. *River of No Return*. Lewiston, Idaho: Bailey-Blake Printing Company, 1935.

Bancroft, Caroline. *Denver's Lively Past*. Boulder, Colo.: Johnson Publishing Company, 1959.

———. *Gulch of Gold*. Denver: Sage Books, 1958.

Barlow, Jeffrey, and Christine Richardson. *Chinese Doctor of John Day*. Portland: Binford and Mort, 1979.

Barrett, Velma, and Hazel Oliver. *Odessa: City of Dreams, a Miracle of the Texas Prairies*. San Antonio, 1966, 166.

Barth, Gunther. *Bitter Strength: A History of Chinese in the United States, 1850–1870*. Cambridge, 1964.

BeDunnah, Gary P. *The History of the Chinese in Nevada, 1855–1904*. San Francisco: R&E Research Associates, 1973.

Beebe, Lucius, and Charles Clegg. *Virginia and Truckee: A Story of Virginia City and Comstock Times*. Stanford, Calif.: Stanford University Press, 1949.

Bennett, Estelline. *Old Deadwood Days*. New York: Charles Scribner's Sons, 1935.

Bennett, Marion T. *American Immigration Policies: A History*. Washington, D.C., 1963.

Bird, Annie Laurie. *My Home Town*. Caldwell, Idaho: The Caxton Printers, Ltd., 1968.

Bluden, Caroline, and Mark Elvin. *Cultural Atlas of China*. New York: Facts on File, 1983.

Bowles, Samuel. *Our New West, Records of Travel between the Mississippi River and the Pacific Ocean*. Hartford, Connecticut, 1869.

Boyd, Joseph H. *Reminiscenses of Joseph H. Boyd*, arranged by William S. Lewis. Seattle: University of Washington Press, 1924.

Bradley, Anita. *Trans-Pacific Relations of Latin America*. New York: Institute of Pacific Relations, 1942.

———. *Trans-Pacific Relations of Latin America*. New York: International Secretariat, Institute of Pacific Relations, 1942.

Broaddus, J. Morgan. *The Legal Heritage of El Paso*, ed. Samuel D. Myers. El Paso: Texas Western College Press, 1963, 134.

Bromley, Isaac H. *The Chinese Massacre at Rock Springs, Wyoming Territory, September 2, 1885.* Boston: Franklin Press, 1886.

Brown, Jesse, and A. M. Williard. *The Black Hills Trails.* Rapid City: Rapid City Journal Company, 1924.

Burkhardt, V. R. *Chinese Creeds and Customs.* Hong Kong: The South China Morning Post, Ltd., 1953.

Bushnell, John E. *The History of Westminster Presbyterian Church.* Minneapolis: Lund Press, 1938.

Casey, Robert J. *The Black Hills and Their Incredible Characters.* Indianapolis: Bobbs-Merrill Co., 1949.

Caurus, Paul. *Chinese Life and Customs.* Chicago: Open Court Pub. Co., 1907.

Chan, Loran Briggs. *Sagebrush Statesman: Tasker L. Oddie of Nevada.* Nevada Studies in History and Political Science, no. 12. Reno: University of Nevada Press, 1973.

Chan, Sucheng. *This Bittersweet Soil: The Chinese in California Agriculture, 1860–1910.* Berkeley and Los Angeles: University of California Press, 1986.

Chen, Jack. *The Chinese of America: From the Beginnings to the Present.* San Francisco: Harper & Row, 1981.

Chen, Kwong Min. *Mei-chou hua ch'iao t'ung chien [A general history of the Chinese overseas in america].* New York: Overseas Chinese Culture Publishing Co., 1950.

Chen, Ta. *Emigrant Communities in South China.* English edition by Bruno Lasket. New York: Institute of Pacific Relations, 1940.

Cheng, Tien-fang. *Chinese Immigration.* New York: Holt, 1909.

Cheng-tsu, Wu. *Chink.* New York: World Publishing Co., 1972.

Chinn, Thomas. *A History of the Chinese in California.* San Francisco: Chinese Historical Society of America, 1969.

Chinn, Thomas W., H. Mark Lai, and Philip P. Choy, eds. *A History of the Chinese in California: A Syllabus.* San Francisco: Chinese Historical Society of America, 1969.

Chiu, Ping. *Chinese Labor in California, 1850–1880: An Economic Study.* Madison: State Historical Society of Wisconsin, 1963.

Chu, Daniel, and Samuel Chu, Ph.D. *Passage to the Golden Gate: A History of the Chinese in America to 1910.* Garden City, N.Y.: Doubleday, 1967.

Clark, Walter Van Tilburg, ed. *The Journals of Alfred Dolen, 1849–1903,* 3 vols. Reno: 1973.

Clemens, Samuel Langhorne (Mark Twain). *Roughing It.* Hartford, Conn.: American Publishing Co., 1872; New York: New American Library, 1962.

Clowser, Don C. *Deadwood . . . The Historic City.* Deadwood: Fenwyn Press Books, 1969.

Condit, Ira M. *The Chinaman As We See Him.* Chicago: Fleming H. Revell Company, 1900.

Conlin, Joseph R. *Bacon, Beans and Galantines: Food and Foodways on the Western Mining Frontier.* Reno: University of Nevada Press, 1986.

Coolidge, Robert. *Chinese Immigration.* New York: Henry Holt and Co., 1909.

Copper Camp: Stories of the World's Greatest Mining Town, Butte, Montana. Compiled by Members of Writers Program of the Works Project Administration in the State of Montana. New York: Hastings House, 1943.

Corral, Ramón. *Memoria de la aministración pública del Estado de Sonra, presenada a la Legislatura del mismo por el Gobernador Ramón Corral,* 2 vols. Guaymas: Imprenta de E. Gaxiola, 1891.

Cortbitt, Duvon C. *A Study of the Chinese in Cuba, 1847–1947.* Wilmore, Ky.: Asbury College, 1971.

Courtwright, David. *Dark Paradise.* Cambridge, Mass.: 1922.

Cross, Ira B. A *History of the Labor Movement in California.* Berkeley, 1935.

Culin, Stewart. *The Gambling Games of the Chinese in America.* Publications of the University of Pennsylvania, Series in Philology, Literature and Archaeology, vol 1, no. 4. Philadelphia: University of Pennsylvania Press, 1891; Las Vegas: Gambler's Book Club, 1969.

———. *The Phing or "Patriotic Rising," a Secret Society among the Chinese in America.* San Francisco: R&E Research Associates, 1970.

Daniels, Roger. *Asian America: Chinese and Japanese in the United States since 1850.* Seattle: 1988.

Davis, E. D. *The First Five Years of the Railroad Era in Colorado, June 19, 1867 to June 19, 1872.* Golden, Colo.: Sage Books Incorporated, 1948.

Davis, Fei-Lung. *Primitive Revolutions of China.* Honolulu: University Press of Hawaii, 1979.

d'Easum, Dick. *Fragments of Villainy.* Boise, Idaho: Statesman Printing Company, 1959.

Dicker, Laverne Mau. *The Chinese in San Francisco: A Pictorial History.* New York: Dover, 1979.

Dillon, Richard H. *The Hatchet Men: The Story of the Tong Wars in San Francisco's Chinatown.* New York: Coward-McCann, 1962.

Dobi, Charles C. *San Francisco's Chinatown.* New York: 1936.

Donaldson, Thomas. *Idaho Yesterdays.* Caldwell, Idaho: The Caxton Printers, Ltd., 1941.

Donelly, Thomas C., and Arthur N. Holcombe. *Rocky Mountain Politics.* Albuquerque: University of New Mexico Press, 1940.

Dorfles, Gilo. *Kitsch: An Anthology of Bad Taste.* London: Studio Vista Ltd., 1969.

Eaves, Lucile. A *History of California Labor Legislation, with an Introductory Sketch of the San Francisco Labor Movement.* Berkeley: The University Press, 1910.

Edson, Christopher. *The Chinese in Eastern Oregon, 1860–1890.* San Francisco: R&E Research Associates, 1974.

Elsehsohn, Sister M. Alfreda. *Idaho Chinese Lore.* Cottonwood: Idaho Collection of Benedictine Sisters, 1970.

Espinoza, José Angel. *El ejemplo de Sonora.* Mexico, D.F. 1932.

Farrar, Nancy. *The Chinese in El Paso.* El Paso: Texas Western Press, 1972.

Fong, N. G. *The Chinese in New Zealand: A Study of Assimilation.* Hong Kong: Hong Kong University Press, 1959.

Fossett, Frank. *Colorado, Its Gold and Silver Mines.* New York: C.G. Crawford, 1880.

———. *Colorado: A Historical, Descriptive and Statistical Work on the Rocky Mountain Gold and Silver Mining Region.* Denver: Daily Tribune Steam Printing House, 1876.

Galloway, John Debo. *The First Transcontinental Railroad.* New York: Simmons-Boardman, 1950.

Gardner, A. Dudley, and Verla R. Flores. *Forgotten Frontier: A History of Wyoming Coal Mining.* Boulder, Colo.: Westview Press, 1989.

Gem State Author's Guild. *Starlight and Syringa.* Pocatello, Idaho: Gateway Printers, Inc. 1959.

Genthe, Arnold, and Will Irwin. *Old Chinatown.* New York: M. Kennerley, 1913.

Getting Together. *Chinese-American Workers: Past and Present.* San Francisco: Getting Together, 1970.

Greever, William S. *The Bonanza West: The Story of the Western Mining Rushes, 1848–1900.* Norman: University of Oklahoma Press, 1963.

Gulick, Sydney L. *American Democracy and Asiatic Citizenship*. New York: Funk and Wagnalls Company, 1919.

Hafen, LeRoy R., ed. *Colorado and Its People, A Narrative and Topical History of the Centennial State*. New York: Lewis Historical Publishing Company, 1948.

Haney, Kenneth, ed. *Gold Rush by Sea from the Journal of Garrett W. Low*. Philadelphia: University of Pennsylvania Press, 1941.

Hansen, Gladys C., and William F. Heintz. *The Chinese in California: A Brief Bibliographic History*. Portland Oregon: 1970.

Hart, Arthur A. *Basin of Gold: Life in Boise Basin, 1862–1890*. Idaho City, Historical Foundation, 1986.

Harte, John Bret. *Portraits of a Desert Pueblo*. Woodland Hills, Calif.: Windsor, 1980.

Helper, Hinton. *Land of Gold*. Baltimore: H. Taylor, 1855.

Henderson, Charles W. *Mining in Colorado, A History of Discovery, Development, and Production*. Washington, D.C.: Government Printing Office, 1926.

Hiatt, Isaac. *Thirty One Years in Baker County*. Baker City, Ore.: Abbott and Foster Publishers, 1893.

Hildebrand, Lorraine B. *Straw Hats, Sandals, and Steel: The Chinese in Washington State*. Tacoma: Washington State American Revolution Bicentennial Commission, 1977.

History of Union Pacific Coal Mines 1869–1940. Omaha, Nebr.: The Colonial Press, 1940.

Hollon, W. Eugene. *Frontier Violence: Another Look*. New York: Oxford University Press, 1974.

Holt, Hamilton, ed. *The Life Stories of Undistinguished Americans*. New York: James Pott and Company, 1906.

Hoy, William. *The Chinese Six Companies*. San Francisco: Chinese Consolidated Benevolent Association, 1942.

Hunt, Michael H. *The Making of a Special Relationship: The United States and China to 1914*. New York: Columbia University Press, 1983.

Inglis, C. et al., eds. *Asians in Australia: The Dynamics of Migration and Settlement*. Singapore: Institute of Southeast Asian Studies, 1992.

Jackson, W. Turrentine. *Treasure Hill: Portrait of a Silver Mining Camp*. Tucson: University of Arizona Press, 1963.

Jacobs, Orange. *Memoirs*. Seattle: Lowman & Hanford, 1908.

Jamieson, Tulitas. *Tuliitas of Torréon: Reminiscences of Life in Mexico*. El Paso: Texas Western Press, 1969.

Jenks, Jeremiah W., and W. Jett Lauck. *The Immigration Problem*. New York: Funk and Wagnalls Company, 1926.

Johnson, David Alan. *Founding the Far West: California, Oregon, and Nevada, 1840–1890*. Berkeley: 1992.

Johnson, Kenneth M, ed. *San Francisco As It Is: Gleanings from the 'Picayune.'* Georgetown, Calif.: 1964.

Jung-pang Lo, ed. and trans. *K'ang Yu-wei: A Biography and a Symposium*. Tucson, 1967.

Kane, Harry Hubbell. *Opium-smoking in America and China*. New York: Arno, 1976.

King, Owang, and Arthur Bassett. *Report of Messrs. Owang King and Arthur Bassett, Representatives of His Excellency, Minister Chang Yin Tang in an Investigation Made in Conjunction with Licenciado Antonio Ramos Pedrueza, Representative of His Excellency, Francisco L. de la Narra, President of Mexico, of the Facts Relating to the Massacre of Chinese Subjects at Torreón on the 15th of May, 1911*. Mexico: American Book and Printing Company, 1911.

Kinnear, George. *Anti-Chinese Riots at Seattle, Wn., February 8th, 1886.* Seattle, Wash.: privately printed, Feb. 8, 1911.

Kneiss, Gilbert H. *Bonanza Railroads.* Stanford, Calif.: Stanford University Press, 1941.

Konovitz, Milton R. *The Alien and the Asiatic in American Laws.* Ithaca, N.Y.: Cornell University Press, 1946.

Kraut, Alan M. *The Huddled Masses: The Immigrant in American Society, 1880–1921.* Arlington Heights, Ill.: 1982.

Kung, S.W. *Chinese in American Life: Some Aspects of Their History, Status, Problems, and Contributions.* Seattle: University of Washington Press, 1962.

Kwung, S.W. *Chinese in American Life.* Seattle: University of Washington Press, 1962.

Lai, Hum Mark, Joe Huang, and Don Wong. *The Chinese of America, 1785–1890.* San Francisco, 1980.

Lai, Mark H., and Philip P Choy. *Outlines: History of the Chinese in America.* San Francisco, 1973.

Lamar, Howard R. *The Reader's Encyclopedia of the American West.* New York: 1977.

Lee, Rose Hum. *The Chinese in the United States of America.* Hong Kong University Press, 1960.

Light, Ivan H. *Ethnic Enterprises in America: Business and Welfare among Chinese, Japanese, and Blacks.* Berkeley: University of California Press, 1972.

Ling, Lew, ed. *The Chinese in North America: A Guide to Their Life and Progress.* Los Angeles: East-West Culture Publishing Association, Inc., 1946.

Liu, Pei Chi. *Meiguo huaqiao shi [A history of the Chinese in the United States of America, 1848–1911].* Taipei: Overseas Chinese Affairs Commission, 1976.

Lo, Jung-Pang, ed. *Facts and Figures about Mexico.* Mexico: National Railways of Mexico, 1911.

———, ed. and translator. *Kang Yu-Wei: A Biography and a Symposium.* Tucson: University of Arizona Press for the Association of Asian Studies, 1967.

Lockley, Fred. *Oregon Folks.* New York: The Knickerbocker Press, 1927.

Loewen, James W. *The Mississippi Chinese: Between Black and White.* Cambridge, Mass.: 1971.

Lord, Eliot. *Comstock Mining and Miners.* Berkeley: Howell-North, 1959, reprint of 1883.

Lyman, George. *The Saga of the Comstock Lode: Boom Days in Virginia City.* New York: Charles Scribner's Sons, 1934.

Lyman, Stanford M. *Chinese Americans.* New York, 1974.

———. *The Asian in the West.* Reno: University of Nevada Social Science and Humanities Publication No. 4, 1970.

Macfie, Matthew. *Vancouver Island and British Columbia.* London: Longman, Green, Longman, 1865.

MacInnes, Tom. *Oriental Occupation of British Columbia.* Vancouver: Sun, 1927.

MacNair, Harley F. *The Chinese Abroad: Their Position and Protection: A Study in International Law and Relations.* Taipei: Ch'eng Wen Publishing Company, 1971.

Matthews, Mrs. Mary M. *Ten Years in Nevada.* Buffalo, N.Y.: Baker, Jones, & Co., 1880.

McClellan, R. Guy. *The Golden State: A History of the Region West of the Rocky Mountains.* San Francisco: Flint & Co., 1974.

McClennan, Robert. *The Heathen Chinee: A Study of American Attitudes toward China, 1890–1905.* Columbus: Ohio State University Press, 1969.

McConnell, Virginia. *Bayou, Salado: The Story of South Park.* Denver: Sage Books, 1966.

McKenzie, R. D. *Oriental Exclusion.* Chicago: University of Chicago Press, 1927.

McLeod, Alexander. *Pigtails and Gold Dust.* Caldwell, Idaho: Caxton Printers, 1948.

McWilliams, Carey. *Brothers Under the Skin,* revised edition. Boston: Little, Brown and Company, 1951.

Mears, Elliott Grinnell. *Resident Orientals on the Pacific Coast: Their Legal and Economic Status.* Chicago: University of Chicago Press, 1928.

Memoria, hechos relativos a la matanza de chinos en Torreón y el protocol de 16 diciembre de 1911, prometiendo indemnización por la matanza. n.p.: n.d.

Miller, Stuart. *The Unwelcome Immigrant: The American Image of the Chinese.* Berkeley: University of California Press, 1969.

Minke, Pauline. *Chinese in the Mother Lode 1850–1870.* San Francisco: R&E Research, 1974.

Murray, Pauli, comp. and ed. *States' Laws on Race and Color.* Cincinnati, Woman's Division of Christian Service, Board of Missions of the Methodist Church, 1955.

Myrick, David F. *Railroads of Nevada and Eastern California,* 2 vols. Berkeley, Calif.: Howell-North Books, 1962.

Nee, Victor G., and Brett de Bary Nee. *Longtime Californ': A Documentary Study of an American Chinatown.* New York, 1951.

Nichols, Dorothy Young. *Virginia City . . . in My Days: A Memory Album,* ed. Halmar F. Moser. Placerville: privately printed, 1973.

Paher, Stanley W. *Nevada Ghost Towns and Mining Camps.* Berkeley, Calif.: Howell-North Books, 1970.

Parker, Watson. *Gold in the Black Hills.* Norman: University of Oklahoma Press, 1966.

Parkhill, Forbes. *The Wildest of the West.* Denver: Sage Books, 1957.

Patterson, Edna B., Louise A. Ulph, and Victor Goodwin. *Nevada's Northeast Frontier.* Sparks, Nev.: Western Printing and Publishing Co., 1969.

Paul, Rodman W. *California Gold.* Lincoln: University of Nebraska Press, 1967.

———. *Mining Frontiers of the Far West, 1848–1880.* New York: Holt, Rinehart, and Winston, 1963.

Perkin, Robert, L. *The First Hundred Years: An Informal History of Denver and the Rocky Mountain News.* New York: Doubleday & Co., 1959.

Pioneer Nevada. Reno: Harold's Club, 1956.

Potter, Alvina N. *The Many Lives of the Lynx: A Century of Mining on Lynx Creek between 1863 and 1963.* Prescott, Ariz.: n.p., 1964.

Rak, Mary Kidder. *The Border Patrol.* Boston: Houghton, Mifflin, 1938.

Rand, Helen B. *Gold, Jade, and Elegance.* Baker, Ore.: Hells Canyon National Recreation Area Planning Team, United States Forest Service, 1978.

Reed, S. G. *A History of Texas Railroads and of Transportation Conditions under Spain and Mexico and the Republic and the State.* Houston, 1941, 197–198.

Rogers, Franklin R., ed. *The Pattern for Mark Twain's Roughing It: Letters from Nevada by Samuel Orion Clemens.* University of California English Studies, no. 23. Berkeley: University of California Press, 1961.

Sam, Wong, compiler. *An English-Chinese Phrase Book Together with the Vocabulary of Trade, Law, etc. Also a Complete List of Wells, Fargo, & Co.'s Offices in California, Nevada, etc.* San Francisco: 1875.

Sandmeyer, Elmer Clarence. *The Anti-Chinese Movement in California.* Urbana, Ill.: University of Illinois Press, 1939.

Sawyer, Raymon I. *Reno, Where the Gamblers Go!* Reno: Sawston Publishing Co., 1976.

Saxton, Alexander. *The Indispenisble Enemy: Labor and the Anti-Chinese Movement in California.* Berkeley, 1971.

Schrank, Jeffrey. *Snap, Crackle, and Popular Taste: The Illusion of Free Choice in America.* New York: Dell Publishing Co., Inc., 1977.

Schurz, William L. *The Manila Galleon.* New York: 1939.

Shang-ying, Wu. *Mei-kuo hua-ch'iao pai-nien chi-shih* [*One hundred years of Chinese in the United States and Canada*]. Hong Kong: published by Wu Shang-ying, 1954.

Shepperson, Wilbur S. *Restless Strangers: Nevada's Immigrants and Their Interpreters.* Reno: University of Nevada Press, 1970.

Smith, Duane A. *Rocky Mountain Mining Camps.* Bloomington: Indiana University Press, 1967.

Spencer, J. E. *Asian East by South.* New York: Joh Wiley and Sons, Inc., 1954.

Spring, Agnes W. *The Cheyenne and Black Hills Stage and Express Routes.* Glendale, Calif.: Arthur H. Clarke Co., 1949.

Steiner, Stan. *Fusang: The Chinese Who Built America.* New York: Harper Colophon Books, 1980.

Steinfield, Melvin. *Cracks in the Melting Pot: Racism and Discrmination in American History.* Beverly Hills, Calif.: Glencoe Press, 1970.

Stevenson, Robert Louis. *Across the Plains.* London: Chatto & Windus, 1905.

Stewart, Watt. *Chinese Bondage in Peru: A History of the Chinese Coolies in Peru, 1849–1874.* Durham, N.C.: Duke University Press, 1951.

Stewart, William M. *The Threatened Invasion.* Reno, Nev.: Evening Gazette Print, 1886.

Sulentic, Joe. *Deadwood Gulch: The Last Chinatown.* Deadwood, S.D.: Deadwood Gulch Art Gallery, 1975.

Summerhayes, Martha. *Vanished Arizona.* Philadelphia: Lippincott, 1908.

Sung, Bettie Lee. *Mountain of Gold: The Story of the Chinese in America.* New York, 1971.

Taylor, John. *A Kid on the Comstock: Reminiscences of a Virginia City Childhood,* ed. Dolores Bryant Waldorf. Palo Alto, Calif.: American West Publishing Company, 1970.

Telemaque, Eleanor Wong. *It's Crazy to Stay Chinese in Minnesota.* Nashville, Tenn.: T. Nelson, 1978.

Ten Broek, Jacobus, Edward N. Barnhart, and Floyd W. Matson. *Prejudice, War, and the Constitution.* Berkeley: University of California Press, 1958.

Terry, Charles E., M.D. *The Opium Problem.* New York: 1922.

Terry, T. Philip. *Terry's Mexico: Handbook for Travellers.* Boston: Houghton Mifflin, 1909.

Ting, Wen-chiang. *Liang jen-kung hsien-sheng nien-p'u ch'ang pien ch'u-kao* [*First Draft of an Unabridged Chronological Biography of Lang Ch'i-ch'ao*], 3 vols. Taipei: n.p., 1958.

Tsai, Shih-Shan Henry. *China and the Overseas Chinese in the United States, 1868–1911.* Fayetteville: University of Arkansas Press, 1983.

———. *The Chinese Experience in America.* Bloomington: Indiana University Press, 1971.

Vélez, Ildefonso Villarello. *Historia de la Revolución Mexicana en Coahuila.* Mexico: Talleres Gráficos de la Nación, 1970.

Walker, Henry P., and Don Bufkin. *Historical Atlas of Arizona.* Norman: University of Oklahoma Press, 1979.

Wallnofer, Heinrich, and Anna von Rottauscher. *Chinese Fold Medecine.* New York: Crown, 1965.

Warner, F.W. *Montana and the Northwest Territory.* Chicago: Blakely, Brown, and March Printers, 1879.

Webb, George. *A Pima Remembers*. Tucson: University of Arizona Press, 1959.

Wei Min She Labor Committee. *Chinese Working People in America*. San Francisco: United Front Press, 1974.

Wells, Mariann Kaye. *Chinese Temples in California*. San Francisco: R&E Research Associates, 1971.

Wells, Merle W. *Gold Camps and Silver Cities: Nineteenth Century Mining in Central and Southern Idaho*, 2nd ed. Moscow, Idaho: Idaho Dept. of Lands, Bureau of Mines and Geology, 1983.

Western Historical Publishing Company. *History of Baker, Grant, Malheur, and Harney Counties* (Oregon). n.p.: Western Historical Publishing Company, 1902.

Whitlock, V. H. *Cowboy Life on the Llano Estacado*. Norman: University of Oklahoma Press, 1970.

Wilfley, Lebbeus, and Arthur Bassett. *Memorandum on the Law and the Facts in the Matter of the Claim of China against Mexico for Losses of Life and Property Suffered by Chinese Subjects at Torreón on May 13, 14, and 15, 1911*. Mexico: American Book and Printing Company, 1911.

———. *Memorandum Showing Extent of Destruction of Life and Property of Chinese Subjects During the Recent Revolution in Mexico and Mexico's Responsibility Therefore, Together with Citations of Authorities*. Mexico: American Books and Printing Comapany, 1911.

Wittke, Carl. *We Who Built America*. Cleveland: Western University Press, 1939.

Wong, Karen. *Chinese History in the Pacific Northwest*. Seattle: 1972.

Wright, William (Dan De Quille). *The Big Bonanza*. Hartford, Conn.: American Publishing Co., 1876; New York: Alfred Knopf, 1947.

Wu, Hsien-tzu. *Chung kuo chu hsien-cheng tang shih* [*A history of the Chinese Democratic Constitution Party*]. San Francisco: n.p., 1952.

Wynne, Robert Edward. *Reaction to the Chinese in the Pacific Northwest and British Columbia, 1805–1910*. New York: Arno Press, 1979.

Xiang-yue, Mu. *Ou-chu wu-shi zi-shu* [The autobiography of Mu Xiang-yue]. Shanghai, 1926.

Yu, Yuan-tse. *Mo-hsi-ke Hua-chi-ao Shih-hua* [*Historical sketch of overseas Chinese in Mexico*]. Taipei: Overseas Chinese Library Publication Service, 1954.

Zauner, Phyllis and Lou Zauner. *Carson City Nevada*. South Lake Tahoe, Calif.: E-Z Publishing Co., 1977.

Zo, Kil Young. *Chinese Emigration into the United States, 1850–1880*. New York: Arno Press, 1978.

ARTICLES

" 'She will strike about three . . .': Steamboating in Hell's Canyon." *Idaho Yesterdays* 1, no. 2 (Summer 1957): 6–9.

"A Chinese Romance." *Daily Denver Tribune*. 1 June 1874.

"Chinese in Early Days." *Sacramento Bee*. 21 January 1886.

"Convention between the Governments of Mexico and China for the Payment of an Indemnity." *Supplement to the American Journal of International Law* 8 (January 1914): 147–150.

"David Thomas Story." *Wyoming Press*. 15 April 1931.

"Robertson County: Chinese Farmers of 1870's." (Texas Historical Commission, Austin)

"The Credit Situation in Guaymas, Mexico." *Commerce Reports* 45 (November 9, 1931): 313.

"The Passing of the Pioneer." *The Trail* (State Historical Society of Colorado) 12 (November 1919): 28.

Stewart. "Social Organizations of the Chinese in America." *American Anthropology* 4: 347–351.

Bing Chong. "The Chinese Store as a Social Institution." *Social Process in Hawaii* 7 (1928): 290–299.

Adler, Lee. "Anaconda Closure Doesn't Dampen Yerington's Spirit." *Nevada State Journal* (Reno). 2 July 1978.

Allen, J.S. "Yavapai Inferno: The Story of the Great Prescott Fire." *Arizona Highways*. May 1941.

Anderson, David L. "The Diplomacy of Discrimination: Chinese Exclusion, 1876–1882." *California History* (Spring 1978): 32–45.

Anderson, Harold P. "Wells Fargo and Chinese Customers in Nineteenth-Century California." In *Eastern Banking: Essays in the History of the Hong Kong and Shanghai Banking Corporation*, ed. Frank H.H. King. London: The Athlone Press, 1983.

Arnold, Hazel C. "Sun Yat-sen in Denver." *The Colorado Magazine* 19 (September 1942): 197–198.

Berg, Fred M. (ed.), *Ethnic Heritage in North Dakota* (Washington, D.C.: Attiyeh Foundation, 1983): 143.

Black, Doris. "The Black Chinese." *Sepia* 24 (January 1975): 18–24.

Blackburn, George M., and Sherman L. Ricards. "The Prostitutes and Gamblers of Virginia City, Nevada 1870." *Pacific Historical Review* 48, no. 2 (May 1979): 239–258.

Blue, Verne. "Mining Laws of Jackson County, 1860–1876." *Quarterly* Oregon (Historical Quarterly) 23 (June 1922): 140.

Boletín Oficial 35 (February 1913): 118–122.

Brawley, S. "'No White Policy' in NZ: Fact and Fiction in New Zealand's Asian Immigration Record, 1946–1978." *New Zealand Journal of History* 27, no. 1 (1993): 16–36.

Bright, Verne. "Blue Mountain Eldorados: Auburn, 1861." *Oregon Historical Quarterly* 62 (September 1961): 236.

Briscoe, Edward Eugene. "Pershing's Chinese Refugees in Texas." *Southwestern Historical Quarterly* 62 (April 1959): 467–488.

Brooking, T., and R. Rabel. "Neither British nor Polynesian: A Brief History of New Zealand's Other Immigrants'." In *Immigration and National Identity in New Zealand: One People, Two Peoples, Many Peoples?*, ed. S.W. Greif. Palmerston North: Dunmore Press, 1995.

Browne, J. Ross. "A Peep at Washoe." *Harper's New Monthly Magazine* 22 (December 1860): 1–17; (January 1861): 145–162; (February 1861): 289–305.

Buell, Paul D., and Christoper Muench. "A Chinese Apothecary in Frontier Idaho." *The Annals of the Chinese Historical Society of the Pacific Northwest 1983*.

California History, Special Issue: "The Chinese Who Built California."

Carter, Greg Lee. "Social Demography of the Chinese in Nevada: 1870–1880." *Nevada Historical Quarterly* 18 (Summer 1975): 77.

Cassidy, Belle. "Recollections of Early Denver." *Colorado Magazine* 29 (January 1952): 54–55.

Champion, George W. "Remembrance of South Park." *Colorado Magazine* 40 (January 1963): 29.

Chan, Loren B. "Example for the Nation: Nevada's Execution of Gee Jon." *Nevada Historical Society Quarterly* 18 (Summer 1975): 90–106.

Chan, Sucheng. "Chinese Livelihood in Rural California: The Impact of Economic Change, 1860–1880." *Pacific Historical Review* 53 (August 1984): 273–307.

Chandler, Allison. "The Story of Como and King Park, Colorado." *The Denver Westerners Monthly Roundup* 19 (February 1963): 1.

Chang-Rodriguez, E. "Chinese Labor Migration into Latin America in the Nineteenth Century." *Revista de Historia de América* 46 (December 1958): 375–397.

Cheng, Lucie. "Free, Indentured, Enslaved: Chinese Prostitutes in Nineteenth-Century America." In *Labor Immigration Under Capitalism*, ed. Lucie Cheng and Edna Bonacich. Berkeley and Los Angeles: University of California Press, 1984.

Chinn, Thomas W. "Notes of California Chinese, 1935–1941." *Chinese Historical Society of America Bulletin* 7 (December 1972): 7.

———. "Observations: 1935–1941." *Chinese Historical Society of America Bulletin* 7 (December 1972): 7.

Chiu-thai, Yen. "The Chinese in Phoenix." *Phoenix* 5 (January 1970): 38.

Cole, Cheryl L. "Chinese Exclusion: The Capitalist Perspective of the *Sacramento Union*, 1850–1882." *California History* 57 (Spring 1978): 18–31.

Constant, Rezin H. "Colorado as Seen by a Visitor of 1880." *Colorado Magazine* 12 (May 1935): 107.

Coolidge, Mary R. "Chinese Labor Competition on the Pacific Coast." *Annals* (American Academy of Political and Social Science) 34 (1909): 12.

Courtland, David. "Opiate Addiction in the American West, 1850–1920." *Journal of the West* 21, no. 3 (1982): 25.

Covarrubias, Jose. "La inmigracion china, considerada desde los puntos de vista intelectual y moral." In *Varios informes, sobre tierras y colonizacion*. Mexico: Imprenta y Fototopia de la Secretaria de Fomenta, 1912.

Crane, Paul, and Alfred Larson. "The Chinese Massacre." *Annals of Wyoming* 12 (January 1940): 47–55.

Crossen, Forest. "Recollections of J. G. Jones." *Boulder Daily Camera*. 3 August 1953.

Culin, Stewart. "Chinese Secret Societies in the United States." *Journal of American Folk-Lore* 3, no. 1 (1890a): 39–43.

———. "Customs of the Chinese in America." *Journal of American Folk-Lore* 3, no. 1 (1890b): 191–200.

Cumberland, Charles C. "The Sonora Chinese and the Mexican Revolution." *Hispanic American Historical Review* 40 (May 1960): 191–211.

Cutting, Henry C., compiler. *The Compiled Laws of Nevada in Force from 1861–1900 (Inclusive)*. Carson City, Nev.: Andrew Maute, 1900.

Dai, Bingham. "Opium Addiction: A Socio-psychiatric Approach." In *Contributions to Urban Sociology*, ed. Ernest W. Burgess and Donald J. Bogue. Chicago: University of Chicago Press, 1964.

Daniels, Roger. "American Historians and East Asian Immigrants." *Pacific Historical Review* 43 (November 1974).

De Falla, Paul M. "Lantern in the Western Sky." *Historical Society of Southern California Quarterly* 42, no. 1 (1960): 58.

Derig, Betty. "The Chinese of Silver City." *Idaho Yesterdays* 2, no. 4 (Winter 1958–1959): 2–5.

Derug, Betty. "Celestials in the Diggings." *Idaho Yesterdays* (Fall 1972): 2.

Dorland, C. P. "The Chinese Massacre at Los Angeles." *Historical Society of Southern California Annual* 3 (Los Angeles 1894): 25.

Dubs, H. H. "The Chinese in Mexico City in 1635." *Far Eastern Quarterly* 1 (1942): 387–389.

DuFault, David. "The Chinese in the Mining Camps of California: 1848–1870." *The Historical Society of Southern California Quarterly* 41, no. 2 (July 1959):155.

Esvelt, John P. "Upper Columbia Placering." *Pacific Northwesterner* 3 (1959): 6.

Everett, Milliard F. "Memories of Joseph Emerson Smith." *Denver Catholic Register,* 13 February 1941.

Fielder, Mildred. "Wong Family of Deadwood." *Wi-Iyohi* 13, no. 11 (1 Feburary 1960): 1.

Flaherty, Stacy A. "Boycott in Butte." *Montana the Magazine of Western History* (Winter 1987): 35–47.

Fong, Laurence Michael. "Desert Crossing: Migrations and Settlements of Early Chinese in Arizona." In *Papers of the Second National Conference on Chinese American Studies.* San Francisco: 1980.

———. "Sojourners and Settlers: The Chinese Experience in Arizona." *Journal of Arizona History* 21, no. 2 (1980): 22–56.

Fritz, Christian. "Bitter Strength (k'u-li) and the Constitution: The Chinese before the Federal Courts in California." *The Historical Reporter* (Autumn 1980): 2–15.

Gardner, A. Dudley. "Chinese Emigrants in Southwest Wyoming, 1868–1885." *Annals of Wyoming* 63, no. 4 (Fall 1991): 139–144.

Georgetta, Clel. "Sheep in Nevada." *Nevada Historical Society Quarterly* 8 (Summer 1965): 15–39.

Gilliam, E. W. "Chinese Immigration." *North American Review* 143 (1886): 32.

Goldman, Marion S. *Gold Diggers and Silver Miners.* Ann Arbor: University of Michigan Press, 1981.

———. "Sexual Commerce on the Comstock Lode." *Nevada Historical Society Quarterly* 21 (Summer 1978): 110.

Greenwood, Roberta S. "The Chinese on Main Street." In *Archaeological Perspectives on Ethnicity in America,* ed. Robert L. Schuyler. Farmingdale, N.Y.: Baywood, 1980.

Gulick, Bill. "Murder in Hells Canyon: Dam Is Reminder of Brutal Episode." *Seattle Times Magazine.* 1 July 1973, 8–9.

Haley, S. Evelts. "Mounted Chinese Inspector." In *Jeff Milton: A Good Man with a Gun.* Norman: University of Oklahoma Press, 1948.

Halseth, A., and Bruce A. Glasrud. "Anti-Chinese Movements in Washington, 1885–1886: A Reconsideration." In *The Northwest Mosaic: Minority Conflicts in Pacific Northwest History,* ed. James A. Halseth and Bruce A. Glasrud. Boulder: Pruett Publishing Co., 1959.

Hart, Philip D. "Chinese Community in Lovelock, Nevada: 1870–1940." In *Report of Archaeological and Historical Investigations at Ninth and Amherst, Lovelock, Nevada,* ed. E. M. Hattori, M. K. Rusco, and D. R. Tuohy. Carson City: Nevada State Museum, 1979.

Hayes, Jim. "Auburn—A Ghostly Gold City of Oregon." *Daily Oregonian.* 5 November 1933, magazine section, 3.

Hazlett, Fanny G. "Historical Sketches and Reminiscences of Dayton, Nevada." *Nevada Historical Society Papers* 3 (1921–22): 21–22.

Hill, Herbert. "Anti-Oriental Agitation and the Rise of Working Class Racism." *Society* 20, no. 2 (January–February 1973): 46.

Hu-Dehart, Evelyn. "Immigrants to a Developing Society: The Chinese in Northern Mexico." *Journal of Arizona History* 21, no. 3 (Autumn 1980): 275–312.

Huie, Wing Young. "Port Cities People: Joe Huie." In *Lake Superior Port Cities* 1, no. 2 (1979): 9–12.

Ip, M. "Chinese New Zealanders: Old Settlers and New Immigrants." In *Immigration and National Identity in New Zealand: One People, Two Peoples, Many Peoples?*, ed. S.W. Greif. Palmerston North: Dunmore Press, 1995.

Jacques, Leo, and M. Dambourges. "Have Quick More Money Than Mandarins: The Chinese in Sonora." *Journal of Arizona History* 17 (Summer 1976): 208–218.

———. "The Chinese Massacre in Torreon (Coahuila) in 1911." *Arizona and the West* 16, no. 3 (Autumn 1974): 233–246.

Johnson, Dana Leigh. "Equal Rights and the 'Heathen "Chinee"': Black Activism in San Francisco: 1865–1875." *Western Historical Society Quarterly* 11, no. 1 (January 1980): 57–68.

Karlin, Jules. "The Anti-Chinese Outbreak in Tacoma, 1885." *Pacific Historical Review* 23 (August 1954): 271–283.

———. "The Anti-Chinese Outbreaks in Seattle, 1885–1886." *Pacific Northwest Quarterly* 29 (April 1948): 103–130.

———. "The Indemnification of Aliens Injured by Mob Violence." *Southwestern Social Science Quarterly* 25 (1945): 235–246.

Kraus, George. "Chinese Laborers and the Construction of the Central Pacific." *Utah Historical Quarterly* 37, no. 1 (1969): 41–57.

Kuo, Chia-ling. "The Chinese on Long Island—A Pilot Study." *Phylon* 31 (Fall 1970): 280–289.

Lai, H. M. "Chinese." In *Harvard Encyclopedia of American Ethnic Groups*, ed. Stephan Thernstrom. Cambridge, Mass., 1980.

Laurie, Clayton D. "'The Chinese Must Go': The United States Army and the Anti-Chinese Riots in Washington Territory, 1885–1886." *Pacific Northwest Quarterly* 81, no. 1 (January 1990).

Laurier Papers. MG26 G I(6), Vol 764, N2179930. Public Archives of Canada, Ottawa.

Lee, Rose Hum. "The Decline of Chinatowns in the United States." *American Journal of Sociology* 54 (1949): 422–432.

Lewis, Georgia. "The Dragon That Rides the Wind." *Nevadan Magazine, Las Vegas Review Journal.* 5 March 1972.

Lo, Jung Pang. "Chinese Reform in Idaho." *Idaho Yesterdays* 5, no. 1 (Spring 1961): 20–21.

Lockley, Fred. "Reminiscences of Captain William P. Gray." *Quarterly* (Oregon Historical Society) 14 (December 1913): 326.

Loomis, C. Grant. "Chinese Lore from Nevada, 1867–1878." *California Folklore Quarterly* 5 (January–April 1946): 185–196.

Lowe, Sharon. "Pipe Dreams and Reality: Opium in Comstock Society, 1860–1887." *Nevada Historical Society Quarterly* 36, no. 3 (Fall 1983): 178–193.

Lyman, Stanford J. "Strangers in the City: The Chinese in the Urban Frontier." In *Roots: An Asian American Reader*, eds. Amy Tachiki et al. Los Angeles, 1971.

Lyman, Stanford M. "Marriage and Family among Chinese Immigrants to America, 1850–1906." In *The Asians in the West.* Reno: University of Nevada Press, 1970.

MacArthur, Walter. "Opposition to Oriental Immigration." *Annals of the American Academy of Political and Social Science* 34 (1909): 239–246.

Magnaghi, Russell M. "Virginia City's Chinese Community, 1860–1880." *Nevada Historical Society Quarterly* 24 (Summer 1981): 130–157.

MarDock, Julian. "The Levee: A Nostalgic Look at Tyler's Railside Business District." *Chronicles of Smith County, Texas* 10 (Spring 1971): 44.

Mark, Gregory Lee. "Racial, Economic, and Political Factors in the Development of America's Drug Laws." *Issues in Criminology* 10 (Spring 1975): 65.

McClure, A. K. "Wilbur Fisk Sanders." *Contributions to the Historical Society of Montana*, 10 vols. Boston: J.S. Canner, 1966; original in 1917.

McGraw, John H. "The Anti-Chinese Riots of 1885." *Washington State Historical Society Publications* 2 (1915): 388–397.

Mei, June. "Socioeconomic Organization of Emigration: Guandong to California, 1850–1882." In *Labor Immigration under Capitalism: Asian Workers in the United States before World War II*, ed. Lucie Cheng and Edna Bonacich. Berkeley and Los Angeles: University of California Press, 1984.

Miller, B. F. "Nevada in the Making: Being Pioneer Stories of White Pine County and Elsewhere." *Nevada State Historical Society Papers* 4 (1923–1924): 360.

Mullam, Captain John. "From Walla Walla to San Francisco." *Walla Walla Statesman* (Oregon). 29 November 1862.

Murphey, Rhoads. "Boston's Chinatown." *Economic Geography* 28 (July 1952).

Navarro, Moisés González. "Xenofobia y xenofilia en la Revolución Mexicana." *Historia Mexicana* 18 (April–May 1969): 591.

Newlands, Francis G. "A Western View of the Race Question." *Annals of American Academy of Political and Social Science* 34 (September 1909): 50.

Olsen, John W. "An Analysis of East Asian Coins Excavated in Tucson, Arizona." *Historical Anthropology* 71, no. 2 (1983): 41–55.

Ong, Paul. "An Ethnic Trade: The Chinese Laundries in Early California." *The Journal of Ethnic Studies* 8 (Winter 1981): 95–113.

———. "Chinese Laundries as an Urban Occupation in Nineteenth-Century California." *Annals of Chinese Historical Society of the Pacific Northwest* (1983): 68–85.

———. "Chinese Laundries as an Urban Occupation in Nineteenth-Century California." *Annals of Chinese Historical Society of the Pacific Northwest* (1983): 68–85.

Orbeck, Betty, ed. "Moving West with the Texas and Pacific: From the Pages of the *Dallas Weekly Herald*." *The Permian Historical Annual* 13 (December 1973).

Ourada, Patricia K. "The Chinese in Colorado." *Colorado Magazine* 29 (1952): 2767–2777.

Owens, Kenneth. "Pierce City Incident, 1885–1886." *Idaho Yesterdays* 3, no. 3 (Fall 1959): 9.

Paladin, Vivian, ed. "Henry N. Blake: Proper Bostonian, Purposeful Pioneer." *Montana the Magazine of Western History* 14 (October 1964): 55.

Palat, Ravi Arvind. "Curries, Chopsticks and Kiwis: Asian Migration to Aotearoa/New Zealand." In *Nga Pataj: Racism and Ethnic Relations in Hotearoa/New Zealand*, eds. P. Spoonley, C. Magherson, A. D. Pearson. Palmerston North: Dumore Press, 1996.

Palmer, H. S. "Remarks upon the Geography and Natural Capabilities of British Columbia and the Condition of Its Principal Gold Fields." *Journal of the Royal Geographical Society* 134 (1894): 194.

Parker, Charles Franklin. "Chinee Boy." *Arizona Highway*, September 1941.

Paul, Rodman W. "The Origin of the Chinese Issue in California." *Mississippi Valley Historical Review* 25 (September 1938): 181–196.

People, Newsletter of the University of Texan Cultures, II (January–February, 1972), 2, 7.

Perkins, Clifford. "Recollections of a Chinese-Immigration Inspector." In *Arizona Memories*, ed. Anne Hodges Morgan and Rennard Strickland. Tucson: University of Arizona Press, 1984.

Prazniak, Roxann. "The Chinese in Woodland, California." In *The Chinese Laundry on Second Street: Papers on Archaeology at the Woodland Opera House Site*. California Archaeological Reports no. 24. Sacramento: California Department of Parks and Recreation, 1984.

Quellmalz, Carl Robert. "Late Chinese Provincial Export Wares." *Oriental Art* 22, no. 3 (1976): 289–298.

Quinn, Larry D. "Chink Chink Chinaman: The Beginnings of Nativism in Montana." *Pacific Northwest Quarterly* 58 (April 1967): 82–89.

Reese, James V. "The Early History of Labor Organization in Texas, 1838–1876." *Southwestern Historical Quarterly* 72 (July 1968).

Richards, Kent D. "Insurrection, Agitation, and Riots: The Police Power and Washington Statehood." *Montana the Magazine of Western History* 37 (Autumn 1987): 10–21.

Roberts, Shirley J. "Minority-Group Poverty in Phoenix: A Socio-Economic Survey." *Journal of Arizona History* 14, no. 4 (Winter 1973): 347–362.

Rocha, Guy Louis. "Radical Labor Struggles in the Tonopah-Goldfield Mining District . . . 1922." *Nevada Historical Society Quarterly* 20 (Spring 1977): 26.

Rohe, Randall E. "After the Gold Rush: Chinese Mining in the Far West, 1850–1890." *Montana the Magazine of Western History* 32, no. 4 (1982): 2–19.

Rusco, Mary K. "Counting the Lovelock Chinese." In *Report of Archaeological and Historical Investigations at Ninth and Amherst, Lovelock, Nevada*, ed. E. M. Hattori, M. K. Rusco, and D. R. Tuohy. Carson City: Nevada State Museum, 1979.

———. "Chinese in Lovelock, Nevada: History and Archaeology." *Halcyon* (1981): 141–151.

———. "Counting the Lovelock Chinese." *Nevada Historical Society Quarterly* 24 (Winter 1981): 319–328.

Santagadea, Luis Millones. "Los Chinos en el Perú: cuatro siglos de migración y adaptión en el area andina." In *Minortás Étnicas en el Perú*, Serie de Antropología, Departamento de Ciencias Sociales, Pontifica Universidad Católica de Perú. Lima, 1973.

Sargent, A. A. "The Wyoming Anti-Chinese Riot." *Overland Monthly* 6 (1885): 507–512.

Schwantes, Carlos A. "Protest in a Promised Land: Unemployment, Disinheritance, and the Origin of Labor Militancy in the Pacific Northwest, 1885–1886." *Western Historical Quarterly* 13 (1982): 373–390.

Seager, Robert, II. "Some Denominational Reaction to Chinese Immigration to California." *Pacific Coast Historical Review* 28 (1959): 49–66.

Sedgewick, C. P. "Persistence, Change, and Innovation: The Social Organization of the New Zealand Chinese, 1866–1976." *Journal of Comparative Family Studies* 16, no. 2 (1985): 205–229.

Seward, George F. "Mongolian Immigration." *North American Review* 134 (1882): 562–577.

Shepperson, Wilbur S. "Immigrant Themes in Nevada Newspapers." *Nevada Historical Society Quarterly* 12 (Summer 1969): 20.

———. "Sir Charles Wentworth Dilke: A Republican Baronet in Nevada." *Nevada Historical Society Quarterly* 3 (October–December 1960): 19.

Shewin, H. "Observations on the Chinese Laborer." *Overland Monthly* 7 (1886): 91–99.

Sincock, Bob. "'Case Is Closed': Fifty Years Ago Snake River Flowed Blood and International Complications Lingered Long." *Portland Oregon Journal.* 18 September 1938. (newspaper clipping in WPA Historical Records Survey, BX 66–29, UO.

Siu, Paul E. P. "The Isolation of the Chinese Laundryman." In *Contributions to Urban Sociology,* ed. Ernest W. Burgess and Donald J. Bogue. Chicago: University of Chicago Press, 1964.

———. "The Sojourner." *American Journal of Sociology* 58, no. 1 (1952): 34–44.

Smith, Duane A. "The Caribou—A Forgotten Mine." *Colorado Magazine* 39 (1962): 52.

Smith, W. C. "Changing Personality Traits of Second Generation Orientals." *American Journal of Sociology* 33 (1928): 922–929.

Spier, Robert E. G. "Food Habits of Nineteenth-Century California Chinese." *California Historical Society Quarterly* 37, no. 1 (1958): 79–84; 37, no. 2 (1958): 129–136.

———. "Tool Acculturation among 19th Century Chinese." *Ethnohistory* 5 (Spring 1958): 101–102.

Spoehr, Luther W. "Sambo and the Heathen Chinee: Californians Racial Stereotypes in the Late 1870's." *Pacific Historical Review* 42 (May 1973): 185–204.

Stratton, David H. "The Snake River Massacre of Chinese Miners, 1887." In *A Taste of the West: Essays in Honor of Robert G. Athearn,* ed. Duane E. Smith. Boulder, Colo.: Pruett Publishing Company, 1987.

Strobridge, William F. "Chinese in the Spanish American War and Beyond." *Papers of the Second National Conference on Chinese American Studies.* San Francisco: 1980.

Swartout, Robert R., Jr. "Kwantung to Big Sky: The Chinese in Montana, 1864–1900." *Montana the Magazine of Western History* 38, no. 1 (Winter 1988): 42–53.

———. "In Defense of the West's Chinese." *Oregon Historical Quarterly* 83 (Spring 1982): 25–36.

Thomas, David G. "Memories of the Chinese Riot." *Annals of Wyoming* 19–20 (1947–1948): 105–111.

Townley, John M. "The Tuscarora Mining District." *Northeastern Nevada Historical Society Quarterly* 2 (Summer and Fall 1971): 26.

Trimble, William J. "The Mining Advance into the Inland Empire." *Bulletin of the University of Wisconsin,* no. 638. History Series 3 (1914): 58.

Twain, Mark. "Disgraceful Persecution of a Boy." In *Mark Twain on the Damned Human Race,* ed. Janet Smit. New York: Hill and Wang, 1962.

Tzu-Kuei, Yen. "Rock Springs Incident." *Chinese Studies in History* 8, no. 3 (Spring 1974): 51–66.

Ulloa, Berta. "Las relaciones mexicano-norteamericanas, 1910–1911." *Historia Mexicana* 15 (July–September 1965), 44.

Vanderburg, William A. "Placer Mining in Nevada." *University of Nevada Bulletin* 30 (1936): 158.

Wallace, Mildred Young. "I Remember Chung." *Journal of Arizona History* 20, no. 1 (Spring 1979): 35–46.

Walter, Townsend. "Gold Mountain Guests: Chinese Migration to the United States, 1848–1882." *Journal of Economic History* 37 (March 1977): 264–267.

Washington, Booker T. "The Race Problem in America." *Independent* (July–December 1911): 909–913.

Webster, Helen. "The Chinese School of the Central Presbyterian Church of Denver." *Colorado Magazine* 40, no. 1 (1963): 57–64; 2 (April 1963): 132–136.

Weigle, Gilbert G. "Youth's Love of Slave Girl Starts Death." *San Francisco Examiner*, 28 August 1921.

Weisenburger, Paul. "God and Man in a Secular City." *Nevada Historical Society Quarterly* 14 (Summer 1971): 6.

Westermeier, Therese S. "Colorado Festivals." *Colorado Magazine* 28 (July 1951): 180.

White, W. Thomas. "Race, Ethnicity, and Gender in the Railroad Work Force: The Case of the Far Northwest, 1883–1918." *Western Historical Quarterly* 16 (1985): 265–283.

Wilcox, W. P. "Anti-Chinese Riots in Washington." *The Washington Historical Quarterly* 20, no. 3 (July 1929): 204–212.

Willmott, W. E. "Some Aspects of Chinese Communities in British Columbia Towns." *British Columbia Studies* 1 (Winter 1868–1869): 28.

Wonder, Alice E. "Chinatown, at Fairplay, as It Was in Early Days." *Park County Republican and Fairplay Flume* (Colorado). Summer Tourist Edition, 1956.

Wong, H. K. "Forging a Link." *Chinese Historical Society of America Bulletin*, 15 January 1966.

Woo, Kenny. "The Chinese Colony in San Antonio." *The Junior Historian of the Texas State Historical Association* 15 (January 1955): 6–8, 12.

Woodell, Thomas M. "Un-Organizations: The Family Associations of the Chinese." In *The Folklore of Texan Cultures*, ed. Francis Edward Abernethy and Dan Beaty. Austin, 1974.

Worley, B. "Five Hundred Chinese Refugees." *The Overland Monthly* 71 (April 1918).

Wortman, Roy T. "Denver's Anti-Chinese Riot, 1880." *Colorado Magazine* 42 (Fall 1965): 285–291.

Wu, Ching-ch'ao. "Chinese Immigration in the Pacific Area." *The Chinese Social and Political Science Review* 12 (October 1928): 553.

Wu, Paak-shing. "China's Diplomatic Relations with Mexico." *China Quarterly* 4 (Summer 1939): 1–20.

Wunder, John R. "Chinese in Trouble: Criminal Law and Race on the Trans-Mississippi West Frontier." *Western Historical Quarterly* 17 (January 1986): 25–41.

———. "Law and Chinese in Frontier Montana." *Montana the Magazine of Western History* 30 (Summer 1980): 18–30.

———. "The Chinese and the Courts in the Pacific Northwest: Justice Denied?" *Pacific Historical Review* 52 (May 1983): 191–211.

———. "The Courts and the Chinese in Frontier Idaho." *Idaho Yesterdays* 25 (Spring 1981): 23–32.

Wynne, Robert R. "American Labor and the Vancouver Anti-Oriental Riot." *The Northwest Mosaic: Minority Conflicts in Pacific Northwest History*, ed. James A. Halseth and Bruce A. Glasrud. Boulder: Pruett Publishing Co., 1959.

Young, F. G. "Why Oregon Has Never Had an Oriental Problem." *Annals of American Academy of Political Science and Social Science* 34 (1909): 306–310.

Yu, Connie Young. "The Chinese in American Courts." *Bulletin of Concerned Asian Scholars* 4 (Fall 1972).

Zhu, Liping. "How the Other Half Lived: Chinese Daily Life in Boise Basin Mining Camps." *Idaho Yesterdays* 38, no. 4 (Winter 1995): 20–28.

Index